Mary Boykin Chesnut's A Diary from Dixie *is probably one of the two most important journals kept by an American in the nineteenth century. When Harvard University Press learned that the book was out of print and C. Vann Woodward's long-awaited definitive edition of the* Diary *would not be ready for some time, the editors decided to put the book back into print to serve scholars and students during the interim period.*

—*Publisher's Note*

MARY BOYKIN CHESNUT

A DIARY FROM

DIXIE

by

Mary Boykin Chesnut

with a Foreword

by

EDMUND WILSON

Edited by

BEN AMES WILLIAMS

Harvard University Press
Cambridge, Massachusetts
London, England

Printed in the United States of America

Second printing, 1982

Library of Congress Cataloging in Publication Data

Chesnut, Mary Boykin Miller, 1823–1886.
A diary from Dixie.

Reprint of the 1949 ed. published by Houghton Mifflin, Boston.
Includes index.
1. Chesnut, Mary Boykin Miller, 1823–1886. 2. United States—History—Civil War, 1861–1865—Personal narratives—Confederate side. 3. Confederate States of America—History—Sources. 4. Southern States—Biography. I. Williams, Ben Ames, 1889–1953. II. Title.
E487.C52 1980 973.7'82 79-28592
ISBN 0-674-20290-2 (cloth)
ISBN 0-674-20291-0 (paper)

Foreword

In his brilliant study, Patriotic Gore: Studies in the Literature of the American Civil War (1962), *Edmund Wilson discussed the work of writers involved in the sectional conflict. The following excerpt is from Wilson's chapter titled "Three Confederate Ladies," which discusses, in addition to the diary of Mary Boykin Chesnut, the Civil War memoirs of Kate Stone and Sarah Morgan.*

Publisher's Note

Mrs. James Chesnut, . . . whose journal has been published as *A Diary from Dixie,* . . . a woman of exceptional intelligence, was surrounded by all that the Confederacy could show of most cultivated and most distinguished. The father of Mary Chesnut's husband was a rich South Carolinian, who owned five square miles of plantations, but the son had studied law and gone into politics. Like his father, he had been educated at Princeton, and he had travelled with his wife in Europe. He had served in the United States Senate from 1858, stoutly defending slavery, and, in the autumn of 1860, even before the secession of his State, had been the first Southern senator to resign from the Senate. He had, the following year, taken part in the convention that drafted the ordinance of secession and in the Congress of the Confederate States that drafted their constitution. It was he who had been sent to Major Anderson to demand the surrender of Fort Sumter, and, as an aide with the rank of colonel on the staff of Jefferson Davis, he was close to the Confederate government all through the Civil War and was entrusted with many missions which brought him in touch with the military as well as with the political aspects of the conflict.

Mrs. Chesnut had thus the advantage of living much at the headquarters of the Confederacy, first in Montgomery, Alabama; then, when its capital was shifted, in Richmond, Virginia, where she had for her daily associates the Davises and the Lees, all sorts of incapacitated or visiting army officers — the "first families" of South Carolina and Virginia — and such literary men as the South had produced, the novelist William Gilmore Simms and the poet Paul Hamilton Hayne. Yet we are struck, as we read these two diaries, Miss Morgan's and Mrs. Chesnut's, as well as other Southern documents of the period, by the recurrence of the same family names. Sarah Morgan in Baton Rouge is related to and knows the same families as the Chesnuts in Richmond a thousand miles away. The world that we have here to deal with — the world of that fraction of the ruling class that is at all public-spirited and well-educated — is, as Olmsted says, extremely limited; and how far this element was from being capable of influencing the policy or saving the fortunes of the South may be seen in an appalling and a heartbreaking way in the chronicle of Mrs. Chesnut's diary.

This diary is an extraordinary document — in its informal department, a masterpiece; and on that account, one cannot do it justice by merely running through its record as we have done with that of Sarah Morgan. Mrs. Chesnut is a very clever woman, who knows something of Europe as well as of Washington and who has read a good deal of history as well as of other kinds of literature. Not only is she fully aware of the world-wide importance of the national crisis at one of the foci of which she finds herself; she has also, it would seem, a decided sense of the literary possibilities of her subject. The very rhythm of her opening pages at once puts us under the spell of a writer who is not merely jotting down her days but establishing, as a novelist does, an atmosphere, an emotional tone. A hundred and fifty thousand words of the four hundred thousand words that Mrs. Chesnut wrote were first published in 1904, and this book was read many years after by the late Ben Ames Williams, in preparation for a novel he was writing — *House Divided* — which was to deal with the Civil War. For his purposes, Mr. Williams, as he tells us, laid it heavily under contribution, and even introduced a character that was based on Mrs. Chesnut herself. It would seem to have been injudicious to attempt to exploit for fiction a work that is already a work of art; but Mr. Williams was not at that time in a position to appreciate fully how much a work of art it was. When his interest in Mrs. Chesnut led him to look up her original fifty notebooks, he discovered whole episodes, including the important one of "Buck" Preston and General Hood, as well as elements of the social picture — the ignominies and cruelties of slavery — which the editors had suppressed; and he now tried to do the writer justice by bringing out, in 1949, a new edition of her diary twice as long as the original one. This still left a hundred thousand words unpublished, and the interest of the document as we know it suggests that it might be worth while eventually to print the whole text.

Mr. Williams, in thus cutting down this text, has perhaps, however, pointed it up, and his instincts as a writer of fiction may have led him, by pulling it together, to help the large canvas compose. Yet the diarist's own instinct is uncanny. Starting out with situations or relationships of which she cannot know the outcome, she takes advantage of the actual turn of events to develop them and round them out as if she were molding a novel. One of her most effective performances is her handling of the episode mentioned above — the affair of "Buck" Preston and General Hood. The teen-age belles of the South had sometimes incongruous nicknames. The elaborate chivalric gallantry of young gentlemanhood and young ladyhood was likely to have been preceded by a somewhat rough-and-tumble plantation childhood. Buck Preston had been given this nickname because one of her middle names was Buchanan (another beauty was known as "Boozer"). She was actually a lovely young girl, who had, Mrs. Chesnut tells us, "a mischievous gleam in her soft blue eyes; or are they gray, or brown, or black as night? I have seen them of every color varying with the mood of the moment." (Another Southern lady who knew the Prestons — Mrs. Burton Harrison, in her *Recollections Grave and Gay* — describes Buck and her two sisters as "like goddesses upon a heaven-kissing hill, tall and stately, with brilliant fresh complexions, altogether the embodiment of vigorous health.") Buck, Mrs. Chesnut says, was "the very sweetest woman I ever knew, had a knack of being fallen in love with at sight, and of never being fallen out of love with." But so many of her soldier lovers have been killed in battle or fatally wounded — "Ransom Calhoun, Bradly Warwick, Claude Gibson, the Notts," Mrs. Chesnut enumerates them — that people are beginning to feel that it is bad luck to fall in love with her. Colonel "Sam" Hood from Kentucky (his real name was John Bell Hood), a West Pointer just turned thirty, has already served in Texas and California and has been seriously wounded in fighting the Indians. He has been put in command of the "Texas Brigade" and, as the result of distinguishing himself at Gaines's Mill and Antietam, has been advanced to the rank of major general. But he has lost his right leg at Chickamauga, and he is obliged to retire to Richmond. He had "won his three stars," says Mrs. Chesnut, under the formidable and uncouth Stonewall Jackson, and it was Jackson who had requested his promotion. "When he came in with his sad face," she writes, " — the face of an old crusader who believed in his cause, his cross and his crown — we were not prepared for that type as a beau ideal of wild Texans. He is tall, thin, shy, with blue eyes and light hair, a tawny beard and a vast amount of it, covering the lower part of his face. He wears an appearance of awkward strength. Someone said that his great reserve of manner he carried only into the society of ladies. Mr. Venable added that he himself had often heard of the light of battle shining in a man's eyes, but he had seen it only once. He carried orders to Hood from General Lee, and found him in the hottest of the fight. The man was transfigured. 'The fierce light of his eyes,' said Mr. Venable, 'I can never forget.' "

Hood, too, falls in love with Buck Preston, and his long and adoring suit becomes a great subject of interest to their friends and a source of suspense for the reader. Will she or will she not marry him? Her parents are opposed to the match, for reasons which are not made clear, though one gathers that he is somehow not suitable, certainly not "first family." "He does not," says a fellow officer, "compare favorably with General Johnston, who is decidedly a man of culture and literary attainments." And, besides, he has only one leg. There follows a scene in which the girls of the neighborhood, rather gruesomely, complain of their mutilated lovers: "After some whispering among us, Buck cried: 'Don't waste your delicacy! Sally is going to marry a man who has lost an arm, so he is also a maimed soldier, you see; and she is proud of it. The cause glorifies such wounds.' Annie said meekly: 'I fear it will be my fate to marry one who has lost his head!' 'Tudy has her eye on one who lost an eye!' What a glorious assortment of noble martyrs and heroes! The bitterness of this kind of talk is appalling." Yet everybody has to respect Sam Hood, who, with his tough Texas training, contrasts with many other of the Confederate officers by reason of his professional pertinacity — what the officer quoted above speaks of as his "simple-minded directness of purpose"; and this he brings, also, to the courtship of Buck.

One gets, in general, from Mrs. Chesnut an impression that is not reassuring of the leaders of the army of secession. She quotes General Winfield Scott, the hero of the Mexican War, a Virginian who had stood by the Union, on the qualities of Southern soldiers: Scott feels, she says, that "we [the Southerners] have courage, woodcraft, consummate horsemanship, and endurance of pain equal to the Indians, but that we will not submit to discipline. We will not take care of things, or husband our resources. Where we are, there is waste and destruction. If it could all be done by one wild desperate dash, we would do it; but he does not think we can stand the long black months between the acts, the waiting! We can bear pain without a murmur, but we will not submit to being bored."

Even the high officers share these qualities: they have carried into the army the same disposition that has made the young men fight so many duels. They mostly belong to the same social world, and they know each other too well. They are touchy and jealous of one another. If they don't like the way they are treated, they are apt to get angry and sulk, and to try to get themselves transferred. The rich planter Wade Hampton, who is not a West Pointer, complains to Mrs. Chesnut that one of his brigades has been taken from him and given to Fitzhugh Lee, Robert E. Lee's nephew, and that when he had appealed to Robert E., threatening to resign from the service, the latter had "told him curtly: 'I would not care if you went back to South Carolina with your whole division.' Wade said that his manner made this speech immensely mortifying . . . It seems General Lee has no patience with any personal complaints or grievances. He is all for the cause, and cannot bear officers to come to him with any such matters as Wade Hampton had come about." She does not approve of this pettiness; yet she betrays, in an account of a visit to the Richmond fortifications, how difficult it is for the Southerners of the stratum to which she belongs to realize their responsibilities, as members of a collective enterprise, to take one another seriously: "Mr. Mallory offered me his arm, and we set off to visit and inspect the fortifications of this, our 'Gibraltar of the Jeems,' of whose deeds they are so proud. It holds its own against all comers. Everywhere we went, the troops presented arms, and I was fool enough to ask Mr. Mallory why they did that. With a suppressed titter he replied: 'I dare say because I am at the head of the Navy Department.' "

General Hood's adoration of Buck Preston and the uncertainty of her final acceptance of him become, in this situation, a kind of symbol for the general failure of the South; and it is significant that Mrs. Burton Harrison, the wife of Jefferson Davis's secretary and a friend of Mrs. Chesnut's, should also treat the wooing of Buck Preston, a "fair and regal being," as a subject of major interest. Fascinated, like these ladies, we follow Mrs. Chesnut's account of Buck's vacillations between hot and cold. "Buck saw me sending a rice pudding to the wounded man — it seems he cares for no other dainty — whereupon she said, in her sweetest, mildest, sleepiest way: 'I never cared particularly about him, but now that he has chosen to go with those people [we are not told who they were], I would not marry him if he had a thousand legs, instead of having just lost one.' " Yet somehow she becomes engaged to him: "Such a beamingly, beautiful, crimson face as she turned to me, her clear blue eyes looking straight in mine. 'Do you believe I like him now?' 'No.' She did not notice my answer." But Buck long continues to sustain her role: "Mrs. Preston was offended by the story of Buck's performance at the Iveses'. General Breckenridge told her 'it was the most beautifully unconscious act I ever saw.' The General was leaning against the wall, Buck standing guard by him. The crowd surged that way, and she held out her arm to protect him from the rush. After they had all passed, she handed him his crutches, and they, too, moved slowly away. Mrs. Davis said: 'Any woman in Richmond would have done the same joyfully, but few could do it so gracefully.' Buck is made so conspicuous by her beauty, whatever she does cannot fail to attract attention." Their story runs all through the frivolities — the dinners and the suppers and the amateur theatricals — with which, at once desperate as their situation worsened and unwilling to face its dangers, they continue to amuse themselves. As the result of an evening party cut short by the cook's getting news that her son has just been killed at the front — "Instead of a tray of good things, came back that news to the Martins!" — Mrs. Chesnut, like Kate Stone, is reminded of the French Revolution and says that they now understand the French prisoners who continued to flirt and dance while they were waiting for the tumbril to come for them.

But the devotion of the crippled Hood still persists through all the intrigue and quarrelling which, in the final phases of the war, demoralize the Confederate government. In this government, the fatal incapacity of the Southerners for agreeing or working together becomes even more apparent than in the conduct of the war itself. The passion for independence which with masters of a subject race so often takes the form of wrongheadedness, of self-assertion for its own sake, of tantrums, this self-will that has made an issue, and that is now making a cult, of states' rights, is now provoking certain elements to rebel against the Confederacy itself. President Davis is constantly opposed and denounced in a way that Mrs. Chesnut thinks scandalous, and the various departments of the government have now become quite insubordinate. The great irony is that the recalcitrance of the Southerners against any sort of central control, which has led them to secede from the Union, is also — since they refuse to submit to the kind of governmental coercion that will enable the North to win — obstructing their success with the war. President Davis is doing his best to put through the same war measures as Lincoln — conscription, the suspension of habeas corpus, and even, in the final year, the emancipation of the slaves — but all these are either burked or evaded. The big planters will not allow the government to interfere in any way with their Negroes, even to send them, as James Chesnut advocates, to work on the fortifications. When the crisis becomes alarming, when the need for taking a stronger line is a matter of life or death, the cry goes up at once that Jefferson Davis wants to make himself a dictator, a despot like Abraham Lincoln.

We come to feel that Hood's patient unwavering purpose to induce Buck Preston to marry him is doomed as the Confederacy is. It is like one of those relationships in Chekhov that we know can never come to anything and that, with Chekhov — and we cannot be sure that Mrs. Chesnut is not just as much aware of what her story implies — are meant to imply the impotence and the impending ruin of Russian society. General Hood is sent back to the Army at the beginning of 1864, and he is obliged to retreat, under Johnston, before Sherman, who is marching on Atlanta. When the insecure Jefferson Davis, against the advice of Hood, decides to remove Johnston and put Hood in his place, the latter is left to face Sherman alone. We have already seen him, helpless but proud, exchanging polemics with his terrible opponent over the latter's deportation of the people of Atlanta. The supplies that are needed do not arrive, and the morale of the army is lost. After defeat in a couple of battles, the General is obliged to give up the campaign, and he resigns his command in January, 1865. "The Hood melodrama is over," Mrs. Chesnut ambiguously writes in March, "though the curtain has not fallen on the last scene. Hood stock going down. When that style of enthusiasm is on the wane, the rapidity of its extinction is marvellous, like the snuffing out of a candle; one moment here, then gone forever."

In May, after Appomattox, Buck Preston makes a rather queer attempt to explain things to Mrs. Chesnut — "The music and the moonlight, and that restful feeling of her head on my knee, set her tongue in motion" — though she cautions the older lady that if she should write about the affair in her diary, she must say, "This is translated from Balzac." It had begun with "those beautiful, beautiful silk stockings." Buck had exposed them to view by warming her feet at the fender. Her admirer had always raved about his mistress's foot and ankle (*mistress* in the gallant old sense), but up to now he had treated her with reverence, had never gone further than to kiss her hand. Now he seized her and kissed her throat. She was shocked, and poor Hood had been humble. "He said it was so soft and white, that throat of mine," and put "a strong arm" around her waist so tight that she could not leave the room. "He said that, after all, I had promised to marry him, and that that made all the difference." But the girl could not see it that way, and now she makes a point of wearing boots and never warming her feet, and she wears, also, "a stiff handkerchief close up around my throat." "You see," she says to Mrs. Chesnut, "I never meant to be so outrageously treated again . . . Yet now, would you believe it, a sickening, almost an insane longing comes over me just to see him once more, and I know I never will. He is gone forever. If he had been persistent, if he had not given way under Mamma's violent refusal to listen to us, if he had asked *me!* When you refused to let anybody be married in your house, well, I would have gone down on the sidewalk, I would have married him on the pavement, if the parson could be found to do it. I was ready to leave all the world for him, to tie my clothes in a bundle and, like a soldier's wife, trudge after him to the ends of the earth."

But now it is too late. When we get our last glimpse of Buck Preston, she is travelling in Europe with her married sister; they are going to spend the winter in Paris.

Another of Mrs. Chesnut's main subjects is the plantation of her husband's parents at Camden, South Carolina, where she is sometimes obliged to stay and where she suffers acutely from boredom. She suffers also from the irking constraint imposed upon her by her ninety-year-old father-in-law, an opinionated austere old man who, even when deaf and blind, still keeps such a strong hand on his immense domain that he never has trouble with his slaves. This household of the old-world Chesnuts reminds one of the Bolkónskys of *War and Peace* (comparisons with Russia seem inevitable when one is writing about the old South). The father, presiding at dinner, as "absolute a tyrant as the Tsar of Russia," with his constantly repeated axioms and his authoritarian tone, is a less piquant Bolkónsky *père*. James, Jr., is an equally distinguished and equally conscientious, if not equally dashing, André; Miss Chesnut, his sister, may figure as a cool-headed and penurious, a less sympathetic

Princess Marie. But there is also a dowager Mrs. Chesnut, originally from Philadelphia, who was married in 1796 and falls easily into telling people about "stiff stern old Martha Washington" and describing the Washingtons' drawing room. The younger Mrs. Chesnut likes her mother-in-law, who has evidently more human warmth than the other members of the family and who, though never buying books herself, borrows them from other people and reads them in enormous quantities; but, in general, the younger woman finds Mulberry, the Chesnut estate, both oppressive and melancholy. "My sleeping apartment is large and airy, with windows opening on the lawn east and south. In those deep window seats, idly looking out, I spend much time. A part of the yard which was once a deer park has the appearance of the primeval forest; the forest trees have been unmolested and are now of immense size. In the spring, the air is laden with perfumes, violets, jasmine, crab apple blossoms, roses. Araby the blest never was sweeter in perfume. And yet there hangs here as on every Southern landscape the saddest pall. There are browsing on the lawn, where Kentucky bluegrass flourishes, Devon cows and sheep, horses, mares and colts. It helps to enliven it. Carriages are coming up to the door and driving away incessantly."

The Chesnut Negroes are faithful; they have been well trained and well treated. Yet everyone is rather uneasy. Mrs. Chesnut the younger herself has, like Kate Stone, a horror of slavery. When she sees a mulatto girl sold at auction in March, 1861, "My very soul sickened," she writes, and a few days later, when, with a visiting Englishwoman, she is again passing the auction block, "If you can stand that," she says to her companion, "no other Southern thing need choke you." And "I wonder," she is soon reflecting, "if it be a sin to think slavery a curse to any land. Men and women are punished when their masters and mistresses are brutes, not when they do wrong. Under slavery, we live surrounded by prostitutes, yet an abandoned woman [a white one, she means] is sent out of a decent house. Who thinks any worse of a Negro or mulatto woman for being a thing we can't name? God forgive us, but ours is a monstrous system, a wrong and an iniquity! Like the patriarchs of old, our men live all in one house with their wives and their concubines; and the mulattoes one sees in every family partly resemble the white children. Any lady is ready to tell you who is the father of all the mulatto children in everybody's household but her own."

This problem of the mixture of white and black blood, so systematically suppressed by Southern writers — "the ostrich game," Mrs. Chesnut calls this — she treats with remarkable frankness and exclaims at the hypocrisy of the Chesnuts in locking up the novels of Eugène Sue, and even a Gothic romance by the Carolinian Washington Allston, when the colored girls of the household are more or less openly promiscuous. "I hate slavery," she writes at the beginning of the war. "You say there are no more fallen women on a plantation than in London, in proportion to numbers; but what do you say to this? A magnate who runs a hideous black harem with its consequences under the same roof with his lovely white wife, and his beautiful and accomplished daughters? He holds his head as high and poses as the model of all human virtues to these poor women whom God and the laws have given him. From the height of his awful majesty, he scolds and thunders at them as if he never did wrong in his life. Fancy such a man finding his daughter reading *Don Juan*. 'You with that immoral book!' And he orders her out of his sight. You see, Mrs. Stowe did not hit the sorest spot. She makes Legree a bachelor."

Encountering such passages, we wonder whether the prudery of Buck Preston with her fiancé may not be something more than a curious local development of the nineteenth-century proprieties, something more than a romantic convention derived from the age of chivalry. That Buck Preston was not unusual in her reluctance to let men see her feet is shown by another anecdote, this time about James Chesnut's young nephew: "Today he was taking me to see Minnie Hayne's foot. He said it was the smallest, the most perfect thing in America! Now, I will go anywhere to see anything which can move the cool Captain to the smallest ripple of enthusiasm. He says Julia Rutledge knew his weakness, and would not show him her foot. His Uncle James had told him of its arched instep and symmetrical beauty. So he followed her trail like a wild Indian, and when she stepped in the mud, he took a paper pattern of her track, or a plaster cast; something that amazed Miss Rutledge at his sagacity." And Mrs. Chesnut herself, though she is not disinclined to flirt as the younger ladies do and occasionally provokes jealous scenes on the part of Mr. Chesnut, is offended by risqué stories and horrified by current French novels (which, nevertheless, she continues to read); will not allow legs to be mentioned; and cannot digest the news, brought back by a traveller from Europe, that the sternly moralistic George Eliot has been living in sin with George Henry Lewes.

One is forced to the conclusion that the pedestalled purity which the Southerners assigned to their ladies, the shrinking of these ladies themselves from any suggestion of freedom, were partly a "polarization" produced by the uninhibited ease with which their men could go to bed with the black girls. There is an atmosphere of tittering sex all through Mrs. Chesnut's chronicle, yet behind it is a pride that is based on fear and that sometimes results in coldness. Mrs. Chesnut, who was married at seventeen, has obviously no passionate interest in her husband, yet though Chesnut has, we gather, amused himself with occasional love affairs — not, so far as one is told, with blacks but with white women of inferior social status — she has never dared to take a lover. To allow oneself to weaken in this direction would be to associate oneself with the despised and dreaded slave girls who were bearing their masters' half-breeds, to surrender one's white prestige. The gaiety and ease of these ladies must have always masked a fundamental, a never-relaxing tension.

Mrs. Chesnut, in this intimate record, drops the mask and expresses herself with more candor than was usual for Southern ladies, even, as one imagines, in the working of their own minds. Her attitude toward Harriet Beecher Stowe is strikingly different, for example, from that of most Southerners of Mrs. Chesnut's own day or, indeed, of any day. Grace King, the New Orleans historian and novelist, born in 1852, writes in her autobiography of the "hideous, black, dragonlike book that hovered on the horizon of every Southern child" but which in her own family was never allowed to be mentioned. Mrs. Chesnut takes this horror more coolly and shows a strong interest in *Uncle Tom's Cabin.* In March of 1862 she rereads it, and at any instance of cruelty to slaves she is likely to mention that Mrs. Stowe would be delighted to hear of it. "I met our lovely relative," she writes in May, 1864, "the woman who might have sat for Eva's mother in *Uncle Tom's Cabin.* Beautifully dressed, graceful, languid, making eyes at all comers, she was softly and in dulcet accents regretting the necessity of sending out a sable Topsy to her sabler parent, to be switched for some misdemeanor. I declined to hear her regrets as I fled in haste." She says of the grandfather of one of her friends that he used to "put Negroes in hogsheads, with nails driven in all round, and roll the poor things downhill."

Her own point of view is vigorously expressed in November, 1861, in an outburst against Mrs. Stowe. Mrs. Stowe, she declares, and Greeley and Thoreau and Emerson and Sumner "live in nice New England homes, clean, sweet-smelling, shut up in libraries, writing books which ease their hearts of their bitterness against us. What self-denial they do practice is to tell John Brown to come down here and cut our throats in Christ's name. Now consider what I have seen of my mother's life, my grandmother's, my mother-in-law's. These people were educated at Northern schools, they read the same books as their Northern contemporaries, the same daily papers, the same Bible. They have the same ideas of right and wrong," while they of the South are doomed to "live in Negro villages," the inhabitants of which "walk through their houses whenever they see fit, dirty, slatternly, idle, ill-smelling by nature. These women I love have less chance to live their own lives in peace than if they were African missionaries. They have a swarm of blacks about them like children under their care, not as Mrs. Stowe's fancy painted them, and they hate slavery worse than Mrs. Stowe does. . . . The Mrs. Stowes have the plaudits of crowned heads; we take our chances, doing our duty as best we may among the woolly heads. My husband supported his plantation by his law practice. Now it is running him in debt. Our people have never earned their own bread. Take this estate, what does it do, actually? It all goes back in some shape to what are called slaves here, called operatives or tenants or peasantry elsewhere. I doubt if ten thousand in money ever comes to this old gentleman's hands. When Mrs. Chesnut married South, her husband was as wealthy as her brothers-in-law. How is it now? Their money has accumulated for their children. This old man's goes to support a horde of idle dirty Africans, while he is abused as a cruel slave-owner."

In this she is unfair to the New Englanders: she forgets that Elijah Lovejoy has been murdered for his Abolitionist agitation, that Garrison has been dragged through the streets of Boston and Whittier stoned by a mob in New Hampshire, and that Sumner has had his head broken and been incapacitated for two years by a furious South Carolinian; and she of course had not the least idea of the years of anxiety and hardship which, in the case of Harriet Beecher Stowe, had produced her explosive book. Yet there is plenty of evidence in Mrs. Chesnut's diary that slavery had become to the Southerners a handicap and a burden. At one point she makes the assertion that "not one third of our volunteer army are slave-owners" and that "not one third of that third fail to dislike slavery as much as Mrs. Stowe or Horace Greeley."

Mrs. Chesnut notes again and again the apparent impassivity of the Negroes in relation to what is going on. "We have no reason to suppose a Negro knows there is a war," she is still able to write in November, 1861. "I do not speak of the war to them; on that subject, they do not believe a word you say. A genuine slave-owner, born and bred, will not be afraid of Negroes. Here we are mild as the moonbeams, and as serene; nothing but Negroes around us, white men all gone to the army." Yet one of their neighbors, a Cousin Betsey, has been murdered only a few weeks before. This old lady, whose domestic servants are said to have been "pampered" and "insubordinate," has been smothered in her bed by two of them after her son has promised them a thrashing. The elder Mrs. Chesnut, a Northerner, had been frightened in her youth by the stories of the Haiti rebellion, and, as a result, now treats every Negro "as if they were a black Prince Albert or Queen Victoria." She makes her daughter-in-law uneasy by incessantly dwelling, as the younger woman says, "upon the transcendent virtues of her colored household, in full hearing of the innumerable Negro women who literally swarm over this house," then by suddenly saying to the family at dinner, " 'I warn you, don't touch that soup! It is bitter. There is something wrong about it!' The men who waited at table looked on without a change of face." But the staff of the Chesnut household finally begins to crack in an unexpected place. James Chesnut is very much dependent on his Negro valet Lawrence, who is always at his side, always, says Mrs. Chesnut, with "the same bronze mask," who darns socks and has made Mrs. Chesnut a sacque, who is miraculous in his resourcefulness at producing, despite wartime shortages, whatever is wanted in the way of food — even to that special rarity, ice for mint juleps and sherry cobblers. But in February, 1864, while the Chesnuts are living in Richmond, Lawrence turns up at breakfast drunk. When he is ordered to move a chair, he raises it over his head and smashes the chandelier. His master, whose self-control is always perfect, turns to his wife and says, "Mary, do tell Lawrence to go home. I am too angry to speak to him!" But Lawrence "will soon be back," Mrs. Chesnut confides to her diary, "and when he comes he will say: 'Shoo! I knew Mars' Jeems could not do without me!' And indeed he cannot."

In the meantime Colonel Higginson and his fellow Yankees were exploring the abandoned plantations of the South Carolinian Sea Islands. We hear something from Mrs. Chesnut of the families to which these had belonged. Of the Middletons, on whose place Charlotte Forten had admired the magnolia tree and from whose house she had taken the bathtub, Mrs. Chesnut writes as follows: "Poor Mrs. Middleton has paralysis. Has she not had trouble enough? . . . Their plantation and house at Edisto destroyed [it had actually been plundered but not destroyed], their house in Charleston burned, her children scattered, starvation in Lincolnton, and all as nothing to the one dreadful blow — her only son killed in Virginia. Their lives are washed away in a tide of blood. There is nothing to show they were ever on earth." And of another expropriated family from the coastland taken over by the Northerners: "Captain Barnwell came to see us," she writes. "We had a dinner for them at Mulberry. Stephen Elliott was there. He gave us an account of his father's plantation at Beaufort, from which he has just returned: 'Our Negroes are living in great comfort. They were delighted to see me, and treated me with overflowing affection. They waited on me as before, gave me beautiful breakfasts and splendid dinners; but they firmly and respectfully informed me: "We own this land now. Put it out of your head that it will ever be yours again."' "

The Negroes on the Chesnut plantation, with the exception of one boy who goes off with the Yankees, all, however, remain loyal to the family when Sherman's army comes through Camden. This has not always been the case with the slaves of their neighbors, and an annoying problem presents itself when the black women run away and drop off their children beside the road. It is with somewhat mixed feelings that their former owners greet the efforts of a well-meaning person who has collected these abandoned babies and brought them back in a cart. The soldiers of the Northern army have bayoneted the runaway women if they proved to be an encumbrance; eighteen corpses are found. And the Chesnuts have been fortunate, also, in that their house has not been burned down. Neither James nor his wife was then at home. He had sent her to North Carolina to be out of the line of Sherman's march, and they had been fully prepared to lose everything. But when at last they make their way back to Camden, through a countryside with no sign of habitation except the "tall, blackened chimneys," they find that the house is still standing, though the horses have all been driven off and the road to Charleston is strewn with their books and letters and papers. One side of the house has been badly damaged: every window broken, every bell torn down, every door smashed in, and every piece of furniture demolished. But this wreckage had been arrested when Sherman, in one of his relentings, decided that it had gone far enough. "It was a sin," he had told his soldiers, "to destroy a fine old house like this, whose owner was over ninety years old." Miss Chesnut has behaved splendidly. When a Yankee officer entered and sat down at the fire to warm himself, she said to him "politely," " 'Rebels have no rights. But I suppose you have come to rob us. Please do so and go. Your presence agitates my blind old father.' The man had jumped up in a rage: 'What do you take me for? A thief?' " Miss Chesnut is proud of the fact that they have lost, aside from the horses, the smashed furniture and the scattered books, only two gold-headed canes and two bottles of champagne.

The old man survived everything with dignity. His wife, also over ninety, had died before the final disaster. His daughter-in-law remembers having seen him in the mornings sauntering down the wide corridor from his own to his wife's bedroom, with a large hairbrush in his hand. He would take his stand on the rug before the fire in her room and, as he brushed his few remaining white locks, would roar out to her his morning compliments so loudly that it shook the panes in the windows of the room above. One morning, after her mother-in-law's death, Mary Chesnut, passing the door of Mrs. Chesnut's room, saw her father-in-law kneeling and sobbing beside the empty bed. When we hear of him last, he is ninety-three, but "apparently as strong as ever and certainly as resolute of will." His Negro servant Scipio has never deserted old Chesnut: "six feet two, a black Hercules and as gentle as a dove in all his dealings with the blind old master, who boldly strides forward, striking with his stick to feel where he is going." "Partly patriarch, partly *grand seigneur*," his daughter-in-law sums him up, "this old man is of a species that we will see no more; the last of the lordly planters who ruled this Southern world. His manners are unequalled still, but underneath this smooth exterior lies the grip of a tyrant whose will has never been crossed."

On the eve of Lee's surrender, when Mary Chesnut has taken refuge in North Carolina, her husband comes to see her and tells her than many of their own fellow-Southerners are rejoicing over the ruin of the planter class. "They will have no Negroes now to lord it over!" he says he has heard one of them say. "They can swell and peacock about and tyrannize now over only a small parcel of women and children, those only who are their very own family."

Contents

	INTRODUCTION	xxiii
I	CHARLESTON	1
II	MONTGOMERY	5
III	CAMDEN	23
IV	CHARLESTON	27
V	CAMDEN	41
VI	MONTGOMERY	45
VII	CAMDEN	53
VIII	RICHMOND	65
IX	FAUQUIER WHITE SULPHUR SPRINGS	76
X	RICHMOND	81
XI	CAMDEN	134
XII	COLUMBIA	178
XIII	CAMDEN	181
XIV	COLUMBIA	185
XV	FLAT ROCK	274
XVI	MEMORIES	277
XVII	CAMDEN	318
XVIII	RICHMOND	321
XIX	CAMDEN	403
XX	COLUMBIA	416
XXI	LINCOLNTON, N.C.	478
XXII	CHESTER	507
XXIII	CAMDEN	527
	INDEX	549

Introduction

In preparation for writing *House Divided*, and during the progress of the work, I added to my library many books dealing with civilian life in the South during the War of the Sixties. *A Diary from Dixie*, by Mary Boykin Chesnut, was the fourth out of more than three hundred such purchases, and the second of these books which I read. During the actual writing of *House Divided*, I never began a new chapter without first looking into the Diary to see what Mrs. Chesnut had had to say about the period with which I was about to deal.

As a consequence, anyone who read the novel will find in the Diary much that is familiar. More than that, the reader of *House Divided* and of this Diary will soon begin to recognize a strong resemblance, spiritually and psychologically, between Mrs. Chesnut and Cinda Dewain. They might have been sisters; and certainly many of their experiences and their thoughts were shared.

So when I was invited to edit a new edition of the Diary, which would include passages that had been eliminated from the earlier edition, I eagerly accepted the task. According to the Introduction to the earlier edition, this Diary was first edited by Mrs. Chesnut herself. She had written it from day to day during the war, on whatever scraps of paper were available; but after the War, being an intelligent woman, she knew that the Diary should be preserved in some orderly form. So she set herself the task of transcribing the original in a series of small notebooks, and — doubtless eliding some portions as she went along — she did so.

The original edition of the Diary filled some four hundred book pages. I anticipated that the complete diary would be somewhat longer; but I was not prepared for the actuality. The original edition contained about 150,000 words; the manuscript copy of the complete

Diary contains nearer 400,000. Since Mrs. Chesnut herself made the first copy from the original, the magnitude of the task suggests the vigor of her character.

Mrs. Chesnut died in 1886, bequeathing the Diary — which filled about fifty notebooks — to her friend Isabella D. Martin. In 1904, Miss Martin and Myrta Lockett Avary edited the Diary for publication. The portions which they eliminated — either because they might offend persons then living, or because they shocked the editors, or because they presented a picture of conditions under slavery which the editors hoped might be forgotten — proved when the whole Diary was copied to be its most interesting passages. The romance of General Hood and "Buck" Preston, for instance, is barely hinted at in the published Diary, though in the complete version it flavors scores of pages; the most human and appealing passages in letters written by Mrs. Jefferson Davis were elided; while the occasional faintly off-color but deliciously amusing remarks of Mrs. Chesnut or her friends vanished completely.

The complete Diary reveals to the present editor a hitherto undiscovered country; a Southern society where remote and untouchable ladies in crinoline relish a scandalous piece of gossip or a *risqué* jest, and where gentlemen may share these well-spiced conversations. Here are men and women of flesh and blood, infinitely more human in their faults and their fancies, their flirtations and frivolities, their sins and their sorrows, their laughter and their tears than the lay figures which march solemnly through the pages of so many books of fact or fiction dealing with the Southern scene. The old woman who held a Bed of Justice every Monday morning and switched her slaves with a lively zeal, the slaves who murdered their mistress, the beautiful young lady nicknamed "Boozer" who was thought capable of marrying the whole Union army, the flirtations of Department clerks and Confederate officers away from home, the idyllic beauty of life on Mulberry plantation and why Mrs. Chesnut hated it, the lively and heart-warming story of the deep fine love between Mrs. Chesnut and her husband, the hopes of 1861 that became the fears of 1864 and the hunger and hardship and despair of 1865, the scars left by Sherman on the Southern scene and the Southern mind and heart, the war within a war between Jeff Davis and his enemies, the noble and the base, the cruel and the tender, the weaklings and the strong; they are all here in abounding measure.

If the only true history concerns itself not so much with what statesmen and generals *did* at a given time as with what men and women *were*, then this Diary is a masterpiece of history in the highest and fullest sense.

The writer of fiction based on history is free, as long as he seeks out and respects the truth, to supplement that truth with details based on probabilities and supplied by his imagination. But to be able to do that, he must be familiar not only with what is historically recorded as having happened in his period; he must seek to know what ordinary people during that period were thinking. Such diaries as that of Mrs. Chesnut are, to this end, invaluable.

They are, by the same token, rare; for Mrs. Chesnut was a rare woman. As a diarist she had unusual qualifications. In the first place, she was well informed; she knew most, if not all the leaders of the Confederate Government, and of the Confederate Army; she knew the way of life of the well-born and the wealthy southern planter; she knew not a little about the way of life of poorer white people; and she knew the Negro. In the second place she was intelligent, and she thought her own thoughts. In the third place, she was articulate, expressing herself easily and clearly. And finally, she was an interesting individual, a devoted wife and a loyal friend without being blind to the faults of her husband, or of her friends — or of herself. She had a bluntness which must have dealt many wounds, and a warmth which must have made it easy to forgive her blunt speech.

She was well and widely read. She knew Shakespeare, Thackeray, George Eliot, Eugène Sue, Coleridge, Lady Mary Montagu, Oliver Wendell Holmes, Milton, Schiller; she was able to compare Bulwer's translation of Schiller with those made by Coleridge, Mrs. Austin and Carlyle; she speaks of reading "Fanny." "There can be no worse book than 'Fanny,' " she says; and having shortly before that re-read *Uncle Tom's Cabin* she adds in characteristic vein: "It is not nastier or coarser than Mrs. Stowe, but then it is not written in the interests of philanthropy!" She read Russell's *India* and remarked: "Saintly folks, these English, when their blood is up." She read *Les Miserables;* she thought of writing a novel, of translating a French play; having read *Romola*, she refused to believe that George Eliot was a "fallen woman." She thought *Romola* a better novel than *Adam Bede* or *Silas Marner;* she discussed the relative merits of Milton and Goethe; she read Dumas's *Maîtres d'Armes* in the original French.

But her principal interest was people, so this diary is a completely human document, and one which deserves immortality. An afternoon with Mr. Pepys or with John Evelyn, if I could have them for the asking, would not tempt me; but I would give a good deal to listen for an afternoon to Mrs. Chesnut.

She was, above all, the chronicler of the contemporary. Someone asked her: "Why do you write in your diary at all, if as you say you have to contradict today what you wrote yesterday?" She replied: "Because I like to tell the tale as it was told to me. I write current rumour. I do not vouch for anything." Her Diary is invaluable as a record of what people believed and felt and said, not years after the fact, but at the time.

This version of the Diary is approximately twice as long as the original Appleton edition; but even this is not complete, since the present editor has elided many poems and quotations, and condensed or omitted most of the letters which Mrs. Chesnut transcribed. Also he has blue-pencilled incidents lacking either human or historical interest. These cuts have been particularly extensive after the assassination of Lincoln. By these various eliminations, the Diary has been reduced in length approximately one fourth. The attempt has been to make the Diary easily readable, without doing violence to Mrs. Chesnut's own words; so occasionally a noun or a verb has been supplied, or a phrase inserted or transposed; and the dashes which were her usual form of punctuation have been replaced by more conventional marks. Negro dialect has been left as she wrote it.

There are hundreds of names in the Diary, and perhaps one third of the individuals who here have speaking parts are familiar to students of the period. To identify by footnotes every governor who is mentioned, and every member of the President's cabinet or his military family would clutter the book and weary the reader, so footnotes have been held to a minimum; but some who appear in this Diary chiefly because they were among Mrs. Chesnut's friends and intimates may here be mentioned. The order is, of course, alphabetical.

Boykin: Ten Boykins are named. The Boykin plantation was near Mulberry, the Chesnut plantation south of Camden; and the two families were intimate.

Brewster: This gentleman, a Texan who had held office in his home state, seems to have served for a while on General Hood's staff; but beyond that, though he appears scores of times in Mrs. Chesnut's pages, he seems to have been undistinguished.

Clay: Clement Clay of Alabama served in the United States Senate, succeeding Jere Clemens in 1853; and Mrs. Clay wrote her reminiscences of the period under the title: *A Belle of the Fifties.*

Hampton: General Wade Hampton was, before the War, perhaps the wealthiest man in the South. He became one of the Confederacy's great cavalry leaders. The editor has never before seen in print any hint of his rebuff by General Lee, which is here recorded. During Reconstruction, his wisdom and his organizing capacities were largely responsible for the re-establishment of settled government in South Carolina. Eleven members of the family are mentioned by Mrs. Chesnut. Millwood, the splendid Hampton mansion five miles from Columbia, was burned by Sherman's soldiers.

Martin: Isabella Martin, the "irrepressible Isabella" of the Diary, was the daughter of the Reverend William Martin, who was a founder of the first Wayside Hospital in Columbia. Mrs. Chesnut's regard for her was evidenced when she bequeathed to Miss Martin the original Diary.

Preston: Sally Buchanan Campbell Preston, under her nickname, "Buck," probably appears in the Diary more frequently than any other of Mrs. Chesnut's friends. She was the daughter of General John S. Preston of Columbia, Chief of the Conscript Bureau during the later years of the War. Her mother and her sister Mary, who married Dr. John Darby, were equally Mrs. Chesnut's friends.

Randolph: Mrs. George W. Randolph was the wife of the third Confederate Secretary of War, who had distinguished himself by his handling of the artillery in the skirmish at Big Bethel in June, 1861.

Wigfall: Louis T. Wigfall was United States Senator from Texas, resigning when Texas seceded. His daughter Louise, the beautiful "Louly" of the Diary, married D. Giraud Wright and wrote her memoirs under the title, *A Southern Girl in '61.*

Williams: Mrs. David R. Williams was Mrs. Chesnut's beloved sister "Kate." The present Mr. and Mrs. David R. Williams live at Mulberry Plantation; and it is largely through their interest and co-operation that this complete edition of the Diary is published.

Mrs. Chesnut has drawn, in the Diary, her own portrait. She was born in 1823 and was the daughter of Stephen Decatur Miller, a distinguished South Carolinian who served his state as Governor, in the National House of Representatives, and in the Senate. In 1840, when she was seventeen, she married James Chesnut, Jr. He was the son of Colonel James Chesnut, and was destined to a distinguished career in public life which culminated in his appointment to the United States Senate, and in his military service of the Confederacy as an aid to President Davis and as a Brigadier General.

He and Mrs. Chesnut had no children. From the time of their marriage until Mr. Chesnut's appointment to the Senate, a year or two before the War, they lived at Mulberry Plantation, the home of General Chesnut's father and mother, just outside Camden, South Carolina. After the War they built Sarsfield, near Mulberry. General Chesnut died there in 1885, Mrs. Chesnut in 1886.

B. A. W.

July 1949

I

Charleston

FEBRUARY 15th, 1861. — I came to Charleston on November 7th and then went to Florida to see my mother. On the train, just before we reached Fernandina, a woman called out: "That settles the hash!" Tanny touched me on the shoulder and said: "Lincoln's elected." "How do you know?" "The man over there has a telegram." Someone cried: "Now that the black radical Republicans have the power I suppose they will Brown * us all."

I have always kept a journal, with notes and dates and a line of poetry or prose, but from today forward I will write more. I now wish I had a chronicle of the two delightful and eventful years that have just passed. Those delights have fled, and one's breath is taken away to think what events have since crowded in.

It was while I was in Florida, on November 11th that (alas!) my husband resigned his seat in the Senate of the United States. I might not have been able to influence him, but I should have tried.

In Florida I spent two weeks amid hammocks and everglades, oppressed and miserable. One evening while we were at dinner, Stephen brought in some soldiers from an encampment near there, the Montgomery Blues. The poor fellows said they were "very soiled blues." They had been a month before Fort Pickens and not allowed to attack it. Colonel Chase, who commanded the Alabama troops there, they accused of too great affection for the Fort. He built it himself, and

*John Brown's seizure of Harper's Ferry and his attempt to set up a slave republic had revived throughout the South the ever-present fear of a slave rebellion.

could not bear it should be proved not impregnable. Colonel Lomax telegraphed Governor Moore if he might not try "Chase or no Chase." The Governor of Alabama was inexorable. They said "we have been down there and worked like niggers, and as soon as the fun seems about to begin, we are replaced by regulars." Sadly discomfited they were. My mother packed a huge hamper of eatables for the Colonel, and the subalterns amiably played a game of billiards. I dare say they would fight, as they eat, like Trojans.

Colonel Chase had blazed out a road behind them. The Montgomery Blues had gone there to take Fort Pickens, and here was a road ready for them to retreat if they were attacked! They resented the insulting insinuation which they scented in the "blazing" of that road. Indeed it was not needed, if they felt an inclination to run. Stephen took a servant there who had never seen anything larger than a double barrel shotgun. When they fired the evening gun, he dashed off for home and got there by daybreak next day, cured of all tendency toward soldiering forever.

I saw a few men running up a wan Palmetto flag, and shouting, though prematurely: "South Carolina has seceded!" I was overjoyed to find Florida so sympathetic, but Tanny told me the young men were Gadsdens, Porchers and Gourdins, names as inevitably South Carolinian as Moses and Lazarus are Jewish.

In Charleston my room was immediately above the dining-room where Mayor Bartow and a delegation from Savannah were having a supper given to them. The noise of the speaking and cheering was pretty hard on a tired traveller. Suddenly I found myself listening with pleasure. Voice, tone, temper, sentiment, language, all were perfect. I sent Tanny to see who it was that spoke. He came back saying, "Mr. Alfred Huger, the old postmaster." He may not have been the wisest or wittiest man there, but he certainly made the best after-supper speech.

We went to Camden. I travelled with a racking headache and a morphine bottle — and with Colonel Colcock and Judge Magrath, who were sent to Columbia by their fellow-citizens in the Low Country to hasten the slow movement of the wisdom assembled in the State Capital. Their message was, they said: "Go ahead, dissolve the Union, and be done with it, or it will be worse for you." The fire in the rear is hottest; and yet people talk of the politicians leading! Everywhere that I have been, people have been complaining bitterly of slow and luke warm public leaders.

It is hard for me to believe these people are in earnest. They are not putting the young, active, efficient, in place anywhere. Whenever there is an election, they hunt up some old fossil who was ages ago laid on the shelf. There never was such a resurrection of the dead and forgotten. This does not look like business. My first doubts came when I saw who were elected to any office and that efficiency was never thought of but political maneuvering still ruled. My father was a South Carolina nullifier, Governor of the state at the time of the nullification row, and then United States Senator; so I was of necessity a rebel born. My husband's family being equally pledged to the Union party rather exasperated my zeal. Yet I felt a nervous dread and horror of this break with so great a power as the United States, but I was ready and willing. South Carolina had been rampant for years. She was the torment of herself and everybody else. Nobody could live in this state unless he were a fire-eater. Come what would, I wanted them to fight and stop talking. South Carolinians had exasperated and heated themselves into a fever that only blood-letting could ever cure. It was the inevitable remedy. So I was a seceder.

This Judge Magrath who travelled with us is a local celebrity of whom likenesses were suspended, in the frightfullest signpost-style of painting, across various thoroughfares in Charleston. The happy moment seized by the painter to depict him was while Magrath was in the act of dramatically tearing off his robes of office in rage and disgust at Lincoln's election. The painting is in vivid colors, the canvas huge, and the rope hardly discernible. He is depicted with a countenance flaming with contending emotions — rage, disgust and disdain.

At Kingsville we encountered James Chesnut,* who had resigned his seat in the United States Senate. Said someone spitefully: "Mrs. Chesnut does not look at all resigned." For once in her life, Mrs. Chesnut held her tongue. She was dumb. In going back to Mulberry to live, she was indeed offering up her life.

Secession was delayed because the men, who are all, like Governor Pickens, "insensible to fear," are very sensible in case of smallpox. There being now an epidemic of smallpox in Columbia, they adjourned to Charleston. While we were in Camden we were busy and frantic with excitement, drilling, marching, arming, and wearing blue cockades. Red sashes, guns and swords were ordinary fireside accompaniments. So wild were we, I saw at a grand parade of the home guard a

* Kingsville was the junction point where two railroads, one from Wilmington and one from Charleston, met on their way to Columbia.

woman, the wife of a man who says he is a secessionist *per se*, driving about to see the drilling of this new company, although her father was buried the day before.

We soon returned to Charleston and I spent Christmas at Combahee, a beautiful country seat. Mrs. Charles Lowndes was sitting with us when Mrs. Kirkland brought in a copy of the Secession Ordinance. I wonder if my face grew as white as hers. She said after a moment: "As our day, so shall our strength be." They say I had better take my last look at beautiful Combahee. It is on the coast, open to gunboats.

Two days after Christmas, Mrs. Gidière came in quietly from her marketing and in her neat, incisive manner exploded this bombshell: "Major Anderson has moved into Fort Sumter,* while Governor Pickens slept serenely." The row is fast and furious now. State after state is taking its forts and fortresses. They say if we had been left out in the cold alone, we might have sulked a while; but back we would have had to go, and would merely have fretted and fumed and quarrelled among ourselves. We needed a little wholesome neglect. Anderson has blocked that game, but now our sister states have joined us, and we are strong. I give the condensed essence of the table-talk: "Anderson has united the Cotton States. Now for Virginia! Anderson has opened the ball." Those who want a row are in high glee. Those who dread it are glum and thoughtful enough.

Yet we can still smile at a good joke. Tom River has a horn blown every morning before day to wake up his people. Dr. Tom and Sally have no clock, so when they hear the horn, they get up and prepare breakfast. Some time ago — they generally go to bed at dark — they heard the horn, got up and cooked their breakfast and ate it, and still had to wait for day. You can imagine those two sitting by the fire, with little to say, waiting and waiting! The horn had been blown at ten o'clock at night for a Negro to take a dose of medicine.

We go now to Montgomery, the capital of the Confederacy.

* Major Anderson, in the view of many Southerners, committed an act of aggression when, on December 26, 1860, he abandoned Fort Moultrie, which he considered an untenable position, and under cover of darkness moved his entire command a quarter of a mile across Charleston Harbor to garrison Fort Sumter.

II

Montgomery

FEBRUARY 19th, 1861. — The brand new Confederacy is making or remodelling its Constitution. Everybody wanted Mr. Davis to be either General-in-Chief or President. Keitt and Boyce and a party preferred Howell Cobb for President, and the fire-eaters *per se* wanted Barnwell Rhett.

I am despondent once more. If I thought them in earnest because at first they put their best in front, what now? We have to meet tremendous odds by pluck, activity, zeal, dash, endurance of the toughest, military instinct. We have to choose born leaders of men, who could attract love and secure trust. Everywhere political intrigue is as rife as in Washington.

Cecil's saying of Sir Walter Raleigh that he could "toil terribly" was an electric touch. Above all, let the men who are to save South Carolina be young and vigorous. While I was reflecting on what kind of men we ought to choose, I fell on Clarendon; and it was easy to construct my man out of his portraits. What has been, may be again, so the men need not be purely ideal types.

Mr. Toombs * told us a story of General Scott and himself. He said he was dining in Washington with Scott, who seasoned every dish and every glass of wine with the eternal refrain, "Save the Union; the Union must be preserved." Toombs remarked that he knew why the Union was so dear to the General, and illustrated his point by a steamboat anecdote; an explosion, of course. While the passengers were struggling

* Robert Toombs, then Confederate Secretary of State, was the only man in that first cabinet who opposed the attack on Sumter. He predicted that the attack would unite the North and prove fatal to the Confederacy.

in the water a woman ran up and down the bank crying: "Oh, save the red-headed man!" The red-headed man was saved, and his preserver, after landing him, noticed with surprise how little interest in him the woman who had made such moving appeals seemed to feel. He asked her, "Why did you make that pathetic outcry?" She answered: "Oh, he owes me ten thousand dollars." "Now, General," said Toombs, "the Union owes you seventeen thousand dollars a year!" I can imagine the scorn on old Scott's face.

I do not allow myself vain regrets or sad forebodings. This Southern Confederacy must be supported now by calm determination and cool brains. We have risked all, and we must play our best, for the stake is life or death.

FEBRUARY 25th. — I find everyone working very hard here. As I dozed on the sofa last night, I could hear the scratch, scratch of my husband's pen as he wrote at the table until midnight.

After church today, Captain Ingraham called. He dared to express regrets that he had had to leave the United States Navy. He had been stationed for two years in the Mediterranean, where he liked best to be, and meant to take his daughters to Florence. Then came Abraham Lincoln, and rampant Black Republicanism, and he must leave all that for South Carolina. He says we lack everything necessary in naval gear to retake Fort Sumter.

At dinner Judge Withers * was loudly abusive of Congress. He said: "They have trampled the Constitution underfoot! They have provided President Davis with a house!" He was disgusted, too, with the folly of parading the President at the inauguration in a coach drawn by six white horses. Mrs. Fitzpatrick made herself conspicuous by being the only lady who sat with the Congress. After the inaugural, she poked Jeff Davis in the back with her parasol that he might turn and speak to her. What a woman!

What a pity the Judge will be so harsh and abusive! He frightens me. Today he called the people he represents, the Kershaw District, fools and knaves. Mr. Chesnut lost his patience at last and said: "If I thought so, I would resign and not represent such people. I would not hold office an hour with such an opinion of my countrymen."

*Judge Thomas J. Withers was an intimate friend of Stephen Decatur Miller, Mrs. Chesnut's father; and he married Elizabeth Boykin, who was Mrs. Chesnut's aunt. His high temper and his sarcastic tongue were as famous as his kind heart and his affectionate nature. He, Joseph Kershaw and James Chesnut were members of the Secession Convention.

A Mr. Martin came in with the latest news, a telegram from Governor Pickens to the President. "A war steamer is lying off the Charleston bar laden with reinforcements for Fort Sumter, and what must we do?" Answer: "Use your own discretion!" Pickens's discretion! There is faith for you.

Trescot writes that on the 22nd, Anderson fired thirty-four guns for all the original United States, in utter scorn of our Confederate States. Insolent wretch! I do not write to Trescot, because he was too "Frenchy" in some of his anecdotes to me. My silence is forever.

Everybody who comes here wants an office, and the many who are disappointed raise a cry of corruption against the few who are successful. I thought we had left all that in Washington.

"Constitution" Browne says he is going to Washington for twenty-four hours. I mean to send five dollars by him to Mary Garnett for bonnet ribbons. If they take him up as a traitor, he may cause a civil war. Mr. Chesnut told him not to make himself a bone of contention.

Everybody means to go into the army. If Sumter is attacked, then Jeff Davis's troubles will begin. The Judge says a military despotism would be best for us, anything to prevent a triumph of the Yankees. All right, but every man objects to any despot but himself.

FEBRUARY 26th. — Mr. Chesnut returned from what he called a perfectly delightful dinner with the Louisiana delegation. "Constitution" Browne is appointed Assistant Secretary of State, and so does not go to Washington. There was at the breakfast table the man who advertised for a wife, with the wife so obtained. She was ugly as sin.* We dine at Mr. Pollard's and go to a ball afterward at Judge Bibbs's. The New York Herald says Lincoln stood before Washington's picture at his inauguration, which was taken by the country as a good sign. They must be frantic for a good sign!

FEBRUARY 27th. — Mr. De Leon called, fresh from Washington, and says General Scott is using all his power and influence to prevent officers from the South resigning their commissions, promising that they shall never be sent against us in case of war. Captain Ingraham, in his short, curt way, said: "That will never do. If they take their government's pay they must do its fighting."

Dined at the Pollards'. Very pleasant, but I can give a better dinner than that! Mr. Robert Barnwell took me down. I sat with a Mr. Robert Smith, who had a pretty wife opposite. He told me several funny tales and is very handsome, but he told me he was a little tight

* Former editors of the Diary changed this to "She was not pretty."

when something or other happened! I always feel as if a man had no moral sense of right or wrong, or even decency, when he alludes to his own intoxication. Came home and found the Judge and Governor Moore waiting to go with me to the Bibbs's. There Mrs. Hunter told us a joke that made me sorry I had come.

FEBRUARY 28th. — In the drawing-room a Mrs. Saxon abused South Carolina till she found I was a South Carolinian and took it back. She spoke of her letters being printed, but she used "incredible" for "incredulous," and "was" for "were." A fine writer she must have been.

We laughed over a piece in the New York Herald today which said James Chesnut, Jr., was the only son of one of the wealthiest Carolinians, that his father owned a thousand Negroes and could not in a day ride over his lands.

Mr. Chesnut and I a day or two ago discovered a nice book shop. I went there this morning and bought "Evan Harrington" and two numbers of Blackwood's — and passed Edward Taylor twice, but fortunately he did not know me!

Brewster says the war specks are growing in size. Nobody at the North, or in Virginia, believes we are in earnest. They think we are sulking and that Jeff Davis and Stephens are getting up a very pretty little comedy. The Virginia delegates were insulted at the peace conference; Brewster said, "kicked out." He says every word the papers tell about Lincoln's vulgarity is true, and his wife and son are as bad.

Yesterday after dinner a Mrs. Lafayette Borland Harns called, a beautiful woman. I met her twenty years ago when I was coming back from Mississippi, and I remember now her amazement at the attentions Robert Campbell, then unmarried, devoted to me in spite of her attractions. I never was handsome and I wonder what my attraction was, for men did fall in love with me wherever I went.*

I went to supper with Governor Moore. The old sinner has been making himself ridiculous with that little actress Maggie Mitchell. Then Mr. Mallory called. I like him in spite of his unpleasant reputation. He is witty, and seems to have a high opinion of me, but: Captain Ingraham told Mr. Chesnut that he was so notoriously dissolute that a woman was compromised to be much seen with him.

* In a footnote dated 1875, Mrs. Chesnut herself wrote: "Reading this Journal, I find I was a vain and foolish old woman, to record silly flattery of myself; in short, an old idiot."

The Judge thought Jefferson Davis rude to him when the latter was Secretary of War. Mr. Chesnut persuaded the Judge to forego his private wrong for the public good, and so the Judge voted for him; but now his old grudge has come back with an increased venomousness. What a pity to bring the spites of the old Union into this new one! Men are willing to risk an injury to our cause, if they may in so doing hurt Jeff Davis.

MARCH 1st. — Dined today with Mr. Hill from Georgia, and his wife. After he left us she told me he was the celebrated individual who refused to fight a duel with Stephens. She seemed very proud of him for his conduct in the affair. Ignoramus that I am, I had not heard of it.

Mr. Hill and Judge Withers joked each other, after the fashion of elderly persons, about telling their wives of their flirtations. I drove with Jesse James and we picked up a Mrs. Willie Knox whose husband beats her. She was wishing he would go to Pensacola and be shot!

Brewster says Lincoln passed through Baltimore disguised, and at night, and that he was wise to do so, for just now Baltimore is dangerous ground. Senator Stephen A. Douglas told Mr. Chesnut that "Lincoln is awfully clever," and that he had found him a heavy handful.

Went to pay my respects to Mrs. Jefferson Davis. She met me with open arms. We did not allude to anything by which we are surrounded. We eschewed politics and our changed relations. I came home and went to bed after a chat with Mr. Chesnut, which after all is the best fun.

MARCH 3rd. — Everybody of my world in fine spirits. They have one and all spoken in the Congress to their own perfect satisfaction.

The Montgomery Blues are here now. They have presented Stephen with a silver dipper in appreciation of his hospitality when they camped near his home. They were drilling in front of this house. Several of us were in the piazza, second story. To my amazement, the Judge took me aside, and after delivering a panegyric upon himself (and here comes the amazement) he praised my husband to the skies, and said he was the fittest man of all for a foreign mission. Aye, and the farther away they send us from this Congress the better I will like it.

I found Thackeray's "Virginians" very dull. "Vanity Fair" is the best he has done yet, though I'm not sure I don't prefer "Henry Esmond."

Mr. Mallory is not yet confirmed as Secretary of the Navy. The judge thinks Mr. Mallory is attentive to me because he wishes to propitiate Mr. Chesnut and himself and get their votes. As if he were half as attentive to me as he used to be in Washington! I will not let him be, since I have heard of his character! He told me a thing I before suspected from what I saw myself, the affair between Holt and Mrs. Phillips. What a mad, bad woman she is. These men who so often dine here are so clever and witty. No wonder the solemnity and trifles of Mulberry bored me so. But I have to smooth things among them sometimes. I wish Mr. Mallory would not tell me so much of his own flirtation with Mrs. Phillips. I do not think it is as innocent as he pretends, but it is none of my business.

Mrs. Fitzpatrick — the jolly old girl, handsome as ever — was there with her stepson, who is none the less interesting that he has jilted Sally Elmore Taylor.

Saw Mr. Clemens and Nick Davis, social curiosities, since they are anti-secession leaders; then George Sanders and George Deas. The Georges are of the opinion that it is folly to try and take back Fort Sumter from Anderson and the United States; that is, before we are ready. They saw in Charleston the devoted band prepared for the sacrifice, ready to run their heads against a stone wall. Daredevils they were. They had dash and courage enough, but science only could take that Fort; and the Georges shake their heads.

March 4th. — The Washington Congress, they say, has passed peace measures.

At last, according to his wish, I was able to introduce Mr. Hill of Georgia to Mr. Mallory; also Governor Moore and Brewster. The latter is the only man I know in this democratic subdivided republic without a title of some sort. I was the only lady. I must say the stories were rich and racy, though rather strongly spiced for my presence. Mr. Mallory's were the best. They say his mother was a washerwoman, but he is the most refined in the group who surround me here, except my husband. As to the washerwoman mother, "Why not?" demanded the Judge. "She taught him not to go with the great unwashed. Cleanliness next to Godliness, you know."

I have seen a Negro woman sold upon the block at auction. I was walking. The woman on the block overtopped the crowd. I felt faint, seasick. The creature looked so like my good little Nancy. She was a bright mulatto, with a pleasant face. She was magnificently gotten up in silks and satins. She seemed delighted with it all, sometimes ogling the bidders, sometimes looking quite coy and modest; but her mouth never relaxed from its expanded grin of excitement. I dare say the poor thing knew who would buy her. My very soul sickened. It was too dreadful. I tried to reason. "You know how women sell themselves and are sold in marriage, from queens downwards, eh? You know what the Bible says about slavery, and marriage. Poor women, poor slaves."

My latest book, "Evan Harrington," is splendid. One sentence: "Like a true English female, she believed in her own inflexible virtue, but never trusted her husband out of sight."

The New York Herald says: "Lincoln's carriage is not bomb-proof, so he does not drive out." Two flags and a bundle of sticks have been sent him as a gentle reminder. The sticks are to break our heads.

The English are gushingly unhappy as to our family quarrel. Magnanimous of them, for it is their opportunity.

Brewster called Madame Bodisco, who married the English Captain last winter, a Leviathan of Loveliness.

Mr. Mallory came and I said to him: "Be seated. Florida land claims shall not prevent a little chat tonight." The others soon left and the Judge stayed as usual, and had most of the talk, but Mr. Mallory told of the effect upon him of a beautiful woman in Washington who had a claim against the government. The Judge is not a proper person to trust a love tale with; so I left him to his ill-chosen confidant. He must have been intoxicated to have told such a tale either before me or the Judge. Though he said very little, his story might mean a quantity. Mr. Chesnut was making such a stamping overhead that I knew his patience at my long stay was exhausted. I found that Mr. Chesnut was hurt because Mr. Hill said he kept his own counsel. Mr. Chesnut thinks himself an open, frank, confiding person, and he asked me if he was not. Truth required me to say that I knew no more what he thought or felt on any subject now than I did twenty years ago. Sometimes I feel that we understand each other a little, but then up goes the iron wall once more. I don't mean that for a moment he ever gives you the impression of an insincere, or even a cold person; but he is reticent, and like the Indian, too proud to let the world know he feels. I wish he went to church. He is so much finer than the men who do.

MARCH 5th. — We stood on the balcony to see our Confederate Flag go up. Roar of cannon. Miss Sanders complained, and so did Captain

Ingraham, of the deadness of the mob. "It was utterly spiritless," she said. "No cheering, or so little; no enthusiasm." Captain Ingraham suggested: "Gentlemen are apt to be quiet. This was a thoughtful crowd. The true mob element with us just now is hoeing corn." And yet, it is uncomfortable that the idea has gone abroad that we have no joy, no pride in this thing. The Band was playing "Massa's in the Cold, Cold Ground."

Major Deas was busy telling us why he came south. "The New York clubs were so unpleasant now for Southern men," although he had always lived at the North. Respect for his Deas and Izard blood had been so dinned in his ears by his relatives, he could not fail to feel altogether Southern.

Mr. Chesnut told Mr. Mallory that the Senate had confirmed his nomination as Secretary of the Navy. They were standing at my back, I was leaning over the balustrade, watching the Flag. Mr. Mallory did not interrupt what he was saying to me, but continued in the same placid voice. I did not find this very civil to Mr. Chesnut, so I turned. "Had you heard that important fact before?" "No." "And yet you took no notice of Mr. Chesnut's making himself the bearer of good news to you?" The Secretary of the Navy smiled and thanked me with a profound bow. Afterwards Mr. Chesnut told me that Florida, Mr. Mallory's own state, went against him.

Captain Ingraham pulled out of his pocket some verses sent him by a Boston girl. It amounted to this, well rhymed in; that she held a rope ready to hang him, yet still shed tears when she remembered his heroic rescue of Koszta.* Koszta, the rebel! And she calls us rebels too! Depends upon who one rebels against, whether it is heroic to save or not.

Miss Tyler, daughter of ex-President Tyler, ran up our Flag.

I read Lincoln's Inaugural. Comes he in Peace, or comes he in War? Or to tread but one measure as young Lochinvar?

At Mrs. Davis's reception today, it was crowded; too many men of note to attempt to name them. We laughed at the hospitable, non-committal Governor Fitzpatrick. In Washington he was always urging

* Martin Koszta, a Hungarian revolutionist in 1848, came to the United States and took the first steps toward naturalization. On a business trip to Smyrna in 1853, he was seized and imprisoned aboard an Austrian man of war. Captain Ingraham, commanding an American vessel, demanded his release, and was subsequently supported by the State Department. The case established a precedent.

us to come down here and see him at his own home. Now, in Montgomery, when he is so near at hand, he says: "The roads are so bad. . ." Hence our small joke.

Lincoln's aim is to seduce the Border States.

Mr. Barnwell and Mr. Miles called. They showed me some lines, comic enough. Conrad of Louisiana and Barnwell Rhett * of South Carolina are always at words, everlasting speakers and wranglers. The parson being absent, someone suggested The Honorable Barnwell Rhett should lead the prayers. These verses made fun of the suggestion, remarking that in case the Lord did not answer Barnwell Rhett, Conrad certainly would. This helped to pass an evening call merrily. Also they cited Simon Suggs to the Judge, who is always vaunting his own probity and sneering at the venality of everybody else. Simon was always saying: "Integrity is the post I ties to." At camp meeting he got religion, handed round the hat, took the offering to the Lord down into the swamp to pray over it, untied his horse and fled with it, hat, contribution and all.

The Judge laughed loudest of any, and said for a while he would keep all hints of his transcendent honesty to himself. Of course, only political honesty was in question. It seems there is a great difference, but I do not seem to see it.

These people — the natives, I mean — are astounded that I calmly affirm in all truth and candor that if there were awful things in society in Washington, I did not see or hear of them. One must have been hard to please who did not like the people I knew in Washington.

Mr. Chesnut has gone with a list of names to the President: De Treville, Kershaw, Baker, Robert Rutledge. I hope there will be good places in the Army for our list.

An adventure today. A devout lady, one who holds Washington and worldly dissipation in holy horror, dreaded the effect of these Congressmen here. They might make Montgomery a second Washington. When she asked, as they all do, "How do you like Montgomery?" I replied: "Charming! I find it charming!" General Bonham stared. He has been made Commander in Chief of the South Carolina Army. "I will not be fobbed off with that rubbish," he says. "The Governor

* Robert Barnwell Rhett of South Carolina, an orator rivalled only by Yancey of Alabama, was sometimes called The Father of Secession. After secession became a fact, his political influence waned and he was at last completely discredited, even in his own state.

can do all that." He laughs at such a position. "Where is the South Carolina Army that I am to be General of?" he asks, and echo answers, "Where?"

A lady asked me to go with her to make a few visits. A plain-spoken old lady * took my arm as we left her drawing-room; and, restraining me, inquired: "Why are you in such company?" "Why not? She is lovely and pious, and so clever." "Yes, but talked about, you know." "No indeed, I did not know." "It is her pastor. He prays with her, and now he stays with her!" By this time the culprit was safely in her carriage, and the chorus around me was in full blast. I put my hands to my ears and flew out of it all. They screamed after me: "A word to the wise is sufficient!" Now they tell me that my old-lady-informant's baby was born too soon after her marriage. Was there ever such a world?

George Sanders came in, and someone said in an undertone: "The age of chivalry is not past." "What do you mean?" "That man was nominated by President Buchanan for a foreign mission. Some Senator stood up in his place and read a very abusive paper printed by this office-seeker, abusive of a woman, and signed by his name in full. So we would have none of him. His chance was gone forever."

MARCH 8th. — Judge Campbell † of the Supreme Court has resigned. Lord! How they must all have hated to do it. Now we may be sure the bridge is broken. And yet in the Alabama Convention they say Reconstructionists abound and are busy.

Met a distinguished gentleman whom I knew when he was in more affluent circumstances. I was willing enough to speak to him, but when he saw me advancing for that purpose, he suddenly dodged round

* After Mrs. Chesnut had copied her original diary, she destroyed most of that original; but one or two notebooks escaped. In the original of this passage, decidedly more scandalous than her later version, she used names; and she included a reference to a recent bride whose neighbors were "counting months on their fingers."

† Judge Campbell, an Alabama man, acted as an intermediary between commissioners sent by the Confederacy and Secretary of State Seward. Seward assured him that the Government intended to evacuate Fort Sumter on March 15 or soon after; he subsequently repeated these assurances. Early in April, a month after this entry in the diary, Judge Campbell wrote Mr. Seward asking whether this promise would be kept. Mr. Seward replied, on April 7: "Faith as to Sumter fully kept. Wait and see." Next day a message from President Lincoln, announcing that the Fort would be provisioned — and so, obviously, would not be evacuated — was delivered to Governor Pickens of South Carolina and to General Beauregard. The attack on the Fort resulted.

a corner. It was William, Mrs. DeSaussure's *ci devant* coachman. I remember him on his box, driving a pair of handsome bays, dressed sumptuously in blue broadcloth and brass buttons; a stout, respectable, fine looking, middle-aged mulatto. Then, night after night, we met him as fiddler-in-chief at all our parties. He sat in solemn dignity, making faces over his bow and patting his foot with an emphasis that shook the floor. We gave him five dollars a night. That was his price. His mistress never refused to let him play for any party. He had stable boys in abundance. What was his grievance? He was far above any physical fear for his sleek and well fed person. How majestically he scraped his foot, as a sign that he was tuned up and ready to begin.

Now, he is a shabby creature indeed. He must have felt his fallen fortunes when he met me, one who knew him in his prosperity. He ran away, this stately yellow gentleman, from wife and children, home and comfort. My Polly asked him why. "Miss Liza was good to you, I know." "Yes, but Marster was so mean. He wasn't bad, he was mean. In the twenty years I lived in his yard he never gave me a four pence. That is, in money." I wonder who owns him now. He looked forlorn. He has not bettered himself!

I asked Governor Cobb who that beautiful Juliet was, to whom he seemed playing Romeo on the balcony. Mr. Chesnut was shocked at my levity, but Governor Cobb was vastly amused at my question.

Mrs. Fitzpatrick wanted the Postmaster Generalship for the Governor. It was offered to Wirt Adams, who declined to accept it, and now Reagan of Texas has it. This blessed American freedom to go straight to the top of the tree, if you are built for climbing.

March 9th. — Governor Moore brought in, to be presented to me, the President of the Alabama Convention. It seems I knew him before. He said he danced with me at a dancing school ball when I was in short frocks, sash, flounces and wreath of roses. He was one of those clever boys of our neighbors in whom my father saw promise of better things. I was enjoying his conversation immensely, for he was praising my father without stint, when the Judge came in breathing fire and fury. Congress has incurred his displeasure. We are abusing one another as fiercely as ever we abused Yankees. It is disheartening.

Mrs. Childs was here tonight (Mary Anderson from Statesburg) with several children. She is lovely. Her hair is piled up on the top of her head. Fashions from France still creep into Texas across the Mexican border. Mrs. Childs is fresh from Texas. Her husband is an artillery officer, or was. They will be glad to promote him here.

These people were so amusing, so full of western stories. Dr. Boykin behaved strangely. All day he has been gayly driving about with us, and never was a man in finer spirits. Tonight in this brilliant company he sat dead still as if in a trance. Once he waked somewhat. A high public functionary came in with a present for me, a miniature gondola. A perfect Venetian specimen, he said — and said it again and again. In an undertone Dr. Boykin muttered: "That fellow has been drinking." "Why do you think so?" I replied, quite shocked at his rude speech. "Because he has told you exactly the same thing four times."

Wonderful! Some of these great statesmen always tell me the same thing, and have been telling me the same thing ever since we came here.

Mrs. Childs has the sweetest Southern voice, absolute music. But then she has all of the high spirit of those sweet-voiced Carolina women too.

Then Mr. Browne came in with his fine English accent, so pleasant to the ear. He tells us that Washington is not reconciled to the Yankee régime. Mrs. Lincoln means to economize. She informed the major-domo that they were poor, and hoped to save twelve thousand dollars every year from their salary of twenty thousand. Mrs. Browne said Mr. Buchanan's farewell was far more imposing than Lincoln's inauguration.

Mrs. Gwinn sheds many tears; but she will not come South (small blame to her).

So many of these Congressmen have been, and are, Methodist or Baptist preachers. A bad mixture of trades. Tom Cobb, the best of men, in his capacity of preacher is a furious Sabbatarian and tries to have the cars stopped on Sunday. In his capacity of Georgia politician, he went off today, Sunday, to attend a political convention.

I have had a delightfully affectionate long letter from my husband's father. It is refreshing to find he likes me so well.

March 11th. — The drawing-room tonight was full of judges, governors, senators, generals, congressmen. They were exalting John C. Calhoun's hospitality. He allowed every visitor to stay all night at his house, but one ill-mannered person refused to attend family prayers. Mr. Calhoun said to the servant: "Saddle that man's horse and let him go." I remarked that I believed in Mr. Calhoun's profuse hospitality, but not in his family prayers. Mr. Calhoun's piety was of the most philosophical type.

Then I told a story which I picked up in a life of Franklin. He stole it from Jeremy Taylor, who filched it Heavens knows where. Abraham drove out an Eastern traveller because he blasphemed the living God. At night an angel came in quest of the aforesaid guest. "I sent him forth in the wilderness for taking the Lord's name in vain." The affable Archangel answered: "Thus saith the Lord your God; have I borne with this man, lo these many years, and you could not bear with him one night?" The Judge commended me for a quotation aptly used. His good words being, like the Angel's visits, few and far between, are highly esteemed. But our brides were shocked by his anecdote of a pair who quarrelled on a bridge, and the man said, blubbering: "Nancy, take the baby. I will drown myself." But she said: "No, take the baby with you! I want none of your breed left!" What a tale!

The latest news is counted good news; that is, the last man who left Washington tells us that "that serpent, Seward" is in the ascendancy. He is thought to be the friend of peace.

Miss Lane has eleven suitors. One is described as likely to win, but he is too heavily weighted; he has been married before and goes about with children, and he has two mothers. There are limits! Two mothers-in-law!!

Mr. Ledyard spoke to Mrs. Lincoln for the doorkeeper, who almost felt he had a vested right, having been there since Jackson's time, but met with the answer: she had brought her own girl, she must economize.

Mr. Ledyard thought the twenty thousand (and little enough it is) was given to the President of those United States to enable him to live in a proper style, and to maintain an establishment of such dignity as befits the head of that great nation. It is an infamy to economize with the public money and to put it in one's private purse. It puts the nation to an open shame. One would suppose this money was given them as a reward of merit for getting a plurality of votes.

Mrs. Browne was walking with me, while we were airing our indignation against Mrs. Lincoln and her shabby economy. The New York Herald says three only of the *élite* Washington families attended the inauguration ball. The *élite* are so called by the Herald; Parkers, Greens, and I forget who.

Mr. Buchanan and his Secretary of the Interior * had a controversy

* Jacob Thompson of Mississippi, while still Secretary of the Interior under President Buchanan, had early in 1861 gone to Raleigh to urge North Carolina to secede. The "point of personal veracity" may have arisen over Mr. Thompson's statement that the President knew and permitted this action.

on a point of personal veracity. Mr. Browne was cut by President Buchanan for supporting Jake Thompson. Mr. Thompson made me shudder, when I met him in Washington, saying coarsely: "My son can't git shet of the chills." Mrs. Thompson was covered with diamonds. The night before the Jake Thompsons left Washington, they dined at the White House and took an affectionate farewell — as good as acknowledging that the President was right in calling him a liar! Mrs. Browne said: "When Mrs. Thompson told me that, I could not believe my ears. President and Mrs. Buchanan had cut our acquaintance because Mr. Browne denied that Mr. Thompson told a lie. Mrs. Thompson said she felt so ashamed of it she hoped no one would hear of it, knowing the light it would cast upon the controversy."

Mr. Browne told a funny story of American awkwardness in handling titles. A raw statesman inquired of him: "Shall I call Lord Morpeth "My Lord," "The Lord," or "Oh Lord"? That was on the way down the Potomac to Mt. Vernon. Coming back, the American had been made so easy in his mind by mint juleps that he slapped the noble stranger on the back and called him Moppy!

Mrs. Browne was telling how her English friends last summer derided her. "Oh, you are a Yankee girl." She answered: "The Southern people hate Yankees worse than you do." Just then our walk led by that sale of Negroes; the same place that I saw before. "If you can stand that, no other Southern thing need choke you," I said. She said not a word. After all, it was my country and she was an English woman. There are ugly sights all over the world. I could see she was sorry for me in her heart.

The Judge has just come in. He says that last night after Dr. Boykin left came a telegram. His little daughter Amanda had died suddenly. Queer! In some way he must have known it; he changed so suddenly and seemed so careworn and unhappy. He believes in clairvoyance, in magnetism and all that. Certainly there was some terrible foreboding on his part.

March 14th. — "Now this is positive," they say. "Fort Sumter is to be relieved, and we are to have no war." Poor Sumter. Relieved? Not half as much as we would be! After all, this is far too good to be true. If there be no war, how triumphant Mr. Chesnut will be. He is the only man who has persisted from the first that this would be a peaceful revolution. Heaven grant it may be so!

Mr. Browne told us that in the interest of peace, Lincoln came through Baltimore locked up in an Adams Express car. A noble entrance into the government of a free people! He wore a Scotch cap. Baltimore "Plug Uglies" have a bad name.

The women here crowd on all sail. They are covered with jewelry — diamonds especially — from breakfast on to midnight. A man told me: "Lord S——, my sister's fiancé says. . ." [Mrs. Chesnut herself elided the remark, and added:] I was so taken aback by the fact that he was to be "brother-in-law to a three-tailed Bashaw," and that his sister was engaged to a live Lord, that I forgot to ask what the Lord said unto her regarding jewelry in the morning.

Mrs. Davis said to a lady * here of her own age, who was hinting at what she would do if she were a widow: "What! When we see all you could do in your youth and beauty? If your husband is the best you could do when you were fresh and young, what better chance could you hope for now that you are old?" And Madame Flibbertygibbet deserved every word of it.

We went to the Congress. Governor Cobb, who presides over that august body, put Mr. Chesnut in the chair and came down to talk to us. Jolly old soul, he is. He thought that "Romeo and Juliet" scene from the balcony that we interrupted needed an explanation. He told us why the pay of Congressmen was enacted in secret session and why the amount of it was never divulged; to prevent the lodging house and hotel people from making their bills of a size to cover it all. "The bill was sure to correspond with the pay," he said.

In the hotel parlor we had a scene. Mrs. Scott was describing Lincoln, who is of the cleverest Yankee type. She said: "awfully ugly, even grotesque in appearance. The kind who are always at corner stores sitting on boxes, whittling sticks, and telling stories as funny as they are vulgar." Here I interposed to sigh: "But Douglas said one day to Mr. Chesnut 'Lincoln is the hardest fellow to handle I have ever encountered yet.' " Mr. Scott is from California. He said: "Lincoln is an utterly American specimen, coarse, rough and strong. A good-natured, kindly creature, and as pleasant tempered as he is clever. And if this country can be joked and laughed out of its rights, he is the kind-hearted fellow to do it. Now if there be a war and it pinches the Yankee pocket, instead of filling it —" Here a shrill voice came from the next room (which opened upon the one we were in, by

* In the original, quoting the remark, Mrs. Chesnut says: "As Mrs. Jeff Davis once said to me . . ."

folding doors thrown wide open). "Yankees are no more mean and stingy than you are. People at the North are as good as people at the South." The speaker advanced upon us in great wrath. Mrs. Scott apologized and made some smooth, polite remarks, though evidently much embarrassed; but the vinegar face and curly pate refused to receive any concession. She said: "That comes with a very bad grace after what you were saying," and she harangued us loudly for several minutes. Someone in the other room giggled outright. We were quiet as mice. Nobody wanted to hurt her feelings; she was one against so many. If I were at the North I should expect them to belabour us, and should hold my tongue. We separated from the North because of incompatibility of temper. We are divorced, North from South, because we have hated each other so. If we could only separate politely, and not have a horrid fight for divorce.

This poor exile had already been insulted, she said; she was playing Yankee Doodle on the piano before breakfast to soothe her wounded spirits, and the Judge came in and calmly requested her to "leave out the Yankee while she played the Doodle." He said the Yankee end of it did not suit our climate, was totally out of place and had got out of its latitude.

Mrs. Davis does not like her husband being made President. People are hard to please. She says, "General of all the Armies would have suited his temperament better." And then Mrs. Watkins came in to deplore her husband's having been made Adjutant General of the Alabama contingent.

A man said today: "This is nothing. It will soon blow over. It's only a fuss gotten up by that Charleston clique." * Toombs asked him to show his passports, for a man who uses such language is a suspicious character.

Captain Smith Lee wishes "South Carolina could be blown out of water." He does so hate the disrupting of his dearly beloved Navy.

We went to return a call. There they were.† Madame, old, ugly, rich, clever, red hair and blue blood. An heiress, she was. He young, worthless, handsome, good name, good office, small pay. Now she hangs on his arm. He is not allowed to dance with anyone but his wife! She never loses sight of him. He looks dogged and desperate.

* In the original notes, George Sanders was the speaker, and "clique" was "mob."

† In this and the passages immediately following, Mrs. Chesnut does not name the persons to whom she refers.

"Look at them. After all, he earns his money as the Bible says it shall be done, by the sweat of his brow. Any man who had married her money would have to do that." I am reminded that in the world we live in, they who wreck character are not as calumnious as they who are simply idle. The men and the women who have nothing to do, do mischief.

Frightful scene. At this our first call we found the household quarrelling. They did not pay us the compliment to suspend the little unpleasantness for our benefit. On the contrary they seemed to welcome us as witnesses. One called aloud, "By your coming you have averted a tragedy." The other vowed to God with arms extended "that she was a lone woman"! (Here her voice became a scream.) "She had no husband to defend her, but she hoped God might strike her dead if—etc., etc." Here, as she attempted to leave the room, she gave such a lurch I thought God had taken her at her word; but she turned to us, all tears and smiles, and said: "It is only I am so rickety in my legs."

We waited for many days before we had strength to attack our list of "calls to be returned" again.

I met a recent bride, Mrs. Elsbury. She was so very large and handsome and strong; so calm, so covered with a tangle and frizzle frazzle of finery. Silent and grave, she found it all she could do to take care of her cloud of drapery in the crowd. She guarded her dress with her hands, and as it was caught by the passersby, with quiet dignity she unhooked herself. On every side, the tag end of her costume required to be detached from man or woman. Her occupation being to take care of her clothes, like the unkind Jew in the parable, I passed by on the other side.

I wonder if it be a sin to think slavery a curse to any land. Men and women are punished when their masters and mistresses are brutes, not when they do wrong. Under slavery, we live surrounded by prostitutes, yet an abandoned woman is sent out of any decent house. Who thinks any worse of a Negro or mulatto woman for being a thing we can't name? God forgive us, but ours is a monstrous system, a wrong and an iniquity! Like the patriarchs of old, our men live all in one house with their wives and their concubines; and the mulattoes one sees in every family partly resemble the white children. Any lady is ready to tell you who is the father of all the mulatto children in everybody's household but her own. Those, she seems to think, drop from the clouds. My disgust sometimes is boiling over. Thank God for my country women, but alas for the men! They are probably no worse than men everywhere, but the lower their mistresses, the more degraded they must be.

I think this journal will be disadvantageous for me, for I spend my time now like a spider spinning my own entrails, instead of reading as my habit was in all spare moments.

III

Camden

March 18th, 1861. — The day before we left Montgomery, in the midst of a red-hot patriotic denunciation of a great many people South, and everybody North, someone threw open the folding doors suddenly, to be sure that the next room contained no spies nor eavesdroppers. An unexpected tableau; a girl resting in a man's arms, he kissing her lips at his leisure or pleasure. They were on their feet in an instant. She cried, "Oh, he is my cousin! He is married. He is taking me home from school." In her innocence she seemed quite cool about it. He knew better, and was terribly embarrassed. He might well be ashamed of himself.

Governor Moore came and prosed until I yawned myself out. Smith Lee wishes South Carolina blown out of water, the horrid traitor! Mr. Mallory imitated Mr. Holt in love with Mrs. Phillips, like an old pelican slightly ill from eating too much fish. That was exquisite!

We went to a party with the Brownes. At first we stood alone and were gazed at, not pinched as was the Prince. I know my dress was the prettiest in the room. Mrs. Taylor told me her legs behaved so comically because of a weakness in them.

John Chesnut * is a pretty soft-hearted slave owner. He had two Negroes arrested for selling whiskey to his people on his plantation, and buying stolen corn from them. The culprits in jail sent for him.

* John Chesnut was her husband's brother, but this may refer to Johnny, his son, of whom she often speaks. "Old Mr. Chesnut," in the following paragraph, was her husband's father.

He found them (this snowy weather) lying in the cold on a bare floor, and he thought that punishment enough, they having had weeks of it. But they were not satisfied to be allowed to evade justice and slip away. They begged him (and got it) for five dollars to buy shoes to run away in. I said "Why, that is flat compounding a felony." Johnny put his hands in the armholes of his waistcoat and stalked majestically before me. "Woman, what do you know about Law?"

Mrs. Reynolds stopped the carriage today to tell me Kitty Boykin is to be married to Savage Heyward. He has ten children already. These people take the old Hebrew pride in the number of children they have. True colonizing spirit, no danger of crowding here, inhabitants are wanted. Old Mr. Chesnut said today: "Wife, you must feel that you have not been useless in your day and generation. You have now twenty-seven great grandchildren."

MARCH 22nd. — Trying to forget my country's woes, I read the life of Lord Dundonald today. The man is so charming, till the cold wave comes. The shock! A hero must be like Caesar's wife. His hands must be clean from money, or the suspicion of it. A hero who cheats? In money matters! ! !

At my aunt's, I heard her coachman give her a message. "The ladies say I must tell you they father is behaving shamefully. He is disgracing hisself. He had not tasted whiskey for 15 years. He took some as physic a month ago, and he ain't drawed a sober breath since."

MARCH 24th. — I was mobbed yesterday by my own house servants. Some of them are at the plantation, some hired at the Camden Hotel, some here at Mulberry. They agreed to come in a body and beg me to stay at home, to keep my own house once more, and said I ought not to have scattered and distributed them every which way.

I have not been a month in Camden since 1858, so a house here would be for their benefit solely. I asked my cook if she lacked anything on the plantation at the Hermitage.

"Lack anything? I lack everything. What is cornmeal and bacon, milk and molasses? Would that be all you wanted? Ain't I bin living and eating exactly as you does all these years? When I cook fer you didn't I have some of all? Dere now!"

So she doubled herself up laughing, and they all shouted: "Missis, we is crazy for you to stay home."

Armsted, my butler, said he hated the Hotel. Besides, he heard a man there abusing "Marster," but Mr. Clyburn took it up and made him stop short. Armsted said he wanted Marster to know Mr. Clyburn was his friend, "would let nobody say a word behind his back agin him."

Stay here? Not if I can help it! "Festers in provincial sloth." That's the Tennyson way of putting it.

I did Mrs. Browne a kindness. I told those women in Montgomery she was childless now, but that she had lost three children. I hated to leave her all alone. Women have such a contempt for a childless wife. Now they will be all sympathy and kindness. I took away her "reproach among women." Mrs. Chesnut was bragging to me one day, with exquisite taste — to me, a childless wretch — of her twenty-seven grandchildren; and Colonel Chesnut, a man who rarely wounds me, said to her: "You have not been a useless woman in this world." But what of me! God help me, no good have I done to myself or anyone else with the power I boast of so, the power to make myself loved. Where am I now? Where are my friends? I am allowed to have no children.

We came along on Sunday with a Methodist parson, who is also a member of the Congress. Someone said he was using his political legs; his pulpit feet would not move on a Sabbath day.

A man claimed acquaintance with me because he has married an old school friend of mine. "At least she is my present wife." Whispered the Light Brigade: "Has he had them before, or means he to have them hereafter?" We had no time to learn; but our parson friend gravely informed us: "If he is the man I take him to be, he has buried two."

One of our party so far forgot his democratic position toward the public as to wish aloud: "Oh that we had separate coaches, as they have in England; that we could get away from these whiskey-drinking, tobacco-chewing rascals and rabble." All with votes!! Worse, all armed! A truculent crowd, truly, to offend! But each supposed he was one of the gentlemen, to be separated from the others.

The day we left Montgomery a man was shot in the street for some trifle. Mr. Browne was open mouthed in his horror of such ruffian-like conduct. They answered him: "It is the war fever. Soldiers must be fierce. It is the right temper for the times cropping out."

There was tragedy on the way here, too; a mad woman taken from her husband and children. Of course she was mad, or she would not have given her grief words in that public place. Her keepers were along. What she said was rational enough, pathetic, at times heartrending. It excited me so I quietly took opium. It enables me to retain every particle of mind or sense or brains I have, and so quiets my nerves that I can calmly reason and take rational views of things otherwise maddening.

Then a highly intoxicated parson was trying to save the soul of a "bereaved widow," so he addressed her always as "my bereaved friend and widow." The devil himself could not have quoted Scripture more fluently. After the opiate I diligently read my book.

March 19th. — Mulberry. Snow a foot deep. Winter at last, after months of apparently May or June weather. Even the climate, like everything else, is upside down. After that den of dirt and horror, Montgomery Hall, how white the sheets look. Luxurious bed linen once more, and delicious fresh cream with my coffee. I breakfast in bed.

Duelling has been rife in Camden. William M. Shannon challenges Leitner. Rochelle Blair is Shannon's second; Artemus Goodwyn is Leitner's. My husband has been riding hard all day to stop the foolish people. More cropping out of the war spirit, the Western man would say. Mr. Chesnut did arrange the difficulty. There was a Court of Honor and no duel. Mr. Leitner struck Mr. Shannon at a Negro trial. That's the way the row begins. Everybody knows of it. We suggested that Judge Withers should arrest the belligerents. Dr. Boykin and Joe Kershaw were aiding Mr. Chesnut to put an end to this useless risk of life.

IV

Charleston

March 26th, 1861. — Charleston. Yesterday we came down here by rail — as the English say. Such a crowd of Convention men. John Manning dashed in to beg me to reserve the seat by me for a young lady under his charge. "*Place aux dames*," said my husband politely, and went off to seek a seat somewhere else. As soon as we were fairly under way, Governor Manning came back and threw himself cheerfully down in the vacant place. After arranging his umbrella, overcoat, etc., to his satisfaction he coolly remarked: "I am the young lady." He is the handsomest man alive (now that poor William Taber is killed in a duel), and he can be very agreeable. That is, when he pleases. He does not always please.

He seemed to have made his little maneuver principally to warn me of impending danger to my husband's political career. "Every election now will be a surprise. New cliques are not formed yet. The old ones are principally bent upon displacing each other."

"But the Yankees! Those dreadful Yankees!"

"Oh, never mind! We are going to take care of home folks first. How will you like to go back to Mulberry and mind your own business?"

"If I only knew what that was, my business!"

Our round table consists of the Judge, Langdon Cheves, Trescot and ourselves. Here are four of the cleverest men we have. Such very different people, as opposite in every characteristic as the four points of the compass. Langdon Cheves and my husband have more ideas and feelings in common. Mr. Petigru * said of that brilliant Trescot: "He is a man without indignation." Trescot and I laugh at everything.

The Judge, from his life as solicitor and then on the Bench, has learned to look for the darkest motives for every action. His judgment on men and things is always so harsh it shocks and upsets even his best friends. Today he said: "Your conversation reminds me of a flashy second-rate novel." "How?" "By the quantity of French you sprinkle over it. Do you wish to prevent us from understanding you?" "No," said Trescot. "We are using French against Africa. We know the black waiters are all ears now, and we want to keep what we have to say dark. We can't afford to take them in our confidence, you know."

This explanation Trescot gave with great rapidity and many gestures toward the men standing behind us. Still speaking the French language, his apology was exasperating. So the Judge glared at him and in unabated rage turned to talk with Mr. Cheves, who found it hard to keep a calm countenance.

On the Battery with the Rutledges, Captain Hartstein was introduced to me. He has done some heroic thing, brought home some ship or other, is a man of mark. Afterwards he sent me a beautiful bouquet; not half so beautiful, however, as Mr. Robert Gourdin's, which already occupied the place of honor on my center table.

What a dear, delightful place Charleston is.

A lady (who shall be nameless because of her story) came to see me today. Her husband has been on the Island with the troops for months. She has just been down to see him. She meant only to call on him, but he persuaded her to stay two days. She carried him some clothes, made by his old pattern. Now they are a mile too wide.

"So much for a hard life!" I said.

"No, no! They are jolly down there. He has trained down, says it is good for him. He likes the life." Then she became confidential — and it was her first visit and I was a perfect stranger. She had no clothes down there, pushed in that manner under Achilles's tent, but she managed. She tied her petticoat around her neck for a nightgown!!

March 28th. — Governor Manning came to breakfast at our table.

* James Louis Petigru was a distinguished Charleston lawyer, who in spite of the fact that he opposed to the end secession and disunion, retained the affection and respect of all who knew him.

The others had breakfasted hours ago. I looked at him in amazement. He was in full dress, ready for a ball, swallow-tail and all. "What is the matter with you?" "Nothing. I am not mad, most noble Madam! I am only going to the photographer. My wife wants me taken — *thus!*"

He insisted on my going, too, and we captured Mr. Chesnut and Governor Means. The latter presented me with a book, a photo book in which I am to pillory all celebrities.

Dr. Gibbes says the Convention is in a snarl. It was called as a Secession Convention. A secession of places seems to be what it calls for first of all. It has not stretched its eyes out to the Yankees yet; it has them turned inward still. Introspection is its occupation.

Last night as I turned down the gas I said to myself: "Certainly this has been one of the pleasantest days of my life." I can only give the skeleton of it, so many pleasant people, so much good talk; for after all it was all talk, talk, talk! And yet the day began rather dismally. Mrs. Capers and Mrs. Tom Middleton came for me, and we drove to Magnolia Cemetery to see the Vanderhorst way of burying the dead. One is embalmed, kept life-like by some process, dressed as usual, can be seen through a glass case. I did not look. How can anyone?

I did see William Taber's broken column. It was hard to shake off the blues after this graveyard business.

The others were off at a dinner party. I dined *tête-à-tête* with Langdon Cheves, so quiet, so intelligent, so very sensible withal. There never was a pleasanter person, or a better man, than he. While we were at table, Judge Whitner, Tom Frost and Isaac Hayne came and broke up our deeply interesting conversation — for I was hearing what an honest and a brave man feared for his country. And then the Rutledges dislodged the newcomers and bore me off to drive on the Battery. On the staircase we met Mrs. Izard who came for the same purpose. On the Battery, Governor Adams stopped us to say that he had heard of my saying he looked like Marshall Pelissier, and he came to say that at last I had made a personal remark which pleased him! When we came home, Mr. Isaac Hayne and Chancellor Carroll called to ask us to join their excursion to the Island forts tomorrow. With them was William Haskell. Last summer at the White Sulphur, he was a pale, slim student from the University; today he is a soldier, stout and robust. A few months in camp, soldiering in the open air, has worked this wonder. This camping out proves a wholesome life after all. Then those nice, sweet, fresh, pure-looking Pringle girls. We had a charming topic in common, their clever brother Edward.

There are people who already say that the detestable hotels at Montgomery * will drive the Congress elsewhere. I have a letter from Eliza B. [Browne?], who is still there. She says:

Sad, sore and manifold as are the privations at the "Hall," I have persuaded Mr. B. to bear them in preference to embarking on the unknown sea of troubles called Montgomery housekeeping. At any moment that you have nothing better to do, think of me in that brilliant saloon, with tiny dishes of every sort before me, covered with all imaginable species of parboiled viands, and all called by courtesy eatables. Or you can see me in the luxurious chamber of the second floor with the asthmatic hair cloth sofa and the little painted rocking chair. And yet I am quite contented, much preferring the "Hall" to the misery of keeping house with the servants of other people.

Since you left, gaiety of every description has fled the city. The Ware ball was the last festivity of the season. Perhaps after Lent, they of the fashionable world will begin anew and try to eclipse that incomparable entertainment.

Mr. Mallory got a letter from a lady in Washington a few days ago, who said that there had recently been several attempts to be gay at Washington, but that they proved dismal failures. The black Republicans were invited, came, stared at their entertainers and at their new Republican companions, and looked unhappy while they said they were enchanted. They showed no ill temper at the hardly stifled grumbling and growling of our friends, who thus found themselves forced to meet their despised enemy. I had a letter from the Gwinns today. They say Washington is like Goldsmith's Deserted Village.

MARCH 31st. — My 38th birthday, but I am too old now to dwell in public on that unimportant circumstance.

A long dusty day on those windy Islands? Never! So I was up early to write a note of excuse to Chancellor Carroll. My husband went. I hope Anderson will not pay them the compliment of a salute with shotted guns as they pass Fort Sumter, as pass they must!

Here I am interrupted by an exquisite bouquet from the Rutledges. Are there such roses anywhere else in the world?

Now a loud banging at my door. I get up in a pet, and throw it wide open. "Oh," said John Manning. "Pray excuse the noise I

* Montgomery was at first the capital of the Confederacy; not till after Sumter and the secession of Virginia was the capital moved to Richmond.

made. I mistook the number. I thought it was Rice's room, that is my excuse. But now that I am here, come go with us to Quinby's. Everybody will be there. To be photographed is the rage just now."

We had a nice open carriage, and we made a number of calls — Mrs. Izard, the Pringles, the Tradd Street Rutledges — my handsome ex-Governor doing the honors gallantly. He had ordered dinner at six, and we dined *tête-à-tête*. If he should prove as great a captain in ordering his line of battle as he is in ordering a dinner, it will be as well for the country as it was for me today.

Fortunately for the men, the beautiful Mrs. Joe Heyward sits at the next table, so they take her beauty as one of the goods the Gods provide, and it helps to make life pleasant, with English grouse and venison from the West, not to speak of the salmon from the Lakes which began the feast. They have me to listen, an appreciative audience, while they talk; and they have Mrs. Joe Heyward to look at.

Beauregard called. He is the hero of the hour. That is, he is believed to be capable of great things. A hero worshipper was struck dumb because I said that so far he has only been a Captain of artillery or engineers or something. I did not see him. Mrs. Wigfall did, and reproached my laziness in not coming out.

At church today I saw old Negro mammys going up to the communion in their white turbans. Being at the Lord's table — so called, even then — black, white and brown must still separate according to caste.

The morning papers say Mr. Chesnut made the best shot on the Island yesterday. It was target practice. No war yet, thank God. Likewise they tell me he has made a capital speech in the convention. He came home enraged and accused me of flirting with John Manning. I went to bed in disgust. I am ordered now not to walk on the Battery with gentlemen! I assured him I do not tell him everything.

"Of the fullness of the heart the mouth speaketh," says the Psalmist, but it is not so here. Our hearts are in doleful dumps, and yet we are as gay, as madly jolly as the sailors who break into the strong room when the ship is going down. First came our great agony. We were out alone. We longed for some of our big brothers to come out and help us. Well, they are out; but now it is Fort Sumter and that ill-advised Anderson. There stands Fort Sumter, and thereby hangs peace or war.

Wigfall says that before he left Washington, Governor Pickens and

Trescot were openly against Secession. Trescot does not pretend to like it now, but Governor Pickens is fire-eater down to the ground. "At the White House Mrs. Davis wore a badge 'Jeff Davis no seceder,' " says Mrs. Wigfall. Captain Ingraham comments in his rapid way, words tumbling over each other out of his mouth: "Charlotte Wigfall meant that as a fling at those people, but I think better of men who stop to think. It is too rash to rush on as some do." "And so," adds Mrs. Wigfall, "the eleventh-hour men are rewarded, but I say the half-hearted are traitors in this row."

April 3rd. — Met the lovely Lucy Holcombe, now Mrs. Governor Pickens, last night at the Isaac Haynes's. Old Pick has a better wig. I saw Miles begging in dumb show for three violets she had in her breast-pin. She is silly and affected, looking love into the eyes of the men at every glance.

"And you who are laughing in your sleeve at the scene! Where did you get that huge bunch?" "Oh, there is no sentiment when there is a pile like that of anything!" "Oh! Oh!"

And so we fool on into the black cloud ahead of us.

April 4th. — Mr. Hayne said his wife moaned over the hardness of the chaperone seats at St. Andrew's Hall at a St. Cecilia ball. She was hopelessly deposited there for hours. "But the walls are harder, my dear. What are your feelings to those of the poor old fellows leaning against the walls, watching their beautiful young wives waltzing as if they could never tire, in every man's arms in the room. Watch their haggard, weary faces! The old husbands have not exactly a bed of roses; their wives twirling in the arms of young men, they hugging only the wall!"

At church I had to move my pew. The lovely Laura was too much for my boys. They all made eyes at her, and nudged each other, and she gave them glance for glance. Wink, blink and snigger as they would, she liked it.

While we were at supper at the Haynes's, Wigfall was sent for to address a crowd before the Mills House piazza. So let Washington beware. We were sad that we could not hear the speaking, but the supper was a consolation; *pâté de foie gras*, *salade*, *biscuit glacé* and *champagne frappé*.

A ship was fired into yesterday and went back to sea. Is that the first shot? How can one settle down to anything? One's heart is in one's mouth all the time. Any minute, the cannon may open on us, the fleet come in.

APRIL 6th. — The plot thickens, the air is red-hot with rumors. The mystery is to find out where these utterly groundless tales originate.

In spite of all, Tom Huger came for us and we went on the *Planter* to take a look at Morris Island and its present inhabitants. Mrs. Wigfall and the Cheves girls, Maxcy Gregg and Colonel Whiting, John Rutledge of the Navy, Dan Hamilton and William Haskell. John Rutledge was a figurehead to be proud of. He did not speak to us, but he stood with a Scotch shawl draped about him, as handsome and stately a creature as ever Queen Elizabeth loved to look upon.

Then came up such a wind we could not land. I was not too sorry. Though it blew so hard (I am never seasick), Colonel Whiting explained everything about the Forts and what they lacked in the most interesting way, and Maxcy Gregg supplemented his report by stating all of the deficiencies and shortcomings on land.

Beauregard is a demigod here to most of the natives, but there are always some who say "wait and see." They give you to understand that Whiting has all the brains now in use for our defence. He does the work, Beauregard reaps the glory.

Things seem to draw near a crisis. Colonel Whiting is clever enough for anything; so we made up our minds today, Maxcy Gregg and I. Mr. Gregg told me that my husband was in a minority in the Convention. So much for cool sense, when the atmosphere is phosphorescent.

Mrs. Wigfall says we are mismatched; that she should pair with my cool, quiet, poised Colonel, and that her stormy petrel is but a male reflection of me.

APRIL 8th. — Yesterday, Mrs. Wigfall and I made a few visits. At the first house they wanted Mrs. Wigfall to settle a dispute. "Was she indeed fifty-five?" Fancy her face when more than ten years were bestowed upon her so freely.

Then Mrs. Gibbes asked me if I had ever been in Charleston before. Says Charlotte Wigfall, to pay me for my snigger when that false fifty-five was flung in her teeth: "And she thinks this is her native heath and that her name is McGregor!"

Allan Green came up to speak to me at dinner, in all of his soldier's toggery. It sent a shiver through me.

Tried to read Margaret Fuller Ossoli, but could not. The air is too full of war news and we are all so restless.

Went to see Miss Pinckney, one of the last of the 18th Century Pinckneys. She inquired particularly about a portrait of her father, Charles Cotesworth Pinckney, which she said had been sent by him to my husband's grandfather. I gave a good account of it. It hangs in the place of honor in the drawing-room at Mulberry. She wanted to see my husband, for "his grandfather, my father's friend, was one of the handsomest men of his day."

We came home, and soon Mr. Robert Gourdin and Mr. Miles called. Governor Manning walked in, bowed gravely, seated himself by me, and said, in mock heroic style and with a grand wave of his hand: "Madame, your country is invaded." When I had breath to speak, I asked: "What does he mean?" "He means this. There are six men-of-war outside the Bar. Talbot and Chew have come to say that hostilities are to begin. Governor Pickens and Beauregard are holding a Council of War." Mr. Chesnut then came in. He confirmed the story. Wigfall next entered in boisterous spirits. He said "there was a sound of revelry by night . . ."

In any stir or confusion my heart is apt to beat so painfully. Now the agony was so stifling that I could hardly see or hear. The men went off almost immediately, and I crept silently to my room where I sat down to a good cry.

Mrs. Wigfall came in and we had it out, on the subject of civil war. We solaced ourselves with dwelling on all its known horrors, and then we added some remarks about what we had a right to expect with Yankees in front and Negroes in the rear. "The slave owners must expect a servile insurrection, of course," said Mrs. Wigfall, to make sure that we were unhappy enough.

Suddenly loud shouting was heard. We ran out. Cannon after cannon roared. We met Mrs. Allan Green in the passageway with blanched cheeks and streaming eyes. Governor Means rushed out of his room in his dressing gown and begged us to be calm. "Governor Pickens has ordered, in the plenitude of his wisdom, seven cannon to be fired as a signal to the 7th Regiment. Anderson will hear, as well as the 7th Regiment. Now you go back and be quiet. Fighting in the streets has not begun yet." So we retired. Dr. Gibbes calls Mrs. Green, Dame Placid. There was no placidity today, no sleep for anybody last night. The streets were alive with soldiers and other men shouting, marching, singing. Wigfall, the "stormy petrel," was in his glory, the only thoroughly happy person I saw. Today things seem to have settled down a little. One can but hope. Lincoln or Seward have made such silly advances, and then far sillier drawings back. There may be a chance for peace after all.

Things are happening so fast. My husband has been made an aide-de-camp of General Beauregard. Three hours ago we were quietly packing to go home. The Convention had adjourned. Now he tells me the attack upon Fort Sumter may begin tonight.

It depends upon Anderson and the fleet outside. John Manning came in with his sword and red sash, pleased as a boy to be on Beauregard's staff while the row goes on. He has gone with Wigfall to Captain Hartstein with instructions.

Mrs. Hayne called. She had, she said, but one feeling; pity for those who are not here.

Jack Preston, Willie Allston — "the take-life-easy," as they are called — with John Green, "the big brave," have gone down to the Island and volunteered as privates. Seven hundred men were sent over. Ammunition wagons rumbling along the streets all night. Anderson burning blue lights; signs and signals for the fleet outside, I suppose.

Today at dinner there was no allusion to things as they stand in Charleston Harbor, but there was an undercurrent of intense excitement. There could not have been a more brilliant circle. In addition to our usual quartette (Judge Withers, Langdon Cheves and Trescot), our two Ex-Governors dined with us; Means and Manning. These men all talked so delightfully, and for once in my life I listened.

That over, business began in earnest. Governor Means had found a sword and a red sash and brought them for Colonel Chesnut, who has gone to demand the surrender of Fort Sumter.

And now, patience! We must wait. Why did that green goose Anderson go into Fort Sumter? Then everything began to go wrong. Now they have intercepted a letter from him urging them to let him surrender. He paints the horrors likely to ensue if they will not. He ought to have thought of all that before he put his head in the hole.

APRIL 12th. — Anderson will not capitulate!

Yesterday was the merriest, maddest dinner we have had yet. Men were more audaciously wise and witty. We had an unspoken foreboding it was to be our last pleasant meeting. Mr. Miles dined with us today. Mrs. Henry King rushed in. "The news? I come for the latest news! All of the men of the King family are on the Island," of which fact she seemed proud.

While she was here, our peace negotiator or our envoy came in; that is, Mr. Chesnut returned. His interview with Colonel Anderson had been deeply interesting but he was not inclined to be communicative, and wanted his dinner. He felt for Anderson. He had telegraphed to President Davis for instructions as to what answer to give Anderson. He has now gone back to Fort Sumter with additional instructions. When they were about to leave the wharf, A. H. Boykin sprang into the boat in great excitement. He thought himself ill used; a likelihood of fighting and he to be left behind.

I do not pretend to go to sleep. How can I? If Anderson does not accept terms at four o'clock, the orders are he shall be fired upon.

I count four by St. Michael's chimes, and I begin to hope. At half past four, the heavy booming of a cannon! I sprang out of bed and on my knees, prostrate, I prayed as I never prayed before.

There was a sound of stir all over the house, a pattering of feet in the corridor. All seemed hurrying one way. I put on my double-gown and a shawl and went to the house top. The shells were bursting. In the dark I heard a man say: "Waste of ammunition!" I knew my husband was rowing about in a boat somewhere in that dark bay, and that the shells were roofing it over, bursting toward the Fort. If Anderson was obstinate, Mr. Chesnut was to order the Forts on our side to open fire. Certainly fire had begun. The regular roar of the cannon, there it was! And who could tell what each volley accomplished of death and destruction.

The women were wild, there on the house top. Prayers from the women and imprecations from the men; and then a shell would light up the scene. Tonight, they say, the forces are to attempt to land. The *Harriet Lane* had her wheel house smashed and put back to sea.

We watched up there, and everybody wondered why Fort Sumter did not fire a shot. Today Miles and Manning, Colonels now, and aids to Beauregard, dined with us. The latter hoped I would keep the peace. I gave him only good words, for he was to be under fire all day and night, in the bay carrying orders.

Last night — or this morning, truly — up on the house top, I was so weak and weary I sat down on something that looked like a black stool. "Get up, you foolish woman! Your dress is on fire," cried a man; and he put me out. It was a chimney, and the sparks caught my clothes; but my fire had been extinguished before it broke out into a regular blaze.

Do you know, after all that noise, and our tears and prayers, nobody has been hurt. Sound and fury signifying nothing! A delusion and a snare!

Louisa Hamilton comes here now. This is a sort of news center. Jack Hamilton, her handsome young husband, has all the credit of a famous battery which is made of railroad iron. Mr. Petigru calls it The Boomerang, because it throws the balls back the way they came. So Louisa Hamilton tells us. She had no children during her first marriage; hence the value of this lately achieved baby. To divert Louisa from the glories of "the Battery" of which she raves, we asked if the baby could talk yet. "No, not exactly, but he imitates the big gun. When he hears that, he claps his hands and cries 'Boom Boom.' " Her mind is distinctly occupied by three things; Lent Hamilton, whom she calls "Randolph," the baby, and the big gun — and it refuses to hold more.

Pryor * of Virginia spoke from the piazza of the Charleston Hotel. I asked what he said. Louisa, the irreverent woman, replied: "Oh, they all say the same thing, but he made great play with that long hair of his, which he is always tossing aside."

Somebody came in just now and reported Colonel Chesnut asleep on the sofa in General Beauregard's room. After two such nights he must be so tired as to be able to sleep anywhere.

Just bade farewell to Langdon Cheves. He is forced to go home, to leave this interesting place. He says he feels like the man who was not killed at Thermopylae. I think he said that that unfortunate had to hang himself when he got home for very shame; maybe fell on his sword, which was a strictly classic way of ending matters.

I do not wonder at Louisa Hamilton's baby. We hear nothing, can listen to nothing. Boom Boom goes the cannon all the time. The nervous strain is awful, alone in this darkened room.

"Richmond and Washington Ablaze," say the papers. Blazing with excitement! Why not? To us these last days' events seem frightfully great. We were all, on that iron balcony, women. Men we only see now at a distance. Stark Means marching under the piazza at the head of his regiment held his cap in his hand all the time he was in sight. Mrs. Means was leaning over, looking with tearful eyes. "Why did he take his hat off?" said an unknown creature. Mrs. Means stood straight up. "He did that in honor of his mother. He saw me." She is a proud mother, and at the same time most unhappy. Her lovely daughter Emma is dying before her eyes of consumption. At that moment, I am

* Roger Pryor, as vigorous in his advocacy of secession as were Rhett and Yancey, after the War organized in Petersburg a memorial service for Abraham Lincoln. In 1866, he was practicing law at 95 Liberty Street, New York City.

sure Mrs. Means had a spasm of the heart. At least she looked as I sometimes feel. She took my arm and we came in.

APRIL 13th. — Nobody hurt, after all. How gay we were last night. Reaction after the dread of all the slaughter we thought those dreadful cannons were making such a noise in doing. Not even a battery the worse for wear.

Fort Sumter has been on fire. He has not yet silenced any of our guns, or so the aids — still with swords and red sashes by way of uniform — tell us. But the sound of those guns makes regular meals impossible. None of us go to table, but tea trays pervade the corridors going everywhere. Some of the anxious hearts lie on their beds and moan in solitary misery. Mrs. Wigfall and I solace ourselves with tea in my room. These women have all a satisfying faith. "God is on our side," they cry. When we are shut in, we, Mrs. Wigfall and I, ask: "Why?" Answer: "Of course, He hates the Yankees! You'll think that well of Him."

Not by one word or look can we detect any change in the demeanor of these Negro servants. Lawrence sits at our door, as sleepy and as respectful and as profoundly indifferent. So are they all. They carry it too far. You could not tell that they even hear the awful noise that is going on in the bay, though it is dinning in their ears night and day. And people talk before them as if they were chairs and tables, and they make no sign. Are they stolidly stupid, or wiser than we are, silent and strong, biding their time.

So tea and toast come. Also came Colonel Manning, A.D.C., red sash and sword, to announce that he had been under fire — and didn't mind! He said gayly: "It is one of those things! A fellow never knows how he will come out of it until he is tried. Now I know I am a worthy descendant of my old Irish hero of an ancestor, who held the British officer before him as a shield in the Revolution and backed out of danger gracefully!" We talked of St. Valentine's Eve, of the Maid of Perth, and the drop of the white doe's blood that sometimes spoiled all.

The war steamers are still there outside of the Bar. And there were people who thought the Charleston Bar "no good" to Charleston. The Bar is our silent partner — a sleeping partner — yet in this fray it is doing us yeoman service.

APRIL 15th. — I did not know that one could live such days of excitement. They called: "Come out! There is a crowd coming." A mob, indeed; but it was headed by Colonels Chesnut and Manning.

The crowd was shouting and showing these two as messengers of good news whom they were escorting to Beauregard's Headquarters. Fort Sumter had surrendered! Those up on the housetop shouted to us: "The Fort is on fire." That had been the story once or twice before.

When we had calmed down, Colonel Chesnut, who had taken it all quietly enough, if anything more unruffled than usual in his serenity, told us how the surrender came about.

Wigfall was with them on Morris Island when he saw the fire in the Fort, jumped in a little boat, and with his handkerchief as a white flag, rowed over to Fort Sumter. Wigfall went in through a porthole. When Colonel Chesnut arrived shortly after, and was received by the regular entrance, Colonel Anderson told him he had need to pick his way warily, for it was all mined. As far as I can make out, the Fort surrendered to Wigfall. But it is all confusion. Our flag is flying there. Fire engines have been sent to put out the fire. Everybody tells you half of something and then rushes off to tell someone else, or to hear the last news.

In the afternoon Mrs. Preston, Mrs. Joe Heyward and I drove around the Battery. We were in an open carriage. What a changed scene! The very liveliest crowd I think I ever saw. Everybody talking at once, all glasses still turned on the grim old Fort.

Russell, the English reporter for the Times, was there. They took him everywhere. One man studied up his Thackeray to converse with him on equal terms. Poor Russell was awfully bored, they say. He only wanted to see the Forts and get news that was suitable to make an interesting article. Thackeray was stale news over the water.

Mrs. Frank Hampton and I went to see the camp of the Richland troops. South Carolina College had volunteered to a boy. Professor Venable (The Mathematical) intends to raise a company from among them for the war, a permanent company. This is a grand frolic, no more — for the students at least!

Even the staid and severe-of-aspect Clingman is here. He says Virginia and North Carolina are arming to come to our rescue; for now the United States will swoop down on us. Of that we may be sure. We have burned our ships. We are obliged to go on now. He calls us a poor little hot-blooded, headlong, rash and troublesome sister state.

General McQueen is in a rage because we are to send troops to Virginia.

There is a frightful Yellow Flag story. A distinguished potentate and militia power looked out upon the bloody field of battle, happening to stand always under the waving of the Hospital Flag. To his numerous other titles they now add Y.F.

Preston Hampton in all the flush of his youth and beauty — he is six feet in stature, and after all only in his teens — appeared in lemon-colored kid gloves to grace the scene. The camp in a fit of horse play seized him and rubbed them in the mud. He fought manfully but took it all, naturally, as a good joke.

Mrs. Frank Hampton knows already what civil war means. Her brother was in the New York Seventh Regiment so roughly received in Baltimore. Frank will be in the opposite camp.

V

Camden

April 20th, 1861. — Mulberry. Home again. In those last days of my stay in Charleston I did not find time to write a word. And so we took Fort Sumter, *nous autres.* We, Mrs. Frank Hampton and others and I, took it in the passageway of the Mills House, between the reception room and the drawing-room. There we held a sofa against all comers. That was after we found out that bombarding did not kill anybody. Before that we wept and prayed and took our tea in groups, in our rooms away from the haunts of men.

Captain Ingraham and his kind took Fort Sumter from the Battery, with field glasses, and figures made with ten sticks in the sand to show what ought to be done.

Wigfall, Chesnut, Miles, Manning; they took it rowing about in the Harbour in small boats from Fort to Fort under the enemy's guns, bombs bursting in air.

And the boys and men who worked those guns so faithfully at the Forts; they took it too, their way.

Old Colonel Beaufort Watts told me many stories of the *jeunesse dorée* under fire. They took it easily as they do most things. They had cotton bag bomb-proofs at Fort Moultrie, and when Anderson's shot knocked them about someone called out: "Cotton is falling." Down went the kitchen chimney and loaves of bread flew out. They cheered gaily: "Bread stuffs are rising." Willie Preston fired the shot which broke Anderson's flagstaff. Mrs. Hampton from Columbia telegraphed him: "Well done, Willie!" She is his grandmother, the wife or widow of General Hampton of the Revolution, and the mildest, sweetest, gentlest of old ladies. It shows how the war spirit is waking us all up.

Colonel Miles (who won his spurs in a boat, so William Gilmore Simms * said) gave us this characteristic anecdote. They met a Negro out in the Bay rowing towards the city with some plantation supplies. "Are you not afraid of Colonel Anderson's cannon?" "No, sar, Marse Anderson ain't dars'nt to hit me. He know Marster wouldn't 'low it."

I have been sitting idly today looking out upon this beautiful lawn, wondering if this can be the same world I was in a few days ago. After the smoke and the din of the battle, a calm.

Arranging my photograph book. First page, Colonel Watts. Here goes a sketch of his life, romantic enough, surely. Beaufort Watts, bluest blood, gentleman to the tips of his fingers, chivalry incarnate, and yet this was his fate. He was given in charge a large amount of money, in bank bills. The money belonged to the State and he was only to deposit it in the bank. On the way he was obliged to stay over one night. He put the roll on a table at his bedside, locked himself in and slept the sleep of the righteous. Lo, next day when he awaked, the money was gone. Well, all who knew him believed him innocent, of course. He searched, and they searched, high and low; but to no purpose — the money had vanished. A damaging story, in spite of previous character; a cloud rested on him.

Many years after, the house where he had taken that disastrous sleep was pulled down. In the wall, behind the wainscoting, was his pile of money. How the rats got it through so narrow a crack it seemed hard to realize. Like the hole mentioned by Mercutio, it was not as deep as a well nor as wide as a barn door, but it did for Beaufort Watts until it was found. Suppose that house had been burned, or the rats had gnawed up the bills past recognition? The people in power understood how this proud man suffered these many years, in silence, while men looked askance at him. They tried to repair the small blunder of blasting a man's character. He was made Secretary of Legation to Russia. He was afterwards made Consul at Sante Fé de Bogotá. And then when he said he was too old to wander so far afield, they made him Secretary to all the governors of South Carolina, in regular succession.

I knew him more than twenty years ago as Secretary to the Governor. He was a made-up old battered dandy. He was the soul of honour,

* William Gilmore Simms was perhaps the most distinguished Southern novelist of the day.

and his eccentricities were all humored. His misfortune had made him sacred. He stood hat in hand before the ladies, and bowed as I suppose Sir Charles Grandison might have done. It was hard not to laugh at the purple and green shades of his too-black hair. He came at that time to show me the sword presented to Colonel Shelton for killing the only Indian who was killed in the Seminole War. We bagged Osceola and Micanopy under a flag of truce; that is, they were snared, not shot on the wing.

To get back to my knight errant. He knelt, handed me the sword, and then kissed my hand. I was barely sixteen, and did not know how to behave under the circumstances. He said, leaning on the sword: "My dear child, learn that it is a much greater liberty to shake hands with a lady than to kiss her hand. I have kissed the Empress of Russia's hand, and she did not make faces at me."

He looks now just as he did then. He is in uniform, covered with epaulettes and aiguillettes, shining in the sun; and with his plumed hat he reins up his war steed and bows low as ever.

Now I will bid farewell for a while, as Othello did, to all the pomp and circumstance of glorious war, and come down to my domestic strifes and troubles. I have a sort of volunteer maid, the daughter of my husband's nurse, dear old Betsey. She waits on me because she so pleases. Besides, I pay her. She belongs to my father-in-law, who has too many slaves to care very much about their way of life.

So Maria Whitaker came, all in tears. She brushes hair delightfully, and as she stood at my back I could see her face in the glass. "Maria, are you crying because all this war talk scares you?" said I. "No ma'am." "What is the matter with you?" "Nothing more than common." "Now listen, let the war end either way and you will be free. We will have to free you before we get out of this thing. Won't you be glad?" "Everybody knows Marse Jeems wants us free, and it is only old Marster holds hard. He ain't going to free anybody, anyway. You see . . ."

And then came the story of her troubles. "Now Miss Mary, you see me married to Jeems Whitaker yourself. I was a good and faithful wife to him, and we were comfortable every way, good house, everything. He had no cause of complaint. But he has left me." "For Heaven's sake! Why?" "Because I had twins. He says they are not his, because nobody named Whitaker ever had twins."

Maria is proud in her way, and the behavior of this bad husband has nearly mortified her to death. She has had three children in two years.

No wonder the man was frightened! But then Maria does not depend on him for anything. She was inconsolable, and I could find nothing better to say than: "Come now, Maria! Never mind, your old Missis and Marster are so good to you. Now let us look up something for the twins." The twins are named John and Jeems, the latter for her false loon of a husband. Maria is one of the good colored women. She deserved a better fate in her honest matrimonial attempt. They do say she has a trying temper. Jeems was tried, and he failed to stand the trial.

Note the glaring inconsistencies of life. Our Chatelaine locked up Eugène Sue, and returned even Washington Allston's novel with thanks and a decided hint that it should be burned; at least it should not remain in her house. Bad books are not allowed house room except in the library and under lock and key, the key in the Master's pocket; but bad women, if they are not white and serve in a menial capacity, may swarm the house unmolested. The ostrich game is thought a Christian act. These women are no more regarded as a dangerous contingent than canary birds would be.

If you show by a chance remark that you see that some particular creature more shameless than the rest has no end of children and no beginning of a husband, you are frowned down. You are talking on improper subjects. There are certain subjects pure-minded ladies never touch upon, even in their thoughts. It does not do to be so hard and cruel to the poor things. It is best to let them alone, if they are good servants otherwise. Do not dismiss them. All that will come straight as they grow older. And it does. They are frantic, one and all, to be members of the church, and the Methodist Church is not so pure-minded as to shut its eyes. And it has them up and turns them out with a high hand if they are found going astray as to any of the Ten Commandments.

VI

Montgomery

April 27th, 1861. — Here we are in Montgomery again. Robert Barnwell came with us. His benevolent spectacles give him a most Pickwickian expression. We Carolinians revere his goodness above all things. Everywhere the cars stopped, the people wanted a speech. There was one stream of fervid oratory. We came along with a man whose wife lived in Washington, and he was bringing her to Georgia as the safest place.

The Alabama crowd are not as confident of taking Fort Pickens as we were of taking Fort Sumter. Baltimore is in a blaze. They say Colonel Ben Huger is in command there. General Lee, son of Light Horse Harry Lee, has been made General in Chief of Virginia. With such men to the fore we have hope. The New York Herald says: "Slavery must be extinguished, if in blood."

Mr. Chesnut has gone with Wade Hampton to see President Davis about the Legion which Wade wants to get up. The Herald thinks we are shaking in our shoes at their great mass meeting; but we are jolly as larks, all the same.

The President came across the aisle to speak to me at church today. He was very cordial and I appreciated the honour.

Mr. Mallory has a daughter here, and a granddaughter. Miss Mallory married a nice Connecticut Yankee. Poor man, he is a fish out of water here.

Wigfall is black with rage at Colonel Anderson's account of the fall of Sumter. Wigfall did behave so magnanimously, and Anderson does not seem to see it in that light. "Catch me risking my life to save him again," says Wigfall. "He might have been man enough to tell the truth to those New Yorkers, however unpalatable to them a good word for us might have been. We did behave well to him. The only men of his killed, he killed himself, or they killed themselves, firing a salute to their old striped rag."

Mr. Chesnut was delighted with the way Anderson spoke to him when he went to demand the surrender. They parted quite tenderly. Anderson said: "If we do not meet again on earth I hope we may meet in Heaven." How Wigfall laughed at the thought of Anderson greeting Chesnut in the other world.

What a kind welcome these old gentlemen gave me. One, more affectionate and homely than the other, slapped me on the back. Several bouquets were brought me, and I put them in water around my plate. Then General Owens gave me some violets, which I put in my breastpin. "Oh," said my Gutta Percha Hemphill, "if I had known how those were to be honored, I would have been up at daylight seeking the sweetest flowers." Governor Moore came in, and of course seats were offered him. "This is the most comfortable chair," cried an overly polite person. "The most comfortable chair is beside Mrs. Chesnut," said the Governor, facing the music gallantly; and he sank into it gracefully. Well done, old fogy!

Browne said: "These Southern men have an awfully flattering way with women." "Oh, so many are descendants of Irishmen, and some blarney remains yet, even and in spite of their grey hairs." For it was a group of silver-grey flatterers. "Yes, blarney as well as bravery comes in with the Irish."

At Mrs. Davis's reception, dismal news; civil war seems certain. At Mrs. Toombs's reception, Mr. Stephens came to sit by me. Twice before we have had it out on the subject of this Confederacy, once on the cars coming from Georgia here, and once at a supper when he sat next to me. Today he was not cheerful in his views. I called him half-hearted and accused him of looking back. Man after man came and interrupted the conversation, but we held on. He was deeply interesting, and he gave me some new ideas as to our dangerous situation. Fears for the future, and not exultation at our successes, pervade his discourse.

Dined at the President's. Never had a pleasanter day. She is as witty as he is wise. He was very agreeable; he took me in to dinner. The talk was of Washington, nothing of our present difficulties.

A General Anderson from Alexandria — DC, I think — was in doleful dumps. He says the North is so much better prepared than we are. They are organized, or will be, by General Scott. We are in wild confusion. Their arms are the best in the world; we are wretchedly armed. And so on. L. G. Washington was quite as much of a Job's comforter.

Mr. Mallory complained of the Judge to me, as if I were responsible for what he says. Mr. Mallory thinks it ill bred, to say the least, to come to one of Mr. Davis's Cabinet and abuse him. Who doubts it? Ill bred is a mild word.

Mrs. Walker, resplendently dressed — she is one of those gorgeously arrayed persons who fairly shine in the sun — tells me she mistook the inevitable Morrow for Mr. Chesnut. "Pass over the affront to my power of selection." I told her. "It was an insult to the Palmetto Flag. Think of a South Carolina Senator like that!"

They come rushing in from Washington with white lips, crying: "Danger, danger." It is very tiresome to have these people always harping on this. "The enemy's troops are the finest body of men we ever saw." Why did you not make friends of them, I feel disposed to say. We would have war, and now we seem to be letting our golden opportunity pass. We are not preparing for war. Talk, talk in the Congress; lazy legislation; and rash, reckless, headlong, devil-may-care, proud, passionate, unruly raw material for soldiers.

They say we have among us a regiment of spies — men and women — sent here by the wily Seward. Why? Our newspapers tell every word that there is to be told, by friend or foe.

Had a two-hour call from the Honorable Barnwell Rhett. His theory is that all would have been right if we had taken Fort Sumter six months ago. He made it very plain to me, but I forget why it ought to have been attacked before.

At another reception, Mrs. Davis was in fine spirits. Russell of the London Times wondered how we had the heart to enjoy life so thoroughly, when all the northern papers said we were to be exterminated in such a short time.

MAY 9th. — Virginia's Commissioners * are here. Mr. Staples and Mr. Edmonston came to see me. "They say Virginia has no grievance;

* Virginia had passed an Ordinance of Secession on April 17, and had been admitted to the Confederacy on May 6. The Commissioners came to discuss the removal of the capital to Richmond.

she comes out on a point of honor. Could she stand by and see her sovereign sister states invaded?"

"Sumter" Anderson has been offered a Kentucky regiment. Can they raise a regiment in Kentucky against us?

General Beauregard and his aid, John Manning (the last left him of the galaxy who surrounded him in Charleston), have gone Heaven knows where; but out on a war path, certainly. Governor Manning called himself "the last rose of summer," left blooming alone of that fancy staff.

Ben McCulloch, the Texan Ranger, is here; and Mr. Ward, my Gutta Percha friend's colleague from Texas. Mr. Senator Ward in appearance is the exact opposite of Mr. Senator Hemphill. The latter has a face as old and dried as a mummy, and the color of tanned leather, with a thousand wrinkles; but he has the hair (or wig) of a boy of twenty. Mr. Ward is fresh and fair, with blue eyes and a boyish face; but his head is white as snow. Whether he turned it white in a single night or by slower process I do not know; but it is strangely out of keeping with his clear young eyes. He is thin, and has a queer stooping figure. This story he told me. On a western steamer there was a great crowd, and no unoccupied berth or sleeping place of any sort whatsoever in the gentlemen's cabin. Saloon, I think they call it. He had taken a stateroom, 110; but he could not eject the people who had seized it and were asleep in it. Neither could the Captain. It would have been a case of revolver, or of an eleven-inch bowie knife. Near the ladies' saloon, the steward said aloud: "This man is 110, and I cannot find a place for him. Poor fellow."

A peep-out of bright eyes. "Steward, have you an old man 110 years old out there? Let us see him. He must be a natural curiosity." "We are overflowing," said the steward. "Poor old 110! We can't find a place for him to sleep." "Poor old soul. Bring him in here; we will take care of him." "Stoop and totter," whispered the steward to Mr. Ward, "and go in."

"Ah," said Mr. Ward, "how those houris patted and pitied me and hustled me about and gave me the best berth. I tried not to look. I knew it was wrong, but I did." He saw them doing their back hair. He was lost in amazement at the collapse when the huge hoop skirts fell off, unheeded on the cabin floor. Then one beauty who was disporting herself near his curtain suddenly caught his eye. She stooped and hastily gathered up her belongings. "I say, Stewardess, your old a hundred and ten is a humbug. His eyes are too blue for anything!" And she fled as he shut himself in, nearly frightened to death.

I forget how it ended. There was so much laughing at his story I did not hear it all. So much for hoary locks and their reverence-inspiring power.

I have made the acquaintance of a clever woman; Mrs. McLane, née Sumner, daughter of the General, not the Senator. They say the Senator avoids matrimony. "Slavery is the sum of all evil," he says, so he will not reduce a woman to slavery. There is no slave, after all, like a wife.

Mrs. Ellis — niece of Mr. King, Minister to France and all that — Mr. Sumner asked her to marry him. I wish she had, if only to know what he would have done with her plantation and her hundreds of Negroes. She is a rich widow, and charming.

Russell, the wandering Englishman, was telling how very odd some of our plantation habits were. He was staying at the house of an ex-Cabinet Minister. Madame would stand on the back piazza and send her voice three fields off, calling a servant. Now that is not a Southern peculiarity. Our women are soft and sweet, low-toned, indolent, graceful, quiescent! But I dare say there are bawling, squalling, vulgar people everywhere.

MAY 13th. — We came down on the boat to that God-forsaken landing, Portland.* Found everybody drunk, that is, the three men who were there. At last secured a carriage to carry us to my brother-in-law's house. Mr. Chesnut had to drive seven miles, in pitch dark, over an unknown road. My heart was in my mouth, which last I did not open. Suddenly, at our elbow, it seemed: "Who's there?" "Where is my carpet bag?" said Mr. Chesnut to me as quickly. "Under your feet." "Law now, is that Mars' Jeems Chesnut?" called out a Negro in joyful manner. "Yes." "Law, Mars' Jeems, I knowed your voice the first word you said. Don't you know me? I'm Jonas. I drove Mr. William Lang's carriage out there in Camden. Why I 'member you jist as well."

So it was all smooth again. Jonas showed us the right road, asking thousands of questions. Mr. Chesnut carefully moved the carpet bag from under our feet and said: "There is scarcely any danger greater than trampling on two revolvers, not to speak of the jolts and bangs of this rough road." He solemnly requested me never again to meddle

* Mrs. Chesnut's mother lived near Portland, Alabama, with another daughter.

with his pistols. "I thought you would want them at hand." But I was utterly subdued by darkness and fright, and I promised hereafter to leave his carpet bag where he put it himself.

Next day a patriotic person informed us that so great was the war fever only six men could be found in Dallas County, and I whispered to Mr. Chesnut: "We found three of the lone ones *hors de combat* at Portland." So much for the corps of reserves, alcoholized patriots!

Saw for the first time the demoralization produced by hopes of freedom. My mother's butler (whom I taught to read, sitting on his knife board) contrived to keep from speaking to us. He was as efficient as ever in his proper place, but he did not come behind scenes as usual and have a friendly chat. He held himself aloof so grand and stately that we had to send him a "tip" through his wife, Hetty, Mother's maid, who showed no signs of disaffection. She came to my bedside next morning with everything that was nice for breakfast. She had let me sleep till midday and embraced me over and over again. I remarked: "What a capital cook they have here." She curtsied to the ground. "I cooked every mouthful on that tray. As if I did not know what you liked to eat, since you was a baby."

May 19th. — Back in Montgomery. Mrs. Fitzpatrick said Mr. Davis is too gloomy for her. He says we must prepare for a long war and unmerciful reverses at first, because they are readier for war, and so much stronger numerically. Men and money count so in war. "As they do everywhere else," said I, doubting her accurate account of Mr. Davis's spoken words, though she tried to give it faithfully. We need patience and persistence. There is enough and to spare of pluck and dash among us; the do-and-dare style.

I drove out with Mrs. Davis. She finds playing Mrs. President of this small Confederacy slow work, after leaving friends such as Mrs. Emory, Mrs. Joe Johnston and the like in Washington. I do not blame her. The wrench has been awful with us all. But we don't mean to be turned into pillars of salt.

Mr. Mallory came for us to go to Mrs. Toombs's reception. Mr. Chesnut would not go, and I decided to remain with him, and it proved a wise decision. First Mr. Hunter came. In college they called him, from his initials, R.M.T., Run Mad Tom Hunter. Just now I think he is the sanest, if not the wisest, man in our newborn Confederacy. I remember when I first met him. He sat next to me at some state dinner in Washington. Mr. Clay had taken me in to dinner, but he seemed quite satisfied that my other side should take me off his hands. Mr. Hunter did not know me, nor I him. I suppose he inquired or looked at my card lying on the table, as I did his. At any rate we began a conversation which lasted steadily through the whole thing from soup to dessert. Mr. Hunter, though in evening dress, presented a rather tumbled-up appearance. His waistcoat wanted pulling down and his hair wanted brushing. He delivered unconsciously that day a lecture on English literature which if printed I still think would be a valuable addition to that literature. Since then I have always looked forward to a talk with the Senator from Virginia with undisguised pleasure. Next came Mr. Miles, and Mr. Jamison of South Carolina. The latter was President of our Secession Convention. Also he has written a life of Du Guesclin. Not so bad.

So my unexpected reception was of the most charming, as the French say. Judge Frost came a little later. They all remained until the return of the crowd from Mrs. Toombs's.

These men are not sanguine. I can't say without hope exactly. They are agreed in one thing; it is worth while to try a while, if only to get away from New England. Captain Ingraham was here too. He is South Carolina to the tips of his fingers, but he has it as a dyed-in-the-wool part of his nature to believe the United States Navy can whip anything in the world. All of these little inconsistencies and contrarieties make it very exciting. One never knows what talk any one of them will make at the next word.

MAY 20th. — Lunched at Mrs. Davis's. Everything nice to eat, and I was ravenous. (For a fortnight I have not gone to the dinner table. Yesterday I was forced to dine on cold asparagus and blackberries, so repulsive in aspect was the other food they sent me.) And she was as nice as the luncheon. When she is in the mood, I do not know so pleasant a person. She is awfully clever, always. We talked of this move from Montgomery to Richmond. Mr. Chesnut opposes it violently because this is so central a position for our government. Then he wants our troops sent into Maryland to make our fight on the border, and to encompass Washington. I think these uncomfortable hotels will move the Congress. Our statesmen love their ease. And it will be so hot here in summer. "I do hope they will go," Mrs. Davis said. "The Yankees will make it hot for us, go where we will; and if war comes . . ." "It has come," said I. "Yes, I fancy these dainty folks may even live to regret the fare of the Montgomery hotels!" "Never."

Mr. Chesnut has three distinct manias. The Maryland scheme is one, and he rushes off to Jeff Davis, who I dare say has fifty men every day come to him with infallible plans to save the country. If only he can keep his temper. . . . Mrs. Davis says he answers all in softly modulated, dulcet accents.

But of Mr. Chesnut's three crazes: Maryland to be made seat of the war, old Morrow's idea of buying up steamers abroad for our coast defences, and last of all — but far from the least — we must make much cotton and send it to England as a Bank to draw on.* The very cotton we have now, if sent across the water, could be a gold mine to us.

* The question whether, by shipping cotton to England before the Northern blockade became effective, the South could have financed the war, has been argued pro and con, North and South, for almost ninety years. It was not attempted, largely because many Southern politicians thought that by keeping their cotton at home the South could bankrupt the North and force England to recognize the Confederacy. "Cotton is King" was the slogan; and many Southerners, knowing no other commodity, believed that cotton made the world go 'round, and that by refusing to grow or ship cotton they could bring the world to its knees.

VII

Camden

May 22nd, 1861. — Mulberry. We came here with R. M. T. Hunter and Mr. Barnwell, who has excellent reasons for keeping the cotton at home, but I forget what they are. Generally we take what he says, and also Mr. Hunter's wisdom, as unanswerable. Not so Mr. Chesnut, who growls at both, much as he likes them. Also we had Tom Lang and his wife, and Dr. Boykin. Surely there never was a more congenial party. The younger men had been in the South Carolina College while Mr. Barnwell was President. Their love and respect for him was immeasurable, and he benignly received it, smiling behind those spectacles.

Met John Darby in Atlanta and told him he was Surgeon of the Hampton Legion, which delighted him. He had had adventures. He had remained a little too long in the Medical College in Philadelphia, where he was some kind of a professor; and they were within an ace of hanging him as a Southern spy. "The rope was ready," he chuckled. We had only a few moments on the platform to interchange confidences. At Atlanta, when he unguardedly said he was fresh from Philadelphia, he had barely escaped another lynching. There he was taken up as a Northern spy. "Lively life among you, both sides," he said, hurrying away; and I moaned: "There was John Darby, like to have been killed by both sides, and no time to tell me the details." What marvellous experiences a little war begins to make.

May 27th. — They look for a fight at Norfolk. Beauregard is there. I think if I were a man I'd be there too. Also, Harper's Ferry is to be attacked. At Alexandria, the Confederate Flag has been cut down by a man named Ellsworth, who was in command of Zouaves. Jackson was the name of the person who shot Ellsworth in the act.

Sixty of our Cavalry have been taken by Sherman's Brigade. Deeper and deeper we go in.

Thirty of Tom Boykin's company have come home from Richmond, objecting that they went as a rifle company and were then armed with muskets. They were sandhill tackeys,* those fastidious ones, not very anxious to fight with anything or in any way, I fancy. Richmond ladies had come for them in carriages, feted them, waved handkerchiefs to them, and brought them dainties with their own hands, in the faith that every Carolinian was a gentleman, and every man south of Mason and Dixon's line a hero. These returned warriors are not exactly descendants of the Scotch Hay who fought the Danes with his plough share, or the oxen's yoke, or anything that could hit hard and come handy.

Johnny † has gone as a private in Gregg's regiment. He could not stand it at home any longer. Mr. Chesnut was willing for him to go, because those sandhill men said: "This is a rich man's war," and that the rich men could be officers and have an easy time, and the poor ones be privates. So he said: "Let the gentlemen set the example; let them go in the ranks." So John Chesnut is a gentleman private. He took his servant with him, all the same.

Read "Say and Seal" today. Interesting. Piety and pie-making equally so. As George Herbert says, housemaid's duties are made divine when a beautiful girl does broom work, sweeping, dusting, kneading dough. The hero is a Christian, armed with texts. He kisses close and often, and calls down a blessing from Heaven on every embrace, and every caress is chronicled and sanctified by scriptural

* The "sandhill tackeys" were men, poor by comparison with the planters, who owned or lived on small farms, where the soil was usually unfruitful, in the low rolling hills between Camden and Columbia.

† Johnny Chesnut was Mrs. Chesnut's nephew. When, soon after the fall of Sumter, Maxcy Gregg's regiment was ordered to Virginia, several companies refused to go, saying they had enlisted for service in South Carolina. The companies which did agree to go were promised that when their enlistments expired, on June 30, they would be disbanded; and this was done. Their arrival in Richmond had been marked by such an ovation as Mrs. Chesnut describes; when they went home, three weeks before the battle at Manassas, they were abused as cowards and renegades.

reference. The hero stands by the heroine lovingly and watches her get breakfast, dinner and supper. He admires her butter-making, scrubbing, making up beds, and all the honest work she glories in; but strange to say, he stops her from dressmaking. Why? One must draw the line somewhere, I suppose! The book has human interest, and one reads on; still, why should her dressmaking outrage him so?

Johnny reproved me for saying: "If I were a man I would not sit here and dawdle and drink and drivel and forget the fight going on in Virginia." He said it was my duty not to talk so rashly and make enemies. He says he had the money in his pocket to raise a company last fall, but it has slipped through his fingers, and now he is a common soldier. "You wasted it, or spent it foolishly." "I do not know where it has gone. There was too much consulting over me; too much good counsel was given to me, and everybody gave me different advice." "Don't you ever know your own mind?" "We will do very well in the ranks, men and officers all alike. We know everybody."

So I repeated Mrs. Lowndes's solemn words when she heard that South Carolina had seceded alone. "As thy days, so shall thy strength be." I don't know exactly what I meant, but thought I must be impressive, as he was going away. Saw him off at the train. Forgot to say anything then, but cried my eyes out.

Sent Mrs. Wigfall a telegram: "Where shrieks the wild Sea Mew?" She answered: "Sea Mew at the Spotswood Hotel. Will shriek soon. I will remain here. C. U. Wigfall."

JUNE 4th. — Davin! Have had a talk concerning him today with two opposite extremes of people. Old Mrs. Chesnut praises everybody, good and bad. "Judge not," she says. She is a philosopher. She would not give herself the pain to find fault. The Judge abuses everybody, and he does it so well! Short, sharp and incisive are his sentences, and he revels in condemning the world *en bloc*, as the French say. So nobody is the better for her good word, or the worse for his bad one. In Camden I found myself in a flurry of women, all excited over Davin. "Traitors" they cried. "Spies! They ought to be hanged!" "Davin is taken up! Dean and Davis, they are his accomplices!" "What has Davin done?" "He'll be hung; never you mind." "For what?" "They caught him walking on the trestle work in the swamp, after no good, you may be sure." "They won't hang him for that." "Hanging is too good for him!" "You wait till Colonel Chesnut comes! He is a lawyer," I said gravely. "Ladies, he will disappoint you. There will be no lynching if he goes to that meeting today. He will not move a step, except by *Habeas Corpus*, and trial by jury, and a quantity of bench and bar to speak long speeches."

Mr. Chesnut did come, and gave a more definite account of poor Davin's precarious situation. They had intercepted a treasonable letter of his at the Post Office. I believe it was not a very black treason after all. At any rate, Colonel Chesnut spoke for him with might and main at the meeting. It was composed (the meeting) of intelligent men with cool heads; and they banished Davin to Fort Sumter. The poor Music Master can't do much harm in the casemates there! He may thank his stars that Mr. Chesnut gave him a helping hand. In the red-hot state our public mind now is in, short shrift for spies!

Judge Withers said that Mr. Chesnut never made a more telling speech in his life than he did to save this poor Frenchman for whom Judge Lynch was ready.

As for me, I had never heard of Davin in my life until I heard he was to be hung.

Judge Stephen A. Douglas, the little giant, is dead; one of those killed by the war, no doubt; trouble of mind.

Twenty-eight hundred men have been taken from Bragg at Pensacola, so it seems trouble is looked for at Richmond.

Charleston people are thin-skinned. They shrink from Russell's touches. I find his criticisms mild. I expected so much worse. Those Englishmen come, somebody says, with their three P's; Pen, Paper, Prejudices; and I dreaded some of those after dinner stories. About that day in the Harbour, he let us off easily. He says our men are so fine-looking. Who denies it? Not one of us. Also, that it is a silly impression which has gone abroad that men cannot work in this climate. He says we live in the open air and work like Trojans at all manly sports, riding hard, hunting, playing at being soldiers.

These fine manly specimens have been in the habit of leaving the coast when it became too hot there; and also of fighting a duel or two if kept too long sweltering in a Charleston inn. The handsome youths whose size and muscle he admired so much as they prowled around the Mills House would not relish hard work in the fields between May and December. "Gifts are various," and we give it up. Negroes stand a tropical or semi-tropical sun at noonday better than white men. But fighting is different. Our men will not mind sun, or rain, or wind, then.

Major Emory, when he was ordered West, placed his resignation in the hands of his Maryland brothers. After the Baltimore row, the brothers sent it in; but then, after all, Maryland declined to secede. Mrs. Emory, who is at least two thirds of that co-partnership — old Franklin's granddaughter, and true to her blood — tried to get it back. Mr. Lincoln refused, point-blank, though it is said she went on her knees. That I do not believe. The Franklin race are stiff-necked and stiff-kneed, not much given to kneeling to God or man, from all accounts.

Mrs. Mallory was with her husband in Montgomery. She is a Spanish Creole, and one can see she has been a beauty. Now she is a grandmother, pure and simple. Her name is Angela, and we give it angelically, *à l'anglais.* Mr. Mallory, who is very proud of her, gave the Spanish pronunciation — *Anhla.* We failed to reproduce the sound in his fashion, and Mr. Browne said it was because Mallory did it principally with his nose — *Anhla!*

Polly, my old South Carolina maid, was inclined to give me all of the hotel scandal; and black enough it was. Her kitchen stories took away the last iota of my appetite. One day she came with eyes and mouth wide open. "Well, I believe it now! Things is upside down. I see a yaller gal slap a white child she was nussing!" "What did you say to her, Polly?" "I said, Lord gal, if Miss Sally Hamilton was to see you —" I laughed aloud. I am afraid the girl, who is half Indian, did not understand the extent of that threat. Then said Polly: "They got no sense, niggers ain't. When you got in that open carriage with that lady, what does that impident man do? When he sees me up at the window, he begin to holler and bawl at me! And ladies in the carriage! His Missis didn't say a word. I was that 'stonished and outdone, if I could er found a rock handy I'd a liked to chunked him off that box. Him talking on his box, and his Missis in de carriage!" I had shared Polly's astonishment. "Wealth without civilization," I thought.

JUNE 10th. — Have been looking at Mrs. O'Dowd as she burnished the "Major's arms" before Waterloo; and I have been busy too. My husband has gone to war. He is to join Beauregard, somewhere beyond Richmond. I feel blue-black with melancholy; but I used not one word to prevent his going, because I knew he ought to be there. I hope to be in Richmond before long myself. That is some comfort.

Privateering is all the talk in Charleston; the *Savannah* taken as a prize of war; the Mercury assures the enemy that its vengeance will be fearful if a hair of their heads is hurt, poor boys.

Carried a packet of papers to Wm. E. Johnson, President of the Bank. He was quite confidential. His wife, all the world knows, is a thousand times too good for him. She is good, he is clever. He told me in his queer plaintive voice: "My wife is a good creature, but there is nothing in her. She is honest and simple minded, that's all. Simple hearted too."

The war is making us all tenderly sentimental. No casualties yet, no real mourning, nobody hurt; so it is all parade, fuss and fine feathers. There is no imagination here to forestall woe, and only the excitement and wild awakening from everyday stagnant life is felt; that is, when one gets away from the two or three sensible men who are still left in the world.

Miss McEwen tells me of a pretty picture. Mrs. Kershaw has had her Joe's hair made into bracelets and necklace. She sits with bare neck and sleeveless arms, with one hand resting on a beloved offspring caressingly. Lovely arms and neck, doubtless; I remember she had a thoroughly graceful figure.

When Beauregard's report of the capture of Fort Sumter was printed, Willie Ancrum said: "How is this? Tom Ancrum and Ham Boykin's names are not here! We thought from what they told us that they did most of the fighting."

Colonel Magruder has done something splendid on the Peninsula. Bethel is the name of the battle. Three hundred of the enemy killed, they say.

Our Great Republic? I remember the proverb: "Slow to grow, long to last; quick to grow, quick to pass." Maybe the model Republic will be like its Grand Maternal Great Britain; regularly mined, every now and then. But what an immense amount of mining it takes to hurt her at all. For there she stands.

The old Spanish proverbs seem to stick in my mind. "A frightened partridge is half cooked," and "In every day's journey, there are three leagues of heartbreak."

Our people, Southerners, I mean, continue to drop in from the outside world; and what a contempt those who have seceded a few days sooner feel for those who have just come.

A Camden notable called Jim Villepigue said in the street today: "At heart Robert E. Lee is against us; that I know." * What will not people say in war times? Also, he said that Colonel Kershaw wanted General Beauregard to change the name of the stream near Manassas

* It was true that General Lee had opposed disunion; equally true that he had long ago freed his own slaves. Loyalty to his state, not to the Confederacy, led him to draw his sword.

Station. Bull's Run is so unrefined. Beauregard answered: "Let us try and make it as great a name as your South Carolina Cowpens."

Old Mrs. Chesnut, born in Philadelphia, cannot see what right we have to take Mt. Vernon from our Northern sisters. She thinks that ought to be common to each party. We think they will get their share of this world's goods, do what we may; and we will keep Mt. Vernon if we can.

At Bethel a poor young soldier was found with a bullet through his heart and a Bible in his pocket, marked: "From the Bible Society to the defender of his country." If the Bible can't prevent war, how is it to stop a bullet?

Johnny, the gentleman private, has sent for his man William and a baggage wagon; and he shall have both.

Mr. Kirkland trumped Jim Villepigue's trick. He says: "General Lee will surely be tried for a traitor." "Why, in Heaven's name?" "He is blazing out a path behind them in case of a retreat. To talk of retreat is treason, disheartening the soldiers."

No comfort in Mr. Chesnut's letter from Richmond. Unutterable confusion prevails, and discord already.

In Charleston, a butcher has been clandestinely supplying the Yankee fleet outside of the Bar with beef. They say he gave the information which led to the capture of the *Savannah.* They will hang him. Mr. Petigru alone, in South Carolina, has not seceded. When they pray for our President, he gets up from his knees. He might risk a prayer for Mr. Davis, though I doubt if it would do Mr. Davis any good. Mr. Petigru is too clever to think himself one of the righteous, whose prayers avail so overly much. Mr. Petigru's disciple, Mr. Bryan, followed his example. Mr. Petigru has such a keen sense of the ridiculous, he must be laughing in his sleeve at the hubbub this untimely trait of independence has raised.

Harper's Ferry has been evacuated, and we are looking out for a battle at Manassas Station. I am always ill. The name of my disease is a longing to get away from here, and go to Richmond. Good Lord, forgive me! Your commandment I cannot keep. How can I honor what is so dishonorable, or respect what is so little respectable, or love what is so utterly unlovely. Then I must go, indeed; go away from here.*

* Here, and elsewhere in the Diary, there are suggestions that Mrs. Chesnut, like many another daughter-in-law, was not always happy with her husband's father and mother.

Read Cooper's Naval History all day. A good book to give one a proper estimate of one's foes.

JUNE 19th. — In England, Mr. Gregory and Mr. Lyndsey rise to say a good word for us. Heaven reward them, and shower down its choicest blessings on their devoted heads — as the fiction folks say. Barnwell Heyward telegraphed me to meet him at Kingsville; but I was at Cool Spring and all my clothes at Sandy Hill, so I lost that good opportunity of the very nicest escort to Richmond.

Kate's German tutor today asked me if when I did not appear my time was given up to reading. "No, far from it. While out of sight today I made a pudding, and put the finishing touches to a jar of pickles. Then Molly's baby is ill. Nancy's died last week, so we have a kind of baby epidemic. I had to see the cows fed in Molly's place. She milks and the cow boy is very trifling and inefficient. So I was busy enough."

The German announced that he was careless what he ate; I quoted in an undertone the solemn belief of a Low Country gentleman: "Any man who pretends that he does not care for a good dinner is either a d——d liar or a d——d fool."

Tried to rise above the agonies of everyday life to read Emerson. Too restless. Manassas on the brain.

Saw, today, Napoleon's advice. Two armies always frighten one another. The best general is he who knows how to take advantage of the first panic. Napoleon ought to know. Russell's letters are filled with rubbish about our wanting an English prince to reign over us. He actually intimates that the noisy arming, drumming, marching, proclaiming at the North scares us. Yes, as the making of faces, and turning somersaults of the Chinese scared the English.

Mr. Binney * has written a letter. It is in the Intelligencer. He offers Lincoln his life and fortune. All that he has is put at Lincoln's disposal to conquer us. Queer. We only want to separate from them, and they put such an inordinate value on us that they are willing to risk all, life and limb and all their money, to keep us; they love us so.

Mr. Chesnut is accused of firing the first shot †; and his cousin, an

* Horace Binney was a Philadelphia lawyer, brother-in-law of old Mrs. Chesnut.

† The question of who fired the first shot at Fort Sumter rests on the broader question: which battery fired first? There was even a quibble: which projectile first reached the Fort? Edmund Ruffin, of Virginia — he and Rhett and Yancey and Pryor did more than any other four men to bring about secession — is usually

ex-West Pointer, writes in a martial fury. They confounded the best shot made on the Island the day of our picnic with the first shot at Fort Sumter. That is claimed by Captain James. Others say it was one of the Gibbses. But Anderson fired the train which blew up the Union, when he slipped into Fort Sumter that night at a time when we expected to talk it all over.

I have a letter from my husband, and one from Mrs. Bradford, from Talladega, Alabama. Mrs. Bradford says, underscoring every other word:

My dear Madam:

This being the day set apart by our noble President for prayer for our Southern Confederacy, the interest of our section has come up before my mind in all its bearings, and although I am utterly opposed to women taking any part in affairs publicly, I am a great advocate for their influence in the right time and right direction.

Occupying the position you do, you and the other ladies of the Congress and of the Cabinet have it in your power to give tone to society for all time to come. I trust in God, you will exert it in the right way, and I believe you will. The ladies of your State I have always admired. There is a well assured confidence of position about them, and therefore, they are plain and unassuming. This elegant simplicity is so desirable, that I trust it will be kept up in our higher fashionable circles.

As Congress has taken its departure from Montgomery I do not know that I shall ever see it in session again — but my heart goes with it. You may consider yourself fortunate in being the wife of one of that noble body, the first Southern Congress. My husband was not a member; but he was a delegate to Charleston, to Richmond, and to Baltimore, and claimed his share in bringing about the glorious result.

I am a plain, old-fashioned woman, and do not go into fashionable company, but I do trust that good sense and Christian simplicity will long be the standards in our "Southern Courts and firesides," and that our women may be as good as our men are brave.

Now that war is actually going on and its stern realities are upon us, there is no danger of little things engrossing our attention. When it is over and prosperity reigns, then will come the danger.

---

accorded the "first shot" distinction. He was at the time sixty-seven years old; but he joined The Palmetto Guards, and the company voted to him the honor of firing the first gun from their battery.

May we, as Patrick Henry said, "profit by the example," and learn wisdom from our old and now broken-down Washington Society.

Yours respectfully,
Louisiana Bradford

No comment needed. My husband writes from headquarters at Manassas Junction:

My dear Mary:

I wrote you a short letter from Richmond last Wednesday, and came here next day. Found the camp all busy and preparing for a vigorous defense. We have here at this camp seven regiments, and in the same command, at posts in the neighborhood, six others; say ten thousand good men. The General and the men feel confident that they can whip twice that number of the enemy, at least.

I have been in the saddle for two days, all day, with the General; to become familiar with the topography of the country, the posts he intends to assume, and the communications between them.

We learn General Johnston has evacuated Harper's Ferry and taken up his position at Winchester, to meet the advancing column of McClellan, and to avoid being cut off by the three columns which were advancing upon him. Neither Johnston nor Beauregard consider Harper's Ferry as very important in strategic point of view. I think it most probable that the next battle you will hear of will be between the forces of Johnston and McClellan.

I discover that our generals have not a very high opinion of the efficiency of the Administration, especially the War Department. I think what we particularly need is a head in the field, a Major General to combine and conduct all the forces, as well as plan a general and energetic campaign. Still we have all confidence that we will defeat the enemy whenever and wherever we meet in general engagement. Although the majority of the people just around here are with us, still there are many who are against us.

Send me, by whomever may come this way first, my large sponge, and my gun with the strap on it, with some buckshot and a box of caps to fit it.

I have been to Kershaw Camp. Tell Mr. Team I saw his son. They are all well, except a few cases of measles. His son is quite well, and satisfied. When you write, direct to me at Headquarters of General Beauregard, Virginia. God bless you.

Yours, James Chesnut, Jr.

My mare is lame. I am riding a horse captured from the United States Dragoons at Fairfax. He is a fine charger.

Just now I called to mind that last delightful luncheon at Mrs. Davis's. She said I was like Cuddie Headrig in Scott's novel. "I remembered her always at meal time." In Montgomery that was. If my lady correspondent who writes with such a craze for Republican simplicity could have seen her that day. Maggie Howell and herself were hemming kitchen towels, though I am afraid it was a sporadic effort.

In that Presidential Mansion outside of the Constitution — which has broken the Judge's heart and blighted his faith in any political honesty whatever — one always found at meal time a charming hostess, kind, clever and hospitable. And then she had so good a cook! I had taken into my inmost being a perfect loathing for everything in those hot and unsavory hotels.

Mary Hammy and myself are off for Richmond. Reverend Meynardie of the Methodist persuasion goes with us. We are to be under his care.

Isaac Hayne, the man who fought a duel with Ben Allston across the dinner-table, and yet lives, is the bravest of the brave. He attacks Russell, the London Times correspondent, in the Mercury, for saying we wanted an English prince to the fore. Not we, indeed! Every man wants to be at the head of affairs himself. If he cannot be King himself, why then a republic of course. It was hardly necessary to do more than laugh at Russell's absurd idea. He writes candidly enough of the British in India. We can hardly expect him to suppress what is to our detriment.

JUNE 22nd. — Making ready for Richmond. Last night I was awakened by loud talking and candles flashing everywhere, tramping of feet, growls dying away in the distance, loud calls from point to point in the yard. Up I started, my heart in my mouth. Some dreadful thing had happened, a battle, a death, a horrible accident. Mrs. Chesnut was screaming aloft, that is from the top of the stairway, hoarsely like a boatswain in a storm. Colonel Chesnut was storming at the sleepy Negroes, looking for fire, with lighted candles, in closets. I dressed and came upon the scene of action. "What is it? Any news?" "No, no, only Mamma smells a smell. She thinks something is burning, somewhere." The whole yard was alive, literally swarming. There are sixty or seventy people kept here to wait upon this household, two thirds of them too old or too young to be of any use. But families remain intact. Mr. Chesnut has a magnificent voice. I am sure it can be heard for miles. Literally he was roaring from the piazza, giving orders to the busy crowd who were hunting the smell of fire.

Mrs. Chesnut is deaf, so she did not know what a commotion she was creating. She is very sensitive on the subject of bad odors. Candles have to be taken out of the room to be snuffed. Lamps are extinguished only in the porticos or further afield. She finds violets oppressive, can only tolerate a single kind of sweet rose. Tea roses, she will not have in her room.

She was totally innocent of the storm she had raised, and now in a mild sweet voice was suggesting places to be searched. I was weak enough to laugh hysterically. The bombardment of Fort Sumter was nothing to this.

As I said, this yard is a Negro village. For them, taxes are paid, and doctors' bills. They earn their daily bread, and their large families get food and clothes and house rent, by "waiting in the house." They rapidly increase and never diminish in numbers. Maria's three children in two years bear witness to their powers that way, and is a suggestive fact; and her new free husband is "as good as white, but not quite," Rachel says. "No wonder Jeems Whitaker deserted her, and lef ole Missis to support her."

This village is just outside of the palings. After this alarm, enough to wake the dead, the smell was found; a family had been boiling soap, and around the soap pot they had swept up some woolen rags. Raking up the fire to make all safe before going to bed, the rags were heaped up with the ashes; and the faint smoldering tainted the air — at least to Mrs. Chesnut's nose, two hundred yards away or more. After much mumbling and grumbling, things settled down; and the deadly quiet reigned once more.

Yesterday, some of the Negro men on the plantation were found with pistols. I have never seen aught about any Negro to show that they knew we had a war on hand, in which they have an interest.

Mrs. John DeSaussure bade me good-bye and God bless me. I was touched. Camden people never show any more feeling or sympathy than red Indians, except at a funeral. It is expected of all to howl then. If you don't "show feeling," indignation awaits the delinquent.

VIII

Richmond

June 27th, 1861. — I am in Richmond. Mr. Meynardie was perfect in the part of travelling companion. He had his pleasures too. The most pious and eloquent of parsons is human, and he enjoyed the conversation of the "eminent persons" who turned up on every hand and gave their views freely on all matters of state.

Mr. Lawrence Keitt joined us *en route.* With him were his wife and baby. We don't think alike, but Mr. Keitt is always original and entertaining. Already he pronounced Jeff Davis a failure, and his cabinet a farce. "Prophetic?" I suggested, since he gave his opinion before the administration had fairly got under way. "A foregone conclusion," he replied. He was fierce in his fault-finding as to Mr. Chesnut's vote for Jeff Davis. He says Mr. Chesnut over-persuaded the Judge, and those two turned the tide, at least with the South Carolina delegation. We wrangled, as we always do. He says Howell Cobb's common sense might have saved us. He was a Cobb* man. I averred that Jeff Davis would save us.

* The election of Jefferson Davis as Provisional President of the Confederacy was the result of a misunderstanding. Georgia had three candidates; Howell Cobb, Robert Toombs, and Alexander Stephens. Toombs was the general choice of the delegates from other states; Cobb they distrusted. Under the impression that Georgia would go for Cobb, the other states organized a "Stop Cobb" move and agreed on Jefferson Davis. Only his own state, Mississippi, opposed the choice, preferring to keep Davis as commander of Mississippi's armed forces. Georgia, for the sake of unanimity, yielded her own claims. Not till too late was it discovered that Georgia's candidate was not Cobb but Toombs. Toombs would have been acceptable.

Two quiet unobtrusive Yankee school teachers were on the train. I had spoken to them, and they had told me all about themselves, so I wrote on a scrap of paper: "Do not abuse our home and house so before these Yankee strangers going North. Those girls are school mistresses returning from whence they came."

In the cars there were soldiers everywhere. Keitt quoted a funny Georgia man who says we try our soldiers if they are hot enough before we enlist them. If when water is thrown on them they do not sizz, they won't do; their patriotism is too cool.

Our journey was a lively one, though fearfully hot and dusty. Every woman from every window of every house we passed waved a handkerchief — if she had one — at the soldiers. This fluttering of white flags from every side never ceased from Camden to Richmond. Parties of girls came to every station simply to look at the troops passing. They always stood (the girls, I mean) in solid phalanx; and as the sun was generally in their eyes, they made faces. Mary Hammy never tired of laughing at this peculiarity of her sister patriots.

At the depot in Richmond, Mr. Mallory, with Wigfall and Garnett, met us. We had no cause to complain of the warmth of our reception. Our rooms had been taken at the Spotswood, but the people who were in the rooms engaged for us had not departed at the time they said they were going. They lingered among the delights of Richmond, and we knew of no law to make them keep their words and go. Mrs. Preston has gone for a few days to Manassas, so we took her room.

Mrs. Davis, as kind as ever, met us in one of the corridors and asked us to join her party and to take our meals at her table. Mrs. Preston came back and we moved into a room so small there was only space for a bed and a washstand with a glass over it. My things were hung up out of the way on nails behind the door.

As soon as my husband heard we had arrived, he came too. After dinner he sat smoking with the solitary chair of the apartment tilted against the door as he smoked, and my poor dresses were well fumigated. I remonstrated feebly. "War times," he said. "Nobody is fussy now. When I go back to Manassas tomorrow you will be awfully sorry you snubbed me about those trumpery things up there." So he smoked the pipe of peace, for I knew that his remarks were painfully true. As soon as he was once more under the enemy's guns, I would repent in sackcloth and ashes. He came, by order of the General, for more ammunition. General Joe Johnston says he has not ammunition sufficient to enable him to attack Generals Cadwallader and McClellan.

The President said at table: "Whoever is too fine — that is, so fine that we do not know what to do with him — we send him to Beauregard's staff!" It is truly a wonderful collection of ex-Governors, Generals, and United States Senators.

Mrs. McLane is here. Mrs. Davis always has clever women around her. They gravitate to her. Captain Ingraham came with Colonel Lamar. The latter said he could only stay five minutes; he was obliged to go back at once to his camp. This was a little before eight o'clock; but at twelve he was still talking to us on that sofa. We taunted him with his fine words to the FFV crowd before the Spotswood. He had said: "Virginia has no grievance. She raises her strong arm to catch the blow aimed at her weaker sisters." He liked it well, however, that we knew his speech by heart.

Here is a letter from Mr. Chesnut, sent here from Camden, since it arrived there after we had left that hot hole.

Richmond, June 12th, 1861

My dear Mary,

I got here last night very much worried by heat, dust, etc., and found the greatest difficulty to get a place to sleep. This city is crowded, and the hotels are overflowing. I have to remain here today because my horse could not be transported yesterday from Petersburg. I left her there last night with Lawrence, to come on this morning, and they have arrived safely. My hands were so full with the four Negroes, all green except Lawrence, that I had no time to take a meal from the time I left Kingsville until I got here. The Negroes had to lie on the trunks all night in the hall of the hotel; and I sent them to the camp this morning by a private soldier, Hinson of Kennedy's company. I will leave in the morning myself.

Yesterday we heard that Magruder's command at Bethel Church on the York had several engagements with the enemy and repulsed them each time with loss on the Federal side; but we do not know the exact truth yet. Reinforcements were sent from here last night; the New Orleans Zouaves. Cash and Bacon's regiments are still here, and will move to Manassas tomorrow; fine bodies of men, both. You must not be surprised if you hear of an advance into Maryland or a flank movement in the rear of McClellan's command. Beauregard's command will be the advancing column.

We have just heard of the landing of Federal Forces at Hilton Head. If true, it is only as I predicted.

Henry Marshall of Louisiana and myself are sleeping in the same bed, and others in the same room. Richmond is hot and comfortless. I will prefer the Camp, where I will be tomorrow night.

Love to all. As ever. Your

James Chesnut, Jr.

This Spotswood is a miniature world. The war topic is not so much avoided. Everybody has some personal dignity to take care of, and everybody else is indifferent to it. A Richmond lady told me under her breath that Mrs. Davis had sent a baby's dress to her friend Mrs. Montgomery Blair,* and Mrs. Blair had responded: "Even if the men kill one another, we will abide friends to the bitter end, the grave." I said nothing, because I will be taken aside and told by somebody else: "That Blair story is all false, made up by these malicious, gossipy women." In this wild confusion, everything likely and unlikely is told you, and then everything is as flatly contradicted.

Trescot was telling us how they laughed at little South Carolina in Washington, and said it was almost as large as Long Island, which is hardly more than a tail-feather of New York. Always there is a child who sulks and won't play; that was our rôle. And we were posing as San Marino and all model-spirited though small Republics. He tells us that Lincoln is a humorist. He sees the fun of things. He thinks if they had left us in a corner or out in the cold awhile, pouting, with our fingers in our mouth, by hook or by crook they would have got us back; but Anderson spoiled all.

The Russian Minister called us the subjects of Pickens The First.

June 28th. — Louis Wigfall kept Mr. Chesnut a day longer. Also, Mr. Henry Marshall had him busy getting guns, tents and the like for Gregg's Regiment. If Pickens will let them keep what they have, Mr. Marshall, because of his love and faith in Maxcy Gregg, will be security for them. Well, he is so rich.

I have worked like a beaver, or rather a mole, for my friends; and here

* Montgomery Blair was Postmaster General in Lincoln's cabinet. The suggestion is of course that Mrs. Davis was "corresponding with the enemy."

is a letter from the first one who has thanked me, seeing shrewdly my finger in the pie.

Waco, Texas, June 21st, 1861

Honorable James Chesnut
Dear Sir:

I have just received notice of my appointment as District Attorney for the Western District of Texas. Knowing that you have been instrumental in my favor in this matter, and learning from the Honorable John Hemphill that Mrs. Chesnut also expressed much interest in my appointment, I write this note to acknowledge my obligation to you both, and promise you that zeal and inclination shall not be wanting in the discharge of the duties which the office may impose upon me.

Your friend, respectfully,
John C. West

In Mrs. Davis's drawing-room last night, the President took a seat by me on the sofa where I sat. He talked for nearly an hour. He laughed at our faith in our own prowess. We are like the British; we think every Southerner equal to three Yankees at least, but we will have to be equivalent to a dozen now. After his experience of the fighting qualities of Southerners in Mexico, Mr. Davis believes that we will do all that can be done by pluck and muscle, endurance and dogged courage, dash and red-hot patriotism, and yet his tone was not sanguine. There was a sad refrain running through it all. For one thing, either way, he thinks it will be a long war. That floored me at once. It has been too long for me already. Then he said that before the end came we would have many a bitter experience. He said only fools doubted the courage of the Yankees, or their willingness to fight when they saw fit. And now we have stung their pride, we have roused them till they will fight like devils. He said Mr. Chesnut's going as aide-de-camp to Beauregard was a mistake, and that he ought to raise a regiment of his own.

Mrs. Bradley Johnson is here, a regular heroine. She outgeneralled the Governor of North Carolina in some way and has got arms and clothes and ammunition for her husband's regiment. There was some joke. The regimental breeches were all wrong, but a tailor righted that; hind part before, or something odd.*

* The ladies who cut the cloth for the trousers cut out only right legs; it was necessary to secure an additional supply of cloth and cut out left legs before the trousers could be made.

Captain Hartstein came today with Mrs. Bartow. Colonel Bartow commands a Georgia regiment now in Virginia. He was the Mayor of Savannah who helped to wake the patriotic echoes the livelong night under my sleepless window in Charleston in November last. His wife is a charming person, witty and wise, daughter of Judge Berrian. She had on a white muslin apron with pink bows on the pockets. It gave her a gay and girlish air, and yet she must be as old as I am.

Mr. Lamar, who does not love slavery any more than Sumner does — nor more than I do — laughs at the compliment New England pays us. We want to separate from them, to be rid of Yankees forever, at any price; and they hate us so. Yet they would clasp us — or hook us, as Polonius has it — to their bosoms with hooks of steel. We are an unwilling bride. I think incompatibility of temper began when it was made plain to us that we get all the opprobrium of slavery while they, with their tariff, get the money there is in it.

Mr. Lamar says the young men are light-hearted because there is a fight on hand, but those few who look ahead, the clear heads, they see all the risk, the loss of land, limb and life; of home, children and wife. Yet as in the brave days of old, they take it for their country's sake.

June 29th. — Mrs. Preston, Mrs. Wigfall, Mary Hammy and I drove in a fine open landau to see the *Champ de Mars*. It was a grand tableau out there. Mr. Davis rode a beautiful grey horse. His worst enemy will allow that he is a consummate rider, graceful and easy in the saddle; and Mr. Chesnut, who has talked horse with his father ever since he was born, owns that Mr. Davis knows more about horses than any man he has met yet. General Lee was there with him, also Joe Davis, and Wigfall was acting as Mr. Davis's aid.

Poor Mr. Lamar has been brought from his camp; paralysis, or some sort of stroke. Every woman in the house is ready to rush into the Florence Nightingale business. I think I will wait for a wounded man before I make my first effort as Sister of Charity. Mr. Lamar sent for me. As everybody went, Mrs. Davis setting the example, so did I. He will not die this time. Will men flatter and make eyes until their eyes close in death? Except that he was in bed, with some learned professor at his bedside, and that his wife has been telegraphed for, he was the same old Lamar of the drawing-room.

It is pleasant at the President's table. My seat is next to Joe Davis, with Mr. Browne on the other side, and Mr. Mallory opposite. There is a great constraint, however. As soon as I came, I repeated what a

North Carolina man said on the cars; that North Carolina had 20,000 men ready and they were kept back by Mr. Walker.* The President caught something of what I was saying and asked me to repeat it, which I did, although I was scared to death. The President said: "Madame, when you see that person, tell him his statement is false. We are too anxious here for troops to refuse a single man who offers himself, not to speak of twenty thousand men."

Silence prevailed. Now when I take my seat, my grace is a prayer to God that I may not put my mouth in at the wrong place or time.

Uncle H—— gave me three hundred dollars for his daughter Mary's expenses, making four in all that I have of hers. He also paid me one hundred, which he said he owed my husband for a horse. I thought it an excuse to lend me money, though I told him I had enough and to spare for all my needs until my Colonel came home from the wars.

Ben Allston, the Governor's son, is here and came to see me. He does not show much of the wit of the Petigrus; a pleasant person, however. Mr. Brewster and Wigfall came at the same time, the former chafing at Wigfall's anomalous position here. Mr. Wigfall was calm and full of common sense; a brave man, and without thought of any necessity for displaying his temper. He said: "Brewster, at this time, before the country is strong and settled in her new career, it would be disastrous for us, the head men, to engage in a row among ourselves." Brewster begged him to remember what Governor Houston had said when he heard that Wigfall was elected Senator from Texas. "Thank God this country is so great and strong that it can bear even that!" Mr. Brewster declared he thought this country already strong enough to bear a rupture between Mr. Davis and Mr. Wigfall. He did not think it would be too much for the country.

Mr. Wigfall took it all in high good humor.

I thought I had two new books. One was "The Crossed Path" by Wilkie Collins, but "Basil" was its old name. It is too good to be forgotten. As "Basil" I think I read it twenty years ago. Frank Sumter brought it to me, and I had the benefit of his brilliant criticism. The other old friend with a new name is Kingsley's "Westward Ho!," well-remembered.

As I was fanning the prostrate Lamar, I repeated Mr. Davis's conversation of the night before. "He is all right. The fight had to come. We are men, not women. The quarrel had lasted long enough. We

* Leroy Pope Walker of Alabama was the first Confederate Secretary of War.

hate each other, so the fight had to come. Even Homer's heroes, after they had stormed and scolded enough, fought like brave men, long and well." He said, too: "If the athlete Sumner had stood on his manhood and training and struck back when Preston Brooks assailed him,* Preston Brooks's blow need not have been the opening skirmish of the war. Sumner's country took up the fight because he did not. Sumner chose his own battlefield, and it was the worse for us. What an awful blunder that Preston Brooks business was!"

I told Lamar how Mr. Chesnut laughed when he remembered the Town and Gown fights (Students and Snobs, so called then) at Princeton, and now heard our people say that Northern men would not fight. Lamar said Yankees did not fight for the fun of it; they always made it pay or let it alone. Wigfall said to the Pennsylvania Cameron in the Senate, who announced himself as furiously out on a war path: "The profit will accrue."

All are dissatisfied with Walker as Secretary of War. Rhymes they make: "Double U, Double U, I will trouble you," and so on.

A comic coincidence. We were in the aforesaid landau. Today I paid for it, five dollars an hour. Yesterday, Mrs. Preston had it. Mrs. Wigfall, as we neared home, was giving us a bit of Spotswood gossip. Wife ill, and also jealous; husband's room with no outlet but through hers. There he was incarcerated; or so the ladies said who nursed her. We declined to believe the tale. Just then one of the windows above us was cautiously opened and the military man in question put himself halfway out of the window and silently and energetically kissed his hand to us. Mrs. Wigfall was triumphant at this circumstantial evidence of the truth of her story. She said: "If they give him a looking glass and

* The incident occurred in 1856. In the course of debate, Senator Sumner of Massachusetts criticized Senator Butler of South Carolina. Preston Brooks, a nephew of Senator Butler, and himself a member from South Carolina of the House of Representatives, went to the Senate Chamber, where Sumner was seated at his desk. He carried a stout cane, and after a preliminary word or two, struck Sumner with it. Half-stunned by the first blow, Senator Sumner nevertheless sprang to his feet with such violence that his desk was ripped from the floor; but Mr. Brooks, keeping out of his reach, continued to strike the Senator with his cane until Sumner fell bleeding and unconscious. His head was cut and gashed; he had suffered a severe concussion and an injury to his spine. Brooks received a vote of censure from the House, resigned, and went home to be eulogized and honored — and triumphantly re-elected. Sumner's injuries were so severe that it was four years before he could resume his seat in the Senate. Mr. Lamar's criticism of Sumner — his point is that Sumner should have challenged Mr. Brooks — represented the vocal Southern attitude toward the affair. Mr. Brooks died in the January following.

a bottle of hair dye, he will be content. He will not find he is locked in till dinner time." "Shall we not kiss hands back to him?" said polite little Mamie Hammy. "No need, he is only thinking of himself. Besides, they would see us, and so find him out too. You see, he is behind bars."

Met Keitt and Boyer in the corridor with muskets, or rifles, something murderous in aspect. They were en route to Manassas.

Met Mr. Lyon. News indeed! A man here in the midst of us, taken with Lincoln's passports in his pocket; a palpable spy. Mr. Lyon said he would be hanged — in all human probability, that is.

My husband writes:

If you and Mrs. Preston can make up your minds to leave Richmond and can come up to a nice little country house near Orange Court House, we could come to see you frequently, while the Army is stationed here. It would be a safe place for the present, near the scene of action and directly in the line of news from all sides.

So we go to Orange Court House.

Read about Souluque,* the Haytian man. His story has a wonderful interest just now. Slavery has to go, of course, and joy go with it. These Yankees may kill us, and lay waste the land for a while; but conquer us? Never!

JULY 4th. — Russell abuses us in his letters from New Orleans. People here care a great deal for what Russell says because he "represents the Times," and the London Times reflects the sentiment of the English people. How we do cling to the idea of an alliance with England or France. Without France, even Washington could not have done it. Somebody said today: "Is not the South as much our country, and as able to declare its independence, as the colonies? We were not even Colonies from New England." "Might makes right" was the answer.

Prince Polignac dined with the President today. He was *triste* and silent, his English not being too ready. When he was here before, they said he mistook Mrs. Browne for Mrs. Davis, after which *gaucherie* doubtless he feels it necessary to be cautious in his approaches.

We drove to the Camp to see the President present a flag to the Maryland Regiment. Having lived on the battlefield (Kirkwood) near Camden, we have an immense respect for the Maryland line. When

* Souluque, born a slave, in 1849 became Emperor of Haiti.

our militia ran away, Colonel Howard and the Marylanders held their own against Rawdon and Cornwallis, and every place near there is named for some captain killed in our defence. Kirkwood, Hobkirk, DeKalb! The last, however, was a Prussian Count.

Near our carriage there stood the very handsomest man I ever saw. He seemed madly excited, and hurrah-ed himself hoarse. Some cool citizen asked: "Where are you from?" "Baltimore." So the men there are as handsome as the women, if this be a specimen.

We brought home a spy, a spy on our side, just from the other side. A very good-looking creature too. He is on General Johnston's staff.

A letter from my husband written June 22nd has just reached me. He writes:

My heart was made glad by the sight of your handwriting in the letter brought to me yesterday by James Villepigue. It was the first time I had heard from home, and it lifted me out of the despond to which I was fast falling. Until day before yesterday I had been actively in the field, but so many persons were daily brought into camp that the General thought it expedient to bring into requisition my services as Judge Advocate. So I have been confined to the Court tent for two days. I do not like the duty. We are very strongly posted, and well entrenched, and have now at our command about 15,000 of the best troops in the world. We have, besides, two batteries of artillery, and a regiment of cavalry, and daily expect a battalion of flying artillery from Richmond. We have sent forward seven regiments of infantry and rifles toward Alexandria. Our outposts have felt the enemy several times, and in every instance the enemy recoils or runs. General Johnson has had several encounters with the advancing columns of the other army, and with him too the enemy, although always superior in numbers, are invariably driven back.*

There is great deficiency in the matter of ammunition. General Johnston's command, in the very face of overwhelming numbers, have only 30 rounds each. If they had been well provided in this respect, they could and would have defeated Cadwallader and Patterson with great ease. I find the opinion prevails throughout the Army that there is great imbecility and shameful neglect in the War Department.

Unless the Republicans fall back we must soon come together on both lines, and have a decided engagement. But the opinion prevails here that Lincoln's army will not meet us if they can avoid it. They have already fallen back before a slight check from 400 of Johnston's men. They had 700 and were badly beaten.

* This letter is quoted as suggesting the lack of precautions for "security" during the War.

You have no idea how dirty and irksome the camp life is. You would hardly know your best friend in camp guise. The weather is exceedingly hot and dusty. We send three miles for water. With most of them, ablution is limited to face and hands, which rarely show the proper application of water.

I write upon my knee, at present, as our table is otherwise employed. As always, your James Chesnut, Jr.

Noise of drums, tramp of marching regiments all day long, rattling of artillery wagons, bands of music, friends from every quarter coming in. We ought to be miserable and anxious, and yet these are pleasant days. Perhaps we are unnaturally exhilarated and excited.

Just now Major George Deas made Mrs. Joe Johnston very unhappy. He said "a battle is looked for at any minute between Patterson and General Johnston, and Johnston lacks ammunition." Mrs. Johnston said: "If my Joseph is defeated, I will die!" Mrs. Davis said: "Lydia, beware of ambition!"

A young Carolinian with queer ideas of a joke rode his horse through the barroom of this hotel. How he scattered people and things right and left! Captain Ingraham was incensed at the bad conduct of his young countryman. "He was intoxicated, of course," said Captain Ingraham. "But he was a splendid rider."

Today some Virginia women called Maxcy Gregg's regiment cowards, because when their enlistments were up, they disbanded, with a battle looked for daily. It was hard to bear with patience. Maxcy Gregg won't stay long in any situation where he can be called a coward. John Chesnut was a private in that regiment. He goes back at once, as a private in a cavalry company, Boykin's Rangers.

Today we drove out to the camp of the Hampton Legion. How very nice our Carolina gentry are. Today I found them charming. Indeed, I felt so proud of them.

I heard some people in the drawing room say: "Mrs. Davis's ladies are not young, are not pretty," and I am one! The truthfulness of the remark did not tend to alleviate its bitterness. We must put Maggie Howell and Mary Hammy in the foreground, as youth and beauty are in request. At least they are young things, bright spots in a sombre-tinted picture.

The President does not forbid our going to Orange Court House, but he is very much averse to it. We are consequently frightened by our own audacity, but we are wilful women, and so — we go.

IX

Fauquier White Sulphur Springs

July 6th, 1861. — We are at the Springs. Mr. Brewster came from Richmond with us. Mr. Mallory sent for our luncheon the very largest box of crystallized fruit ever seen out of a confectionary shop, enough and to spare for us all for weeks. Keitt and Boyce came armed for the slaughter of birds; also Mr. Clingman of North Carolina. And the cars were jammed with soldiers to the muzzle. They were very polite and considerate and we had an agreeable journey in spite of heat, dust and crowd.

Robert Barnwell was with us. He means to organize a hospital for sick and wounded. There was not an inch of standing room even. So sultry, so close, but everybody in tip-top spirits.

Mrs. Preston and Mr. Chesnut met us at Warrenton. We saw across the lawn, but not to speak to them, some of Judge Campbell's family. There they wander disconsolate, just outside of the gates of their paradise. A resigned Judge of the Supreme Court of the United States! Resigned and for a cause that he is hardly more than half in sympathy with. His is one of the hardest cases.

A woman at table said triumphantly: "I hear they are starving in Charleston." Mary Hammy meekly responded: "No, they have the whole rice crop of last year yet." "They have plenty to eat on hand then?" "Yes, thank you."

July 7th. — This water is making us young again. How these men enjoy the baths. They say Beauregard can stop sixty thousand Yankees; and that many are coming. Women from Washington come riding into our camp, beautiful women. They bring letters done up in their back hair, or in their garments. "They are spies," spitefully we suggested. "They are for sale. Maybe they are fooling you. Seward can outbid you." "Never. These are patriotic creatures, risking every thing for their country." "For men," I added.

An antique female with every hair curled and frizzed is said to be a Yankee spy. She sits opposite to us. Brewster solemnly wondered, with eternity and the judgment to come so near at hand, how she could waste her few remaining minutes curling her hair. He bade me be very polite, for she would ask me questions. When we were walking away from table I demanded his approval of my self-control under such trying circumstances. It seems I was not as calm and forbearing as I thought myself. Brewster answered with emphasis: "Do you always carry brickbats like that ready in your pocket for the first word that offends you? You must not do so when you are with spies from the other side." "I do not feel at all afraid of their hearing anything through me, for I do not know anything." Brewster relented. "I did like your discourse, however, that last brickbat especially." [Mrs. Chesnut does not quote her conversational "brickbat."]

Girls here are enthusiastic. All wear Palmetto Cockades.

Our men could not tarry with us in these cool shades and comfortable quarters. They have gone back to Manassas, and the faithful Brewster with them, to bring in the latest news. They left us in excellent spirits, which we shared until they were out of sight. We went with them to Warrenton, and there heard that General Johnston was in full retreat, and that a column was advancing upon Beauregard. So we came back all forlorn. If our husbands are taken prisoners, what will they do with them? Are our husbands soldiers? Or traitors? *

Mrs. Ould read us a letter from Richmond. How horrified they are there at Joe Johnston retreating. The enemies of the War Department accuse Walker of not sending Joe Johnston ammunition in sufficient quantities, and say that is the real cause of his retreat. How will they not make the ears of that slow coach, the Secretary of War, burn!

Read Rutledge, but it is pretty hard to fix one's attention. Mrs. Preston's maid, Maria, has a way of rushing in. "Don't you hear the cannon?" We fly to the windows, lean out to our waist and pull all the hair away from our ears, but cannot hear anything.

* The possibility that in case of defeat Southern leaders would be hung as traitors was in many minds throughout the War.

Lincoln wants four hundred millions of money, and men in proportion. Can he get them? He will find us a heavy handfull.

Midnight. I hear Maria's guns.

We are always picking up some good thing of the rough Illinoisian's saying. Lincoln objects to some man: "Oh, he is too *interruptious*." That is a horrid style of man or woman. The Interruptious! I know the thing, but had no name for it before.

JULY 9th. — Our battle summer, so called. May it be our first and our last!

After all, we have not had any of the horrors of war. Could there have been a gayer or pleasanter life than we led in Charleston? And Montgomery! How exciting it all was there. So many clever men and women, congregated from every part of the South. To be sure, flies and mosquitoes and a want of neatness and a want of good things to eat did drive us away. In Richmond, the girls say it is perfectly delightful. We find it so too, but the bickering and quarrelling has begun there.

At table today we heard Mrs. Davis's ladies described. They were said to wear red frocks and flats on their heads. We sat mute as mice. One woman said she found that the drawing-room of the Spotswood was so warm, so stuffy and stifling. "Poor soul," murmured the inevitable Brewster. "And no man came to air her in the moonlight. Why didn't somebody ask her out on the piazza to see the comet?" Heavens above, what philandering there was done in the name of the comet. When you stumbled on a couple in the piazza they lifted their eyes, and "Comet" was the only word you heard!

Mary Hammy — no doubt she had seen the comet repeatedly — said severely: "You are like Cousin Mary. She laughs at everything. She even laughs at General Washington." "Never!" "Well then, at his statue prancing on that monument!" "The horse may prance, but he is bowing. What does she say amuses her?" "Oh, he looks like the top of the castors, and the great Virginians around him on their pedestals like the cruets; vinegar cruet, pepper pot, all that!" "That is only when you go too near. At a distance it is sublime!" "She is worse about Henry Clay." "What? In his bower in the corner of the park?" "Yes, that small summer house of his. He in his swallow-tail white marble coat, with the collar halfway up the back of his head; and his marble trousers fit so badly. Oh, what a shame to make a great man so absurd. And oh, that mouth! Surely they had no right to do him so." Thus we joke.*

*** The reference is to statuary in Capitol Square in Richmond.**

Brewster had a paper from Washington with terrific threats of what they will do to us. Threatened men live long. There was a soft and sweet and low and slow young lady opposite to us. She seemed so uncertain of anything that Mr. Brewster called her Miss Albina McClush, who always asked her maid, when a new book was mentioned: "Seraphina, have I perused that volume?"

Van Dorn has come, and the men said: "Earl Van Dorn will fight. We don't like retreaters." The Prestons are Joe Johnston's * cousins, and they were indignant, since he only retreats for want of arms and ammunition.

Mary Hammy, having a fiancé in the wars, is inclined at times to be sad and tearful. Mrs. Preston quoted her Negro nurse to her. "Never take any more trouble in your heart than you can kick off at the end of your toes."

JULY 11th. — We did hear cannon today.

The woman who slandered Mrs. Davis's court — of which we are honorary members — by saying they, well, were not young, and that they wore gaudy colors, and dressed badly: I took an inventory of her charms today. She is darkly, deeply, beautifully freckled, and she wears a wig which is kept in place by a tiara of mock jewelry, and she has the fattest of arms and wears black bead bracelets!

The one who is under a cloud, shadowed as a Yankee spy, today confirmed our worst suspicions. She exhibited unholy joy as she reported seven hundred sick soldiers in the hospital at Culpepper and that Beauregard had sent a flag of truce to Washington. "Ladies," said Mr. Brewster to us, "Do you know you are only thirty miles from Washington?"

What a night we had! Maria had seen suspicious persons hovering about all day, and Mrs. Preston saw a ladder which could easily be placed so as to reach our rooms. Mary Hammy saw lights glancing about among the trees, and we all heard guns. So we sat up most of the night. Consequently I am writing in bed today.

A letter from my husband, our orders to move on:

My dear Mary:

Here we are still, and no more prospect of movement now than when I last

* General Johnston was among the half dozen ablest Confederate generals, and his retreats often paid better dividends than the victories of other commanders; but the South resented them. Popular criticism of his strategy and tactics, when in 1864 it led to his removal from command, contributed to the fatal loss of Atlanta and the Confederate disaster at Franklin.

wrote you. It is true, however, that the enemy is advancing slowly in our front and we are preparing to receive him. He comes in great force, being more than three times our number. The camp is greatly revived by the fine rain which fell yesterday. Everything looks fresh and clean, and we will be free from dust for a few days.

When do you go down? Don't stay longer than Saturday. The enemy might make a flank movement and cut you off, by taking the railroad.

When you go to Richmond, inquire of the tailors called Shafer and Company, just below the Exchange, for my coat and pants which I ordered to be made. Keep them for me. Drop us a line daily.

Yours, J. Chesnut Jr.

Our clothes are at the washerwoman's but we won't let a trifle like that keep us. To tell the truth, we are terrified women and children, and that touch about the flank movement will send us flying to Richmond. But is Richmond safe?

The spy, so called, gave us a parting shot. She said Beauregard arrested her brother so that he might take a fine horse aforesaid brother was riding. Why? Beauregard could have at a moment's notice any horse in South Carolina — or Louisiana, for that matter — at a word. The brother was arrested and sent to Richmond, and "will be acquitted as they always are," said Brewster. They send them first to Richmond to see and hear everything there; then they acquit them, and send them out of the country by way of Norfolk to see everything there. But after all, what does it matter? The Yankees have no need of spies. Our newspapers keep no secrets hid. The thoughts of our hearts are all revealed. Everything with us is open and above board. At Bethel, the Yankees fired too high, and every daily is jeering them about it even now. They'll fire low enough next time, but no newspaper man will be there to get the benefit of their improved practice! Alas!

X

Richmond

July 13th, 1861. — Brewster beguiled the journey back to Richmond with stories from Texas, before it was annexed. His daughters are in a convent somewhere, being educated; but he is a vestryman — how he came to be one Heaven knows — of an Episcopal Texas Church. A pious Philadelphian sent them a silver communion service, but they could not take it out of the Custom House for want of funds to pay duty on it. So a judge and some lawyers played cards all night. The man who won the money dedicated it to good works, and delivered the communion service from its durance vile and gave it to the church. Then, after all that, before it was used, the church was struck by lightning and knocked into flinders. "That's the way in Texas, no fooling with a thing, good or bad," said Brewster.

Furthermore he took out a letter, addressed to Wigfall, which Brewster carefully preserved because it was from a high public functionary; and in the letter fire was spelled fiar, like liar, and drum, drumb, like crumb.

Here in Richmond we feel safe and comfortable, for we cannot be flanked! Mr. Preston met us at Warrenton. Mr. Chesnut doubtless had too many spies to receive from Washington, galloping in with the exact number of the enemy done up in their hair. Wade Hampton is here, and Dr. Nott also. Everybody is here, *en route* for the army, or staying for the meeting of Congress.

Lamar is out on crutches. His father-in-law, once known only as the humorist Longstreet, author of "Georgia Scenes," but now a staid Methodist, has outgrown the follies of his youth. He bore Lamar off today. They say Judge Longstreet has lost the keen sense of fun that illuminated his life in days of yore.* Mrs. Lamar and her daughter were here.

The President met us so cordially, but he laughed at our sudden retreat, our baggage lost and so on. He had tried to keep us from going, had said it was a dangerous experiment. I dare say he knows more about the situation of things than he chooses to tell us.

Today in the drawing-room I saw a *vivandière*, in the flesh. She was in the uniform of her regiment, but wore Turkish pantaloons. She frisked about in her hat and feathers, did not uncover her head as a man would have done, played the piano, sang war songs. She had no drum but she gave us a rataplan! She was followed at every step by a mob of admiring soldiers and boys.

Yesterday as we left the cars we had a glimpse of war. It was the saddest sight; the memory of it is hard to shake off. Sick soldiers, not wounded. There were quite two hundred lying about as best they might on the platform. Robert Barnwell was there doing all he could. Their pale ghastly faces!! So here is one of the horrors of war we had not reckoned on. There were many good men and women with Robert Barnwell, doing all the service possible in the circumstances.

When I was writing just now of the sick soldiers a card was brought me from Mr. Ould. Then they said Hugh Rose had called. In the drawing-room I saw no Hugh Rose, but Mr. Ould joined me. We sat opposite the door. I happened to look up and saw Mr. Chesnut with a smile on his face, watching us from the passageway. I flew across the room and as I got halfway saw Mrs. Davis touch him on the shoulder. She said he was to go at once into Mr. Davis's room, where General Lee and General Cooper were. After he left us, Mrs. Davis told me General Beauregard had sent Mr. Chesnut here on some army business.

July 14th. — Mr. Chesnut was closeted with the President and the Generals all the afternoon. The news does not seem pleasant. At least he is not inclined to tell me any of it. He satisfied himself with telling me how sensible and soldierly this handsome General Lee is. General Lee's military sagacity was his theme. Of course the President

* Augustus Baldwin Longstreet, at the outbreak of hostilities, was President of the University of South Carolina in Columbia. He had been a passionate advocate of secession until it became clear that secession meant war; then, too late, he tried to avert the catastrophe. General James Longstreet was his nephew. When General Longstreet's father died, Judge Longstreet took the boy into his home and was thereafter like his father.

dominated the party, as well by his mind as by his position. I did not care a fig for a description of the war council. I wanted to know what is in the wind now.

JULY 16th. — Dined today at the President's table. Joe Davis, the nephew, asked me if I liked white port wine. I said I did not know, all that I had ever known had been dark red; so he poured me out a glass and I drank it. It nearly burned up my mouth and throat. It was horrid, but I did not let him see how it annoyed me. I pretended to be glad that anyone found me still young enough to play a practical joke upon me. It was thirty years since I had thought of such a thing.

Met Colonel Baldwin in the drawing room and pointed significantly to his Confederate buttons and grey coat. At the White Sulphur last summer he was a Union man to the last point. "How much have you changed beside your coat?" "I was always true to our country. She leaves me no choice now." Mrs. McLane pitched into Juliet, said she was "free of her love" because of her Southern blood. She was answered: "Free love is a Northern persuasion. There is no free-love sect out of New England." We are always ready for combat here on any subject, if only North and South are the points of the compass touched upon.

As far as I can make out, Beauregard sent Mr. Chesnut to the President to gain permission for the forces of Joe Johnston and Beauregard to join, and unite to push the enemy — if possible — over the Potomac. Now every day we grow weaker and they stronger, so we had better give a telling blow at once. Already we begin to cry out for more ammunition, and already the blockade is beginning to shut it all out.

A young Emory here. His mother writes to him to go back. Her Franklin blood certainly calls him with no uncertain sound to the Northern side, while his fatherland is wavering and undecided, split in half by factions. Mrs. Wigfall says he is half inclined to go. She wondered that he did not. With a father in the enemy's army, he will always be "suspect" here, let the President and Mrs. Davis do for him what they will.

I did not know there was such a "bitter cry" left in me; but I wept my heart away today when my husband went off. Things do look so black.

When Mr. Chesnut comes here he rarely brings his body servant. A Negro man, Lawrence, has charge of all Mr. Chesnut's things, his watch, his clothes. Two or three hundred gold pieces lie in the tray of his trunk. All these, he tells Lawrence to bring to me if anything happens to him, but I said: "Maybe he will pack off to the Yankees, and freedom, with all that money." "Fiddlesticks! He is not going to leave me for anybody else. After all, what can he ever be, better than he is now, a gentleman's gentleman?" I said: "He is within sound of the enemy's guns, and when he gets to the other army he is free." Maria said of Mr. Preston's man: "What he want with anything more? Don't he live jest as well as Mars John do, now?"

Mr. Davis is in wretched health. That is a great misfortune to us. He has trouble enough, anxiety, responsibility; and then his unlucky nervous irritation doubles the trouble.

Today I was ill. Mrs. Ould kindly insisted on my taking something to ease my pain. She seized upon a small laudanum bottle. "The very thing." She dropped ten drops, and I drank it with a grave face. I had filled that vial with Stoughton bitters just before leaving home. I have no intention of drugging myself now. My head is addled enough as it stands, and my heart beats to jump out of my body at every sound. Mrs. Davis came in and sat for some time. She has so preoccupied an air, I am sure something is going wrong. Mrs. McLane, Mrs. Joe Johnston, Mrs. Wigfall, they all came. I am sure so many clever women could divert a soul *in extremis.*

The Hampton Legion is all in a snarl about I forget what. Standing on their dignity, I suppose. I have come to detest a man who says: "My own personal dignity and self-respect requires . . ." I long to say: "No need to respect yourself until you can make other people do it."

A quiet moment, a knock, a basket of delicious peaches. My misery took the form of no appetite at breakfast, but it failed to quench my taste for peaches, so I enjoyed them thoroughly.

JULY 19th. — Beauregard telegraphed yesterday, they say, to General Johnston: "Come down and help us, or we will be crushed by numbers." The President telegraphed General Johnston to move to Beauregard's aid.

At Bull's Run, Bonham's Brigade, Ewell's, Longstreet's, encounter the foe and repulse him. Six hundred prisoners sent here. Yesterday afternoon, thanks to the fact that it was bitters in that vial and not laudanum, and a light dinner of peaches, I arose — as the Scripture says — and washed my face and anointed my head and went down stairs. At the foot of them stood General Cooper, radiant, one finger nervously arranging his shirt collar — or adjusting his neck to it — after his fashion. "Your South Carolina man, *bon homme*, has done a capital thing at Bull's Run, driven back the enemy if not defeated him, killed and prisoners, etc." But poor Garnett * is killed, cowardice or treachery on the part of natives up there, or some of Governor Letcher's appointments to military posts. I hear all these things said. I do not understand, but it was a fatal business.

Mrs. McLane says she finds we do not believe a word of any news unless it comes in this guise: "A great battle fought; not one Confederate killed; enemy's loss in killed, wounded, and prisoners taken by us immense!"

Today we were to go with Mr. Mallory to see the new ship, *Patrick Henry*, but wild horses could not drag us an inch from here now. To this spot all telegrams tend, the President being here.

I was in hopes there would be no battle until Mr. Chesnut was forced to give up his amateur aid-ship to come and attend to his regular duties in the Congress.† Keitt has come in. He says Bonham's great battle was a skirmish of outposts. Joe Davis, Jr., said: "Would Heaven only send us a Napoleon!" "Not one bit of use. If Heaven did, Walker would not give him a commission."

We got the very latest news from Mrs. Davis. She was in Mrs. Preston's room last night until one o'clock. We were screaming together like a flock of chickens that a hawk has scared. Mrs. Davis and Mrs. Joe Johnston, her dear Lydia, were in fine spirits. The effect upon the rest of us was evident. We rallied visibly.

South Carolina troops pass every day. They go by with a gay step. Tom Taylor and John Rhett bowed to us from their horses, as we leaned out of the windows. Such shaking of handkerchiefs. We are forever at the windows.

Mrs. McLane was harping on the perfect right every man had to be true to his own side. "Who denies it?" says Brewster. "But I think the President makes a blunder when he puts place and power in the hands of Northern men. They will be true to their own, not to us. At best, they are always suspect."

Last night the Tuckers were here. John Randolph's half-nephew, Randolph Tucker, is a humorist of the first class.

Bonham's battle was not such a mere skirmish. We took three rifled cannon and six hundred stands of arms. Mr. Davis has gone to

* General Garnett fell in battle at Cheat Mountain, in western Virginia. General McClellan was the commander of the Northern forces; and his success in the west led presently to his appointment to command the Union army in the east.

† Mr. Chesnut, who had been the first Southerner to resign from the United States Senate, was at this time a provisional member of the Confederate Senate.

Manassas. He did not let Wigfall know he was going. That ends the duration of Wigfall's aid-ship.

No mistake today. I was too ill to move out of my bed, so they all sat in my room. Mrs. McLane came in with a splendid baby, her sister's. Mrs. Long, her sister, married a Virginian of that name. Miles says she is a fascinating woman. A new beauty, an expression I did not think her capable of, was in Mrs. McLane's face. Her tenderness and love and pride in that baby! Women need maternity to bring out their best and true loveliness.

JULY 22nd. — Mrs. Davis came in so softly that I did not know she was here until she leant over me, and said: "A great battle has been fought. Jeff Davis led the center, Joe Johnston the right wing, Beauregard the left wing of the Army. Your husband is all right. Wade Hampton is wounded. Colonel Johnson of the Legion is killed and so are Colonel Bee and Colonel Bartow. Kirby Smith is wounded or killed." I had no breath to speak, and she went on in that desperately calm way to which people betake themselves when under greatest excitement. "Bartow was rallying his men, leading them into the hottest of the fight. He died gallantly at the head of his regiment. The President telegraphs me only that 'it is a great victory.' General Cooper has all the other telegrams." Still I said nothing. I was stunned, and then I was so grateful. Those nearest and dearest to me were still safe. Then she began in the same concentrated voice to read from a paper she held in her hand: "Dead and dying cover the field . . . Sherman's battery taken . . . Lynchburg regiment cut to pieces . . . Three hundred of the Legion wounded . . ."

They got me up. Times were too wild with excitement to stay in bed. We went into Mrs. Preston's room and she made me lie down on her bed. Men, women and children streamed in. Every living soul had a story to tell. "Complete victory" you heard everywhere. We had been such anxious watchers. The revulsion of feeling was almost too much to bear.

A woman from Mrs. Bartow's county was in a fury because they stopped her as she rushed to be the first to tell Mrs. Bartow that her husband was killed. It had been decided that Mrs. Davis was to tell her. Poor thing, she was lying on her bed when Mrs. Davis knocked. "Come in" she called, and when she saw it was Mrs. Davis she sat up ready to spring to her feet. But there was something in Mrs. Davis's pale face that took the life out of her. She stared at Mrs. Davis and then sank back and covered her face with her shawl. "Is it bad news for me?" Mrs. Davis did not speak. "Is he killed?" Today she told me: "As soon as I saw Mrs. Davis's face, I knew."

Maria, Mrs. Preston's maid, is furiously patriotic for South Carolina. She came into my room crying indignantly: "These colored people say it's printed in the papers here that the Virginia people done it all. Now Mars' Wade Hampton had so many of his men killed, and he wounded, it stands to reason South Carolina was no ways backwards!"

Mrs. —— was making her moan, crying: "My husband is ordered off with his regiment and I can't even see him." "Indeed you can," said Mary Hammy briskly, and then suddenly subsided in confusion. Someone had made her a sign to hold her tongue. The Spotswood is built round a hollow square, and our rooms overlooked the billiard room on the opposite side of the inner yard. This much lamented husband had been there in evidence for several days, and in a condition! But I suppose he respected Madame too much to make his appearance as he was. When she left us, Mary Hammy inquired naïvely: "Why did you not let me relieve her mind?" "Because she would a thousand times rather think him under the enemy's guns than here right under her in the basement, and as he is!"

"You see, Mary," said Mrs. Mallory, "women like men with winning ways, but not spending days at the card table to exercise them!"

"Oh, oh!" said Mary Hammy. "Everybody seems to be giving me new ideas on the mysteries of matrimonial life. I thought she wanted to know he was safe!"

Judge Nisbett and others were grieving over Georgia's loss in Bartow, saying everything that was good of him, when a military funeral passed the hotel. As that march came wailing nearer, Mrs. Bartow fainted. The empty saddle and the led war horse; we saw and heard it all. Now it seems we are never out of the sound of the Dead March in Saul. It comes and it comes until I feel inclined to close my ears and scream.

Dr. Nott said Congressman Ely * came down to see the fun, came out

* Congressman Alfred Ely of New York was one of that large number of ladies and gentlemen who came out from Washington to witness the expected victory at Manassas. Finding himself under fire, he took shelter behind a tree, and stayed there until captured by the advancing Confederates in their pursuit of the broken Union army. He was taken to Richmond and held prisoner for five months. In prison he had many callers, Southern gentlemen who had served with him in the National House of Representatives; but also it was a popular diversion in Richmond to go down to the prison and see the Yankee Congressman! His journal of his captivity — although he says history will certainly call First Manassas a drawn battle — is temperate in tone.

for wool and got shorn. He was taken prisoner. Dr. Nott said he himself slept under the same tree with Joe Johnston. Cried out a shrill female voice: "Mrs. Johnston, don't you wish it had been you?" Dr. Nott said Mr. Davis got there too late. The foe began to fly just as he arrived.

Mrs. S——, with a magnificent solitaire in each ear, and tears as large and as clear in her eyes, is mad with anxiety. No word can she hear of her husband. He's alive. If he were dead she would be broken up by the Dead March under her windows. He's alive and she knows it, for all those wet eyes of hers. Her claret cup is perfection. She is brewing some now.

Yesterday Mrs. Singleton and ourselves sat on a bedside and mingled our tears for those noble spirits, John Darby, Theodore Barker, James Lowndes. Today we find we wasted our grief. They are not so much as wounded. They were supposed to have fallen in the face of the enemy, with flags in their hands, leading their men. Someone objected: "But Dr. Darby is a surgeon!" Someone else replied: "He is as likely to forget that as I am. He is grandson of Colonel Thomson of the Revolution, called, by way of a pet name by his soldiers, 'Old Danger.'" Thank Heaven, they are all quite alive, and we will not cry next time until officially notified.

July 24th. — Here Mr. Chesnut opened my door and walked in. Of the fullness of the heart the mouth speaketh. I had to ask no questions. He gave me an account of the battle as he saw it, walking up and down my room, occasionally seating himself on a window sill, too restless to remain still. He told what regiments he was sent to bring up. He took the orders to Colonel Jackson, whose regiment stood so stock still under fire that they are called a stone wall! Also, they call Beauregard "Eugene," and Johnston "Marlboro." Mr. Chesnut rode with Lay's cavalry after the retreating enemy, following them until midnight. Then there came such a rain as is only known in semi-tropical lands.

In the drawing room Colonel Chesnut was the "belle of the ball," they crowded him so for news. He is the first arrival from the field of battle that they could get at; handle, so to speak. But the women had to give way to the dignitaries of the land who were as filled with curiosity as the women themselves; the Cobbs, Captain Ingraham, etc.

Wilmot DeSaussure says Senator Wilson * of Massachusetts came

* Senator Wilson was an anti-slavery leader, and a United States Senator from 1855 till 1873 when he was inaugurated Vice President under General Grant. He

to Manassas en route to Richmond, with his dancing shoes ready for the festive scene which was to celebrate a triumph.

They brought me a Yankee soldier's portfolio from the battlefield. The letters were franked by Senator Harlan (of Iowa). One might shed a few tears over some of the letters. Women — wives and mothers — are the same everywhere. But what a comfort the spelling was! We were willing to admit the Yankees' universal free school education puts them ahead of us in a literary way of speaking, but these letters do not attest that fact. The spelling is comically bad, though not so bad as Wigfall's man, who spelled fire "fiar," like "liar."

JULY 27. — Mrs. Davis's drawing-room last night was brilliant, and she was in great form. Outside, a mob collected and called for the President, and he spoke. He is an old war horse and scents the battle from afar. His enthusiasm was contagious. They called for Colonel Chesnut, and he gave them a capital speech too. As we sometimes say: "It was the proudest moment of my life." Me, the woman who writes here. I did not hear a great deal of it, for always when anything happens of any moment my heart beats up in my ears; but the distinguished Carolinians that crowded round me told me how good a speech he made. I was dazed.

Mrs. McLane was very angry with Joe Davis. He forgot her presence and wished "all the Yankees were dead." Somebody said he did remember her presence, for the habit of our men was to call them "dam Yankees." Mrs. Davis was at her wit's end what to do with Joe Davis, for she is devoted to Mrs. McLane. There goes — as I write — the Dead March, for some poor soul. Mrs. Davis asked us all what to do about Joe, and Mrs. Wigfall said when her children were small she broke them of using bad words by washing their mouths with soap and water to cleanse them. But Joe Davis is not small! Then somebody told a story. A little girl came running to tell on her brother. "Oh Mamma, Charlie is using bad language, curse words!" "What is it?" "He says: 'Dam Yankees are here, prisoners.' " But Charlie protested: "Well Mamma, is not that their name? I never hear them called anything else."

Today the President told us at dinner that Mr. Chesnut's eulogy of Bartow in the Congress was highly praised. Two eminently satisfactory

---

was active in the political organization of Southern Negroes after the War; and it was a speech he delivered in New Orleans in 1867, and which General Longstreet heard, which led Longstreet to adhere to the Republican party and resulted in his ostracism in the South, and his appointment to Federal office by General Grant.

speeches in twenty-four hours is doing pretty well. Last night while those splendid descriptions of the battles were being given from our windows to the crowd below, I said: "Then, why do we not go on to Washington?" "You mean why did they not? The time has passed, the opportunity is lost." Mr. Barnwell said to me: "Silence, we want to listen to the speaker!" And Mr. Hunter smiled compassionately. "Don't ask awkward questions!"

Mr. Chesnut said: "They were lapping round Hampton and I saw they would flank us. Then that fine fellow Elzey came in view. At first we thought it was the enemy,* and we had our hands full before. Then the wind spread Elzey's flag, and as that joyful sight relieved my mind, I saw confusion in the enemy's wagon train, and their panic began."

Elzey and Kirby Smith came down the turnpike at the very nick of time. Still, the heroes who fought all day and held the Yankees in check deserve credit beyond words, or it would all have been over before the Joe Johnston contingent came. The eleventh-hour men claim all the credit, and they who bore the heat and brunt and burden of the day do not like that. Everybody said at first: "Pshaw! There will be no war." Those who foresaw evil were called ravens, ill fore-boders. Now the same sanguine people all cry: "The war is over!" They are the very same who a few days ago were packing to leave Richmond! Many were ready to move on when the good news came. There are such owls everywhere. But to revert to the other kind, the safe and circumspect; they say very little, but that little shows they think the war barely begun. There was no great show of victory on our side until two o'clock, but when we began to win, we did it in double quick time.

I was talking with Mr. Clingman and the friendly Brewster when a United States surgeon on parole came to see Mrs. McLane. A terrible Confederate female of ardent patriotism and a very large, damp mouth said: "How I would like to scalp that creature!" "A descendant of Pocahontas, evidently," said Brewster with a faint smile. "She must mean Mrs. McLane, who has a beautiful head of hair. The man is

* The first Confederate Flag, the "Stars and Bars" had three stripes, two red and one white, with seven stars on a blue field. After this incident at Manassas the "Battle Flag" was adopted as more easily recognized. It was red, crossed by diagonal blue bars containing thirteen stars. In May, 1863, a National Flag, a white field with the "Battle Flag" in the corner was designed; but because when it drooped this looked like a flag of truce, this was modified in March, 1865, by adding a red bar on the end opposite the staff.

shorn to the quick, no hair to get a purchase to tear his scalp off." Mr. Clingman could not look more disgusted than he always does.

Arnold Harris told Mr. Wigfall the news from Washington last Saturday. For hours the telegraph reported at rapid intervals, "great victory," "defeating them at all points." About three o'clock, the telegrams began to come in on horseback, and after two or three o'clock there was a sudden cessation of all news. About nine, messengers came on foot or on horseback, wounded, weary, draggled, footsore, panic stricken, spreading in their path on every hand terror and dismay. That was our opportunity! Wigfall says there was nothing to stop us, and when they explain why we did not go on, I understand it all less than ever. But we will dilly dally, and Congress will orate, and generals will parade, until they get up an army three times as large as McDowell's that we have just defeated.

Trescot says this victory will be our ruin. It lulls us into a fool's paradise of conceit at our superior valor, and the shameful farce of their flight will wake every inch of their manhood. It was the very fillip they needed.

There are gentlemen here who know their Yankees well, and they say if the thing begins to pay — Government contracts and all that — we will never hear the end of it until they get their profit in some way out of us. They will not lose money by us, of that we may be sure. Trust Yankee shrewdness and greed for that.

There seems to be a battle raging at Bethel, but no mortal here can be got to think of anything but Manassas. Mrs. McLane says she does not see that it was such a great victory; and even if it be so great, how can one defeat hurt a nation like the North. John Waters fought the whole battle over for me. Now I understand it. Before this, nobody could take time to tell the thing consecutively, rationally and in order. The crowd came to get Mr. Davis to speak to them. They wanted to hear all about it again. Afterwards they called for Chesnut of South Carolina, who could not be found. He had retired into Mrs. Preston's room.

Mr. Venable said he did not see a braver thing than the cool performance of a Columbia Negro. He brought his master a bucket of ham and rice which he had cooked for him, and he cried: "You must be so tired and hungry, Marster. Make haste and eat." This was in the thickest of the fight, under the heaviest of the enemy's guns. The Federal Congressmen were making a picnic of it. Their luggage was all ticketed to Richmond.

Cameron has issued a Proclamation. They are making ready to come after us on a magnificent scale. They acknowledge us at last as foemen worthy of their steel. The Lord help us, since England and France won't — or don't. If we could only get a friend outside, and open a port.

Mr. Mason came and would march me in state on his arm into Mrs. Davis's drawing-room. Maxcy Gregg and Mr. Miles were with me when Mr. Mason and Mr. Seddon called. They meekly followed, and I looked back and wished I was with the unobserved rear guard. Mr. Mason is a high and mighty Virginian. He brooks no opposition to his will.

One of these men told me he had seen a Yankee prisoner who asked him what sort of a diggins Richmond was for trade. He was tired of the old concern and would like to take the oath and settle here.

They brought us handcuffs found in the debacle of the Yankee army. For whom were they? Jeff Davis, no doubt, and the ringleaders. Tell that to the Marines! We have outgrown the handcuff business, on this side of the water.

Russell, the Englishman, was in Alexandria. Why did we not follow him there? That's the question!

After the little unpleasantness between Mrs. Davis and Mrs. Wigfall there was a complete reconciliation, and Mrs. Wigfall in all amity presented Mrs. Davis with the most hideous Chinese mandarin I ever saw!

Dr. Gibbes says he was at a country house near Manassas when a Federal soldier who had lost his way came in exhausted. He asked for brandy, which the lady of the house gave him. Upon second thought he declined it; she brought it to him so promptly, he said, he thought it might be poisoned. Certainly, his mind was! She, naturally, was enraged. "Sir, I am a Virginia woman. Do you think I could be as base as that? Here Tom! Bill! Disarm this man! He is our prisoner." The Negroes came running, and the man surrendered without more ado. Another Federal was drinking at the well. A Negro girl said: "You go in and see Missus." The man went in, and she followed crying triumphantly: "Look here, Missus, I got a prisoner too!" The Negroes were not ripe for John Brown, you see. This lady sent in her two prisoners, and Beauregard complimented her on her pluck and patriotism and presence of mind.

These Negroes were rewarded by their owners. Now if slavery is as disagreeable as we think it, why don't they all march over the border where they would be received with open arms. It amazes me. I am always studying these creatures. They are to me inscrutable in their ways, and past finding out.

Dr. Gibbes says the faces of the dead on the battlefield have grown as black as charcoal, and they shine in the sun. Now this horrible vision of the dead on the battlefield haunts me.

Old Ruffin * has promised me a John Brown pike, and Dr. Gibbes a handcuff for my very own; trophies for future generations. I suppose they see I do not believe any stories of pikes or handcuffs, or of a cage for Jeff Davis.

These young men say the war is doing them good. Hugh Rose, who has a room in this hotel, offered to share it with his father. It was that or the street for the old gentleman, so great is the crowd. They seem to think it an act of superhuman virtue "to have your father in your room."

Somebody sent me a caricature of Jeff Davis trying to throw sand in John Bull's eyes, and to stuff wool in his ears.

There are so many wonderful tales here about everybody. One about that strange looking man, Clingman, I thought funny enough. Dancing is a serious business with him. Some young lady spoke to him while he was dancing with her. "Pray withhold all remarks," he said. "It puts me out. I cannot do two things at once. If you must talk, I shall have to stop dancing." When he was presented to Miss Lane, he bowed low and immediately held his nose. Holding it firmly, he said: "Pardon me, I will retire now. I may come back and make a few remarks." He had bowed so low his nose began to bleed, and he had to hold it with all his might. Fancy Miss Lane's face! She is the very queen of the proprieties. I cannot imagine her laughing in the wrong place or at the wrong time, and yet she must have laughed then. Stories of Clingman abound. He cut his throat because he was not as clever as Mr. Calhoun and made a failure there too, for it was sewed up and he still lives!

Here is one of Mr. Chesnut's anecdotes of the Manassas. He had in

* This is the same Edmund Ruffin who fired the first gun at Sumter. As a part of his campaign to persuade the South to secede, he had sent to the capital of each Southern state pikes with which he said John Brown had proposed to arm revolting slaves at Harper's Ferry. The story of the pikes, like the story of "thirty thousand handcuffs," and of a cage for Jefferson Davis, which the Union Army was said to have brought to Manassas, were widely circulated, and widely believed. Mrs. Chesnut says she did not believe the stories, and she was a sensible woman. Such propaganda is of course a commonplace in every war.

his pocket a small paper of morphine. He put it there to alleviate pain. Ever since Tom Withers's frightful fractured leg, when the doctors would not give him anodyne enough to put him to sleep and quiet his agony for a time at least, Mr. Chesnut always carried morphine powders in his pocket. These he gave Tom Withers in the night, in spite of the faculty; and the soothing of that poor boy's anguish he considered one of the good deeds of his life. Now a man was howling with pain on the outskirts of the battlefield. He was, by the way, the only one Mr. Chesnut heard that made any outcry that day, be their wounds as grievous as they might. This man proved to be only a case of pain in the stomach. Him Mr. Chesnut relieved with the opiate, and passed on rapidly where he was sent. Later in the day he saw a man lying under a tree who begged for water. He wore the Federal uniform. As Mr. Chesnut carried him the water, he asked where he was from. The man refused to answer. "Poor fellow, you have no cause to care about all that now. You can't hurt me and God knows I would not harm you. What else do you want?" "Straighten my legs. They are doubled up under me." The legs were smashed. Mr. Chesnut gave him some morphine to let him know at least a few moments of peace. He said to me: "This is my first battle. I hope my heart will not grow harder."

Clingman said he credited the statement that they wanted water, for he remembered the avidity with which he drank water himself from dirty pools.

Captain Ingraham told Captain Smith Lee: "Don't be so conceited about your looks. Mrs. Chesnut thinks your brother Robert a handsomer man than you." I did not contradict the statement, and yet it was false. This is how I saw Robert E. Lee for the first time. I had heard of him, strange to say, in this wise. Though his family, who then lived at Arlington, called to see me in Washington because of Mrs. Chesnut's intimacy with Nelly Custis in the old Philadelphia days, and because Mrs. Lee was Nelly Custis's niece, I had not known the head of the Lee family. He was somewhere with the Army. Last summer at the White Sulphur, I met Roony Lee and his wife, that sweet little Charlotte Wickham, and I spoke of Roony with great praise. Mrs. Izard said: "Don't waste your admiration on him. Wait till you see his father! He is the nearest to a perfect man I ever saw." "How?" "Every way. Handsome, clever, agreeable, high bred!" Now, here in Richmond, Mrs. Stanard came for Mrs. Preston and me, to drive to the camp. She was in an open carriage. A man riding a beautiful horse joined us. He wore a hat with somehow a military look to it. He sat his horse gracefully, and he was so distinguished at all points that I very much regretted not catching the name as Mrs. Stanard gave it to us. He, however, heard ours, and bowed as gracefully as he rode; and the few remarks he made to each of us showed he knew all about us. But Mrs. Stanard was in ecstasies of pleasurable excitement. I felt she had bagged a big fish, since just then they abounded in Richmond. We chatted lightly and I enjoyed it, since the man and horse and everything about them was perfection. As he left us, I said eagerly: "Who is he?" "You did not know? Why, that was Robert E. Lee, the first gentleman of Virginia."

All the same, I like Smith Lee better; and I like his looks too. Besides, I know him well. Can anyone say they know his brother? I doubt it! He looks so cold, quiet and grand.

Dr. Moore was made Surgeon General. Dr. Gibbes has the sulks.

Kirby Smith is our Blucher. He came on the field in the nick of time, as at Waterloo; but now we are as the British who do not remember Blucher. With them it is all Wellington. Every individual man I see fought and won the battle, from Kershaw up and down; all the eleventh-hour men won the battle, turned the tide. The Marylanders, and Elzey and Company, one never hears of them; or one hears as little as one hears of Blucher in the English Waterloo stories.

I have had a painful adventure, in a small way. The poor soul who was debarred the pleasure of rushing to Mrs. Bartow with the news of her husband's death — they call her "bad-accident maker" — came into my room. She was with us when Adele spoke of "That woman Cousin Mary calls 'Bad Accident.' " I quickly asked the poor creature: "Is it true your son has met with a bad accident? We are so sorry to hear it." "Oh yes, it is a dreadful wound. He was punched in the side by the butt end of a musket." The deep and absorbing interest I evinced in that wound, and the frowns that I gave Adele when I could turn my head, and Adele's reckless making of comic faces over her blunder; it was decidedly overheating, at this state of the thermometer!

Mary Stark wrote me a long letter from Columbia. She said: "Old Scott! I only wish every disaster on that battlefield could be photographed on his heart and brain, so that mortification, remorse and shame might balance in some degree the horrors he has brought on our country." She urges me to write again and often. I write now only for needed things, and to people who can perhaps supply them. Thus I wrote to Harriet: "Today Mrs. George Randolph, who is President of the Ladies' Association here, tells me she needs arrowroot and tannic acid, and there is none to be found. Tomorrow I am going the rounds of the hospitals with her. Whatever you have, send direct to Mrs. G. Randolph, Franklin Street, Richmond. Always send by express. She is the head, and distributes to Winchester, Culpeper and every other place where things are needed. Ask Kate Williams to get us arrowroot from Florida." And I added, to encourage her: "Everyone who comes from Manassas brings a fresh budget of news. We are still finding batteries, rifles and muskets. We had eighteen cannon on our side and we captured 63 (pretty good for beginners), mostly rifled cannon. The Negroes come in loaded like mules. One man brought four overcoats, and when they cheered him he said: 'You never mind. I done give the best one to Marster.' Mrs. Randolph says: 'I think many comforts were captured. I know 52 barrels of white sugar were taken.' "

Mr. Venable was praising Hugh Garden and Kershaw's regiment generally. This was delightful, since they are my friends and neighbors at home. I showed him Mary Stark's letter. At the bottom of our hearts we believe every Confederate soldier to be a hero, *sans peur et sans reproche.*

Things must be on a pleasanter footing. Why? I met the President in the corridor. He took me by both hands. "Have you breakfasted? Come in and breakfast with me." Alas, I had had my breakfast and he said, laughing at his own French: "*Ici on suis facher, de tout mon cœur.*" When he jokes it is a good sign.

At the public dining-room, where I had taken my breakfast with Mr. Chesnut, Mrs. Davis came to him while we were at table. She said she had been to our rooms. She wanted Wigfall hunted up. Mr. Davis thought Chesnut would be apt to know his whereabouts. I ran to Mrs. Wigfall's room. She told me she was sure he could be found with his regiment in camp, but Mr. Chesnut did not have to go to the camp, for Wigfall came to his wife's room while I was there. Mr. Davis and Wigfall would be friends if . . . if . .

The Northern papers say we hung and quartered a Zouave, cut him in four pieces, and that we tie prisoners to a tree and bayonet them. In other words, we are savages! It ought to teach us not to credit what our papers say of them. We are absolutely treating their prisoners as well as our own men. In fact it is complained of here. I am going to the hospitals here for the enemy's sick and wounded to see for myself.

Trescot says many leaders here hate Jeff Davis. He says disintegration has already begun. Mr. Davis's enemies ask: Why did we not follow the flying foe across the Potomac? That is the question of the hour, even in the drawing-room, among those of us who are not contending as to "who took Rickett's Battery?" Allan Green, for one, took it. Allan told us that finding a portmanteau with nice clean shirts, he was so hot and dusty he stepped behind a tree and put on a clean Yankee shirt, and was more comfortable.

I was made to do an awfully rude thing. Trescot wanted to see Mr. Chesnut on particular business. I left him on the stairs, telling him to wait for me there, and that I would be back in an instant. Mr. Chesnut listened until I had finished my story, then locked the door and put the key in his pocket. He said I should not be running up and down stairs on Trescot's errands. Today I saw Trescot. He waited on the stairs an hour, he said. He was very angry, you may be sure.

The New York Tribune soothes the Yankee self-conceit, which has received a shock, by saying we had 100,000 men on the field at Manassas. We had about 15,000 effective men in all. And then the Tribune tries to inflame and envenom them against us by telling lies as to our treatment of prisoners. They say when they come against us next it will be in overwhelming force. I long to see Russell's letter to the Times about Bull's Run and Manassas.* It will be rich and rare. In Washington, it is all crimination and recrimination. Well, let them abuse one another to their hearts content.

JULY 31. — Dined at the President's table, and for the last time. Tomorrow we move to the Arlington. We had tea with Mr. Mason and others. Mr. Chesnut accounted for his turning his back on us and talking to Mrs. Long with such earnestness by saying: "I had to do it, to keep her from hearing Mr. Mason. He was wishing all the Yankees dead, and all of you were forgetting that that sort of thing must be unpleasant to her."

Men or women from the North who are here, married to Southern

* A Southern account of this first major battle of the War, published in 1862, called it "The Battle of Young's Branch"; but either "Manassas" or "The Manassas" was at first more common in the South, "Bull Run" in the North. Antietam — Sharpsburg, and Stone's River — Murfreesboro were other instances where nomenclature varied, and still does. One critic of *House Divided* objected that the author did not always name the battles he described. Presumably that critic visualized General Lee as announcing one morning to his army: "We are now about to fight the Battle of the Seven Days." "Bull Run," the Northern name for this first encounter, had in view of the Northern panic connotations so obvious that it was to a considerable extent adopted by the amused Southerners, but usually, as in this case, Bull's Run refers to the skirmish a few days before the actual battle.

people, must have a trying time; and ours in the same scrape at the North, ditto. Bad words for the enemy in everybody's mouth, and people do not like to hear their native land vilified.

August 1st. — At Arlington House. Everybody now is abusing the Spotswood, where I had no end of a good time.

Captain Boykin of Boykin's Rangers has appointed John Chesnut First Lieutenant, Thurston Second Lieutenant, and Guerard Third.

Mrs. Wigfall with the "Lone Star" flag in her carriage called for me. We drove to the Fair Grounds. Mrs. Davis's landau with her spanking bays rolled along in front of us. The Fair Grounds are still covered with tents and soldiers. As one regiment moves off to the Army, a fresh one from home comes to be mustered in and takes its place.

The President with his aids dashed by. My husband was riding with him. The President presented the flag to the Texans. Mr. Chesnut came to us for the flag and bore it aloft to the President. We seemed to come in for part of the glory. We were too far off to hear the speech, but Jeff Davis is very good at that sort of thing, and we were satisfied that it was well done. Heavens! How that redoubtable Wigfall did rush those poor Texans about. He maneuvered and marched them until I was weary for their sakes. Poor fellows! It was a hot afternoon, the thermometer in the nineties.

Mr. Davis uncovered to speak, but Wigfall replied with his hat on. Is that military? I read somewhere that a high and mighty nobleman would not take his hat off in the King's presence. He maintained he had a right to wear it. The King acknowledged the ancestral right, but — pointing right and left — remarked: "No one has a right to keep his hat on in a room where there are ladies." The King had him then, you see.

At the Fair Grounds there was much music and mustering and marching, much cheering and flying of flags, much firing of guns and all that sort of thing; a gala day with a double-distilled Fourth of July feeling. In the midst of it all a messenger came to tell Mrs. Wigfall that a telegram had been received saying her children were safe across the lines, in Gordonsville. That was something to thank God for, without any doubt. These two little girls came from somewhere in Connecticut where they had been with Mrs. Wigfall's good sister, the only person in the world except Susan Rutledge who ever seemed to think I had a soul to be saved! Now suppose Seward had held Louisa and Fanny as hostages for Louis Wigfall's good behavior. Eh?

That bold Brigadier, the Georgia General Toombs, charging about too recklessly, got thrown. His horse dragged him up to the wheels of our carriage. For a moment it was frightful. Down there among the horse's hoofs was his face turned up towards us, purple with rage. His foot was still in the stirrup, and he had not let go the bridle. The horse was prancing over him, rearing and plunging, and everybody hemming him in, and they seemed so slow and awkward about it. We felt it an eternity, looking down at him and expecting him to be killed before our very faces. However, he soon got it all straight, and though awfully tousled and tumbled, dusty, rumpled and flushed, with redder face and wilder hair than ever, he rode off gallantly, having to our admiration bravely remounted the recalcitrant charger.

If I were to pick out the best-abused man in Richmond, now when all catch it so bountifully, I should say Mr. Commissary General Northrop was the most cursed and vilified. He is held accountable for everything that goes wrong in the Army. He may not be efficient, but his having been a classmate and crony of Jeff Davis at West Point points the moral and adorns the tale. I hear that alluded to oftenest of his many crimes. They say Beauregard writes that his Army is upon the verge of starvation; and here in Richmond every man, woman and child is ready to hang to the very first lamp post anybody of whom the Army complains. Every Manassas soldier is a hero, dear to our patriotic hearts. Put up with any neglect of the heroes of the 21st July? Never!

And now they say we did not move on right after the flying foe because we had no provisions, no wagons, no ammunition, and so on. Rain, mud, and Northrop; these restrained us. But then where were the enemy's supplies that we bragged so of bagging? Echo answers where!

No, we lacked the will to push on; for when there is a will there is a way. We stopped to plunder that rich convoy, and somehow for a day or so everybody thought the war was over and paused to rejoice. Or so it appeared here.

All this was our dinner-table talk today. Mr. Mason dined with us and Mr. Barnwell sits by me always. The latter reproved me sharply for saying these things, but Mr. Mason laughed at "this headlong, unreasonable woman's harangue," and spoke of "female tactics and their war ways." He called it table talk, but this month's mismanagement cannot be remedied, maybe not for years, "and it may be forever" — as the song says! A freshet in the autumn does not compensate for a drought in the spring. Time and tide wait for no man, and there was a tide in our affairs which might have led to Washington. We did not take it, and so lost our fortune; this nobody could deny!

We hear two South Carolinians have been hung by the Yankees; and a Virginia woman said: "The President threatens to hang four Yankees for these two; a crazy threat." Carolinians are beginning to brag "like dogs begin to bark and bite, for 'tis their nature to!" Mr. Barnwell says "Gamecock" would have been a good name for the whole state. We are game; we fight to the bitter end. But we are too ready to begin a fight, and why must we flap our wings and crow so loud? Now we go in for claiming the credit of turning the tide of battle on the 21st, when we were being pressed back by the weight of heavier columns. Suddenly there was a panic and we raced them back across the Potomac. Now who killed cock robin? "I," said the sparrow, "with my bow and arrow." At any rate, cock robin has flown. Write *requiescat in pace*, on a heavy tombstone, with no fear of *resurgam*.

Dr. Gibbes tells a story, sad enough. He was seated with a friend of his from Columbia, a lady who could hear nothing of her husband, so she came to find out what she could for herself. They were occupying chairs placed in the corridor, and some Columbia men came strolling by. Dr. Gibbes went to speak to them. "What brought you down from the Army? I thought furloughs were not so easy to get." "Oh, we came to bring poor Smith's body." So Dr. Gibbes had to hurry back and lead the unhappy woman into a room, or she would have met these men and heard of the death of her husband there out in that thronged passageway.

AUGUST 3rd. — Went to the Library of the Capitol with Mr. Brewster. The librarian said I must have a separate order from some Senator for every two books that I wanted. Mr. Boyce was there, and Mr. Hunter and Mr. Hemphill, so I got four books.

Little Fanny Wigfall, a mere mite of a thing, Wigfall's offspring, heard someone say on the cars as she came from Connecticut: "We are now in Virginia." She sprang to her feet. "And now I may be permitted to express my political sentiments," she cried.

Mr. Brewster told me that the northwest part of South Carolina had been without a showing for so long a time they were restive. Mr. Chesnut being from the east made it a bad lookout for him at the next election. "It is very hard to be beaten for anything, by anybody, or in any way," I sighed. "Yes," said the plain-spoken Brewster. "We might bear the disappointment of our friends, but the exultation of one's enemies — who can bear it?"

McClellan virtually supercedes the titan Scott. Physically, General Scott is the largest man I ever saw. Mrs. Scott said: "Nobody but his wife could ever know how little he was!" And yet they say old Winfield Scott could have organized an army for them, if they had had patience. They would not give him time.

The President and family have moved into their own house, the Brockenbrough Mansion.* The unmannerly papers call Mrs. President Davis "portly and middle-aged."

Miss Garnett, Mrs. Singleton's governess — no relative to our Garnetts — is an Irishwoman. She met Dick Manning, who said: "I did not think you would kiss me now. I am such a big boy!" "Yes, indeed," she retorted. "I would not mind if you were twice as big!" Once when Governor Manning began to pay himself some of the highest compliments, Miss Garnett said: "Oh! I see your trumpeter is dead." "What do you mean?" "Have you not to blow your own trumpet?" Someone said: "My mother even wears a pistol now." "What for?" "For runaway Negroes, disorderly soldiers, men coming from nobody knows where." Miss Garnett replied: "I am thoroughly afraid of a pistol, not the least in the world afraid of a man." Nor need she have been!

Burwell Boykin, son of Burwell Boykin of Mount Pleasant, died of typhoid fever. My sister writes: "So we have lost our best man, the very best man I ever knew, the kindest. One of the largest slave owners in the county, in attending to his plantation Negroes among whom this fever raged, he caught it and died." So many escape the dangers and perils of the battlefield, only to die in their peaceful homes. This one could ill be spared. We need just such a well-balanced character, just such a fearless good man at home, where there are now so few left, and so many women and children and Negroes.

Dr. Boykin wants the Kirkwood Rangers, of which he is First Lieu-

* The White House of the Confederacy, built in 1816 by Dr. John Brockenbrough — of whom John Randolph of Roanoke said "That gentleman stands A1 among men" — after changing hands several times, was sold in 1861 to the city of Richmond. The city proposed to offer it to Mr. Davis as his residence; but he declined to accept it till the Confederacy rented the house for his use. After the fall of Richmond, President Lincoln visited the mansion. Subsequently it came to be used as a school building, till in 1890 it was bought by popular subscription and converted into the present Museum.

tenant, mustered into service. Also he says in a letter that Colonel Chesnut must raise a cavalry regiment. The aforesaid Colonel has gone to see what he can do to pacify Toombs and Maxcy Gregg. South Carolina troops and Georgians have been fighting on the cars over watermelons which were being brought here as a present for Mrs. Davis.

Prince Jerome has gone to Washington. Yankees, so far, are as little trained as we are; but suppose France takes the other side and we have to meet disciplined and armed men, soldiers who understand war, Frenchmen with all the *élan* of which we boast.

Ransom Calhoun, Willie Preston and Dr. Nott's boys are here. These foolish, rash, hair-brained Southern lads have been within an ace of a fight over their camping ground with a Maryland company. That is too Irish, to be so ready to fight anybody, friend or foe. They are thrilling with fiery ardor. The red-hot Southern martial spirit is in the air. These young men, however, were all educated abroad; and it is French or German ideas that they are filled with. The Marylanders were as rash and reckless as themselves, and had their coattails ready for anybody to tread on, Donnybrook Fair fashion. One would think there were Yankees enough and to spare for any killing that was to be done. It all began about picketing their horses. These quarrelsome young soldiers have lovely manners. They are so sweet tempered here among us at the Arlington.

After twelve o'clock last night Mr. Barnwell sent for Mr. Chesnut, who told me to go to the door and say he was in bed and asleep; and he made his words good in a few seconds. I had a new novel, so they doubtless saw a light in my dressing room.

August 4th. — Mine is a heavy, heavy heart. Of all our sorrows, memory is the worst. Another missive from Jordan is querulous and fault-finding. Things are all wrong. But here they seem to feel that the war is over, except the President and Mr. Barnwell, and all the foreboding such as Captain Ingraham. He thinks it has only begun.

Mr. Chesnut told me about the trouble last night, the Maxcy Gregg-Toombs imbroglio. Davis, a Georgian, killed Axson, a Carolinian, on the cars in a quarrel which grew out of watermelons. Two Carolinians were mixed up in the row and Gregg will not surrender them to Toombs and Georgia reprisals.

Another outburst from Jordan. He says Beauregard is not seconded properly. To think that any mortal general (even though he had sprung up in a month or so from Captain of Artillery to General) could be so puffed up with vanity, so blinded by a false idea of his own consequence, as to intimate that men would sacrifice their country, injure themselves, and ruin their families to spite the aforesaid general. Conceit and self-love can never reach a higher point than that! They give you to understand Mr. Davis does not like Beauregard; in point of fact they fancy he is jealous of him. They say that rather than let Beauregard make a good showing, Mr. President — who would be hanged, at the very least, if things go wrong — will cripple the army. Mr. Mallory says: "How we would laugh! But you see it is no laughing matter to have our fate in the hands of such self-sufficient, vain Army idiots." Beauregard called Joe Kershaw a militia idiot, so the amenities of life are spreading.

In the meantime we seem to be lying on our oars, debating in Congress while the enterprising Yankees are doubling and quadrupling their Army at their leisure. A knack of hoping is a great blessing in private life, but a too hopeful Congress is a positive misfortune. Every day regiments march by. The town is crowded with soldiers. These new ones are running in, fairly. They fear the war will be over before they get a sight of the fun. Every man from every little country precinct wants a place in the picture.

AUGUST 5th. — The North requires 600,000 to invade us. Truly we are a formidable power! The New York Herald says it is useless to move with a man less than that. England has made it all up with them, or rather she will not break with them. Jerome Napoleon also is in Washington, and not our friend.

At the Spotswood, the want of dignity in Government officials would entrance Mrs. Bradford. Madame —— has children, mostly babies, with a little black Topsy to mind them. Topsy is clad, as Topsy always is on the stage, in one straight homespun garment. She shares the general spanking which besets the olive branches, or so Trescot tells us. He objects to the chastisement of the infantry because he cannot sleep for the howling. Topsy seems happy as the day is long, and so are the objects of her ward and guard. One is ill just now. Madame —— says, with a whimper: "They just simply will play in the dreen!" No affectation of high life in all that!

Dr. Gibbes is a bird of ill omen. Today he tells me eight of our men have died at the Charlottesville Hospital. It seems sickness is more redoubtable in an army than the enemy's guns. There are 1100 there *hors de combat*, and virulent typhoid fever among them. They want money, clothes, nurses; so I am writing right and left calling for help from the sister societies at home. The good and patriotic women at home are easily stirred to this work.

Mary Hammy has many strings to her bow; a fiancé in the Army and Dr. Berrian in town. Today she drove out with Major Smith and Colonel Hood; and yesterday Custis Lee was here. But she is a prudent little puss and needs no good advice — if I were one to give it.

Today I had a passage at arms with Mrs. Smith Lee, *née* Mason. She assaulted Mr. Miles for saying that it was no new thing for him to hate the Star Spangled Banner and that he had always looked on it as it floated over the Custom House at Charleston, or over the forts, as a symbol of oppression. She does not take to the new order of things kindly, says she was "dragged away from Washington and across the Long Bridge, kicking."

Toombs and Maxcy Gregg snarl as hotly as ever over Axson dead and Davis threatened. We got the worst of it. Our man Axson was killed, and all the protocols in the world will not bring him to life, but Maxcy Gregg is grinding his teeth savagely.

Lawrence does all our shopping. All of his master's money was in his hands until now. I thought it injudicious, when gold is at such a premium, to leave it lying loose in the tray of a trunk, so I have sewed it up in a belt which I can wear in an emergency. The cloth is wadded, and my diamonds are there too. The belt has strong strings, so it can be tied under my hoops, around my waist, if the worst comes to the worst. Lawrence wears the same bronze mask with no sign of anything he may feel or think of my latest fancy. Only, I know he asks for twice as much money now when he goes to buy things; at least twice as much as he used to take when it was lying in the tray for him to do as he pleased with it. Which reminds me of the saying that "honesty sometimes keeps a man from growing rich, as civility often keeps him from being witty." Many a good laugh has to be suppressed for fear of hurting people's feelings. Wit is a rare article, after all is said and done.

I went to Miss Sally Tompkins's * hospital, and there I was rebuked, and I felt I deserved it. I asked: "Are there any Carolinians here?" She replied: "I never ask where the sick and wounded come from."

AUGUST 8th. — Wilmot DeSaussure makes an admirable salad dressing for our tomatoes; and I am so hot, so tired, so feverish I care

* Miss Sally Tompkins, immediately after Manassas, established a hospital in the Robertson house at the corner of Main and Third Street; and without help from the Government made it so useful that she was given a commission in the Army. She was the only woman thus honored by the Confederacy.

for nothing else. Today I saw a sword captured at Manassas. The man who brought the sword was taken prisoner by the Yankees in the early part of the fray. They stripped him, took his sleeve buttons, and were in the act of despoiling him of his boots when the rout began, and the play was reversed.

Wade Hampton denounced those men taken prisoner so early in the day, called them cowards and liars.

Commodore Barron came with glad tidings. We had taken three prizes at sea, and brought them in safely; one was laden with molasses, one with sugar, one with salt and fruit. Miss Barron has a letter from Washington. It says "Tilly Emory reads us the most amusing letters from our little stockade," as she calls the blockaded and shut in and ably guarded Confederacy. Mr. Smith Lee says indignantly: "Who writes those letters?"

Mr. Lyon told us Lord Dundas pronounced the blockade incomplete. Commodore Barron said: "Such a speech will only make the Yankees stricter, and cause them to double the ships on guard duty."

Captain Ingraham did not see how they could keep up a stricter watch. His heart is torn in twain. The United States Navy has been his supreme affection, his first thought and duty. Patriotism now calls him to turn and fight against his first love. When I tell him he ought to have brought his ships in with him, he is amazed. "That would have been treason," he cries. I say: "Not so, not more than coming yourself. The ships were ours, as much as you were ours. Half of everything was ours. We paid our taxes, kept up the revenue." He smiles in pity at a woman pretending to understand things; but I say: "We were a co-partnership. When we dissolved it, we had a right to divide assets. Our money helped to build ships, and the tariff in some inscrutable way took all our money. We had a right to share and share alike all public property."

Mr. Meynardie first told us how pious a Christian soldier was Kershaw; how he prayed, got up, dusted his knees and led his men on to victory with a dash and courage equal to any Old Testament mighty man of war. Then came John Green, and he reversed the picture. "When Kershaw saw the Legion give way he cried: 'Damn you, you shameful cowards, turn back or I'll fire on you.' " He used some mighty fanciful profanity, got up in the fury of the moment; but the classic English 'damn' covers it all.

"Impossible," I protested, and repeated what Mr. Meynardie had just told us. "Besides, there will be blood shed if they hear you say they fled at Manassas; and after all, who kept the enemy at bay until Kirby Smith arrived? For pity's sake, be magnanimous. You are all brave enough!"

Mrs. Sam Jones — called Becky, by her friends and cronies, male and female — said that Mrs. Pickens had confided to someone that Mrs. Wigfall described Mrs. Davis to her as a coarse western woman. At first Mrs. Joe Johnston called Mrs. Davis "a western belle"; but when the quarrel between Johnston and the President broke out, Mrs Johnston took back the "belle" and substituted "woman."

Mrs. Johnston was on her way to see Mrs. Rickett, who is sharing her husband's prison. Rickett's battery is principally famous for the number of heroes who took it. I know of twenty or more — Captains, Colonels, Majors, even privates — who captured Rickett's Battery.

Dr. Gibbes today was furious. He said: "Walker's slowness will cost thousands of lives." "Slowness in promoting Dr. Gibbes," we whispered to each other, Mrs. Preston and I.

Here is Governor Manning's account of Prince Jerome Napoleon: "He is stout, and he is not handsome. Neither is he young, and as he reviewed our troops he was terribly overheated." He says the Prince seldom speaks. "But I heard him say '*En Avant*.' That I can testify of my own knowledge; and I was told he had been heard to say, with unction, '*Allons*' more than once." The sight of the battlefield had made the Prince seasick, and he received gratefully a draught of fiery whiskey.

Beauregard is half Frenchman, and speaks French like a native; so one awkwardness was done away with. Governor Manning remarked that it was a comfort to see Beauregard speak without the agony of finding words in a foreign language, and forming them with damp brow; a fate which befell others who spoke "a little French." The Prince said one more battle would end the conflict. May he prove a prophet.

Scott's favorite aid, to us bequeathed so unwillingly, distinguished himself. The aforesaid fiery whiskey was to blame. He sat on the dinner table after dinner, kicking his heels against the table legs, with his back to the Prince. Later, when they were all riding around, he got into everybody's way and General Beauregard said to Joe Heyward: "Get him off, somehow." Joe Heyward made short work of it. He seized the horse by the bit and roughly backed the animal down in a ditch, then called to some soldiers: "Come here and carry off this fellow." Captain Heyward was too well bred to be ruffled by any such trifle. His face betrayed no emotion. But Governor Manning said: "In our hearts we were crying, 'Well done, Joe.' "

Mrs. Johnston and Mrs. Rickett have fraternized and wept together. One heartless being asked Mrs. Johnston if she found the prisoner in irons, and being answered in the negative cried with indignation: "Oh I only hope he was tied to the bedpost by a light chain." Such chaffing was in bad taste, but it continued. Mrs. Rickett was offered a private apartment, but she sought a martyr's crown. She said she came to nurse her husband, and to be with him. She wished to look after the wounded, and to share the privations of the prisoners. I should think she has had a fine opportunity of testing her zeal, occupying a room with half a dozen men. I tell the tale as it is told to me.

General and Mrs. Cooper came to see us. She is Mrs. Smith Lee's sister. They were talking of old George Mason. In Virginia, his was a name to conjure with. George Mason violently opposed the extension of slavery. He was a thorough aristocrat, and gave as his reason for refusing the blessing of slaves to the new states in the Southwest and Northwest that vulgar new people were unworthy of so sacred a right as that of holding slaves. It was not an institution intended for such people as they were. Mrs. Lee remarked: "What good does it do my sons to be Light Horse Harry Lee's grandsons, and George Mason's? I do not see that it helps them at all." When Mrs. Lee and the Coopers had gone, what a rolling of eyes and uplifting of hands! Fitzhugh Lee and Roony are being promoted hand over fist; and Custis Lee is A.D.C. to the President, they say because his father wishes it. If he prefers to be in active service, that matters not; he must stay where he can do most good. Thus ran the drawing-room hum at the Arlington.

Russell, the Times man, gives a ludicrous account of Senator Wilson's flight from the battlefield on the 21st of July. A friend in Washington writes me that we might have walked into Washington any day for a week after Manassas, such was the consternation and confusion there. Now, she says troops are literally pouring in from all quarters, and she thinks we have lost our chance forever.

Mrs. Wigfall said triumphantly that Cobb, Hammond, Keitt, Boyce and Banks were in the coalition against Jeff Davis, although Clay of Alabama was still his personal friend. Wigfall, fresh from the Army, stroked his beard and said nothing. He has too much common sense not to see how quarrelling among ourselves must end.

Alex Haskell,* Gregg's aide-de-camp, who has all human perfections except that he stammers fearfully in speech — though he fights without let or hindrance — is engaged to be married to Rebecca Singleton. We are all glad of it.

Mary Hammy has gone to stay at the President's for a few days with Maggie Howell. Mrs. Davis paid Mary a compliment. "She is a girl any mother might be proud to have brought up." Mrs. Davis is utterly upset. She is beginning to hear the carping and fault-finding to which the President is subjected. There must be an opposition in a free country, but it is very uncomfortable. United we stand, divided we fall. She showed us in the New York Tribune an extract from an Augusta, Georgia, paper. "Cobb is our man. Davis is at heart a reconstructionist."

We may be flies on the wheel — we know our insignificance — but Mrs. Preston and myself have entered into an agreement and our oath is recorded on high. We mean to stand by our President, and to stop all fault-finding with the powers that be, be they Generals or Cabinet Ministers. We can be magnanimous, even if we are feeble!

August 13th. — Mr. Robert Barnwell says the Mercury influence began this opposition to Jeff Davis before he had time to do wrong. They were offended not with him so much as with the man who was put in what they considered Barnwell Rhett's rightful place. The latter had howled nullification and secession for so long that when he found his ideas taken up by all the Confederate world, he felt he had a vested right to the leadership. Mr. Barnwell says: "If this influence combines with the Davis people in South Carolina, Mr. Chesnut will not be sent back to the Senate. He is now the breakwater between those two extremes." If that happens, think of being again immured in Camden; those long, long weary days, outside friendship with only a handful of people, and no intercourse with those who up to this time have been my world.

There is here a handsome Spaniard, or rather a Cuban, leader of rebellion there too. He is said to be so like Beauregard as to be mistaken for him. This Gonzales, besides his fine person, has a fine voice. He sings divinely. Tonight he told me that General Robert E. Lee was

* The letters and diary of Alexander Cheves Haskell, edited by his daughter, Mrs. Louise Haskell Daly, present what is probably the most vivid picture of cavalry tactics and cavalry action on the Southern side during the war.

fencing with Rosencrantz * in the western mountains of Virginia. General Lee's daughters are staying with Mrs. Stanard. Mrs. Smith Lee has come here to the Arlington. Nine funerals passed here Sunday.

I went to Miss Sally Tompkins's Hospital today. Mrs. James Alfred Jones and Mrs. Carter were assisting Miss Tompkins.

Jordan, Beauregard's A.D.C., still writes to Mr. Chesnut that the mortality among the raw troops in camp is fearful. Yet everybody seems to be doing all they can. Think of the British sick and wounded away off in the Crimea. These people are only a half a day's journey by rail from Richmond.

With a grateful heart I record the Davis reconciliation with the Wigfalls. They dined at the President's yesterday, and the little Wigfall girls stayed all night.

Seward is fêting the outsiders; Napoleon, the cousin of the Emperor, and Russell of the omnipotent London Times. But there is no outside to our Confederate stockade.

Mr. Clayton reports to us a speech of Vice-President Stephens. He said that "the revolution had only begun, and that if we were wise in our conduct, we should soon have Washington, and some of the Northern states would join us." Certainly we undervalued ourselves. We had no idea they would consider it such a disaster to lose us. They abused us and called us so worthless, seemed to find us a disgrace they would be glad to shake off. Or so we had every reason to think!

AUGUST 14th. — Boykin's Rangers are in tantrums now because Joe Kershaw says he won the battle, that the Rangers came too late! It was suggested that this may not be our very last battle, and that Boykin and his Rangers may yet figure in the Gazette to their hearts' content. Joe writes his own praise.

Last night there was a crowd of men to see us, and they were so clever and so critical. I made a futile effort to record their sayings, but sleep and heat overcame me and today I can hardly remember a word. But I remember one of Mr. Mason's stories, a thing he heard on the cars. That is one of our sources of "reliable information." A man entered, of very respectable appearance, and standing in the gangway he announced: "I am just from the seat of the war." Newspaper men heard him. "Is Fairfax Courthouse burned?" they asked. "Yes, burnt yesterday." "I am just from there," one objected. "Left it standing all

* The usual Confederate way of spelling "Rosecrans."

right an hour or so ago." "Oh," explained the man who was 'just from the seat of the war,' "I must do them justice to say they burned only the Tavern. They did not want to tear up and burn anything but the railroad." "There is no railroad at Fairfax Courthouse," objected the man just from Fairfax. "Oh! Indeed!" said 'the seat of the war,' "I did not know that. Is that so?" And he coolly seated himself and began talking of something else.

We had a more reliable style of witness last night who described Cash's interview with Congressman Ely. Cash was for short work. "Take him back and shoot him!" This was by no means Ely's idea of war. Of course, Cash was stopped in time.* Our informant, General Cooper's son, said Ely, a Negro and a parson were kept all night in a stable, and the parson howled and cried. Next morning they were in the wagon and someone called: "Give the Negro a good master and a good whipping, and hang the Congressman and the parson." Poor Ely nearly died of terror. Our people are lashing themselves into a fury against the prisoners. Only the mob in any country would do that. Decency and propriety will not be forgotten, and the prisoners will be treated as prisoners of war ought to be in a civilized country.

Prince Napoleon, in compliment no doubt to his English speaking hosts, said "Damn" more than once. At least, credible witnesses so testify.

August 15th. — Mrs. Randolph came, and with her the Freelands, Rose and Maria. The men rave over Mrs. Randolph's beauty, call her a magnificent specimen of the finest type of dark-eyed, rich and glowing Southern womankind. Clean brunette she is, with the reddest lips, the whitest teeth, and glorious eyes. There is no other word for them. Having given Mrs. Randolph the prize among Southern beauty, Mr. Clayton said Prentiss was the finest Southern orator. Mr. Marshall and Mr. Barnwell dissented. They preferred William C. Preston. Mr. Chesnut had found Colquitt the best, or at least the most effective stump orator.

Henry Dean Nott, just from Paris via New York, says New York is ablaze with martial fire. At no time during the Crimean War was

* Congressman Ely, in his published narrative, says that his captors at Manassas took him to Colonel E. B. C. Cash of a South Carolina Regiment, who "drawing his pistol and pointing it directly at my head replied: 'G—d d—n your white-livered soul! I'll blow your brains out!' " According to Mr. Ely, the Confederate captain restrained Colonel Cash and apologized for his actions, saying "he was very much excited and had been drinking."

there ever in Paris such a show of soldiers preparing for the war as he saw in New York. The face of the earth seemed covered with marching regiments. We heard from Captain Buchanan, of Maryland, the reverse of this appalling picture of New York as an armed camp. Captain Buchanan saw the disbanded regiments going home and rejoicing on their way.

The debate about who won our battle still goes on. Mr. Chesnut finds all this very amusing, as he posted many of the regiments, and all the time was carrying orders over the field. The discrepancies of all these private memories amuse him; but he smiles and lets every man tell the tale his own way. Certainly too much modesty does not oppress us. Mr. Barnwell says: "Fame is an article usually homemade. You must write your own puffs, or superintend their manufacture; and you must tell the newspapers to print your own military reports. No one else will give you half the credit you take to yourself. No one will look after your fine name before the world with the loving interest and faith you have in yourself." This thing of telling a lie until you believe it! They say George the Fourth actually believed he had been at Waterloo disguised as a major.

AUGUST 16th. — Russell's letters are becoming utterly abominable, but not half so bad as his accounts of the British in India. Those Indian letters show us British philanthropy when their blood is up! Imagine! An inferior race to rise against them! According to the admirers of John Brown, the East Indians treated the English women and children just as they had cause to do.

We hear news of a victory, this time in Missouri, far enough off for us to believe anything we choose.

Mary Hammy says 'Shot Pouch' Walker has the handsomest A.D.C. she ever saw, and that Gonzales is splendid in grey or in blue, I forget which, but the uniform he wore today.

Captain Shannon of the Kirkwoods called and stayed three hours. He has not yet been under fire, but is keen to hear or to see the flashing of the guns. He is proud of himself and proud of his company, but proudest of all that he has no end of the bluest blood of the Low Country in his troop. FFC's, he says, of the first water. He seemed to find my knitting a pair of socks every day for the soldiers droll. He has been so short a time from home he does not know how the poor soldier needs them. He was so overpoweringly flattering to my husband that I found him very pleasant company.

I read "Oliver Twist" again.

August 18th. — Found it quite exciting to have a spy drinking his tea with us, perhaps because I knew his profession. I did not like his face. He is said to have a scheme by which Washington will fall into our hands like an overripe peach.

Miss Sally Tompkins laughed at Mrs. Carter, who is so handsome. The wounded men could not help looking at her, and one was not so badly off but that he burst into flowery compliment! Mrs. Carter turned scarlet with surprise and indignation. Miss Sally Tompkins said, "If you could leave your beauty at the door, and bring in only your goodness and your energy."

I found that Mary Hammy is competent to pronounce on a man's comeliness. Walker's A.D.C. is all she said he was, a picture of manly beauty. Captain Haseltine, who breakfasted with me, thought women attached too much importance to men's outside show. Hm-m!

Governor Means, means to be a Brigadier. Governor Manning has gone home with similar intentions, I fancy. The day for high and mighty A.D.C.'s is over. War means business now, and a young and a trained staff is desirable.

Mrs. Wynne said: "England and France recognized us yesterday!" She said she had it from a sure hand. A prophet he must be too, as it takes some little time to get the news. Some suggested the spirits had brought the news, up the table legs no doubt. They annihilate time and space, even if they don't make two lovers happy. The newspapers contain news from over the water that is encouraging. Some of the Yankee prisoners of a better sort are publishing letters in the Herald denying the stories of their ill treatment here. I doubt if they are happy, all the same, or that our prisoners in their hands are on a bed of roses.

Mr. Barnwell urges Mr. Chesnut to remain in the Senate. He says Mr. Chesnut can do his country more good by wise counsel where it is most needed. I do not say to the contrary. I dare not throw my influence on the army side, for if anything happened!

Why am I so frightfully ambitious? I will try from henceforth to care only for my country's salvation.

Mr. Miles told us last night that he had another letter from General Beauregard. The general wants to know if Mr. Miles has delivered his message to Colonel Kershaw. Mr. Miles says he has not done so, neither does he mean to do it. They must settle their matters of veracity according to their own military etiquette. It is a foolish wrangle. Colonel Kershaw ought to have reported to his commander-in-chief, and not made an independent report and published it.

Yesterday in the Congress, Mr. Chesnut spoke against confiscation. I know he is right, though I can't say I understand it all. Then there is sequestration, that I will give the go-by. I understand it less than the other thing. I hate all bankruptcy and cheating creditors, at home and abroad. Today he is ill in bed, the confiscation effort too much for him maybe. While he has fever, he gives me all the reasons why the confiscation act conflicts with the law of nations.

Today at dinner an awkward scene. How I wished Mr. Chesnut had been there. He has so much tact as a pacificator. If General Walker and Honorable Robert Barnwell were but as common folk, I should say "words had passed," and ugly ones. It happened thus. Two Yankee officers who fought or figured at Manassas have since deserted and come over to us. I can understand how deserters should be detestable, come they from East or West, North or South. They, the deserters, are going with our army. General Walker said: "If I had had a brother killed at Manassas, I would shoot down these men at sight." Mr. Barnwell gave that little twittering nervous laugh of his. "And then you'd be hanged." "Never. Twenty thousand Georgians are here. They would create a counter-revolution before they would permit a hair of my head to be touched." Mr. Barnwell repeated his offensive little laugh. "Nevertheless, you would be hanged. You ought to be hanged if you commit murder."

This he fired off at regular intervals, and 'Shot Pouch' Walker literally raved. "No, no! My Georgians would know the reason why," etc. Mr. Barnwell grew very quiet, but continued his fatuous smile, and to the last stuck to his original preposition: "You'd be hanged." This made me wretched. Mr. Barnwell was right, but why would he say it any more? I was so uncomfortable that as soon as silence prevailed, I left the table. I made a good deal of commotion on purpose, dropped things to be picked up, fan, handkerchief, all to divert them from their madness or folly. A man is always in such a fuss about his dignity, what is due his own self-respect and so forth, and so contemptuous of feminine folly!

Our Government declines to adopt the Washington spy's plot, and the spy's scheme to blow up the Capital by inside and social influence has fallen through.

The New York Tribune is so unfair. It began howling to get rid of us. We were so wicked. Now that we are so willing to leave them to their over-righteous self-consciousness, they cry "crush our enemy or they will subjugate us." The idea, that we want to invade or to subjugate! We would only be too grateful to be left alone. Only let us alone. We ask no more, of Gods or men.

A general belief says: "This war is an attempt to extend the area of slavery." Can that be? When not one third of our volunteer army are slave owners? And not one third of that third fail to dislike slavery as much as Mrs. Stowe, or Horace Greeley. And few have found their hatred or love of it remunerative as an investment.

The heat and the excitement and a sort of slow fever subdues me quite, and takes away all appetite, leaving me to live on tomatoes alone, and Wilmot DeSaussure's salad dressing. Today he had so much politics to whisper to me that I forgot even the tomatoes — raw. It was all about the rapid growth of the party forming against Mr. Davis.

Our soldiers rest all their disasters upon Commissary Northrop. They say the army at Manassas is paralyzed by illness. From the New York Herald we see that in Washington they are calling for all sorts of regiments, from anywhere and anybody, anything.

The impressible, the notorious A. D. Banks indulged in a private street fight yesterday. Have not heard who his antagonist was.

Nat Willis is still peeping around the world. This time he saw Lincoln changing his shirt, and he describes it. That is one of Nat's small ways of singing and stinging. The great Illinoisian took exactly twenty-two minutes to dress, by Willis's watch, all at an open window, with Franklin's air bath thrown in. Picture Lincoln adonizing! They say Lincoln is frightfully uncouth and ugly, with the keenest sense of vulgar humor.

It is General Lee's army now who are abusing Northrop. They can't move for want of commissary stores. That terrible Northrop!

I went to the hospital with a carriage load of peaches and grapes, and made glad the hearts of some men thereby. When my supply gave out, those who had none looked so wishfully as I passed out that I made a second raid on the market. Those eyes sunk in cavernous depths haunted me as they followed me from bed to bed.

In the hospital I met Anthony Kennedy from Camden. He coolly helped himself and ate my soldier's peaches, as if peaches grew on trees here free to all.

Wilmot DeSaussure harrowed my soul by an account of a recent death by drowning on the beach at Sullivan's Island. A Mr. Porcher, who was trying to save his sister's life, lost his own and his child's. People seem to die out of the army quite as much as in it.

Mrs. Randolph presided in all her beautiful majesty at an aid association. The ladies were old ones, and all wanted their own way. They were cross-grained and contradictory, and the blood would mount rebelliously into Mrs. Randolph's clear-cut cheek, but she held her own with dignity and grace. One of the causes of disturbance was that Mrs. Randolph proposed to divide everything sent in equally with the Yankee wounded and sick prisoners. Some were enthusiastic from a Christian point of view; some shouted in wrath at the bare idea of putting our noble soldiers on a par with Yankees, living, dying or dead. Shrill and long and loud it was; fierce dames, some of them; august, severe matrons who evidently had not been accustomed to hear the other side of any argument from anybody, and who were just old enough to find the last pleasure in life in power — the power to make their claws felt. Those old ladies each had philanthropic schemes, but they held to their own and would listen to no other. Maybe such warmth will hurry on the good work.

AUGUST 23rd. — A brother of Dr. Garnett has come fresh and straight from Cambridge, and he says that recruiting up there is dead. He came by Cincinnnati and Petersburg; says all the way it was so sad and mournful and quiet that it looked like Sunday. Meantime the camp is a hospital; that terrible sickness continues there, and with it the abuse of the persons in power. They seem to hold the War Department responsible. As if they could help it!

I asked Mr. Brewster if it were true Senator Toombs had turned Brigadier. "Yes, soldiering is in the air. Everyone will have a touch of it. Toombs could not stay in the Cabinet." "Why?" "Incompatibility of temper. He rides too high a horse for so despotic a person as Jeff Davis."

Gonzales lit my candle for me, and at the foot of the stairs gave me a box of quinine pills for my husband, whose fever lingers still. These foreigners have a way of doing things, gracious and graceful.

Oh such a day! Since I wrote this morning I have been with Mrs. Randolph to all the hospitals. I can never again shut out of view the sights I saw of human misery. I sit thinking, shut my eyes and see it all. Thinking, yes, and there is enough to think about now, God knows! Long rows of ill men on cots; ill of typhoid fever, of every human ailment; wounds being dressed; all horrors to be taken in at one glance.

At the Alms house, Dr. Gibson is in charge. He married a Miss Ayer of Philadelphia. He is fine-looking and has charming manners, the very beau-ideal of a family physician, so suave and gentle and pleasant. The Sisters of Charity are his nurses. That makes all the difference in the world. They told us Mrs. Rickett was there. Mrs. Randolph did not ask for her. One elderly sister, withered and wrinkled and yet with the face of an angel, spoke severely to a young surgeon. "Stop that sky-larking," she said; and he answered: "Where have you sent that pretty Sister you had here yesterday? We all fell in love with her." We had the joke all to ourselves, however. She did not see it; but after a while she said: "*Honi soit qui mal y pense.*" The wounded soldiers enjoyed every word that was said.

Then we went to the St. Charles. Horrors upon horrors again. Want of organization, long rows of men dead and dying; awful smiles and awful sights. A boy from home had sent for me. He was lying on a cot, ill of fever. Next him a man died in convulsions while we stood there. I was making arrangements with a nurse, hiring him to take care of this lad. I do not remember any more, for I fainted. The next I knew, the doctor and Mrs. Randolph were having me, a limp rag, put into the carriage at the door of the hospital. Fresh air, I dare say, brought me to! First of all we had given our provisions to our Carolinians at Miss Sally Tompkins'. There they were nice and clean, and merry as grigs.

As we drove home, we brought the doctor with us, I was so upset. He said: "Look at that Georgia regiment marching there. Look at their servants on the sidewalk. I have been counting them, making an estimate. There is sixteen thousand dollars worth of Negro property which can go off on its own legs to the Yankees tomorrow whenever it pleases."

Russell, I think in his capacity of Englishman, despises both sides. He derides us equally, North and South. He prefers to attribute Bull's Run to Yankee cowardice rather than to Southern courage. He gives no credit to either side. After all, we are mere Americans!

August 24th. — Today, the wife of the kind surgeon of yesterday called. Whenever I see much of a man and he immediately sends his wife to make my acquaintance I know it is a compliment. It is the pleasantest kind of flattery.

Mr. Miles and Mr. Mason came to go with us to the President's reception. Mr. Miles is going home with Mr. Mason, who lives near

Winchester. There revels the Yankee Banks. Should he capture William Porcher Miles, what fun for them! Think of the scorn our friend Miles heaped upon Congressman Ely. The same cup to his own lip would be bitter. Mrs. Davis asks me to luncheon on Monday, and the President said I must make Mr. Chesnut ride with him every evening. Such extraordinary gowns! A grass-green dress with a gold belt, and gold wheat in the fair one's hair. You see, I did go to the reception.

A fiasco; an aide-de-camp was engaged to two young ladies at the same time. They had quarrelled, but they made friends unexpectedly, and his treachery was revealed under that august roof. Fancy the row when it all came out.

When we left the reception, we found our coach but no coachman. When he was found he was not in a condition to drive, so one of the gentlemen of our party took his place and drove us home. At home we found James Lowndes awaiting us. He said that we had already reaped one good result from the war. The orators, the spouters, the furious patriots who were so wordily anxious to do or die for their country, now either had not tried the battlefield at all, or had precipitately left it at their earliest convenience. So he thought we were rid of them for a while, but I doubt it.

I have just read John Bright's speech for the Union in the British Parliament. He is so dead against us. Reading this does not brighten one.

AUGUST 25th. — Mr. Barnwell says democracies lead to untruthfulness. To be always electioneering is to be always false; so both we and the Yankees are unreliable when we narrate our own exploits. How about Empires? Were there ever more stupendous lies than the Emperor Napoleon's? He went on: "People dare not tell the truth in a canvass. They must conciliate their constituency, and everybody in a democracy always wants an office." I said: "At least everybody in Richmond just now seems to want one." Never heeding interruptions, he went on: "As a nation, the English are the most truthful in the world." I retorted: "And so are our country gentlemen. They own their constituents, at least in some of the parishes, where there are so few white people, only immense estates and Negroes. Thackeray tells of the lies on both sides in the British wars with France, England kicking quite alongside of her rival in that fine art. They lied then as fluently as Russell does now about us."

Mr. Clayton, Assistant Secretary of State, says we spend two millions a week. Where is all that money to come from? They don't want us to plant cotton, but to make provisions. Now cotton always means money, or did when there was an outlet for it and anybody to buy it. Where is money to come from?

A rose by any other name; that is our Florence Nightingale, Miss Sally Tompkins. Went to her hospital today. I came home tired to death. I took down my hair, had it hanging over me in a crazy-Jane fashion. I sat still, hands over my head, half undressed but too lazy and sleepy to move. I was in a rocking chair by an open window taking my ease and the cool night air. Suddenly, the door opened and Captain —— walked in. He was in the middle of the room before he saw his mistake. He stared — transfixed, as the novels say — and I dare say I looked an ancient Gorgon. Then, with a more frantic glare, he turned and fled without a word. I got up and bolted the door after him, and then I looked in the glass and laughed myself into hysterics. I will never forget to lock the door again. Of course it does not matter. I looked totally unlike the person bearing my name who, covered with lace caps, etc., frequents the drawing room. I doubt if he knows me again.

AUGUST 26th. — I have ardent symptoms of that hospital slow fever, such headaches, and I am so miserably nervous and depressed.

A polite little Southerner said to Mrs. Foster: "How do you do, Ma'am." She responded in a voice of thunder: "How dare you speak to me! You rebel!" The Southerner was meek and easily frightened, and he cowered in silence. As he came through North Carolina, a woman came aboard the cars. She surveyed the Yankee prisoners, then told them solemnly: "If you kill all of our men, remember, there are the women; and they will run you out with broomsticks." And the virago in her fierceness looked quite equal to the performance of her threat.

"The Terror" has full swing at the North now. All papers favorable to us have been suppressed. How long would our mob stand a Yankee paper here? But newspapers against our Government, such as the Examiner and the Mercury, flourish like green bay trees.

A man up to the elbows in finance said today: "Clayton's story is all nonsense. They did pay out two millions that week, but they paid the soldiers. They don't pay the soldiers every week." "Not by a long shot," cried a soldier laddie, with a grin.

Someone, reading this, asked me: "Why do you write in your diary at all, if, as you say, you have to contradict every day what you wrote yesterday?" "Because I like to tell the tale as it is told to me. I write current rumor. I do not vouch for anything."

Mr. Chesnut went off to see Jeff Davis. He means to take a Colonelcy of Cavalry if they will give it to him. But Jeff Davis was ill in bed; he did not see him.

Wilmot DeSaussure is in ecstacies over a cooking stove invented by the soldiers. It is cut out of the earth on hillsides, chimney and all. Only it is a fixture. They have not faith to move mountains, so must leave the hillside, with its stove cut therein, when they change camp. He thinks I would be a valuable adjunct to Mr. Chesnut's cavalry regiment if I went along and superintended the cuisine. It would add so much to the strength of the army if the men were decently, properly fed.

We went to Pizzini's, that very best of Italian confectioners. From there we went to Miss Sally Tompkins's Hospital, loaded with good things for the wounded. The men under Miss Sally's kind care looked so clean and comfortable; cheerful, one might say. They were pleasant and nice to see. One, however, was dismal in tone and aspect, and he repeated at intervals with no change of words in a forlorn monotone: "What a hard time we have had since we left home." But nobody seemed to heed his wailing, and it did not impair his appetite.

Mrs. Toombs is raging. She is so anti-Davis she will not even admit that the President is ill. "All humbug." "But what good would pretending to be ill do him?" "That reception now, was not that a humbug? Such a failure. Mrs. Reagan could have done better than that!"

Mrs. Walker is a Montgomery beauty with such magnificent dresses — she was an heiress — but she is dissatisfied with Richmond, seems to be accustomed to be a belle. As she is as handsome and well-dressed as ever, it must be the men who are all wrong!

Mrs. Smith Lee says of Southern women that she does not like their languor and easy-going ways; their low voices; their laziness. She would have them like the morning Hamlet saw the ghost, "with an eager and a nipping air." Now there was Loulou Corcoran, loud talking, rough spoken, like the rest of us in Washington. Her grandmother was loud and hearty and strong. Have you seen her now that she is Loulou Eustis, since she has spent a winter with the Eustises in New Orleans? She is as soft and sweet and faint voiced and languid and fine lady as any Eustis of them all; gentle, and quiet, and aggravating as those Southern women all are. And she takes it easy. We thought she would worry about her father. Not at all! She is not the least uneasy. Fine ladies don't fret and make any disturbance; but a year ago she would have howled, or we would have found her unfeeling.

Someone asked me: "Did you give Lawrence that fifty-dollar bill to go out and change? Suppose he takes himself off to the Yankees?" "Well, he would leave us with not too many fifty-dollar bills. He is not going anywhere, however. I think his situation suits him."

That wadded belt of mine, with the gold pieces quilted in; it has made me ashamed more than once. I leave it under my pillow, and my maid finds it and hangs it over the back of a chair, in evidence as I reenter the room after breakfast. I forget and leave my trunk open, and Lawrence brings me the keys, and tells me: "You oughten to do so, Miss Mary." And Mr. Chesnut leaves all his little money in his pockets, and Lawrence says that's why he can't let anyone but himself brush Mars' Jeems clothes.

Beauregard asked Colonel Kershaw how he came to send his military report to the Mercury before he sent it to the Commander-in-Chief. Colonel Kershaw said he did it because Burnett Rhett wished him to, so the Mercury could have the report as soon as possible! So Theo Barker told us today. He does Beauregard's French shrug of the shoulders to perfection.

I heard the wife of a high public functionary say today: "No use to talk to me. If one of them Yankees kills my husband, I'll kill one of them certain and sure." I repeated this to Mrs. Davis, who moaned: "And we were to leave all vulgarity behind us in Washington!"

Here comes the London Post, said to be the mouthpiece of the men in power there. In it I read: "The Southern States of America have achieved their independence." Also came a Scotch paper which has the very best account of us yet published across the water.

AUGUST 27th. — Toady Barker and James Lowndes came today. A man told James Lowndes: "All that I wish on earth is to be at peace, and on my own plantation." Mr. Lowndes said quietly: "I wish I had a plantation to be on, but just now I can't see how anyone would feel justified in leaving the army." The gentleman who had been answered so completely by James Lowndes answered spitefully: "Those women who are so frantic for their husbands to join the army would no doubt like them killed!" Things were growing rather uncomfortable, but an interruption came in the shape of a card. An old classmate of Mr. Chesnut's, Captain Archer, just now fresh from California, followed his card so quickly that Mr. Chesnut had hardly time to tell us that in Princeton College they called him Sally Archer, he was so pretty. He is good looking still, but the service and consequent rough life have destroyed all softness and girlishness. He will never be so pretty again.

Today I saw a letter from a girl crossed in love. Her parents object to the social position of her fiancé; in point of fact, they forbid the banns. She writes: "I am misserable." Her sister she calls a "mean retch." For such a speller, a man of any social status would do. They ought not to expect so much for her. If she wrote her "pah" a note I am sure that "stern parient" would give in.

I am miserable too today, but with one "s." The North is consolidated. They move as one man, with no states but with the army organized by the central power.

We see people here everywhere; I wonder why they let them stay. They are not true to us. Mr. Chesnut says I am like the man in the French convention who howled by the hour for the arrest of everyone. But Governor Letcher says: "Through the treachery of the guides, General Lee's plan for surprising Rosencrantz miscarried." I said: "I hope they hanged the guides!" "You hard-hearted, blood thirsty woman!" Custis Lee was present. He said simply: "I have heard nothing from my father."

I do not know when I have seen a woman without knitting in her hand. "Socks for the soldiers" is the cry. One poor man said he had dozens of socks and but one shirt. He preferred more shirts and fewer stockings. It gives a quaint look, the twinkling of needles, and the everlasting sock dangling. A Jury of Matrons, so to speak, sat at Mrs. Greenhow's. They say Mrs. Greenhow furnished Beauregard with the latest news of the Federal movements, and so made the Manassas victory a possibility. She sent us the enemy's plans. Everything she said proved true, numbers, route and all.

It is a despotism over there now, with Seward the despot; but our men say it enhances our chances three to one. David Power they outraged to the point of driving him in to us. They have arrested Wm. B. Reed and Miss Winder, she boldly proclaiming herself a secessionist. Why should she seek a martyr's crown? Writing people love notoriety. It is so delightful to be of enough consequence to be arrested. I have often wondered if such incense was ever offered as Napoleon's so-called persecution and alleged jealousy of Madame de Staël.

Today our assemblage of women, Confederate, talked pretty freely. Let us record some samples. "You people who have been stationed all over the United States and have been to Europe and all that; tell us home-biding ones. Are our men worse than the others? Does Mrs. Stowe know? You know what I mean?" "No, our men are no worse. Lady Mary Montagu found we were all only men and women, everywhere. But Mrs. Stowe's exceptional cases may be true. You can pick out horrors from any criminal court record or newspaper in any country." "You see, irresponsible men do pretty much as they please."

Russell now, to whom London and Paris and India were everyday sights — and every night too, streets and all: for him to go on in indignation because there were women in Negro plantations who were not vestal virgins! Negro women are married, and after marriage behave as well as other people. Marrying is the amusement of their life. They take life easily. So do their class everywhere. Bad men are hated here as elsewhere.

I hate slavery. You say there are no more fallen women on a plantation than in London, in proportion to numbers; but what do you say to this? A magnate who runs a hideous black harem with its consequences under the same roof with his lovely white wife, and his beautiful and accomplished daughters? He holds his head as high and poses as the model of all human virtues to these poor women whom God and the laws have given him. From the height of his awful majesty, he scolds and thunders at them, as if he never did wrong in his life. Fancy such a man finding his daughter reading "Don Juan." "You with that immoral book!" And he orders her out of his sight. You see, Mrs. Stowe did not hit the sorest spot. She makes Legree a bachelor.

Someone said: "Oh, I know half a Legree, a man said to be as cruel as Legree. But the other half of him did not correspond. He was a man of polished manners, and the best husband and father and church-member in the world." "Can that be so?" "Yes, I know it. And I knew the dissolute half of Legree. He was high and mighty, but the kindest creature to his slaves; and the unfortunate results of his bad ways were not sold. They had not to jump over ice blocks. They were kept in full view, and were provided for, handsomely, in his will. His wife and daughters, in their purity and innocence, are supposed never to dream of what is as plain before their eyes as the sunlight. And they play their parts of unsuspecting angels to the letter. They profess to adore their father as the model of all earthly goodness."

"Well, yes. If he is rich, he is the fountain from whence all bessings flow."

"The one I have in my eye, my half of Legree, the dissolute half, was so furious in his temper, and so thundered his wrath at the poor women that they were glad to let him do as he pleased if they could only escape his everlasting fault-finding and noisy bluster."

"Now, now, do you know any woman of this generation who would stand that sort of thing?"

"No, never, not for one moment. The make-believe angels were of the last century. We know, and we won't have it. These are Old World stories. Women were brought up not to judge their fathers or their husbands. They took them as the Lord provided, and were thankful."

"How about the wives of drunkards? I heard a woman say once, to a friend, of her husband, as a cruel matter of fact without bitterness and without comment: 'Oh, you have not seen him. He is changed. He has not gone to bed sober in thirty years.' She has had her purgatory, if not what Mrs. —— calls 'the other thing,' here in this world. We all know what a drunken man is. To think that for no crime a person may be condemned to live with one thirty years."

"You wander from the question I asked. Are Southern men worse because of the slave system, and the facile black women?"

"Not a bit! They see too much of them. The barroom people don't drink, the confectionary people loathe candy. Our men are sick of the black sight of them!"

"You think a nice man from the South is the nicest thing in the world?" "I know it. Put him by any other man and see!" "And you say there are no saints and martyrs now; those good women who stand by bad husbands? Eh?" "No use to mince matters. Everybody knows the life of a woman whose husband drinks."

"Some men have a hard time, too. I know women who are — well, the very devil and all his imps." "Ah, but men are dreadful animals." "Seems to me those of you who are hardest on men here are soft enough with them when they are present. Now everybody knows I am 'the friend of man' and I defend them behind their backs as I take pleasure in their society, well, before their faces."

Our tongues went on. We heard that Mr. Mason * is going to be sent to England. My wildest imagination will not picture Mr. Mason

* James Mason, former United States Senator from Virginia, set out with John Slidell on a mission to England. They travelled on the British steamer Trent, and when she was stopped and searched by a Union vessel, Mason and Slidell were taken to Boston and imprisoned. The resulting diplomatic interchange brought England and the United States close to a severing of relations before the United States yielded.

as a diplomat. He will say 'chaw' for 'chew,' and he will call himself 'Jeems,' and he will wear a dress coat to breakfast. Over here, whatever a Mason does is right in his own eyes. He is above law. Somebody asked him how he pronounced his wife's maiden name. She was a Miss Chew from Philadelphia.

"The finest and best of women! I don't care how he pronounces the nasty thing, but he will do it; I mean, chew tobacco. In England a man must expectorate like a gentleman, if he expectorates at all." "They say the English will like Mr. Mason; he is so manly, so straightforward, so truthful and bold. A fine old English gentleman — so said Russell — but for tobacco."

And so on for hours.

August 29th. — No more feminine gossip, but the licensed slanderer, mighty Russell of the Times, says the battle of the 21st was fought at long range: 500 yards apart were the combatants. The Confederates were steadily retreating when some commotion in their wagon train frightened the Yankees and they made tracks. In good English, they fled amain; and on our side we were too frightened to follow them, or — in high flown English — to pursue the flying foe. In spite of all this, there are glimpses of the truth sometimes. And the story reads to our credit, with all its sneers and jeers. When he speaks of the Yankees' cowardice, falsehoods, dishonesty, and braggadocio, the best words are in his mouth. He repeats the thrice told tale, so often refuted and denied, that we were harsh to wounded prisoners. Dr. Gibson told me that their surgeon general has written to thank our surgeons. He says: "I know in that hospital with the Sisters of Charity, they were better off than our own men at the other hospitals. That I saw with my own eyes."

Our party of matrons had their shot at those saints and martyrs, the imprisoned Mrs. Greenhow and Mrs. Phillips. These poor souls are jealously guarded night and day. It is a hideous tale. Mrs. Lee punned upon the old expression. "Think of ladies of their age being confined!" Some say Mrs. Greenhow had herself confined and persecuted so that we might trust her the more. The Manassas men swear she was our good angel, but the Washington women say she was up for sale to the highest bidder, always — and they have the money on us.

Women who come before the public are in a bad box now. False hair is taken off and searched for papers. Pistols are sought for with crinolines reversed, bustles are suspect. All manner of things, they say, come over the border under the huge hoops now worn; so, they are ruthlessly torn off. Not legs but arms are looked for under hoops, and sad to say are found. Women are used as detectives and searchers, to see that no men come over in petticoats. So, the poor creatures coming this way are humiliated to the deepest degree. To men war brings glory, honor, praise and power — if they are patriots. To women, daughters of Eve, punishment comes in some shape, do what they will.

Mary Hammy's eyes were starting from her head with amazement while a very large and very handsome South Carolinian talked rapidly. "What is it?" asked I, after he had gone. "Oh, what a year can bring forth. Last summer, you remember how he swore he was in love with me? He told you, he told me, he told everybody; and even if I did refuse to marry him, I believed him. Now he says he has seen, fallen in love with, courted, married another person; and he raves of his little daughter's beauty. Yet they say time goes slowly," said Mary Hammy, with a sigh of wonder.

Mrs. Frank Hampton said you could not flirt with those South Carolinians. They would not stay at the tepid degree of flirtation. "They grow so horridly in earnest before you know where you are."

A hospital nurse from North Carolina says she likes everything Confederate except the "assisting surgeons." She does not like their ways. "They take the white sugar and give the patients moist brown. They take the lemons and give the sick men citric acid. And, as for the whiskey and brandy, many a man has died because the surgeon did not leave, from his own toddy, whiskey enough to keep a typhoid case alive.'

At our feminine pow-wow, someone asked: "Do you think two married people ever lived together without finding each other out? I mean, knowing exactly how good or how shabby, how weak or how strong, and above all how selfish each was?" "Yes, unless they are dolts they know to a tittle. But if they have common sense, they make believe and get on so-so." Like the Marchioness and her orange peel wine in Old Curiosity Shop.

Mr. Barnwell was ill today. When Lawrence brought me the milk and rice which I had prepared my way, I made him take part of it to Mr. Barnwell. Lawrence came back delighted. "Miss Mary, he eat it like he was famished. Nothing here is like home cooking."

A violent attack upon the North today in the Albion. They mean to let freedom slide a while, until they subjugate us. The Albion says they use letters *de cachet*, passports and all the despotic apparatus of regal governments. Russell hears the tramp of the coming man, the king or the kaiser, the tyrant that is to rule them. Is it McClellan? Little

Mac? We may tremble when he comes. We have only "the many-headed monster," armed democracy. Our chiefs quarrel among themselves.

My experience does not coincide with the general idea of public life; I mean the life of a politician or statesman. Peace, comfort, quiet, happiness, I have found away from home. Only your own family, those nearest and dearest, can hurt you. Wrangling, rows, heart-burnings, bitterness, envy, hatred, malice, unbrotherly love, family snarls, neighborhood strife and ill blood — a lovely brood I have conjured up. But they were all there, and for these many years I have almost forgotten them. I find them always alive and rampant when I go back to semi-village life. For after all, though we live miles apart, everybody flying round on horses or in carriages, it amounts to a village community. Everybody knows exactly where to put the knife.

The Adonis of an A.D.C. says, as one who knows, that "Sumter" Anderson's heart is with us, that he will not fight the South. After all that has been said and done, that sounds like nonsense. Also, he told me something of that Garnett who was killed at Cheat Mountain. He has been an unlucky man clear through. In the army before the war, the A.D.C. had found him proud, reserved and morose, as cold as an icicle to all; but for his wife and child, he was a different creature. He adored them and cared for nothing else. One day he went off on an expedition. They were gone six weeks. It was out in the northwest, and the Indians were troublesome. When he came back, his wife and child were underground. He said not one word; but they found him more frozen and stern and isolated than ever, that was all. The night before he left Richmond, he said in his quiet way: "They have not given me an adequate force. I can do nothing. They have sent me to my death." It is acknowledged that he threw away his life. "A dreary-hearted man" said the A.D.C., "and the unluckiest."

On the front steps every evening we take our seats and discourse at our pleasure. A nicer or more agreeable set of people were never assembled than our present Arlington crowd. Tonight it was Yancey who occupied our tongues. Send a man to England who had killed his father-in-law in a street brawl! That was not knowing England or Englishmen, surely. Who wants eloquence? We want somebody who can hold his tongue. People avoid great talkers, men who orate, men given to monologue, as they would avoid fire, famine or pestilence. Yancey will have no mobs to harangue. No stump speeches will be possible, but only a little quiet conversation with slow, solid, common-sense people who begin to suspect as soon as any flourish of trumpets meet their ear. If he uses fine words, who cares for that over there.

"Which will the English bear best; Mr. Mason's tobacco, or Yancey's murder?" "We will wait and see."

Then the Navy men came under discussion. They are like the people St. Paul cited, "who were sawn asunder." There is an awful pull in their divided hearts. Faith in the United States Navy was their creed, and their religion, and now they must fight it and wish it ill luck. Commodore Barron has left us. He has hoisted his flag in the good ship *Manassas*, not half so grand a vessel as his beloved and lost *Wabash*, but he is proud of her. Commodore Barron when he was a middy accompanied Phil Augustus Stockton to claim his bride. He, the said Stockton, had secretly married an heiress, Sally Cantey. They were married by a magistrate and she returned to Mrs. Grélaud's boarding school until it was time to go home to Camden. Lieutenant Stockton was the handsomest man in the Navy, and irresistible. The bride was barely sixteen. And now he was to go down South among those fire eaters and claim her; and Commodore Barron, then his intimate friend, went as his backer. They were to announce the marriage and defy the guardians. Commodore Barron said he expected a rough job of it all, but they were prepared for all risks. "You expected to find us a horde of savages, no doubt." "We did not expect to get off under a half dozen duels." They looked for insults from every quarter. They found in Camden a polished and refined people who lived in princely fashion, and they were received with a cold and stately and faultless politeness which made them feel as if they had been sheep-stealing. The young lady had confessed to her guardians, and they were for making the best of it; above all, for saving her name from all scandal or publicity. Colonel John Boykin took young Lochinvar to stay with him. Colonel Deas sent for a parson and made assurance doubly sure by marrying them over again. Then there came balls and parties and festivities no end. Commodore Barron was enchanted with the easy-going life of these people. With dinner parties the finest in the world, deer- and fox-hunting, dancing, pretty girls, and everything that heart could wish; but then, said the Commodore: "The better it was, and the kinder the treatment, the more ashamed I grew of my business down there. After all, it was stealing an heiress, you know."

I told him how the same fate still haunted that estate. Mr. Stockton sold it to a gentleman, who sold it again to an old man who had married when near eighty and who left it to the daughter born of that marriage late in life. This child of his old age naturally was left an orphan quite young. At fifteen she was carried off and married by a boy of seventeen, a canny Scotchman. The young couple lived to grow up, and it was after all a happy marriage. (This last heiress left six children, so the estate will be divided and no longer tempt fortune hunters.) The Commodore said: "To think we two youngsters, in our blue uniforms, went down to bully those people!" He was much more at Colonel Chesnut's, Mrs. Chesnut being a Philadelphian. He was at ease with them, and said it was the most thoroughly appointed establishment he had ever visited.

Went with the Leviathan of Loveliness to a ladies' meeting. No scandal today, no wrangling, all harmonious. Everybody was knitting; I dare say that soothing occupation helped our perturbed spirits to be calm.

Mrs. C.——, the Leviathan aforesaid, is lovely, a perfect beauty. Said Brewster: "In Circassia, think what a price would be set upon her. There, beauty sells by the pound!"

Coming home I had the following conversation. "Mrs. —— says we have an institution worse than the Spanish Inquisition, worse than Torquemada and all that sort of thing."

"What does she mean?"

"It is your own family she calls the familiars of the Inquisition. She declares they set upon you, fall foul of you, watch and harrass you from morn till dewy eve. They have a perfect right to your life, night and day unto the fourth and fifth generation. They drop in at breakfast. 'Are you not imprudent to eat that?' 'Take care now, don't overdo it. I think you eat too much, so early in the day.' And they help themselves to the only thing you care for on the table. They abuse your friends and tell you it is your duty to praise your enemies. They tell you all of your faults candidly, because they love you so. That gives them a right to speak, the family interest they take in you. You ought to do this, you ought to do that. And then, the everlasting 'you ought to have done' that comes near making you a murderess — at least in heart. 'Blood's thicker than water,' they say, and there is where the longing to spill it comes in. No locks or bolts can keep them out! Are they not your nearest family? They dine with you, dropping in after you are at soup; they come after you have gone to bed. All the servants have gone away, and the man of the house in his night shirt-tail, standing sternly at the door with the huge wooden bar in his hand, nearly scares them to death, and you are glad of it."

"Private life, indeed!" She says her husband entered public life and they went off to live in a faraway city. There for the first time in her life she knew privacy. She never will forget how she jumped for joy as she told her servant not to admit a soul until after two o'clock in the day. There she was free indeed. She could read and write, stay at home, or go out at her own sweet will. She had no longer to sit for hours with her fingers between the leaves of a frantically interesting book, while her kin slowly drivelled nonsense by the yard. Waiting, waiting, yawning! Would they never go? Then, for hurting you, who is as likely as a relative? They do it from a sense of duty. For stinging you, for cutting you to the quick, who is like one of your own household? In point of fact, only they can do it. They know the spot and how to hit it, every time. You are in their power. She says: "Did you ever see a really respectable, responsible, revered and beloved head of a family, who ever opened his mouth at home except to find fault. He really thinks that in life all enjoyment is sinful. He is there to prevent the women from such frivolous things as pleasures." *

At home, I sat placidly rocking in my chair by the window when Mary Hammy rushed in, literally drowned in tears. I never saw so drenched a face in my life. My heart stopped still.

"Commodore Barron is taken prisoner. The Yankees have captured him and all his Lieutenants. Poor Imogene — and there is my father, scouting about the Lord knows where. I only know he is in the advance guard. The Barron's turn has come. Mine may come any minute. Oh, Cousin Mary, when Mrs. Lee told Imogene, she fainted! Those poor girls, they are nearly dead with trouble and fright."

"Go straight back to those children. Nobody will touch a hair of their father's head. Tell them I say so. The Yankees are not savages, quite. This is civilized war, you know."

When she came in, throwing her bad news at my head, I nearly suffocated; but as she wept and wailed, my senses came back to me. Mrs. Eustis knows her world better. Mrs. Lee said to her yesterday: "Have you seen those accounts of arrests in Washington?"

Mrs. Eustis answered calmly: "Yes, I know all about it. I suppose you allude to the fact that my father has been imprisoned. I have no fear for my father's safety."

* This sounds like Mrs. Chesnut's own words. It is curious, since she often spoke of the Union in terms of a family — the "sister states," the South as an unwilling bride — that she did not here suggest the analogy. It was because North and South were so closely akin that each could so wound the other.

Mrs. Lee added hastily: "I did not know Mr. Corcoran had been arrested or I never would have said a word to you on the subject."

More trouble. Fort Hatteras has given up. When Commodore Barron was here three weeks ago, he foretold this disaster, as poor Garnett did his, if adequate measures were not taken to strengthen him; but not the slightest heed did Mr. Mallory pay to his words. Commodore Barron continued to say, day and night while he was here: "This point needs as effective a force to hold it as Fortress Munroe, or Fort Pickens, or Charleston. But they leave it to take its chance."

August 31st. — Fever every day now. Captain Ingraham refuses to remember all of Commodore Barron's Cassandra talk. No wonder, since he was one of those who refused to hear or heed him. The poor Barron children came to tea. The pale faces and red eyes of those girls were too much for me. I dare not look again. It was hard work keeping back a good cry myself.

They say we have driven back two regiments at Manassas, but here we have Hatteras on the brain. It is useless to try and interest anyone in anything else.

Congress adjourns today. Jeff Davis is ill. We go home on Monday, if I am able to travel. I already feel the dread stillness and torpor of our Sahara at Sandy Hill creeping into my veins. It chills the marrow of my bones. Now for good neighborly hate. I am revelling in the noise of city life, but I know what is before me; nothing more cheering than the cry of the poor whippoorwill, will break the silence at Sandy Hill, except that as night draws on the screech owl will add his moanful note.

Commodore Barron's little son was in my room. A nice boy. He went out on a shopping expedition for me, brought me some wool for my knitting. He was so pleased; he called himself my "Confederate Agent." I sent him again for a vast amount of confectionary, some to carry home to Kate's children and some for himself — but he does not know that.

Jenny Barron, Jenny Cooper, and Mary Hammy have gone to have their photographs taken as "Tricoteuses," each armed with their knitting. It will be a lovely group.

September 1st. — At the Arlington, with fever still. There has not been an unpleasant person at this house, and not one of those disagreeable small wars that made the Spotswood so hot.

North Carolina writes for arms for her soldiers. Have we any to send? No. Brewster, the plain-spoken, says: "The President is ill, and our affairs are in the hands of noodles. All the Generals away with the armies, nobody here, General Lee in western Virginia," etc. The devil is sick, the devil a saint would be! Lord how are they increased that trouble me? Many are they that rise up against me! I will not be afraid for the thousands of the people that have set themselves against me round about. Up Lord and help me!

Sunday, and a beautiful night. I look down from my windows high, and the south wind blows softly.

SEPTEMBER 2nd. — Arlington House. Sam Slick says "Young people never care for religion unless they are sick or sorry." Here is an old person who was both yesterday, and I see by the page before me that I was very piously inclined. I am far better off than the wives and children of those men in Yankee dungeons, or the womenkind of the men who lie sick or wounded in hospitals, or in camp. But this plan of thinking, or thanking God, fills me with utter despondency.

Mr. Miles says he is not going anywhere at all, not even home. He is to sit here permanently, chairman of a committee to overhaul camps, commissariats, etc.

We composed our ideas of Mr. Mason, on whom we agreed perfectly. In the first place he has a noble presence. He is really a handsome man, a manly old Virginian, straightforward, brave, truthful, clever, the beau-ideal of an independent, high-spirited FFV. If the English value a genuine man, they will have it. In every particular he is the exact opposite of Talleyrand. True, he has some peculiarities. For instance, he has never had an ache or a pain himself, his physique is perfect, and he loudly declares that he hates sick people. Sickness seems to him an unpardonable weakness. Again, he loathes mountains. "What are they good for? What do you see pretty in rocks and forlorn trees, and how can you care to scramble over rough ground, uphill all the time, nothing but rocks and snakes." We agreed that we adored Mr. Mason.

Today when Mr. Mallory came, Imogene Barron entered the room with her sad face, to get, as she said, all the comfort she could from the Secretary of the Navy. "Could he find anyone to exchange prisoners and so release her father?" He answered: "I would give all Richmond for him!"

So many people came to tell me goodbye, and I had fever as usual today; but in the excitement of this crowd of friends the invalid forgot fever. Mr. Chesnut held up his watch to me warningly, and intimated "it was late indeed for one who had to travel tomorrow." So, as the

Yankees say after every defeat, I "retired in good order." Not quite, for I forgot handkerchief and fan. Gonzales rushed after and met me at the foot of the stairs. In his foreign, pathetic, polite, high-bred way, he bowed low and said he had made an excuse of the fan and handkerchief, for he had a present to make me. And "then, though startled and amazed, I paused and on the stranger gazed." Alas, I am a woman approaching forty, and the offering proved to be a bottle of Cherry Bounce. Nothing could have been more opportune, and with a little ice, etc., helped, I am sure, to save my life on that dreadful journey home.

No discouragement now felt at the North. They take our forts and are satisfied for a while. Then the English are strictly neutral. Like the woman who saw her husband fight the bear: "It was the first fight she ever saw that she did not care who whipped."

Mrs. Lee gave us an anecdote of one of the incarcerated ladies, the wife of a celebrated lawyer; a lawyer who was employed to defend Sickles, when he killed Phil Barton Key. This lawyer's wife patted Sickles on the back and said: "Now we have got you off this time. Now you be a good boy."

Here is the end of Mr. Chesnut's Colonelcy of Cavalry. Mr. Davis tells him that while he was ill, Secretary of War Walker took it on himself to order an election * for Colonels of the two regiments Mr. Davis intended to give Tom Drayton and Mr. Chesnut. This election was ordered without consulting the President. Mr. Davis, however, urges Mr. Chesnut to remain in the Congress; says he will be needed there. If all the men of sense go into the army, what will become of the legislative branch? Brains in the conduct of affairs is a great want now.

Mr. Davis was very kind about it all. He told Mr. Chesnut to go home and have an eye to all the state defences, etc. And that he would give him any position he asked for if he still wished to continue in the army. Now this would be all that heart could wish, but Mr. Chesnut

* Until the spring of 1862, officers in the Confederate Army below the rank of General were elected by popular vote. Since an efficient officer was not necessarily popular, this was a serious detriment. Thus shortly before the Battle of Williamsburg, Colonel William E. Jones, a West Pointer and a stern disciplinarian, was defeated for reelection by Fitzhugh Lee, who was at that time more distinguished as a gallant and as grandson of Light Horse Harry Lee than as a soldier. Both men subsequently had distinguished military careers, but the results of the system of election were not always so happy.

will never ask for anything. I am certain of very few things in life now, but this is one of them. Mr. Chesnut will never ask mortal man for any promotion for himself, or for one of his own family.

Mrs. Joe Johnston told us of the appeal made by General Scott to her husband, to stay in the Union Army. General Scott also spoke to Mrs. Johnston. "Get him to stay with us. We will never disturb him in any way." "My husband cannot stay in an army which is about to invade his native country." "Then let him leave our army, but do not let him join theirs." She answered: "This is all very well, but how is Joe Johnston to live? He has no private fortune, and no profession, or no profession but that of arms."

Someone wrote: "Whosoever attempts to put down what fifteen or twenty women say when they get together will write one of the worst books in the world." She means the silly rot, super silly. All the same, I am always putting down what they say. They always decry and abuse men, while men praise women. But then when twenty men are together, without any women, I am not there; so I can't say they don't get even with us. My mother once accused my father of flattering all women, whenever he approached them. "Not flattery at all," he said. "I tell them the truth, that they are clever and good and pretty, and they like to hear it." "But all women are not good and pretty." "Ah, but I never go near the bad and ugly ones."

At any rate, the men who form my circle of friends have very different topics of conversation from the womenfolk. With Mary Hammy's swarm of gay and gallant beaux, splendid in their martial array and in the highest spirits, it is all love and war.

XI

Camden

September 9th, 1861. — Mulberry. Home again. We left Richmond September 3. At Wilmington met George Deas fretting and fuming. We came with the Moses family, mother and son; also a young Haynesworth, a wounded soldier they were taking care of. They averred we had fifteen thousand such as he — wounded, sick and sore — in Virginia. The patriarch Moses said we had lost eight thousand men on the 21st July. Mr. Chesnut answered, "No, nearer five thousand." "Well, well," said old Moses, nowise inclined to be obstinate about it. Team and his wife, who went to nurse their son, have brought home his dead body.

I came home with the fever in full possession of me and found this beautiful country place, with its placid outlook, by no means the abode of innocence and peace. The tales told around my sickbed made me draw up the sheets over my head in shame and disgust. No fear I should repeat them, as I heard that frantic women do. I recalled what I have seen somewhere: "The most unhappy people are the people who have bad thoughts."

Dr. Boykin, now Lieutenant of Cavalry, came to see me once, and said it was only a case for nursing and went his way with his company to Virginia. My sister Kate came. She is my ideal woman, the most agreeable person I know in the world, with her soft, low and sweet voice, her graceful gracious ways and her glorious grey eyes into which I looked as we confided our very souls to each other. Being Lieutenant of Kirkwood Rangers has routed all of the country doctor left in Dr. Boykin. Few and brief were the words he said to Kate, as to my case;

but he made up for that by the jolly camp stories he told, and the joyous atmosphere of certain success that he was taking to the wars.

God bless old Betsy's yellow face. She is a nurse in a thousand, and would do anything for "Mars' Jeems' wife." My small ailments in all this comfort set me mourning over the dead and dying soldiers I saw in Virginia. How feeble my compassion proves, after all.

Reverend John Johnson presented the Rangers with a flag. H. G., in costume, a veiled prophet, had the management of it and a front place in the picture. She was veiled because of something the matter with her face just now. She got up tableaux and a concert. John Boykin Lee called to request Mr. Chesnut to use all of his influence in high places — to get John Boykin Lee a commission. Naturally he does not want to stay in the ranks.

I wonder why the Rangers are so daft to go to Virginia. They will be wanted here. The fleet which is to land an immense invading force is looked for daily. Port Royal, they say, will be invaded by an overwhelming army, and our army will be attacked from that quarter. The Mercury explains to them, while it is warning us, that the tides now are high enough to bring in any vessel of their Navy.

The mother of that poor lad I went to see die at the tobacco factory in Richmond met me. She says he is the same boy sent to Miss Henrietta's school. It is a nice thing when the grateful hearts remember, and the idle people who did the kind act forget. At any rate, I had forgotten, until she said her son's only claim on me was that I had helped him before. It was gratifying; that I will admit. Now they are raising money to bring his body home. Too late. A little of it would have made him comfortable, and maybe saved his life. When I think of the filth and squalor in which I found him, his clothes unchanged for weeks, an atmosphere of horror on every side, wounded men parked in rows like sardines in a box. No wonder I fainted! But now we are efficient at last, and have money to bring home the body! Oh, in this world, if we could only know in time!

I handed my husband's father a letter from his grandson in the army, thinking he would be glad to learn something of one of them. At one time they seemed all in all with him; but that was before they developed exactly what material they were made of — and though sometimes hope told a flattering tale, we had no children. They were to carry on his line and inherit the estates he loves so well. Now he is under no delusion. He said, as he folded up the missive from the seat of war: "With your husband, we die out. He is the last of my family." This old man of ninety years was born when it was not the fashion for a gentleman to be a saint, and being lord of all he surveyed for so many years, he lived irresponsibly in the center of his huge domain. It is wonderful he was not a greater tyrant. The softening influence of that angel wife no doubt. Saint or sinner, he understands the world about him — *au fond.*

There stands Gonzales's big black bottle that saved my life — possibly. How sentimentally he handed it to me, Cherry Brandy to a woman of forty. Of all that hot, dirty, stifling journey home I remember little, but this stands out; they were discussing Miles and his interview with Congressman Ely. Someone cried: "And Miles is the best-mannered man I know." "Of course," said Mr. Chesnut. "In fencing as in fighting, one is taught to salute politely one's antagonist." " 'Rudeness comes easy,' said someone, 'when you hate people.' " I remembered Commodore Barron's account of their reception when they faced the chivalry here so gallantly in quest of the stolen bride.

In Missouri, Ben McCulloch caught a Dutch parson in the act of making some men take the oath of allegiance to the Union. He ordered him "to take his Bible again in his hand and unswear them as quick as possible!" It is encouraging when one hears of a piece of fun, however broad. If one can afford to laugh, things are mending.

Kentucky does not mean to come to us, but neither does she mean to free her slaves. They will let her keep what she will, if she keeps the peace. She means to keep her slaves, at any rate.

Have had a violent attack of something wrong about my heart. It stopped beating, then took to trembling and creaking and thumping like a Mississippi high-pressure steamboat; and the noise in my ears was more like an ammunition wagon rattling over the stones in Richmond. That was yesterday, and yet I am alive. That kind of thing makes one feel very mortal.

Russell writes how disappointed Prince Jerome Napoleon was with the appearance of our troops and that he did not like Beauregard at all. Well, I give Bo'gar' up to him; but how a man can find fault with our soldiers as I have seen them individually and collectively in Charleston, Richmond, and everywhere, that beats me. Looks are not everything.

I reflect sadly on this collection of money to send for that poor boy's body, now that he is dead. The money, sent in time, might have saved his life; for he died of neglected typhoid fever, not of wounds incurred in battle.

September 18th. — Yesterday was rather rough on a convalescent.

We had actually a reception, six men and a boy. Two of the interesting creatures came to ask for overseers' places, and sat for hours. One of the men was Jackson Revel, a sandhill neighbour from his youth upwards. The young ladies of this house taught him to read, and his son is named for my husband. Oh, the leisure these people have! Some of these stupid, slow, heavy-headed louts sat from twelve o'clock till five; and Mr. Chesnut would never have forgiven me if I had shown impatience. The boy came to beg, while his mother and sisters sat at the gate. Mr. Chesnut was in imminent danger of going mad, but they sat steadfast. All remained to dinner, boy included, even though he knew his family waited all day at the gate. Then after dinner the two Workmans came. They told us of the family camping outside, impatient for their son.

The Yankees in their papers claim every victory, but if they were fairly victorious would not they be down upon us, instead of hovering around the coast or dancing along the border line? They are like a man who wants to rob a house but prudently stands beyond the fence because there is a bad dog in there.

The British are the most conceited people in the world, the most self-sufficient, self-satisfied and arrogant; but each individual man does not blow his own penny whistle. They brag wholesale. Our people send forth their own reports of their prowess. "I did this!" "I did that!" I know they did it, but I hang my head. In Tarleton's Memoirs, in Lee's and in Moultrie's, in Lord Rawdon's letters, self is never brought to the front. I have been reading them over, and I admire their modesty and good taste as much as I do their courage and cleverness. That kind of British eloquence takes me.

Our name has not gone out of print. Today the Examiner, as usual, pitches into the President. It thinks "Toombs, Cobb, Slidell, Lamar or Chesnut would have been far better." Considerable choice among that lot! Certainly five men more utterly dissimilar were never named in the same paragraph.

SEPTEMBER 19th. — Sandy Hill.* A small war in the Ladies Aid Society. Harriet is President, Sue Bonney Vice-President; and already secession is in the air, a row all the time in full blast. At first there were nearly a hundred members, eighty or ninety always present at a meeting. Now ten or twenty are all that they can show. The worst is they have forgotten the hospitals, where they really could do so much good,

* Sandy Hill, like Mulberry, was one of old Mr. Chesnut's plantations near Camden. Others were Sarsfield, Cool Spring, Knight's Hill and The Hermitage, none far away.

and have gone off to provision and clothe the army, where their help is a drop in the bucket, or in the ocean.

A painful piece of news came to us yesterday. Our cousin, Mrs. Witherspoon of Society Hill, was found dead in her bed. She was quite well the night before. Killed, people say, by family troubles; by contentions, wrangling, ill blood among those nearest and dearest to her. She was a proud and high-strung woman, of a warm and tender heart, truth and uprightness itself. Few persons have ever been more loved and looked up to. A very handsome old lady, of fine presence, dignified and commanding. "Killed by family troubles!" So they said when Mr. John N. Williams died, so Uncle John said yesterday of his brother Burwell. "Death deserts the army," said that quaint old soul, "and takes fancy shots of the most eccentric kind nearer home."

The high and disinterested conduct our enemies seem to expect of us is involuntary and unconscious praise. They pay us the compliment to look for from us — and execrate us for the want of it — a degree of virtue they were never able to practice themselves. They say our crowning misdemeanour is to hold in slavery still those Africans they brought over here from Africa, or sold to us when they found to own them did not pay. They gradually slid them off down here, giving themselves years to get rid of them in a remunerative way. We want to spread them too, west and south, or northwest, where the climate would free them or kill them; would improve them out of the world as the Yankees do Indians. If they had been forced to keep them in New England, I dare say they would have shared the Indians' fate; for they are wise in their generation, these Yankee children of light. Those pernicious Africans!

Mr. Chesnut and Uncle John, both *ci-devant* Union men, are now utterly for State's Rights.

Queer how different the same man appears, viewed from different standpoints. "What a perfect gentleman! So fine looking, high-bred, distinguished, easy, free and above all graceful in his bearing. So high-toned! He is always indignant at any symptom of wrong-doing. He is charming, the man of all others I like to have strangers meet, a noble representative of our country." "Yes, every word you say is true. He is all that. But then the other side of the picture is true too. You always know where to find him! Wherever there is a looking glass, a bottle or a woman; there will he be also." "My God! And you call yourself his friend." "Yes, but I know him down to the ground."

This conversation I overheard from an upper window while I was looking down on the piazza below. They were discussing a complicated character with what Mrs. Preston calls the refinement spread thin, skin deep only.

Kate came down, as fresh, as sweet, as smiling as a spring morning. She is the proudest and happiest mother. "Mary, tell Auntie your analysis of character at ——'s house." "Oh," said the loveliest blonde with the blackest blue eyes, not yet ten years old: "She likes everybody. She is happy and she wants her children to be happy. He dislikes every living soul outside of their own house, and he is miserable if he can't make everybody as wretched as he is."

An iron steamer has run the blockade at Savannah. We raise our wilted heads like flowers after a shower. This drop of good news revives us.

SEPTEMBER 21st.* — Last night when the mail came in, I was seated near the lamp. Mr. Chesnut, lying on a sofa at a little distance, called out to me: "Look at my letters and tell me whom they are from?" I began to read one of them aloud. It was from Mary Witherspoon, and I broke down; horror and amazement was too much for me. Poor cousin Betsey Witherspoon was murdered! She did not die peacefully in her bed, as we supposed, but was murdered by her own people, her Negroes. I remember when Dr. Keith was murdered by his Negroes, Mr. Miles met me and told me the dreadful story. "Very awkward indeed, this sort of thing. There goes Keith in the House always declaiming about the 'Benificent Institution' — How now?" Horrible beyond words! Her household Negroes were so insolent, so pampered, and insubordinate. She lived alone. She knew, she said, that none of her children would have the patience she had with these people who had been indulged and spoiled by her until they were like spoiled children, simply intolerable. Mr. Chesnut and David Williams have gone over at once.

I went up to see Caroline Perkins. Her mother would not permit me to see her. Priscilla has spent her life in mourning. Gloom hangs over her like a pall. This beautiful French young thing, does Priscilla expect to make her as miserable for life as she now is? The mother will never understand the daughter. She may, however, shut her up and

* The pages covering the period from September 24, 1861, to February 20, 1862, presumably because the notebooks in which they were written were not found, were not included in the original edition of *A Diary From Dixie;* but much of their matter, and particularly the record of the murder of Mrs. Witherspoon by her own slaves, is too important to any full picture of the South to be omitted.

mope her to death. The child is young. She can throw off any grief now, if they will only let her alone. Mr. Perkins asked Judge Withers if he did not think Caroline should wear widow's caps. "That young thing!" I said, "I wonder they don't shave her head and make her rend her garments and sit in sack cloth and ashes."

SEPTEMBER 24th. — The men who went to Society Hill (the Witherspoon home) have come home again with nothing very definite. William and Cousin Betsey's old maid, Rhody, are in jail; strong suspicion but as yet no proof of their guilt. The neighborhood is in a ferment. Evans and Wallace say these Negroes ought to be burnt. Lynching proposed! But it is all idle talk. They will be tried as the law directs, and not otherwise. John Witherspoon will not allow anything wrong or violent to be done. He has a detective there from Charleston.

Hitherto I have never thought of being afraid of Negroes. I had never injured any of them; why should they want to hurt me? Two thirds of my religion consists in trying to be good to Negroes, because they are so in our power, and it would be so easy to be the other thing. Somehow today I feel that the ground is cut away from under my feet. Why should they treat me any better than they have done Cousin Betsey Witherspoon?

Kate and I sat up late and talked it all over. Mrs. Witherspoon was a saint on this earth, and this is her reward. Kate's maid Betsey came in — a strong-built, mulatto woman — dragging in a mattress. "Missis, I have brought my bed to sleep in your room while Mars' David is at Society Hill. You ought not to stay in a room by yourself these times." She went off for more bed gear. "For the life of me," said Kate gravely, "I cannot make up my mind. Does she mean to take care of me, or to murder me?" I do not think Betsey heard, but when she came back she said: "Missis, as I have a soul to be saved, I will keep you safe. I will guard you." We know Betsey well, but has she soul enough to swear by? She is a great stout, jolly, irresponsible, unreliable, pleasant-tempered, bad-behaved woman, with ever so many good points. Among others, she is so clever she can do anything, and she never loses her temper; but she has no moral sense whatever.

That night, Kate came into my room. She could not sleep. The thought of those black hands strangling and smothering Mrs. Witherspoon's grey head under the counterpane haunted her; we sat up and talked the long night through.

The Judge thought as Uncle Hamilton Boykin had given ten thousand dollars to raise the company called Boykin's Rangers, and then subscribed twenty thousand more to the Confederacy, William E. Johnson ought not to be allowed to unseat him as Senator. That is it, then. This is the upshot of all those whispers forever being poured in my ears as to A. Hamilton Boykin's unpopularity. The cat is out of the bag. They want his seat in the State Senate. That's the outcome of it all.

Went over just now to have a talk with that optimist, my mother-in-law. Blessed are the pure in mind, for they shall see God. Her mind certainly is free from evil thoughts. Someone says, the most unhappy person is the one who has bad thoughts. She ought to be happy. She thinks no evil. And yet, she is the cleverest woman I know. She began to ask me something of Charlotte Temple (I call her this to keep back her true name). "Has she ever had any more children?" "She has one more." "Is she married?" "No." "Is she a bad girl, really?" "Yes." "Oh! Don't say that. Poor thing! Maybe after all she is not really bad, only to be pitied!" I gave it up. I felt like a fool. Here was one thing I had made sure of as a fixed fact. In this world, an unmarried girl with two children was, necessarily, not a good woman. If that can be waved aside, I give up, in utter confusion of mind. Ever since she came here sixty or seventy years ago, as a bride from Philadelphia, Mrs. Chesnut has been trying to make it up to the Negroes for being slaves. Seventeen ninety-six, I think, was the year of her marriage. Today someone asked her about it, when she was describing Mrs. Washington's drawing-room to us. Through her friendship for Nelly Custis, and living very near, and stiff, stern old Martha Washington not liking to have her coach horses taken out for trifles, and Mrs. Cox letting Nelly Custis and Mary Cox have the carriage at their pleasure, Mrs. Chesnut was a great deal thrown with the Washington household. Now she eloquently related for the hundredth time all this. "How came you to leave that pleasant Philadelphia and all its comforts for this half civilized Up-Country and all the horrors of slavery?" "Did you not know that my father owned slaves in Philadelphia? In his will he left me several of them." In the Quaker City, and in the lifetime of a living woman now present, there were slave holders. It is hard to believe. Time works its wonders like enchantment. So quickly we forget.

Grandma is so awfully clever, and you can't make her think any harm of anybody. She is a resolute optimist. A caller, speaking of "Charlotte Temple," said it was better for the world to call a fallen woman by her proper name. It might be unchristian and nasty; but it was better, just as it was better for the world to hang a murderer, however unpleasant for the individual. She said she did not believe in seduced women. They knew the consequences. To smile amiably, and with a lovely face and a sweet voice to call evil good, would hardly do for everybody to try, if there was to be any distinction made between right and wrong.

Mrs. Chesnut has a greediness of books such as I never saw in anyone else. Reading is the real occupation and solace of her life. In the soft luxurious life she leads, she denies herself nothing that she wants. In her well-regulated character she could not want anything that she ought not to have. Economy is one of her cherished virtues, and strange to say she never buys a book, or has been known to take a magazine or periodical; she has them all. They gravitate toward her, they flow into her room. Everybody is proud to send, or lend, any book they have compassed by any means, fair or foul. Other members of the family who care nothing whatever for them buy the books and she reads them.

She spends hours every day cutting out baby clothes for the Negro babies. This department is under her supervision. She puts little bundles of things to be made in everybody's work basket and calls it her sewing society. She is always ready with an ample wardrobe for every newcomer. Then the mothers bring their children for her to prescribe and look after whenever they are ailing. She is not at all nervous. She takes a baby and lances its gums quite coolly and scientifically. She dresses all hurts, bandages all wounds. These people are simply devoted to her, proving they can be grateful enough when you give them anything to be grateful for. Two women always sleep in her room in case she should be ill, or need any attention during the night; and two others sleep in the next room — to relieve guard, so to speak. When it is cold, she changes her night clothes. Before these women give her the second dress, they iron every garment to make sure that it is warm and dry enough. For this purpose, smoothing irons are always before the fire, and the fire is never allowed to go down while it is cool enough for the family to remain at Mulberry. During the summer at Sandy Hill it is exactly the same, except that then she gets up and changes everything because it is so warm! It amounts to this, these old people find it hard to invent ways of passing the time, and they have such a quantity of idle Negroes about them that some occupation for them must be found. In the meantime, her standing employment is reading, and her husband is driving out with a pair of spanking thoroughbred bays, which have been trained to trot as slowly as a trot can be managed.

OCTOBER 1st. — Went to the Ladies Aid Society. My initiation fee was ten dollars. Everybody was knitting, quantities of things were being packed and bailed up to send off. These good people are not gushing "ladies in stays, as stiff as stones." Kate came in, bowing and smiling on every side. Dear graceful sister, you make these wooden pegs stiffer than ever. Someone (a man, of course) said she was like a beautiful deer among stolid cattle, chewing the cud as those cows were.

Dr. Young, just from Richmond, reports the President ill and gone off with his physician to a farm, and things in a distracted state consequently.

—— is in ecstasies over the senseless abuse heaped upon Jeff Davis. I have to swallow a great deal, for with her at least I must hold my tongue. It is my duty not to quarrel there, but how I longed to say, "Oh, please keep your private spites until we are out of the woods. It is a hopeless business, if we cannot work together for one year in peace. Republics, everybody jawing, everybody putting their mouths in, nothing sacred, all confusion of babble, crimination and recrimination — republics can't carry on a war!"

One begins to understand the power which the ability to vote gives the meanest citizen. We went to one of Uncle Hamilton's splendid dinners, plate, glass, china, and everything that was nice to eat. In the piazza, when the gentlemen were smoking after dinner, in the midst of them sat Squire MacDonald, the well-digger. He was officiating in that capacity at Plain Hill, and apparently he was most at his ease of all. He had his clay pipe in his mouth, he was cooler than the rest, being in his shirt sleeves, and he leaned back luxuriously in his chair tilted on its two hind legs, with his naked feet up on the bannister. Said Louisa — "Look, the mud from the well is sticking through his toes! See how solemnly polite and attentive Mr. Chesnut is to him!" "Oh, that's his way. The raggeder and more squalid the creature, the more polite and the softer Mr. Chesnut grows."

OCTOBER 3rd. — The Mercury correspondent from Richmond grows more audacious. Last night, we read of his hopes that: "When another battle was won we would not have to wait half a year for waggons, or for Jeff Davis to recover his health, or for Beauregard to write a fancy report of the battle."

Dr. Deas brought us confirmation of Price's victory away off somewhere; but then here is Port Royal under our noses — they can take their revenge there. Yesterday, the Mercury called their attention to Wilmington, which it said was totally undefended and crammed with military stores. Lila Davis, commenting on this, said her Uncle George wrote they would not be ready for the enemy at Wilmington for a fortnight. Let us hope the enemy will have sufficient polite consideration to wait that time. We always lie on our oars until they can complete all of their preparations to annihilate us. We told Dr. Deas: "If the Confederacy had chosen to elect Barnwell Rhett President instead of Jefferson Davis, or had Mr. Davis made Barnwell Rhett Secretary of State, we might have escaped one small war at least; the war the Mercury was now waging with the Administration."

October 4th, Friday. — Edward Haile was awfully shocked when Mr. Chesnut said any man who came out of this war without being ruined in his estate would be lucky. Mr. Haile said: "Why, I went into it meaning to double mine, and so I will, so help me God." Said Kate: "Somehow I never associate the name of God with doubling fortunes."

Edward Haile said that the government at Richmond had given the States notice they must take care of themselves. Easy enough to say, not so easy to do. How can they? They have stripped themselves of men and money for the armies of the Confederacy.

The New York Herald prophesies that the north will be too hot for Beecher and Greeley if we are victorious; and yet would either of them be received with open arms here? Never! Also, the Herald is delighted to hear of our internal dissensions and divisions, says it is an omen of good for them. The Inquirer grows sarcastic and advises us to win the spoils before we proceed to divide them.

Last night my husband was saying his father's twenty thousand acres of unoccupied land might be cut up into small farms and make us a much more prosperous country. The swamp lands are only utilized now for the black man, a creature whose mind is as dark and unenlightened as his skin. This kind of talk is fearfully distasteful to the old gentleman. His idea of the whole duty of man is that he should keep his estate intact as he received it from his father, and go on buying out the neighbours and enlarging his borders.

October 7th. — Mrs. Davis and Mrs. Joe Johnston have been upset — the former not exactly in a situation to abide upsets without harm to herself.* Mrs. Johnston's arm is broken. I have written to each of the errant ladies. My whole mind was riveted upon the dangers that encompass our men. I never dreamed our womenfolk were in any danger of life or limb.

* William Howell Davis was born a few weeks later.

An appalling list of foreigners in the Yankee army, just as I feared; a rush of all Europe to them, as soon as they raised the cry that this war is for the extirpation of slavery. If our people had read less of Mr. Calhoun's works, and only read the signs of the times a little more; if they had known more of what was going on around them in the world.

And now comes back on us that bloody story that haunts me night and day, Mrs. Witherspoon's murder. The man William, who was the master spirit of the gang, once ran away and was brought back from somewhere west; and then his master and himself had a reconciliation and the master henceforth made a pet of him. The night preceding the murder, John Witherspoon went over to his mother's to tell her of some of William's and Rhody's misdeeds. While their mistress was away from home, they had given a ball fifteen miles away from Society Hill. To that place they had taken their mistress's china, silver, house linen, etc. After his conversation with his mother, as he rode out of the gate, he shook his whip at William and said: "Tomorrow I mean to come here and give every one of you a thrashing." That night Mrs. Witherspoon was talking it all over with her grandson, a half-grown boy who lived with her and slept indeed in a room opening into hers. "I do not intend John to punish these Negroes. It is too late to begin discipline now. I have indulged them past bearing. They all say I ought to have tried to control them, that it is all my fault." Mrs. Edwards, who was a sister of Mrs. Witherspoon, sometime ago was found dead in her bed. It is thought this suggested their plan of action to the Negroes. What more likely than she should die as her sister had done! When John went off, William said: "Listen to me and there will be no punishment here tomorrow." They made their plan, and then all of them went to sleep, William remaining awake to stir up the others at the proper hour.

What first attracted the attention of the family to the truth about her death was the appearance of black and blue spots about the face and neck of the body of their mother. Then someone, in moving the candle from the table at her bedside, found blood upon their fingers. Looking at the candlestick, they saw the print of a bloody hand which had held it. There was an empty bed in the entry, temporarily there for some purpose, and as they were preparing to lay her out, someone took up the counterpane from this bed to throw over her. On the under side of it, again, bloody fingers. Now they were fairly aroused. Rhody was helping Mary Witherspoon, a little apart from the rest. Mary cried: "I wish they would not say such horrid things. Poor soul, she died in peace with all the world. It is bad enough to find her dead, but nobody ever touched a hair of her head. To think any mortal could murder her. Never! I will not believe it!" To Mary's amazement, Rhody drew near her and, looking strangely in her eyes, she said: "Miss Mary, you stick to dat! You stick to dat!" Mary thrilled all over with suspicion and dread.

There was a trunk in Mrs. Witherspoon's closet where she kept money and a complete outfit ready for travelling at any moment; among other things, some new and very fine night gowns. One of her daughters noticed that her mother must have opened that trunk, for she was wearing one of those night gowns. They then looked into the closet and found the trunk unlocked and all the gold gone. The daughters knew the number of gold pieces she always kept under lock and key in that trunk. Now they began to scent mischief and foul play in earnest, and they sent for the detective.

The detective dropped in from the skies quite unexpectedly. He saw that one of the young understrappers of the gang looked frightened and uncomfortable. This one he fastened upon, and got up quite an intimacy with him; and finally, he told this boy that he knew all about it, that William had confessed privately to him to save himself and hang the others. But he said he had taken a fancy to this boy, and if he would confess everything, he would take him as State's evidence instead of William. The young man fell in the trap laid for him and told every particular from beginning to end. Then they were all put in jail, the youth who had confessed among them, as he did not wish them to know of his treachery to them.

This was his story. After John went away that night, Rhody and William made a great fuss. They were furious at Mars' John threatening them after all these years. William said: "Mars' John more than apt to do what he say he will do, but you all follow what I say and he'll have something else to think of beside stealing and breaking glass and china. If ole Marster was alive now, what would he say to talk of whipping us!" Rhody always kept the key to the house to let herself in every morning, so they arranged to go in at twelve, and then William watched and the others slept the sleep of the righteous. Before that, however, they had a "real fine supper and a heap of laughing at the way dey'd all look tomorrow." They smothered her with a counterpane from a bed in the entry. They had no trouble the first time, because they found her asleep and "done it all 'fore she waked." But after Rhody took her keys and went into the trunk and got a clean night gown — for they had spoiled the one she had on — and fixed everything, candle, medicine and all, she came to! Then she begged them hard for life. She asked them what she had ever done that they should want to kill her? She promised them before God never to tell on them. Nobody should ever know! But Rhody stopped her mouth with the counterpane, and William held her head and hands down, and the other two sat on her legs. Rhody had a thrifty mind and wished to save the sheets and night gown, so she did not destroy them. They were found behind her mantelpiece. There the money was also, all in a hole made among the bricks behind the wooden mantelpiece. A grandson of Rhody's slept in her house. Him she locked up in his room. She did not want him to know anything of this fearful night.

That innocent old lady and her grey hair moved them not a jot. Fancy how we feel. I am sure I will never sleep again without this nightmare of horror haunting me.

Mrs. Chesnut, who is their good angel, is and has always been afraid of Negroes. In her youth, the San Domingo stories were indelibly printed on her mind. She shows her dread now by treating every one as if they were a black Prince Albert or Queen Victoria. We were beginning to forget Mrs. Cunningham, the only other woman we ever heard of who was murdered by her Negroes. Poor cousin Betsey was goodness itself. After years of freedom and indulgence and tender kindness, it was an awful mistake to threaten them like children. It was only threats. Everybody knew she would never do anything. Mr. Cunningham had been an old bachelor, and the Negroes had it all their own way till he married. Then they hated her. They took her from her room, just over one in which her son-in-law and her daughter slept. They smothered her, dressed her, and carried her out — all without the slightest noise — and hung her by the neck to an apple tree, as if she had committed suicide. If they want to kill us, they can do it when they please, they are noiseless as panthers. They were discovered because, dressing her in the dark, her tippet was put on hindpart before, and she was supposed to have walked out and hung herself in a pair of brand new shoes whose soles obviously had never touched the ground.

We ought to be grateful that anyone of us is alive, but nobody is afraid of their own Negroes. I find everyone, like myself, ready to trust their own yard. I would go down on the plantation tomorrow and stay there even if there were no white person in twenty miles. My Molly and all the rest I believe would keep me as safe as I should be in the Tower of London.

Romeo was the Negro who first confessed to the detective; then Rhody, after she found they had discovered the money and sheets where she had hidden them. William and Silvie still deny all complicity in the plot or the execution of it.

John Williams has a bride! Has she not married South at a fine time? She is terrified, and who can blame her? It will be a miracle if she don't bolt altogether. The very name of Society Hill is enough to scare the life out of anyone. To expect the bride to come back, simply because her husband was here, and with details of that black tragedy ringing in her ears; indeed it was too much. I dare say she would as soon take up her abode in Sodom or Gomorrah.

It was Rhody who pointed out the blood on the counterpane. They suppose she saw it, knew they would see it, and did it to avert suspicion from herself.

October 11th. — Read a letter from Robert J. Walker — not Le Roy P. — aloud, and very loud indeed it had to be, for old Colonel Chesnut is so very deaf. My breath was wasted after all, for he remarked: "For a Secretary of War to the Confederacy, some of those sentiments sounded very odd." The old gentleman is ninety, but he wants to know everything that is going on. He is blind, but he takes interest in the affairs of the world with wonderful tenacity.

October 13th. — Mulberry. We went in the afternoon to the Negro church on the plantation. Manning Brown, a Methodist minister, preached to a very large black congregation. Though glossy black, they were well dressed and were very stylishly gotten up. They were stout, comfortable looking Christians. The house women, in white aprons and white turbans, were the nicest looking. How snow white the turbans on their heads appeared! But the youthful sisters flaunted in pink and sky blue bonnets which tried their complexions. For the family, they had a cushioned seat near the pulpit, neatly covered with calico. Manning Brown preached Hell fire so hot, I felt singed, if not parboiled. I could not remember any of my many sins that were worthy of an eternity in torment; but, if all the world's misery, sin, and suffering came from so small a sin as eating that apple, what mighty proportions mine take!

Jim Nelson, the driver, the stateliest darky I ever saw, tall and straight as a pine tree, with a fine face, and not so very black but a full-blooded African, was asked to lead in prayer. He became wildly excited, on his knees, facing us with his eyes shut. He clapped his hands at the end of every sentence, and his voice rose to the pitch of a shrill shriek, yet was strangely clear and musical, occasionally in a plaintive minor key that went to your heart. Sometimes it rang out like a trumpet. I wept bitterly. It was all sound, however, and emotional pathos. There was literally nothing in what he said. The words had no meaning at all. It was the devotional passion of voice and manner which was so magnetic. The Negroes sobbed and shouted and swayed backward and forward, some with aprons to their eyes, most of them clapping their hands and responding in shrill tones: "Yes, God!" "Jesus!" "Savior!" "Bless de Lord, amen," etc. It was a little too exciting for me. I would very much have liked to shout, too. Jim Nelson when he rose from his knees trembled and shook as one in a palsy, and from his eyes you could see the ecstasy had not left him yet. He could not stand at all, and sank back on his bench.

Now all this leaves not a trace behind. Jim Nelson is a good man, honest and true; but those who stole before, steal on, in spite of sobs and shouts on Sunday. Those who drink, continue to drink when they can get it. Except that for any open, detected sin they are turned out of church. A Methodist parson is no mealy-mouth creature. He requires them to keep the Commandments. If they are not married — and show they ought to be — out of the church they go. If the married members are not true to their vows and it is made plain to him by their conduct, he has them up before the church. They are devoted to their church membership and it is a keen police court.

Suddenly, as I sat wondering what next, they broke out into one of those soul-stirring Negro camp-meeting hymns. To me this is the saddest of all earthly music, weird and depressing beyond my powers to describe.

I have a letter from Wilmot DeSaussure dated Charleston, 4 October 1861. He says he cannot give all the news, because "the Father of Lies" has not remained wholly with our adversaries, but has entered largely into Confederate service, so that the news of today proves on tomorrow wholly untrue. "In Charleston little is heard of except the blockading fleet, and preparations for war at home and abroad. The fleet has within the last week been increased to four vessels, and it is generally believed the increase has been made to intercept Messieurs Mason and Slidell. The preparations for war are seen in the continued drilling of troops, in the foundries where ordnance stores in prodigious quantities are being cast, in all the varied workshops where munitions, implements and equipment can be made. Vast piles of clothing are being prepared for the troops, both in Virginia, and in service along the coast of our own State. Batteries are erected at all of the inlets which have any draft of water, and heavy guns mounted and being mounted. About seven thousand men are placed along the seaboard, three thousand in camp in the interior. Three thousand are held in Charleston ready to be used in any direction required.

"The continued attacks of the Mercury upon Mr. President Davis are making something of a party against him. The policy which prevents forward movements by our army does not meet the approval of this party. Far removed from the seat of war, they deem themselves more competent to judge of what is proper to be done than those who are bearing the brunt. I do not hear of any opposition to Mr. W. Porcher Miles for Congress, and do not think any could be successful. Mr. Barnwell Rhett will certainly be pressed by his friends, and will, I think, be as certainly defeated.

"Scandal is dead at present so that I cannot give you a word. Mrs. DeSaussure says she has some, but as she has not confided it to me, I cannot tell it. With her eight children about her, and scandal dead, she certainly has been ingenious in finding it!" Thus he writes.

October 15th. — They say the long looked-for battle of Port Royal is raging. I tore up four white counterpanes to send to the hospitals for bandages, and I am picking to pieces all my worsted curtains, to make shirts for the soldiers.

Kate came. We knitted away at our socks and she gave various items of news. Hatteras is evacuated. Mason and Slidell have left Charleston for Nassau or some British Port. News came yesterday that we had driven back an invading squadron on the Potomac, at what loss we know not yet. At Annapolis their steamers swarm, armed and manned. When will they land? Miss Denie McEwen, sister-in-law to the telegraph operator, says Captain Ingraham and a lot of old sea dogs have gone with Mason and Slidell to take command of a fleet of iron-clad steamers. The name of the port where this imaginary flotilla rides at anchor is not given. An article in the Courier, as mischievous as the Mercury, shows how utterly undefended Fort Sumter was last summer and how thin the defenses are now. Somebody suggested it was a ruse to tempt the enemy in to his ruin. We think it sheer stupidity to make this public statement, and that it is in all probability perfectly true.

I was shocked to hear that dear friends of mine refused to take work for the soldiers because their seamstresses had their winter clothes to make. I told them true patriotesses would be willing to wear the same clothes until our seige was raised. They did not seem to care. They have seen no ragged, dirty, sick and miserable soldiers lying in the hospital, no lack of woman's nursing, no lack of woman's tears, but an awful lack of a proper change in clean clothes. They know nothing of the horrors of war. One has to see to believe. They take it easy, and are not yet willing to make personal sacrifices. The time is coming when they will not be given a choice in the matter. The very few stay-at-home men we have are absorbed as before in plantation affairs; cotton-picking, Negro squabbles, hay stealing, saving the corn from the freshet. They are like the old Jews while Noah was building the Ark.

Woe to those who began this war, if they were not in bitter earnest. Lamar (L. Q. C., and the cleverest man I know) * said in Richmond in one of those long talks of ours: "Slavery is too heavy a load for us to carry." We agreed to take up Davie Crockett's slogan: "My country! May she be right, but my country right or wrong!" Russell does not see why we cannot be subjugated.

OCTOBER 18th. — Mrs. Witherspoon's death has clearly driven us all wild. Mrs. Chesnut, although she talks admirably well and is a wonderfully clever woman, bored me by incessantly dwelling upon the transcendant virtues of her colored household, in full hearing of the innumerable Negro women who literally swarm over this house. She takes her meals in her own rooms, but today came in while we were at dinner. "I warn you, don't touch that soup! It is bitter. There is something wrong about it!" The family answered her pleasantly, but continued calmly to eat their soup. The men who waited at table looked on without change of face. Kate whispered: "It is cousin Betsey's fate. She is watching every trifle, and is terrified." My husband gave his mother his arm, and she went quietly back to her room. Afterwards Kate said to me: "She is afraid they will poison us. Did you ever hear the story of Dr. Keith?" "No." "He is the first and only man I have ever heard of being poisoned by Negroes. I have

* Few Southerners could match the long and honorable career of L. Q. C. Lamar of Mississippi. Born in 1825, he served before the War in the National House of Representatives. During the War he was Lieutenant Colonel and then commander of the Nineteenth Mississippi till illness forced him to resign. After the War he was a leader in restoring orderly government in Mississippi; he served in the National House and then in the United States Senate, and Grover Cleveland appointed him Secretary of the Interior, and later Associate Justice of the United States Supreme Court. No man worked harder to end the "bloody shirt" era in American politics.

often wondered they did not, if half the stories people tell of bad masters are true. Dr. Keith was one of the kindest of men and masters, but he was passionate and impulsive and not warranted to act reasonably if he was too much excited about anything. He had some chronic ailment, was always ill, and a friend said: 'Keith, yours is a queer case. I begin to think these villainous Negroes are trying to poison you. Come with me to my house and see if a change will do you any good.' Dr. Keith promised to be prudent and to come the next day. As soon as his friend left, a Negro woman brought him a cup of tea. In stirring it, a white powder became evident, settled in the bottom of the cup. In a moment he believed what his friend had suspected. He dashed the tea in her face. 'You ungrateful beast, I believe you are trying to poison me.' Next morning he was found with his throat cut from ear to ear. Afterward, it was discovered that they were putting calomel in his coffee every morning. The woman was hung, but two of the men were allowed to escape."

October 20th. — The Mercury today was utterly exasperating in its taunts and abuse of the Confederate Government. Simply atrocious! Could they not wait one year? There are the Yankees to abuse, if our newspapers would only let loose their vials of wrath on them, and leave us until the fight is over a united people. It is our only hope. We have *élan* enough and to spare, if we only had patience and circumspection. The idea is that in pluck and dash our strength lies, but the newspapers are trying to take the heart out of us. If they persuade us that everybody in office is fool, knave, or traitor, how can we go on? I agree with Carlyle that "a few able editors hung might save us yet." Mr. Miles says: "Ah, Mrs. Chesnut, but it must be so; her Majesty's Government, and her Majesty's Opposition. One is as true and loyal as the other."

"It won't do here," I insisted. "The wounded men, the sick men, the widows and orphans must feel pretty flat when they read in the Examiner and the Mercury that they were done to death by their own inefficient government! Everyone should do all they can to keep up the fire of our enthusiasm."

"And those who play disheartening slander and abuse as if from a hose upon this fire, they ought to be burned alive as traitors," said Kate, the meek and sweet-voiced, coming in with her soft footfalls.

Our friend Senator Wilson (of Massachusetts) has a regiment. In making a speech to it, he scorns long range. "Give them the bayonet!" Come closer in your wrath, I say. Why not give us the awl? Our poor

Negroes have had enough paper-soled shoes from his factory, thanks to his sympathetic awl!

Today I read La Martini's "Geneviève." He cites the servants of Augustus Caesar's time, to prove fidelity among that class. Also, during the French Revolution, nine out of ten were faithful unto death. Now we are here at Sandy Hill half a dozen of the whites, or dominant class, and sixty or seventy Negroes, miles away from the rest of the world.

Old Mr. Chesnut said his wife must know everything, so my husband had to write several sheets of paper filled with poor Mrs. Witherspoon's tragedy. We thought it could so easily have been kept from Mrs. Chesnut's ears, she is so deaf; but his father ordered it otherwise, and now she is simply overwrought on the subject. I have never known her so nearly thrown from her balance, for she is a calm, philosophical personage.

Hume says: "Mighty governments are built up by a great deal of accident, with a very little of human foresight and wisdom." We have seen the building of one lately, with no end of Jefferson and a constant sprinkling of Calhoun, etc. Which is the wisdom, where is the accident or the foresight? One thing Mrs. Browne and I once discussed. There were in Richmond and in Montgomery, the safe, sober, second thoughts of the cool, wise morning hours. But in the smoking Congresses where women were not came what we called "Ideas preserved in alcohol"; wild schemes, mad talk, exaggerated statements — inflamed and irrational views of our might and the enemy's weakness! . . . If "*In Vino Veritas*," God help us. I care no more for alcoholized wisdom than I do for the chattering of blackbirds. But the great statesmen and soldiers deliberately drink down their high inheritance of reason, and with light hearts become mere gabbling geese. Alcohol! Pfaugh!

Thank God for pine knots! Gas and candles and oil are all disappearing in the Confederacy. Lamb thinks that for social purposes, candles are so much better than the garish light of the sun. Imagine the unsocial nights of our ancestors in their dark caves. They must have laid about and abused one another in the dark. No, they went to sleep! And women then were too much slaves to dream of curtain lectures, which is one form of lying about and abusing one another in the dark. What repartees could have passed when you had to feel around for a smile, and had to handle your neighbour's cheek to see if he understood you.

OCTOBER 24th. — At Bonney's store I heard that at Leesburg

"Shanks" Evans had defeated the Yankees and taken three hundred prisoners; and they left five hundred dead on the field, besides a great number who were drowned. Allowing for all exaggeration, it must be a splendid victory. Among the prisoners were ten officers.

Mrs. Ben Lee gave us an account of the last ship which ran the blockade. The ship was entrusted by the blockaders with letters for New York, which being brought into Charleston, were opened. These letters told that our coast was to be attacked simultaneously from separate points; Bull's Bay, and Port Royal, and I forget the other point. This was to prevent our concentrating to defend any particular place. Mrs. Lee's husband is in the army. She looked so lovely. Her dress was exquisite, and her one thought is clothes. I fled; and yet she is beautiful as a picture.

My next visit was hard on the chivalry. Johnny lent Kate his house fully furnished. She did not know that the furniture was his brother's, which Johnny thought he had bought, and considered the purchase as a matter settled. The Florida brother, in a huff, sent word to have everything of his taken out of that house; so without one word of warning, the wagons came. Thus one of the fairest ladies of the land, and her children — her husband away in the wars — was left on bare boards. And so I found her. Indignant was a faint word to express her state of mind. It was a case of pure spite, so it must have been women's work. Kate was principally concerned at the amount of mortification Johnny would feel. There was not a stick of furniture or anything in the house, only her trunks and her children.

October 25th. — The Witherspoons are here. Mary repeated what she heard her Negroes say: "Let us go to that hanging; it's a warning to us all."

Lawrence, Mr. Chesnut's man, is an excellent tailor; not a bad accomplishment for a valet. He darns stockings beautifully. Mrs. Clay never tired of laughing at the picture he made, seated cross-legged on Mr. Chesnut's trunk, darning. His master never trusted to Lawrence's tailoring before, but now it will be a great comfort. He is making me a sacque at present.

The Yankees' principal spite is against South Carolina. Fifteen war steamers have sailed — or steamed — out against us. Hot work will be cut out for us whenever they elect to land. They hate us, but they fear us too. They do not move now until their force is immense; overwhelming is their word. Enormous preparations and a cautious approach are the lessons we taught them at Manassas.

And now we have many little wars beside the great one. The Judge is raging in tantrums. He speaks to me, but he has ceased to look at me. It is months since I have caught his eye. The President writes asking for particulars of that famous interview on the 13th July. There were present Colonel John S. Preston, General Lee, General Cooper, Mr. Chesnut and the President. General Beauregard says he sent to the President, by his aid, Colonel Chesnut, a plan of battle which the President rejected. Are we going to be like the Jews when Titus was thundering against their gates? Quarrelling among ourselves makes me faint with fear. I wrote out a copy of Mr. Chesnut's report to Beauregard, written while the guns were firing on the 18th. Surely Beauregard, by stopping a man to write that day, showed he wanted his justification prepared *en cas*. He looked out for his own fame, the eyes of posterity and all that. I remember Mr. Chesnut's talk when he came back to our rooms, his praise of General Lee's clear soldierly views, and his disgust because I would interrupt him to say "how handsome General Lee was, such a splendid looking soldier, but that I liked Smith Lee best."

The Mississippi Regiment which faced the enemy so gallantly at Leesburg was the same which behaved not so well on the 21st July — something like Frederick the Great at his first battle. They asked, this time, for a place of danger and difficulty, so that they might redeem themselves and the name of their regiment.

NOVEMBER 6th. — Mr. Chesnut has gone to Charleston, and Kate to Columbia, on her way to Flat Rock. Partings are sorrowful things now. I read Mrs. Shelley's book, "The Last Man." It is written to sell. A filthy man, but the book is not so bad. She used Byron and Shelley and wrote of things she knew.

As for the dunderheads here, I can account for their stolidity only in one way. They have no imagination. They cannot conceive what lies before them. They can only see what actually lies under their noses. To me it is evident that Russell, the Times correspondent, tries to tell the truth, unpalatable as it is to us. Why should we expect a man who recorded so unflinchingly the wrong-doing in India, to soften matters for our benefit, sensitive as we are to blame. He described slavery in Maryland, but says that it has worse features further South; yet his account of slavery in Maryland might stand as a perfectly accurate picture of it here. God knows I am not inclined to condone it, come what may. His work is very well done for a stranger who comes and in his haste unpacks his three P's — pen, paper, and prejudices — and hurries through his work.

So, the mighty Scott has resigned; our six-feet-six general. He stood a head and shoulders above the multitude, and little McClellan is to try on his boots.

November 8th. — The Reynolds came and with them terrible news. The enemy are landing at Port Royal. I ordered the carriage and rushed off to Camden to hear the worst. John MacPherson DeSaussure confirmed the bad news, but it did not affect his spirits, which are always light and airy. He held us there, not like the Ancient Mariner — for he lacks the glittering eye — but literally he laid hold of the carriage door and stood between the wheels thereof. He wanted us to hear what a fine crop Harry was making, as if all that mattered now. Met Aunt S. B. matching ribbons at Miss McEwen's. She said: "If this is true, Mr. B. will go at once to Charleston," and then dismissed the subject from her mind and conversation. Mr. B. would settle it. It was his business, not hers — there is faith for you! I do not know where my husband is. He went to Charleston a week ago; but, at his approach, the sun and moon do not stand still.

Miss McEwen told me they were very unhappy at the Judge's, because Mr. K was down there in the midst of it all. I drove up there at once and found them at dinner and in fine spirits. The Judge opened fire on me, talking about the "meanness and dishonesty, the corruption and depravity of all men." I said: "I don't know how anyone dares speak ill of our soldiers, dying, fighting, lying in the hospitals suffering a thousand martyrdoms. Here we are in slippers and dressing-gowns, snug fires, good dinners. Our men are as good as they are brave."

"Have you heard aught in this house disrespectful in regard to the Confederate Army?" asked the Judge angrily. "Have you heard one word?"

"You said 'all men' were rogues and rascals. Well, all of our men are in the army! If you mean to abuse only those who shirk the fighting, I beg your pardon."

Aunt B. said amicably: "Come in and sit down. Why do you stand off there? You make us uncomfortable." "No, thank you. I do not wish to take a seat. Under the guns at Port Royal would be pleasant compared to my warm reception here."

All this because we will not join in the scandalous abuse of Jeff Davis, and indeed of everybody but the Judge's own family.

There was a striking picture upstairs. A perfect beauty is an uncommon sight, and here was one; nobody denies that. It is her profession, and yet she can't bear to go out and show herself. She is as beautiful as flesh and blood ever gets to be, and she is always exquisitely dressed. Today it was soft mull muslin, all fluffy and fluted and covered with Valenciennes lace. She said she did not expect to ask anyone into her room and she did not mean to leave it. She was in a terrible fret. The trimming they had brought her from Camden to finish her baby's fine frock did not suit her taste at all. We had a few minutes' polite conversation on immaterial subjects, and I left her as I found her, in a rage of disappointment about that trimming.

At the gate, I took the reins so that Armsted might open the gate. When he came again to the carriage, he looked in and asked gently: "Why do you come here, my Missis? They make you cry so. Please don't come any more." For I was sobbing to break my heart. The apathy at the telegraph office was worse. As I drove down the street, I said to myself: "Never mind. Those people and their inconceivable indifference, they are only civilians. Our men are in the army."

I forgot one thing. As I went upstairs, the Judge shouted after me: "I forgot to tell you Orr and Pickens have coalesced against Mr. Chesnut. It is a settled bargain between them." Then followed a roar of laughter at my probable discomfiture.

A letter from John Preston, the stateliest cavalier of them all, who is now in Charleston, says: "Last Sunday I received a telegram from General Beauregard urging me to meet Mr. Miles in Richmond instantly. This morning Mr. Miles explained to me that the General and the President may be at sword's points in the matter which Mr. Chesnut brought down before the Battle of Manassas.

"Great terror prevailing here, and no preparation, neither troops nor defences! I believe the Fort could be taken in six hours. This war will have to be continued above tide water, as it was in the Revolution. Wherever they can float and fight, they are our masters. I believe they will have Charleston within thirty days.

"General Lee * is here visiting the defences. He does not seem in

* General Lee was not put in command of the Army of northern Virginia until months later. After the collapse of his campaign in Western Virginia, he was sent to Charleston to organize the coast defense there.

particularly good humor concerning things here. It seems to me there is miserable confusion, ignorance and inefficiency in every department; my only consolation is the consciousness of my own ignorance, in which I may make false estimates."

It was utter defeat at Port Royal. DeSaussure's and Dunavant's regiments were cut to pieces. General Lee sent them, they say. *Preux chevalier*, booted and bridled and gallant rode he, but so far his bonnie face has only brought us ill luck.

Camden people do not in the least take in what it means to have one's country successfully invaded; and I know now what it means when people say one's heart is like lead in one's bosom.

Papers say Pillow has had a victory away off somewhere. Far away news, I care not for it!

NOVEMBER 11th. — Yesterday Mr. John DeSaussure came, absolutely a lunatic, his preposterous and ill-timed gayety all gone. He was in a state of abject fright because the Negroes show such exultation at the enemy's making good their entrance at Port Royal. I cannot see any change in them, myself; their faces are as unreadable as the Sphinx. Certainly they are unchanged in their good conduct. That is, they are placid, docile, kind and obedient — and as lazy and dirty as ever. So, as far as man can destroy, that beautiful Beaufort is gone! Mrs. Elliott and Mrs. Cuthbert, and Septima Washington; how those women used to rave to me of that bay, to say their homes were in the very garden spot of the world, an earthly paradise.

Last night Rochelle Blair came to say there was a despatch from Governor Pickens for my husband. They wanted Colonel Chesnut's address.

NOVEMBER 12th. — That telegram to Mr. Chesnut was a grand secret, surely. Judge Withers knew it, so I heard in the street. I will not write it, even, for everybody reads my journal as it lies on the table in my room. I went to the turn-out at Mulberry for Mr. Chesnut. Minnie F. says they are hanging Negroes in Louisiana and Mississippi like birds in the trees, for an attempted insurrection; but out there they say the same thing of South Carolina, and we know it is as quiet as the grave here, and as peaceful. We have no reason to suppose a Negro knows there is a war. I do not speak of the war to them; on that subject, they do not believe a word you say. A genuine slave owner, born and bred, will not be afraid of Negroes. Here we are mild as the moonbeams, and as serene; nothing but Negroes around us, white men all gone to the army.* Mrs. Reynolds and Mrs. Withers, two of the very kindest and most considerate of slave owners, aver that the joy of their Negroes at the fall of Port Royal is loud and open; but there is no change of any kind whatever with ours.

A man named Parker has got home from Beaufort. Two Camden men were killed. Parker says it was all a botch on our side. General Drayton ordered DeSaussure's regiment to an island, to draw off attention from Drayton's maneuvers around the Fort. DeSaussure, finding his men cut to pieces for no earthly good, cried: "Save yourselves," and now they are scattered from Richmond to Montgomery. Parker speaks, not I. He may be good authority. I know not.

For the first time, the Examiner is on Jeff Davis's side, condemning 'Shot Pouch' Walker for making a difficulty about which regiment he should take. The President is accused of making a place for his brother-in-law, Dick Taylor. After all, it is only transferring Walker, a Georgian, to a Georgia regiment, and giving Walker's regiment, which is from Louisiana, to Dick Taylor of that ilk. Walker says he has disciplined and trained this regiment, and now Dick Taylor will have all the benefit of his work. Forgetting their country, quarrelling for their own glory! For shame!

Mrs. Reynolds's conversation with her jet-black butler, Ammon. "Missis, at Beaufort they are burning the cotton and killing the Negroes. They do not mean the Yankees to have cotton or Negroes." She tried to make him understand, in vain: "Would I kill you, or let anybody else kill you? You know nobody kills Negroes here. Why will you believe they do it there?" "We know you won't own up to anything against your side. You never tell us anything that you can help." Ammon has been that nuisance, a pampered menial, for twenty years. The summer after we were married, when Mr. Chesnut was a candidate for the Legislature, he had to risk his election to defend Ammon, who was brought before a magistrate for insulting some gentleman of the town; and Mr. Chesnut got him off scatheless — to the regret of most people. His insolence has always been intolerable. The Chesnut Negroes are spoiled to a degree; but then they have such good manners, they are so polite you forget everything else. And they make you so comfortable, if you can afford ten to do the work of one servant.

* Mrs. Chesnut, it is fair to say, doth protest too much. The fear of a slave insurrection — reawakened so short a time before by the murder of Mrs. Witherspoon — lay always like a slumbering ember in the subconscious mind. An instance of violence by slaves against their masters anywhere in the South not infrequently set off an epidemic of arrests and hangings elsewhere in the Southern States.

My husband is at home again. Yesterday at Kingsville he met Governor Pickens's telegram, telling him to seize all salt for the use of the army. So he came home to see about it, but not to seize it, I hope. And also, Governor Pickens directed him to raise another regiment here immediately.

East Tennessee against us makes it as hot for Kate at Flat Rock as she was here.

Charleston is being fortified on the land side. When the enemy overran James Island, the Negro men went to the Fleet, but the women and children came to us. So many more mouths to feed, a good way to subdue us by starvation. How they laugh at our calamity, and mock when our fear cometh. The enemy grins at us. We grinned so when they ran at Manassas.

Mr. Preston again telegraphs for Mr. Chesnut to go back to town about this Davis-Beauregard imbroglio. I do not seem to feel that it is a life and death business that Beauregard should be misunderstood. Let him stand to his guns. There is fighting enough to do ahead of him. Bygones can take care of themselves.

November 17th. — Old Mr. Chesnut's library is on the first floor, my husband's a beautiful room in the third story, overlooking this beautiful lawn and grand old oaks. Up here, all is my very own. Here I sit and make shirts for soldiers, knit, or read, or write in my journal as I see fit. I am under my own vine and fig tree, out of the way of all callers or intruders, of all that goes on downstairs.

John DeSaussure says he means in case of trouble to take refuge under the Federal Flag with his cotton and his Negroes; and he is fool enough to think they will let him keep them.

November 19th. — I opened Sir Thomas Browne idly. The first sentence my eye fell upon was: he could never persecute anyone for what he thought, for how did he know that he might not think so too, tomorrow. So I read on, and I have stuck to Sir Thomas Browne like a leech, ever since.

November 20th. — Slidell and Mason seized under the flag of England. Something good is obliged to come from such a stupid blunder. The Yankees must bow the knee to the British, or fight them. As I read the Northern newspapers, the blood rushes to my head. In the words of the fine fiction writers, my cheek is mantling with shame. Anyhow, down they must go to Old England, knuckle on their marrow bones, to keep her on their side — or barely neutral. Seward is too smart a Yankee to undertake the British Lion, with us on his hands. The England of history cannot let this insult to her flag pass.

So our hope and fear alternates. The Mercury sees no cause for war on the British part; the Richmond Examiner sees every cause for it. Somehow it is borne in on me that it does not so much matter what the Mercury or the Examiner think. It is what England will think.

Suppose Mr. Mallory had taken up poor old Morrow's idea, so fiercely backed by Mr. Chesnut, and got all of those iron steamers to defend our rivers and our coast? It was spoken of in time. We could have armed and manned them then, and sent cotton to pay for them.

Six companies have already been offered Mr. Chesnut for his regiment. Yesterday he heard from Massey of Lancaster. Now another troop offers itself, Captain McIlvaine's Cavalry. The Captain came in person, and then Captain Boykin in full uniform.

Mary DeSaussure was grieving over Colonel DeSaussure's mischance. "He is a lion," she cries. "There never was so brave a man." Then she went for Johnny. He sent a message to "Henry DeSaussure's wife." "I have a name, I hope!" she said, her Irish blood flaming in her face. Here we agitate ourselves for such trifles.

Being told last night that my conversation was like the bluster of Barnwell Rhett, I kept up here. All day I have looked out from my window high upon the sky, with a secret chuckle at the inanity that I was escaping. Old Mr. Chesnut tramped about and said, "Without the aid and countenance of the whole United States, we could not have kept slavery. I always knew that the world was against us. That was one reason why I was a Union man. I wanted all the power the United States gave me, to hold my own!"

As for them, there is no limit to their recruiting. The whole world is open to them. England is patting both sides on the back. She loves to see a Kilkenny cat fight. After all, she is not dying for the want of our cotton. She is prospering, and pampering her Indian cotton, and will magnanimously accept any apology for the Mason and Slidell affair that smart Yankee Seward tenders her. Captain Boykin said: "Noise from below never moved England. She would stand firm if all her manufacturers starved. When her plans and her policy were fixed, millions of discontents might go to the devil for her."

Read Dickens's "Pictures from Italy." Pleasant company in my airy retreat.

Last January I sent for all the English reviews, Blackwoods, Atlantic, Harper, Cornhill. I just threw away my subscription money. Everything stopped with Fort Sumter. How I miss that way of looking out into the world. The war has cost me that. How much more? I can't for the life of me see how my last night's conversation recalled Barnwell Rhett's bluster. All the same, Mr. Chesnut intended to insult me, and I cannot get over my sulks easily.

November 24th. — During the hymn at church, I could have rested my head on the cushion and sobbed and shrieked like a new convert at a revival camp meeting. But not an eyelash moved. So much for civilized self-control.

November 25th. — Mr. Chesnut has gone to Richmond, and now there is nothing but frizzle frazzle talked in this house. To me this calm, monotonous baby talk is maddening.

A painful raising of old ghosts, looking over and destroying letters all day. I find people writing to me as my dearest friends whose very names and existence I have long forgotten.

Kingsley's "Two Years Ago" is a capital work of the imagination. There will never be an interesting book with a Negro heroine down here. We know them too well. They are not picturesque. Only in fiction do they shine. Those beastly Negress beauties are only animals. There is not much difference, after all, between the hut where all ages, sizes and sexes sleep promiscuously, and our Negro cabins.

Now for a story taken down from Maria's lips; she who is left forlorn for the sad and involuntary crime of twins. For "Jeems" Whitaker is still unapproachable in his ire.

Martha Adamson is a beautiful mulattress, as good looking as they ever are to me. I have never seen a mule as handsome as a horse, and I know I never will; no matter how I lament and sympathize with its undeserved mule condition. She is a trained sempstress, and "hired her own time, as they call it; that is, the owner pays doctor's bills, finds food and clothing, and the slave pays his master five dollars a month, more or less, and makes a dollar a day if he pleases. Martha, to the amazement of everybody, married a coal-black Negro, the son of Dick the Barber, who was set free fifty years ago for faithful services rendered Mr. Chesnut's grandfather. She was asked: How could she? She is so nearly white. How could she marry that horrid Negro? It is positively shocking! She answered that she inherits the taste of her white father, that her mother was black.

The son of this marriage — a bright boy called John — is grown, reads and writes. The aforesaid Martha is now a widow. Last night there was a row. John beat a white man, who was at his mother's. Poor Martha drinks. John had forbidden Mr. T—— to bring whiskey to the house, and he found him seated at table with his mother, both drunk. So he beat him all the way home to his own house. The verdict of the community: "Served him right!" Maria's word: "White people say, 'Well done, John! Give it to him!' "

NOVEMBER 28th. — "Ye who listen with credulity to the whispers of fancy" — pause, and look on this picture and that.

On one side Mrs. Stowe, Greeley, Thoreau, Emerson, Sumner. They live in nice New England homes, clean, sweet-smelling, shut up in libraries, writing books which ease their hearts of their bitterness against us. What self-denial they do practice is to tell John Brown to come down here and cut our throats in Christ's name. Now consider what I have seen of my mother's life, my grandmother's, my mother-in-law's. These people were educated at Northern schools, they read the same books as their Northern contemporaries, the same daily papers, the same Bible. They have the same ideas of right and wrong, are high-bred, lovely, good, pious, doing their duty as they conceive it. They live in Negro villages. They do not preach and teach hate as a gospel, and the sacred duty of murder and insurrection; but they strive to ameliorate the condition of these Africans in every particular. They set them the example of a perfect life, a life of utter self-abnegation. Think of these holy New Englanders forced to have a Negro village walk through their houses whenever they see fit, dirty, slatternly, idle, ill-smelling by nature. These women I love have less chance to live their own lives in peace than if they were African missionaries. They have a swarm of blacks about them like children under their care, not as Mrs. Stowe's fancy painted them, and they hate slavery worse than Mrs. Stowe does. Book-making which leads you to a round of visits among crowned heads is an easier way to be a saint than martyrdom down here, doing unpleasant duty among the Negroes with no reward but the threat of John Brown hanging like a drawn sword over your head in this world, and threats of what is to come to you from blacker devils in the next.

The Mrs. Stowes have the plaudits of crowned heads; we take our chances, doing our duty as best we may among the woolly heads. My husband supported his plantation by his law practice. Now it is running him in debt. Our people have never earned their own bread. Take this estate, what does it do, actually? It all goes back in some shape to what are called slaves here, called operatives, or tenants, or peasantry elsewhere. I doubt if ten thousand in money ever comes to this old gentleman's hands. When Mrs. Chesnut married South, her husband was as wealthy as her brothers-in-law. How is it now? Their money has accumulated for their children. This old man's goes to support a horde of idle dirty Africans, while he is abused as a cruel slave owner. I say we are no better than our judges in the North, and no worse. We are human beings of the nineteenth century and slavery has to go, of course. All that has been gained by it goes to the North and to Negroes. The slave owners, when they are good men and women, are the martyrs. I hate slavery. I even hate the harsh authority I see parents think it their duty to exercise toward their children.

But what good does it do to write all that? I have before me a letter I wrote to Mr. Chesnut while he was on our plantation in Mississippi in 1842. It is the most fervid abolition document I have ever read. I came across it while burning letters the other day, but that letter I did not burn.

NOVEMBER 29th. — How disheartened I am! I have just seen Kirkland, with his bad Low Country news. Low Country gentlemen curse Lee and Drayton alike. Only Mr. Barnwell stands by Jeff Davis. While they were pitching into the President, I said my say, not fearing consequences. The Reverend Mr. Hay gave me a benignant smile of approbation, but he did not by words fly in the face of the hysteria there present. Of course, the Judge told me for the hundred thousandth time the story of the house in Montgomery, rented for Jeff Davis unconstitutionally. Thus they waste time killing dead snakes, while the live ones are rattling.

NOVEMBER 30th. — Tobin named his company the Chesnut Rangers. Mr. Chesnut forgot to answer his letter telling of the compliment for a fortnight; and now, Lo, we see in the papers that he has changed the name. It is now "Hammond Huzzars." Huzza!

My Molly came to complain, with a black catalogue of crimes urged against Team, the overseer; crimes against me, not against "cullud people." She brings me for my butter so much more butter than I expected, but she says Team takes as much as he pleases and he will not pay her for it. She says the poultry business pays splendid. She has not lost a chicken. "Nobody will steal Missis's chickens." But she says Team proclaims aloud that if one of Molly's Missis's chickens is stolen, Molly will rush out and seize in the place of it the very first cbicken she sees, no matter who it belongs to. That makes it the interest of all "not to tetch Missis's chickens." "But," says Molly, "he takes my butter and yo things. His wife has grown so fat she has to go through the big gate. The little one is too narrow for her now. No wonder. Sundays, they puts two of yo hams on their dinner table. Yes Missie, two hams they eats!"

Yes, how I envy those saintly Yankee women, in their clean cool New England homes, writing books to make their fortunes and to shame us. The money they earn goes to them. Here every cent goes to pay the factor who supplies the plantation. Mrs. L—— is a Yankee woman who married a Southern clergyman, and has always been harder on Negroes than any native. She can't get over the idea that they ought to behave like white people. If they will not work, the benificent whip must make them do it, she says.

Mr. John Raven Matthews has burned his cotton, his gin houses and his Negro houses. The Moscow idea is rampant. How old Mr. Chesnut sneers whenever he hears of "another such fool as that." He is deaf and blind and ninety years old, but he hears everything, and his comments are racy indeed. The papers are read to him in a shrieking voice every night. He dozes until you stop, then he wakes and sternly demands: "What's the matter? Who told you to stop?" Sometimes he breaks out in talk of his own. "I was always a Union man. The world's against us. But for the strong power of the United States, repressing insurrections and keeping the hands of outsiders off, we would not keep slavery a day. The world will not tolerate a small slave power."

The Negroes say of my husband: "Mars' Jeems, he don't care for Niggers. He'll git rid of the trouble of 'em, soon as they are hisen. Not a bit like ole Marster. He hole 'em tight. Ole Marster, he know what Niggers worth. Mars' Jeems never in dis world will he worry his head wid dem." Old Mr. Chesnut loves his laugh at his heir's expense, but he sees his fine estates slipping away from him. These are his Gods; he worships his own property. George the II's name is attached to the Mulberry patent. They were granted their lands, mostly, so they came cheap. Cheaper still came the slaves from Yankee slave ships. Then the big fish ate up all the little ones, so the great estates grew up here. I mean the large plantations. There are only two or three of such in every district. There is no primogeniture law, and no subdivision of estates. This one has been kept together by three generations of only sons.

When this establishment at Mulberry breaks up, the very pleasantest, most easy-going life I ever saw will be gone. Mrs. Chesnut, with all her angelic mildness and sweetness, has a talent for organizing, training, making things comfortable, moving without noise and smoothly. He roars and shouts if a pebble of an obstacle is put in his way. Somehow I find her the genius of the place.

My sleeping apartment is large and airy, with windows opening on the lawn east and south. In those deep window seats, idly looking out, I spend much time. A part of the yard which was once a deer park has the appearance of the primeval forest; the forest trees have been unmolested and are now of immense size. In the spring, the air is laden with perfumes, violets, jasmine, crabapple blossoms, roses. Araby the blest never was sweeter in perfume. And yet there hangs here as on every Southern landscape the saddest pall. There are browsing on the lawn, where Kentucky bluegrass flourishes, Devon cows and sheep, horses, mares and colts. It helps to enliven it. Carriages are coming up to the door and driving away incessantly.

But I take this easy-going life coolly. I would sleep upon bare boards, if I could once more be amidst the stir and excitement of a live world. These people have grown accustomed to dullness. They were born and bred in it. They like it as well as anything else.

Mrs. Chesnut tells us that fifty or sixty years ago she was never satisfied unless she went North every summer. A tolerably troublesome job that must have been, four weeks to her home in Philadelphia with coach and four, baggage wagons, children, nurses, outriders. After all her outspoken praises of Negroes, she would never trust her children except to a white head nurse. Fortunately she found a good one, who remained with her until the poor old soul died. The maids here dress in linsey-woolsey gowns and white aprons in the winter, and in summer in blue homespun. These deep blue dresses and white turbans and aprons are picturesque and nice-looking; but on Sundays their finery is excessive and grotesque. I mean their holiday church and outdoor get-up. Whenever they come about us they go back to the white apron uniform.

My dear old maid is as good as gold, and pretty much of that color. She chooses to wait on us because "she nussed Mars' Jeems." She only attends to me here. She never leaves home. She is as noiseless in her ministrations as the white cat. She brings water and builds up a fire, lets that burn down to warm the room, then makes a positive bonfire and says shrilly: "Ain't you gwine to get up? First bell for breakcous done ring." If I disregard this mandate, she lets me sleep as long as I please and brings a nice breakfast to my bedside.

While I loiter over my breakfast, she gets my room in what she calls "apple pie" order. When I am in my dressing room and bath, she sweeps and dusts, cleaning and getting things to rights by magic, with no trouble or disorder. Mrs. Chesnut had the art of training servants, but an immense income is consumed by the young and old unprofitable Negroes.

From my window high (I sit here in the library alone a great deal), I see carriages approach. Colonel Chesnut drives a pair of thoroughbreds, beauties, mahogany bays with shining coats and arching necks. It is a pleasure to see Scip drive them up. Tiptop and Princess are their names. Mrs. Chesnut has her carriage horses and a huge family coach for herself, which she never uses. The young ladies have a barouche and their own riding horses. We have a pair, for my carriage; and my husband has several saddle horses. There are always families of the children or grandchildren of the house visiting here, with carriage and horses, nurses and children. The house is crammed from garret to cellar without intermission. As I sit here writing, I see half a dozen carriages under the shade of the trees, coachmen on their boxes, talking, laughing. Some are "hookling," they call it. They have a bone hook something like a crochet needle, and they hook themselves woolen gloves. Some are reading hymn books or pretending to do so. The small footmen are playing marbles under the trees. A pleasant, empty, easy-going life, if one's heart is at ease. But people are not like pigs; they cannot be put up and fattened. So here I pine and fret.

I have been reading and destroying old letters, many from M. K., and from Caroline P. Like Wolsey, I tear my hair and cry: "If I had served my God, as I have served you." They both bow politely when they pass me. No wonder that I find no place for the word gratitude in this world, but in the dictionary.

DECEMBER 2nd. — Met Louisa Salmond at the gate, going on a visit of condolence to Aunt Mary L. I had not seen her since Lemuel's death, so was easily persuaded to join the expedition. On the front seat was old Penny, Mrs. Salmond's maid. Louisa said Penny had elected herself to be their bodyguard, and ever since Dr. S. had gone to the wars, Penny had deserted her comfortable quarters, and left her warm bed to sleep on the floor and take care of them. Little Maggie calls Penny our Beauregard.

At Aunt Mary's everything was quiet and sad. Once only there was a bitter word. Aunt Mary said with an outburst of grief: "I never see a coffin leave this house but I wish I was in it!"

Once more I have been under grape and chain shot. I stood it until forbearance ceased to be a virtue, and then I gave back shot for shot. I do not think I was ever so angry in my life. My country and everybody in it was abused, suspected, assigned such despicable motives, and there sat the comfortable cynic, calling himself the only true patriot. In times like these, there he sat in his warm, soft dressing gown, sleeping sweetly at night and eating of the best, his taste studied in every particular. Must I stay there and hear him malign and vilify the unfortunates who are lying in snow and mud, risking life and limb, deserting home, wife, children, worldly goods, perilling all — yes, maybe their very souls — for what they believe their own country, and no Yankee land. A Union! Let them call it an empire, a kingdom. We in this Union would be an unwilling bride, a Union where one party is tied and dragged in, if he can be well drubbed first!

My interlocutor hated the Union enough, and admired our army *en masse*, but he gave each individual man the meanest motive.

DECEMBER 6th. — A heavy fall, but no bones broken. That was my way with this Senatorship. I wanted that and nothing else — until my husband was sent to Washington. Then — but that is my private howl! Words are vain. Mr. A. H. Boykin refused to allow Mr. Barnwell's and Mr. Chesnut's names to be put up together. He thought that as Mr. Chesnut was the incumbent, he should be elected first. Mr. Barnwell's friends then coalesced with Orr, and now those two are our Senators. To ride a high horse so foolishly at this time! And when Mr. Davis, and Mr. Barnwell himself, had urged Mr. Chesnut to remain in the Congress, and so he let everyone who pleased take the offices he could have had in the army.

This is Governor Manning's account of the fiasco. He said: "It is Ham Boykin's extraordinary handling of his friend's election." And Mr. Boykin says: "What troubles me so is that I see it was my fault."

This vote shows how the wind blows. Orr is and always was a Union man, and so was left out in the first Congress. Mr. Barnwell is sent because otherwise he has no way to support his family. He is one of the unhappy ones whose estate and whose home was destroyed at Beaufort. Besides, does it not read as a vote of disapprobation? Mr. Chesnut was the first man to resign, when Lincoln was made President. They seem now to prefer the men who were slowest to move off from the old Union!

Last night I read the most bravely indelicate letter from Mrs. Greenhow. She wants us to know how her delicacy was shocked and outraged, and that could be done only by most plain-spoken revelations. For eight days she was kept in full sight of men, her rooms wide open, and sleepless sentinels watching by day and by night. Soldiers, tramping by, looked in at her by way of amusement. Beautiful as she is, even at her time of life, few women like all the mysteries of their toilette laid bare to the public eye. She says she was worse used than Marie Antoinette, when they snatched a letter from the poor queen's bosom.

Mr. Team was here today. He is a stalwart creature, a handsome old man, perhaps the finest black eyes I ever saw. He has been an overseer all his life. Most people detest overseers, but Mr. Team is an exception. He has the good will and respect of all the world; of our small world, I mean. How those magnificent eyes blazed today. He is disgusted at the way Mr. Chesnut has been left out in the cold. He said today: "In all my life I have only met one or two womenfolk who were not abolitionists in their hearts, and hot ones too. Mrs. Chesnut is the worst. They have known that of her here for years." We told him Uncle Tom's story, as invented or imagined by Mrs. Stowe. He said he had not seen many of that sort. If there were any, "money couldn't buy 'em." We said: "Daddy Abram was as good." "I never knew a Negro to be murdered or burnt. But, if the Marsters are bad or drunken, look out. Slavery is a thing too unjust, too unfair to last. Let us take the bull by the horns, set 'em free, let 'em help us fight, to pay for their freedom."

Old Mr. Chesnut did not hear, and I noticed no voice was raised to enable him to hear. He is a Prince of Slaveholders, and so he will die. His forefathers paid their money for them, and they are his by that right divine — he thinks. Our votes are not counted. We are women, alas!

Team said: "Slavery does not make good masters." Then he told a tale of a woman so lazy she tied her child to her back and jumped in the river. She said she did not mean to work, nor should her child after her! He had had us crying over his stories, but now we laughed, so that we might not cry.

The Southern landscape is always sad. Now the freshet is up on every side, and the river comes to our doors. The lower limbs of the trees dip mournfully in the water. Many sheep and cattle have been driven up. This house is a Noah's Ark, and their lowing and bleating adds to the general despairing effect. We are surrounded by water on three sides. This is not at all like the Sandy Hill house, with all its God-forsaken make-shift wretchedness. Here everything is fresh, bright, cool, sweet-scented; and a mocking bird is singing and a woodpecker at work — or a yellow hammer, for I cannot see the small bird which is making such a noise. I hear loud laughing among the Negroes, and every sound comes up of a jolly contented life. There is neither silence nor solitude. All the same, it is mournful; a 'dismal swamp' feeling hangs around us still.

Another Russell letter says the Yankees are satisfied they will get what cotton they want; the almighty dollar always wins its way. That was written before Port Royal. Russell thinks he knows the fervid beating of this strong Southern heart, and that we will destroy everything before their approaching footsteps. He finds our courage a fact past controversy, and says that if our money was as palpable a fact, as visible to the naked eye as our soldierly qualities, no mortal could doubt the issue of this conflict.

December 8th. — My husband is ill in Richmond with pneumonia. Mrs. Huger found him in his room forgotten by all (Lawrence was not there) and nearly dead, his dinner of three days before beside his bed untouched. She and her daughter nursed him through it. He will be home today or tomorrow. He takes the Senator business coolly. His consolation is, he has been put aside by the same wise body which put in Pickens.

I do not think anybody would mind the troubles of life, if nobody felt bound to talk it over with us. The triumph of one's enemies does not approach in annoyance the condolence and sympathy of one's voluble friends.

The circuit rider is here. (I mean the colored church.) He looks into everything, and if commandments are not kept, he turns out church members. They dislike to be up before the church and excommunicated more than aught else in the world, so it is a wholesome discipline. Mr. Shuford, the man who has charge here now, was my nearest neighbor in Kirkwood; so I know him, and also Mrs. Shuford and the little Shufords, well. We went to church in the grove. There was a Negro wedding after service. When Mr. Shuford preached I saw from whence Jim Nelson got his ideas of eloquence, though he improved on his model. Mr. Shuford begins each sentence in a low chanting voice, distinct enough; then he works himself up, shuts his eyes, clenches his fists, and the end of the sentence might be addressed to a congregation over the river, so loud and shrill is the shriek. It is like nothing I have ever heard, except calling the ferry man. And oh, the bridal party, all as black as the ace of spades. The bride and her bridesmaids in white swiss muslin, the gayest of sashes, and bonnets too wonderful to be described. They had on red blanket shawls, which they removed as they entered the aisle, and seemed loath to put on when the time came to go out, so proud were they of their finery. Gibbes Carter arose amidst the ceremony and threw a red shawl over the heads of the congregation to a shivering bridesmaid. The shawl fell short and wrapped itself about the head of a sable dame comfortably asleep. She waked with a snort; struggled to get it off her head with queer little cries: "Lord ha' mussy! What dis here now?" There was a decided tendency to giggle, but they were too well-bred to misbehave in church, and soon it was unbroken solemnity. I know that I shook with silent laughter long after every dusky face was sober and respectable. The bride's gloves were white and the bridegroom's shirt bosom was a snowy expanse, fearfully like Johnny's Paris garments, which he says disappear by the dozen. This one had neat little frills and a mock diamond of great size in the middle.

Maria was hard on Mr. Shuford as she combed my hair at night. She likes Manning Brown. "He is ole Marster's nephew, a gentleman born, and he preaches to black and to white just the same. There ain't but one gospel for all. He tells us 'bout keeping the Sabbath holy, honoring our fathers and mothers, and loving our neighbors as ourselves. Mr. Shuford he goes for low life things, hurting people's feelings. 'Don't you tell lies! Don't you steal!' Worse things, real indecent. Before God, we are white as he is, and in the pulpit he no need to make us feel we are servants."

I took up the cudgels for Mr. Shuford. Years ago I went to see some sick Negroes, and I left the carriage at the overseer's house and with my basket went down the line on foot. I passed what I knew to be an unoccupied house and heard coming from it queer sounds, so I softly drew near. It was Mr. Shuford teaching the little Negroes. They were answering all together, and seemed to know their catechism wonderfully well. I sat there listening more than an hour. I know how hard it is to teach them, for I have tried it, and I soon let my Sunday School all drift into singing hymns. I determined to wait until they developed more brains, but Mr. Shuford's patience was sublime. How he wrestled in prayer for those imps of darkness, and he thought only God saw or heard him. I do not believe a genuine follower of

Christ can be a soldier. It is a trade which calls for all that he forbids. There!

Mr. Shuford unconsciously took a shot at us. "Go to, you rich men. Weep, howl, for your miseries have come upon ye." Hitherto I have felt so poor, and have fancied my life so devoid of pleasure that I was inclined to grumble at providence. Today under Mr. Shuford's ministrations I began to tremble, to shiver. Maybe, after all, we were the rich who were threatened with howling.

I went whimpering to Mr. Chesnut. He said coolly: "Let the galled jade wince!" He said the saddle was on the other horse; that his Negroes owed him about fifty thousand dollars now for food and clothes. "Why the lazy rascals steal all of my hogs, and I have to buy meat for them, and they will not make cotton. Well, if they don't choose to make cotton, and spin it and weave it, they may go naked for me. There are plenty of sheep. Let them shear the sheep and spin that too." That means I must look after the spinners and weavers, and it can be done easily. Everybody else is beginning to do it.

One joke at Mr. Chesnut's expense always made him very angry. At an agricultural dinner, Mr. Taylor told the story. "Chesnut offered his crop to his overseer for his wages. The overseer answered: 'La, Colonel, you don't catch me that way!' "

He is like his mother in feeling, but he likes to be thought like his father, whose bark is worse than his bite. How men can go blustering around, making everybody uncomfortable, simply to show that they are masters and we are only women and children at their mercy! My husband's father is kind, and amiable when not crossed, given to hospitality on a grand scale, jovial, genial, friendly, courtly in his politeness. But he is as absolute a tyrant as the Czar of Russia, the Khan of Tartary, or the Sultan of Turkey. The best description of Mrs. Chesnut is: "She likes everything and everybody better than they deserve, and praises them beyond what they merit."

All proud persons are much attached to the "*Convenances*," without a due respect for which a person meaning to be civil is often very impertinent. A refugee, Mr. Stephen Robinson, said on the cars as he came up that he chose Camden because he knew so many people here. It would be jolly. "Who do you know?" "Old Colonel Chesnut. Mr. Tom Lang. Miss Susan and Murray Lang." He was told that the list did not have a jolly sound. Colonel Chesnut, over ninety, deaf and blind, is not very available for social purposes, and Mr. Lang has been dead for several years. That left only Susan and Murray!

DECEMBER 13th. — Charleston is in flames, one part of the city utterly destroyed. On the night of the eleventh, we had here a furious windstorm. We rather enjoyed it, in the interest of the Yankee Fleet outside of the Bar there. As the blast howled, we said: "How now, blockaders?" Evil thoughts are like chickens; they come home to roost. When the telegram came today, I was too much shocked to speak. Suffering, death and destitution on every side. In all this confusion they might attack us. What then!

Old Colonel Chesnut said: "Charleston has been twice burned down before in my recollection." He described the other two fires. He seemed greatly relieved that the Yankees had no hand in it.

Everybody reads my journal, but since I have been making sketches of character at Mulberry I keep it under lock and key. Yesterday I handed this book to my new little maid, Ellen, who is a sort of apprentice under Betsey, trying to learn her trade. When I gave Ellen the book, I pointed to an *armoire*. She mistook the direction of my finger and took it into Miss S. C's room, where she laid it on the table. Today, I looked for it in the *armoire*, and it was gone. "Ellen, where is the book I write in? I gave it to you." She flew into Miss S. C's room, which happened to be empty just then, and brought it. Words were useless! In my plain speaking and candour, what have I not said, intending no eye save mine to rest upon this page. The things that I cannot tell exactly as they are, I do not intend to tell at all.

Old Colonel Chesnut will lend the Sandy Hill house to refugees, because the Charleston catastrophe was a visitation from God; but he has no patience with people who run away from their homes and destroy them to spite the Yankees.

DECEMBER 14th. — More news of the Charleston fire. Carolina Institute, where secession was signed, burned down, and so did Mr. Petigru's house; so being antisecession does not save. The fire, like the rain, falls on the just and the unjust. The fire appeared simultaneously in several places.

John DeSaussure has sent a hundred bales of cotton to be sold. He says he knows his factor will slip it into Old England or into New England.

Horace Greeley says in his Tribune: "South Carolina is the meanest and the vainest state in the Union, and nobody will feel any compunction at laying it waste." So he does not count us out of the Union yet.

Who is it that says: "After forty we repent, but we never reform." Still, I am under that awful age.

The lesson of today in church, as the parson read it, was a little alarming. It was from Isaiah and applied so clearly to Charleston and its fire and destruction. "All things are less dreadful than they seem." After church, Mrs. Roper said: "Not a house left on Logan Street except Tom Frost's." The Judge gravely replied: "That is a reward for his marrying an Up Country girl, and for such a pious mother-in-law."

It is amazing that so clever a man should not be able to see how senseless is his cynical abuse of everybody. Today it was the South Carolina Legislature. He called it the weakest, stupidest, most venal body of men ever assembled. He said that Johnston complained that his family used so many pounds of butter and so many pounds of tea a week that he asked Johnston if they gave tea and butter to his horses; and he quoted Kate Williams: "Complaining of the foolish extravagance of your family is a vulgar parvenue way of bragging about your money."

DECEMBER 16. — One of the complaints of Mr. Chesnut since his defeat is that the only night he was in Columbia, he stayed in his own room and did not go to see anybody. He thought it unseemly to electioneer for such a place as Senator. The Legislators thought otherwise; thought he was too grand and that a taking down would do him good.

Boxes upon boxes of provisions and clothes are being sent to the needy and burnt out in Charleston, while Northern newspapers are gloating over our misfortunes and fiery destruction.

Mrs. Davis's new baby is called William Howell.

England demands that Mason and Slidell be replaced under the aegis of her flag. Lord Lyons talks of breaking the blockade. France is counted on to do whatever England does. Troops are ordered to Canada.

A letter from S.R.R. in Charleston says: "Thanks for your kind note today, dear Mrs. Chesnut. Comfortable clothing will be a great help; and for the children, anything that you can spare.

"Charleston looks like a mutilated body! Your first impulse would be to turn away and hide your face!

"The fire began in a Negro house next to the Blind Factory, through carelessness, and the wind rose with the flames, until it got beyond control. Picture to yourself Mr. Alfred Huger seated on the steps of the Poor House next morning with only a blanket around him. That was his gesture! There was Mrs. Wm. Huger's house in Broad Street out of the way of the wind, where he could have been comfortable and private — as he was afterward. He would not allow his furniture, etc., to be saved in time; thought the house was safe. While it was burning, he remained opposite in an armchair with his desk in his lap.

"I wonder if the Yankees think as Job's friends did? We don't!"

This and much more; so we are comparatively well off here, even without being again Senator, eh?

DECEMBER 22nd. — Anniversary of secession. The reality is not as dreadful as the anticipation. I have seen not half as much as I dreaded of fire and sword, bad as it is.

Lord Lyons demands his passports. That is a ray of sunshine, a patch of blue sky in a clouded heaven. "Passports, or Mason and Slidell!" That is Lord Lyons's word. The Mercury, whose first instinct is always to insult and alienate and drive off our friends, says England does this because she wants tobacco and cotton; that she does not resent the insult to her flag. Fortunately, neither the Queen nor the Emperor is, I dare say, a subscriber to the daily Mercury.

We dined with Hamilton Boykin, who thinks he has quite repaired his shortcomings in the Senator's election when he says: "Really James, I think it was all my fault. You see I lost my temper!" It was not an agreeable subject, and we said nothing, literally. "Let it drop, for pity's sake," thought I.

The conversation turned on Joe Johnston. Says Mr. Hamilton Boykin: "Now we all know Sid Johnston, the General's brother. Never in his life could he make up his mind that everything was so exactly right that the time to act had come. Joe Johnston is that way too. Wade Hampton brought him here to hunt. We all liked him, but as to hunting, there he made a dead failure. He was a capital shot, better than Wade or I; but with Colonel Johnston — I think he was Colonel then — the bird flew too high or too low, the dogs were too far or too near. Things never did suit exactly. He was too fussy, too hard to please, too cautious, too much afraid to miss and risk his fine reputation for a crack shot. Wade and I bulged through the mud and water, briars and bushes, and came home with a heavy bag. We shot right and left, happy-go-lucky. Joe Johnston did not shoot at all. The exactly right time and place never came.

"Unless his ways are changed, he'll never fight a battle. You'll see. He is as brave as Caesar, an accomplished soldier, but he is too particular. Things are never all straight. You must go ahead at a venture to win." And much more said he.

Christmas day, 1861. — We did not exactly achieve a victory at Dranesville, for Frank English was killed. His father wrote to Mr. Chesnut to get a discharge for him, his health was so feeble. He is discharged now, poor boy, from this earth and its troubles.

The Negroes who murdered Mrs. Witherspoon were tried by the law of the land, and were hung. A man named Wingate with a John Brown spirit — namely, that Negroes were bound to rise and kill women — made himself Devil's counsel and stood by the Negroes clear through. At the hanging, he denounced John Witherspoon bitterly, and had high words with George Williams. Afterwards, George Williams, having raised a company, was made Captain of it. The men were actually on board the train, and Captain Williams was sitting in a chair ready to jump on board when the whistle blew. Wingate came behind him, rested his gun on the back of the chair, and shot him dead, there before the very faces of his soldiers. It was very hard to rescue Wingate from the hands of George's men, who wanted to shoot him instantly, and no wonder. The people who laud and magnify John Brown's philanthropy must adore Wingate. He was lodged in jail. George Williams leaves his young wife with two babies, the eldest not two years old. Widows and orphans; it becomes easy to be that now.

The servants rushed in with "Merry Christmas," "Christmas Gift," etc. I covered my face and wept.

Mr. Chesnut, in good spirits, is trying a new horse. As long as he has a dollar left in the world it will go into horseflesh. If fate will leave him a fine horse to ride, she can never utterly depress him otherwise.

At our Christmas dinner, the Hugers were here, a charming mother and daughter. Meta, the clever, addressed her whole conversation to Mr. Chesnut and myself. She talked incessantly, but was interesting always. The family were all gathered, of course, and the table was very long. The others sat stiff and lifeless as pins stuck in rows, showing only their heads. Meta affected me as champagne does one lately unaccustomed to that exciting beverage. Here I am surrounded by — what shall I say? Well, something as dull as ditch water.

There was everything at that table. Romeo is a capital cook, and the pastry cook was good, with her plum puddings and mince pies. There was everything there that a hundred years or more of unlimited wealth could accumulate as to silver, china, glass, damask; but without Meta? Well I hate to think what it would have been.

Here is a word from Mrs. Huger on matrimony. "There is not six months difference between a beauty and an ugly woman. In that time, the husband has totally forgotten her looks either way, has grown callous from habit. After the first year, no man can tell whether he married for love or money. It is what a woman really is, not what he supposed her to be, that makes it good or bad for her in the end."

Meta retorted: "Ah, but Mamma, that is taking the end of the matrimonial six months for granted. But without beauty, it is hard for a woman to begin that six months ordeal."

DECEMBER 30th. — Prince Albert is dead! Comes the selfish thought — will that affect us? No; he has had the absolute wisdom to efface himself, and by so doing he brought no trouble upon his devoted wife. As kings and queens go, what a happy couple, as if it had been love in a cottage. My democratic husband loves to tell how the gay young girl queen graciously returned his bows in the park, the year before she was married.

More gossip of the crowned heads. Mrs. Huger says a Frenchman told her that the Prince Royal was an Imperial necessity, a supposititious heir, better than none. She says Eugènie introduced hoop skirts to hide a lack, not an exuberance, of figure.

I went to Kirkwood and gave Captain DePass's company my fifty pairs of drawers and socks and shirts. He sent a letter of warm and heartfelt thanks.

XII

Columbia

JANUARY 1st, 1862. — We came over to Columbia today on the train. There were Mrs. Huger, Meta, Tanny Withers and Franklin J. Moses. Tanny Withers is a boy with the war spirit so prematurely developed that he brickbatted his teacher, Barnwell Stewart, so he is sent to a military academy to try what that discipline will do for him. He regards the fight with Barney Stewart with great complacency. The difference in age and size was as much against him, and in Barney's favor, as it is against us in our present combat with the United States. The schoolboys' applause was balm to Tanny's bruises.

I made the journey pleasantly located on a trunk (it was a freight train and had no seats), surrounded by little Negroes, pumpkins, boxes, bags, etc. We found Mr. Chesnut dressed and on the wing to a dinner at the Prestons'. And we, to waste no time after the social desert of Sahara of Camden, went to tea at the Greens'. We plunged into society at once, only to be told our men were losing hope and heart because there have been so many blunders on the coast.

JANUARY 3rd. — I went to drive with Mrs. Preston, and met Colonel Preston in full uniform. He is a splendid specimen of humanity. It is a little too much that so handsome a man — six feet four — should be clever and charming in like degree. As Swift defines aristocracy, he had the three essentials; brains, blood, wealth. Also, he is as lucky in his wife and children. One would think he had nothing to wish for in this world; but he is a bitter, a disappointed man. The popular breath cares for none of these things, and he is ambitious for what the popular vote alone can give; political distinction. Yet he does seem to have so many things which dwarf these poor democratic holders of high station into nonentity, nearly.

JANUARY 4th. — On Pinckney Island, the Negroes have been reinforced by runaways and outlaws, and they are laying in supplies, getting in provisions, selecting a king, etc.

JANUARY 5th. — I saw Mr. Keitt as I came up, and we had a long talk. I leaned over the banister and he looked up. I like him. He is quick as a flash. No one gets the better of him; and though he covers himself with words, the longest and the finest, like a garment, still there is the strongest common sense always at the bottom of it all. Whenever I leave Mr. Keitt I have something to tell as good and as self-evident as a proverb; something original and new that I had never thought of before.

Mr. Chesnut is to be Colonel of a regiment and Keitt the Lieutenant Colonel, or so he said. "No," I replied. "Never. Before you're done, you will put him in some political hole, smother him with fine words, and march off with the regiment. See if you don't!"

"You are awfully spiteful," he retorted. "All women are. Besides, your program is too good to be true."

JANUARY 7th. — Now they say there is to be a Council of Safety, a bundle of sticks and crutches for old Pickens. If I were asked to go into such a council, I would throw the nasty office in their faces. Today we dined with Governor Pickens. Mrs. Pickens was bitter against the convention for giving Governor Pickens these guardians, or this guard of honor, or this council, call it what you will. It means that Governor Pickens has been felt to need aid and counsel.

JANUARY 8th. — A pleasant day at the Prestons'. We went to dinner with Governor Manning. Those beautiful girls declaimed for us in French, early in the evening. Later we went to Mrs. Herbemont's. Two or three events in one day! Dinners! Parties! After life at Mulberry, it is a waking up. Here, there are absorbing interests for all. There, old Mr. Chesnut's health, what he eats, what she says; that and nothing more.

JANUARY 9th. — I called on Mrs. Pickens and we flattered each other as far as that sort of thing can be done. She is young, lovely, clever, and old Pick's third wife. She cannot fail to hate us, since Mr. Chesnut * is now put as a sort of watch and ward over her husband.

* He had been named head of the Council of Safety.

Mrs. Harry Middleton, who is English, mistook Governor Manning for Mr. Chesnut. Then she asked me: "Is he as handsome as that?"

"No," answered Mrs. Manning with emphasis.

"But ever so much cleverer," I replied as emphatically.

"How you American women praise your husbands," said Mrs. Middleton, and I retorted:

"Life is, I dare say, pretty much the same game everywhere. Whatever one says of one's husband here is always repeated to him by some shabby women present. They like to lay a trap for you!"

XIII

Camden

JANUARY 11th, 1862. — Back at Mulberry, I have a headache, yet I had not an ache or a pain in Columbia. It is the dullness striking in.

Colonel Chesnut is so quiet and comfortable. He has forgotten the war. He is busy making another will, telling each Negro to whom he intends to leave him or her — as if there were no Yankees. Some startling shock will come and wake us up again. Yet even this, this cold beneficence, seizes my praise, when I reflect on those who sigh with sympathy for the wretched, yet shun them, nursing their delicious solitude in slothful loves and dainty sympathies.

At the convent in Columbia, where I went with Mary P., I fancied the Mother Superior had a hope of Mary's going over to them. Ellen Spann had just been made a nun, and taking the vows at this time, she turned the attention of idle heads and restless hearts to the repose and safety of the Cloister.

The nuns told us how their veils cured headaches; that they were cool in summer and warm in winter. One said that before she took the veil she was a martyr to dyspepsia, but she had never felt a twinge since she left the world.

Mrs. Preston was not alarmed for Mary's orthodoxy, and least of all that she would join a convent. She said Mary loved the world too well.

Ransom Calhoun is under arrest for writing an insulting letter either to or about General Ripley.

Coming home, General Hardee told us a significant fact. On board were the bodies of two men. These dead men had been bringing Negroes from the coast, Negroes who did not want to come. The men laid down their guns and went to sleep. The Negroes took the guns, shot the owners of them, and went back to the Yankee fleet.

Oh, the amount of virulent nonsense I have had to hear and bear today. Among other things, to hear Mr. Chesnut called a First Consul, to hear that this was the beginning of the Bastille and the guillotine. "But Mr. Chesnut is so mild," suggested the speaker's daughter. "He is not the least likely to do anything horrid!" Answer: "They chose their mildest men for triumvirs in France, and you see what came of it." I said nothing. Things looked a little mixed.

This pleasant Sabbath day, I read Gideon's battle of Manassas and the rewards thereof: of how they told the timorous to depart, and of the thirty thousand, twenty thousand left silently in the night; and of the tribe of Ephraim, who did not come to fight the Amalekites, but who found it easy and pleasant to fight their brethren afterwards for the spoils.

But nothing will ever equal that "first sprightly running" of our foes, at our Manassas.

JANUARY 13th. — Mr. Chesnut is gone. I was ill but I did not say so, as he had to go, and had better go with an easy conscience, which might not have been the case if he had left me in bed. I kept up the game to the last; sang out to him from the piazza as he drove off: "Ladies! Beware of the gay young knight who loves and who rides away."

So they have fobbed Mr. Chesnut off with this trouble-bringing — and no glory-giving — office on the Council, and Keitt takes his regiment, as I foresaw. To say "I told you so" does not comfort me. Far from it. His Colonel's uniform came home today.

While we were in Columbia, our General Kershaw, of boundless ambition, was told that he was to have a serenade. He gathered together the sleepy ladies at the hotel. "Keep awake, there is to be a serenade tonight for me!" He made ready his fiery eloquence. But alas, none came to serenade him.

I read "Castle Richmond." In this one thing, Trollŏpe manages his elderly lady-in-love better than Thackeray. In Esmond, marrying your mother-in-law was painfully revolting to me, a discordant note which continued to vibrate throughout Esmond — which is, after all, the best of Thackeray's.

JANUARY 15th. — Mrs. Pringle's little grandchild is dead! Lovely little thing, away from her parents.

Mrs. K's new baby is called Ethel Newcome. Shabby genteel names from novels make a child a laughing stock.

JANUARY 16th. — Mrs. Henry DeSaussure is hard on men who do not fight and die for their country.

So far, the Union estimates it has lost 22,000 men. That is a flea bite for them. They hardly feel it. They can waste life at their own sweet will.

They were rating two of Mr. Chesnut's nephews for not being in the army. I said of one: "His lungs are weak. I heard that when he married. Unsound, they said he was."

"Then why did my niece marry him?"

"Because he was sound on the goose," I placidly explained.

"What does she mean?" the lady demanded, and her daughter said: "Oh Mamma, don't you know that slang expression? It means he had a plantation and no end of Negroes."

"Do you mean" — turning to me savagely — "to insinuate that my niece married from mercenary motives?"

"Did you mean to insult and slander my nephew-in-law when you said he shirked the army?" It was as broad as it was long.

I heard loud talking below, so threw down my book and flew. I arrived not a second too soon. Old Mr. Chesnut was mistaking my guest, Mrs. Roper, for Mrs. Hocot, the turpentine man's wife; and she was losing her patience in futile explanation.

Driving out today I passed the awkward squad. They were drilling. The order must have been "wipe your noses"; they were doing so thoroughly well, every handkerchief in air. It was hopelessly wet under foot, and a mild soaking drizzle seemed to be seeking every pore.

Last night I sat up until one o'clock, reading a very bad book, but it was enchanting because its portraiture of the absurdities of village life is so finely illustrated to me daily, to me who suffer under it so. For example, think of the emptiness of life here in war times. Mr. Hay, the reverend gentleman, tells a story nearly a month old against the Ropers; that they sat by a pump and ate apples on Christmas day, in the streets of Camden, streets as desert as Sahara!

JANUARY 20th. — I have a neuralgia of the eyes, have wept and prayed, cannot see to read or to work, only tears and despair. I feel abandoned of God and man, here in this dismal swamp. That cry on the Cross must have come from the mortal part of our Savior, the cruelest pang a mortal can feel: "My God! My God! Why hast thou forsaken me?"

The R.'s, Harriet's pinks of perfection, are here. They have enlivened things somewhat. They disapprove of me highly, and primly let me see it, with that eternal chorus of astonishment: "Why Aunt Mary!" But they are so quiet and ladylike, so polite and so little interfering. People who interrupt, people who ask questions, people who interfere perpetually in trifles, they make life difficult. Lincoln's idea, "I hate an interruptious fellow," is not half a bad description.

Team was here. Mr. Chesnut lent his Gold Branch plantation to the Trapiers and Jenkins. "Jenkins," said Team, "is a parson. Two of his Niggers run away a'ready. They are from the ocean wave. They call our river — the big Wateree — a spring branch. They swim like ducks across the river. They laughs at ferries and bridges and toll gates. Did you all ever have a runaway?"

"Never," said Mr. Chesnut. "It's pretty hard work to keep me from running away from them! Have these Negroes gone back to the fleet at Beaufort?"

"Straight as the crow flies."

XIV

Columbia

JANUARY 24th, 1862. — I am here at Mrs. Preston's. Mr. Chesnut was seized with a new freak today. He drew me out, and Mrs. Venable's ready laugh drew me on. I did more than my share of the talking, felt ashamed of myself, and expected a lecture such as I am accustomed to. Late at night, when we were seated alone in the upper piazza which opens out of our rooms, Mr. Chesnut said gravely: "This has been a very happy day."

There was a story, at dinner, of Mrs. Scott. She did not accept Winfield Scott until after many offers on his part and refusals on hers. Finally, after her marriage, someone said: "And so you married Captain Scott after all?" "No, I refused Captain Scott to the last. I accepted the General." But after a brief matrimonial experience she kept the broad Atlantic between them. Mrs. Scott could not be accused of the crime of proximity. I heard today for the first time of a post office which was closed and its postmaster dismissed. The poor man asked why. Too great proximity to another post office was the answer. He expostulated earnestly with the Department. Pecuniarily he did not mind — so far, the office had only brought him in sixty-two and one-half cents a month — but to be accused of the crime of proximity was more than he could bear, and he would not stand it! Neither would Mrs. Scott.

Ex-President Tyler is dead, Zollicoffer dead and defeated. East Tennessee and the part of North Carolina which borders on East Tennessee is gone. How down-hearted are we, who were so happy yesterday.

John Frierson has sent his wooden leg to the hospital! They ought to exercise it! Dr. Gibbes told us: "A wonderful machine it is, and a queerer present!" *

Edmund Rhett is queer about women and matrimony and money.† Surely women have a right to a maintenance, even when they are penniless girls before the wedding and bring no dowry. We had our share of my father's estate. It came into our possession not long after we were married, and it was spent for debts already contracted. A man with a rich father is offered every facility for plunging in debt head foremost. That being the case, why feel like a beggar, utterly humiliated and degraded, when I am forced to say I need money? I cannot tell, but I do; and the worst of it is, this thing grows worse as one grows older. Money ought not to be asked for, or given to a man's wife as a gift. Something must be due her, and that she should have, and with no growling and grumbling nor warnings against waste and extravagance, nor hints as to the need of economy, nor amazement that the last supply has given out already. What a proud woman suffers under all this, who can tell? One thing is sure. Nothing but the direst necessity drives her to speak of an empty purse. What a world of heart-burning some regular arrangement of pin money must save.

From this, for many a day, I will be saved by my belt of gold. Besides, the two Mollys bring me their butter and chicken money. We run that business on shares.

Mr. Chesnut thinks I will never be willing to go home again. This is certainly a charming house, the very kindest and most agreeable people I ever knew. And there is everything to tempt an invalid's capricious appetite — and I am ill, there is no denying that — oysters, game, etc. That soup *à la reine* today! I think it had everything nice in the world in it.

JANUARY 29th. — Went to a party at Dr. Gibbes's last night. Mr. Venable solemnly made Governor Gish tell over and over again his pun, of which the Governor was so proud. A poor woman came to him. "I am forced to drink Rio coffee." "Do not bewail your fate,

* The gift would not have seemed a "queer present" later in the war, when there were thousands of soldiers who had lost a leg, and when properly made artificial limbs had to be run through the blockade from England.

† The general legal principle of the times, in Virginia and elsewhere, North and South, was expressed in the phrase: "A husband and wife are one person, and that person is the husband." Broadly speaking, the only married women who had property were widows who had inherited from their husbands.

Madame. There are those who drink rye!" It seems people parch rye and drink it for coffee.

The Governor's lady was there. She received in state, and did not rise from her chair as we spoke to her. We are only of the Governor's Council! Young Moses, Franklin Jr., is Secretary to Governor Pickens. He hung over the lovely Lucy, standing or bending over her from the back of her chair. It suggested the Devil whispering in Eve's ear, in the primeval days. Mr. Chesnut has taken a senseless aversion to little Moses and says: "He is a liar, a sneak, has no moral sense; in a word, a true son of old Franklin Moses."

FEBRUARY 11th. — I am at Congaree House, able to write again after an illness. It came to a point while I was dining at Mrs. Ben Taylor's. Now, after several weeks, dawdling on, kept alive by opium, once more I am on my feet.

While I was ill, an amusing thing happened. I have nervous fainting fits. Mrs. Preston, at whose home I was staying, had left Mary beside my bed and had gone down to the very end of that beautiful garden to look after a cow with which something was amiss. All at once, Mary came flying to her: "Come! Come! Mrs. Chesnut is dying, if not dead." "Who is with her?" "Nobody." "Did you leave her?" cried Mrs. Preston, coming back at full speed. "Surely, Mamma," whimpered Mary, as white as the wall herself, "you would not have me stay there to see her die!"

Confederate affairs are in a blue way. Roanoke taken, Fort Henry on the Tennessee open to them, and we fear for the Mississippi River too. We have evacuated Romney — wherever that is. New armies and new fleets are swarming and threatening everywhere. We ought to have as good a conceit of ourselves as they have of us, and to be willing to do as much to save ourselves from a nauseous Union with them as they are willing to do by way of revengeful coercion in forcing us back. England's eye is scornful and scoffing as she turns it on our miseries. I have nervous chills every day. Bad news is killing me.

Mr. Chesnut had a jolly good time in Charleston, dining with the Jourdins. He came home very unexpectedly; having heard I was ill. He pretends to be as hopeful as ever. I fancy he takes that tone with my wildly excited nerves. Something must be done to soothe them. I do not credit anything but his good intention, and so he fails to comfort me.

W. R. T——, the man John Chesnut, the black freedman, beat for drinking at his house and at table with his colored mother, now is made a member of the convention in place of Judge Withers! What a triumph to the Judge in his scorn of Kershaw District! Mr. T—— is stupid, dissipated, and all that that other story implies. The Judge is of the very best culture we have, with a moral standing as pure as ever sported the ermine. He is a little bitter of speech, a little hard of judgment; but Heavens! The difference between that first choice of theirs and this one. This new man was selected by the people still left in Kershaw District; the-stay-at-homes. The best and bravest are in the army, of course.

I hear from the Spotswood talk of painted Jezebels as of yore, of men seen in rooms where to be is folly. The talk is not to be believed. No mortal does believe any of the nasty nonsense, but they say Generals are called in to settle it all, and duels after the war are among the possibilities.

Dr. Gibbes has accused Colonel Preston of being too kind to Yankee prisoners, too lenient, and not half strict enough in his guard. As if anybody ever expected Mr. Preston to be hard on prisoners! However, Columbia is stirred to its depths.

FEBRUARY 13. — I read a book, utterly abominable — no gainsaying that — Balsac's "La Cousine Bette." And yet a book can be worse.

At this Congaree House, Mrs. Preston still takes charge of my diet; for fever comes as it listeth still and long nervous depressions follow. As I lie here in bed I think of this man who has displaced the Judge, this representative of the stay-at-homes. Judge Withers was acknowledged to be the best judge on the Bench, of as high and pure a character as any in America. Fault-finding was his only fault, useless and uncalled for, but mostly only a bad habit. It is nearly nineteen hundred years since the mob voted for Barrabas, not Jesus, yet still we believe the mob is the best of all powers to rule by its votes. Salvation, we believe, is to come to us by the votes of the mob.*

At first I did not believe the crowd were in earnest, loud as they cried. I could not think they meant war, when at the head of every important state office they put unearthed fossils and incapables. When it came to a one-man power, the mob howled. To hear the discontented talk you would think we had invented Jeff Davis since secession; yet he was our leader in the Senate at Washington, and so acknowledged

* The movement toward universal manhood suffrage, which began about 1850 to accelerate throughout the South, was generally deplored by men of property; the fact that Lincoln believed in popular sovereignty was a basic reason for the resentment with which Southern political leaders viewed his election.

then by the Joe Johnstons and Barnwell Rhetts, who seem to think now that their enemies found him to perplex and annoy them.

Everybody believes that when the time comes the right man to save the country will step forward. Well, let him step! The time has come for him, if ever.

I see cheerful and comfortable Yankee prisoners every day. They seem to be laughing at us, so sure are they that their time is at hand. The jail is opposite Mrs. Togno's School, where I go so often for Kate Withers. One of the girls (Ida DeSaussure, at least, acknowledged it, though many did it) waved her handkerchief to a prisoner, because he looked so sorrowful up there. They knew women were kind to our men wherever they were. Madame was told of it, and she raised an awful shindy against the girls. "Treason" was the mildest word in her mouth!

North Carolina papers shower brickbats on Jeff Davis. They taunt him with only remembering North Carolina when he wants more troops.* Now that I am old, I want peace most of all things; and yet I can only hear of wars and rumors of wars. Mr. Chesnut says: "Would you prefer a disgraced country as your home?" "No! Never!"

FEBRUARY 16th. — Awful newspapers today. Fort Donelson they call a drawn battle. You know that means that we have lost it! That is nothing — they (the Yankees) are being reinforced everywhere! Where are ours to come from, unless they wait and let us grow some.

A Negro girl who brought a note from Madame Togno was in a great state of excitement. She had witnessed a frightful outrage on the street. She was so graphic, she had to be silenced. She said a drunken soldier assaulted "a lady, a real lady dressed fine. She fought like a tigress, and two Negroes ran to her help, but the soldier drew his pistol and held the lady by one leg and his pistol in the other hand, and such a crowd was tearing up, and she was yelling like a stuck pig, and dancing and prancing!" The ladies in the drawing room made allowance for the luxuriant black imagination. The soldier was carried off to the guardhouse. The unknown lady in fine clothes went her way at double-quick speed. It is hard to be forced to think ill of a soldier, drunk or sober.

FEBRUARY 17. — Our men were depressed today. "Men can find

* Virginia and North Carolina, two great states which steadily refused to secede until after Sumter President Lincoln turned to coercion, supplied about equal numbers to the Southern armies; their regiments formed the bulk of the Army of Northern Virginia.

honorable graves, but we do not see what is to become of the women and children." "Has it come to that?" "Oh, no, we are sure to get through. Never fear. It will be all right." So they put on their military cloaks and left me to sad thoughts. Then Mrs. Preston sent me oysters, toast, and jelly; and almost simultaneously came Mrs. Ben Taylor's tray, biscuits, butter, fruit! Can one eat with one's heart in one's mouth, as those men left me?

Youth is a blunder, manhood a struggle, old age is one long regret!

I was crushed at a report that Cedar Keys is gone and that they have Nashville, with thousands upon thousands of our few and precious soldiers. John McRae says it is not true, but John Manning hates Jeff Davis so that he rejoices in anything which will prove a discomfiture to him. Just as the election of W. R. T. was nuts * to the Judge. It pleased him so to find the people of Kershaw District as shabby as he had always proclaimed them. "When the district disgraces itself, you see my bad opinion of it is justified."

FEBRUARY 19th. — Fancied I was very ill, so Mr. Chesnut loitered about the house all day. John Manning prayed Jeff Davis would go to the front and be taken prisoner. They say Governor Pickens is in an awfully bad humor; but also they say Nashville is not taken, and when he hears that he may recover his spirits.

About Nashville, I declined to believe the good news. Mr. Chesnut said with dignity, his military cloak thrown over his arm: "My dear wife, do you think I would deceive you?" I laughed in his face. "To think of trying the 'mutual confidence' dodge on me!" I cried.

Today I read a French play, but everything is flat after "Mariage de Figaro," which was yesterday's *bonne bouche*, and the day before, "Barbier de Seville." The Prestons have sent me Beaumarchais's works, and a pile of Scribe, to beguile the slow and solitary hours when I do not leave my bed.

FEBRUARY 20th. — Had an appetite for my dainty breakfast. Always breakfast in bed now. But then, my Mercury contained such bad news. Fort Donelson has fallen, but no men fell with it. It is prisoners for them that we cannot spare, or prisoners for us that we may not be able to feed. They lost six thousand, we two thousand; I grudge that proportion. We have Buckner, Beauregard, and Albert

* "Nuts to the Judge!" This expression, in Mrs. Chesnut's original manuscript, suggests that some slang is older than we suppose.

Sidney Johnston. With such leaders and God's help we may be saved from the hated Yankees; who knows?

FEBRUARY 21st. — A crowd collected here last night and there was a serenade. I am like Mrs. Nickleby, who never saw a horse coming full speed but she thought the Cheerybles had sent post-haste to take Nicholas into co-partnership. So I got up and dressed, late as it was. I felt sure England had sought our alliance at last, and we would make a Yorktown of it before long. Who was it? Will you ever guess? — Artemus Goodwyn and General Owens, of Florida.

Just then, Mr. Chesnut rushed in, put out the light, locked the door and sat still as a mouse. Rap, rap, came at the door. "I say, Chesnut, they are calling for you." At last we heard Janney (hotel-keeper) loudly proclaiming from the piazza that "Colonel Chesnut was not here at all, at all." After a while, when they had all gone from the street, and the very house itself had subsided into perfect quiet, the door again was roughly shaken. "I say, Chesnut, old fellow, come out — I know you are there. Nobody here now wants to hear you make a speech. That crowd has all gone. We want a little quiet talk with you. I am just from Richmond." That was the open sesame, and today I hear none of the Richmond news is encouraging. Colonel Shaw is blamed for the shameful Roanoke surrender.

Toombs is out on a rampage and swears he will not accept a seat in the Confederate Senate given in the insulting way his was by the Georgia Legislature. He calls it shabby treatment, and adds that Georgia is not the only place where good men have been so ill used.

The Governor and Council have fluttered the dovecotes, or, at least, the tea-tables. They talk of making a call for all silver, etc. I doubt if we have enough to make the sacrifice worthwhile, but we propose to set the example.

Wade Hampton claims Cheves McCord's company for his legion, so Cheves leaves the state also. We are so weak already, that we gaze with longing eyes at any company of soldiers marching away from us.

FEBRUARY 22nd. — What a beautiful day for our Confederate President to be inaugurated! * God speed him; God keep him; God save him!

* Unfortunately, the weather in Richmond on this inauguration day was not like that in Columbia. The Square in front of the Capitol was a sea of mud, and rain fell so steadily and so hard that although the Square was packed with people, few could hear Mr. Davis's inaugural address.

Mrs. Chesnut knows nothing of man and wife being one. I sent for a carriage blanket, calling it mine. She sent me a shabby old shawl and a message: There was a blanket, or a rug, there of James's, but she saw nothing of mine. I wrote back that she did not understand marital rights. He would call that dreadful old shawl his, if he wanted it; so, whoever she thought the carriage blanket belonged to, she had better send it or I would get an order from the Governor and Council for it. I told her to read the marriage ceremony: "Mine is thine, thine is mine" (which, however, is not in it). But "with all my worldly goods" certainly includes carriage rugs!

John Chesnut's letter was quite what we needed. In spirit it is all that one could ask. He says, "Our late reverses are acting finely with the army of the Potomac. A few more thrashings and every man will enlist for the war. Victories made us too sanguine and easy, not to say vainglorious. Now for the rub, and let them have it!"

A lady wrote to Mrs. Bunch: "Dear Emma: When shall I call for you to go and see Madame de St. André?" She was answered: "Dear Lou: I cannot go with you to see Madame de St. André, but will always retain the kindest feeling toward you on account of our past relations," etc. The astounded friend wrote to ask what all this meant. No answer came, and then she sent her husband to ask and demand an explanation. He was answered thus: "My dear fellow, there can be no explanation possible. Hereafter there will be no intercourse between my wife and yours; simply that, nothing more." So the men meet at the club as before, and there is no further trouble between them. The lady upon whom the slur is cast says, "and I am a woman and can't fight."

February 23rd. — While Mr. Chesnut was in town I was at the Prestons'. John Cochran and some other prisoners had asked to walk over the grounds, visit the Hampton Gardens, and some friends in Columbia. After the dreadful state of the public mind at the escape of one of the prisoners, General Preston was obliged to refuse the request. Mrs. Preston and the rest of us wanted him to say "Yes," and so find out who in Columbia were his treacherous friends. Pretty bold people they must be, to receive Yankee invaders in the midst of the row over one enemy already turned loose amid us.

General Preston said: "We are about to sacrifice life and fortune for a fickle multitude who will not stand up for us at last." The harsh comments made as to his lenient conduct to prisoners have embittered him. I told him what I had heard Captain Trenholm say in his speech. He said he would listen to no criticism except from a man with a musket on his shoulder, and who had beside enlisted for the war, had given up all, and had no choice but to succeed or die.

FEBRUARY 24th. — Congress and the newspapers render one desperate, ready to cut one's own throat. They represent everything in our country as deplorable. Then comes someone back from our gay and gallant army at the front. The spirit of our army keeps us up after all. Letters from the army revive one. They come as welcome as the flowers in May. Hopeful and bright, utterly unconscious of our weak despondency.

FEBRUARY 25th. — They have taken at Nashville more men than we had at Manassas; there was bad handling of troops, we poor women think, or this would not be. Mr. Venable added bitterly, "Giving up our soldiers to the enemy means giving up the cause. We cannot replace them." The Up Country men were Union men generally, and the Low Country were seceders. The former growl; they never liked those aristocratic boroughs and parishes, they had themselves a good and prosperous country, a good constitution, and were satisfied. But they had to go — to leave all and fight for the others who brought on all the trouble, and who do not show too much disposition to fight for themselves.

That is the extreme Up Country view. The extreme Low Country says Jeff Davis is not enough out of the Union yet. His inaugural address reads as one of his speeches did four years ago in the United States Senate.

A letter in a morning paper accused Mr. Chesnut of staying too long in Charleston. The editor was asked for the writer's name. He gave it as Little Moses, the Governor's secretary. When Little Moses was spoken to, in a great trepidation he said that Mrs. Pickens wrote it, and got him to publish it; so it was dropped, for Little Moses is such an arrant liar no one can believe him. Besides, if that sort of thing amuses Mrs. Pickens, let her amuse herself.

MARCH 5th. — Mary Preston went back to Mulberry with me from Columbia, for a few days there. She found a man there tall enough to take her in to dinner — Tom Boykin, who is six feet four, the same height as her father. Tom was very handsome in his uniform, and Mary prepared for a nice time, but he looked as if he would so much rather she did not talk to him, and he set her such a good example, saying never a word.

Old Colonel Chesnut came for us. When the train stopped, Quashie, shiny black, was seen on his box, as glossy and perfect in his way as his blooded bays, but the old Colonel would stop and pick up the dirtiest little Negro I ever saw who was crying by the roadside. This ragged little black urchin was made to climb up and sit beside Quash. It spoilt the symmetry of the turn-out, but it was a character touch, and the old gentleman knows no law but his own will. He had a biscuit in his pocket which he gave this sniffling little Negro, who proved to be his man Scip's son.

I was ill at Mulberry and never left my room. Doctor Boykin came, more military than medical. Colonel Chesnut brought him up, also Team, who said he was down in the mouth. Our men were not fighting as they should. We had only pluck and luck, and a dogged spirit of fighting, to offset their weight in men and munitions of war. I wish I could remember Team's words; this is only his idea. His language was quaint and striking — no grammar, but no end of sense and good feeling. Old Colonel Chesnut, catching a word, began his litany, saying, "Numbers will tell," "Napoleon, you know," etc., etc.

At Mulberry the war has been ever afar off, but threats to take the silver came very near indeed; silver that we had before the Revolution, silver that Mrs. Chesnut brought from Philadelphia.

Wade Manning came to see his cousin. Without emulating Mrs. Stowe, how can I tell Wade's tales? He is miserable where he is. Those Preston and Hampton boys loathe slavery and all its concomitants. Zack Cantey and Dr. Boykin came back on the train with us. Wade Hampton is their hero. For one thing he is sober. Wigfall and Whiting are all tarred with the same stick; and the pity of it! They are capable of the greatest things.

Letters came to the Council warning them to watch Mrs. Henry Duncan. Our men cannot be made to watch and worry women.

Reading Creasy's "Decisive Battles." Also I have Theo Hook *in extenso*, and Mr. Browning, so I am provisioned for a siege. Theo Hook's book is London in the year 1996, "The Progress of Philanthropy." The Duke of Bedford's family servants, having long been equal, grew superior to their masters. Then the upward progress grew so rapid that coach horses found out their rights and their mights, and kicked against the traces. The old grey mare protested and refused to go between the shafts, as that amounted to servitude, disguise it as you will. Lady Bedford begged and implored the Duke that she might be allowed to seize the opportunity, while a few unenlightened horses still remained, to fly. They had still some dull horses who could be prevailed upon to drag them off, and out of the country. It all means holding up hands in holy horror of us because of African slavery.

Sweet May Dacre. Lord Byron and Disraeli make their rosebuds Catholic; May Dacre is another Aurora. I like Disraeli because I find so many clever things in him. I like the sparkle and the glitter. Lord Lyons has gone against us. Lord Derby and Louis Napoleon are silent in our hour of direst need. People call me Cassandra, for I cry that outside hope is quenched. From the outside, no help indeed cometh to this beleaguered land.

MARCH 7th. — David Williams adds not to our encouragement. It is bluer, or blacker, in Florida than here, he says. He was answered: "As for the particular settlement to which you refer, they are in no danger. They have not taken up arms against the United States. They have not aided or abetted us. They can point to all that, when Yankees come along." David, though in the army himself, found this saying bitter as applied to his friends and neighbors.

At tea, I introduced David to our party, Governor Gist, Judge Glover — and stopped there, because I had not warned him, and it was dangerous to say suddenly: "Colonel Quattlebaum!" He might laugh.

Judge Withers is denouncing Governor and Council to all his Grand Juries. He tells them they are living under a despotism. It does not matter if we get out of the scrape, and if we do not, he will perhaps find harder work to do than going round the country criticizing and abusing his friends.

Edward Boykin bragged; they said he was no saint, but he had made the women and children God had given him happy. There was no happier family than his in the world. There was no skeleton in his closet!

MARCH 9th. — "Can it be possible," said Halcott Green, "that Colonel Chesnut is opposed to the aggressive policy?" " 'Aggress' did you say? Why, we have not men to defend." Then he said in our game of *rouge et noir*, the run had been upon the black lately, but luck must turn. Today he stopped me at the church door. "The run on the red has begun!" And he told the wonderful *Merrimac** news.

Mrs. Middleton was dolorous indeed. General Lee had warned the planters about Combahee, etc., that they must take care of themselves now; he could not do it. Confederate soldiers had committed some

* Mrs. Chesnut refers, of course, to the success of the Merrimac against the Union fleet at Newport News. This occurred on March 2; so the news was, presumably, five days in reaching Columbia.

outrages on the plantations and officers had punished them promptly. She poured contempt upon Yancey's letter to Lord Russell. It was the letter of a shopkeeper, not in the style of a statesman at all.

We called to see Mary McDuffie (Mrs. Wade Hampton). She asked Mary Preston what Dr. Boykin had said of her husband as we came along in the train. She heard it was something very complimentary. Mary P. tried to remember, and to repeat it all. "For one thing," she said lightly, "Dr. Boykin said you could always find Uncle Wade sober." "That's horrid news. I notice they never promote any but topers to be brigadiers."

Mary M. was amazed to hear of the list of applicants for promotion. One delicate-minded person accompanied his demand for advancement by a request for a written description of the Manassas battle; he had heard Colonel Chesnut give such a brilliant account of it in Governor Cobb's room.

The Judge saw his little daughter at my window and he came up. He was very smooth and kind. It was really a delightful visit; not a disagreeable word was spoken. He abused no one whatever, for he never once spoke of anyone but himself, and himself he praised without stint. He did not look at me once, though he spoke very kindly to me.

March 10th. — Second year of Confederate independence. I write daily for my own diversion. These *memoires pour servir* may at some future day afford facts about these times and prove useful to more important people than I am. I do not wish to do any harm or to hurt anyone. If any scandalous stories creep in they can easily be burned. It is hard, in such a hurry as things are now, to separate the wheat from the chaff. Now that I have made my protest and written down my wishes, I can scribble on with a free will and free conscience.

Congress at the North is down on us. They talk largely of hanging slave owners. They say they hold Port Royal, as we did when we took it originally from the aborigines, who fled before us; so we are to be exterminated and improved, *à l'Indienne*, from the face of the earth.

Medea, when asked: "Country, wealth, husband, children, all are gone; and now what remains?" answered: "Medea remains." There is a time in most men's lives when they resemble Job, sitting among the ashes and drinking in the full bitterness of complicated misfortune.

March 11th. — A freshman came quite eager to be instructed in all the wiles of society. He wanted to try his hand at a flirtation, and requested minute instructions, as he knew nothing whatever: he was so very fresh. "Dance with her," he was told, "and talk with her; walk with her and flatter her; dance until she is warm and tired; then propose to walk in a cool, shady piazza. It must be a somewhat dark piazza. Begin your promenade slowly; warm up to your work; draw her arm closer and closer; then, break her wing."

"Heavens, what is that — break her wing?" "Why, you do not know even that? Put your arm round her waist and kiss her. After that, it is all plain sailing. She comes down when you call, like the coon to Captain Scott: 'You need not fire, Captain,' etc."

The aspirant for fame as a flirt followed these lucid directions literally, but when he seized the poor girl and kissed her, she uplifted her voice in terror and screamed as if the house was on fire. So quick, sharp, and shrill were her yells for help that the bold flirt sprang over the banister, upon which grew a strong climbing rose. This he struggled through, and ran toward the college, taking a bee line. He was so mangled by the thorns that he had to go home and have them picked out by his family. The girl's brother challenged him. There was no mortal combat, however, for the gay young fellow who had led the freshman's ignorance astray stepped forward and put things straight. An explanation and an apology at every turn hushed it all up.

Now, we all laughed at this foolish story most heartily. But Mr. Venable remained grave and preoccupied, and was asked: "Why are you so unmoved? It is funny." "I like more probable fun; I have been in college and I have kissed many a girl, but never a one scrome yet."

Mrs. McCord, the eldest daughter of Langdon Cheves, got up a company for her son, raising it at her own expense. She has the brains and energy of a man. Today she repeated a remark of a Low Country gentleman, who is dissatisfied: "This Government (Confederate) protects neither person nor property." Fancy the scornful turn of her lip! Someone asked for Langdon Cheves, her brother. "Oh, Langdon!" she replied coolly. "He is a pure patriot; he has no ambition. While I was there, he was letting Confederate soldiers ditch through his garden and ruin him at their leisure."

Cotton is five cents a pound and labor of no value at all; it commands no price whatever. People gladly hire out their Negroes to have them fed and clothed, which latter cannot be done. Cotton Osnaburg at thirty-seven and a half cents a yard leaves no chance to clothe them. Langdon was for martial law and making the bloodsuckers disgorge their ill-gotten gains. We, poor fools, who are patriotically ruining ourselves, will see our children in the gutter while treacherous dogs of millionaires go rolling by in their coaches — coaches that were acquired by taking advantage of our necessities.

This terrible battle of the ships — *Monitor*, *Merrimac*, etc. All hands on board the *Cumberland* went down. She fought gallantly and fired a round as she sank. The *Congress* ran up a white flag. She fired on our boats as they went up to take off her wounded. She was burned. The worst of it is that all this will arouse them to more furious exertions to destroy us. They hated us so before, but how now?

In Columbia I do not know a half-dozen men who would not gaily step into Jeff Davis's shoes with a firm conviction that they would do better in every respect than he does. The monstrous conceit, the fatuous ignorance of these critics! It is pleasant to hear Mrs. McCord on this subject, when they begin to shake their heads and tell us what Jeff Davis ought to do.

MARCH 12. — Today's paper calls enlisting students: "exhausting our seed corn." All right, but how about preserving land wherein to plant your corn? Your little corn patch seems slipping away from you. You need boys, yes and even women's broomsticks, when the foe is pulling down your snake fences.

In the naval battle the other day we had twenty-five guns in all. The enemy had fifty-four in the *Cumberland*, forty-four in the *St. Lawrence*, besides a fleet of gunboats, filled with rifled cannon. Why not? They can have as many as they please, the whole boundless world being theirs to recruit in. Ours is only this one little spot of ground — the blockade, or stockade, which hems us in with only the sky open to us. For all that, how tender-footed and cautious they are as they draw near.

An anonymous letter purports to answer Colonel Chesnut's address to South Carolinians now in the army of the Potomac. The man says, "All that bosh is no good." He knows lots of people whose fathers were notorious Tories in our war for independence, and made fortunes by selling their country. Their sons have the best places, and they are cowards and traitors still. Names are given, of course.

Floyd and Pillow * are suspended from their commands because of Fort Donelson. The people of Tennessee demand a like fate for Albert

* John B. Floyd was in command at Fort Donelson; Gideon J. Pillow his second in command. They escaped from the Fort before its surrender. Floyd was Secretary of War of the United States from 1857 till secession; and the charge was often made — probably without real foundation — that he shipped arms from Northern to Southern arsenals in anticipation of secession.

Sidney Johnston. They say he is stupid. Can human folly go further than this Tennessee madness?

MARCH 13th. — Mr. Chesnut fretting and fuming. From the poor old blind bishop downward, everybody is besetting him to let off students, theological and other, from going into the army. One comfort is that the boys will go. Mr. Chesnut answers: "Wait until you have saved your country before you make preachers and scholars. When you have a country, there will be no lack of divines, students, scholars to adorn and purify it." He says he is a one-idea man. That idea is to get every possible man into the ranks.

Professor Le Conte is an able auxiliary. He has undertaken to supervise and carry on the powder-making enterprise, the very first attempted in the Confederacy, and Mr. Chesnut is proud of it. It is a brilliant success, thanks to Le Conte.

Mr. Chesnut receives anonymous letters urging him to arrest the Judge as seditious. They say he is a dangerous and disaffected person. His abuse of Jeff Davis and the Council is rabid. Mr. Chesnut laughs and throws the letters into the fire, "Disaffected to Jeff Davis!" says he. "Disaffected to the Council, that doesn't count. He knows what he is about; he would not injure his country for the world."

Read "Uncle Tom's Cabin" again. These Negro women have a chance here that women have nowhere else. They can redeem themselves — the "impropers" can. They can marry decently, and nothing is remembered against these colored ladies. It is not a nice topic, but Mrs. Stowe revels in it. How delightfully Pharisaic a feeling it must be to rise superior, and fancy we are so degraded as to defend and like to live with such degraded creatures around us — such men as Legree and his women.

The best way to take Negroes to your heart is to get as far away from them as possible. As far as I can see, Southern women do all that missionaries could do to prevent and alleviate evils. The social evil has not been suppressed in old England or in New England, in London or in Boston. People in those places expect more virtue from a plantation African than they can insure in practice among themselves, with all their own high moral surroundings — light, education, training, and support. Lady Mary Montagu says, "Only men and women at last." "Male and female created he them," says the Bible. There are cruel, graceful, beautiful mothers of angelic Evas North as well as South, I dare say. The Northern men and women who came here were always hardest, for they expected an African to work and behave as a white man. We do not.

I have often thought from observation truly that perfect beauty hardens the heart; and as to grace, what so graceful as a cat, a tigress, or a panther. Much love, admiration, worship hardens an idol's heart. It becomes utterly callous and selfish. It expects to receive all and to give nothing. It even likes the excitement of seeing people suffer. I speak now of what I have watched with horror and amazement.

Topsys I have known, but none that were beaten or ill-used. Evas are mostly in the heaven of Mrs. Stowe's imagination. People can't love things dirty, ugly, and repulsive, simply because they ought to do so, but they can be good to them at a distance; that's easy. You see, I cannot rise very high; I can only judge by what I see.

March 14th. — Thank God for a ship! It has run the blockade with arms and ammunition.

There are no Negro sexual relations half so shocking as Mormonism; and yet the United States Government makes no bones of receiving Mormons into its sacred heart. Mr. Venable said England held her hand over "the malignant and the turbaned Turk" to save and protect him, slaves, seraglio, and all. But she rolls up the whites of her eyes at us when slavery, bad as it is, is stepping out into freedom every moment through Christian civilization. They do not grudge the Turk even his bag-and-Bosphorus privileges. To a recalcitrant wife it is, "Here yawns the sack; there rolls the sea," etc. And France, the bold, the brave, the ever free, she has not been so tender-footed in Algiers. But then the "you are another" argument is a shabby one. "You see," says Mary Preston sagaciously, "we are white Christian descendants of Hugenots and Cavaliers, and they expect of us different conduct."

Went in Mrs. Preston's landau to bring my boarding-school girls here to dine. At my door met J. F., who wanted me then and there to promise to help him with his commission or put him in the way of one. At the carriage steps I was handed in by Gus Smith, who wants his brother made commissary. The beauty of it all is they think I have some influence, and I have not a particle. The subject of Mr. Chesnut's military affairs, promotions, etc., is never mentioned by me. If I told him these men wanted my influence with him, I think he would be in a fury. They think he listens to me. He does not.

When we came home, there stood Warren Nelson, propped up against my door, lazily waiting for me, the handsome creature. He said he meant to be heard, so I walked back with him to the drawing-room. They are wasting their time dancing attendance on me. I cannot help them. Let them shoulder their musket and go to the wars like men.

After tea came "Mars' Kit" — he said for a talk, but that Mr. Preston would not let him have, for Mr. Preston had arrived some time before him. Mr. Preston said "Mars' Kit" thought it "bad form" to laugh. After that you may be sure a laugh from "Mars' Kit" was secured. Again and again, he was forced to laugh with a will. I reversed Oliver Wendell Holmes's good resolution — never to be as funny as he could. I did my very utmost.

Mr. Venable interrupted the fun, which was fast and furious, with the very best of bad news! Newbern shelled and burned, cotton, turpentine — everything. There were 5000 North Carolinians in the fray, 12,000 Yankees. Now there stands Goldsboro. One more step and we are cut in two. The railroad is our backbone, like the Blue Ridge and the Alleghenies, with which it runs parallel. So many discomforts, no wonder we are down-hearted.

MARCH 17th. — Back to the Congaree House to await my husband, who has made a rapid visit to the Wateree region. As we drove up Mr. Chesnut said: "Did you see the stare of respectful admiration E. R. bestowed upon you, so curiously prolonged? I could hardly keep my countenance." "Yes, my dear, I feel the honor of it, though my individual self goes for nothing in it. I am the wife of the man who has the appointing power just now, with so many commissions to be filled. I am nearly forty, and they do my understanding the credit to suppose I can be made to believe they admire my mature charms. They think they fool me into thinking that they believe me charming. There is hardly any farce in the world more laughable."

Last night a house was set on fire; last week two houses. "The red cock crows in the barn!" Our troubles thicken, indeed, when treachery comes from that dark quarter.

When the President first offered Johnston Pettigrew a brigadier-generalship, his answer was: "Not yet. Too many men are ahead of me who have earned their promotion in the field. I will come after them, not before. So far I have done nothing to merit reward." He would not take rank when he could get it. I fancy he may cool his heels now waiting for it. He was too high and mighty. There was another conscientious man — Burnet, of Kentucky. He gave up his regiment to his lieutenant colonel when he found the lieutenant colonel could command the regiment and Burnet could not maneuver it in the field.

He went into the fight simply as an aid to Floyd. Modest merit just now is at a premium.

William Gilmore Simms is here; read us his last poetry; have forgotten already what it was about. It was not tiresome, however, and that is a great thing when people will persist in reading their own rhymes.

At daylight there was a loud knocking at my door. I hurried on a dressing-gown and flew to open the door. "Mrs. Chesnut, Mrs. M. says please don't forget her son. Mr. Chesnut, she hears, has come back. Please get her son a commission. He must have an office." I shut the door in the servant's face. If I had the influence these foolish people attribute to me why should I not help my own? I have a brother, two brothers-in-law, and no end of kin, all gentlemen privates; and privates they would stay to the end of time before they said a word to me about commissions.

Mary P. was giving Wade Manning's story of his Aunt Camilla's Bed of Justice. The lady is of the stoutest, with a fiery red face and straggling grey hair. Her room opens on a stairway up and down which all the world goes, and is obliged to go, for it is the only staircase in the house. With her door wide open, she sat in bed with a bundle of switches; and every Monday morning, everybody in the yard was there to give an account of their deeds or misdeeds for the past week. They were mustered in a row and waited. She solemnly rehearsed their misdemeanors. Some were adroit enough to avert their fate. Those whom she condemned stepped up to the bedside and received their punishment, screaming, howling and yelling to the utmost of their ability to soften her heart. She belabored them with her night cap flying, and her gown in horrid disarray from the exercise of her arm. Wade found her dreadful to think of as he fled from the sight and sound. Peace once restored and everybody once more at the daily avocations, they were as jolly as larks, with perspiration streaming. Wade moaned: "It shocks and makes me miserable, but they don't seem to mind a switching, Cousin Mary, not ten seconds after it is over! And this is the place my father sends me to be educated!"

Mary C. said to Mr. Venable: "I would like that story of Wade's to be *bestowed.* What would she think of it or make of it?" "Mrs. Stowe would feel exactly as we do; but then she would take an extraordinary freak of nature as a specimen of a class, a common type." "Wade says everybody at breakfast was as jolly, as pleasant, as smiling as if there had been no human tornado raging a few minutes before." "The be-switched and all?" "Yes, the howlers and all." "Don't take on so," said Mr. Venable. "A fat old thing like her can't hurt much."

They asked me if I had ever heard of this Devil's Matins before. "Yes, but I heard it was a daily service." "Oh, no, no," said Wade. "Once a week is as much as mortal could bear, of a row such as that in any house."

It is only on Mondays. One woman knows how to escape the switches; she says she gathers up all the scandals of the town. "Missus is too keen to hear the news to trouble me. I brings her plenty 'bout everybody, specially them she don't like."

After a long talk we were finally disgusted, and the men went off to the bulletin board. Whatever else it shows, good or bad, there is always woe for some house in the killed and wounded. We have need of stout hearts. I feel a sinking of mine as we drive near the board.

MARCH 18th. — My war archon is beset for commissions, and somebody says "for every one given, you make one ingrate and a thousand enemies."

As I entered Miss Mary Stark's I whispered: "He has promised to vote for Louis." What radiant faces! To my friend, Miss Mary said, "Your son-in-law, what is he doing for his country?" "He is a tax collector." Then spoke up the stout old girl: "Look at my cheek; it is red with blushing for you. A great, hale, hearty young man! Fie on him! Fie on him! For shame! Tell his wife; run him out of the house with a broomstick; send him down to the coast at least." Fancy my cheeks! I could not raise my eyes to the poor lady, so mercilessly assaulted. My face was as hot with compassion as the outspoken Miss Mary pretended hers to be with vicarious mortification.

Went to see sweet and saintly Mrs. Bartow. She read us a letter from Mississippi — not so bad: More men there than the enemy suspected, and torpedoes to blow up the wretches when they came. Next to see Mrs. Izard. She had with her a relative just from the North. This lady had asked Seward for passports, and he told her to "hold all, open and safe." Today Mrs. Arthur Hayne heard from her daughter that Richmond is to be given up. Mrs. Buell is her daughter.

Met Mr. Chesnut, who said: "New Madrid has been given up." I do not know any more than the dead where New Madrid is. It is bad, all the same, this giving up. I can't stand it. The hemming-in process is nearly complete. The ring of fire is almost unbroken.

Mr. Chesnut's Negroes offered to fight for him if he would arm them. He pretended to believe them. He says one man cannot do it. The whole country must agree to it. He would trust such as he would select, and he would give so many acres of land and his freedom to each one as he enlisted.

Mrs. Albert Rhett came for an office for her son John. I told her Mr. Chesnut would never propose a kinsman for office, but if anyone else would bring him forward he would vote for him certainly, as he is so eminently fit for position. Now he is a private.

The church was crowded today, but only one man, Hallcot Green. It is plain why there is no marrying nor giving in marriage in Heaven. The church is the gate to Heaven, and the church is usually filled with women only, going up there.

MARCH 19th. — He who runs may read. Conscription * means that we are in a tight place. This war was a volunteer business. Tomorrow conscription begins — the last resort. The President has remodelled his Cabinet, leaving Bragg for North Carolina. His War Minister is Randolph of Virginia. A Union man *par excellence*, Watts, of Alabama, is Attorney General. And now, too late by one year, when all the mechanics are in the army, Mallory begins to telegraph Captain Ingraham to build ships at any expense. We are locked in and cannot get "the requisites for naval architecture," says a magniloquent person.

Henry Frost says all hands wink at cotton going out. Why not send it out and buy ships? "Every now and then there is a holocaust of cotton-burning," says the magniloquent. Conscription has waked the Rip Van Winkles. The streets of Columbia were never so crowded with men. To fight and to be made to fight are different things.

To my small wits, whenever people were persistent, united, and rose in their might, no general, however great, succeeded in subjugating them. Have we not swamps, forests, rivers, mountains — every natural barrier? The Carthaginians begged for peace because they were a

* There has been no attempt to footnote in detail the progress of the war; but a summary may here be in order. After Manassas, the South as a whole relaxed. Some thought the war was over; some adopted the position: "We beat them once; we can do it again." From the summer of 1861 till the spring of 1862, the North worked furiously in preparation for a new campaign, the blockade was made increasingly effective; and a series of military and naval successes, of which Grant's campaign up the Tennessee was perhaps the most important, steadily weakened the Southern position. In the spring of 1862, the Southern armies were shrinking, term-expired men were refusing to re-enlist, farmer-soldiers went home to plant a crop and did not return; and only the adoption of conscription kept an effective Southern force in the field and made it possible to meet McClellan's advance up the Peninsula.

luxurious people and could not endure the hardship of war, though the enemy suffered as sharply as they did! "Factions among themselves" is the rock on which we split. Now for the great soul who is to rise up and lead us. Why tarry his footsteps?

MARCH 20th. — The *Merrimac* is now called the *Virginia*. I think these changes of names so confusing and so senseless.

I was lying on the sofa in my room, and two men slowly walking up and down the corridor talked aloud as if necessarily all rooms were unoccupied at this midday hour. I asked Maum Mary who they were. "Yeadon and Barnwell Rhett, Jr." They abused the Council roundly, and my husband's name arrested my attention. Afterward, when Yeadon attacked Mr. Chesnut, Mr. Chesnut surprised him by knowing beforehand all he had to say. Naturally I had repeated the loud interchange of views I had overheard in the corridor.

First, Nathan Davis called. Then Gonzales, who presented a fine, soldierly appearance in his soldier clothes; and the likeness to Beauregard was greater than ever. Nathan, all the world knows, is by profession a handsome man.

General Gonzales told us what in the bitterness of his soul he had written to Jeff Davis. He regretted that he had not been his classmate; then he might have been as well treated as Northrop. In any case he would not have been refused a brigadiership, citing General Trapier and Tom Drayton. He had worked for it, had earned it; they had not. To his surprise, Mr. Davis answered him, and in a sharp note of four pages. Mr. Davis demanded from whom he quoted, "not his classmate." General Gonzales responded, "from the public voice only." Now he will fight for us all the same, but will go on demanding justice from Jeff Davis until he gets his dues — at least, until one of them gets his dues, for he means to go on hitting Jeff Davis over the head whenever he has a chance.

"I am afraid," said I, "you will find it a hard head to crack." He replied in his flowery Spanish way: "Jeff Davis will be the sun, radiating all light, heat and patronage; he will not be a moon reflecting public opinion, for he has the soul of a despot; he delights to spite public opinion. See, people abused him for making Crittenden brigadier. Straightway he made him major general, and just after a blundering, besotted defeat, too." Also, he told the President in that letter: "Napoleon made his generals after great deeds on their part, and not for having been educated at St. Cyr, or Brie, or the Polytechnique," etc., etc. Nathan Davis sat as still as a Sioux warrior, not an eyelash moved.

And yet he said afterward that he was amused while the Spaniard railed at his great namesake.

Gonzales said: "Mrs. Slidell would proudly say that she was a Creole. They were such fools, they thought Creole meant —" Here Nathan interrupted pleasantly: "At the St. Charles, in New Orleans, on the bill of fare were 'Creole eggs.' When they were brought to a man who had ordered them, with perfect simplicity, he held them up. 'Why, they are only hens' eggs, after all." What in Heaven's name he expected them to be, who can say?" smiled Nathan the elegant.

One lady says (as I sit reading in the drawing-room window while Maum Mary puts my room to rights): "I clothe my Negroes well. I could not bear to see them in dirt and rags; it would be unpleasant to me." Another lady: "Yes. Well, so do I. But not fine clothes, you know. I feel — now — it was one of our sins as a nation, the way we indulged them in sinful finery. We will be punished for it."

Last night, Mrs. Pickens met General Cooper. Madam knew General Cooper only as our Adjutant General, and Mr. Mason's brother-in-law. In her slow, graceful, impressive way, her beautiful eyes eloquent with feeling, she inveighed against Mr. Davis's wickedness in always sending men born at the North to command at Charleston. General Cooper is on his way to make a tour of inspection there now. The dear general settled his head on his cravat with the aid of his forefinger; he tugged rather more nervously with the something that is always wrong inside of his collar, and looked straight up through his spectacles. Someone crossed the room, stood back of Mrs. Pickens, and murmured in her ear, "General Cooper was born in New York." Sudden silence.

General Cooper, having recovered from that cold blast from the North, was quite genial. He forgot to snuggle his neck in his cravat. He has been in Carolina before on a visit to General Sumter, at High Hills on the Santee; so he has seen the very prettiest part of our country. He thinks Statesburg would, in case of invasion, be a safe place; he found it almost inaccessible, from the necessity of crossing those Santee swamps.

All this was at the Prestons', where we dined. General Hampton and Blanton Duncan were there also; the latter a thoroughly free-and-easy Western man, handsome and clever; more audacious than either, perhaps. He pointed to Buck — Sally Buchanan Campbell Preston. "What's that girl laughing at?" Poor child, how amazed she looked. He bade them "not despair; all the nice young men would not be killed in the war; there would be a few left." For himself, he could give them no hope; Mrs. Duncan was uncommonly healthy. Mrs. Duncan is also lovely. We have seen her.

MARCH 24th. — I was asked to the Tognos' tea, so refused a drive with Mary Preston. As I sat at my solitary casement, waiting for the time to come for the Tognos, I saw Mrs. Preston's landau pass, and Mr. Venable making Mary laugh at some of his army stories, as only Mr. Venable can. Already I felt that I had paid too much for my whistle — that is, the Togno tea. The Gibbeses, Trenholms, Edmund Rhett, were there. Edmund Rhett has very fine eyes and makes fearful play with them. He sits silent and motionless, with his hands on his knees, his head bent forward, and his eyes fixed upon you. I could think of nothing like it but a setter and a covey of partridges.

As to President Davis, Rhett sank to profounder deeps of abuse of him than even Gonzales. I quoted Yancey: "A crew may not like their captain, but if they are mad enough to mutiny while a storm is raging, all hands are bound to go to the bottom." After that I contented myself with a mild shake of the head when I disagreed with him, and at last I began to shake so persistently it amounted to incipient palsy. "Jeff Davis," he said, "is conceited, wrong-headed, wranglesome, obstinate — a traitor." "Now I have borne much in silence," said I at last, "but that is pernicious nonsense. Do not let us waste any more time listening to your quotations from the Mercury."

He very good-naturedly changed the subject, which was easy just then, for a delicious supper was on the table ready for us. But Dr. Gibbes began anew the fighting. He helped me to some *pâté* — "Not *foie gras*," said Madame Togno, "*pâté perdreaux*." Dr. Gibbes, however, gave it a flavor of his own. "Eat it," said he, "it is good for you; rich and wholesome; healthy as cod-liver oil."

A queer thing happened. At the post office a man saw a small boy open with a key the box of the Governor and the Council, take the contents of the box and run for his life. Of course, this man called to the urchin to stop. The urchin did not heed, but seeing himself pursued, began tearing up the letters and papers. He was caught and the fragments were picked up. Finding himself a prisoner, he pointed out the Negro who gave him the key. The Negro was arrested.

Governor Pickens called to see me today. We began with Fort Sumter. For an hour did we hammer at that fortress. We took it, gun by gun. He was very pleasant and friendly in his manner.

James Chesnut has been so nice this winter; so reasonable and considerate — that is, for a man. The night I came from Madame Togno's, instead of making a row about the lateness of the hour, he said he was "so wide awake and so hungry." I put on my dressing-gown and scrambled some eggs there on our own fire. And with our feet on the fender and the small supper-table between us, we enjoyed the supper and glorious gossip. Rather a pleasant state of things when one's own husband is in good humor, and cleverer than all the men outside.

This afternoon, the *entente cordiale* still subsisting, Maum Mary beckoned me out mysteriously; but Mr. Chesnut said: "Speak out, old woman; nobody here but myself." "Mars' Nathum Davis wants to speak to her," said she. So I hurried off to the drawing-room, Maum Mary flapping her down-at-the-heels shoes in my wake. "He's gwine bekase somebody done stole his boots. How could he stay bedout boots?" So Nathan said good-bye. Then we met General Gist, Maum Mary still hovering near, and I congratulated him on being promoted. He is now a brigadier. This he received with modest complaisance. "I knowed he was a general," said Maum Mary as he passed on. "He told me as soon as he got in his room befo' his boy put down his trunks."

As Nathan, the unlucky, said good-bye, he informed me that a Mr. Reed from Montgomery was in the drawing-room and wanted to see me. Mr. Reed had traveled with our foreign envoy, Yancey. I was keen for news from abroad. Mr. Reed settled that summarily. "Mr. Yancey says we need not have one jot of hope. He could bowstring Mallory for not buying arms in time. The very best citizens wanted to depose the State government and take things into their own hands, the powers that be being inefficient. Western men are hurrying to the front, bestirring themselves. In two more months we shall be ready." What could I do but laugh? I do hope the enemy will be considerate and charitable enough to wait for us.

Mr. Reed's calm faith in the power of Mr. Yancey's eloquence was beautiful to see. He asked for Mr. Chesnut. I went back to our rooms, swelling with news like a pouter pigeon. Mr. Chesnut said: "Well! Four hours! A call from Nathan Davis of four hours!" Men are too absurd! So I bear the honors of my forty years gallantly. I can but laugh. "Mr. Nathan Davis went by the five o'clock train," I said; "it is now about six or seven, maybe eight. I have had so many visitors. Mr. Reed, of Alabama, is asking for you out there." He went without a word, but I doubt if he went to see Mr. Reed; my laughing had made him so angry.

Lincoln threatens us with a proclamation abolishing slavery here in the free Southern Confederacy; and they say McClellan is deposed. They want men who will do more fighting — I mean the Government, whose skins are safe — and trust to luck for the skill of the new generals.

MARCH 28th. — We have left the Congaree House for Mrs. McMahan's, and I did leave with regret Maum Mary. She was such a good, well-informed old thing. My Molly, though perfection otherwise, does not receive the confidential communications of new-made generals at the earliest moment. She is of very limited military information. Maum Mary was the comfort of my life. She saved me from all trouble as far as she could. Seventy, if she is a day, she is spry and active as a cat, of a curiosity that knows no bounds, black and clean; also, she knows a joke at first sight, and she is honest. I fancy the Negroes are ashamed to rob people as careless as James Chesnut and myself.

One night, just before we left, Mr. Chesnut had forgotten to tell some all-important thing to Governor Gist, who was to leave on a public mission next day. So at the dawn of day he put on his dressing-gown and went to the Governor's room. He found the door unlocked and the Governor fast asleep. He shook him. Half-asleep, the Governor sprang up and threw his arms around Mr. Chesnut's neck and said: "Honey, is it you?" The mistake was rapidly set right, and the bewildered plenipotentiary was given his instructions. Mr. Chesnut came into my room, threw himself on the sofa, and nearly laughed himself to extinction, imitating again and again the pathetic tone of the Governor's greeting.

Mr. Chesnut calls Lawrence "Adolphe," but says he is simply perfect as a servant. Mary Stevens said: "I thought Cousin James the laziest man alive until I knew his man, Lawrence." Lawrence will not move an inch or lift a finger for anyone but his master. Mrs. Middleton politely sent him on an errand; Lawrence, too, was very polite; hours after, she saw him sitting on the fence of the front yard. "Didn't you go?" she asked. "No, ma'am. I am waiting for Mars' Jeems." Mrs. Middleton calls him now, "Mr. Take-It-Easy."

My very last day's experience at the Congaree. I was waiting for Mars' Jeems in the drawing-room when a lady there declared herself to be the wife of an officer in Clingman's regiment. A gentleman who seemed quite friendly with her, told her all Mr. Chesnut said, thought, intended to do, wrote, and *felt*. I asked: "Are you certain of all these things you say of Colonel Chesnut?" The man hardly deigned to notice this impertinent interruption from a stranger, presuming to speak, but who had not been introduced! After he went out, the wife of Clingman's officer was seized with an intuitive curiosity. "Madam, will you tell me your name?" I gave it, adding, "I dare say I showed myself an intelligent listener when my husband's affairs were under discussion." The man was Mr. Chesnut's secretary, but I had never seen him before.

A letter from Kate says she had been up all night preparing David's things. He had left them for the army that day. Little Serena sat up and helped her mother. They did not know that they would ever see him again. Upon reading it, I wept, and James Chesnut cursed the Yankees.

Here is a story told of Morgan. At Nashville he sat at the table d'hôte just opposite General Buell, the Yankee Commander. He nearly bagged Buell, and would have done so, but the toll-gate keeper warned Buell in time. Next day, the toll-gate keeper committed suicide; at least he was found hanged near his own gate, and nobody did it!

We have here at Mrs. McMahan's our beauty. She is a beauty in spite of her teeth, and her neck is too long and ever so little scraggy. But now all the harm that can be said of her appearance is over, for her eyes are blue and beautiful, her nose straight and perfect, her complexion as exquisite as complexion is ever made. With those violet eyes she looks into the very souls of men, and they come down and surrender as the coon did to Captain Scott. They don't stop to parley. She wears a dagger and has been known to stab a man "for scorning her mother." She gathers around her all the men who will be of use to her; that is, to her husband. She is the most loyal of wives and mothers.

April 1st. — I went with Mr. Chesnut to Governor Pickens's reception; very few men there, but the nicest supper. Fair Lucy was a lovely and a charming hostess. I played whist with Judge Carroll as my partner — against Mrs. Herbement and Mr. H. Middleton. In that company, I actually felt young, comparatively.

Gave the girls a quantity of flannel for soldiers' shirts; also a string of pearls to be raffled for at the Gunboat Fair. Mary Witherspoon has sent a silver teapot.

April 2nd. — Dr. Trezevant, attending Mr. Chesnut, who was ill, came and found his patient gone; he could not stand the news of that last battle. He got up and dressed, weak as he was, and went forth to hear what he could for himself. The doctor was angry with me for permitting this, and more angry with him for such folly. He said: "He will certainly be salivated after all that calomel in this damp weather."

Today, the ladies in their landaus were bitterly attacked by the morning paper for lolling back in their silks and satins, with tall footmen in livery, driving up and down the streets while the poor soldiers' wives were on the sidewalks. It is the old story of rich and poor! My little barouche is not here, nor has James Chesnut any of his horses here; but then I drive every day with Mrs. McCord and Mrs. Preston, either of whose turnouts fills the bill. The Governor's carriage, horses, servants, etc., are splendid — just what they should be. Why not?

APRIL 14th. — Our Fair is in full blast. We keep a restaurant. Our waitresses are Mary and Buck Preston, Isabella Martin, and Grace Elmore.

APRIL 15th. — We have made bushels of money. All the world came. I saw Sue King with an infatuated Gwinn ten or twenty years younger than herself, utterly upset by love and consumption. It was pitiful. Poor young soldier! Last night a beautiful show, cadets and school girls. We had gone in person and begged a holiday for them.

Trescot is too clever ever to be a bore. That was proved today, for he stayed two hours. As usual Mr. Chesnut said "four." He was very surly — calls himself Ex-Secretary of State of the United States of America; now Nothing-in-Particular of South Carolina or of the Confederate States of America. Then he yawned. "What a bore this war is! I wish it was ended, one way or another." He speaks of going across the border and taking service in Mexico. "Rubbish!" I said. "Not much Mexico for you!"

The enemy have flanked Beauregard at Nashville.

There is grief enough for Albert Sidney Johnston * now. We begin to see what we have lost. We were pushing them in the river when he was wounded. Beauregard was lying in his tent at the rear in a green sickness; melancholia, perhaps. No matter the name of the malady. He was too slow to move, and lost us all the advantage gained by our dead hero. Without him, there is no head to our western army. Pulaski fallen! What more is there to fall?

Trescot gave me rough truths to digest. His brains bristle like bayonets, but what a relief! Of late, the sofa pillows have been downy, so

* General Johnston, commanding the successful Confederate attack on the first day at Shiloh, was wounded in the leg; but thinking it a minor wound he stayed in the saddle till, the bullet having cut an artery, he bled to death. General Beauregard, after his long altercation with President Davis, had been sent to the western front and succeeded to command; but Grant, heavily reinforced, was able to turn the tide of battle on the second day.

pestered were we with fools, suave, soft, politely punctilious. I wonder why he hates Mrs. Davis so. Clever people usually gravitate towards her. He says people do not mind Sue King's being fast; they only talk of her flirtations and keep out of her way because she is quarrelsome.

Judge Wardlaw, of his brother-on-the-bench, says: "I knew my friend always would make a fool of himself to amuse the crowd on railroad cars and at tavern dinner tables, but I did not expect him to carry his buffoonery to the bench." This long talk with Judge Wardlaw was a great comfort to me. He thinks my husband is doing great service to his country in his organization of all military matters, his Nitre Bureau, his foundry, etc.*

Gladden, the hero of the Palmetto's in Mexico, is killed. Shiloh has been a dreadful day to us. Last winter Stephen, my brother, had it in his power to do a kindness for Colonel Gladden. In the dark, he heard his name, and that he had to walk twenty-five miles in Alabama mud or go on an ammunition wagon; so he introduced himself to Colonel Gladden and then drove him in his carriage comfortably to where he wanted to go, a night drive of fifty miles for Stephen, for he had the return trip too.

I would gladly go to Liberia, or worse still, to Sahara, than live in a country surrendered to Yankees! Yet the Carolinian says the conscription bill passed by Congress is fatal to our liberties as a people.

Two thousand dollars we made at the Fair. It is for the gunboat.†

A touching letter from Colonel Chesnut of Mulberry says he "fails to please anybody now in his own house but his wife." He says the others think him in his dotage. They are tormenting him to make another will. He makes a heroic resistance. He wants his land to go to his son, but what can a poor old man do? They beset him with the cry that they will be paupers, since Negroes are to be freed, and he has given them only Negroes and bank stock. He says they are tired of waiting for dead men's shoes.

I read "Vanity Fair" once more. I can always reread Thackeray.

Mrs. Starke says: "The French minister is here, on his way to Rich-

* The difficulties which the Confederacy encountered in securing a supply of nitre for the manufacture of powder led to the composition and private publication of two bits of vulgar doggerel on "The Art of Making Saltpetre" which were widely circulated from hand to hand during the war.

† The initial success of the iron-clad *Merrimac* at Hampton roads led to many "Gunboat Fairs" throughout the South; but the results were more important to the ladies who thus found outlet for their patriotism than to the Confederate Navy.

mond to recognize us." That is too good to be true, but in regard to this glorious advent I find it pleasanter to take this lady's word than Mr. Chesnut's, who doubts everything systematically.

I sat up all night and read "Eothen" straight through in our old Wiley and Putnam edition we bought in London in 1845. How could I sleep? The power they are bringing to bear against our country is tremendous. Its might may be irresistible. I dare not think of that.

APRIL 21st. — I have been ill. One day I dined at Mrs. Preston's on *pâté de foie gras* and partridges prepared as I like them. I had been awfully depressed for days, and could not sleep at night, but I did not know that I was bodily ill. Mrs. Preston came home with me. She said emphatically: "Milly, if your mistress is worse in the night send for me instantly." I could not breathe if I attempted to lie down, and very soon I lost my voice. Milly raced out and sent Lawrence for Dr. Trezevant. She said I had the croup. The doctor said "congestion of the lungs." So here I am, laid by the heels.

Battle after battle results in disaster after disaster. Every morning's paper reports enough to kill a well woman, or to age a strong and hearty one.

Isabella was here. She is nothing if not funny. She says her dismay is caused by the thought that the man she is ordained by fate to marry, whoever he is, may be killed before she knows him, or before he knows *it*.

Dr. Trezevant, the kind and sensible physician, comes every day and brings the latest budget of "reliable" reports. Everybody comes, and is kind; most of all, Mrs. McCord and Mrs. Preston.

Today the waters of this stagnant pool were wildly stirred. The President telegraphed for my husband to come on to Richmond and offered him a place on his staff. I was a joyful woman. It was a way opened by providence out of this slough of despond, and out of this Council, whose counsel no one talks. To leave Pickens the First! I thought we were to be lifted up anew; but no! Mr. Chesnut says "his duty is here." I have no talent for self-abnegation. I do not love to be flayed alive. I do not like endless rows of pins stuck into me in this grand court of the Great Buzzfuzzy, and by little Moses who is not even out of the bulrushes yet! I want to go, and Mrs. Preston agrees with me that Mr. Chesnut ought to have gone. Through him the President might hear many things to the advantage of our state.

A letter from Quinton Washington was the best tonic yet. He writes so cheerfully. He says we have fifty thousand men on the Peninsula, and McClellan eighty thousand; but we expect that disparity of numbers. We can stand that.

So much that we believed is not true. McClellan has not been superseded. Also Count Mercier, if he came from France to recognize us, has made no bow to us yet, has not even touched his hat!

April 22nd. — Follies of the wise! From Mrs. McCord today I heard that Dr. Trezevant believes with all his heart, with all his mind, and with all his soul in spirits! He listens with credulity to their rappings and credits every word a medium conveys to him from the spirits. So does Waddy Thompson, my father's friend.

April 23rd. — On April 23rd, 1840, I was married, aged seventeen. Consequently, on the 31st of March, 1862, I was thirty-nine.

Today Mrs. Middleton asked me, sitting here by my bedside, if my husband was annoyed by that newspaper attack in Dr. Gibbes's paper. "Far from it," said I. "He traced it at once to the lowest source, little Moses. And when he spoke to Moses, the miserable little traitor took refuge behind his lady's petticoats."

Mrs. Middleton soon departed. In rushed Mrs. McMahan, our landlady, breathless with haste. "I do hope you did not say anything to Mrs. Middleton that you did not want the Governor's wife to know, because she hardly took time to put on her bonnet before she was off and away down the street to the Pickens'." Which is only two doors off. I said: "If Mrs. Pickens likes that Moses anecdote as well as I do, things will be established on a more satisfactory basis." In utter bewilderment, Mrs. McMahan left me.

I saw a wedding today from my window, which opens on Trinity Church. Nanna Shand married a Dr. Wilson. Then a beautiful bevy of girls rushed into my room, with such a flutter and a chatter. Thank Heaven for a wedding. It is a charming relief from the dismal litany of our daily song.

A letter today from our octogenarian at Mulberry, with his never failing refrain: we can't fight all the world, two and two only make four, numbers will tell, etc. In more personal vein, he says he has lost half a million dollars already, in railroad bonds, bank stock and western notes of hand, not to speak of Negroes to be freed and lands to be confiscated. He takes the gloomiest views of everything.

We are fighting a battle over the new gunboat's name. Dr. Gibbes, Mrs. Pickens's knight errant, wants to call it the *Lucy Holcombe* for her. We wanted to call it *Caroline* for our old darling Mrs. Preston; but if we are to have a female name I say let it be: "*She Devil*," for it is the Devil's own work it is built to do.

Mr. Preston came, more splendid-looking than ever. Better than that, he so very agreeable, so kind, so sensible. He is a great admirer of Mrs. McCord, and I repeated her amazement at the man who found fault with his treatment of Yankee prisoners. She said: "Did he look in Mr. Preston's face and live? I have always treated him as a poodle of the Hamptons. Whenever I saw him, he was walking on his hind legs for their amusement, or rolling off the rug to get out of the way of their feet! He keeps his poodle nature, but I see he has changed masters!"

APRIL 26th. — Doleful dumps, alarm bells ringing! Telegrams say the mortar fleet has passed the forts at New Orleans. Down into the very depth of despair go we.

APRIL 27th. — New Orleans is gone, and with it the Confederacy! Are we not cut in two? The Mississippi ruins us if it is lost. The Confederacy is done to death by the politicians. Those wretched creatures, the Congress, could never rise to the greatness of the occasion. They seem to think they were in a neighborhood squabble about precedence. The soldiers have done their duty. All honor to the army. But statesmen, busy bees about their own places or their personal honor, are too busy to see the enemy at a distance. With a microscope they are examining their own interest or their own wrongs, forgetting the interest of the people they represented. They were concocting newspaper paragraphs to injure the Government. No matter how vital, nothing, nothing can be kept from the enemy. They must publish themselves night and day, and what they are doing for fear omniscient Buncombe will forget them!

This fall of New Orleans means utter ruin to the private fortunes of the Prestons. Mr. Preston came from New Orleans so satisfied with Mansfield Lovell and the tremendous steam rams he saw there. In New Orleans, Burnside offered Mr. Preston five hundred thousand dollars on a debt due from him to Mr. Preston, and Mr. Preston refused to take it. He said the money was safer in Burnside's hands than in his; and so it may prove, ugly as the outlook is now. Burnside is wide awake. He is not a man to be caught napping.

The former Mrs. Judge, now Mrs. Brooks, wants to come and live in Columbia. Live? Death, not life, seems to be our fate now. They have got Beauregard in a *cul de sac*.

Mary Preston was saying she had asked the Hamptons how they

relished the idea of being paupers. Mr. Chesnut came in, saying: "If the country is saved, none of us will care for that sort of thing." He reported a telegram from New Orleans. The great iron-clad *Louisiana* went down at the first shot.

April 29th. — The news from New Orleans is fatal to us. Met Mr. Weston. He wanted to know where he could find a place of safety for two hundred Negroes. I looked in his face to see if he were in earnest, then to see if he were sane. He said there were a certain set of two hundred Negroes that had grown to be a nuisance. Apparently all the white men of the family had felt bound to stay at home to take care of them. There are, apparently, people who still believe Negroes to be property. They are like Noah's neighbors, who insisted that the deluge would only be a little shower after all. These Negroes were Plowden Weston's. He gave Enfield rifles to one of our companies, and forty thousand dollars to another, and he is away with our army at Corinth, so I said: "You may rely upon Mr. Chesnut to assist you to his uttermost in finding a home for these people." Nothing belonging to that particular gentleman shall come to grief, not even if we have to take charge of them on our own place. Mr. Chesnut did get a place for them, as I said he would.

Another acquaintance of ours wanted his wife to go back home. They live in Charleston, and while he is in the army she could protect their property. "Would you subject me to the horrors of a captured and a sacked city?" she demanded. He answered, vacantly staring at her: "What are they?"

We had to go to the Governor's or they would think we had hoisted the Black Flag. They said we were going to be beaten as Cortez did the Mexicans, by superior arms. Mexican bows and arrows made a poor showing in the face of powder and shot. Our enemies have such superior weapons of war. We hardly have any but what we capture from them in the fray. The Saxons and the Normans were in the same plight.

War seems a game of chess. We have knights, kings, queens, bishops, and castles enough, but not enough pawns; and our skillful generals whenever they cannot arrange the board to suit them exactly, burn up everything and march away. We want them to save the country. They seem to think their whole duty is to destroy ships and save the army.

The citizens of New Orleans say they were deserted by the army. Oh, for an hour of brave Andrew Jackson! The citizens sent word to the enemy to shell away, that they did not mean to surrender. Surely this must be that so often cited darkest hour before our daylight.

Last night Governor Pickens sent twice for Colonel Chesnut. He could not be found. The Governor asked: "Has he run away?" I retorted: "If he has, the war is over. This Council is an exigency of the war. While the war lasts, in spite of all I can do or say, he seems inclined to cleave to you."

There is a report abroad that Richmond will be given up,* that Jeff Davis is expected here. Not he! He will be the last man to give up heart and hope!

Mr. Robert Barnwell wrote that he had to hang his head for South Carolina because, he said, we had not furnished our quota of the new levy, five thousand men. Today, Colonel Chesnut published his statement to show that we have sent thirteen thousand, instead of the smaller number required of us; so Mr. Barnwell can hold up his head again!

Men born Yankees are an unlucky selection as commanders for the Confederacy. They believe in the North in a way no true Southerner ever will, and they see no shame in surrendering to Yankees. They are half-hearted clear through; Stephens as Vice-President, Lovell, Pemberton, Ripley. A general must command the faith of his soldiers. These never will, be they ever so good and true.

Today the Courier pitches in, in the same vein; with the native talent, which we undoubtedly possess, to think of choosing Mallory and Walker for Navy and Army. "Whom the Gods would destroy they first make mad!"

APRIL 30th. — The last day of this month of calamities! Lovell left the women and children in New Orleans to be shelled, and took the army to a safe place. I do not understand. Why not send the women and children to the safe place, and let the army stay where the fighting was to be? Armies are to save, not to be saved; at least, to be saved is not the *raison d'être* exactly. If this goes on, the spirit of our people will be broken.

I had a passage at arms. A lady said: "The Up Country are a new people, it seems. The old blood of the cavalier stays near the salt water."

"Yes," I retorted. "I accept the charge. We are new, fresh, not little, nor ugly, nor dwarfed, nor pretentious, nor blind. We are new,

* McClellan's deliberate advance up the Peninsula had created a minor panic; and the abandonment of Richmond was seriously considered.

fresh, handsome, full grown, wealthy, accomplished, agreeable, brave as the bravest!" "Oh, I meant nobody in particular!" "Neither did I." A grave silence, and suddenly a horse-laugh from a listener, in which the interlocutors joined most heartily.

One ray of comfort from Mr. Henry Marshall. "Our army of the Peninsula is fine; it is so good I do not think McClellan will venture to attack it." So mote it be!

MAY 6th. — Why write, when I have nothing to chronicle but disasters; so I read instead, first "Consuelo," then "Columbia." Two ends of the pole, certainly. Then a translated edition of "Elective Affinities." Food enough for thought in every one of this odd assortment of books.

At the Prestons' where I am staying (because Mr. Chesnut has gone to see the crabbed old father, whom he loves, and who is reported ill) I met Mars' Kit [Christopher Hampton]. He tells us Wigfall is out on a warpath, wants them to strike for Maryland. The President's opinion of the move is not given. Also Mars' Kit met the First Lieutenant of the Kirkwoods, E. M. Boykin, and says he is just the same man he was in the South Carolina College. In whatever company you may meet him, he is the pleasantest man there.

Mr. Preston accuses me of degenerating into a boarding-house gossip and I answer triumphantly: "But one you love to gossip with full well."

The Hampton Estate has fifteen hundred Negroes on Lake Washington, in Mississippi; but neither Wade nor Preston, that splendid boy, would lay a lance in rest, or couch it — which is the right phrase? — for the sake of slavery. They hate slavery as we do. Someone asked: "Then what are they fighting for?" "For Southern rights, whatever that is! And they do not want to be understrappers forever for those nasty Yankees."

They talk well enough about it, but I forget what they say. John Chesnut says: "No use to give a reason. A fellow could not stay away you know, not very well." Johnny is not sound on the goose, either;* but then it takes four Negroes to wait on him satisfactorily.

A beautiful and deceitful minx has been here to talk me over. I found her charming while she was here, and utterly forgot my opinion of her while she was beguiling me. She carried off "Elective Affinities."

* In a letter written at about this period and found in a New England attic, and which discussed a candidate for Congress, appears the inquiry: "Is he sound on the old goose question?" This seems to have been a colloquialism of which everyone knew the meaning, so no one troubled to define it!

Now, in cold blood, I think it all over, and I trust her as little as ever. A mischief-making gadfly! Dr. —— has stirred her to this.

A telegram says we repulsed the enemy at Williamsburg. Oh, if we could drive them back to "their ain countree"! Richmond is hard-pressed this day. The Mercury says: "Jeff Davis now treats all men as if they were idiotic insects."

Mary Preston said all sisters quarrelled; but we never quarrel, I and mine. We keep all our bitter words for our enemies. We are frank heathens; we hate our enemies and love our friends. Some people (our kind) can never make up after a quarrel. Let there be hard words only once, and all is over. To us, forgiveness is impossible. Forgiveness means calm indifference, but a philosophic forgiveness of love's wrongs is impossible. Those dutiful wives who piously overlook — well, everything — do not care one fig for their husbands. I settled that in my own mind years ago. Some people think it magnanimous to praise their enemies, and to show their impartiality and justice by acknowledging the faults of their friends. I am for the simple rule, the good old plan. I praise when I love and abuse when I hate!

Mary Preston is translating Schiller. We are familiar with Bulwer's translations, Mrs. Austin's, Coleridge's, Carlyle's; and we show her how each renders the passage she is trying to make into English. At one point of the Max and Thekla scene in "Wallenstein" I like Carlyle best of all, better than Coleridge, though they say Coleridge's "Wallenstein" is the only translation in the world as good as the original. Mrs. Bartow repeated some beautiful scraps of Uhland's which I had not heard before. She is to write them for us.

Oh for peace, and a literary leisure for my old age, unbroken by care and anxiety!

Here is one thing too good to go unrecorded. "Why did you marry him? Candidly answer that." "For love." We had leaned forward to catch the answer to this astounding question; and when it came, with innocent softness and simplicity and a clear blue eye facing the enemy unflinchingly, we owned Mrs. H. —— defeated, routed, horse, foot and dragoons.

Was Williamsburg a victory? John Chesnut is there, in Stuart's Brigade of Cavalry. Quinton Washington writes that the Clays and Mallorys have taken wing for happier climes than Richmond — or safer — just now, at any rate.

A lady today was weeping and lamenting. "How will we feel if death comes, or worse?" She dwelt especially on the "worse." I was stupidly wanting in comprehension, preferred to be taken for a fool rather than indulge her in such horrid talk. Someone said: "Americans will never trouble women. All the horrors of war will fall on our men. It is for them I fear."

I could have driven out delightfully if I could have divided myself in four. The Prestons came for me, Mrs. Singleton came for me, then Mrs. Ben Taylor, and finally Mrs. McCord. I sent the same message to all. I was too ill to leave my bed. Mrs. McCord came up to see for herself, and Mrs. Bartow. With such agreeable people, time flew and I forgot my aches and pains. Mrs. Bartow brought me "Peau de Chagrin."

Another sell-out to the Devil! It is this giving up that kills me. Norfolk, they talk of now. Why not Charleston next? I read in a western letter: "Not Beauregard, but the soldiers who stopped to drink the whiskey they had captured from the enemy, lost us Shiloh." Cock robin is as dead as he ever will be now. What matters it who killed him?

May 12th. — At the Christy Minstrels, with the Togno school girls, a mournful miner sang that his sweetheart Sally sent him to dig for gold in California, promising that then she would marry him. Returning with the gold, he found her married already. Her new flame had red hair. The refrain: "Enough to make a fellow swear; Sally with a baby, and the baby with red hair." Here he wrung tears from the very dirtiest pocket handkerchief any miner ever pocketed. I watched the faces of my well-brought-up boarding-school girls; no expression whatever, except maybe a transient shade of disgust so slight as to be barely perceptible. There they sat, prim, demure and stiff. From the pursed lips of the one nearest me escaped the words, "Very improper!" although the lips moved not.

Mr. Chesnut says he is very glad he went to town, says everything in Charleston is much more satisfactory than it is reported, and that the troops are in good spirits. It will take a lot of ironclads to take that city.

Yeadon told them he had let the Council alone until he found they did not mean to give his men anything. Now they were to look out, since he intended to open his batteries using all his guns.

Isaac Hayne said at dinner yesterday that both Beauregard and the President had a great opinion of Mr. Chesnut's natural ability for strategy and military evolution. Mr. Barnwell concurred. "Then why did not the President offer me something better than an aidship?"

"I heard he offered to make you a general, last year, and you said you would not go over other men's shoulders until you had earned promotion. You are too hard to please." "No. It was not exactly that. I was only offered a colonelcy, and Mr. Barnwell persuaded me to stick to the Senate. Then he wanted my place, and between the two stools, I fell to the ground."

Today our literary lion was on the hunt for plagiarists. "Nothing new under the sun," said Madame Flippant. "Now look what I have been reading today; a queer old flirtation liable to misconstruction. Nausicaa and her maidens washing her regal father's clothes." Came an interruption. "Kings were so common in those days. They were as cheap as South Carolina Colonels, or as Georgia Majors. Maybe it was their way of saying 'squire.' " She went on: "Nausicaa, as we were saying, while washing her father's clothes, found Ulysses without any clothes at all, cast away upon the shore. She lent him some maid's apparel at his own request, and drove back into town with him sitting beside her. But when they get near town, she bethought herself of evil tongues. A young unmarried woman cannot be too particular. So she put him out to walk. Nothing new under the sun, you see."

Someone called from across the room: "What are you laughing at over there?" "The way they gossipped and flirted in the time of Ulysses."

We played whist. It wasn't fair. Two were slightly deaf, and vain old souls who would not put on their spectacles. Then only two spoke French, and somehow a great deal of French was spoken. So they who could see and hear and understand each other in many languages won all the games. It was a poor joke, and one player at least was ashamed of it. We did not play for money, however.

Mrs. M., who is English, remarked: "You lost the sympathy of England when you sent Yancey, a manslayer, as your representative." "England's prudence and her prejudices never interfere when she really wants to do anything." Mrs. M. was in a rage. Her husband said: "Not a word, dear. It is a fair retort. You abused her country, you know."

MAY 13th. — Read Beverly Tucker's "Partisan." Just such a rose-water revolution he imagines as we fancied we were to have, and now the reality is hideous agony.

To wear the color of slaves is the worst. The misery of poverty is alike everywhere; many a person can be beaten with many stripes, by his own family, his father or mother, his schoolmaster, his superior officer by land or sea, his master if he is an apprentice, her husband if she be a woman, or everybody who chooses, if she be a child. Wherever there is a cry of pain, I am on the side of the one who cries.

Now Norfolk is burnt, and the *Merrimac* sunk by our own men, without striking a blow.

A queer episode: Mr. Chesnut had a lovely note asking him to receive the writer at his office on business. As I write a hand exactly like his when I please, he got me to answer the note. At Mrs. Preston's I found the noble master of the house inclined to brag of some mysterious compliment, of being led on. It turned out he had had an exactly similar note. Each of them had an interview, and each made love as best they knew how. "We made all the love possible," they said, "as we were in duty bound."

Hanging all the state officials was proposed. "Save the country that way, and spare the rank and file." "I won't mind," said Mrs. Pickens, radiantly young and beautiful. "Let them hang the Governor, if it can save the state." Whereupon a horse-laugh. This was one of the jokes repeated as having occurred down at the State House. Mrs. Pickens calls the Governor's other wives gone before her, Number One and Number Two. The men say she is as clever as she is handsome. "She put it this way: 'Let them hang an old husband, if that would save the country!' " added Mr. Preston, who is verbally correct always, when he repeats.

The best and the bravest went first. Now the lag-lasts do not want to be conscripted. As officers, they would gladly face the music, but the few that are left are old, or middle-aged, and nothing remains for them but the ranks. They hoped to reap where others had sowed, to win where they did not work. Without a murmur they sent their sons, but they grumbled when asked for money, though they gave it. Kill a man's wife (or son) and he may brook it, but keep your hands out of his breeches pocket. Their own sacred skins they respect, but there was not a regular shrinking until sacred property was touched. This never-to-be-too-much-abused Council wants to take their Negroes and send them to work at the forts; hence these tears. How long before they will lay violent hands on Negroes and put them in the army? The only question now; could they be induced to stand fire, fighting on our side. The Council is in bitter earnest, anxious to fortify the outpost, to prepare for the worst; and the few remaining big braves, the stay-at-homes, thought talk was to do it. Negroes were to stay and work, while they overlooked them. Now they are ready to cut the

Council's throats because the Negroes are to be forced into the army.

MAY 17th. — Oh, the things that I have been said to have said. Dr. Gibbes thinks he heard me make scoffing remarks derogatory to the dignity of the Governor and Council. Mr. Chesnut wrote him a note, that my name was to be kept out of it, that he was never to mention my name again under any possible circumstances. It was all preposterous nonsense, but it annoyed my husband amazingly. He said it was a scheme to use my chatter to his injury. He was very kind about it. He knew my style so well, that he could always tell my real imprudences from what was fabricated for me.

I read a letter from Mr. Venable. He does not see how we could have made a worse mess of it than we did at New Orleans. He could see no reason for burning either the *Louisiana* or the *Mississippi;* and the reckless, wanton waste, and destruction of provisions and ammunition which could so easily have been saved, even after the Yankees were in actual possession of the city.

Re-reading Milton, I see the speech of Adam to Eve in a new light. Women will not stay at home, will go out to see and be seen, even if it be by the Devil himself.

Very encouraging letters from Honorable Mr. Memminger and from L. Q. Washington. They tell the same story in very different words. It amounts to this. Not one foot of Virginia soil is to be given up without a bitter fight for it. We have one hundred and five thousand men in all, McClellan one hundred and ninety thousand. We can stand that disparity.

At the Prestons', Mr. Daniel Blake and his son were talking, and in another part of the room Mr. Chesnut had induced Sally to declaim in French something of Joan of Arc, which she does in a manner to touch all hearts. Mr. Chesnut turned to young Blake, who was listening to one of the other girls chattering, and said with his finger raised: "*Ecoutez!*" Young Blake stared at him a moment in bewilderment, and then gravely got up and began turning down the gas. Isabella said: "Oh, so '*Ecoutez*' means put out the lights!"

Willie Taylor, before he left home for the army, fancied one day — day, remember, not night — that he saw Albert Rhett standing by his side. He recoiled from the ghost in horror. "You need not do that, Willie; you will soon be as I am." Willie rushed into the next room to tell them what had happened and fainted. It had a very depressing effect upon him. The other day he died in Virginia.

MAY 19th. — Mary McDuffie (Mrs. Hampton) is a martyr to truth.

Mr. Pickens said enthusiastically: "I think Wade Hampton the handsomest man in the world, except the Czar-Emperor of Russia." "Do you?" said Mary McDuffie. "I don't." "Oh," said Mrs. Pickens, "I own that I think Governor Pickens very handsome!" "Do you?" said Mary, more surprised than ever. "I don't." Is this a *canard?*

Young Robert Barnwell says the very latest news from Richmond is that Beauregard and Bragg have notified the authorities that they will obey no further orders from Jeff Davis.

MAY 21st. — Mrs. H—— being strong-minded, harangued us. "Now I assert that the theory upon which modern society is based is all wrong. A man is supposed to confide his honor to his wife. If she misbehaves herself, his honor is tarnished. But how can a man be disgraced by another person's doing what, if he did himself (that is, if he committed the same offense), he would not be hurt at all in public estimation. He would only be 'a little gay,' a Sad Dog, a Lothario. If an action did not disgrace him, how could the same action by his wife disgrace her or him?" To all of which we listened in silence. Among other theories of hers: "Women are more dangerous to men at thirty or forty years of age than when younger." There was a sort of dissenting murmur: "If a man's heart is the point upon which the attack is designed, youth is a fatal weapon." Another faint murmur: "The older the men grow, the younger they like their wives."

There is said to be an order from Butler, turning over the women of New Orleans to his soldiers! Thus is the measure of his iniquities filled. We thought that generals always restrained by shot or sword, if need be, the brutal soldiery. This hideous, cross-eyed beast orders his men to treat the ladies of New Orleans as women of the town; to punish them, he says, for their insolence.*

MAY 23rd. — Mem Cohen missed me. The Jewish angel came with healing on her wings; that is, in her hands she bore opium. Two victories for us. Mem says: "Now you will get well."

Jere Clemens has gone to the Yankees. How I wish all of that kind would at once take that road; the ultra-Union men, the half-hearted, the half-handed, the outspoken abusers of our Confederate Government.

MAY 24th. — The enemy are landing at Georgetown. With a little

* General Butler's actual order, issued several weeks after the occupation, was that ". . . hereafter, when any female shall, by word, gesture or movement, insult or show contempt for any officer or soldier of the United States, she shall be regarded and held liable to be treated as a woman of the town plying her vocation." Thereafter, his officers and men suffered no further discourtesy from the women of New Orleans.

more audacity, where could they not land; but we have given them such a scare, they are cautious. If it be true, I hope some cool-headed white men will make the Negroes save the rice for us; it is so much needed. They say it might have been done at Port Royal with a little more energy. South Carolinians have pluck enough, but they only work by fits and starts. There is no continuous effort. They can't be counted on for steady work. They will stop to play, or enjoy life in some shape.

Mr. Chesnut has offended Trescot mortally, for he has given Wilmot DeSaussure the position Trescot asked; so now they have Trescot's pen against them, and they have not made a friend of Wilmot DeSaussure. For the Council is unpopular. It forces men into the ranks, and it sends Negroes away from their master's plantation to work on the coast fortifications. Two-thirds of the time of the Council is taken up hearing excuses from men who do not want to go in the ranks.

Without let or hindrance, Halleck is being reinforced. Beauregard, unmolested, is making some fine speeches and proclamations — while we are fatuously looking for him to make a tiger's spring on Huntsville. Hope springs eternal in the Southern breast.

My Hebrew friend, Mem Cohen, has a son in the war. He is in John Chesnut's company. Cohen is a high name among Jews. It means Aaron. She has long fits of silence, and is absent-minded. If she is suddenly roused she is apt to say, with overflowing eyes and clasped hands: "If it please God to spare his life." Her daughter is the sweetest little thing, and the son is the mother's idol. Mrs. Cohen was Miriam de Leon. I have known her intimately all my life.

Mrs. Bartow, the widow of Colonel Bartow who was killed at Manassas, is now in one of the departments here, cutting bonds, Confederate bonds, for five hundred Confederate dollars a year.* A penniless woman. Judge Carroll, her brother-in-law, has been urgent with her to come and live with them. He has a large family, and she will not be a further burden to him. In spite of all he can say, she will not forego her resolution, and she will be independent. She is a resolute little woman, with the softest silkiest voice and ways, and clever to the last point.

I think I write a plain hand, easy to read. But I sent to Team for

* Scores and perhaps hundreds of Southern women, left without support by the death of their husbands or because their estates were in the enemy's hands, earned a meagre living by cutting or by signing Confederate bonds and notes as the printing presses poured out emergency currency.

some things and he sent me four sugar-cured hams. Now what word of mine he mistook for hams I wonder. In lodgings as I am, I can but give away the hams.

This Columbia is the place for good living, pleasant people, pleasant dinners, pleasant drives. I feel that I have put the dinners in the wrong place. They are the climax of the good things here. This is the most hospitable place in the world, and the dinners are worthy of it. In Washington, there was an endless succession of state dinners. I was kindly used. I do not remember ever being condemned to two dull neighbors; one side or the other was a clever man. So I liked Washington dinners. In Montgomery there were a few dinners, but the society was not smoothed down. It was — such as it was — given over to balls and suppers. In Charleston, Mr. Chesnut went to gentlemen dinners all the time. No ladies present. Flowers were sent to me, and I was taken to drive and asked to tea. There could not have been nicer suppers. In Richmond, there were balls which I did not attend — and very few to which I was asked; but Mr. Chesnut dined out nearly every day.

But then the breakfasts! The Virginia breakfast is a thing *comme il y en a peu* in the world. Always there were pleasant people. Indeed, I have had a good time everywhere; always clever people, and people I liked, and everybody so good to me.

Here in Columbia, the family dinners are the specialty. You call, or they pick you up and drive home with you. "Oh, stay to dinner," and you stay gladly. They send for your husband, and he comes willingly. Then comes apparently a perfect dinner — you do not see how it could be improved — yet they have not had time to alter things or add because of the additional guests. They have everything of the best. Silver, glass, china, table linen, damask, etc. The planters live "within themselves" as they call it; from the plantations come mutton, beef, poultry, cream, butter, eggs, fruits and vegetables. It is easy to live here, with a cook who has been sent to the best eating house in Charleston to be trained. Old Mrs. Chesnut's Romeo was apprenticed at Jones's, in town. I do not know where Mrs. Preston's got his degrees, but he deserves a medal.

And now for a document *à la* Stowe, about Mrs. Preston's butler, William, and his brother John, and his sister Maria. In Richmond, Mrs. Preston always engaged a room next or opposite hers for Maria, who was her maid. Maggie Howell and Mary Hammy were forced to hunt up a recalcitrant maid late at night. They found the maids sleeping under the roof, where it is almost impossible to stand. They were stretched out in that hot, suffocating place, like sardines in a box. "Maria, do you know how blest you are?" said Mary Hammy, after her return to cleaner and cooler regions. "But I must say that in that stifling low room, where our damsel was stowed away with her likes, packed as if in a box, we found them hilarious. The din was so great, we could hardly make ourselves heard."

Maria often smoothed a dress for me. She loved to talk of her marital relations. She was so sad and mysterious in her dark revelations, I cannot make them very clear. She was married, her husband ill-used her; he did something very bad, that is very wrong, and he left her and then he died. She had no children. Then she would go off to her family history, which I had heard from Mrs. Preston when we were at the Fauquier White Sulphur. This is not a pretty story, but Maria told it leaving out all ugly words. Her mother died when they were quite young. She belonged to a Scotchman, a doctor. Her master married a white lady who did not like Maria and her two brothers; but she was not bad to them while her husband lived. Then the Scotchman died, and the widow found these white-fathered children in her yard a blot on the Scotchman's escutcheon. She sent them to Columbia to be sold. They were delighted to be sold, for they hated her worse than she hated them. Mrs. Preston bought them.

Before I knew the history of the Walkers (William, Maria, John), I remember a scene which took place at a ball given by Mrs. Preston while Mr. Preston was in Louisiana. Mrs. Preston was resplendent in diamonds, point lace, velvet train, etc. There is a gentle dignity about her which is very attractive, and her voice is low and sweet, and her will is iron. She is an exceedingly well-informed person, but quiet, retiring and reserved. Her apparent gentleness almost amounts to timidity. At that ball, Governor Manning said to me: "Look at sister Caroline! Does she look as if she had the pluck of a heroine?" "How?" "A little while ago, William came to tell her that his brother John was drunk in the cellar, mad with drink, and that he had a carving knife which he was brandishing in his drunken fury and keeping everybody from their business, threatening to kill anyone who dared to go in the basement. They were like a flock of frightened sheep down there. Caroline did not speak to one of us, but followed William down to the basement, holding up her skirts. She found the servants scurrying everywhere, screaming and shouting that John was crazy and going to kill them. John was bellowing like a bull of Basham, knife in hand, chasing them at his pleasure. Caroline walked up to him. 'Give me that knife.' He handed it to her; she laid it on a table. 'And now come with me,' she said, putting her hand on his collar. She led him away to the empty smoke house, and locked him in and put the key in her pocket; and she returned without a ripple on her placid face to show what she had done. She told me of it, smiling and serene as you see her now."

Before the war shut us in, Mr. Preston sent to the lakes for his salmon, to Mississippi for his venison, to England for his mutton and grouse. But the best dish at all of these houses is what the Spanish call "the hearty welcome." Thackeray says at every American table he was first served with "grilled hostess." At the head of the table sat a person fiery-faced, anxious, nervous, inwardly murmuring like Falstaff "would it were night, Hal, and all were well."

At Mulberry, the house is always filled to overflowing, and one day is curiously like another. People are coming and going, carriages driving up or driving off. It has the air of a watering place where one does not pay, and where there are no strangers. At Christmas, the china closet gives up its treasures. The glass, china, silver, fine linen reserved for grand occasions comes forth. But as for the dinner itself, it is only a matter of great quantity; more turkey, more mutton, more partridge, more fish — and more solemn stiffness. Usually, a half-dozen persons unexpectedly dropping in makes no difference; they let the housekeeper know, that is all.

People are beginning to come here from Richmond. One swallow does not make a summer, but it shows how the wind blows, as these straws do. It does look squally. We are drifting on the breakers. Mem Cohen's son writes a stirring account of the cavalry charge at Williamsburg. Mem's eyes are wonderful to see. She laughs and weeps and reads it all to us.

Mrs. Preston and I have determined that come what will, survive or perish, we will not stand up all day at a table and cut notes apart, ordered around by a department clerk. We will live at home with our families and starve in a body. Any homework we will do, any menial service under the shadow of our own roof tree. But in a department? Never!

We put our trust now in Beauregard and Joe Johnston. Magruder is to supercede Lovell, and Mercer takes Ripley's place. On our side, Yankees are unlucky, to say the least.

May 29th. — Betsey, recalcitrant maid of the W.'s, is sold to a telegraph man. She is as handsome as a mulatto ever gets to be, and clever in every kind of work; but my Molly thinks her mistress very lucky in getting rid of her and says she was a dangerous inmate. But she will be a good cook, a good chambermaid, a good dairymaid, a beautiful clear-starcher, and the most thoroughly good-for-nothing woman I know to her new owners if she chooses. Molly evidently hates her, but thinks it her duty to stand by her color.

Mrs. Gibson, a Philadelphia woman, is true to her husband and children; but she does not believe in us, in the Confederacy. I make allowances for those people. If I had married North, they would have a heavy handful in me just now. Mrs. Chesnut, my mother-in-law, has been sixty years in this country, and she has not changed in feeling one iota. She cannot like hominy for breakfast and rice for dinner, without a relish to give it some flavor. She cannot eat watermelons and sweet potatoes freely as we do. She will not eat hot cornbread at discretion and hot buttered biscuits without any. Mrs. Gibson said her mind was fixed on one point; she never would own slaves. "Who would that was not born to it?" I cried.

We met Mrs. Hampton Gibbes at the door; another Virginia woman as good as gold. She told us Mrs. Davis was delightfully situated at Raleigh.* North Carolinians were so loyal, and so hospitable, she had not been allowed to eat a meal at the hotel. "How different from Columbia," said Dr. Gibbes, looking at Mrs. Gibson, who has no doubt been left to take all of her meals at his house.

"Oh, no," cried Mary. "You do Columbia injustice. Mrs. Chesnut used to tell us that she was never once turned over to the tender mercies of the Congaree cuisine, and at McMahan's it is fruit, flowers, invitations to dinner every day."

After we came away she asked: "Why did you not back me up? Why did you let them slander Columbia?" "It was awfully awkward," I said. "But you see, it would have been worse to let Dr. Gibbes and Mrs. Gibson see how different it was with other people."

Uncle Hamilton Boykin is here, staying at the DeSaussures. He says Manassas was play to Williamsburg. He was at both. He led a part of Stuart's cavalry in the charge at Williamsburg, riding a hundred yards ahead of his company.

Colonel Arthur Manigault writes to his family here: "Beauregard's wife is still in New Orleans and he gnashes his teeth. She will not leave

* Fear for Richmond's safety as the city faced McClellan's slow advance up the Peninsula had led Jefferson Davis to send his family away.

a doctor who — the only one in the world, she thinks — understands her case."

Toombs is ready for another revolution. He curses freely everything Confederate from a president down to a horse boy; and he thinks there is a conspiracy against him in the army. Why? Heavens and earth, why? Let us get through with our Yankee fight first! But if you are too impatient to wait, I will waive rank and go out with you tomorrow morning.

Dr. Berrian shows us how Magruder lisps and swears at the same time, and the combination leads to comical results, as for instance in saying: "Charge, and charge furiously!"

Mr. John Izard Middleton lost two hundred barrels of rice. His wife and daughter were nearly taken prisoners. The Negroes fled to the woods, and the overseer saved the ladies.

JUNE 2nd. — A battle is said to be raging around Richmond. I am at the Prestons. Mr. Chesnut has gone to Richmond on business of the military department. It is always his luck to arrive in the nick of time and be present at a great battle.

Molly heard yesterday that one of her children was ill. Her mother, the best woman in the world, is given nothing else to do but take charge of Molly's children; but Molly went off by the next train. She is to come back or stay as she pleases, for though I cannot well do without her, she would be a nuisance if she were dissatisfied.

News from the battle. Wade Hampton shot in the foot. Johnston Pettigrew killed. The telegraph says Lee and Davis were both on the field, the enemy being repulsed. Each army now burying its dead. That looks like a drawn battle. We haunt the bulletin board.

A clipping:

The Infamous Proclamation of General Butler.

It will be seen by the report in the telegraphic column that General Beauregard, in an address published to his troops, has referred to the infamous and beastly proclamation of Major-General Butler, of New Orleans, with respect to the women of that city. The terms of this proclamation are reported to be of the most outrageous description. It is proposed that the Yankee soldiers shall revenge themselves for any insult or scorn, by word, gesture, or movement, which the women of New Orleans may dare to offer to the invaders of their homes, by being free to treat them in such circumstances as common women or harlots. The proposition in bravery and decency is a hideous, but faithful, characteristic of the Northern mind. If any appeal was wanting to string the nerves of our soldiers, and to make *them dedicate anew all they have of labor, of blood and of life, to the destruction of their enemy, it may be found in the vile and brutal proclamation of the notorious libertine and coward who insults the unhappy fortunes of New Orleans by a proposition to license in its streets crimes as horrible as those of the Sepoys.**

In Saturday's Mercury there was a vindication of Ripley, and a map of all the coast defenses, a map better than the very cleverest spy in the world, without help from our headquarters, could have given to the enemy.

Back to McMahan's. Mem is ill. Her daughter Isabel warns me not to mention the battle raging around Richmond, since young Cohen is in it. She tells me her cousin, Edwin de Leon, is sent by Mr. Davis on a mission to England. Mrs. Preston is anxious about her sons. John is with General Huger at Richmond, Artie in the swamps on our coast with his company.

Robert Barnwell has gone back to the hospital. Oh, that we had given our thousand dollars to the hospital, and not to the gunboat!

"Stonewall Jackson's movements," the Herald says, "do them no harm North, but bring out volunteers there in great numbers." And a Philadelphia paper abused us so fervently I felt all the blood in me rush to my head with rage.

Allan Green said: "Johnston Pettigrew was rash, I suspect." "Could you not find a better word to use? You are speaking of a hero dead upon the field of battle." Then he began to qualify his rash expression.

JUNE 3rd. — Dr. John Cheves is making infernal machines in Charleston, to blow the Yankees up. A pretty name they have, those machines.

Yeadon will be worse than ever, now; for the adopted son whom the Council and my husband would not promote has been killed.

My horses, the overseer says, are too poor to send over. They said in January there was enough corn on the place for two years, but now in June they write that it will not last until the new crop comes in. Somebody is having a good time on the plantation, even if it be not my poor horses.

Mr. Venable is made an aid to Robert E. Lee. He is at Vicksburg. He writes: "When the fight is over here, I will be glad to go to Virginia!"

Miss Bay handed me a Courier and said with an air of surprise:

* Not all Southern newspapers took this view. The Macon, Mississippi, Beacon editorially professed a complete lack of sympathy with the "pretended indignation" at the Butler order, and suggested that no lady would insult Northern soldiers or officers who were in New Orleans only because it was their duty to be there. Any woman who did so, the editor suggested, demeaned herself and deserved harsh treatment.

"There is no attack upon the Council in it." This ever-blooming, elderly Bay blossom! I answered: "Council indeed! And a life or death struggle going on at Richmond. Where will your fine Courier newspaper be if Richmond falls?" I gave her a race last night. I am glad it did not kill her. We walked home together. Suddenly I remembered Mrs. Bartow's adventure, and I fled, leaving her to keep up as best she might. Mrs. Bartow and Dr. Berrian met Treadwell, dreadfully drunk, the night before. They tried to evade him, but he would not let them escape. He was insolent and aggressive. He got in front of them and blocked the way. Dr. Berrian raised his stick, but Treadwell drew a pistol. So did Dr. Berrian. Mrs. Bartow threw her arms around her brother, etc. etc.

Telegrams come from Richmond ordering troops from Charleston. They cannot be sent, for the Yankees are attacking Charleston too, doubtless to prevent reinforcements from being sent from there.

I sat down at my window in the beautiful moonlight and tried hard for pleasant thoughts. A man began to play on the flute with piano accompaniment; first "Ever of Thee I Am Kindly Dreaming"; then "Long, Long, Weary Day." At first I found it but a complement to the beautiful scene, and it was soothing to my wrought-up nerves; but Von Weber's "Last Waltz" was too much. Suddenly I broke down. Heavens, what a bitter cry! Such floods of tears! The wonder is there was any of me left.

I see in Richmond the women go in their carriages for the wounded, carry them home and nurse them. One saw a man too weak to hold his musket. She took it from him, put it on her shoulder and helped the poor wounded fellow along.

If ever there was a man who could control every expression of his emotion, who can play stoic like an Indian chief, it is Colonel Chesnut; but one day when he came home from the Council he had to own a breakdown, or nearly. He was awfully ashamed of his weakness. There was a letter from Mrs. Gaillard asking him to help her, and he tried to read it to the Council. She wanted a permit to go on to her son, who lies wounded in Virginia. He could not control his voice, and there was not a dry eye there. Suddenly one man called out: "God bless the women."

Lewis Young, Johnston Pettigrew's aid, says he left his chief mortally wounded on the battlefield. Left him?

Just before Johnston Pettigrew went to Italy to take a hand there in their war for freedom and self-government, I met him one day at Mrs.

Frank Hampton's. Mr. Pettigrew, Mr. Preston and myself were the only people who dined there that day. Mr. Preston announced the engagement of the beautiful Miss W. to Hugh Rose. I was too annoyed to speak. In his very quick, excited way, Johnston Pettigrew asked, "Why do you say that?" "Well, it seemed to startle you, but it is so. I have never heard it, but I saw it. In London a month or so ago I entered Mrs. Williams's drawing-room. They were seated on a sofa opposite the door. . . ." "That amounts to nothing!" "No, not in itself; but they looked so foolish and so happy. Newly engaged people always look that way." "But they are not!" "Then I am very sorry." "You? Why?" "Because when I see a splendid creature like that unmarried, I think what a deal of happiness some fellow is losing."

Johnston Pettigrew was white and red in quick succession, in a rage of indignation and disgust. "I think this kind of talk a liberty with the young lady's name, and an impertinence in us."

Mr. Hampton said to Mr. Preston afterwards, "They say he is in love with Miss W. himself." I fancy him, left dying! I wonder what they feel, those who are deserted and left to die of their wounds on the battlefield. Hard lines!

Trescot, the very cleverest writer we have, is sulking, though not in his tent like Achilles. Far from it. I am sure he is in some very comfortable house. Mrs. Pickens said, referring to that savage attack upon the fine ladies lolling in their landaus: "Why not? General Washington attended the Assembly Balls, and wanted everything done that could be done to amuse his soldiers and comfort and refresh them, and give them new strength for the fray."

Free schools are not everything. Yankee epistles found in camp show how illiterate they can be, with all their boasted schools. Fredericksburg is spelled "Fretrixbirg," medicine "metson," "to my sweat brother," etc. But now, for the first time in my life, no book can interest me. Life is so real, so utterly earnest. Fiction is so flat comparatively. Nothing but what is going on in this distracted world of ours can arrest my attention for ten minutes at a time. Here is Wigfall's programme; that is, if he had been president. "Every afternoon, business hours over, I would walk down and stand on the pavement before the Spotswood and talk with all comers. How else is one to keep abreast of public opinion?" It was suggested that the Examiner enlightens our President as to what his enemies are saying. "No, no! That is not my idea at all, no one-sided affair, but every side! What everybody is saying! *Vox populi, vox Deo!* One might as well be in a ballroom as shut in that

Brockenbrough House. Now who dares tell the President the truth? Everybody is afraid of him!"

Somebody sniggered and said: "The truth is coming in now, like the Yankee Army from Bull's Run, on horseback, on foot, by land and by water. The very fowls of the air are bringing it. The President must encounter the 'reliable man' even in his rides; and the 'reliable man,' so often quoted but never named, has always the best of bad news in his saddle bags!"

JUNE 4th. — Battles near Richmond, bombardment of Charleston, Beauregard fighting his way out — or in. Thus saith the "reliable man" today.

Mrs. Gibson is at Dr. Gibbes's. Tears are always in her eyes. Her eldest son is Willie Preston's Lieutenant. They are down on the coast. She owns that she has no hope at all. She was a Miss Ayer of Philadelphia. She says: "We may look for Burnside now. Our troops which held him down to his Iron Flotilla have been withdrawn. They are three to one against us now, and they have hardly begun to put out their strength, while in numbers at least we have come to the end of our tether, unless we wait for the yearly crop of boys as they grow up to the requisite age." She would make despondent the most sanguine person alive. She went on: "They have sent for Captain Ingraham from Charleston. In this hour of our sorest need, they want him for a Court-Martial! One would think that could wait. So it was with Captain Hollins. They telegraphed for him. He answered that his presence was absolutely essential at New Orleans. In a few moments, a peremptory reply from the Secretary of the Navy: 'Come on at once.' When he arrived at Richmond, they met him with the news that New Orleans had fallen. In his excitement he rushed into the Executive Office and said outright, without any reserve: 'I believe if I had been there in my proper place this might not have happened.' Jeff Davis buried his face in his hands."

Now remember, I write down all that I hear; and the next day, if I hear that it is not so, then I write down the contradiction too.

"As a general rule," says Mrs. Gibson, "Government people are sanguine, but the son of one high functionary whispered to Mary G., as he handed her into the car, 'Richmond is bound to go!' Do you know, there is only one doctor in Richmond who will take pay from wounded soldiers? The idea now is that we are to be starved out. Shut us in, prolong the agony, it can then have but one end." In her rage she says: "The Baboon's commissary general." "Who is the

Baboon? Lincoln?" "Oh yes, his best friends say the Yankee President is just the ugliest, most uncouth, the nastiest joker, etc."

Governor Pickens has been telegraphed for more men for Stonewall, for fear Fremont may flank him. Down here, we sleep securely, with the serenest faith that Stonewall is to flank everybody, and never to be flanked himself!

Mrs. Preston and I whisper, but Mrs. McCord scorns whisper. She speaks out. She says: "There are our soldiers; since the world began there never were better. But God does not deign to send us a general worthy of them. I do not mean drill sergeants, or military old maids who will not fight until everything is just so. The real ammunition of our war is faith in ourselves and enthusiasm in our cause. West Point sits down on enthusiasm, laughs it to scorn, wants only discipline. And now comes a new danger, these blockade runners. They are filling their pockets, and they gird and sneer at the fools who fight. Don't you see this Stonewall, how he fires the soldiers' hearts? He will be our leader, maybe, after all. They say he does not care how many are killed. His business is to save the country, and not the army. He fights to win, God bless him! And he wins. If they do not want to be killed, they can stay at home. They say he leaves sick and wounded to be cared for by those whose business it is to do so. His business is war. They say he wants to hoist the Black Flag, have a short, sharp, decisive war and end it! He is a Christian soldier."

"Let us drop all talk of the merciful Christ just now!"

"They say Stonewall comes down upon them like a house afire," said Miss Mary Stark.

Mrs. McCord continued: "The great Napoleon knew all about the business of war. He left nothing to chance and worthless undersnappers. He knew every regiment, its exact number, its officers down to the least sergeant and corporal. Now ask a general here for some captain or major in his command. He stares at you. He has lived up in Wigfall's ballroom, high up in the air, too high up for his business." Miriam told us of a Mrs. V—— in Charleston who was more Confederate than the Confederacy. She railed at that ape Lincoln, to whom she owed her devastated plantations; at Lincoln's hordes, his rascals, his traitors, etc. And yet "Spy" was whispered here and there under the breath. "Disguised," they said, because she wore green goggles, and an enormous straw hat. She was queer looking. No wonder they had hard thoughts of her. Then you know we are all crazy with suspicion in war time. Miriam became acquainted with her in this way:

She had a house to rent in town and Mrs. V—— came to rent it; but she was too fluent, and pointed out to Mem the duty of every woman to remain at her post, to succor the ill and the wounded, to cheer, support and stimulate the fainting soldier. Mem was too great a coward to let her know she was leaving her house because she was afraid to stay. She began to talk highfalutin' back to Mrs. V——. As she saw Mem hesitate, Mrs. V—— offered to pay monthly or weekly, in advance. She said women who left their husbands and sons forfeited them to those who stayed and nursed them. At this Dr. Cohen, whose wife had left the city, showed signs of life. "No sir," she said. "This is not for you. I have a splendid husband already, and three more ready to take his place, in case of accident." Dr. Cohen leaned back, showing signs of relief.

She then related to Mem and Dr. Cohen the only personal conflict she had ever engaged in. "At my friend Fillmore's (the ex-President) I met some Connecticut Yankees. One said, of me, to a little girl: 'Don't let that woman touch you. She is a nigger stealer! She whips Negroes for the fun of it, when she is at home!' I struck a heroic attitude. 'Back, Slanderer! At your peril!' She addressed me as a 'nigger stealer.' I fell aboard of her and pommelled her soundly. Up rushed the husband of the creature, coattails pigeoning in the air as he flew and fluttered. 'Do you think this lady is a slave that you beat her?' My hand was in, so I boxed his ears soundly; and I can tell you the pigeon coattails flew away faster than they came."

Mem insisted that she used Mrs. V——'s very words. "Did you rent her your house?" "I was completely cowed. I dared not refuse to rent her my house, not face to face; so I shilly-shallyed. After she left, I sneaked out as best I might! Then it came out that the Vigilance Committee had its eyes on her."

The lady, however, soon procured a house, which was closed from the time she and her party moved into it. She was seen flitting here and there with a man in uniform. She wrote innumerable letters of the most extravagantly patriotic type, which were always mailed in an open and above-board manner by the person in goggles. Of course they were instantly pounced upon by the sagacious Vigilance Committee and opened and read. One day her landlord received a note from Mrs. V—— saying she had gone for a few days to see her husband, whom she heard was in Richmond, and whom she had not seen for fifteen months. She would be back at once. The confiding landlord spoke of this. "Why! Your house is empty, wide open, deserted!" So the landlord sorrowfully went to see for himself. He found on the front steps a congregation of old oyster-women in tears, milkmen in arms, bread-cart left in the lurch. Hers was the perfect and impartial "pay nobody" style. In Richmond, Mem ran across her would-be tenant again. She held her tongue, for the lady was a lioness. "She was seen in the President's carriage. She was herself the President of many associations, at the head of gunboat fairs, making speeches, instituting bazaars. Then, lo, the poor soul was struck down with fever, and it was death at last with whom she made her flitting."

"Oh, Mem, what a shame to have made us laugh like that at the poor thing! It was a farce and all at once the tragedy sweeps in." "Well, in these climes, and these times, that's the way it all ends."

Thus very unexpected things come about. Now these Yankees; they were depicted to us, held up to us in all the colors of the rainbow, marked cowards; but now in their armies, you know they are not acting so very cowardly!

JUNE 5th. — Beauregard retreating and his rear guard cut off. If Beauregard's veterans will not stand, why should we expect our newly levied reserves to do it? Landing on John's Island and James Island, these awful Yankees! The Yankee General who is besieging Savannah announces his orders are to take Savannah in two weeks time, and then proceed to erase Charleston from the face of the earth!

Albert Luryea was killed in the battle of June 1st. Last summer a bomb fell in the very thick of his company. He picked it up and threw it into the water. A bomb! To put your hand on a bomb! Think of that, those of ye who love your life. The company sent the bomb to his father; inscribed on it was "Albert Luryea, bravest where all are brave." Isaac Hayne did the same thing at Fort Moultrie.

We discussed clever women who help their husbands politically. Some men hate every man who says a good word of or to their wives. These lady politicians, if they are young and pretty, always get themselves a little bit talked about. Does anything pay for that? Besides, the most charitable person will think they must be a trifle too kind, to win such devoted adherents.

Wilmot DeSaussure telegraphs for sandbags, cannon-powder and flatboats. Powder sent, the other things not ready. Those rude Yankees; they will not wait until we are properly prepared to receive them. We take it easy, we love the *dolce far niente*. We are the nine Lotus Eaters. We cannot get accustomed to being hurried about things.

This race have brains enough, but they are not active minded. Those old revolutionary characters — Middletons, Lowndeses, Rutledges, Marions, Sumters — they came direct from active-minded forefathers, or they would not have been here. But two or three generations of gentlemen planters and how changed the blood became! Of late, all of the active-minded men who sprang to the front in our government were the immediate descendants of Scotch or Scotch-Irish; Calhoun, McDuffie, Cheves, Petigru — who Huguenotted his name, but could not tie up his Irish. Our planters are nice fellows, but slow to move; impulsive but hard to keep moving. They are wonderful for a spurt, but that lets out all their strength, and then they like to rest.

June 6th. — Paul Hayne, the poet, has taken rooms here. Mr. Chesnut offered to buy me a pair of horses. He says I need more exercise in the open air. "Come now, are you providing me with the means to beat a rapid retreat? I am pretty badly equipped for marching!"

Our commissary here, being a man, telegraphs to General DeSaussure to know of what kind of cloth sandbags ought to be made. Said I: "A woman by this time would have had half of Columbia sewing night and day with their machines, and the other half sending them off, and the other half filling them with sand!" "But," said my husband without a smile, "they will not be filled with sand until they get to the coast. There is sand enough there."

Now, after all, Johnston Pettigrew and Lomax are alive and in a Yankee prison; at least, so says the New York Herald. What fun for Johnston Pettigrew to read his own splendid obituary. They called him eccentric and crank-brained because he was so much in earnest. He did not waste time haranguing about Kentucky resolutions, States Rights, Cotton is King! That fatuous style left the talkers looking like imbeciles when the time for action came, and the time for talk was over. If we ever have a man who will simply state the business at hand, go direct to the point at issue, and not try to enlighten the universal world by a long speech about everything else — he will be our leader. I foresee that when Gabriel blows his horn, elected Americans will all be found on a platform making long speeches.

Mrs. Rose Greenhow is in Richmond. One half of these ungrateful Confederates say Seward sent her. Mr. Chesnut says the Confederacy owes her a debt they never can pay. She warned them at Manassas, and so they got Joe Johnston and his Paladins to appear upon the stage in the very nick of time. In Washington, they said Lord Napier left her as a legacy to the British Legation, and they accepted the gift — unlike the British nation, who would not accept Emma Hamilton and her daughter, Horatia, though they were willed to the nation by Lord Nelson.

A dreadful scene on the cars. Godard Bailey had heard that Mr. Chesnut was appointed one of the new brigadiers; so, calling on Mr. Chesnut by name, he asked to be appointed one of his staff. Somebody asked who Godard Bailey was; another man got up and denounced Godard Bailey bitterly, using the very ugliest and most exasperating epithets. Mr. Bailey drew his pistol. Mr. Chesnut put his hand on it and forcibly prevented his shooting the man who had so gratuitously insulted him!

One of our boarders here is a German woman. She has been very ill and is still very feeble. Dr. Fair attended her, and Mem says Dr. Fair advised the poor woman today to try and speak English, because German was a very heavy language for one as weak as she was. "A very difficult language to speak," he said, turning to Mem. "If not English, then she had better try French, until she gains some strength." And the woman meekly responded: "My own tongue is lighter for me."

And now a heavy blow! General Johnston, the staff upon whom we leaned so heavily, has had his shoulder blade and two ribs broken in battle. Now what are we to do? Who will take command until he gets well? *

Mem came fresh from the hospital, where she went with a beautiful Jewess friend. Rachel, we will call her (be it her name or no) was put to feed a very weak patient. Mem noticed what a handsome fellow he was, and how quiet and clean. She fancied by those tokens that he was a gentleman. In performance of her duties, the lovely young nurse leaned kindly over him and held the cup to his lips. When that ceremony was over and she had wiped his mouth, to her horror she felt a pair of by no means weak arms around her neck and a kiss upon her lips — a kiss which she thought strong indeed! She did not say a word, made no complaint; but she slipped away from the hospital, and hereafter she will put in her hospital work at long range — no matter how weak and weary, sick and sore, the patients may be.

"And," said Mem, "I thought he was a gentleman!"

"Well," I suggested, "A gentleman is a man after all, and she ought not to have put those red lips of hers so near."

When the ironclads attack Drury's Bluff, then Richmond must go. So say Mrs. Gibson's letters.

* General Joseph Johnston, wounded at Seven Pines, was succeeded in command by Robert E. Lee.

June 7th. — Commissary Jones told Mrs. McCord: "Each sandbag costs fifty-five cents." She answered: "You had but to put two lines in the morning paper, and every woman in Columbia would have been there with her needle and scissors, and they would have cost you nothing."

Cheves McCord's battery on the coast has three guns and one hundred men. If this battery should be captured, John's Island and James Island would be open to the enemy, and Charleston utterly exposed. Mrs. McCord spent the morning with me. She knew Mrs. Pickens before her marriage, at the White Sulphur, several years ago. Governor Pickens brought the beautiful belle, Lucy Holcombe, to see her. Lucy the fair was not slow, and low voiced, and languid then; she was bright and fluttering. Unfortunately, Mrs. McCord directed her conversation to Mr. Pickens; and Miss Lucy Holcombe, who was not accustomed to play second fiddle or to be overlooked, was on her high horse.

Apricots, apricots! I am ill, so my friends have showered apricots on me, and I am not too ill to eat them! Far from it.

The Mercury is reduced to a half sheet. Mrs. McCord stopped her paper when it published a map of the coast defences, in defence of Ripley. By the way, that was a false report. General Ripley is not dead. He has been given a command in Longstreet's division.

Wade Hampton writes to Mrs. Hampton that Chickahominy * was not as decided a victory as he could have wished. Fort Pillow and Memphis are given up. Next? And Next? The Provost Marshall in Richmond orders everyone to furnish a bed for a wounded soldier. If they are not given they will be taken.

June 9th. — Bratten, who married Miss Mann, is taken prisoner; Beverly Mann killed; his mother-in-law a few days ago found stone dead in her bed. Misfortunes enough for one family surely. When we read of the battles in India, in Italy, in the Crimea, what did we care? It was only an interesting topic, like any other, to look for in the paper. Now, you hear of a battle with a thrill and a shudder. It has come home to us. Half the people that we know in the world are under the enemy's guns. A telegram comes to you and you leave it on your lap. You are pale with fright. You handle it, or dread to touch it, as you would a rattlesnake, or worse; for a snake could only strike you. How many, many of your friends or loved ones this scrap of paper may tell you have gone to their death.

When you meet people, sad and sorrowful is the greeting. They

* The battle subsequently called Seven Pines.

press your hand, and tears stand in their eyes or roll down their cheeks as they happen to have more or less self-control. They have brothers, fathers, or sons as the case may be in the battle; and this thing now seems never to stop. We have no breathing time given us. It cannot be so at the North, for the papers say gentlemen do not go in the ranks there. They are officers, or clerks of departments. That is why we see so many foreign regiments represented among our prisoners; Germans, Irish, Scotch. But with us, every company in the field is filled with our nearest and dearest as rank and file, common soldiers.

Miriam's story today: A woman she knew heard her son was killed, but had hardly taken in the horror of it when they came to say it was all a mistake. She fell on her knees with a shout of joy. "Praise the Lord, oh my soul!" she cried in her wild delight. The swing back of the pendulum from the scene of weeping and wailing of a few moments before was very exciting. In the midst of this hubbub, the hearse drove up with the poor boy in his metallic coffin.

Does anybody wonder so many women die. Grief and constant anxiety kill nearly as many women as men die on the battle field. Miriam's friend is at the point of death with brain fever; the sudden change from joy to grief was more than she could bear.

Story from New Orleans: As some Yankees passed two boys playing in the street, one of the boys threw a handfull of burnt cotton at them, saying: "I kept this for you." The other, not to be outdone, spit at the Yankees. "And I kept *this* for you." The Yankees marked the house, a corporal's guard came. Madam was affably conversing with a friend. In vain the friend, who was a mere morning caller, protested he was not the master of the house. He was marched off to prison.

The Mississippi is virtually open to the Yankees, and Beauregard has evacuated Corinth.

Stonewall Jackson said in his quaint way: "I like strong drink, so I never touch it!" May Heaven, who sent him to help us, save him from all harm.

Here is how Mr. Moise got his money out of New Orleans. He went to the station with his two sons, who are still small boys. When he got there, the carriage that he expected was not to be seen. He had no money about his person, for he knew he would be searched. Some friend called out: "I will lend you my horse, but then you will be obliged to leave the children." This offer was accepted, and as he rode off one of the boys called out: "Papa, here is your tobacco, which you have forgot." He turned back and his son handed him a roll of tobacco which he had held openly in his hand all the time. Mr. Moise took it and galloped off. In that roll of tobacco was enclosed twenty-five thousand dollars.

At the church door Mr. Preston joined me. Mary McDuffie was ill, he said, and a child of Mr. Frank Hampton was dying. "And now Madam, go home and thank God on your knees that you have no children to break your heart. Mrs. Preston and I spent the first ten years of our married life in mortal agony over ill and dying children." "I won't do anything of the kind. Those lovely girls I see around you now, they make your happiness. They are something to thank God for, far more than anything I have not."

Mrs. McCord has a Frenchman in her hospital so dissatisfied she thinks he is dangerous. She has taken possession of the College buildings for her hospital. After my failure, illnesses and fainting fits, in Richmond, I have deemed it wise to do my hospital work from the outside. I felt humiliated at having to make this confession of weakness to Mrs. McCord.

Mr. Chesnut traced Stonewall's triumphant career on the map. He has defeated Fremont and taken all of his cannon; now he is after Shields. The language of the telegram is vague, saying only: "Stonewall has taken plenty of prisoners." Plenty, no doubt of it; enough and to spare. But if we can't feed our own soldiers, how are we to feed prisoners?

They denounced Toombs in some Georgia paper which I saw today for planting a full crop of cotton. They say he ought to plant provisions for the soldiers.

Now the Guardian must try its hand at betraying us, after the fashion of the Mercury. It calls Federal attention to Columbia, denouncing the Governor and Council for not fortifying it, demonstrating how easily it could be taken, and explaining what a rich prize it would prove if it fell into Yankee possession. We have all noticed that as soon as our newspapers point out some weak point which needs protection, and have gratified their spleen by abusing men in power for not doing their duty in fortifying such a place, the Yankees quietly go there and seize the defenceless spot so indicated to them.

Every man in Virginia and the eastern part of South Carolina is in revolt because old men and boys are ordered out as a reserve corps, and worst of all, sacred property — that is Negroes — are seized and sent to work on the fortifications along the coast.

June 10th. — General Gregg writes that Chickahominy was a victory lost because Joe Johnston received a disabling wound, and General Smith was ill. The subordinates in command had not been made acquainted with the plan of battle.

A letter from John Chesnut says it must be all a mistake about Hampton's wound, for he saw him in the field to the very last; that is until late that night. Hampton writes to Mary McDuffie (Mrs. Hampton) that the ball was extracted from his foot in the field, and that he was in the saddle all day, but that when he tried to take his boot off at night, his foot was so inflamed and swollen, the boot had to be cut away; and the wound proved more troublesome than he had expected.

Mrs. Preston sent her carriage to take us to Mrs. Herbemont's — Mary Gibson calls her Mrs. Bergamot. Miss Bay came down, ever blooming, in a cap so formidable I could but laugh. It was covered with a bristling row of white satin spikes. She coyly refused to enter Mrs. Preston's carriage, but allowed herself to be over persuaded.

Mrs. McCord makes a frightful list of what her hospital needs. Mr. Chesnut does all he can for her. No wonder she is so devoted to him. Her complaints are never without cause, so he gives heed at once.

I am so ill Mrs. Ben Taylor said to Dr. Trezevant: "Surely she is too ill to be going about. She ought to be in bed." "She is very feeble, very nervous as you say; but then she is living on nervous excitement. If you shut her up she would die at once." A prostration of heart is what I have. Sometimes it beats so feebly I am sure it has stopped altogether. Then they say I have fainted, but I never lose consciousness.

Smith is under arrest for disobedience of orders, Pemberton's orders. This is the third general whom Pemberton has displaced within a few weeks, Ripley, Mercer and now Smith. Another boat has escaped to the Yankee fleet. Whatever the Charleston press fails to communicate daily to the Yankees, a boat openly puts out to sea and tells them the latest news.

Mrs. McCord is as little afraid of personal responsibility as the Jacksons, Andrew or Stonewall. She wishes to remedy the present state of things. "Visiting nurses must consult the head nurse before they dare act. The head nurse must see the steward, and the steward must speak to the doctors. All this complicated machinery takes time. They consult among themselves, and waste time, but the poor wounded soldier consults nobody, and dies while they consult."

I see one new light breaking in upon the black question. My Molly says there is not salt enough on the plantation. "Master had sent to the coast, three days' journey, but we don't git enough. There is plenty of bread, and all the people has fine fat hogs; but you see our people are used to salt as much as they choose and now they will grumble." When I told Mr. Chesnut that Molly was full of airs since her late trip home, he made answer: "Tell her to go to the Devil, she or anybody else on the plantation who is dissatisfied! Let them go. It is bother enough to feed and clothe them now." But when he went over to the plantation, he came back charmed with their loyalty to him and their affection for him.

JUNE 11th. — Sixteen more Yankee regiments have landed on James Island. Eason writes: "They have twice the energy and enterprise of our people." I answered: "Wait awhile. Let them alone until climate and mosquitoes and sand flies and dealing with Negroes takes it all out of them."

It is told of Pemberton, probably because he is a Yankee born, that he has stopped the work of obstruction in the Harbor, and that he has them busy making rat holes in the middle of the city for men to hide in. Why? No one knows. All the cannon is on the Battery, but there are no casemates for men to retire into. It is all crimination and recrimination, everybody's hand against everybody else. Pemberton is said to have no heart in this business, so the city cannot be defended.

Stonewall is a regular brick! Going all the time — winning his way wherever he goes.

Governor Pickens called to see me. His wife is in great trouble, anxiety and uncertainty. Her brother and her brothers-in-law are either killed or taken prisoners.

That splendid little boy of Paul Hayne's says he is a Colonel. He pulls out his commission, given him by Governor Pickens, who is his cousin. "You need not show us that," says Miriam Cohen. "All good Carolinians are entitled to take the rank of Colonel if they have property enough. In Alabama, if the boat takes a hundred bales from a man's plantation, he is a Colonel. Before the war it required from three hundred to a thousand bales to make him a general."

Molly is all in tears because I asked her if she were going to turn against me. No, she would follow me to the ends of the Earth; that is, she would if it weren't for her children. But this is the reason she was out of sorts. Jonathan, her father, is driver; that is, he is head man of the colored people. (She never says Negroes. The only nigger is the Devil, that's her idea.) She says the overseer and the headman of the plows connive together to cheat Master outen everything. Master's the best Master the Lord ever sent, but there's so much lying and cheating on the plantation, it's no wonder she came back outer sorts. "Overseer's wife has gotten so fat on yo' substance she can't get through the little gate, and have to open the wagon gate for her. Sometimes of Sundays two hams is put on their table. Dat woman sho to die of fat." So Molly and I are reconciled, and she is as good and as attentive as ever. All the same, she was awfully stuck up when she first came back.

Tom Taylor says Wade Hampton did not leave the field on account of his wound. "What heroism!" "No, what luck! He is the luckiest man alive. He'll never be killed. He was shot in the temple and that did not kill him! His soldiers believe in his luck." Tom Taylor has a glorious beard, but so far no commission.

General Scott, on Southern soldiers, says we have courage, woodcraft, consummate horsemanship, and endurance of pain equal to the Indians, but that we will not submit to discipline. We will not take care of things, or husband our resources. Where we are, there is waste and destruction. If it could all be done by one wild desperate dash, we would do it; but he does not think we can stand the long blank months between the acts, the waiting! We can bear pain without a murmur, but we will not submit to being bored. Now for the other side. They can wait. They can bear discipline. They can endure forever. Losses in battle are nothing to them. Their resources in men and materials of war are inexhaustible, and if they see fit they will fight to the bitter end. A nice prospect for us, as comforting as the old man's croak at Mulberry: "Bad times, and worse coming!"

"We will wear you out," said General Scott. Now Seward says: "We will starve you out." So nobody is allowed to go out of this huge stockade, and they will not even take their prisoners away, but leave them here to help eat us out of house and home.

Mrs. McCord says that in the hospital, the better born — that is, those born in the purple, the gentry, those who are accustomed to a life of luxury — they are better patients. They endure in silence. They are hardier, stronger, tougher, less liable to break down, than the sons of the soil." "Why is that?" "Because of the something in man that is more than the body."

I know how it feels to die. I have felt it again and again. For instance, someone calls out: "Albert Sidney Johnston is killed." My heart stands still. I feel no more. For so many seconds, so many minutes — I know not how long — I am utterly without sensation of any kind, dead. Then there is that great throb, that keen agony of physical pain.

The works are wound up again, the ticking of the clock begins anew, and I take up the burden of life once more. Someday it will stop too long, or my feeble heart will be too worn out to make that awakening jar, and all will be over. I do not think that when the end comes that there will be any difference, except the miracle of the new life throb. Good news is just as bad. "Hurrah — Stonewall has saved us!" Pleasure that is almost pain!

Miriam's Luryea, and the coincidences of his life. He was the hero of the bomb shell. His mother was at a hotel in Charleston. Kind-hearted Anna de Leon Moses gave up her own chamber to her, so that her child might be born in the comfort and privacy of a home. Only our people are given to such excessive hospitality. So little Luryea was born in Anna de Leon's chamber. After Chickahominy, when this man was mortally wounded, Anna, who is now living in Richmond, found him, and again she brought him home, and again she gave up her chamber to him; and as he was born in her room so in her room he died.

JUNE 12th. — Artie Preston writes: "Never you fear, we will hold James Island." Mr. Chesnut is not so hopeful. He said he had supinely let them possess themselves of the best places from which to bombard and assail us. Mr. Preston says we will not be able to fight on equal terms until our press is muzzled or Seward muzzles them.

New England's Butler, best known to us as "Beast" Butler, is famous — or infamous — now. His amazing order to his soldiers, and comments on it are in everybody's mouth. We hardly expected from a Massachusetts man behaviour to shame a Comanche.

One happy moment in Mrs. Preston's life. I watched her face today as she read the morning papers. Willie's battery is lauded to the skies. Every paper gave him a paragraph of praise.

There was a cry of amazement and horror at the breakfast table when someone declared that no noted public character, no highly placed politician, could do anything so wrong as to disgrace him in this state. Mr. Preston was indignant, and eloquent in defence of the state; but Mrs. Preston's voice was heard in her low, distinct tones. "Henry Junius Nite said that. I have often heard him say that moral obliquity was not an obstacle to a man's rise in public affairs in America. Did you ever see a man cut for any offense whatever?" "Yes, cheating at cards, or cowardice."

I have seen only two men in all my life who were sent to Coventry thoroughly and deliberately. One was a fine young officer in all his bravery of naval uniform, travelling with a rich old harridan at her expense. I asked why no one spoke to him, and they gave me no answer but a smile or a shrug of the shoulder. That was at Saratoga. In Washington I saw Mr. Sickles sitting alone on the benches of the House of Representatives. He was as left to himself as if he had smallpox. I spoke of this now. "What had the poor man done?" "Killed Phil Barton Key." "No, no! That was all right. It was because he condoned his wife's profligacy, and took her back." Chorus: "He had a perfect right to shoot down Key at sight and the jury acquitted him."

"An unsavory subject," said Mrs. Preston with a sniff of disgust. "But there are Crawford, Judge O'Neal, Governor Perry and Mr. Petigru. They openly condemn this war, but no hand is lifted to turn them aside from any public praise or honor."

"We know that they are honest. They have a right to their opinion. They do not take sides against us!" "Now listen! Here it all is in a nutshell. Men may be dishonest, immoral, cruel, black with every crime. But take care how you say so, unless you are a crack shot and willing to risk your life in defence of your words. For as soon as one defamatory word is spoken, pistols come at once to the fore. That is South Carolina ethics. If you have stout hearts — and good family connections — you can do pretty much as you please." Thus ran our tongues.

South Carolina was at Beauregard's feet after Fort Sumter, but since Shiloh she has gotten up and now looks askance when his name is mentioned. Without Price or Beauregard, who will take charge of the Western forces? Beauregard has just lost his wife. She was Mrs. Slidell's sister. They say he is horribly depressed, in a sort of green melancholy; yet this is his second experience of wives who die.

"Can we hold out if England and France hold off?" cries Mem. "No, our time has come." "For shame, faint heart! Our people are brave, our cause just, our spirit and our patient endurance beyond reproach." Here came in Mary Cantey's strident voice. "My woman's instinct tells me, all the same, slavery's time has come. If we don't end it, they will."

After all this, I tried to read "Uncle Tom" and could not. It is too sickening. A man sent his little son to beat a human being tied to a tree. It is as bad as Squeers beating Smike. Flesh and blood revolts. You must skip that; it is too bad, like the pulling out of eyeballs in Lear.

Back to lodgings, and an old lady opposite giggled all the time. She was in a muslin print gown and diamonds. I felt uncomfortable, and wondered if there was anything amiss with me. I dressed in the dusk of the evening. Generally I hold Molly responsible that I shall not be a figure of fun, but this afternoon she was not at home. Maybe the old lady is always so. Some women are born with a constitutional titter, and it holds on till they die.

Mr. Preston's story of Joe Johnston as a boy: a party of boys at Abingdon were out on a spree. There were more boys than horses, so Joe Johnston rode behind John Preston, who is his cousin. While going over the mountain, he tried to change horses and get behind a servant who was in charge of them all. The servant's horse kicked up, threw Joe Johnston, and broke his leg. A bone showed itself. "Hello, boys! Come here and look! The confounded bone has come clear through," called out Joe coolly. They had to carry him on their shoulders. As one party grew tired another took him up. They knew he must suffer fearfully, but he was as cool and quiet after his hurt as before. He was pretty roughly handled, but they could not help it. His father was in a towering rage because his son's leg had to be set by a country doctor, and it might be crooked in the process. Before Chickahominy, brave but unlucky Joe had already eleven wounds.

JUNE 13th. — I have been remembering Decca's wedding, which happened last year in September.* We were all lying on the bed or on sofas near it, taking it coolly as to undress. Mrs. Singleton had the floor. "They were engaged before they went up to Charlottesville," she said. "Alexander was on Gregg's staff, and Gregg was not hard on him. Decca was the worst in love girl I ever saw.

"Letters came from Alex, urging her to let him marry her at once, since in war times human events, and even life, were very uncertain. For several days consecutively, Decca cried without ceasing. Then she consented. We were at the hospital. The rooms were all crowded, so Decca and I slept together in the same room. It was arranged by letter that the marriage should take place. Then after a luncheon at her grandfather Minor's, she was to depart with Alex for a few days at Richmond. That was to be their brief slice of honeymoon.

"The day came, the wedding breakfast was ready and so was the bride in all her bridal array. No Alex! No bridegroom! Alas, such is the uncertainty of a soldier's life. The bride said nothing, but she wept like a water nymph. At dinnertime she plucked up heart and at my earnest request she was about to join us. Then we heard the cry:

* Mrs. Chesnut of course does not say so, but her thoughts were certainly prompted by the fact that Decca — Mrs. Alexander Cheves Haskell — was about to have a baby. The baby was born a week later; and Decca, the mother, died on the 26th of June. Mrs. Singleton was Decca's mother.

The bridegroom cometh! He brought his best man, and other friends. We had a jolly dinner. Circumstances over which he had no control had kept him away.

"His father sat next to Decca, and talked to her all the time as if she were already married. It was a piece of absent-mindedness on his part, pure and simple; but it was very trying, and the girl had had a good deal to stand that morning. You can well understand."

Chorus: "Of course! To be ready to be married, and the man not to come! That's the most awful thing of all we can imagine!"

"Immediately after dinner, the belated bridegroom proposed a walk; so they strolled up the mountain for a very short walk indeed. Decca, upon her return, said to me: 'Send for Robert Barnwell. I mean to be married today.' 'Impossible,' I cried. 'There is no spare room in the house, and no getting away from here, the trains are all gone. You know this hospital is crammed to the ceiling.' But she insisted. 'Alex says I promised to marry him today. It is not his fault he could not come before.' I shook my head. 'I don't care,' said the positive little thing. 'I promised Alex to marry him today and I will. Send for the Reverend Robert Barnwell.' So I yielded. We found Robert after a world of trouble, and the bride, lovely in Swiss muslin, was married.

"Then I proposed they should take another walk, and then I went to one of my sister nurses and begged her to take me in for the night, as I wished to resign my room to Mr. and Mrs. Haskell. When the bride came from her walk, she asked: 'Where are they going to put me?' That was all. At daylight next day, they took the train for Richmond, and the small allowance of honeymoon permitted in war time."

Beauregard's telegram: He cannot leave the Army of the West. His health is bad. No doubt the sea breezes would restore him, but he cannot come now. Such a lovely name, Gustave Toutant de Beauregard; but Jackson and Johnston and Smith and Jones will do, and Lee is short and sweet!

Ransom Spann came to see me and stayed several hours. All these wealthy young planters raised companies, often entirely at their own expense. Now the government, to induce the men to re-enlist for the war, gives them leave to choose their own captains; and as a general rule, the former captain is thrown out. He will not go down to the ranks of his own company, so he comes home to hunt another place with a commission attached. It is really very bad. These men have worked for more than a year to discipline and drill a company any man might be proud of; then the strict martinet goes by the board and they elect a captain, a "good fellow," one of themselves who will not be too strict with them. Ransom Spann says in any case he goes straight back to the army. That sort of rough life in the open air agrees with him. He was never so well and hearty in his life.

And if the worst comes? If we fail? He has selected his vocation. He will be a highway robber; he knows the swamps. "And there will be no danger of meeting runaway Negroes then!" "No — that terror of the swamps will be over." "I am too old and too lazy to work. I mean to harry the new inhabitants who will come to replace us."

"Every day," says Miriam, "They come here in shoals, so-called men who say we cannot hold Richmond, we cannot hold Charleston much longer. Wretched beasts, why do you come here? Why don't you stay there, then, and fight? Don't you see that you are yourselves cowards, coming away in the very face of a battle. If you are not liars as to the danger, you are cowards to run away from it!" Thus roars the practical Miriam, growing more furious at each word; but these Jeremiahs laugh. They think she means the others, not present company.

Tom Huger resigned his place in the United States Navy and came to us. The *Iroquois* was his ship in the old Navy. They say as he stood in the rigging after he was shot in the leg, his ship leading the attack upon the *Iroquois*, his old crew in the *Iroquois* cheered him; and when his body was borne in, the Federals took off their caps in respect for his gallant conduct. When he was dying, Meta Huger said to him: "An officer wants to see you. He is one of the enemy." "Let him come in. I have no enemies now." But when he heard the man's name: "No, no! I do not want to see a Southern man who is now in Lincoln's Navy." The union officers attended his funeral.

Paul Hayne began with Carlyle, which led to Emerson. We were having a good time with Longfellow when Miss Bay interrupted. Whenever we are fairly underway, somebody is sure to come and turn the conversation to rubbish.

June 14th. — Drop a tear for Turner Ashby, the hero of the Valley. They say he is killed! All things are against us, Memphis gone, the Mississippi fleet annihilated; and we hear it all as stolidly apathetic as if it were a story of the English war against China, which happened a year or so ago.

Mrs. McCord gives her whole soul to the hospital. The saddest confusion still prevails, she says; insufficient medical aid, few good nurses. Those she hires eat and drink the things provided for the sick and wounded.* She is the woman to put it straight with her good common sense, her great administrative ability, and her indomitable will.

As Mrs. McCord went away, Reverend Mrs. Young came. She wants rooms here. She laid her hand on my arm and said impressively: "You know I must have a room to myself. No third person must come between me and my God!" "Stupid that I am," said the irrepressible Miriam after she left, "I thought she wanted to be alone for her bath, until she uttered the unexpected word."

The sons of Mrs. John Julius Pringle have come. They were left at school at the North. A young Huger is with them. They seem to have had adventures enough; to get here they walked, waded, rowed in boats if boats they could find, swam rivers when boats there were none. Brave lads! One can but admire their pluck and energy. Mrs. Fisher of Philadelphia gave them money to make the attempt to get home.

While the Middletons were here, our venerable Bay blossom flew in and out, popped in, popped out, upon the most preposterous errands. We could hear her ask of all passers in the corridor: "Who are they?" Alas, in this house, nobody could tell her. Finally she came for Mr. Chesnut and Paul Hayne to be witnesses to her will. "I drew it myself," she said. "I am a lawyer's daughter." Mr. Chesnut said: "It is all wrong." "What does it matter? There is nobody to contend for my estate. I have no heirs." "And very few of us will have any estate to contend for, I fear, before long," said he.

JUNE 16th. — Felt suddenly ill in church. As I tried to slip by Mr. Preston unperceived, he looked up, and in his deepest tragic tones asked: "Shall I go with you?" "No," I snapped in a sharp treble. After service, they came to see why I had forsaken them. The heat was so oppressive I should certainly have fainted.

Stuart's cavalry have rushed through McClellan's lines and burned five of his transports. Jackson has been reinforced by 16,000 men, and they hope the enemy will be drawn from around Richmond, and the Valley be the new seat of war. John Chesnut is in Whiting's brigade, which has been sent to Stonewall. Mem's son is with the Boykin Rangers, and she had persistently wept ever since she heard the news. It is no child's play, she says, when you are with Stonewall. He doesn't play at soldiering, doesn't take care of his men at all. He only goes to kill the Yankees.

* The "nurses" in Southern hospitals were usually men; women volunteers gave many merciful attentions to the wounded, but there were few feminine nurses in the modern sense.

Somebody rushed in to tell us that Wade Hampton, who came home last night, says France has recognized us. Now that is a sure thing. Louis Napoleon does not stop at trifles. He never botches his work, he is thorough; so we hope he will not help us with a half-hand.

June 16th. — (Later.) And now not a word of all this is true. Wade Hampton is here, shot in the foot, but he knows no more about France than he does about the man in the moon. A wet blanket he is, just now; Johnston is badly wounded. Lee is called King of Spades, because he has them all once more digging for dear life. Unless we can reinforce Stonewall, the game is up. Our chiefs contrive to dampen and destroy the enthusiasm of all who go near them. So much entrenching and falling back destroys the morale of any army. This everlasting retreating, it kills the hearts of the men. Then we are scant of powder, etc. My husband is awfully proud of Le Conte's powder manufacturing here. Le Conte knows how to do it, and Mr. Chesnut provides him the means to carry out his plans.

The Hampton girls have asked their father's friends, Mr. and Mrs. Rose, and Mr. and Mrs. Alfred Huger to stay with them at Millwood; to spend the summer at any rate. An anecdote of Mrs. Huger, *née* Rutledge: She was proud of her exquisite figure, and the fashion of the day enabled ladies to appear in next to nothing, pink stockinet and a book muslin, classically cut gown, nothing more. It was this liberal display of herself as nature made her that put the final stroke to Jerome Napoleon.

Mr. Venable don't mince matters. "If we do not deal a blow, a blow that will be felt, it will be soon all up with us. The Southwest will be lost to us. We cannot afford to shilly-shally much longer. Thousands are enlisting on the other side in New Orleans. Butler holds out inducements. To be sure, they are principally foreigners who want to escape starvation. Tennessee we may count as gone, since we abandoned her at Corinth, at Fort Pillow and at Memphis. A real man must be sent there, or it is all gone." In my heart I feel: "All is gone now."

They call Mars' Robert "Ole Spade Lee," he keeps them digging so. Mr. Venable said: "General Lee is a noble Virginian. Respect something in this world! As a soldier, he was as much above suspicion as Caesar required his wife to be. If I remember Caesar's Commentaries, he owns up to a lot of entrenching. You let Mars' Robert alone; he knows what he is about."

"How did the Creoles take the fall of New Orleans?" "Men, women, and children ran around distracted, screaming, chattering, gesticulating. There was no head, no order. All was mere confusion and despair." Then he defended Lovell valiantly, for he charged with all our chivalry. "Lovell had only twenty-five hundred regulars to follow him when he left New Orleans. The crack regiments of New Orleans remained. Butler captured twenty thousand men capable of bearing arms, and now they are spading for Butler at Fort Jackson. Many of the wealthiest citizens are there in their shirt sleeves, spade in hand."

"Tell us of the womenfolk. How did they take it?" "They are an excitable race. As I was standing on the levee, a daintily dressed lady picked her way, parasol in hand, toward me. She accosted me with great politeness and her face was as placid and unmoved as in ante bellum days. Her first question. 'Will you be so kind as to tell me what is the last general order?' 'No order that I know of, Madam. General disorder prevails now.' 'Ah, I see. And why are those persons flying and yelling so noisily, and racing in the streets in that unseemly way?' 'They are looking for a shell to burst over their heads at any moment.' 'Ah!' Then, with a curtsey full of dignity and grace, she waved her parasol and departed, but stopped to arrange her parasol at a proper angle to protect her face from the sun. There was no vulgar haste in her movements. She tripped away as gracefully as she came. She was the one self-possessed soul I saw there in New Orleans; but I saw another woman so overheated and out of breath she had barely time to say she had run miles when a sudden shower came up. In a second she was cool and calm. 'My bonnet — I must save it at any sacrifice.' So she turned her dress over her head and went off, forgetting her country's troubles and screaming for a cab."

At Secessionville, we went to drive the Yankees out, and we were surprised ourselves. We lost one hundred, the Yankees four hundred. They lost more men than we had in the engagement. Fair shooting that! As they say in the West, "We whipped our weight in wildcats" and some to spare. Henry King was killed. He died as a brave man would like to die. From all accounts, they say he had not found this world a bed of roses.

I went to see Mrs. Burroughs at the old de Saussure house. She has such a sweet face, such soft, kind, beautiful, dark grey eyes. Such eyes are a poem. No wonder she had a long love story. We sat in the piazza at twelve o'clock of a June day, the glorious southern sun shining his very hottest; but we were in a dense shade. Magnolias were in full bloom; ivy, vines of I know not what, and roses in profusion closed us in. It was a living wall of everything beautiful and sweet. I have been thinking of it ever since. In all this flower garden of a Columbia, this is the most delicious corner I have been in yet.

More talk of Secessionville. Dr. Tennent proved himself a crack shot. They handed him rifles, ready loaded, in rapid succession; and at the point he aimed were found thirty dead men. Scotchmen in a regiment of Federals at Secessionville were madly intoxicated. They had poured out whiskey for them like water.

I got from the Prestons' French library "Fanny," with a brilliant preface by Jules Janin. Now then, I have come to the worst! There can be no worse book than "Fanny." The lover is jealous of her husband. The woman is for the polyandry rule of life; she cheats both and refuses to break with either. But to criticize it, one must be as shameless as the book itself. Of course it is clever to the last degree, or it would be kicked into the gutter. It is not nastier, or coarser, than Mrs. Stowe; but then it is not written in the interest of philanthropy.

June 21st. — Decca Singleton, now Mrs. Haskell of a short year's standing, has a daughter.

Mr. Preston said of Mrs. ——: "I felt so mortified! It must have been my grey hairs. I called upon her. She came down, she said, as soon as she saw my card. She did not make up for me. I know what that means. It means I am an older man than I thought myself. My dear friend, taken *au naturel*, is sallow and freckled, and so careless in her dress! She had a rough-dried yellow gown. Some of the buttons were missing, and she held it together with her hand. But I stayed two hours, because after all, she is so interesting, charming, fascinating."

Mr. Chesnut gave a quite otherwise account of his reception by her. "Her complexion is the loveliest thing I ever saw, a dazzling pink and white. Her gown was miraculous, white muslin with pink ribbon in knots all over it and around it, and a train a yard long. Her beautiful hair was done up in the most intricate style. She was stiff as a stone, did the *grande dame* for me. It was an awful bore. I only stayed a few minutes."

"Oh! Oh!" said Mr. Preston. "Which of us did she mean to flatter? For me she had her hair *à la chinois*, with the two tails of plaits hanging down behind. She has a noble brow — I did not mind its being bare. I am humiliated. I am an old man, and she has found it out. On another visit she sat on the Goggle board and bounced up and down between every sentence. All that was not Goggle was giggle. She does not put on her dignity with me. I don't mind. She is awfully clever.

. . ." "You mean that her eyes are beautifully blue." "Why not? To have such eyes is the cleverest thing a woman can do."

We had an unexpected dinner party today. First Wade Hampton came and Mary McDuffie; then Mr. and Mrs. Rose. I remember that the late Colonel Hampton once said to me a thing I thought odd at the time: "Mr. James Rose, and" — I forget now who was the other — "are the only two people on this side of the water who know how to give a state dinner." Mr. and Mrs. James Rose; if anybody wishes to describe old Carolina at its best, let them try their hands at painting these two people. Wade Hampton still limps a little, but he is rapidly recovering.

Here is what he said, and he has fought so well that he is listened to. "If we mean to play at war as we play a game of chess, West Point tactics prevailing, we are sure to lose the game. They have every advantage. They can lose pawns to the end of time, and never feel it. We will be throwing away all that we had hoped so much from, Southern, hot-headed, reckless gallantry. The spirit of adventure. The readiness to lead forlorn hopes!"

He says England is sending troops to Canada, and that there is a rumor that Lord Lyons has demanded his passports.

Mrs. Rose is Miss Sarah Parker's aunt. Somehow it came out — when I was not in the room, but those girls tell me everything — that Miss Sarah Parker said: "The reason I cannot bear Mrs. Chesnut is that she laughs at everything and at everybody." If she saw me now, she would give me credit for some pretty hearty crying, as well as laughing. It was a mortifying thing to hear about one's self, all the same.

Mr. Preston came in and announced that Mr. Chesnut was in town, that he had just seen Mr. Alfred Huger, who came up on the Charleston train with him. At Mrs. McMahan's, Lawrence said his master had gone to look for me at the Prestons'; and we met Governor Pickens, who showed us telegrams from the President of the most important nature. The Governor added: "And I have one from Jeems Chesnut, but I hear he has followed it so closely that I need not show you that one. My advice to you is to find him, for Mrs. Pickens says he was last seen in the company of two very handsome women." The two beautiful dames Governor Pickens threw in my teeth were almost neighbours; they live only fifteen miles from Camden.

At Mrs. Preston's, it was a feast of apricots. They break them in half, pile them up on a dish, and you eat them as you do peaches, with cream and sugar.

Mary Gibson says her father writes to them that the Confederates can hold Richmond. *Gloria in Excelsis!*

Another personal defeat. Little Kate says: "Oh, Cousin Mary, why don't you cultivate heart. They say at Kirkwood that you had better let your brains alone awhile, and cultivate heart." She had evidently caught up a phrase and repeated it for my benefit. So that is the way they talk of me! The only good of loving anyone with your whole heart is to give that person the power to hurt you! To hear that those people complained of my want of heart; how it hurt!

June 24th. — Mr. Chesnut, having missed the Secessionville fight by half a day, was determined to see the row around Richmond. He went off with General Cooper and Wade Hampton. Mr. Duncan sent them, for a luncheon on board the cars, ice, wine and every manner of good thing.

Mrs. McCord came for me. Mr. Preston heard with dismay her hospital stories. Dismal enough they are. Dr. ——, a good creature, conscientious to the last degree, does his very best; but the Yankee prisoners sent in a round robin begging "for God sake" that he might be called off; that he was killing them off so rapidly by his zeal without knowledge. So they sent him to Mrs. McCord to try his hand there. Mr. Preston "hoped he would turn traitor and go over and give the Yankees the benefit of his skill." "Anything to get rid of him," said Mrs. McCord. "He is so scientific, so obtusely bent upon being of use to his country."

In all this death and destruction, the women are the same; chatter, patter, chatter. They say: "The Charleston refugees are so full of airs." "Airs, airs!" laughed Mrs. Bartow, parodying Tennyson. "Airs to the right of them, airs to the left of them! Someone had blundered."

A democratic landlady in Raleigh who was asked by Mrs. President Davis to have a carpet shaken, shook herself with rage. "You know, Madam, you need not stay here if my carpet or anything else does not suit you."

John Chesnut gives us a spirited account of their ride around McClellan. I sent the letter to his grandfather. He says the women ran out, screaming with joyful welcome, as soon as they caught sight of the grey uniform. They brought handfulls and armfulls of food for them. One grey-headed man, after preparing a hasty meal for them, knelt and prayed for them as they snatched it. They were in the saddle from Friday until Sunday. They were used up, and so were their horses. He writes for clothes and more horses.

Miss S. C. says: "No need to send any more of his fine horses, to be killed or captured by the Yankees." She will wait and see how the siege of Richmond ends, for though in patriotism she is bent, she bears a frugal mind. The horses will go, all the same, as Johnny wants them.

JUNE 25th. — I forgot to tell of Mrs. Pickens's reception for General Hampton. She met him at the door, took his crutch away, putting his hand upon her shoulder instead. "That was the way to greet heroes," she said. Her blue eyes were aflame; and in response, poor Wade smiled and smiled until his face hardened into a fixed grin of embarrassment and annoyance. He is a simple-mannered man, and does not want to be made much of by women. The butler was not in plain clothes, but wore — as the other servants did — magnificent livery brought from the Court of St. Petersburg. One man in gold embroidery. They had Russian tea and champagne; there was a samovar, a thing to make tea in as it is made in Russia. Little Moses was there. For us, they have never put the servants into Russian livery, nor paraded little Moses under our noses; but I must confess, the Russian tea and the champagne always set before us left nothing to be desired.

"How did General Hampton bear his honours?" I asked. "Well, to the last, he looked as if he wished they would let him alone."

Met Mr. Ashmore fresh from Richmond. He says Stonewall is coming up behind McClellan, and then comes the tug of war. He thinks we have so many spies in Richmond, they may have found out our strategic movements and circumvent them.

Mrs. Bartow's story of a clever Miss Toombs: so many men were in love with her, and the courtship, while it lasted, of each one was as exciting and bewildering as a foot chase. She liked the fun of the run, but she wanted something more than to know a man was in mad pursuit of her. That he should love her, she agreed; but she must love him, too, and how was she to tell? Yet she must be certain of it before she said "yes." So, as they sat by the lamp, she would look at him and inwardly ask herself: "Would I be willing to spend the long winter evenings sitting here forever after, darning your old stockings?" "Never," echo answered. "No, no, a thousand times no!" So each man had to make way for another.

Our girls showed me a letter from a gallant soldier boy who talks well enough, but certainly his ideas of spelling are eccentric. "Oh, I am so glad to hear General Hampton's wound is a slit one," he writes. "Slit one? What does he mean?" "Stupid guesser that you are! A slight wound." "I was thinking the General's boot had been slit."

Captain Shurtz has named his company "Chesnut Light Artillery," and in a very handsome letter says: "Thus identifying it with one of the names by which the Revolution was inaugurated." I confess I found all this very fine, and was in a manner bragging of it. "Oh, we know him! He is our cousin! Let us see his initials; yes, there it is! F. C. Shurtz! Frilled Cotton Shirts."

Wade Hampton sat with Mr. Chesnut in a pew in church. In front of them sat a girl with earrings made in the form of golden ladders. Wade perpetrated the following impromptu:

Lydia swears her prudish ear
No word of love shall ever reach.
Then tell, I pray, why doth she wear
What does another lesson teach?
A sign that's plain to every eye
She's not as deaf as any adder;
And he who hopes to climb so high
Has but to use a golden ladder.

Now did he make that in church, or remember it?

JUNE 27th. — We went in a body (half a dozen ladies with no man on escort duty, for they are all in the army) to a concert. Mrs. Pickens came in alone too. She was joined by Secretary Moses and Mr. Follen. Dr. Berrian came to our relief. Nothing could be more execrable than the singing. Financially, the thing was a great success; for though the audience was altogether feminine it was a very large one.

A telegram from Mr. Chesnut says "Safe in Richmond." That is, if Richmond be safe, with all the power of the Union battering her gates. Not a word from Stonewall Jackson, after all! Strange! Dr. Gibson telegraphs his wife: "Stay where you are. Terrible battle looked for here."

Decca Haskell is dead. Poor little darling! Immediately after her baby was born, she took it into her head that Alex was killed. He was wounded, but they had not told her of it. She surprised them by asking: "Does anyone know how the battle has gone since Alex was killed?" She could not read for a day or so before she died — her head was so bewildered — but she would not let anyone else touch his letters, so she died with several unopened ones in her bosom. When Decca died, Mrs. Singleton fainted dead away, but she shed no tears.

We went there. We saw Alex's mother, who is a daughter of Landdon Cheves. Annie was with us. She said: "This is the saddest thing for Alex." "No," said his mother. "Death is never the saddest thing.

If he were not a good man, that would be a far worse thing." Annie in utter amazement whimpered: "But Alex is so good already." "Yes. Seven years ago, the death of one of his sisters, whom he dearly loved, made him a Christian. That death in our family was worth a thousand lives."

One needs a hard heart now. Even old Mr. Shand shed tears. Mary Barnwell sat as still as a statue, as white and stony. "Grief which can relieve itself by tears is a thing to pray for," said Reverent Mr. Shand.

Came a telegram from Hampton: "All well. So far we are successful." * Robert Barnwell had been telegraphed for. His answer came: "Can't leave here. Gregg is fighting across the Chickahominy." Then said Mrs. Haskell: "My son Alex may never hear this sad news," and her lips settled rigidly. Mr. Barnwell's telegram said Lee has one wing of the army, Stonewall the other.

Anne Hampton came to tell us the latest news, that we have abandoned James Island and are fortifying Morris Island; and she says: "If the enemy will be so kind as to wait, we will be ready for them in two months."

Reverend Mr. Shand and that pious Christian woman Mrs. Haskell — who looks into your very soul with those large and lustrous blue eyes of hers — agreed that the Yankees, even if they took Charleston, would not destroy it. I, sinner that I am, think they will.

To go down to meaner themes: The Clarendon attack upon the Council, because the Council wants to organize a reserve corps and wants to send Negroes to relieve the soldiers working on the fortifications. Naturally, Clarendon does not wish to do either. They need not publish that they would like to stay at home. Everybody knows that already. They gave their sons to their country cheerfully, but when the Council calls for men over forty for the reserve corps, and sacred property in the shape of Negroes † for coast defences, a howl arises. They raise the right hand and swear to protect their lives and property from a disorderly soldiery and the Council. And it is all in such fine language too!

* The Seven Days had begun.

† This question of putting Negroes to work on fortifications was always hotly debated, and the proposal was resisted or vetoed with particular firmness in South Carolina. In the last weeks of the war the South organized a few regiments of Negro soldiers, but it was against strong opposition, and if they ever were put into the fighting, the fact was not generally reported. The refusal of their owners to allow Negroes to be used as laborers on military projects is — in a state so vocal for secession and for the war as South Carolina — difficult to understand or to palliate.

There are people here too small to conceive of any larger business than quarrelling in the newspapers. In such times as these, with the wolf at our doors, men safe in their closets writing fiery articles denouncing those who are at work are beneath contempt. I would arrange it so as to catch every man who has leisure to stay at home and abuse his neighbors, and march him off to the war.

June 28th. — In a pouring rain we went to poor Decca's funeral. They buried her in the little white frock she wore when she engaged herself to Alex Haskell, and which she again put on to marry him about a year ago. She lies now in the churchyard, in sight of my window. Is she to be pitied? She said she had had months of perfect happiness. How many people can say that? So many of us live long dreary lives, and happiness never comes at all.

Alfred Brevard was taken prisoner at Chickahominy. He and another badly wounded Confederate were sent off, guarded by one Yankee. Alfred saw at a little distance General Anderson and his staff. He seized the Yankee, held him in a close embrace, and called to his wounded comrade to disarm him. This the other wounded man did, and they went back to General Anderson. When the General asked: "With your tremendous strength, why did you not take the Yankee prisoner in his turn?" Alfred answered: "I was only too glad to be rid of the companionship of the disagreeable creature."

June 29th. — Victory! Victory heads every telegram one reads now on the bulletin board. It is the anniversary of the battle of Fort Moultrie. The enemy went off so quickly; I wonder if it is not a trap laid for us, to lead us away from Richmond, to some place where they can manage to do us more harm.

And now comes the list of killed and wounded.

Victory does not seem to soothe the sore hearts. Mrs. Haskell has five sons facing the enemy's innumerable cannon. Mrs. Preston two. Mrs. C—— has adopted a languid and helpless manner; but she may talk in as silly a manner as she pleases, she will never deceive anybody into thinking her a fool any more. She rejoiced that her sons were too young to be soldiers. Of course, one fretted and worried about one's husband; but then everyone knew husbands had a way of taking care of themselves. Then she gave us the details of the fight. "McClellan is routed, and we have 12,000 prisoners." Prisoners! My God! What are we to do with them? We can't feed our own people!

For the first time since Joe Johnston was wounded at Seven Pines we may breathe freely. We were so afraid of another General, or of a new one. Stonewall cannot be everywhere, though he comes near it. Magruder did splendidly at Big Bethel. It was wonderful how he played his ten thousand before McClellan like fire flies, and utterly deluded him, keeping him down there ever so long. It was partly the Manassas scare we gave them. They will never be foolhardy again. Now we are throwing up our caps for R. E. Lee.

We do hope there will be no more "ifs." "Ifs" have ruined us. Shiloh was a victory — if Albert Sidney Johnston had not been killed. Seven Pines — if Joe Johnston had not been wounded. At Manassas the "ifs" bristled like porcupines. That victory did nothing but send us off into a fool's paradise of conceit, and it roused the manhood of the Northern people. For very shame, they had to move.

A lady interrupted with a story of schoolboys. "Don't call yourself Jule. Give your whole name." "Julius." The next boy, whose name was Bill, called himself "Billious." Then came Tom — "Thomas." Then Jack, who knew no other way to give himself a proper name than "Jackass."

JUNE 30th. — First came Dr. Trezevant, who announced Burnet Rhett's death. "No," said a listener. "No, I have just seen the bulletin board. It is Julius Grimké Rhett." When the doctor went out, it was added: "Howell Trezevant's death on the battlefield is there too. The doctor will see that, as soon as he goes down by the board."

The girls went to see Lucy Trezevant. The doctor was lying still as death on a sofa, with his face covered. They hurried by him to Lucy's room. Mrs. Trezevant is ill in bed.

At church every face was anxious. The battle was a great deliverance, but the list of killed and wounded is to come. And we hear Halleck is ordered up with fifty thousand fresh troops.

A French man-of-war lies at the wharf in Charleston to take French subjects when the bombardment begins. William Mazyck writes: "The enemy's gun boats are shelling and burning, up and down the Santee River. They raise the white flag, and the Negroes rush down to them. The owners might as well have let these Negroes be taken by the Council to work on the fortifications!"

Mrs. McCord, in her outspoken way, was denouncing a surgeon for some malpractice at her hospital. Mrs. Thornwell (Bravo! Old warhorse!) said promptly: "The man is my nephew! My carriage is at the door. Let us go at once and investigate this matter. If these charges be true, I give him up." Mrs. McCord, nothing daunted, went with Mrs. Thornwell. The charges were true, but the delinquent was not Mrs. Thornwell's nephew but an assistant surgeon.

A doctor spoke roughly to a soldier who wanted a wooden leg: "You can do without it. They are too expensive to give to everybody." "Cheer up, and be of good heart," said Mrs. McCord. "My fine fellow, order your wooden leg and send the bill to me." Mrs. Thornwell said she forgave her on the spot; up to that time she had felt a little wrathy as to the reckless arraignment of her nephew.

July 3rd. — My husband writes from Richmond, under date of June 29:

My Dear Mary:

For the last three days I have been witness of the most stirring events of modern times. On my arrival here I found the Government so absolutely absorbed in the great pending battle that it was useless to talk of the special business that brought me. As soon as it is over, which will probably be tomorrow, I think I can easily accomplish all that I was sent for. The President and General Lee are inclined to listen to me, and to do all they can for us.

General Lee is vindicating the high opinion I have ever expressed of him, and his plans and execution of the last great fight will place him high in the roll of really great commanders. The fight on Friday was the largest and fiercest of the whole war; some sixty or seventy thousand of ours engaged, with great preponderance on the side of the enemy. Ground, numbers, armament, were all in his favor, but our men and generals were superior. The higher officers and men behaved with a resolution and a dashing heroism that has never been surpassed in any country or in any age.

Our line, attacking superior numbers and superior artillery impregnably posted, was three times repulsed. Lee, assembling all the generals, told them that victory depended on carrying the batteries and defeating the army before them, ere night should fall. If night came without victory all would be lost. The work must be done by the bayonet. Our men then made a rapid and irresistible charge, without firing a shot, and carried everything. The enemy melted before them and ran with the utmost speed, though of the regulars of the Federal Government.

The fight between the artillery of the opposing forces was terrific and sublime. The field became one dense cloud of smoke, so that nothing could be seen except the incessant flashes of fire through the clouds. They were within sixteen hundred yards of each other and it rained storms of grape and canister. We took twenty-three pieces of their artillery, many small arms and some ammunition. They burnt most of their stores, wagons, etc.

The victory of the second day was full and complete. Yesterday there was little or no fighting, but some splendid maneuvering, which has placed us completely around them. I think the end must be decisive in our favor. We have lost many men and many officers. I hear Alex Haskell and young McMahan are among them, as well as a son of Dr. Trezevant. Very sad indeed. We are fighting again today. I will let you know the result as soon as possible, and I will be at home some time next week. No letter from you yet.

With devotion,

Yours,

James Chesnut, Jr.

A later telegram from my husband said: "Things satisfactory so far. Can hear nothing of John Chesnut. Saw Jack Preston, safe so far. No reason why we should not bag McClellan's army, or cut it to pieces. Have four to six thousand prisoners already." Then Dr. Gibbes rushed in like a whirlwind to say we were driving McClellan into the river.

Edward Cheves, only son of John Cheves, is killed. His sister kept crying: "Oh, mother, what shall we do? Edward is killed!" But the mother sat dead still, white as a sheet, never uttering a word or shedding a tear. Are our women losing the capacity to weep? The father came today, Mr. John Cheves. He has been making infernal machines in Charleston to blow up Yankee ships.

While Mrs. McCord was telling me this terrible trouble in her brother's family, someone said: "Alex Haskell died of grief!" Stuff and nonsense! Alex will never die of a broken heart, take my word for it.

Late bulletins seem to make it clear that after all, McClellan slipped through our fingers. General Huger is blamed. Mem Cohen says she feels like howling like an Irishman at a wake.

Arrived at Mrs. McMahan's at the wrong moment. Mrs. Bartow was reading to the stricken mother an account of the death of her son. The letter was written by a man who was standing by him when he was shot through the head. "My God!" That was all, and he fell dead. James Taylor was color bearer. He was shot three times before he gave in. Then he said, as he handed the colors to the man next him: "You see I can't stand it any longer," and dropped stone dead.

Three hundred of Mr. Walter Blake's Negroes have gone to the Yankees. Remember, oh ye recalcitrant patriots, property on two legs may walk off without an order from the Council to work on fortifications.

Someone asks: "Why do we wail and whimper so in our soft Southern speech, we poor women?" "Because," said Mrs. Singleton, in her quick and emphatic way, "you are always excusing yourselves. Men here are masters, and they find fault and bully you. You are afraid of them, and take a meek, timid, defensive style." Dramatically I explain: "Dogmatic man rarely speaks at home but to find fault or to ask 'why?' Why did you go? — why, for God's sake, did you come? I told you never to do that! Or — I did think you might have done the other! My buttons are off again, and be d——d to them! The coffee is cold! The steak is tough as the Devil! Ham every day now for a week!"

What a blessed humbug domestic felicity is, eh? At every word, the infatuated fool of a woman recoils as if she had received a slap in the face; and she begins to excuse herself for what is no fault of hers, and explains the causes of failure, which he knows beforehand as well as she does. She seems to be expected to put right every wrong in the world.

The Governor had fifteen guns fired for our victory. The Yankee prisoners say Mac has only taken shelter until his reinforcements arrive. Mrs. General Huger, in a letter to Mrs. Preston asks: "Why are Yankee generals on parole walking about the Spotswood, while ours are in Yankee cells on bread and water?"

When the six girls troop in, I wonder if a handsomer group was ever collected in one room. If it were not for this horrid war, how nice it would be here. We might lead such a pleasant life. This is the most perfectly appointed establishment, such beautiful grounds, such flowers and fruits. Indeed, all that heart could wish is here; such delightful dinners, such pleasant drives, such jolly talks, such charming people. But this horrid war poisons everything.

July 5th. — Frank Ravenel killed! Eheu! Drove out with Mrs. "Constitution" Browne, who told us the story of Ben McCulloch's devotion to Lucy Gwynn. Poor Ben McCulloch. Another dead hero. With Mr. Chesnut and Hayne away, now comes another well-timed attack, a meeting denouncing the Council. Hard lines! We have to work double time, to meet our enemies inside of the state, as well as those from without.

I read a book called "Wife and Ward," the scene laid at the siege of Cawnpore. Who knows what similar horrors may lie in wait for us? When I saw the siege of Lucknow in that little theatre at Washington, what a thrill of terror ran through me as those yellow and black brutes came jumping over the parapets! Their faces were like so many of the same sort at home. To be sure, John Brown had failed to fire their hearts here, and they saw no cause to rise and burn and murder us all, like the women and children were treated in the Indian Mutiny. But how long would they resist the seductive and irresistible call: "Rise, kill, and be free!"

We called at the Tognos' but saw no one. No wonder. They say Ascélie Togno was to have been married to Grimké Rhett in August, and now he lies dead on the battlefield. I had not heard of the engagement before I went there.

JULY 8th. — A gunboat captured on the Santee. So much the worse for us. We do not want any more prisoners, and next time they will send a fleet of boats, if one will not do.

The Governor sent me Mr. Chesnut's telegram with a note. "I received the enclosed telegram at twelve o'clock last night, and would have sent it, but it was so late. You will see that you may have the pleasure of his arrival tomorrow. I regret the telegram does not come up to what we had hoped might be, as to the entire destruction of McClellan's army. I think, however, the strength of the war with its ferocity may now be considered as broken."

Our table talk today: this war was undertaken by us to shake off the yoke of foreign invaders, so we consider our cause righteous. The Yankees, since the war began, have discovered it is to free the slaves they are fighting, so their cause is noble. They also expect to make the war pay. Yankees do not undertake anything that does not pay. They think we belong to them. We have been good milk cows, milked by the tariff — or skimmed. We let them have all of our hard earnings. We bore the ban of slavery; they got the money. Cotton pays everybody who handles it, sells it, manufactures it; but it rarely pays the men who make it. Second-hand, the Yankees received the wages of slavery. They grew rich; we grew poor. The receiver of stolen goods is as bad as the thief. That applies to us too. We received the savages they stole from Africa and brought to us in their slave ships.

There was a fair Texan in the Governor's piazza. Like a mermaid, she sat combing her beautiful hair! She does not stop to parley. She says "yes" and flies. I ought to say "dives," as she is a mermaid.

Miriam says that everybody has his best foot foremost at McMahan's because the stray Englishman there is supposed to be writing a book.

JULY 10th. — Mr. Chesnut has come. He believes from what he heard in Richmond that we are to be recognized as a nation by the crowned heads across the waters. Mr. Davis was very kind. He asked my husband to stay at his house, which he did; and he went every day with General Lee and Mr. Davis to the battlefield, as a sort of amateur aid of the President. Likewise, they admitted him to the informal Cabinet meetings at the President's house. He is so hopeful now that it is pleasant to hear him. And I had not the heart to stick the small pins of Yeadon and Pickens in him, not yet a while.

Public opinion is hot against Huger and Magruder for McClellan's escape.

Dr. Gibbes gave me some letters picked up on the battlefield. One, signed "Laura," tells her lover to fight in such a manner that no Southerner could ever taunt them again with cowardice. She speaks of a man she knows "who is still talking of his intention to seek the bubble reputation at the cannon's mouth," and adds: "The miserable coward! I will never speak to him again." Another writes: "If Hell is a thousand times hotter than a Methodist parson paints it, still I hope all Confederates will be sent there." It was a relief to find one silly young person fill three pages with a description of her new bonnet, and of the old bonnet still worn by her rival. Those fiery damsels who goad their sweethearts bode us no good.

Rachel Lyons was in Richmond, hand in glove with Mrs. Greenhow. Why not? "So handsome, so clever, so angelically kind," says Rachel of the Greenhow, "and she offers to matronize me."

Mrs. Phillips, another beautiful and clever Jewess, has been put in prison again by "Beast" Butler for laughing as a Yankee funeral procession went by.

Mr. Chesnut brought Henry DeSaussure's watch for his wife. At Kingsville he met Captain A. H. Boykin, who gave him Lieutenant Boykin's version of Shannon's treachery. Captain Boykin also told of John Chesnut's prank. Johnny was riding a powerful horse captured from the Yankees. The horse dashed with him right into the Yankee ranks. A dozen men galloped after him shouting "Stuart! Stuart!" Johnny had by that time conquered his horse. The Yankees mistook his mad charge for Stuart's cavalry, broke and fled. These daredevil Camden boys ride like Arabs!

Mr. Chesnut says he was riding with the President. Colonel Browne, the President's aid, was along too. General Lee rode up and, bowing politely, said: "Mr. President, am I in command here?" "Yes." "Then I forbid you to stand here, under the enemy's guns. Any exposure of a life like yours is wrong, and this is useless exposure. You must go back." Mr. Davis answered: "Certainly. I will set an example of obedience to orders; discipline must be maintained." But my husband says he did not go back.

Fighting Dick Anderson, one of the playfellows of my childhood, was ordered to keep his corps in reserve. By some mistake he got in advance, was not supported, and got cut to pieces. Mr. Chesnut, when he tells me anything, adds always: "It is dangerous to repeat what you hear. In military circles there is envy, slander, backbiting, and jealousy. Military jealousy is the worst form of that bad passion." This is disheartening, truly.

He met the Haynes in Richmond. They went on to nurse their wounded son, and found him dead. They were standing in the corridor at the Spotswood — although he was staying at the President's, Mr. Chesnut had retained his room at the hotel — so he gave his room to them. Next day when he went back to his rooms he found that Mrs. Hayne had thrown herself across the foot of the bed and never moved. No other part of the bed had been touched. She got up and went away to the cars, or was led. He says these heart-broken mothers are hard to face.

After all, suppose we do all we hoped! Suppose we start up grand and free, a proud young Republic! Think of all these young lives sacrificed! If three survive for one who is killed, what comfort is that? What good will that do Mrs. Hayne, or Mary DeSaussure. The best and the bravest of our generation are being swept away! Henry DeSaussure has four sons left to honor their father's memory and emulate his example; but those poor boys of between eighteen and twenty years of age — Hayne, Trezevant, Taylor, Rhett — their lives are washed away in a tide of blood. There is nothing to show they were even on earth.

At Kingsville, Mr. Chesnut saw a woman with a basin of water and a sponge and an armful of clean linen, going through the cars washing and dressing the soldiers' wounds. The Governor and Council have organized a hospital there. Dr. Gibbes has it in charge. He says he has dressed the wounds of nearly three hundred as they pass along to their homes. What a comfort it must be to them.

Mem Cohen says a Presbyterian pastor is but a man, pious though he be. Some of the busybodies of the house urged him not to tell Mrs. McMahan of her son's death. He waved them back, tell her he would. The young sister flew out with tears streaming from her beautiful eyes. He drew her to him and tenderly kissed her. Then tough old Mrs.

McMahan came slowly forward, bathed too in tears; but he gave her no kiss. Of course it was a false rumor, for the next mail brought a letter from young McMahan, and then they sent him a telegram and he answered: "I am all right. I am quite alive, thank you." But what amused Mem was the tenderness of the Shepherd for the lambs of his flock, rather than for the old ewes.

July 12th. — Our small colonel, Paul Hayne's son, came into my room. To amuse the child I gave him a photograph album to look over. "You have Lincoln in your book! I am astonished at you! I hate him!" And he placed the book on the floor and struck old Abe in the face with his fist.

Our Englishman told me Lincoln had said that had he known such a war would follow his election, he would never have set foot in Washington, nor been inaugurated; that he had never dreamed of this awful, fratricidal bloodshed. That does not seem the true John Brown spirit, but I was very glad to hear it, to hear something from the President of the United States which was not merely a vulgar joke, and usually a joke so vulgar that you are ashamed to laugh — funny as it is!

I have gone back to my books. "Modeste Mignon" and "Eugénie Grandet" I brought from the Prestons'.

Alex Haskell has come. I saw him, about dusk, ride up and go into the graveyard. I shut my window on that side! Poor fellow!

The Yankees call for three hundred thousand more men. That is a compliment to our prowess. We have never yet had that many in the field, all put together. They say Seward has gone to England and that his wily tongue will turn all hearts against us.

Mr. Browne is here. He told us there was a son of the Duke of Somerset in Richmond who laughed his fill at our ragged, dirty soldiers; but he stopped his laughing when he saw them under fire. Our men strip the Yankee dead of shoes, but they will not touch the shoes of a comrade. Poor fellows, they are nearly barefoot.

July 13th. — Halcott Green came to see us. He says Bragg is a stern disciplinarian, but does not in the least understand citizen soldiers. In the retreat from Shiloh, he ordered that not a gun should be fired. A soldier shot a chicken, and then the soldier was shot. "For a chicken!" said Halcott. "A Confederate soldier for a chicken!"

Mrs. McCord's troubles are often amusing. She says a lady who is also a beauty had better leave her beauty with her cloak and hat at the hospital door. One lovely lady asked a rough old soldier, whose wound could not have been dangerous: "Well, my good soul, what can I do for you?" "Kiss me!"

Mrs. McCord's fury was at the woman's telling it. She knew there were women who would boast of an insult, if it ministered to their vanity. She wanted her helpers to come dressed as Sisters of Charity, not as fine ladies. Then there would be no trouble. When she saw them coming in angel sleeves, displaying all of their white arms and in their muslin showing all of their beautiful white shoulders and throats, she felt disposed to order them off the premises.

Mrs. Bartow goes in her widow's weeds. That is after Mrs. McCord's own heart. But Mrs. Bartow has her stories, too. A surgeon said to her: "I give you no detailed instruction. A mother, necessarily, is a nurse." She passed on quietly, "as smilingly acquiescent, my dear, as if I had ever been a mother of anything." Mrs. Bartow stands up at a desk and cuts bonds apart. Miss Carroll calls the ladies who do that "Revenue Clippers."

I walked up and down the college campus with Mrs. McCord. The buildings are all lit up with gas. Soldiers were seated under the elms in every direction, in every stage of convalescence. We could see, through the open windows, the nurses inside, moving about their tasks. It was a strange weird scene.

Last night the Edgefield Band serenaded Governor Pickens. Mr. and Mrs. Harris stepped out on the porch and sang the Marseillaise for them. It is more than twenty years since I last heard her voice. It was a very fine one then, but there is nothing which the tooth of time lacerates more cruelly than the singing voice of women. There is an incongruous metaphor for you!

The Negroes on the coast received the Rutledge's Mounted Rifles apparently with great rejoicings, and the troops were gratified to find the Negroes in such a friendly state of mind; but one servant whispered to his master: "Don't you mind 'em! Don't trust 'em!" So the master dressed himself as a Federal officer and went down to a Negro quarter that night. The very first greeting: "Massa, you come for ketch rebels?" "We show you whey you can ketch thirty tonight." So they took him to the Confederate Camp, or pointed it out; then added: "We kin ketch officer for you whenever you want 'em."

We met Dr. Gibbes weeping and wailing. He is afraid his arm will have to be cut off from some hurt he received in the hospital at Kingsville. If his arm is amputated, I hope it will be buried with all the honours of war, for it was wounded in manful work; in saving life, not taking it.

Bad news. Gunboats pass Vicksburg. The Yankees are spreading themselves over our fair Southern land like red ants. Did you ever see a black ants' nest which red ants had marked for their own?

JULY 21st. — General Huger is sent to inspect ordinance. Is he thus sent to Coventry? Jackson has gone into the enemy's country. Joe Johnston and Wade Hampton are to follow.

I see that Mr. Senator Rice, who sent us the buffalo robes, from his place in the Senate speaks of us as savages, who put powder and whiskey in the soldiers' canteens to make them mad with ferocity in the fight. No, never! We admire coolness here — because we lack it. We do not need to be fired by drink to be brave. My classical lore is small indeed, but I faintly remember something of the Spartans, who marched to the music of lutes. No drum and fife was needed to fillip their fainting spirits. In that, we think we are Spartans. The powder, we cannot spare from our muskets. Alas, we have so little of it, and we need so much.

Mrs. Fisher and Mrs. Izard have instituted a Wayside Hospital,* at the point where all the railroads meet; at the Columbia junction, in fact. I am ready and thankful to help in every way, by subscription and otherwise; but I am too feeble in health to attend in person. All honor to Mrs. Fisher.

Mrs. Carrington is at Mrs. Preston's, nursing a wounded son. "Have you seen him?" "No, the girls say there is nothing to see, that he is reduced to freckles and whiskers!" "For shame! To laugh at a wounded hero."

Mrs. Browne heard a man say, at the Congaree House: "We are breaking our heads against a stone wall. We are bound to be conquered. We cannot keep it up much longer against so powerful a nation as the United States of America. Crowds of Irish, Dutch and Scotch are pouring in to swell their armies. They are promised our possessions, and they believe they will get them. Even if we are successful, we cannot live without Yankees!" "Now," says Mrs. Browne,

* This was the first of many Wayside Hospitals established in the South. Their function was to relieve, in every possible way, wounded soldiers on their way to the regular hospitals or to their homes. Food, refreshment, clean bandages, clean clothing and medical treatment thus provided helped to ameliorate the ordeal of travel on the crowded, dirty and uncertain trains. At the Columbia junction, wounded men might have to wait for days before trains arrived to take them on to their destination.

"I call him a Yankee spy. Why is he not taken up? In the North, Seward's little bell would tinkle, a guard would come, and the Grand Inquisition of America would order that man to be put under arrest in the twinkling of an eye."

Mr. Preston said he had the right to take up anyone who was not in his right place and send him where he belonged. I said: "Then do take up my husband, instantly. He is sadly out of his right place, in this little Governor's Council." Mr. Preston stared at me, and slowly uttered in his most tragic tones: "If I could put him where I think he ought to be!" This I immediately hailed as a high compliment and was duly ready with my thanks, but upon reflection, it is borne in upon me that he might have been more explicit. He left too much to the imagination!

Then Mrs. Browne described the Prince of Wales on his visit to Washington before this war. His manners, it seems, differ from those of Mrs. ——, who arraigned us from morn to dewy eve, and upbraided us with our ill-bred manners and customs. The Prince conformed at once to whatever he saw was the way of those in whose house he was. He closely imitated President Buchanan's way of doing things. He took off his gloves at once, when he saw that the President wore none. (By the by, I remember what a beautiful hand Mr. Buchanan has.) The Prince of Wales began by bowing to the people who were presented to him; but when he saw Mr. Buchanan shaking hands, he shook, too. Smoking affably with Browne in the White House piazza, he expressed his content with the fine segar Browne gave him. The President said: "I was keeping some excellent ones for you, but Browne has got ahead of me." Long after Mr. Buchanan had gone to bed, the Prince ran into his room in a jolly, boyish way. "Mr. Buchanan, I have come for the fine segars you have for me."

The British contingent liked Floyd best of our Cabinet Ministers. Jake Thompson and Howell Cobb were too boisterous; they laughed too loud and too often.

As I walked up to the Prestons' along a beautifully shaded back street, a carriage passed with Governor Means in it. As soon as he saw me, he threw himself half out of the carriage and kissed both hands to me, again and again. It was a whole-souled greeting, and I returned it with my whole heart too. "Good-bye," he cried, and I answered "Good-bye." I may never see him again. I am not sure that I did not shed a few tears. Mr. Preston and Mr. Chesnut were seated in the piazza of the Hampton House as I walked in. I opened my batteries upon them in this scornful style. "You, you cold, formal, solemn, overly polite creatures, so weighed down by your own dignity; you will never know the rapture of such a sad farewell as John Means and I have just interchanged. He was in a hack and I was on the sidewalk. He was on his way to the wars, poor fellow. The hackman drove steadily along in the middle of the street. But for our grey hairs, I do not know what he might have thought of us. John Means does not suppress feelings at the unexpected meeting with an old friend, and a good cry did me good, too! In this life of terror and foreboding we lead, my heart is in my mouth half of the time. But you two, under no possible circumstances could you so forget your manners."

I read Russell's "India" all day. Saintly folks, those English, when their blood is up. Sepoys and blacks we do not expect anything better from, but what an example of Christian patience and humanity the white "angels" from the West set them.

The beautiful Jewess, Rachel Lyons, was here today. She flattered Paul Hayne so audaciously, and he threw back the ball. She is daft about Mr. Chesnut, but Miriam Cohen says she has not learned his hours yet, since so far she has always called to see me when he was away from home. She gave Paul Hayne the benefit of her philosophy. "Married or single, all men are alike to me." She could only marry one of her own faith. She asked me what I understood by the word "flirtation," and answered her own question. "A mere pretense of love-making; a semblance of love, not the reality. As soon as love itself was waked, it was no longer a flirtation. Is kissing legitimate in a flirtation? Some girls say you cannot keep a man off and on, as it is necessary to do in a flirtation, unless you let him kiss you. Indeed, he will kiss you!" Here Mem Cohen's face assumed such a look of amazement and disgust that Miss Lyons brought herself up shortly. "I think such freedoms horrid. I never let men kiss me!"

Today I saw the Rowena to this Rebecca. Mrs. Robert Barnwell called. She is the purest type of Anglo-Saxon, exquisitely beautiful, cold, quiet, calm, lady-like, and fair as a lily, but with the blackest and longest eyelashes, and her eyes so light in color that someone said: "they are the hue of cologne and water." The effect is startling, but lovely beyond words.

If I chronicled all of the good things sent me, I would have time to write nothing else; but the tray of peaches and musk melons which came to me today from Mrs. Guignard is really so great a treat that it deserves honorable mention.

Another style of beauty came today. She was as handsome as any of them, Jew or Gentile, and brilliant in her conversation. But when she thinks she has made a point, she screams with delight and slaps you on the knee.

Blanton Duncan told us a story of Morgan in Kentucky. He walked into a court where they were trying some secessionists. The judge was about to pronounce sentence, but Morgan rose and begged that he might be allowed to call some witnesses. The Judge asked who were his witnesses. "My name is John Morgan, and my witnesses are fourteen hundred Confederate soldiers."

Mrs. Izard witnessed two instances of patriotism among the people we call "sandhill tackeys." One woman, a forlorn, chill, and fever-freckled creature, yellow, dirty, and dry as a nut, was selling peaches at ten cents a dozen. Soldiers collected around her cart. She took the top off and cried: "Eat away. Eat your fill, I never charge our own soldiers anything." They tried to make her take pay, but when she steadily refused it, they cheered her madly and told her: "Sleep in peace. Now we will fight for you, and keep off the Yankees." Another poor sandhill man refused to sell his cows, but gave them to the hospital instead.

I have letters from Harriet Grant and from Mary DeSaussure: The one pitifully asks that my husband try to get some news of Mrs. Brownfields's son, who is reported dead, but whom Mrs. Brownfield still hopes may be alive; the other thanks me for my letter of sympathy and tells me how to send Mr. DeSaussure's watch. Recalling all the ties it dissolves, all the blood it commands to flow, all the healthy industry it arrests, all the mad men it arms, all the victims that it creates, I question whether one man really honest, pure, and humane who has gone through such an ordeal could ever hazard it again unless he is assured victory is secure; yes, and that the object for which he fights will not be wrested from his hands amidst the uproar of the elements that the battle has released.

XV

Flat Rock

August 2nd, 1862. — I am in Flat Rock, North Carolina. I left Mrs. McMahan's to come to this pleasant spot, hoping to find cool weather. I was ill, and it was very hot and disagreeable for an invalid in a boarding house in that climate. The La Bordes, and the McCord girls came part of the way with me.

The cars were crowded, and a lame soldier had to stand, leaning on his crutches in the aisle that runs between the seats. One of us gave him our seat. You may depend upon it, there was no trouble in finding a seat for our party after that feat. Dr. La Borde quoted a classic anecdote. In some Greek assembly, an old man was left standing and a Spartan gave him his seat. The Athenians cheered madly, but they kept their seats. The comment: "Lacedemonians practise virtue, Athenians know how to admire it."

Nathan Davis happened to be at the station at Greenville. He took immediate charge of Molly and myself — for my party had dwindled to that. He went with us to the Granville hotel, sent for the landlord, told him who I was, secured good rooms for us, and saw that we were made comfortable in every way.

At dinner I entered that immense dining-room alone, but I saw friends and acquaintances on every side. My first exploit was to repeat to Mrs. Ives, Mrs. Pickens's blunder in taking a suspicious attitude toward men born at the North, and then calling upon General Cooper to agree with her. Martha Levy explained the grave faces of my audience by telling me that Colonel Ives was himself a New Yorker. My distress was dire.

Mrs. Ives's brother, Senator Semmes of Louisiana,* danced a hoedown for us; a Negro, corn-shucking, heel-and-toe fling with a grapevine twist and all. Martha Levy applauded heartily and cried: "The Honorable Senator from Louisiana has the floor!"

Louisa Hamilton was there. She told me that Captain George Cuthbert, with his arm in a sling from a wound by no means healed, was going to risk the shaking of a stage coach. He was on his way to his cousin William Cuthbert's, at Flat Rock. Now George Cuthbert is a type of the very finest kind of Southern soldier. We cannot make them any better than that. Before the War I knew him. He travelled in Europe with my sister Kate, and Mary Withers. At once I offered him a seat in the comfortable hack Nathan Davis had engaged for me.

Molly sat opposite to me, and when I was so tired she held my feet in her lap. Captain Cuthbert's man sat with the driver, so we had ample room. I was so ill I could barely sit up, and Captain Cuthbert could not use his right hand or arm at all. I had to draw his match and light his segar. He was very quiet, grateful, gentle; I was going to say docile. He is a fiery soldier, one of those whose whole face becomes transfigured in battle — or so one of his men told me, describing his way with his company. He does not blow his own trumpet, but I made him tell me the story of his duel with the Mercury's reporter. He seemed awfully ashamed of wasting time in such a scrape.

That night we stopped at a country house, halfway toward our journey's end. There we met Mr. Charles Lowndes, whose son is with Hampton. General Ripley in his report tried to put a stigma upon his aids, Lowndes and Kirkland, but he failed utterly. Everybody knew them, and knew him; and their behavior since then has made his bad report more absurd still.

First we drove by mistake into Judge King's yard. Our hack man supposed that was the hotel. Then, as the seafaring men say, we "made" the Farmers' Hotel. Burnet Rhett was at the door, caparisoned, horse and man, with as much red and gold artillery uniform as they could bear. His stirrups, Mexican I believe, looked like little side saddles. Seeing his friend and crony George Cuthbert alight and

* The Senator's brother was Admiral Raphael Semmes, commander of the *Alabama*. Mrs. Semmes, the Senator's wife, was one of the most popular hostesses in Richmond during the war. The performance of *The Rivals* at the home of Mrs. Ives, the Senator's sister, which occurred in February, 1864, was the best-remembered social event in the Confederate capital during the War.

leave a veiled lady in the carriage, this handsome and undismayed young artillerist walked round and round the carriage, talked with the driver, and looked in at the doors. Suddenly I bethought me to raise my veil and satisfy his curiosity. Our eyes met, and I smiled. It was impossible to resist his comic disappointment at seeing a woman old enough to be George Cuthbert's mother, with the ravages of a year of gastric fever on her face, and almost fainting with fatigue. He instantly mounted his gallant steed and pranced away to his fiancée. He is to marry the greatest heiress in the state, Miss Aiken. Then Captain Cuthbert told me his name. Elbert Elmore says there is great choice in Rhetts; that a first-rate Rhett is one thing, but a second-rate Rhett is the devil. Captain Cuthbert said this was a first-rate Rhett.

At Kate's, I found Sally Rutledge; and then for weeks, life was a blank. I remember nothing. The illnesses which had been creeping on for so long a time took me by the throat.

Before he left Flat Rock, Captain Cuthbert dined at Kate's, his arm still in a sling. The little girls were so proud that they were allowed to sit by him, cut up his food, and do everything that the want of a right arm made him helpless to do for himself. Captain Cuthbert was wounded at Manassas, but got back in time for Seven Pines.

At Greenville I witnessed the wooing of Barney Heyward, once the husband of the lovely Lucy Izard, now a widower. He was there nursing Joe, his brother. So was the beautiful Henrietta McGruder, now Mrs. Joseph Heyward. Poor Joe died. It was Barney and Tatty Clinch. There is something magnetic in Tatty Clinch's large and lustrious black eyes. No man has ever resisted their influence. She says her virgin heart has never beat one throb the faster for any mortal here below — until now. Barney Heywood is the mortal.

XVI

Memories

August 2, 1862 to October 27, 1863

I destroyed all my notes and journal * covering my arrival at Flat Rock, and what followed, during a raid upon Richmond in 1863; and afterward I tried to fill up the gap from memory. So this is no longer a journal, but a collection of memories. I will tell all I know of that brave spirit, George Cuthbert. During the winter of 1862–63, while I was living at the corner of Clay and Twelfth Streets, he came to see me. The Preston girls were staying at my house then, and it was very gay. We had heard of him as gallantly facing odds at Sharpsburg, and he asked that if he were wounded I should have him brought to Clay Street. He was shot at Chancellorsville, leading his men. The surgeon did not think him mortally wounded. He sent me a message that he was coming at once to our house. He "knew he would soon get well there." Then he asked one of his friends to write a letter to his mother. Afterwards, he said, he had another letter to write, but that he wished to sleep first. At his request they then turned his face away from the light and left him; and when they came again they found him dead. It was bitter cold, and the wounded who had lost so much blood often weakened in that way, lacking warm blankets and all comforts; and many died who might have been saved by one good hot drink or a few mouthfuls of nourishing food.

I remember that while I was in Flat Rock, Daniel Blake drove down

* There is here a hiatus in the Diary, as Mrs. Chesnut explains. In October, 1863, she wrote her memories of the fourteen intervening months. Since they are more important as a picture of the time than as history, no attempt has been made to arrange the incidents she describes in chronological order.

to my sister's, in his heavy substantial English phaeton, with stout and strong horses to match. I went back with him and spent two delightful days at his hospitable mansion. I met there as a sort of chaplain, the Reverend Thomas Davis of Camden. He dealt unfairly by me. We had a long argument, and when we knelt down for evening prayers he prayed for me most palpably. There was I, down on my knees, red-hot with rage and fury. It was a clear case of hitting a fellow when down! Afterwards, the fun of it all struck me, and I found it difficult to keep from shaking with laughter.

While I was still in Flat Rock came the fatal Sharpsburg. My friend Colonel Means was killed on the battlefield. His wife had not recovered from the death of her other child, Emma, who had died of consumption early in the war. She was lying on a bed when they told her of her husband's death. Their son, too, was wounded, but they tried to keep his condition from her. They think now that she misunderstood, and believed him dead too. She threw something over her face, she did not utter one word. She remained quiet so long, and then someone removed the light shawl which she had drawn over her head. She was dead.

These sad, unfortunate memories — let us run away from them.

During the rest of 1862, this is what my husband did. All of our South Carolina troops were in Virginia. He imported arms through the Trenholms,* enough for our men and more, till he had arms to sell to the Confederacy. He laid the foundation of a nitre bed; and the Confederacy sent to Columbia to learn from Professor Le Conte how to begin theirs. My husband bought up all of the old arms and had them altered and repaired. He built ships. He imported clothes and shoes for our soldiers; he imported cotton cards, and set all idle hands carding and weaving. He tried to stop the sale of whiskey. And alas, he committed the unforgiveable offense of sending the sacred Negro property to work on fortifications, away from their owners' plantations.

Sending laggards to the front by conscription, organizing the reserves, taking a part of the Negroes from the crops and sending them to the coast fortifications where they had a chance to run away — these measures raised such a tempest of wrath against the Council that although it would die a natural death in December, the convention

* George A. Trenholm of Charleston, who later served as Secretary of the Confederate Treasury, was head of the firm of Fraser, Trenholm & Company which owned and operated a large fleet of blockade runners.

was called to annihilate it at once; in plain English, to try the Council for its life. But instead, it pronounced a eulogy on the Council and its work. Colonel Chesnut was exonerated from all blame and applauded for the amount of good he had done in so short a time.

Nevertheless, Bonham of Edgefield being made Governor, we left Columbia in a blaze of anger, made a brief stay at home, and then went on to Richmond, Mr. Davis having appointed Colonel Chesnut on his Staff.

We journeyed to Richmond in company with Mrs. Stanard, one of the leaders of society in that city for twenty years, beautiful and agreeable still. Molly, who is a capital cook, besides being so good as a lady's maid, had looked after our lunch basket; and Mr. Chesnut had selected his wine and brandy from his father's cellar. As Mrs. Stanard ate, and sipped the old brandy, she smiled in his face. "My dear friend, if one will eat, they must drink." Mr. Phoenix was along, the man who married Cissy Blake. He drank to some purpose. He simply disappeared. I did not see him go. I looked under the seat to see if there was a hole in the floor of that rickety old car, thinking he had dropped through.

Before we left Columbia, we saw Cheves McCord at his mother's. He had been badly wounded at Second Manassas, in both the head and the leg. Mrs. McCord went at once to Richmond and found he was still near or at Manassas Junction. She went to Mr. Miles to get a passport to go for him. He said the thing was impossible, that the Government had seized all trains, and no passports were being given. "I let him talk," said Mrs. McCord, "for he does it beautifully. But that very night, I chartered a special train and ran down to Manassas and brought back Cheves in triumph. Now he is nearly well, with our home nursing." But he grew restless, and insisted on returning to camp, though he was not fit for duty. The ball had never been removed from his head, and it gave him so much trouble that his servant brought him from the camp back to Richmond. He died that night, at the home of Mrs. Myers, a friend of theirs. I think I shed the bitterest tears that ever came into my eyes for him, cut off so soon, and for his mother!! Not twenty-one yet, his beautiful bride, and his baby unborn.

In Richmond we lodged first at the Ballard house, and then made our home with some "decayed ladies" forced by trouble, loss of property, etc., to receive boarders. A dreadful refuge of the distressed it was. The house was comfortable, and the table good; but you paid the most extravagant price, and you were forced to assume the patient humility of a poor relation; so fine was the hauteur and the utter scorn with which you were treated.

Mr. and Mrs. Davis met us with warmth and cordiality. Once for all let me say, Mrs. Davis has been so kind to me that I can never be grateful enough, yet even without that I should like her. She is so clever, so brilliant, so warm-hearted and considerate toward all who are around her. After becoming accustomed to the spice and spirit of her conversation, when one is away from her, things seem flat and tame for a while.

For the winter of 1862–63, we took a floor in the house of a Mrs. Lyons, at the corner of Clay and Twelfth. We had a drawing-room, dining-room, chamber, and two servants' rooms for Molly and Lawrence. When the Preston girls came to stay with us, we changed the dining-room into an apartment for them. The poor drawing-room saw rare sights. It was the only parlour we had, and the only dining-room; but we danced — to the music of an old ramshackle piano — and had a good time generally. We received there all that the Confederacy had of good and great, from Mr. President Davis, the Lees, and Mr. Hunter, down to the humblest private — who was often our nearest friend or relative. We had no right to expect any better lodgings, for Richmond was crowded to suffocation, with hardly standing room left.

At first Mr. Chesnut was too civil by half. I knew it could not last, his going everywhere with us, to parties, to concerts, to private theatricals, and even to breakfasts. Then he broke down and denounced us for being so dissipated. Mr. Davis came to our relief and sent the recalcitrant head of our household to inspect and report on Charleston and on Southern armies generally.

The night the Preston girls came, they found me dressing for a party at the Semmes and Ives houses. I made them go with me. There was nothing then or ever in the Confederacy so sweet, so lovely, so stately, so accomplished as those young friends of mine. From the time they came until they left one month after, it was one scene of perfect enjoyment. We had no battle — Fredericksburg was over, and the Wilderness not yet dreamed of. The town was filled with our friends, and it was our duty to make our soldiers forget the discomforts of camp when they ran down for a few days. Buck, the very sweetest woman I ever knew, had a knack of being fallen in love with at sight, and of never being fallen out of love with. But there seemed a spell upon her lovers; so many were killed or died of the effects of wounds;

Ransom Calhoun, Braddy Warwick, Claude Gibson, the Notts.

Once she came in and sat on the edge of my bed. A cloud had come over her bright face. "Buck, what makes you so pale, dear, and why have you that black mantle around you on this warm day?" "Why not? I feel so sad. Black suits me. Alfred Rhett has killed Cousin Ransom in a duel." Here she drew the mantle close around her face. "You know, he was so good to me in those years while I was left at school in Paris. How can I forget it all?"

She wore the black mantle several days; but the days were beautiful, and she so young and light-hearted. Her grief was but a summer cloud, fleeting, and leaving no trace behind. "What is the matter with Buck?" John Derby asked. "She has been languishing on that sofa, profoundly indifferent to me, and to the rest of mankind?" "Don't you know her yet? She would not listen to that poor fellow while he was alive, and now that he is dead she is broken-hearted. Let her alone, she will soon recover."

Johnny was asked if he were not succumbing, too, to Buck's fascinations. It was a road they all travelled. "No, never." He looked alarmed at the bare suggestion. "I dare not. I would prefer to face a Yankee battery. They say: 'So and so is awfully in love with Miss Preston.' Then I say: 'Look out! You will see his name next, in the list of killed and wounded.' "

This was very hard on Buck, but our brave young soldiers faced the music gallantly. Let who would die or be killed, there was always a new crop of flourishing dimensions growing vigorously around her. Lovers were never wanting, though she was loyal to the dead and missing. The darling! Who can describe her? This I know; I would not, if I could, have anything altered about her — mentally, morally, physically. Of how many people can one say that?

In Richmond we had delightful teas at Mrs. Stanard's and at Mrs. Randolph's, where statesmen and warriors were invited to meet us without stint, and what few literate they could bag or scare up. Then there were splendid dinners at the McFarland's and Lyons's.

Johnny, now Captain Chesnut of the Dragoons, came for a visit. We managed to get a room for him from Mrs. Lyons. He had two servants, and the girls had theirs. Mr. Chesnut had left Lawrence to cater for us.

Lawrence has simple ideas, but effective. "You give me the money, I'll find everything you want." There is no such word as fail with him. "There ain't nothing to eat in Richmond, not a bit of it; but you give me the money." Molly was housekeeper, cook, anything and everything as the time required.

One night we came from a ball and found Molly and Anne in the drawing-room with a huge fire and the gas lit. "Well, we have had our frolic, too," she said. "Anne and me are going to do all of our clear-starching and ironing in here when you are out of our way. There you go, night after night, with your sinful frolicking!" Molly and Anne were pious Methodists, to whom dancing was a crime against religion. They were our maids. We had washerwomen, with whom we were satisfied, but not so our maids. They turned up their noses at such washing and ironing, but we would never have asked these creatures to wash and iron by day, much less by night. Anne said: "Marster say to our white people, 'For God sake, don't economise in your washerwomen bill!' "

The infant Samuel came, spruce, dapper, pleasant as ever, a perfect magazine of news. After a week or two, adding very much to our company, suddenly he sank beneath our horizon. We heard that a stormy life in front of the Spotswood had led to friends bodily forcing him back to the Army. Then came letters from him, in shoals. One in particular, containing an euphemistic expression which caused me a laugh and a groan: "I could not present myself before you with the flush of wine upon my brow!"

Every night our parlour was crammed to its utmost capacity. John Darby, who appeared simultaneously with the Preston contingent, taught them to play Casino, and that was the favorite game. There was an immense amount of taffy made. We were happy. These were days of unmixed pleasure, snatched from the wrath to come.

Of course, there were never chairs enough. One night we witnessed the republican independence of the Wigfalls. Mr. Hunter of Virginia came in with Miles and Garnett, and L. Q. Washington made a signal to me. I turned and saw that the President of the Confederacy had quietly entered, and was standing in front of the Wigfalls. They kept their seats — and turned their backs on him! It seems incredible! Somebody whispered, as I passed rapidly to that end of the room: "Bully! The Wigfalls are trying to snub Jeff Davis!"

I am sure the President did not notice it, for the rest of us made obeisance before him, as was due to his position. I was proud to receive him in my house as himself, Jeff Davis; the others stood up to receive the head of the Confederacy as well.

Once the President gave us a breakfast. His aids were all there; the

Prestons and myself the only ladies. He was so kind and so amiable and agreeable, we were all charmed; and Buck came away in a very ecstasy of loyalty. As we got into the lonely Clay Street house she hurrahed for Jeff Davis and professed her willingness to fight for him to the death. When Mrs. Davis came home, she gave us a matinée musicale. Miss Hammersmith sang, and Mrs. Dick Anderson. General (Prince) Polignac was there, and some Germans. The Germans played and sang, accompanying themselves on piano and guitar. All the morning I had been reading German with Mary Preston. I asked her now: "What is Miss Hammersmith singing?" "Good Heavens! Don't you know? It is the ballad we were translating just before we came home today." So I found out I did not know as much German as I thought I did.

Buck declaimed "Jeanne d'Arc" and "Dandolo." She has the very sweetest voice, and it is admirably trained. She was so lovely withal, that the Frenchmen and Germans rained compliments upon her, and never left her side again. It was such a comfort, apparently, to find a beautiful American girl who spoke their languages with ease and comfort to herself and to them.

Strange stories get out. At Mrs. Davis's breakfast the foreigners all did something. I was asked wherever I turned: "What did you do?" and more frequently: "What did Mrs. Davis do?" Finally out of patience with so much idle curiosity I cried: "We danced on the tight rope." "Have mercy, dear," whispered Mrs. Davis. "Never say that again. They will believe you. You do not know this Richmond. They swallow scandal with wide open mouths. Their easy credulity is such that next winter they will have the exact length of our petticoats, and describe the kind of spangles we were sprinkled with."

Turkeys were thirty dollars apiece, but Lawrence kept us plentifully supplied and Molly cooked admirably. We lived well, kept open house, indeed. Our friends the soldiers from the army breakfasted, dined, and supped at the corner of Clay and Twelfth Streets. We had sent us from home wine, rice, potatoes, hams, eggs, butter and pickles about once a month. A man came on with all that the plantation could furnish us.

Above us lived a family with an unpronouncable Polish name. They had a young daughter, and men innumerable scampered up the steps used by us in common. One day this young person in the course of a morning call, gave me her heart history. "I was engaged to such a nice young man; but he lost everything in that Yankee raid around

Winchester. Would you have me marry and starve? Never! But they did not leave him enough to buy me shoe strings. Now Mamma is perfectly miserable because I am flirting with a Frenchman; but that Confederate soldier with ninety-five Confederate dollars a month, why, that would not keep me in hairpins."

The Frenchman sat with her one evening on the piazza which opened upon the street. From our parlour we could not see them, but we had no choice but to hear. "Oh, Oh! don't," on her part and "Ah, you naughty girl!" on his. I asked, "What can they be after?" "Not much. They are on the open piazza on a level with the public street," answered Mr. Chesnut shortly, "and I dare say that phrase is the only English the man knows."

Mrs. Lewis of Audley was stripped by the Yankees of all her earthly possessions. It began by degrees. One day a card was brought her: "Mr. John Washington." Now the name of the father of his country opened all doors at Audley, so the gentleman was promptly asked into the drawing room. He proved to be a crow-black Negro. He produced a note from Milroy, the Yankee general. The order ran thus: "Mrs. Lewis must send John Washington's family in one of her carriages. She must also send a white driver, if she wants her horses returned to her; for her slaves are all freed by Lincoln's proclamation and consequently would not return to her." Mrs. Lewis stood at her window and the calvacade filed off. Of course, many of the Negroes refused to leave her.

Rose Freeland, Mrs. Lewis's sister, was a beautiful girl, too. One day the Prestons came flying in, nearly bursting with a secret. They had solemnly promised Rose not to tell, but Rose was engaged to Captain Harrison. He was only to be in town three hours, and now nothing would do him but he must be married and march away. So they hurried off to dress for this sudden and private wedding. As they went off, they said: "Oh! Mrs. Chesnut, his company has orders to march at three. He has only two hours more here. Isn't that terrible?" "Tell that to the Marines! Captain Harrison will invite his superior officer to the wedding, and they will cause his hard heart to relent; see if they don't. Then he will grant Captain Harrison two or three weeks' furlough." They laughed me to scorn, but two weeks afterward the beautiful bride, lovelier than ever, called with her splendid looking husband. He was still to leave the next day!

This was February, 1863. Today I write in October of the same year. Captain Harrison came home to die of his wounds, and Rose and her new-born baby died, too; died with him, one might say. All three lie buried at Hollywood cemetery.

When I first went back to Richmond from Columbia I thought all things were smooth and pleasant once more. The woman's war at the Spotswood was over, the belligerents dispersed; and Joe Johnston had gone West. Soon enough I found out my mistake. The Confederate Congress devoted the winter of 1862 to a hand-to-hand fight with Mr. Davis on account of Mr. Quartermaster General Myers. Then Northrop! What a bone of contention he is! Even if the Army is mistaken, and Northrop is not inefficient, still something ought to be conceded to their prejudices. We need popular enthusiasm to take men triumphantly through such a martyrdom as life in camp surely is to them.

One day I saw Mr. Northrop at the President's. He is an eccentric creature. He said newspapers were not without some good uses. He wore several folded across his chest under his shirt, in lieu of flannel. He said they kept out the cold effectually. Think of him with those peppery articles in the Examiner next his heart. There is abuse of Northrop in some of those papers, that would warm up the spirit of the Angel Gabriel!

Apropos of Daniels * in the Lyons' den. We were to dine at the Lyons' home. Buck was in doleful dumps because of Claude Gibson. She would not go. Mary had a bad cold and a headache, but people do not believe in either colds or headaches when one has accepted an invitation to dinner a week in advance; so Mary was amenable to reason. It was a great affair, that dinner. The magnificent lord of the mansion stood on the hearth rug with his feet wide apart like the Colossus of Rhodes, and he talked amirably, looking three feet over our heads. His beautiful young wife was ill, and did not appear. He took me down to dinner. On the other side of me sat a clever unknown who apparently knew me. Foolishly, I thought this gentleman's name a matter of no importance if only he were agreeable, as indeed he was to the last degree.

He said: "The man opposite, sitting by Miss Preston, is called the best match in Virginia." I looked at Mary, upon whom so high an honour had been conferred, and saw, alas! how the bad headache, though not enough for an excuse, was enough to damage her appearance, when assisted by the bad cold. Her face was scarlet all over, including her eyes. She looked dead sleepy, and that beautiful mouth of hers, the

* Mr. Daniels was editor of the *Examiner*.

ideal cupid's bow in perfection, was now only a round "O" as she tried to draw a breath into her suffocated lungs. What a cruel thing to have brought her out!

My neighbour was bright and clever beyond my wildest hopes. He knew everybody and everything, and his paragraphs were as cool and ready, as incisive and as decisive as the Examiner's. Once when he was particularly epigrammatical, I said: "Don't try that style! That is like the Examiner." Which remark caused him a moment's reflection. Someone had the bad taste to arraign the President to his handsome secretary, Burton Harrison. I said: "How rude! I know how angry Mr. Harrison feels. They do that to me, although I am the wife of one of Mr. Davis's A.D.C.'s."

"And you!" said he, "You hit harder and nearer than an aide-de-camp tonight." "What do you mean?" "In all innocence, of course, for you do not know who I am, apparently; and we have had an altercation!" "Conversation, you ought to say. But you have abused everybody, friend or foe, and you hit so hard I shiver even for my enemies."

He asked with unmoved face: "Do you include the Examiner among those newspapers you denounce as giving aid and comfort to — or doing yeoman service for — the Yankees." "Yes, they are splitting us into a thousand pieces. I think of the editor of the Examiner in his cozy den, in warm dressing-gown and comfortable slippers, with a good fire and a good cigar; and the President for a tidbit to tear and crunch." He looked grimmer than ever. "Did you tell Mrs. Petigru you hoped to see Daniels hanged?" "I do not know. I say too much, as you may have noticed. But you must own that he deserves it. He is a standing vote of dissatisfaction with the Administration. I am for the gentlemen privates! If I were a shouting character, I should say: 'Three cheers for the gentlemen privates! To the lantern for the dissenting editors!' As for Congress, I would blow them from the guns, as the English did the Sepoys — though the Sepoys only did what the English laud and magnify John Brown for trying to get the Negroes to do here." Here I stopped to take breath. After we were once more in the drawing room, someone said: "What a brilliant conversationist Mr. Daniels is!" "Is Mr. Daniels here?" "He sat by you at table."

That was it, then! I had told him, at his own particular request, what a black-hearted traitor he was, and that he should be hung, drawn and quartered, with his head stuck over the gate!

In June, 1863, my mother's illness summoned me back to Alabama.

I had started from Richmond to Flat Rock to escape the hot weather. At one station on the way I saw men sitting on a row of coffins, smoking, talking and laughing, with their feet drawn up tailor fashion to keep them out of the rain. I met Mr. Chesnut at Wilmington. He only crossed the river with me and then went back to Richmond. He was violently opposed to sending our troops into Pennsylvania,* wanted all we could spare sent west to make an end there of our enemies.

Molly sat by me in the cars. She touched me and with her nose in the air, said: "Look, Missis." There was the inevitable bride and groom — I supposed — and the irrepressible kissing and lolling against each other that I had seen so often before. I was astonished at Molly's prudery, but there was a touch which was new; the man required for his peace of mind that the bride should brush his cheek with those beautiful long eyelashes of hers. Molly became so outraged, in her blue-black modesty, that she kept her head out of the window not to see! When we were detained at a little wayside station, this woman made an awful row about her room. She seemed to know me, and appealed to me; said her brother-in-law was adjutant to Colonel Kershaw. Molly said to her: "Ma'am, you had better go yonder where your husband is calling you." The "bride" drew herself up proudly, and with a toss of her head retorted: " 'Husband' indeed! I am a widow. That is my cousin! I loved my husband too well to marry again, ever, ever!" Absolutely, tears came into her eyes. Molly, loaded as she was with shawls and bundles, stood motionless. "After all that gwine on in the cars! If it was me, I'd have let it go it was my husband, nigger as I am!"

I went to Camden, and then to Mrs. Preston's, in Columbia. There I was at ease on a soft bed of every physical comfort, till there came the telegram that I must go to my mother who was ill in Portland. Colonel Goodwyn, his wife, and two daughters were going; so I joined their party. I telegraphed Mr. Chesnut for Lawrence, and he replied by forbidding me to go at all; it was so hot, the cars so disagreeable, fever would be the inevitable result. But I thought it my duty to go to my mother, as I risked nothing but myself.

We had two days of an exciting drama under our very noses, before our eyes. A party had come to Columbia who said they had run the blockade. Colonel Goodwyn asked me on the cars to look around and see if I could pick out the suspected crew. It was easily done. We were all in a sadly moulting condition. We had come to the end of

* The approaching Gettysburg campaign.

our good clothes, and now our only resource was to turn them upside down or inside out, mending and darning and patching. But near me sat a young woman with a travelling dress of bright yellow, a profusion of curls and pink cheeks, delightfully airy and easy in her manners, absorbed in a flirtation with a Confederate Major. He, in spite of his nice new gray uniform and two stars, had a very Yankee face, fresh, clean-cut, sharp, and utterly unsunburned. Two other women faced this man and woman — we knew them to be newcomers by their good clothes.

A man came in and stood up and read from a paper, "The surrender of Vicksburg." I felt a hard blow strike on the top of my head, and my heart took one of its queer turns. I was utterly unconscious, though not long, I dare say. The first thing I heard was the joy and exultation of the Yankee party. Imagine my rage and humiliation! A man apparently slept through everything, always in earshot of this party. Colonel Goodwyn wrote on a blank page of my book that the sleeper was a Richmond detective. A fair and comely youth joined my two, and I heard him tell them in a furtive undertone: "You can trust me. I am from Tennessee. Plenty of good Union people there." I wrote this in my book and gave it to Colonel Goodwyn. He took care that the detective saw it too, in one of his brief waking intervals. "That boy is one of my subalterns," came back to me, written below my foolish evidence.

When finally, hot and tired out, we arrived at West Point, the dusty cars were still, except for the giggling flirtation of Yellow Gown and her Major. From the door at their backs stalked in two of the tallest and sallowest Confederate officers I ever saw. I felt mischief in the air. One of these was lame and leaned heavily on the other. He sat down on the arm of the seat opposite the unconscious Major, and touched his shoulder. The Major was whispering low to his Dulcinea and bent over her to do so. He started and turned quickly to meet the cold stare of that grim and sallow pair of Confederate officers. Instantly every drop of his blood left his face. It became pallid with terror, and a spasm seized his throat. It was a piteous sight, and I was awfully sorry for him at once. I said to Colonel Goodwyn: "Did you see him? He is guilty, look at his face!" "He is not half as pale as you were when you heard Vicksburg had fallen into Yankee hands. Maybe he has something wrong about the heart."

The pseudo-Confederate Major was then asked for his commission. The Confederate officer looked over his papers. "This is an unusual thing. They are filled up and signed by the same hand, and that is not Mr. Seddon's handwriting." The Major said huskily: "I am from Maine, it is true; but I have fought for the Confederacy from the first." He ought never to have breathed the word, Maine, in that crowd. It condemned him then and there. He added: "I have been in the commissary department; got my discharge because of a disease of the heart." Did he hear Colonel Goodwyn's remark to me? He certainly was deadly pale and breathed with difficulty.

The cruel Confederate officer smiled. "In our service, officers are allowed to resign because of any personal disability, but they are not discharged. Tell me where you served as commissary and I will telegraph." There was a great deal more of this painful scene, and then they marched him out of the car.

Poor Yellow Gown's color was fast, she could not lose it; but the whites of her eyes were livid, and her whole face was changed. She wept real tears and wiped them upwards, to spare those cheeks and their false bloom. The detective went out with the party who led the male spy away captive, but he soon returned, no longer in the least sleepy-headed. He told Yellow Gown that the Major was throwing all the blame on her, saying she had tried to seduce him from his allegiance to the Confederate States, had tried to make him a traitor. How she flamed out in her wrath, and vilified the poor Major! "The wretch! I never laid eyes on him till I met him in these cars." And yet they seemed so intimate from the first!

We left them all together, for we got off at Montgomery. There the boat waited for us. The thermometer was high up in the nineties, and they gave me a stateroom over the boiler. I paid out my Confederate rags of money freely to the chambermaid to get out of that oven. Surely, go where we may hereafter, an Alabama steamer in August, lying under the bluff with the sun looking down, will give one a foretaste and almost an adequate idea of what is to come, as far as heat goes. The planks of the floor burned one's feet, there under the bluff at Selma where we stayed nearly all day.

At Portland I met James Boykin, and he rode away, promising to send a carriage for me at once; but he had to go seven miles on horseback before he reached my sister's, and they were to send it. On that lonely riverside, Molly and I remained, with dismal swamps on every side, and immense plantations, and white people few or none. In my heart I knew my husband was right when he forbade me to undertake this journey.

There was one living thing at this little riverside inn, a white man who had a store opposite. And oh! how drunk he was. After dark, hot as it was, Molly kept up a fire of pine knots; for there was neither lamp nor candle in that deserted house. The drunken man reeled over, now and then, with his lantern; and he would stand with his idiotic drunken glaze, solemnly staggering round us and bowing in his politeness until he nearly fell over us. I sprang out of his way, and he asked: "Well, Madame, what can I do for you?" Shall I ever forget the headache of that night, and the fright! My temples throbbed with dumb misery. I sat upon a chair, Molly on the floor with her head resting against my knee. She was as near as she could get to me. I kept my hand on her. "Missis, now I do believe you are scared of that poor drunken thing. If he was sober I could whip him, fair fight; and drunk as he is I kin throw him over the banister if he so much as teches you. I don't value him a button!"

Taking heart from such brave words, I laughed. It seemed an eternity, but the carriage came by ten o'clock, and then, with the coachman as our sole protector, we poor women drove eight miles or more over the carriage road and through long lanes, swamps of pitchy darkness, plantations on every side. It had never crossed my brother-in-law's head to come for me.

As we drew near the house it looked like a graveyard in a nightmare; so sad, so weird, so vague and phantom-like in its outlines.

I found my mother ill in bed, feeble still, but better than I hoped to see her. "I knew you would come," was her greeting with outstretched hands. Then I went to bed in that silent house. A house of the dead, it seemed. I supposed I was not to see my sister until the next day; but she came in, some time after I had gone to bed. She kissed me quickly, without a tear. She was thin and pale, but her voice was calm and kind. As she lifted the candle over her head to show me something on the wall, I saw that her pretty brown hair was white. It was awfully hard not to burst out into violent weeping; she looked so sweet — and yet so utterly broken-hearted. But as she was apparently without emotion, it would not become me to upset her by my tears. Hetty, mother's old maid, brought my breakfast to my bedside. Such a breakfast! Delmonico could do no better. "What a splendid cook you have here," I said. "My daughter Lena is Miss

Sally's cook. She's well enough as times go, but when our Miss Mary comes to see us, I does it myself." And she curtseyed down to the floor. "Bless your old soul," I cried, and she rushed over and gave me a good hug.

She is my mother's factotum and has been her maid since she was bought from a Virginia speculator, she and her mother. She is pampered until she is a rare old tyrant at times. She can do everything better than anyone else and my mother leans on her heavily. Hetty is Dick's wife. Dick is the butler. They have over a dozen children, and take life very easily.

My sister Sally came in before I was out of bed; and she began at once, in the same stony way, pale and cold as ice, to tell me of the death of her children. It had happened not two weeks before. Her eyes were utterly without life, with no expression whatever; and in a composed and sad sort of way she told the tale as if it was something she had read, and wanted me to hear. "My eldest daughter, Mary, had grown up to be a lovely girl. She was between thirteen and fourteen, you know. Baby Kate had her sister's grey eyes. She was evidently going to be the beauty of the family. That is one of my children who has lived and has gone, and you have never seen her at all. She died first, and I would not go to the funeral. I thought it would kill me to see her put under the ground. I was lying down, stupid with grief. Aunt Charlotte came to me after the funeral with the news: 'Mary has that awful disease too.' There was nothing to say. I got up and dressed instantly, and went to Mary. I did not leave her side again, in that long struggle between life and death. I did everything for her with my own hands. I even prepared my darling for the grave. I went to her funeral, and I came home and walked straight to my mother, and I begged her to be comforted. I told her I would bear it all without one word, if God would only spare me the one child left me now."

Sally has never shed a tear, but she seems twenty years older, cold, hard, careworn. With the same rigidity of manner, she began to go over all the details of Mary's illness. "I had not given up hope, no, not at all. As I sat by her side she said: 'Mamma, put your hand on my knees, they are so cold.' I put my hand on her knee and the cold struck to my heart. I knew it was the coldness of death." As she spoke, she put out her hand and fell forward in an agony of weeping. This lasted for hours. The doctor said this reaction was inevitable, that without it she must have died, or gone mad.

While Sally was so bitterly weeping, her little girl, the last of them, a bright child of three or four, crawled into my bed. "Now Auntie," she whispered, "I want to tell you all about Mamie and Katie, but they watch me so; they say I must never talk about them. Katie died because she ate blackberries. I know that. Then Aunt Charlotte read Mamie a letter, and that made her die too. Maum Hetty says they have gone to God, but I know the people saved a place between them in the ground for me."

Once or twice while I was there, this child missed some member of the family, and she came to me to put her little hand in mine and to whisper: "Don't tell Mamma, but I just know. They are dead too!"

Uncle William was in despair at the low ebb of patriotism out there. "West of the Savannah River, it is property first, life next, and honour last." He gave me an excellent pair of shoes. What a gift! For more than a year, I have had none but some dreadful things Armsted made for me, and they hurt my feet so. These do not fit, but that is nothing; they are large enough, and do not pinch anywhere, absolutely a respectable pair of shoes!

Uncle William says the men who went into the War to save their Negroes are abjectly wretched. Neither side now cares a fig for their beloved Negroes, and would send them all to Heaven in hand-baskets, as Custis Lee says, to win the fight.

General Lee and Mr. Davis and our soldiers everywhere want the Negroes to be put in the Army. Mr. Chesnut and Mr. Venable discussed the subject one night. Would they fight on our side, or desert to the enemy? They don't go to the enemy now, because they are comfortable where they are, and expect to be free anyway.

Seeing Dick, the butler here, reminds me that when we were children, our nurses gave us our tea out in the open air on little pine tables, scrubbed white as milk pails. As Dick passed us, with his slow and consequential step, we called: "Do, Dick, come and wait on us." "No, little Missus. I never wait on pine tables. Wait till you git big enough to put your legs under your pa's mahogany."

I taught him to read as soon as I could read myself, perched on his knife board; but he won't look at me now. He looks over my head, he scents freedom in the air. He was always very ambitious. I do not think he ever troubled with books much, but then my father always said that Dick, standing in front of his sideboard, had heard all subjects of earth or Heaven discussed, and by the best heads in our world.

He is proud, too, in his way. Hetty, his wife, complained that the other men servants were too fine in their livery. "Nonsense, old woman! A butler never demeans himself to wear livery. He is always in plain clothes." Somewhere he had picked up that.

He is the first Negro that I have felt a change in. They go about in their black masks, not a ripple or an emotion showing; and yet on all other subjects except the War they are the most excitable of all races. Now Dick might make a very respectable Egyptian Sphynx, so inscrutably silent is he. He did deign to inquire about General Richard Anderson. "He was my young Master once. I always will like him better than anybody else." The Anderson house was next door. When Dick and Hetty married, the two families agreed to sell either Dick or Hetty, whichever consented to be sold. Hetty refused outright, so the Andersons sold Dick, so that he might be with his wife.* This was magnanimous on their part, for Hetty was only a lady's maid, while Dick was a trained butler, on whom Mr. Anderson had spent no end of pains. Of course if they had refused to sell Dick, Hetty would have had to go to them. Mrs. Anderson was very much disgusted with Dick's ingratitude. As a butler, he is a treasure. He is overwhelmed with dignity but that does not interfere with his work at all. My father had a body servant named Simon who could imitate his master's voice perfectly; and he would call out from the yard, after my father had mounted his horse: "Dick, bring me my overcoat! I see you there, sir! Hurry up." When Dick would hurry out, overcoat in hand, and find only Simon, my mother had always to step out and prevent a fight, and Dick never forgave her laughing.

Once, in Sumter, when my father was very busy preparing a law case, the mob in the street annoyed him, and he grumbled about it while Simon made up his fire. Then — he always said that in all his life he had never laughed so heartily — he suddenly heard himself, the Honorable Stephen Decatur Miller, or "Lawyer Miller" as the speaker announced himself in the dark, appeal to the gentlemen to go away and leave a lawyer in peace to prepare his case for the next day. My father said he could have sworn it was his own voice. The crowd dispersed, and some noisy Negroes came along. Upon them Simon rushed with the whip, slashing around in the dark, calling himself "Lawyer Miller," who was determined to have peace. My father heard him come back, complaining: "Them niggers run so fast I never got in a hundred yards of one of them."

When we went to Portland on our way back to the outside world, Mr. N—— was there. He said: "You will never make me believe Edward Boykin likes a soldier's life. He is too fond of his own ease and comfort, and he never will be reconciled to have his property destroyed." He added: "I wish we lived in Florida. It's easy times, they say, down there. They are making money by blockade running, cheating the government and skulking the fight, hiring substitutes. The substitutes run away. On our army list we have fifty thousand missing — and thirty thousand would have saved Vicksburg. There are folks such as you describe everywhere, who love to make money, and have no stomach for the fight."

He himself was there, he said, with a thousand dollars in his pocket to buy another substitute for State service. He has one substitute already, in the Confederate Army, and he has sent all his cotton through McRae and Company to Liverpool. He is busy laying up his treasures where neither Yankees nor Confederates can burn or molest them.

We brought mother away with us. On the boat to Montgomery, there were no staterooms for us, except that mother had one. My aunt and I sat nodding in armchairs, for the floors and sofas were covered with sleepers too. On the floor, on that night so hot that little covering of clothes or anything else could be borne, lay a motley crew, black, white and yellow, in promiscuous style. Children and their nurses, half-bare, were wrapped in profoundest slumber. "No caste prejudices here," said I. "Neither Garrison, John Brown or Garrett Smith ever dreamed of equality more untrammelled." A crow-black, enormously fat Negro man waddled in every now and then to look after the lamps. The atmosphere of that cabin was stifling, and the sight of those obscene birds on the floor did not make it more tolerable. We soon escaped and sat out near the guards. The next day was the very hottest I have ever known; but we had our supreme consolation, watermelons of the very finest, and ice.

A very handsome woman whom I did not know rehearsed our disasters all along the line, and then as if she held me responsible, she faced me furiously. "And where are our big men, our leaders, the men we have a right to look to to save us? They got us into this scrape. Let them get us out of it!" I sympathized with her, and understood her; but I answered lightly: "I do not know the exact size you want them."

In Montgomery, we were so hospitably received. Ye gods! how those women talked! and all at the same time! They put me under the care of General Dick Taylor's brother-in-law, a Mr. Gordon, who married one of the Berangers. A very pleasant arrangement it was for me.

He was kind and attentive and vastly agreeable with his New Orleans anecdotes. On the first of last January, all his servants left him but four. To these faithful few he gave free papers at once, that they might lose naught by loyalty should the Confederates come into authority once more. He paid high wages and things worked smoothly for some weeks. One day his wife saw some Yankee officers' cards on a table, and said to her maid: "I did not know any of these people had called."

"Oh, Missis!" the maid replied, "They come to see me, and I have been waiting to tell you. It is too hard! I cannot do it! I cannot dance with those nice gentlemen at night at our Union Balls and then come here and be your servant the next day. I can't!" "So," said Mr. Gordon, "freedom must be followed by fraternity and equality." One by one, the faithful few slipped away, and the family were left to their own devices. Why not?

When General Dick Taylor's place was sacked, his Negroes moved down to Algiers, a village near New Orleans. An old woman came to Mr. Gordon to say that these Negroes wanted him to get word to "Mars' Dick" that they were dying of disease and starvation; thirty had died that day. Dick Taylor's help being out of the question, Mr. Gordon applied to a Federal officer. He found this one not a philanthropist, but a cynic, who said: "All right; it is working out as I expected. Improve Negroes and Indians off the continent. Their strong men we put in the army. The rest will disappear."

Back in Richmond * I found Molly and Lawrence quarrelling. He declared he could not put up with her tantrums. I asked him, in the interests of peace and a quiet house, to bear with her temper as I did, because she was so good and useful. He was shabby enough to tell her, at their next quarrel, that I had said this. Then the awful reproaches that she overwhelmed me with! She said she was mortified that I had humbled her before Lawrence!

But the day of her revenge came. At Negro balls in Richmond, they

* Before Mrs. Chesnut made the journey to Alabama, the twelve months of the Confederacy's great offensive — from Seven Pines to Gettysburg — had ended. In what follows Mrs. Chesnut frequently writes of events before Gettysburg; and she is often confused as to times and seasons — as for instance in the following pages when a proposed picnic (with its implication of fine weather) was cancelled to watch soldiers march through "snow, sleet and freezing cold." But exact dates are not of first importance, and Mrs. Chesnut's narrative has been allowed to take its course with a minimum of chronological annotation.

were required to carry "passes," and in changing his coat Lawrence forgot his. Next day he was missing, and Molly came to me, laughing to the point of tears. "Come and look, Missy! Here is the fine gentleman, tied between two black niggers and marched off to jail." She laughed and cheered so that she could not stand without holding on to the window. Lawrence as they passed disregarded her and called to me at the top of his voice, "Please, Ma'am, ask Mars' James to come take me out of this. I ain't done nothing."

As soon as Mr. Chesnut came home, I told him of Lawrence's sad fate, and he went at once to his rescue. There had been a fight and a disturbance at the Ball, police were called in, every man was made to show his "pass," and so Lawrence was taken up as having none. He was terribly chap-fallen when he came home walking behind Mr. Chesnut. He is always so respectable and well-behaved, and stands on his dignity.

At the place where Mr. Chesnut found Lawrence, a good Confederate soldier popped up. Dirty, drunk, miserable, the pride of his family at home, and one whose courage and patriotism and every earthly virtue we heard lauded and magnified *ad nauseam*, this man had been taken up for brawling in the street. Mr. Chesnut said he never would forget the shame and despair of the poor fellow's face as he begged to be "gotten out of that." His eyes were bloodshot, his face haggard and soiled, his clothes worse — and all in disorder. Mr. Chesnut freed him.

And now comes a stange story. Today I had a letter from my sister, who wrote to inquire for her old playmate, friend, and even lover, Boykin McCaa. "I had almost forgotten Boykin's existence, but he came here last night. He stood by my bedside and spoke to me kindly and affectionately. I said, holding out my hand: 'Boykin, you are very pale?' He answered, 'I have come to tell you good-bye.' Then he seized both of my hands, and his were as cold and hard as ice. I screamed again and again, my whole household came rushing in, and the Negroes came from the yard. All had been wakened by my piercing shrieks. This dream haunts me."

"Stop," said Mr. Chesnut, and he read from that day's Examiner: "Captain Burwell Boykin McCaa was found dead upon the battlefield. He died leading a cavalry charge, at the head of his company. He was shot through the head." Coincidences are queer, sometimes.

We met the famous Colonel of the Fourth Texas, now a General, by name John Bell Hood. We call him Sam, because his classmates at West Point did so; the cause unknown. Dr. John Darby asked if he might bring him, bragged of him extensively, said he had won his three stars under Stonewall's eye and that he was promoted by Stonewall's request.

When he came with his sad face — the face of an old crusader who believed in his cause, his cross and his crown — we were not prepared for that type as a beau ideal of wild Texans. He is tall, thin, shy, with blue eyes and light hair, a tawny beard and a vast amount of it covering the lower part of his face. He wears an appearance of awkward strength. Someone said that his great reserve of manner he carried only into the society of ladies. Mr. Venable added that he himself had often heard of the light of battle shining in a man's eyes, but he had seen it only once. He carried orders to Hood from General Lee, and found him in the hottest of the fight. The man was transfigured. "The fierce light of his eyes," said Mr. Venable, "I can never forget."

Hood came to ask us to a picnic next day at Drury's Bluff. The naval heroes were to receive us, and then we were to dine at the Texan's camp. We were to have bands of music, dances, turkeys, chickens, buffalo's tongues. But next morning, just as my foot was on the carriage step, the girls standing behind ready to follow me, up rode John Darby in red-hot haste. He threw his bridle to one of the men who was holding the horses and came toward us, clanking his cavalry spurs with a displeasing sound. "Stop! It's all up. We are ordered back to the Rappahannock. The brigade is marching through Richmond now."

So we unpacked, unloaded, dismissed our hacks and sat down with a sigh. "Suppose we go and see them pass along the Turnpike?" The suggestion was hailed with delight, and off we marched. At the Turnpike, we stood on the sidewalk and saw ten thousand men march by. We had seen nothing like this before. Hitherto, it was only regiments, marching spic and span in their fresh smart clothes, just from home on their way to the Army. Here, such rags and tags, nothing alike — most garments and arms had been taken from the enemy — and such shoes! "Oh, our brave boys!" moaned Buck. They had tin pans and pots tied to their waists, bread or bacon stuck on the ends of their bayonets. Anything that could be spiked was bayonetted and held aloft.

They did not seem to know their shabby condition. They laughed and shouted and cheered as they marched by. There was not a disrespectful or a light word to us, but they went for the men huddled behind us, who seemed trying to be as small as possible and to escape observation. They shouted: "Ladies, send those puny conscripts on to their regiments." "Captain, either take off your shoulder straps or come on to the Rappahannock. Maybe you did not know there was fighting going on there." Johnny began to grumble. "This is my first furlough. I have not missed a battle, not one." "Don't answer," John Darby advised. "Those rough and ready Texans will make you rue it, if you give them a chance."

Hood and his staff came galloping up, dismounted and joined us. Mary Preston gave him a bouquet. He unwrapped a Bible which he carried in his pocket — he said his mother had given it to him — and carefully pressed a flower in it. Mary Preston suggested that he had not worn or used the Bible at all, it was so fresh and new and beautifully kept; and his Texans heard her remark and called their jocose comments.

Buck stood somewhat apart as a spectator of this scene. She had refused to appear the night Hood came to tea. Now Dr. Darby introduced the General, and after he had mounted his horse, and before he rode away, Hood looked at her, turning his horse to do so; and he said something to Dr. Darby which caused the latter to smile. The surgeon came back for more adieux, and Buck asked eagerly: "What was that he said to you about me?" "Only a horse compliment. He is a Kentuckian, you know. He said, 'You stand on your feet like a thoroughbred.' "

They marched, these poor creatures, for four days through the snow and sleet and freezing weather — and then they marched back again. Thirty died on that four days' senseless march — senseless as far as we could see.

Mrs. Ould had just received in some occult way a cask of whiskey. She had it rolled out on the sidewalk and gave each half-starved soldier a drink. "Ah, General!" she said, "I wish there was enough for everyone of them!" Mr. Ould came home to dinner that day and wanted his whiskey. "Surely you need not grumble, since I gave it to those poor frozen soldiers?" "But, my dear, out of a cask, you might have saved me a tumbler!"

That night our little parlour was crammed with soldiers. We were playing Casino, Buck winning as usual, and Mary made her plaint: "Everybody gives her cards, but nobody ever gives me anything." The infatuated Dr. Darby placed that beautiful hand of his on his heart, and looked unutterable things. He missed fire because she did not look up from her cards. She did not see the pantomime, but the General did, and asked his surgeon in slow, solemn, practical tones: "Doctor, what does that signal mean?" "Oh," replied the doctor, "I put two fingers on my heart, as a hint she should play the deuce of hearts." That small joke was made to go a long way. Certainly never did a game of casino cause so much uproarious mirth. They were soon ordered to Suffolk, and there one day as the balls were falling fast, Hood came upon John Darby, who said he was keen to move on, he thought the spot too hot for loitering. "I say, Doctor," Hood agreed, "This is not as pleasant as the corner of Clay Street and casino?"

General Hood was wounded at Gettysburg, and was barely well enough to join his command, which was ordered west to Bragg before Chattanooga. Doctor Darby stayed sweet-hearting a day too long in Richmond, basking in the smiles of love and beauty, before he followed them west; and the battle of Chickamauga was won and Hood's leg had been cut off before he got there. The General's life was despaired of, but the surgeon nursed his chief faithfully to recovery.

Major Edward Johnston did not get into the Confederacy until after the first Manassas. He was in the North, and before he could evade that potentate, Seward rang his little bell and sent him to a prison in the harbour of New York. I forget whether he was exchanged or escaped of his own motion; but the next thing I heard of my ante bellum friend, he had defeated Milroy in Western Virginia. For this victory they named him "Allegheny" Johnston.

When he was startled or agitated, he had an odd habit of falling into a state of incessant winking. He seemed persistently winking one eye at you, but he meant nothing by it. In point of fact, he did not know it himself. In Mexico he had been wounded in the eye, and the nerve vibrated independently of its own will. During the winter of 1863 he was on crutches, and when he hobbled down Franklin Street with us, we were proud to accommodate our pace to that of the wounded General. His ankle continued stiff, so when he sat down, another chair was put before him and he stretched his stiff leg on it, straight as a ramrod. At that time he was our only wounded knight, and the girls waited on him, and made life pleasant to him.

One night I listened to two love tales at once, distracted with trying to hear both. William Porcher Miles, in a perfectly modulated voice, in cadenced accents and low tones, narrated the happy end of his affair; he was engaged to sweet little Bettie Bierne! And I gave him my congratulations with all my heart. It was a capital match, suitable every way, good for her, good for him, etc. I was deeply interested in his story; but there was din and discord in the other. Old Edward, our pet general, sat diagonally across the room with one leg straight out like a poker wrapped in red carpet leggings. He was as red as a turkey cock in the face. His head is so strangely shaped, like a cone or an old-fashioned beehive! As Buck said: "There are three tiers of it. It is like the Pope's tiara!" While Mr. Miles was talking to me, there the General sat, with a loud voice and a thousand winks making love to Mary Preston. I make no excuse for listening. It was impossible not to hear. I tried not to lose a word of Mr. Miles's idyl, while the despair of the veteran was thundered in my other ear. I lent an ear to each.

Mary Preston cannot altogether control her own voice, and her shrill screams of negation: "No, no, never!" utterly failed to suppress her wounded lover's obstreperous assertions of his undying affection for her. Buck said afterwards: "We heard every word of it on our side of the room, even when Mamie shrieked to him that he was talking too loud! Mamie, do you think it was kind to tell him he was forty if he was a day?"

But the venerable Edward was not discouraged; he merely changed his aim to a new target. Two days after he was heard to say he was paying attention now to his cousin, John Preston's second daughter; that her name was Sally, but they called her Buck; "Sally Buchanan Campbell Preston, a lovely girl, sir."

With her he now drove, rode, and hobbled on his crutches; he sent her his photograph, and in due time cannonaded her with proposals to marry him.

Buck was never so decided in her "No" as Mary. ("Not so loud, at least," amends Buck, who always reads what I have written, and makes comments of assent or dissent.) One day as they rode down Franklin Street he began to thunder in her ears his tender passion for her. Buck says she knows the people on the sidewalk heard snatches of it, though she rode as rapidly as she could, and begged him not to talk so loud. Finally they dashed up to our door as if they had been running a race, for she had answered him at last by an application of her whip to her horse.

Unfortunate in love but fortunate in war, our General later won new laurels with Ewell in the Valley, and with the Army of the Potomac.

Major Venable, aide-de-camp to General Lee, dined with us and joined Mr. Chesnut in ridiculing the weakness of men who tattled to women secrets of state or important army news. This was apropos of Dick Anderson, the most silent and discreet of men. His wife showed Mrs. Davis and ourselves a letter from him: "Remain in Richmond. We may be ordered there at any moment."

"That's nothing!" I remarked. "The best of men will tell any lie to keep their wives out of camp. Very few men can bear their wives trailing after them to the Army."

Afterwards they discussed the latest secret dispatch of General Lee to Longstreet. "Surely, Sir," said Mr. Venable, in tones of pretended solemn reproach, "You have not told your wife that!"

L. Q. Washington came with some Executive office wit, so called: "Why is C——r like a parenthesis?" "Because he can be left out without injury to the sense of the Administration." "Why is Cl——n like the Merrimac?" "Because he cannot be boarded." It seems the poor man eats so much they will not have him at any price, neither at the public houses or at private boarding houses.

I think I have told how Mr. Miles, so gently o'er me leaning, told of his successful loves, while General Johnston roared with anguish and disappointment over his failures. Mr. Miles spoke of sweet little Bettie Bierne as if she had been a French girl just from a convent, kept far from the haunts of men and just for him. Now Bettie has a younger sister, married and a widow, and a younger still who was grown and going into society four years ago; but one would think to hear him that Bettie had never cast those innocent blue eyes of hers on a man until he came along. Ever since I first knew Miss Bierne, in 1857, when Pat Calhoun was to the fore in her favour, she has been followed by a trail of men as long as a Highland chief's. Every summer at the Springs, her father, old Oliver Bierne, would appear in the ballroom a little before twelve and chase the three beautiful Biernes home before him in spite of all entreaties; and he was said to frown away her too numerous admirers at all hours of the day.

This new engagement was confided to me as a profound secret, so of course, I did not mention it even to my own household. But next day little Allston, Morgan's adjutant, and George Deas called; and as Colonel Deas removed his gloves he said: "Oh, the Miles and Bierne imbroglio, have you heard of it?" "No, what is the row about?" "They are engaged to be married!" "Who told you?" "Miles himself, as we walked down Franklin Street this afternoon." "And did he not beg you not to mention it because Bettie did not wish it spoken of?" "God bless my soul, so he did! And I forgot that part of it entirely."

Colonel Allston begged the stout Carolinian not to take his inadvertent breach of faith too much to heart. Miss Bettie's engagement had already caused him a dreadful night. A young man, who was his intimate friend, came to his room in the depths of despair and handed him a letter from Miss Bierne, the cause of all his woe. Not knowing that she was already engaged to Miles, he had proposed to her in an eloquent letter; and in her reply she politely stated that she was positively engaged to Mr. Miles. Instead of thanking her for putting him at once out of his misery, he considered the reason she gave as triply aggravating; the agony of the love letter and the refusal. "Too late!" he yelled. "Too late, by Jingo!" So much for the secret!

Miss Bierne and I became fast friends, our friendship based upon our mutual admiration for the honored member from South Carolina. Colonel and Mrs. Myers and Colonel and Mrs. Chesnut were the only friends of Mr. Miles who were invited to his wedding. At the church door, the sexton demanded credentials; none but those whose names he held in his hand were allowed to enter. Not twenty people were present; a mere handfull grouped around the altar in that large empty church.

We were among the first to arrive. Then a faint flutter, and Mrs. Parkman, (the bride's sister, swathed in weeds for her young husband who had been killed within a year of her marriage) came rapidly up the aisle alone. She dropped upon her knees in the front pew and there remained, motionless, during the whole ceremony, a mass of black crêpe, and a dead weight on my heart. Then, while the wedding march turned our thoughts from her, the bride advanced in white satin and Point d'Alençon. Mrs. Myers whispered that it was Mrs. Parkman's wedding dress. She remembered the exquisite lace — and she shuddered with superstitious foreboding.

We were to assemble afterwards at Mrs. McFarland's, but we came out to find a sharp shower falling. All horses in Richmond had been impressed for some sudden cavalry necessity a few days before; so I ran between Mr. McFarland and Senator Semmes, with my pretty Paris rose-coloured silk turned over my head to save it. When we arrived at the hospitable mansion, Mr. McFarland took me straight into the drawing-room, man-like forgetting that my ruffled plumes needed a good smoothing and preening.

Mr. Hunter said he had never known Miles to do an inconsiderate, an impolite or a selfish thing. He spoke smilingly of certain gaieties; and Mr. Miles then informed me that a man's wife had nothing to do with his bachelor scrapes. "But for the faith and loyalty due other women, I would not scruple to tell her all of my past life, for it was not her affair at all." Deluded wretch! Jealousy of the past is most women's Hell. It is one of the hopeless irritations, the pest of married life.

We were walking on Franklin Street when a gay, debonair couple dashed by on horseback. "By Heavens, she has pluck! She was confirmed last Sunday, and so was he. And it is a little more than a month since her confinement. She ought not to be on horseback so soon!" "So soon after which? Confinement or confirmation?"

One day in early June, 1863, Mrs. Lee sent for me. She was staying at Mrs. Caskie's. I was taken directly to her room. She was lying in bed. She said before I had taken my seat: "You know there is a fight going on now at Brandy Station." "Yes, we are anxious. John Chesnut's company is there, too." She spoke sadly but quietly. "My son Roony is wounded. His brother has gone for him. They will soon be here, and we will hear all about it, unless Roony's wife takes him to her grandfather's. I, a poor lame mother, am useless to my children." Mrs. Caskie said: "You need not be alarmed. The General said in his telegraph that it was not a severe wound, and you know even Yankees believe General Lee."

Mrs. Lee was right in her fears, for he was taken by his wife to Mr. Carter's, and there he was captured, since it was within the enemy's lines. He is kept as hostage for Yankee miscreants, and now little Charlotte Wickham repents her wilfullness in refusing to let him be brought down to Richmond, and taking him where she did. They say Custis Lee offered himself to the Yankees in place of his brother, since he was a single man with no wife and children to be hurt by his imprisonment, or made miserable by his danger; but the Yankees preferred Roony.

That day Mrs. Lee gave me a likeness of the General, a photograph taken soon after the Mexican War, which she likes better than the later ones. He certainly was a handsome man then, handsomer even than now. I shall prize it for Mrs. Lee's sake, too.

She said old Mrs. Chesnut and her aunt, Nelly Custis, were very intimate during the old Washington administration in Philadelphia days. I told her Mrs. Chesnut had much to tell of the old Revolutionary times. She was one of the "white-robed choir" at Trenton Bridge, which everybody who writes a life of Washington asks her to give an account of.

Mr. Chesnut was sent to see Vallandingham * out of the Confederacy at Wilmington. The Federals had no use for him, so they handed

* Clement L. Vallandingham of Ohio was a States Rights Democrat, and in 1863, after a particularly violent speech against President Lincoln and the Administration, he was arrested, tried and sentenced to prison. President Lincoln commuted this sentence to banishment. Vallandingham returned to Ohio in 1864 and continued his political career.

him over to us, and we are speeding the parting guest. He will never help us against his own people, of that we may be sure.

We came near having a compliment today, but a further development of Dr. Rufus's taste deprived it of all value. "Mrs. Davis, Mrs. Clay, and you," he said, "I do declare you are the cleverest ladies in the Confederacy. Mrs. Clay, I proclaim her supreme for wit and beauty as well as for refinement. Now one of you girls sing 'Lorena.' * Of all the songs I know, it is supreme as to melody, and also for beauty of versification."

We did not sing for him, so he quoted — or rather declaimed — a verse or two. Maggie Howell says there is a girl in large hoops and a calico frock at every piano between Richmond and the Mississippi, banging on the out-of-tune thing and looking up into a man's face, singing that song. The man wears a soiled and battle-stained uniform, but his heart is fresh enough, as he hangs over her, to believe in Lorena. "Is it not lovely?" said our Doctor. Well, the song has not had a fair chance. We hear it squalled so, and to banged accompaniments which are discord itself. We can almost see the heart-broken lover who was constant — twelve into a hundred goes eight times and four over — eight years and four months. Broken-hearted or not, he had the heart to do that sum, or else it was the exigency of the rhyme and meter. Probably that was it, or he would have said "eight or nine years," you may depend on it.

Mrs. Ould and Mrs. Davis came home with me from Mrs. Lee's. Lawrence had a basket of delicious cherries. "If there was only some ice!" I cried. Respectfully Lawrence said: "Give me money and you shall have ice." By the underground telegraph, he had heard of an ice-house across the river, though its fame was suppressed by certain sybarites, as they wanted all the ice. In a wonderfully short time we had mint juleps and cherry coblers.

Altogether it had been a pleasant day, but as I sat alone, laughing lightly now and then at the memory of some funny story, suddenly a violent ring, and a regular sheaf of telegrams were handed me. I could not have drawn away in more consternation if they had been a nest of rattlesnakes.

* "Lorena" was a sentimental ballad, tremendously popular in the South during the War. In one stanza occur the lines:

" 'Tis just a hundred months, Lorena,
"Since first I held thy hand in mine."

It is to this passage that Mrs. Chesnut presently refers.

First, Frank Hampton was killed at Brandy Station. Wade Hampton telegraphed Mr. Chesnut to see Robert Barnwell and make necessary arrangements to receive the body. Since Mr. Chesnut is still at Wilmington, I sent for Preston Johnston, and my neighbour Colonel Patton offered to see that everything proper should be done. That afternoon I walked out alone. Willie Mountford had shown me where the body, all that was left of Frank Hampton, was to lie in state in the Capitol. Mrs. Petticola joined me, and then Mrs. Singleton. Mrs. Singleton said we had better go in and look at him before the coffin was finally closed. How I wish I had not looked! I remember him so well, in all the pride of his magnificent manhood. He died of a sabre cut across his face and head, and was utterly disfigured. Mrs. Singleton seemed convulsed with grief. In all my life I had never seen such bitter weeping. We sat for a long time on the steps of the State House. Everybody had gone and we were utterly alone. We talked of it all. We had gone to Charleston to see Rachel in "Adrienne Lecouvreur," and as I stood waiting in the passage near the drawing-room, I met Frank Hampton bringing his beautiful bride from the steamer. They had just landed. Than at Mrs. Singleton's place in the country we spent a delightful week together. And now — it is only a few years — nearly all that pleasant company are dead; and our world, the only world we cared for is literally kicked to pieces. Mrs. Singleton cried: "We two lone women, stranded here! So alone am I. Robert Barnwell is in a desperate condition, and Mary is expecting her confinement every day."

It was not till I later returned to Carolina that I heard of Robert Barnwell's death and — with scarcely a day's interval — of the deaths of Mary and her new-born baby. Husband, wife and child were buried in the same grave in Columbia. So Mrs. Singleton has three orphans. What a woeful year this was for her. Robert Barnwell had insisted upon being sent to the insane asylum at Staunton. On account of his wife's situation, the doctor also advised it. His brave wife tried to prevent it. She said: "It is only fever! He is too weak to be dangerous, even if it were anything worse." She tried to say good-bye cheerfully, and she called after him: "As soon as my trouble is over, I will come to you at Staunton." At the Asylum, they said it was typhoid fever which caused his mental aberration, and he died the second day after he got there. When the message came from Staunton that it was fever, nothing more, Mrs. Singleton says she will never forget the triumphant expression of Mary's eyes as she cried: "Robert will get well. It is all right." Her face was radiant, blazing with light. That night the baby was born.

Mrs. Singleton got a telegram, "Robert is dead." She was standing at the window while she read it. As for Mary's life being in danger, she had never thought of such a thing. A servant touched her and said, "Look at Mrs. Barnwell." She turned and ran to the bedside. The doctor said: "It is all over! She is dead."

Not in anger, not in wrath, came the Angel of Death that day; he came to set her free from a world grown too hard to bear.

During Stoneman's raid, I burned my journal proper. Molly constantly told me: "Missis, listen to the guns. Burn up everything. Mr. Lyons say they sure to come, and they'll put in their newspapers whatever you write here every day." The guns did sound very near, and when Mr. Chesnut rode up and told me if Mrs. Davis left Richmond I must go with her, I confess I lost my head. So I have lost all but scraps of my journal, and I am very much tempted to copy all of my letters from Flat Rock. I can pick up a handfull of my letters to Mr. Chesnut from every table, or from every coat pocket that goes to the wash. Here is one rejoicing in his determination to resign from the Council, and one congratulating him because General Lee had turned out to be all my husband said he was, even when he was so unpopular and Joe Johnston was still our great God of War; and here is one in which I thanked God on my knees for our Second Manassas, and said: "Julia Rutledge and I had a charming walk last evening, but like all sublunary things, our pleasure has its drawbacks. Red bugs are our bane. They infest the woods here."

And here is a paragraph about Miss Aiken's wedding to Burnet Rhett. "Julia Rutledge was one of the bridesmaids, and we could not for awhile imagine what she would do for a dress. Kate remembered some stuff she had in the house for curtains, bought before the war and laid aside. It was white and sheer — or even a little worse than sheer — but we covered it with no end of beautiful lace. It made a beautiful dress, and how altogether lovely she looked in it! The night of the wedding, it stormed as if the world was coming to an end. She had a Duchess dressing table trimmed with muslin and lace; not one of the shifts of honest poverty, but a millionaire's attempt at being economical. A candle was left too near this light drapery and it took fire. Outside, lightning to fire the world; inside, the bridal chamber ablaze! And enough wind to blow the house down the mountainside. The English maid behaved heroically, and with the aid of Mrs. Aiken and Mrs. Singleton's servants, put the fire out without disturbing the marriage ceremony which was then being performed below. Everything in the bridal chamber was burnt up except the bed, and that was a mass of cinders and smut-flakes of charred and blackened wood. Mrs. Singleton said: 'Burnet Rhett has strong nerves, and the bride is too good to be superstitious.' "

I find a few notes on this summer of 1863. At the President's, a man was telling us how the Yankees had forced him to do something, dragged and kicked him, etc. Mrs. Davis said in her sweetest tones: "I should have died." "Why? Merely because you were kicked?" "No, not exactly that; but I think I should have kicked and fought them, and then they would have killed me. One can die but once."

In Montgomery, on my return from Portland, a Mrs. Johnson spoke of "this horrid, horrid Confederacy!" "Madame," said Mrs. Taylor, "Why horrid Confederacy?" "It is unendurable. My God! This den of thieves! I have lost everything but my virtue. My clothes are all gone. This dress, it is an old toilette table cover! Do you not feel inclined to stick pins in me?"

Someone asked Mrs. Taylor: "What is Joe Johnston doing now?" "Increasing his reputation in the way he made it, retreating and saving his army." "I hope he may save his country."

Mrs. Johnston said of Mrs. Wigfall: "She is unlike the French woman, she adores innocent pleasures and the beauties of nature." Cried Mrs. Taylor: "You call Louis Wigfall an innocent pleasure! And his company a harmless recreation!"

Another scrap of a note, written in Montgomery: "Beauregard is sulking in Charleston. By supreme negligence, he has lost in Morris Island. He is accused of saying they put him in Charleston because he could make no reputation there. Faith, but he can lose what he has! He has lost it! He never had much brains, and now he is losing heart. Johnston is sulking, too. He is sent west, he says, so that they may give Lee the army he trained, and Lee is reaping where he sowed. But then he was backing straight through Richmond, when they stopped his retreating!"

From Richmond I came back to Camden. Bragg, thanks to Longstreet and Hood, had won Chickamauga; so we looked for results that would pay for our losses in battle. Surely they would capture Rosencrantz. But no! There sat Bragg like a good dog, howling on his hind legs before Chattanooga, and some Yankee Holdfast grinning at him from his impregnable heights. Bragg always stops to quarrel with his generals.

Judge Withers, apropos of my selling cotton and carrying supplies to

Richmond, said: "Yes, buy, sell, do as it suits you for the moment. Enjoy the brief interval which remains to you before your ruin comes, for come it must, and before long." Mr. Chesnut, just from Charleston, tells of seeing a general on the Battery utterly intoxicated. He said: "They treated me more as a Yankee spy, at General Beauregard's headquarters, than as an aide-de-camp of the President of the Confederacy."

At Kingsville on my way to Camden, I caught a glimpse of Longstreet's corps going past. God bless the gallant fellows; not one man intoxicated, not one rude word did I hear. It was a strange sight. What seemed miles of platform cars, and soldiers rolled in their blankets lying in rows with their heads all covered, fast asleep. In their grey blankets packed in regular order, they looked like swathed mummies. One man nearby was writing on his knee. He used his cap for a desk, and he was seated on a rail. I watched him, wondering to whom that letter was to go. To his home, no doubt. Sore hearts for him there!

A feeling of awful depression laid hold of me. All these fine fellows going to kill or be killed, but why? A word took to beating about my head like an old song, "The Unreturning Brave." When a knot of boyish, laughing, young creatures passed and a queer thrill of sympathy shook me. Ah, I know how your homefolks feel. Poor children!

The throng was dense. General Kershaw came up to where I was sitting alone and offered to marshall me through; and as I took his arm, Molly at my heels laden with shawls and bags and bundles, my General remembered his Caesar. They did not open out a path for us soon enough to please him. He called out: "These must be citizens, not soldiers. They do not make way for ladies." With what alacrity and smiling faces they moved aside!

Mem Cohen said: "Catch me making myself town talk, grieving for any man, be I ever so much married to him. Oh, this war! The liberty men take! There may be another woman across the way with as good a right to moan as the lawful wife; yes, or better, for he cares for her. And Madame Wife is the only one who never knows her hard fate."

I had another scandalous letter about that sweet, demure widow; the man, an admirable Crichton, lawyer, parson, foreign ambassador, colonel of a Confederate regiment. A wedding. Former wife's death spoken of as "the removal of the sole obstruction!" When the wedding guests assembled, the parties to be married appeared, she, as sweet and modest as ever, leaning on his arm. In lieu of wedding ceremony, he read this long paper, elaborately prepared, explaining that he had been married several weeks, privately married to the lovely being at his side. His love for her had been of so long standing — he could not tell when it began. It seemed to have grown with his growth and strengthened with his strength, etc. This "wedding" scene took place six weeks after his wife's death. The happy pair at once departed from that place, where he was in charge of a church, to his own church. He explained that he married this lady so promptly after his wife's death (a few days) because he was in the army, and death might come to him any day, and it was the only way to leave her his property; and they did not intend to acknowledge the marriage for a year, but circumstances forced his hand.

Another scandal: A father forbade his daughter's marriage. There was a party at the house. He saw something which made him consent at once, and joy go with her! Oh, what could it be that he saw? Yes, stern parent dozing in the piazza, which was not lighted, saw the forbidden man sitting by a window, his back turned to the piazza. Lightly his daughter tiptoed out; she daintily raised the red hair from the back of that stout, freckled neck and kissed it. "If things have gone that far, let her marry!" swore the father.

So much for travelling! I might have stayed at home forever and never have known of girls who kissed the back of horrid men's necks, or widows like the one Molly and I saw with the spy, who brushed with her eyelashes her cousin's cheeks in the public cars. And they talk of American prudery!

Here are some memories of Richmond. Once last winter, persons came to us with such strange stories of Allston, Morgan's man; stories of his father, too, tales of murder — or at least of how he killed people. He had been a tremendous favourite with Mr. Chesnut, who brought him in, leading him by the hand. But in Richmond Mr. Chesnut said: "With these girls in the house, we must be more cautious." I agreed to be coldly polite, after what had been told me. But when he called, I was very glad to see him, utterly forgetting that he was under a ban. We had a long confidential talk. He told me of his wife and children, and of his army career, and he told Morgan stories and grew more and more cordial. So did I. He thanked me for the kind reception given him in that house, told me I was a true friend, and related to me a scrape he was in which if divulged would ruin him, although he was innocent. He begged me not to repeat anything that he had told of his affairs — not even to Colonel Chesnut — which I promised promptly. Then he went away. I sat poking the fire, thinking what a curiously interesting creature he was; this famous Bob Allston! The folding doors slowly opened and Colonel Chesnut appeared. He had come home two hours ago from the War Office with a headache, and had been lying on the sofa behind that folding door listening for mortal hours.

"So this is your style of being coldly polite," he said. Fancy my feelings. "Indeed I forgot all about what they said of him, while he was here. The lies they tell on him never once crossed my mind. He is a great deal cleverer, and I daresay just as good as those who malign him. For one thing, he was smart enough to keep out of the penitentiary, with its striped breeches and cropped hair, where the Yankees have shut up Morgan and his men!"

Mattie Reedy — I knew her as a handsome girl in Washington several years ago — got tired of hearing Federals abuse John Morgan. One day they were worse than ever, and she spoke up. By way of putting a mark against the name of so rude a girl, the Yankee officer said: "What is your name?" "Mattie Reedy now, but by the grace of God, one day I hope to call myself the wife of John Morgan." She did not know him at all, but he heard the story, so he made it a point to find her out; and as she was as pretty as she was patriotic, by the grace of God she is now Mrs. Morgan. These timid Southern women! Under the guns they can be brave enough.

Aunt Charlotte has told me a story of my dear mother. They were up at Shelby, a white man's country where Negroes are hated. These ladies had with them several Negroes who belonged to my Uncle, at whose house they were staying in his absence. A Negro man named John had married in the neighborhood, and for some cause was particularly obnoxious to the local white people. My aunt and my mother, old-fashioned ladies, shrinking from everything outside of their own door, knew nothing of all this. They occupied rooms on opposite sides of an open passageway. Suddenly my aunt heard a terrible noise; apparently a man was running for his life, pursued by men and dogs who were shouting and hallooing and barking. She had only time to lock herself in, utterly cut off from her sister and dumb with terror. There was a loud knocking at the door, men swearing, dogs tearing round, sniffing, racing in and out of the passage, barking like mad. Aunt Charlotte was sure she heard the panting of the Negro as he ran in a few minutes before. What could have become of him? Where could he have hid? The men shook the doors and windows, and loudly threatened vengeance. My aunt pitied her sister, so feeble, so cut off in that room across the passage. This fright must kill her.

The cursing and shouting continued, till a man's voice in harshest accents made itself heard over all. "Leave my house, you rascals! If you are not gone in two seconds I'll shoot." There was a dead silence, except the noise of the dogs. Quickly the men slipped away and once out of gun shot, they began to call their dogs. After it was all over, my aunt crept across the passage. "Sister, what man was it scared them away?" My mother laughed aloud in her triumph. "I am the man." "But where is John?" Then out crept John from a pile of rubbish in the corner of the room, which my mother had thrown over him. "Lord bless you both. Miss Mary opened de door for me, and dey was right behind, running me." Aunt Charlotte says mother is awfully proud of her prowess.

Mother showed moral courage in another way. At the Springs, she found people unkind to Mrs. Lovell because she was a Northern woman, and her husband had lost New Orleans. Soon my mother heard that Mrs. Lovell had an ailing baby. She drove down to the Springs; and saw that it was true. "I was ashamed of our ladies," said my mother, "So before their faces I asked Mrs. Lovell to drive with me every day. It would do the baby so much good, taking it out in the open air."

One day in Richmond, at the President's, General Lee was there, and Constance and Hetty Cary * came in with Miss Sanders. Miss Constance Cary told us about an attempt to get up a supper, the night before, at some high and mighty FFV's house. Several of them went into the kitchen to prepare something to eat, by the light of one forlorn candle. One of the men of the party, not being of a useful temperament, turned up a tub and sat upon it. Custis Lee, wishing to rest, found nothing upon which to rest but a gridiron. Mrs. Davis inquired softly: "Was he tender on the gridiron? He has never been known to be so anywhere else?" As we went away, we could see General Lee holding the beautiful Miss Cary's hands in the passage outside, though we could not hear what she was saying.

Miss Sanders rose to have her part in the picture, and asked Mr.

* Hetty and Jennie Cary came from Baltimore to Richmond soon after the outbreak of the War. Hetty was thereafter Richmond's reigning belle. Jennie had set to music the poem which became the song: "Maryland, my Maryland," and Hetty sang it first in Baltimore, and many times afterward during the War years at social gatherings and in the camps of the army. Hetty's tragic marriage is reported later in Mrs. Chesnut's reminiscences. Constance Cary was their cousin. She married Burton Harrison, who was secretary to Mr. Davis; and after the war she achieved a reputation as a novelist. Her "Recollections, Grave and Gay," is one of the fine social records of the war.

Davis to walk with her into the adjoining drawing room. He seemed surprised, but rose stiffly and with a scowling brow was led off. As they passed where Mrs. Davis sat, Miss Sanders, all sails set, looked back. "Don't be jealous, Mrs. Davis; I have an important communication to make to the President." Mrs. Davis was amused!

Hetty Cary came through the lines from Baltimore. She crossed the Potomac in a little boat, sitting on her trunk. She is engaged to General Pegram, who is promoted regularly after every one of his defeats. That shows what faith they have in him, a conspicuous mark of the confidence his superior officers have in his merits. After one of his catastrophes, he was at home, and there was a party at his mother's house. Suddenly, armed at all points, in full panoply — that is, in a beautiful Baltimore ball dress — the unlooked-for apparition of Hetty Cary dawned upon them. They thought her in Maryland. General Pegram absolutely fell back fainting with joyful emotion. Mr. Venable taunted us. "No man ever fainted for love of you!" And we could not say that one ever did.

Buck and Captain Chesnut rode out, not remembering how cold it is in Richmond, with silk stockings and thin boots. Buck's feet were nearly frostbitten. She was ill, had a bad sore throat; and she lay on the sofa, wrapped in a cashmere shawl and muffled in laces about the face and neck. Our surgeon dropped on his knees by her side. "What is that for?" said the Captain, standing up brusquely. "I mean to try auscultation, percussion, etc., to see if her lungs are affected." "Come now, that sort of thing won't do!" "Miss Sally," said Dr. Darby, "This sort of thing is done everyday. It is strictly professional. I must rest my head against your chest. It is absolutely necessary for a medical diagnosis." "No you don't," said the Captain. "If I had a sore throat, you would drag me to the window, make me stretch my mouth from ear to ear, put a tablespoon down my throat until I choked, make me stick out my tongue, and then order me a nasty gargle. Or more probably you would barely touch my pulse and say, 'Oh, nothing's the matter with you.' Auscultation, and listening under shoulder blades, you keep for the women!" "Nonsense! Miss Sally, let me put my head where I can hear you breathe!" The Captain cried: "Sir! This furniture is rented. I believe it does not belong to Aunt Mary. But if you don't want to see a chair smashed over your head, take care not to move a peg nearer."

The surgeon got up, dusted his knees, and said: "Everybody knows what a narrow-minded donkey you are." The Captain received this compliment smilingly. "You ought to have waited till I went out. The other fellow feels too like a fool, while that auscultation goes on under his very eyes."

During Stoneman's raid — it was Sunday — I was in Mrs. Randolph's pew. The battle of Chancellorsville was raging, and the rattling of ammunition wagons, the tramp of the soldiers, the everlasting slamming of those iron gates of the Capitol Square just opposite the church, all made it hard to attend to the service. Then began a scene calculated to make the stoutest heart quail: the sexton quietly waking up persons, members of whose family had been brought home wounded, dying or dead; and the pale-faced people following the sexton out.

Finally Mr. Minnegerode himself leaned across the chancel rail for a whispered talk with the sexton. Then he, too, disappeared, and the assistant clergyman went on with the communion. At the church door stood Mrs. Minnegerode, as tragically wretched and as wild-looking as Mrs. Siddons. She managed to tell her husband: "Your son is at the station — dead." When these agonized parents reached the station, it was someone else, a mistake; but somebody's son, all the same. Pale and wan came Mr. Minnegerode back to his place within the altar rails.

After the sacred communion was over, someone asked him what it all meant. "Oh, it was not my son who was killed; but it came so near, it aches me yet."

At home I found L. Q. Washington, who stayed to dinner. He and Mr. Chesnut, as I could see, were utterly preoccupied by some event which they did not see fit to communicate to me. Immediately after dinner, Mr. Chesnut lent Mr. Washington one of his horses and they rode off together. I betook myself to my kind neighbors, the Pattons, for information. There I found Colonel Patton gone, too, but Mrs. Patton knew all about the trouble. She said there was a raiding party within forty miles of us, and no troops in Richmond. They asked me to stay to tea, those kind ladies, and in some way we might learn what was going on. After tea, we went out to the Capitol Square, Lawrence and three men-servants going to protect us.

They seemed mustering in the citizens by the thousands. Companies after companies forming, then battalions, then regiments. It was a wonderful sight to us, looking through the iron railing, seeing them fall into ranks. Then we went to the President's. They were at supper. We sat on the white marble steps in front, and General Elzey told me exactly how things stood — and our immediate danger. Pickets were coming in, men were spurring to and from the door as fast as they could ride. Calmly General Elzey discoursed upon our present weakness, and our chances for aid.

After awhile Mrs. Davis came out and embraced me silently. "It is dreadful," I said. "The enemy are within forty miles of us." "Who told you that tale? They are within three miles of Richmond." I went down on my knees like a stone.

She asked me to stay all night there, which I was thankful to do. Officers kept coming and going, and we gave them what hasty refreshments we could from a side table that was constantly replenished. Finally, in the excitement of the scene and the constant state of activity and the constant change of persons, I forgot the danger. The officers told us such jolly stories, and seemed in such fine spirits, that gradually we took heart, too. There was not a moment's rest for anyone.

Early next morning the President came down. He was still feeble and pale from his illness. Custis Lee and Mr. Chesnut loaded his pistols and he drove off in Dr. Garnett's carriage, they on horseback riding alongside. By eight o'clock the troops from Petersburg came in — and the danger was over. They will never strip Richmond of troops this way again. We had a narrow squeeze of it, but we escaped. It was a terrible night, although we made the best of it.

Here is a scrap from the winter of 1862. I have already written of the summers of '63, when Vicksburg did fall. I was walking on Franklin Street, and I met Mr. Chesnut. "Come with me for a few minutes to the War Office, and then I will go home with you." He took me up a dark stairway, and then we went down a long dark corridor and he left me sitting in a window, saying he "would not be gone a second, that he was obliged to go into the Secretary of War's room." There I sat for mortal hours. Men came to light the gas. From the first I put down my veil, so that nobody might know me. Numbers of persons passed whom I knew, but I scarcely felt respectable, seated up there in that odd way, so I said not a word but looked out of the window. Judge Campbell slowly walked up and down with his hands behind him, the saddest face I ever saw. No wonder he was out of spirits that night! Finally Mr. Ould came. I called. He joined me at once, in no little amazement to find me there, and stayed with me until Colonel Chesnut came. In point of fact, I sent him to look up that stray member of my family. When Mr. Chesnut came, he said: "Oh, Mr. Seddon and I got into an argument, and time slipped away. The truth is, I utterly forgot you were there." When we were once more out in the streets he explained:

"Now don't scold me, for there is bad news. Pemberton has been fighting the Yankees by brigades, and he has been beaten every time; and now Vicksburg must go!" I suppose that was his side of the argument with Seddon.

On another occasion I visited the War Office. I went with Mrs. Ould to see her husband. We wanted to arrange a party on the river on the Flag of Truce boat, to visit Claremont and Brandon; but Mr. Chesnut got into one of his too careful fits, said there was risk in it, and so upset all my plans. Just then I was to go up to the John Rutherfords's by the canal boat. That, too, he vetoed as "too risky," as if anybody was going to trouble us!

One day General Edward Johnston was walking with us in the Capitol Square and the Robbs hurried up so as not to miss us. The Robbs wanted us to join a party who were going to Drury's Bluff next day. Joyfully I acceded to their request. Drury's was a place I wished to see. It was our Gibraltar. At the boat next day, we were joined by a very handsome Englishman, who had lost a leg at Seven Pines. He proved himself to be as agreeable as he was good-looking. I was repeatedly told how interesting the scenery was between Richmond and Drury's, but I can't say I remember anything about it.

Captain Smith Lee met us at the Bluff. He was awfully glad to see me, and helped me up the path. Captain Robb called: "I think Captain Lee is carrying you bodily up the bank." That was not quite true, for I am no light weight; but he was helping me to go up slowly. He remembers how my heart beats when I climb. He took us to his quarters, as clean and as neat as a man-of-war's quarterdeck, and there I sat until I got my breath again.

How he pitched into my country! "South Carolina be hanged! She brought us into this snarl. How I did want to stay in the old Navy. But Virginia comes first with us all, you know, so I am here."

He told us he must go to receive a grand party, Secretary of the Navy Mallory, Attorney General Watts, etc. When they arrived, Mr. Mallory offered me his arm, and we set off to visit and inspect the fortifications of this, our "Gibraltar of the River Jeems," of whose deeds they are so proud. It holds its own against all comers. Everywhere we went, the troops presented arms, and I was fool enough to ask Mr. Mallory why they did that. With a suppressed titter he replied: "I dare say because I am at the head of the Navy Department."

These Navy heads came to try a new gun. After our two luncheons we adjourned and they departed to try their gun, whose boom-boom was the solemn accompaniment of our conversation. We dined on Captain Lee's ship, and after dinner, Captain Lee and I walked the quarterdeck for one good hour, and talked of old days in Washington to our heart's content. We kissed our hands to the Secretary of the Navy's party as they steamed by us on their way home. They were in their grand boat. We had betaken ourselves to the small affair which brought us down there. Regretfully we turned our faces home. Arrived at Rockets, we landed and found no carriage to meet us. Then they found one, but the lame Englishman had lost his leg in our cause, so I said I preferred to walk and gave him my seat. Phil Robb and I set off for Clay Street, and for three long miles I dragged my weary limbs along. When we got home, I was utterly worn out, dead beat. Molly scolded me violently, and made me go to bed at once. There I stayed for nearly a week with fever-headaches, tossing around in dreams.

In Columbia one day I met Mrs. S. grieving over the loss of her clothes, her trunk gone astray hopelessly. "You go on as if you had lost a child," I said, and she retorted: "No indeed! There's no embargo on children down here, but clothes once gone are gone forever. One can make shift to live without children, but how can one do without decent clothes?"

In October we were in Camden. Mr. Chesnut was there at home on his way back to Richmond. He was sent by the President on the rounds of the Western armies. He says Polk is a splendid old fellow.

The battle at Chickamauga did not begin until eleven, although Bragg ordered the advance at daylight. Bragg and his generals quarrel. I think a general worthless, whose subalterns quarrel with him. There is something wrong about the man. Good generals are adored by their soldiers; see Napoleon, Caesar, Stonewall, Lee!

Old Sam (Hood) received orders to hold a certain bridge against the enemy, and he had already driven the enemy several miles beyond it while the slow generals were still asleep. Hood has won a victory, though now he has only one leg to stand on. Mrs. McLane writes that it is even worse since Mr. Davis was there. He could not reconcile them. Atlanta is crammed with displaced or dissatisfied generals.

Mr. Chesnut was with the President when he reviewed our army under the enemy's guns before Chattanooga. He said it was a splendid cavalcade. In Atlanta he found the officers so hospitable and friendly that we have just sent a box of old brandy, old wine, and good home-cured hams to them in kind remembrance.

He brought a funny story from their campfires, about a man — call him Jack Brown — who drank fearfully, till suddenly to the surprise of friend and foe he ceased. It was a dream which checked his mad career. He dreamed that he died and went directly to Hell — or Hades, if the first word is too rough for ears polite. The Devil opened the door for him with ready politeness, bowed low, was too civil by half, said he was charmed to see him, said he had been looking for him for some time, knew his habits and knew how quickly that sort of thing brought people to his hospitable abode. Then his Darkness shouted to his imps below: "Hello, down there! Fire up Number Nine for Jack Brown."

Mr. Chesnut said he told Mr. Davis that every honest man he saw out west thought well of Joe Johnston. The President detests Joe Johnston for all the trouble he has given him, and General Joe returns the compliment with compound interest. His hatred of Jeff Davis amounts to a religion. With him it colors all things. Joe Johnston, whether advancing or retreating, is magnetic; he does draw the good will of those by whom he is surrounded. Being such a good hater, it is a pity he had not elected to hate somebody else than the President of our country. He hates not wisely but too well.

Our friend Breckenridge * received Mr. Chesnut with open arms. There is nothing narrow, nothing self-seeking about Breckenridge. He is not one of those who see no good except in his own red-hot partisans.

A country gentleman was here who complained that he had taken provisions to the Atlanta hospitals, including a bag of sugar. When he asked for sugar for his tea, the surgeon answered curtly: "There is none, sir." Afterwards, he dined with a mess, and saw them take the identical bag of white sugar he had carried to Atlanta and mix for their own surgical mouths many a good hot toddy. That sort of thing is human nature at its lowest.

* Vice-President under Buchanan, John C. Breckenridge came South soon after the outbreak of hostilities and joined the Confederate Army.

XVII

Camden

October 27th, 1863. — Now I can give dates once more, and not a jumble of scraps and letters. I resume my journal. Young Wade Hampton has been here for a few days, a guest of our nearest neighbor and cousin Phil Stockton. Wade, without being the beauty or the athlete that his brother Preston is, is such a nice boy. We gave him a small party. What was lacking in company was made up for by the excellence of Colonel Chesnut's old Madeira. Oh, if everything in the Confederacy was as truly good as old Mr. Chesnut's wine cellars! General Joe Johnston, according to Wade, is so careful of his aids that Wade has never seen a battle; he has always happened to be sent afar off when the fighting comes. He says: "No man exposes himself more recklessly to danger than General Johnston, and no one strives harder to keep others out of it; but the business of this war is to save the country, and a commander must risk his men's lives to do it. As the French say, one can't make an omelette without breaking the eggs."

A letter from Johnny in Richmond speaks amusingly of an incident there, concerning a certain lady. "Her dress was none too high in the neck and by no means tight fitting around her lovely, high-born, FFV bosom. The oysters were red hot. One fell! She screamed! B—— dived for it with a fork, fished it up in a trice. There was much confusion of face, and an instantaneous drawing up of her light shawl. With a fork! Imagine! The muff! I should certainly have risked burning my fingers that time!"

November 5th. — Now Johnny is here, and for a week we have had such a tranquil happy time, with both my husband and Johnny at home. Mr. Chesnut spent his time sauntering around with his father, or stretched on the rug before my fire reading "Vanity Fair" and "Pendennis," and we kept Esmond for the last. He owns that he had a good time.

Johnny was happy too. He does not care for books, though he will read a novel now and then, if the girls continue to talk of it before him. He comes pulling his long blonde moustache, irresolutely, as if he hoped to be advised not to read it. "Aunt Mary, will I like this thing?" He was but a baby when his father died; he was a delicate boy, and has never been in robust health in his life. He is fair and frail, tall and thin. His schools were selected with an eye to his health, and finally a private tutor was tried. He took his diploma at the South Carolina College. He keeps his face so absolutely devoid of expression that except upon rare occasions, one knows nothing of his thoughts or feelings. He knows nothing of politics and cares less. Roughing it in camp, instead of killing him as we thought it would, has made him comparatively strong and hardy. He rides like an Arab and loves his horses in the same way. He is devoted to what he calls "good eating." I think he is happiest when he sends one of his fine horses to some girl who is worthy to ride such a horse. She must be beautiful and graceful. Then, superbly mounted, he goes to ride with her. He is sure to go slowly along where everybody can see them, and can admire the horses and the girl. Strange to say, he has not one jot of personal vanity. Being so silent, one does not suspect him of being a close observer, but he is always taking notes; and he is a keen and merciless, caustic and cruel critic of men and manners. Above all things he waits and watches for the shortcomings of women. I do not think he has an idea what we are fighting about, and he does not want to know. He says, "My company . . . my men" with a pride, a faith and an affection which is sublime. He came into his inheritance at twenty-one (just as the war began) and it was a goodly one, fine old houses and an estate to match.

NOVEMBER 23rd. — Yesterday Johnny went to his plantation for the first time since the war began. John Witherspoon went with him and reports hearing: "How you do, Marster! How you come on?" from every side, in the noisiest welcome from the darkies. Johnny was silently shaking black hands, right and left, as he rode into the crowd. As the noise subsided he said to the overseer: "Send down more corn and fodder for my horses." To the driver: "Have you any peas?"

"Plenty, sir." "Send a wagonload down for the cows at Bloomsbury. They have not milk and butter enough there for me. Any eggs? Send down all you can collect. How about my turkeys and ducks? Send them down two at a time. How about the mutton? Fat? That's good. Send down two a week." As they rode home, John Witherspoon remarked: "I was surprised that you did not go into the fields to see your crops." "What was the use?" "And the Negroes, you had so little talk with them." "No use to talk to them before the overseer. They are coming down to see me day and night, by platoons, and they talk me dead. Besides, William and Parish go up there every night, and God knows they tell me enough plantation scandal, the overseer feathering his nest, the Negroes ditto, all at my expense. Between the two fires, I mean to get something to eat while I am here."

He keeps up a racket in the house with his horses, his dogs and his servants; and the everlasting junketting that he has set afloat never ceases. He loves dancing with all his heart. It is a pleasure that he takes soberly, sadly and in earnest. We got up a charming picnic at Mulberry. Everything was propitious, the most perfect of days, the old place in great beauty, those large rooms delightful for dancing, as good a dinner as mortal appetite could crave, the best of fish, fowl, and game, and a cellar that cannot be excelled. In spite of the blockade, Mulberry does the honors nobly yet.

Mrs. Edward Stockton drove down with me. She helped me with her taste and tact in arranging things. We had no trouble, however. All of the old servants scented the prey from afar off, and they literally flocked in and made themselves useful.

Johnny enjoys life thoroughly. He loves dancing as well as riding and fighting, swimming, horses, jumping fences or fox hunting. He sneers at women — being now a few years over twenty — and he has been idiotically in love with one woman all his life. Her presence brings a hectic flush in his pale face, as clear and distinct as a girl's; but that subject is taboo, for of course she loved another. "You see," he says, "I am not a marrying man. My people, they say: 'Marster, why don't you marry and leave a young missy here to look after we?' I say: 'She'd not stay here and look after you! Never! She'd be trotting after me in the army, bothering everywhere.' Lord, what a nuisance they are. Now you just wait. After this cruel war is over, then look out."

XVIII

Richmond

NOVEMBER 28th. — Our pleasant home sojourn was soon broken up. Johnny had to go back to duty, and Mr. Chesnut was ordered by the President to make a second visit to Bragg's army. So we came here, where the Prestons had taken apartments for me. Molly was with me. Adam Team, with Isaac McLaughlin's help, came with us to take charge of the eight huge boxes of provisions I brought from home. Isaac is a servant of ours, the only one Mr. Chesnut ever bought in his life. His wife belonged to Reverend Thomas Davis, and Isaac to somebody else. This owner of Isaac's was about to go west, and Isaac was distracted. They asked one thousand dollars for him. He is a huge creature, really a magnificent specimen of a colored gentleman. His occupation had been that of a stage driver. Now he is a carpenter, or he will be someday. He is awfully grateful to us for buying him, and is really devoted to his wife and children, though he has a strange way of showing it, for he has a mistress — which fact Molly never failed to grumble about, as soon as his back was turned. "Great big good-for-nothing thing! Come a-whimpering to Marster to buy him for his wife's sake, and all the time he carrying on wid dat —" "Oh Molly stop that."

I was daft with delight to get away from home. My last public act before leaving Camden was to matronize a party down at my mother's old home, seven miles from town. After dinner, Uncle John came to me with tears in his eyes. I had not asked him to say grace before dinner! Such a thing had never happened in that house before! He was cruelly mortified at my heathenism. In vain I said: "But it is only a picnic, a stand-up meal. Nobody asks grace at a picnic!" "Your mother's house . . ." he repeated, over and over. I was sorry to have hurt his feelings and it spoiled all my pleasure.

Mr. Davis visited Charleston and had an enthusiastic reception, Beauregard, Rhetts, Jordan to the contrary notwithstanding. He described it all to Mr. Preston. Mr. Aiken's perfect old Carolina style of living delighted him; those old grey-haired darkies and their automatic, noiseless perfection of training. One does miss that sort of thing. Your own servants think for you, they know your ways and your wants, they save you all responsibility even in matters of your own ease and well-being. The butler at Mulberry would be miserable, and feel himself a ridiculous failure, were I ever forced to ask him for anything.

November 30th. — On the way to Richmond, I had an adventure at Kingsville. Of course, I know nothing of children; in point of fact I'm awfully afraid of them. Mrs. Edward Barnwell came with us from Camden. She had a magnificent boy of two years old. Now don't expect me to reduce that adjective, for this little creature was a wonder of childlike beauty, health and strength. Why not? If like produces like, with such a handsome pair to claim as father and mother? The boy's eyes alone would make any girl's fortune.

At first he made himself very agreeable, repeating nursery rhymes and singing. Then something went wrong. Suddenly he changed to a little fiend, he fought and kicked and scratched like a tiger, he did everything that was naughty, and he did it with a will, as if he liked it. His lovely Mamma, with flushed cheeks and streaming eyes, implored him to be a good boy.

We stopped at Kingsville. I got out first, and then Mrs. Barnwell's nurse, who put the little man down by me. "Look after him a moment," she begged. "I must help Mrs. Barnwell with the bundles." She stepped hastily back on board and the cars moved off and ran down a half mile to turn. I trembled in my shoes before this child! No man could ever frighten me so. If he should choose to be bad again! It seemed an eternity while I waited for that train to turn and come back again. My little charge took things quietly. For me he had a perfect contempt, and of me no fear whatever. I was his abject slave for the nonce. He stretched himself out lazily, at full length; and then he pointed downwards. "Those are great legs," said he, solemnly looking at his own. I immediately joined him in admiring them enthusiastically. Near him he spied a bundle. "Pussycat tied up in that bundle!" He was up in a second, and pounced upon it. If we were to be taken up as thieves, no matter; I dared not meddle with that child, I had seen what he could do. In the bundle there were several cooked sweet potatoes, tied up in an old handkerchief, the property of some Negro, probably. He squared himself off comfortably, broke one in half and began to eat. Evidently he had found what he was fond of. In this posture of events, Mrs. Barnwell found us. She came with comic dismay in every feature. She did not know what our relations might be when she came back to us, feared we might have undertaken to fight it out alone as best we might. The old nurse cried: "Lawsy me!" with both hands uplifted. Without a word I fled. In another moment the Wilmington train would have left me.

We broke down only once between Kingsville and Wilmington; but between Wilmington and Weldon we contrived to do the thing so effectually as to have to remain twelve hours at that forlorn station. The one room that I saw was crowded with soldiers. Adam Team succeeded in routing out two chairs for me. Upon one I sat, and put my feet on the other. Molly sat flat on the floor, resting her head against my chair. I woke cold and cramped. An officer — he did not give his name, but said he was from Louisiana — came up and urged me to go near the fire. He gave me his seat by the fire, where I found an old lady and two young ones, with two men in the uniform of common soldiers. We talked as easily to each other all night as if we had known each other all our lives. We discussed the war, the army, the news of the day. No questions were asked, no names given; there was no personal discourse whatever, and yet if these men and women were not gentry and of the best sort, I do not know ladies and gentlemen when I see them.

Being a little surprised at the want of interest Adam Team and Isaac showed in my well-being, I walked out to see, and I found them working like beavers. They had been at it all night. In the breakdown, my boxes were smashed. They had first gathered up the contents, and now were trying to hammer up the boxes so as to make them once more available.

At Petersburg, a smartly dressed female came in, looked around at the crowd, then asked for the seat by me. Now Molly's seat was paid for the same as mine, but she got up at once, gave the lady her seat and stood behind me. I am sure Molly believes herself my bodyguard, as well as my servant. The lady, having arranged herself comfortably in Molly's seat, began in plaintive accents to tell her melancholy tale. She was a widow, she had lost her husband in the battle around Richmond. Soon someone going out, a man offered her a vacant seat; and straight as an arrow she went in for a flirtation with the polite gentleman. Another person said to me, a perfect stranger: "Well look yonder! As soon as she began whining about her dead beau, I knew she was after another one." "Beau indeed!" cried another listener. "She said it was her husband!" "Husband or lover, it's all the same. She won't lose any time. It won't be her fault if she don't have another one soon."

But the grand scene was the night before. The cars were crowded with soldiers, of course, and not a human being that I knew. An Irish woman, so announced by her brogue, came in. She marched up and down the car, loudly lamenting the want of gallantry in the men who would not make way for her. Two men got up and gave her their seats, saying it did not matter, they were going to get out at the next stopping place.

She was gifted with the most pronounced brogue I ever heard, and she gave us a taste of it. She continued to say that the men ought all to get out of that, that the car was "shuteable" only for ladies. She placed on the vacant seat next to her a large looking-glass, and she continued to harangue us until she fell asleep. A tired soldier, coming in and seeing what he supposed to be an empty seat, quietly slipped into it. Crash went the glass, the soldier groaned, the Irish woman shrieked. The man was badly cut by the broken glass upon which he sat, but she did not mind that; she was simply a mad woman, she shook her fist in his face, said she was a lone woman and he had got in that seat for no good, how did he dare, etc. I do not think the man uttered a word. The conductor took him into another car to have pieces of glass picked out of his clothes, and she continued to rave. Adam Team shouted aloud and laughed as if he were in the Hermitage swamp. The woman's unreasonable wrath and absurd accusations were comic, of course.

Soon the car was silent and I fell into a comfortable doze. I felt Molly give me a gentle shake. "Listen Missis! Hear how loud Mars' Adam Team is talking, and all about old Marster and our business, and to strangers. It's a shame." "Is he saying any harm of us?" "No, Ma'am, not that. He is a-bragging for dear life, how old de ole Marster is, and how rich he is, and all that. I gwine tell him stop." Up stalked Molly. "Mars' Adam, Missis say please don't talk so loud. When people travel they don't do that-a-way."

It reminded me of Mrs. Frank Hampton's explanation of why she wanted to know Mr. Chesnut. Bill Dogan has a laugh that nothing rivals in sound but the falls of Niagara, the very noisiest laugh ever known in this continent. He has been laughing for twenty years, for he is a good fellow, and people considered him as inevitable as one of the forces of nature. He joined Frank Hampton and Mr. Chesnut on the street in Columbia, shouting with glee, running first one side of them and then the other with a story at which he alone laughed, bumping them out of the straight path, stepping in front of them and walking backward, trampling on their toes, sticking his face in theirs as he roared to force them to listen to them. Frank Hampton took him as calmly as the east wind, which he would try and get out of the way of; but not so Mr. Chesnut. He said: "Mr. Dogan, do go and walk on the other side of the street. I never can bear a man to make me conspicuous by noise in a public place." And with a loud laugh, as though at the funniest of all ideas, Dogan went.

After Molly had disposed of Adam Team's narrative, she politely offered me some luncheon from her basket. She said she had cooked some things she knew I liked, broiled chicken, and turnovers as light as a feather. But then she cried, looking all around: "Land, Missis, where is my basket? There ain't no niggers to steal in this car!" She was as loud and violent as the Irish woman. "Sholy, white gentlemen ain't stolen a servant's basket of vittles." She was raging. "White mens, which of you stole my chicken?" I touched her. "Sit down and hold your tongue." She went down like a shot, and I said: "Who is making a noise now? You are as bad as Adam Team or the Irish woman."

When we got up to leave the car, Molly's empty basket was found beside her. Two men had pretended to sleep through Molly's vociferations when she missed her basket. I suspected those hungry individuals, but kept my thoughts to myself. When Molly told Sally Preston, instead of going off in sympathetic abuse of the soldiers who made a raid on her basket, Sally paid Molly this compliment. "And did you worry Mrs. Chesnut that way by making a fuss? You know, Molly, I have told you over and over, you are a good soul, but your manners are atrocious." To which Molly responded by the broadest grins of delight. She is absolutely devoted to Sally, and Sally has undertaken to teach her better manners.

I found Mr. Preston's man Hal at the depot with a carriage to take me to my Richmond house. Mary Preston had rented these apartments for me. I found my dear girls there, with a nice fire, and everything looked so nice and inviting to the weary travellers. Mrs. Grundy, who occupies the lower floor, sent me such a real Virginia tea; hot cakes, rolls, etc. Think of living in the house with Mrs. Grundy, and having no fear of what Mrs. Grundy will say.

Now Mr. Chesnut has come and likes the house and the Grundys. Already he has bought Grundy's horse for sixteen hundred Confederate dollars cash. He is nearer to being contented and happy than I ever saw him. He has not established a grievance yet, but I am on the lookout daily. He will soon find out whatever there is wrong about Cary Street.

Ives, the aide-de-camp, is out of favor. He opens too many of Mrs. Davis's private letters, by mistake. "By mistake," said Mr. Chesnut. "Of course! Can anyone doubt it?" "Yes, by mistake, as you say," I agreed. "But do you and Custis Lee and John Taylor Wood and Mr. Browne ever make that mistake?"

Hood is here at somebody's house. Buck saw me sending a rice pudding to the wounded man — it seems he cares for no other dainty — whereupon she said, in her sweetest, mildest, sleepiest way: "I never cared particularly about him, but now that he has chosen to go with those people, I would not marry him if he had a thousand legs, instead of having just lost one." Marry him? But I asked no questions!

I gave a party. Mrs. Davis was very witty, the Preston girls very handsome, Isabella's fun fast and furious. No party could have gone off more successfully, but my husband decides we are to have no more festivities; says this is not the time or the place for such gaieties.

Maria Freeland is perfectly delightful on the subject of her own wedding. She is ready to the last piece of lace, but her hard-hearted father says "No." She adores John Lewis; that goes without saying. She does not pretend, however, to be as much in love as Mary Preston. In point of fact, she never saw anyone before who was. But she is as much in love as she can be with a man who, though he is not very handsome, is as eligible a match as a girl could make. He is all that heart could wish, and he comes of such a handsome family. His mother, Esther Maria Coxe, was the beauty of a century; and his father was a nephew of General Washington. I think he is far better looking than John Darby or Mr. Miles. She always intended to marry better than Mary Preston or Bettie Bierne.

Lucy Haxall is positively engaged to Captain Coffey, an Englishman. She is sure she will marry him. It is her first fancy. "And she is over thirty," says Grundy, her brother-in-law.

Mr. Venable of Lee's staff was at our party, so out of spirits. He knows everything that is going on, so his depression bodes us no good.

Today General Hampton sent Mr. Chesnut a fine saddle that he had captured from the Yankees in battle array. Mrs. Scotch Allan, Edgar Allan Poe's patron's wife, sent me cream and Lady Cheek apples from her farm. John R. Thompson, the sole literary fellow I know in Richmond, sent me "Leisure Hours in Town" by "A Country Parson."

Mr. Chesnut says he hopes I will be contented, because he came here this winter to please me. If I could have been satisfied at home, he would have resigned his aidship and gone into some service in South Carolina. I am a good excuse, if good for nothing else.

Our old tempestuous Keitt breakfasted with us yesterday. I wish I could remember half of the brilliant things he said. Mr. Chesnut has now gone with him to the War Office. Colonel Keitt thinks it is time he was promoted. He wants to be a Brigadier. Stephen Elliott is promoted, and who deserves it more? My husband has certainly been a friend to the Elliotts. He found that fine fellow Stephen Elliott's papers pigeon-holed, wrapped up in his father's application for a chaplainship. And he lent them Sandy Hill; he would take no rent from a family doing their duty to the country as were the Elliotts.

Now Charleston is bombarded night and day. It fairly makes me dizzy to think of that everlasting racket they are beating about people's ears down there. We hear that Bragg is defeated, and separated from Longstreet — and Rosencrantz not taken after all! One begins each day with "What bad news next, I wonder?"

NOVEMBER 30th. — Anxiety pervades. Lee is fighting Meade, Bragg falling back before Grant, Longstreet — the soldiers call him Peter the Slow — sitting down before Knoxville.

At Mrs. Huger's to see Ellie Preston, and Mrs. Huger said: "Hard measure had General Huger. One man may steal a horse, but the other must not look over the hedge Was General Huger * ever behind time as Bragg and Longstreet are, always?"

General Bragg's aids advised Preston Johnston to do as they did, to destroy nine out of every ten letters sent the general by non-combatants, women and children. Mr. Johnston was horrified. Women and children are sacred to him, and their complaints come nearer his ear than any. "How many of such letters do you show the President?" asked Mrs. Davis gravely. "Oh, about one in sixty." "General Lee requires us to answer every letter," said Mr. Venable, "and to do our

* Mrs. Huger refers to the fact that General Huger's tardiness was sometimes blamed for the failure to destroy McClellan's army during the Seven Days.

best to console the poor creatures whose husbands and sons are fighting the battles of their country. Some women wrote to complain of Stuart, whose horse the girls bedecked with garlands, and said he was in the habit of kissing girls. They thought General Stuart should be forbidden to kiss one unless he could kiss all."

Someone, a happy young bride, called her husband: "Peedee." I said: "That is the Indian name of one of our rivers. We have Pee Dee, Santee, Wateree and Congaree." This sober remark was received with a burst of derision. "P.D. means 'precious darling,' just as D.C. means 'delicious creature'!"

December 2nd. — Bragg begs to be relieved from his command. The army will be relieved to get rid of him. He has a winning way of earning everybody's detestation. Heavens, how they hate him! Hardee declines even a temporary command of the Western Army. Preston Johnston has been sent out there post-haste, not even allowed time to go home and tell his wife good-bye.

The first of December, we went with a party of Mrs. Ould's planning to see a French Frigate which lay at anchor down the river. The French officers went down on board our boat. At half past seven, in that bitter cold, Molly had a scalding hot cup of coffee for me, and a good fire in the dining-room. Then we had to wait one mortal hour for Maggie Howell and the Prestons. Colonel Preston always says: "While I wait for you, my dears, I spend the time in thinking of all your faults." Mrs. Myers joined in, with a black feather flapping over her beautiful eyes. Mrs. Randolph, at that early hour, looked more magnificently handsome than ever. The Lees were along.

The French officers were not in the least attractive, neither in manner nor appearance; but the ladies were most attentive to them, and showered bad French upon them with a lavish hand. The French Frigate was a dirty little thing, though Dr. Garnett was so buoyed up with hope that the French were coming to our rescue that he would not let me say, as I wished to: "An English man-of-war is the cleanest thing known in the world." Mr. Ould said as we went to dinner on our own steamer: "They will not drink Mr. President's health. They do not acknowledge us to be a nation. So mind, none of you say 'Emperor,' not once!" Dr. Garnett interpreted the laws of national politeness otherwise. He stepped forward, his mantle fairly distended with so much French, saying: "Vieff l'Emporer!" But silence prevailed.

The Lieutenant's name was Rousseau, and on the French Frigate, lying on one of the cabin tables, was a volume of Jean Jacques's works — side by side, strange to say, with a map of South Carolina. This Lieutenant was asked by Mary Lee to select some lady, that she might introduce him. He answered, "I choose you," with a look that was a benediction and a prayer.

Preston Hampton was the handsomest man on board, and as lazy and as sleepy as ever. He said of the Frenchmen: "They can't help not being good-looking, but with all the world open to them, why do they wear such shabby clothes?" At dinner he stood behind my chair, a great hungry six-foot-two boy. I asked for everything on the table, and passed it over my shoulder to Preston, who stood at ease and ate at his leisure. So now I am in a fine condition for Hetty Cary's Starvation Party, where they will give thirty dollars for the music, and not a cent for a morsel to eat. Preston said contentedly: "I hate dancing, and I hate cold water, so I will eschew the festivity tonight!" At the park, the Governor Letcher party clung together and sang without ceasing. Dr. Garnett in a patronizing way said he played a poor game of whist, but quite good enough to play with ladies. The ladies beat the braggart with ease, and triumphed as only women can.

I found John R. Thompson at our house when I got home, so tired. He brought me the last number of Cornhill. He knew how much I was interested in Trollope's story, "Framley Parsonage."

Next day I went to tell Mrs. Davis all about the river expedition. I met Mrs. Wigfall, who asked me with a sneer if the distance between Cary Street and the White House was not disagreeable to me. Wigfall, without giving me an opportunity to reply, began: "They say Benjamin wrote the President's message. Never! Jeff Davis writes his own messages!" He gave Mrs. Wigfall and myself no time to spar.

Young Hudson was there. He went with me last spring, that moonlight night — shall I ever forget the pain and fear of it all — to see Stonewall Jackson lying in state at the Capitol.

DECEMBER 4th. — I bought yesterday at the Commissary's one barrel of flour, one bushel of potatoes, one peck of rice, five pounds of salt beef, and one peck of salt, all for fifty dollars. In the street, a barrel of flour sells for one hundred and fifteen dollars.

DECEMBER 5th. — Wigfall was here last night. He began by wanting to hang Jeff Davis. Mr. Chesnut managed him beautifully, and he soon ceased to talk that virulent nonsense, and calmed down to his usual strong common sense. I knew it was quite late, but I had no idea of the hour till Mr. Chesnut beckoned me out. "It is all your fault."

"What?" "Why will you persist in looking so interested in all Wigfall is saying? Don't let him catch your eye! Look in the fire. Did you not hear it strike two?" This attack was so sudden, so violent, so unlooked for, that I could only laugh hysterically. However, as an obedient wife, I went back gravely, took my seat, and looked into the fire. I dare not even raise my eyes to see if my husband also looked in the fire. Wigfall soon tired of so tame an audience and took his departure.

General Lawton was here last night. He superseded Colonel Myers last winter, in spite of Miles with the Congress at his heels. He was one of Stonewall's generals, so I listened with all my ears. "Stonewall could not sleep, so every two or three nights you were waked up by orders to have your brigade in marching order before daylight, and to report in person to the Commander. Then you were marched a few miles out and then a few miles in again." "A little different from the western stories, and some generals nearer Richmond asleep several hours after they have been expected to attack." General Lawton said: "The restless, discontented spirits move the world. All this of Stonewall's was to make us always ready, ever on the alert; and the end of it was this. Jackson's men had gone half a day's march before Pete Longstreet waked and breakfasted." He added: "I think there is a popular delusion about the amount of praying Jackson did. He certainly preferred a fight on Sunday to a sermon. Failing to manage a fight, he loved next best a long Presbyterian sermon, Calvinistic to the core.

"He had no sympathy with human infirmity. He was a one-idea man. He looked upon broken-down men and stragglers as the same thing. He classed all who were weak and weary, who fainted by the wayside, as men wanting in patriotism. If a man's face was white as cotton and his pulse so low that you could not feel it, he merely looked upon him impatiently as an inefficient soldier, and rode off out of patience. He was the true type of all great soldiers. He did not value human life where he had an object to accomplish. He could order men to their death as a matter of course. Napoleon's French conscription could not have kept him supplied with men, he used up his command so rapidly. Hence, while he was alive there was more pride than truth in the talk of his soldiers' love for him. They feared him, and obeyed him to the death; faith they had in him, a faith stronger than death. But I doubt if he had their love, though their respect he did command. And now that they begin to see that a few years more of Stonewall Jackson would have freed them from the yoke of the hateful Yankee, they deify him. They are proud to have been one of the famous Stonewall Brigade, to have been a brick in that wall.

"But be ye sure, it was bitter hard work to keep up with Stonewall Jackson, as all know who ever served with him. He gave his orders rapidly and distinctly, and rode away without allowing answer or remonstrance. When you failed, you were apt to be put under arrest. When you succeeded, he only said 'good.' "

Again the Examiner publishes the story of Mr. Davis's cotton remaining unburned. This was settled last year. Mr. Davis's cotton was burnt, and all the world knows it; but the Examiner knows that the everlasting harping on this sort of thing must annoy Mr. Davis, so it persists.

I spent seventy-five dollars today for a little tea and sugar. I have five hundred left. Mr. Chesnut's pay never has paid for the rent of lodgings since the war began. But John Thompson sent me Blackwood's Magazine, and Mr. Davis gave me a love of a parasol, so this was a day to be marked in white.

DECEMBER 7th.—Judge Campbell has come from Alabama bringing a supply of butter and hams, given him by Mrs. Fitzpatrick. Neither Clay nor Fitzpatrick returned to the Senate. Mr. Chesnut came in with a dreadful tale just now. I have wept so often for things that have never happened, that I withhold my tears now for a dead certainty. Today a poor woman threw herself on her husband's coffin and kissed it. She was weeping bitterly, and so did I, in sympathy. Mr. Chesnut could see me and everyone he loved hung, drawn and quartered without moving a muscle; he could have the same gentle operation performed on himself and make no sign. When through my tears I told him so, he answered, in unmoved tones: "So can any civilized man! Savages, Indians at least, are more dignified in that particular than we are. Hysterical grief never moves me. It annoys me. You think yourself a miracle of sensibility, but self-control is what you need. That is all that separates you from those you look down upon as unfeeling."

Gloom and unspoken despondency hangs like a pall everywhere. Today I saw an account of the sale of Judge Campbell's, Dr. Garnett's and Colonel Ives's houses in Washington. Patriotism is a pretty heavy load to carry sometimes.

I am reading the life of Savonarola. I am absorbed in it up to the ears, body and soul given up to Savonarola. John Thompson sent me the book to tune me up for "Romola."

There cannot be a Christian soldier. Kill or be killed; that's their trade, or they are a failure. Stonewall was a fanatic, the exact character we wanted, willing to raise the Black Flag. He knew that to achieve our liberty, to win our battles, men must die.

DECEMBER 9th. — Today the girls were to come here before luncheon. Mary arrived first. She is the punctual member of the family. As I was giving Lawrence some orders in the dining-room, she called out suddenly: "Come here, Mrs. Chesnut. They are lifting Hood out of his carriage, here at your door." Everybody had been to see General Hood except the Prestons and myself, so he came here. Mrs. Grundy promptly had him borne into her drawing-room, which was on the first floor. Mary Preston and I ran down and greeted him as cheerfully and as cordially as if nothing had happened since we last saw him standing before us.

He was lying on a sofa with a carriage blanket thrown over him. Soon the party was all assembled. Had he heard of the party, or was this a casual coincidence? Mary Preston assisted me in behaving as if nothing was the matter, but the others were hopelessly depressed. They looked as if it would be a luxury to pull out their handkerchiefs and have a good cry. Our wounded friend Sam watched the door wishfully. To end suspense, he asked: "How is Buck?" "Better, but she has been ill in bed for several days."

Heavens, how he was waited upon! Some cut-up oranges were brought him, and he said: "How kind people are! Not once since I was wounded have I ever been left without fruit, hard as it is to get now." "The money value of friendship is easily counted now," said someone. "Oranges are five dollars apiece." Many persons called, among them Mrs. Randolph. Sam whispered: "She is handsomer than ever." Whispered Brewster: "He knows a pretty woman when he sees one."

There had been never a sigh nor a word of sympathy until newcomers were all condolence and tears; it was "leg," "leg," "leg." Old Sam groaned, and Mary Preston made a gesture of despair. Mrs. Mallory came in and in warm terms hailed him as a martyr to his country! The Wigfalls were here too.

"I do not mean to stay at home," said Sam, who by this time had a hectic flush of fever on his face. "This is the first house I have had myself dragged to. I mean to be as happy a fool as a one-legged man can be. But send me off now. So many strangers scare me. I can't run now as I did before."

DECEMBER 10th. — At Mrs. Preston's, I met Mrs. Huger, who was miserable because she heard General Lee was to be sent west. Hood was there, Buck talking to him with tears not quite in her eyes but audible in her voice.

Mrs. Davis and Mrs. Lyons came. We had luncheon brought in for them, and then we walked home with Mrs. Davis. We met the President riding alone. Surely that is wrong. It must be unsafe for him, when there are so many traitors, not to speak of bribed Negroes. But Burton Harrison says he prefers to go alone, and there is none to gainsay him.

My husband laid the law down last night. I felt it to be the last drop in my full cup. "No more feasting in this house! This is no time for junketing and merry-making. There is a positive want of proper feeling in the life you lead." "You said you brought me here to enjoy one winter before you took me home and turned my face to a dead wall." But he is the master of the house. To hear is to obey.

DECEMBER 14th. — Mrs. Ould, who lunched with us at Mrs. Davis's, told of Mrs. Stanard's wedding finery, which has come by flag of truce, by favor of "Beast" Butler. I saw Mrs. T. D. there, and asked about her pretty little girl that we knew on Sullivan's Island. "Dead!" Never will I ask again for anyone I do not see. The horror of this wrong-timed question hung round me all day.

I drove out with Mrs. Davis. She had a watch in her hand which some poor dead soldier wanted sent to his family. First we went to her mantua-maker; then we drove to the Fair Grounds, where the band was playing. Suddenly she missed the watch! She remembered having it when we came out of the mantua-maker's. We drove back instantly, and there the watch was lying, near the steps of the little porch in front of the house. No one had passed in, or no one had seen it. "Blessed chance!" she cried.

She rates Fitzhugh Lee far above Hood as a commander.

Preston Hampton went with me to see Conny Cary. The talk was frantically literary, which Preston thought hard on him.

Sunday, Christopher Hampton walked to church with me. Coming out, General Lee was slowly making his way down the aisle, bowing royally right and left, when he happened to look our way. He bowed low and gave me a charming smile of recognition. I was ashamed of being so pleased. I blushed like a school girl.

We went to the White House and they gave us tea. The President said he had been on the way to our house, coming with all the Davis family to see me, but the children became so troublesome that they turned back. Just then little Joe rushed in and insisted on saying his prayers at his father's knee, then and there. He was in his night clothes.

I was having such a good time, seated between Mr. Preston and Mr. Hunter, two of the most agreeable men I know and the cleverest. Christopher Hampton was there too. Mr. Chesnut, not having any such pleasant companions, grew restless and routed me out to go home. When we were on the pavement, Mrs. Davis called from the window to me that she had something to say. I stopped and Mr. Chesnut came back, saying: "Are you waiting for Kit Hampton?" When he saw how angry I was, he said: "Can't you take a joke?"

Mr. Venable says Buck can't help it; she must flirt. He does not think she cares for the man, it is just sympathy with the wounded soldier, poor helpless Hood.

At dinner, Mr. Hunter said: "The parsons tell us every Sunday that the Lord is on our side. I wish, however, he would show his preference for us a little more plainly than he has been doing lately."

December 19th. — A box has come from home for me. Taking advantage of this good fortune and a full larder, I have asked Mrs. Davis to dine with me Wednesday next. Garnett dined with us today. He says it is the Senate which cross-hobbles Mr. Davis, that the House is not so bad. The House is against Memminger; they are lukewarm as to any scheme of financial reform, because they know Memminger will spoil it, do what they may.

Hood came to ask me to give him a Casino party, and Mr. Chesnut readily agreed to it. Our resolution not to see company, he seems to have forgotten.

For my dinner, Wade Hampton sent me a basket of game. We had Mrs. Davis, and Mr. and Mrs. Preston. After dinner we walked to the church to see the Freeland-Lewis wedding. Mr. Preston had Mrs. Davis on his arm. Mr. Chesnut, Mrs. Preston, Burton Harrison and myself brought up the rear. Willie Allen joined us — and we had the pleasure of waiting one good hour. Then the beautiful Maria, loveliest of brides, sailed in on her father's arm.

After the ceremony, such a kissing, up and down the aisle! The happy bridegroom kissed so wildly that several girls complained; but he said how was he to know Maria's kin that he ought to kiss. It was better to show too much affection for his new relations than too little.

My dinner satisfied me, but my husband found fault. He said it was ill-served, that the kitchen was too far off, that things were cold; above all, that the dining-room was too small. "We must give it up! No more dinners!"

Brewster, in a soaking rain, ran in to say that General Hood was below in a carriage, and wanted me to go to a taffy-pulling at the Preston's. I came home and slept like a log.

DECEMBER 21st. — Joe Johnston is made Commander in Chief of the Army of the West. General Lee had this done.

Mrs. Stanard came. She could not understand why I had not called on her; she was still more amazed that Mr. Chesnut had not done so. "While you were gone, it was so different. He lived opposite. He put out a fire — at least it was nearly a fire!" When the bells began to ring he ran over and caught her with only one stocking on! She was trying to huddle on the other. . . .

Then Miss Agnes Lee and "Little Robert" (as they fondly call General Lee's youngest son, in this hero-worshipping community) called. They told us the President, General Lee and General Elzey had gone out to look at the fortifications around Richmond. Mr. Chesnut came home saying he had been with them, and had lent General Lee his grey horse.

I met Mrs. Lawson Clay, who says she is coming here tonight for eggnog and Casino. I stopped then at the Prestons' and Isabella wrote a note for me to Shirley Carter and Robert Lee, and then I asked Maggie and Burton Harrison. As I was driving with Mrs. Davis, I told her what a scrape I was in. My husband had positively ordered me to give no more tea parties, and he is decidedly master of his own house. To be sure, I had game, partridges, etc., that General Hampton had sent me, and no end of eggs and butter from home, and brandy from home for the eggnog and apple toddy. She laughed at my difficulties, said she was to have a grand dinner for the splendid cavalcade which had left her house for the ride round the fortifications, and she would make it a point to keep Mr. Chesnut there to dinner and as long after as possible. That was the only way she could help me out of this trouble of my own making.

Mary Preston and Brewster made the eggnog. Burton Harrison came after it was all gone. L. Q. Washington and some men who called at the Prestons' and heard they were here followed them. Maggie Howell brought Captain Fearn. Mr. Chesnut escaped from Mrs. Davis — he did not go to her house at all — so she failed to capture him. He came straight home and found the party in full blast. He did not know a word about it. How could he? It grew up after he left home. I trembled in my shoes.

He behaved beautifully, however. If he had refused to dine at the President's because he wished to attend a party at my house, he could not have done better. He seemed to enjoy the whole thing amazingly, played Casino with Mrs. Lawson Clay, looked after Hood, etc.

Today he spoke to me. I was very penitent, subdued, submissive, humble; and I promised not to do so any more. "No more parties," he said. "The country is in danger. There is too much levity here." So he laid down the law.

Mrs. Howell says a year ago on the cars a man said: "We want a Dictator." She replied: "Jeff Davis will never consent to be a Dictator." The man turned sharply toward her. "And pray who asks him? Joe Johnston will be made Dictator by the Army of the West." But of late the Army of the West has not been in a condition to dictate to friend or foe. Certainly Jeff Davis did hate to put Joe Johnston at the head of what is left of it. Detached from General Lee, what a horrible failure, what a slow old humbug is Longstreet. The Manigault pamphlet shows the small calibre of the little Beauregard. Oh for a day of Albert Sidney Johnston, out west; and Stonewall, if he could only come back to us here!!!

Sam, the wounded knight, came for me to drive. I felt I would soon find myself chaperoning some girl, but I asked no questions. He improved the time between Cary and Franklin Streets by saying: "I do like your husband so much." "So do I," I replied simply.

Buck was ill in bed — or so William said at the door — but she recovered her health and came down for the drive in black velvet and ermine, looking queenly. Then, with the top of the landau thrown back, wrapped in furs and rugs, we had a long drive on that bitter cold day.

Yesterday as we were coming back from the Fair Grounds, Sam, the wounded knight, asked Brewster what were the symptoms of a man's being in love. Sam said he did not know what they were. At seventeen, he had fancied himself in love, but that was "a long time ago." Brewster descanted on the symptoms of love. "When you see her, your breath is apt to come short. If it amounts to mild strangulation, you have it bad. You are stupidly jealous, glowering with jealousy, and with a gloomy, fixed conviction that she likes every fool you meet better than she does you. This is especially true of people that you know she has a thorough contempt for. That is, you knew it before you lost your head. I mean before you fell in love. The last stages of unmitigated spooniness I will spare you," said Brewster, with a wave of the hand. "They are too much to inflict on a gay young party." "Well," said Sam, drawing a breath of relief, "I have felt none of these things so far, and yet they say I am engaged to four young ladies. That's a liberal allowance, you will admit, for a man who cannot walk without help."

"To whom do they say you are engaged?" asked Buck, staring at the horses' heads. "Miss Wigfall is one." "Who else?" "Miss Sally Preston." * Buck did not move an eyelid. She still watched the horses' heads, and he asked: "Are you annoyed at such a preposterous report?" "No." Brewster, aside to me: "God help us! He is going to say everything right out here before our faces." Buck continued coolly: "Richmond people are liberal, as you say. I never heed these reports. They also say I am engaged to Shirley Carter, and to Phil Robb." Sam said viciously: "I think I will set a man-trap near your door and break some of those young fellows' legs."

After she had been deposited safely at home, Sam said, with what seemed a little like one of Brewster's symptomatic strangles: "Well, those young soldiers, they are men who dare hope for something in this world." I said never a word.

Next day we called on our way from church to see Mrs. Wigfall. She was ill, but Mr. Wigfall insisted upon taking me into the drawing-room to rest a while. He said Louly was there. So she was; and so was Sam, the wounded knight, stretched full length on a sofa with a rug thrown over him. Wigfall said to me: "Do you know General Hood?" "Yes." Sam laughed with his eyes, as I looked at him; but he did not say a word. I felt it a curious commentary upon the reports he had spoken of the day before. Louly Wigfall is a very handsome girl.

Wigfall, as he escorted me to the door, said: "They say you make short work of a civilian who makes fun of a wounded soldier, eh? (I nodded my head.) But Brewster says that yesterday, when you left with Hood in the carriage, Preston asked if he should have a doctor for the party when you got back, since it was freezing out of doors, and the drive was madness. You agreed, and said you would not risk freezing even for any two-legged animal in the world."

I felt faint. "Mr. Wigfall," I said, "you have been too long in Texas. Your jokes are too rough. Where is your American prudery, to talk before ladies of legs, off or on. And never did I dream that people

* Miss Sally Preston was, of course, Buck.

would say such things about a man's horrible mutilation before his face." "You intimate I am ill-bred." "It is the cruelest behavior in the world." "You don't know how the camp hardens a fellow," he retorted. "The General don't mind it a button. I know what I am about. He was pleased." I doubt that statement.

Brewster is the man who is described in Blackwood's Magazine, by a travelling Englishman, as seated in the piazza reading a Greek play, with his chair tilted and his feet on the banister. Brewster is the most careless creature. He may have Godliness but he has not the next thing to it. Isabella quotes a remark made by my husband. "Colonel Chesnut looked at Mr. Brewster's hands at dinner. Then he said gravely: 'My dear fellow, if you have such an aversion to water, why not grabble in a little clean sand?' "

L. Q. Washington remarked that "Byron believed good blood showed itself in small hands and feet." His own feet are huge, his hands very small and well shaped. He grew enthusiastic in his description of Mary Preston's hands, and someone went to the card table to verify his eulogy, and came back in amazement; for John Darby's hands are smaller and whiter and better shaped than hers, and Hood's are prettier and smaller than any of them.*

I said: "John Chesnut wears six and a half ladies' gloves. It is his only vanity."

"And these are not effeminate men," drawled Washington. "Two of them are stalwart fellows, and one is shot to pieces."

"Captain Chesnut is effeminate in his appearance," I admitted. "Such a pale face, such light hair, so soft and silky, and a Roman nose."

"Well, that is aristocratic too," Washington agreed.

"Let Johnny alone," said Buck. "General Young says he is as bold and reckless a dragoon as ever sat in a saddle."

Then she went across the room with Captain Robb, and they sat down by our wounded General Sam, who said at once: "I was beginning to think you meant to let me go away without a word. I cannot run after you now. I depend upon the charity of my friends. Now, eyes right! I really have something to tell you."

Captain Robb protested impatiently, for surely wounded major

* One piece of circumstantial evidence as to the smallness of many masculine hands a hundred years ago: Many Colt percussion revolvers made between 1836 and 1860 have trigger guards so small that a large man today finds it difficult to put his finger on the trigger.

generals are an intolerable bore: "No, look here to the left. I too have a word to say to you."

Buck was intensely amused. She is lovely at such times, with that mischievous gleam in her soft blue eyes; or are they grey, or brown, or black as night? I have seen them of every color, varying with the mood of the moment.

Mary Preston reproved her mother and myself sharply. We went to the Monumental Church. The preacher was so dull, and we sat afar off, very near the door, so we bad old women fell to whispering, and even to noiseless laughter. We enjoyed our scolding, too, as we walked home.

DECEMBER 24th. — Buck and I were out walking today and Brewster joined us. Buck looked up at the sky. "I wrote a note to Captain Robb this morning to beg him to excuse me. The weather would not permit me to ride. Now it has turned out such a beautiful day. If he had any sense, he would come after all." When we arrived at the Prestons, there stood Captain Robb, impatiently waiting.

"Captain," said Brewster, with an urbane wave of the hand, "you have been tested and you have borne the test nobly."

As we walked, Brewster reported a row he had had with General Hood. Brewster had told those six young ladies at the Preston's that "old Sam" was in the habit of saying he would not marry, even if he could, any silly, sentimental girl who would throw herself away upon a maimed creature such as he was. When he went home, he took pleasure in telling Sam how the ladies complimented his good sense. The General rose in his wrath and threatened to break his crutch over Brewster's head. To think Brewster was such a fool as to go about repeating to everybody poor Sam's whimperings.

I was at Mrs. Preston's when Brewster came in with what he called a Texican. Brewster was Secretary of War, or something, in the government of Texas while it was a lone state, after it had thrown off the yoke of Mexico and was not yet annexed to the United States. The Texican wore shiny, wrinkly new black broadcloth. "One touch of nature makes the world akin." I saw him glance with dismay at Brewster's hands, when Brewster offered to help beat up the eggnog, so I knew he was a nice fellow. Then somebody declaimed the "Charge of the Light Brigade." That was nearly the death of the Texican.

I had a run for it to get home in time for dinner. There is but one certain thing in this distracted world. I never keep my husband waiting at that hour. I was taking my seat at the head of the table, when the door opened and Brewster walked in unannounced. He took his stand in front of the open door, with his hands in his pockets and his small hat pushed as far back as it could get from his forehead. "What, you are not ready yet? The generals are below. Did you get my note?" "No." I begged Mr. Chesnut to excuse me and rushed off to put on my bonnet and furs. I met the girls coming up with a strange man, but the flurry of two major generals was too much for me. I forgot to ask his name. They went up to dine with my husband in my place. He sat eating his dinner, with Lawrence's undivided attention given to him, amid this whirling and eddying in and out. Mary Preston and I went to drive with the generals. The new one proved to be Buckner, who is a Kentuckian. These men told us they slept together the night before Chickamauga. (It seems that *legs* can't be kept out of our conversation now.) General Buckner said: "Once before, I slept with a man, and he lost his leg next day; so I had made a vow never to do so again. When Sam and I parted that morning we said: 'You or I may be killed, but the cause will be safe all the same.' "

After we returned home, everybody came in to tea. Mr. Chesnut was in a famous good humor and we had an unusually gay evening. It was very nice of him to take no notice of my conduct at dinner, for certainly it had been open to criticism, and all the comfort of my life depends upon his being in a good humor.

I have met the Prussian, Major Von Borcke. He has been shot through the throat, and whistles when he tries to speak. He rides with Stuart. Stuart's men — and therefore Johnny — have been out in all this freezing weather for fifty-six hours at a time, without food or sleep. Poor Johnny! If they will only give him a furlough at Christmas, won't we feast him!

Mrs. Clay and Captain Seabrook came for tea. She is so bright and so pretty, and my husband was devoted to her. I said, after they left: "Your plan for the solitary life in Richmond seems to have failed."

CHRISTMAS DAY, 1863. — Letters from Camden say Emma Stockton was found dead in her bed. Emma Lee is married to Barney Stewart. And poor Rose Freeland. Not one year ago, she came to see us; Dr. Harrison and his beautiful bride. Now husband, wife and child are all gone, wiped out, nothing to show they have ever lived.

We dined at the Prestons'. I wore one of my handsomest Paris dresses (from Paris before the war). Three magnificent Kentucky generals were there, and Senator Orr from South Carolina, and Mr. Miles. General Buckner repeated a speech of Hood's to him, to show how friendly they were. Sam said: "I prefer a ride with you to the company of any woman in the world." Buckner's answer: "I prefer your company to that of any man, certainly." This was the standing joke of the dinner. It flashed up in every form. Poor Sam got out of it so badly, if he got out of it at all. General Buckner said patronizingly: "Lame excuses, all of them. Hood never gets out of any scrape unless he can fight his way out."

General Buckner had seen a Yankee cartoon in which angels were sent down from Heaven to bear up Stonewall's soul. They could not find it, and flew back sorrowing, but when they got to the Golden Gate above they found that Stonewall, by a rapid flank movement, had already cut a way in.

Somebody confessed they used half corn and half coffee as a beverage; but it was always popcorn, for while they roasted it, the corn popped out.

Others dropped in after dinner, some without arms, some without legs, and Von Borcke, who cannot speak because of the wound in his throat. Isabella said: "We have all kinds now, but a blind one." Poor fellows, they laugh at wounds, and yet can show many a scar."

We had for dinner oyster soup — *soup à la reine;* it has so many good things in it — besides boiled mutton, ham, boned turkey, wild ducks, partridges, plum pudding, sauterne, burgundy, sherry and Madeira. There is life in the old land yet!

After dinner we invited home two wounded, homeless men; Alex Haskell, who has lost an eye, and Hood. They had heard that lovely little Charlotte Wickham, Roony Lee's wife, is dying — with her husband in a Yankee prison. I had described to Mr. Chesnut the behavior of the Texican when he heard Buck recite "The Charge of the Light Brigade" for the first time, so he tried it on Hood. Hood was excited beyond anything I ever imagined. He sat straight up, his eyes were flaming and scintillating; and he made a gesture, which Mr. Chesnut said was like the motion of a soldier receiving his orders in a battle, at the end of every line.

While Alex Haskell and my husband sat over their wine, Sam gave me an account of his discomfiture at Buck's gentle hands. He said he could not sleep after it, that it was the hardest battle he had ever fought in his life. "And I was routed! She told me there was no hope. You know, at Petersburg, on my way to the western army, she half-promised me to think of it. She would not say 'yes,' but she did not say 'no'; that is, not exactly. At any rate, I went off saying 'I am engaged to you,' and she said, 'I am not engaged to you.' After I was so fearfully wounded, I gave it up; but then since I came home I have — hoped."

"Do you mean to say that you had proposed to her before that conversation in the carriage, when you asked Brewster the symptoms? I like your audacity!"

"Oh, she understood; but it is all up now. She says '*no*.' I asked her about her engagement to Ransom Calhoun. She explained it all, and then I said he was a classmate of mine and had made me his confidant. 'Heavens,' she said, laughing in my face. 'If I had only known that, what a different story I would have told you.' I do not know what this laugh and confession meant; but somehow, after that, I did not care so much for the 'no' as I did before."

December 28th. — Mrs. Roony Lee is dead. One of her babies died too. She was not twenty-three. He is a prisoner still.

December 29th. — I am always mum when conundrums have the floor, but they are a favorite amusement with the six girls at the Prestons'. I found one and took it to them. What are the points of difference between the Prince of Wales, an orphan, a bald-headed man, and a gorilla? Answer: The Prince of Wales is an heir apparent. The orphan has ne'er a parent. The bald-headed man has no hair apparent. The Gorilla has a hairy parent.

The girls drew straws to decide which should be allowed to walk home with my husband. After all, I believe he likes this life that he grumbles so much at. At any rate, he likes the company of those girls, and no wonder; they are devoted to him. Nevertheless, he says I am extravagant. "No, my friend, not that! I had fifteen hundred dollars, and I have spent every cent of it in my housekeeping, not one *sou* for myself, not one *sou* for dress or any personal want whatever." Yet he called me "hospitality run mad."

I have just happened on a letter written by me to Mrs. Davis, dated last September. "I am living a thoroughly out-doors life this heavenly weather. I am on a visit to my husband's father, so I have a carriage and horses and nothing else; but I wish with all my heart that I was once more on foot, and so very uncomfortably lodged as I was in Richmond.

"We are busy looking after poor soldiers' wives. (I mean the wives of poor soldiers.) There are no end of them, and they never have less than nine or ten children. They are borrowing for the unreturning brave, hoping they will return and support their large families once more.

"The whole duty here consists in abusing Lincoln and the Yankees, praising Jeff Davis and the army of Virginia, and wondering when this horrid war will be over. There is not one of us who seems to believe for a moment that we will ever again have an ache or a pain or a trouble or a care, if peace were once proclaimed and a triumphant Southern Confederacy were waving its flag in defiance of the world. What geese we are!

"There is another party, politicians and men with no stomach for fighting, who find it easier to cuss Jeff Davis and stay at home than to go to the front with a musket. They are the kind who came out almost as soon as they went into the war, dissatisfied with the way things were managed. Joe Johnston is their polar star, the redeemer!"

We had enough of them in South Carolina, God knows; but Alabama was worse, and Georgia under Joe Brown does not even cover itself with a Joe Johnston make-believe.

JANUARY 1st, 1864. — God help my country! I think we are like the sailors who break into the spirits closet when they find out the ship must sink. There seems to be for the first time a resolute determination to enjoy the brief hour, and never look beyond the day.

I now have no hope. "Have you any of old Mr. Chesnut's brandy here still? It is a good thing never to look beyond the hour. Lawrence, take this key, look in such a place for a decanter marked . . ." etc.

General Hood is an awful flatterer; I mean an awkward flatterer. I told him to praise my husband to someone else, not to me. He ought to praise me to somebody who would tell my husband, and then praise my husband to another person who would tell me. Man and wife are too much one person to receive a compliment straight in their face that way, and do it gracefully.

Here is a list of the half-hearted ones; at least we all know they never believed in this thing. Stephens, the Vice-President, is Number One. Ashman Keitt. Boya of the South Carolina delegation. Orr. He was lugged in awfully against the grain. And then look at our wisdom! Mr. Mason! We grant you all you are going to say; he is a grand old Virginia gentleman, straightforward, honest-hearted, blunt, high-headed and as unchangeable in his ways as the Rock of Gibraltar. But Mr. Hunter, you need not shake your wise head. You know it set all the world a laughing when you sent Mr. Mason abroad as a Diplomat! The English can't stand chewing tobacco, yet they say that at the lordliest table, Mr. Mason will turn round halfway in his chair and spit in the fire!

Jack Preston says the parting of high Virginia with its sons at the station is a thing to see; tears streaming from each eye, a crystal drop; from the corner of each mouth a yellow stream of tobacco juice.

We all know General Lee and General Huger's hearts were rent asunder when they had to leave the old army. And did not Mrs. Johnston tell us how General Scott thought to save the melancholy, reluctant, slow Joe for the Yankees; but he came to us.

One more year of Stonewall would have saved us. Chickamauga is the only battle we have gained since Stonewall died; and no results, as usual. Stonewall was not killed by a Yankee. He was shot by his own men. Now that is hard.

"General Lee can do no more than keep back Meade," said someone. "One of Meade's armies, you mean," I retorted. "They double their numbers on him when he whips one of them."

General Edward Johnston says he got Grant a place because he could not bear to see an old army man driving a wagon. That was when he found him out west. Grant had been put out of the army for habitual drunkenness. He is their best man, a bull-headed Suwarrow. He don't care a snap if his men fall like the leaves. He fights to win, that chap; he is not distracted by a thousand side issues; he does not see them. He sees only in a straight line. Like Louis Napoleon, from a battle in the gutter he goes straight up.

And like Lincoln, we have ceased to carp at him because he is a rough clown, no gentleman, etc. You never hear now of his nasty fun, but only of his wisdom. It doesn't take much soap and water to wash the hands that hold the rod of empire. They once talked of Lincoln's drunkenness too. Now, since Vicksburg, they have not a word to say against Grant's habits. He has the disagreeable habit of not retreating before our irresistible veterans! You need not be afraid of a little dirt on the hands which wield a Field Marshall's baton, either.

Thus runs our table-talk. General Lee and Albert Sydney Johnston; they show blood and breeding; they are of the Bayard, the Philip Sydney order of soldier. But if General Lee had Grant's resources, he would have bagged the last Yankee or had them all safe back in Massachusetts. You mean, if he had not the weight of the Negro question on his shoulders? No, I mean if he had Grant's unlimited allowance of the powers of war, men, money, ammunition, arms.

They say all Yankees are splay-footed. As they steadily tramp this way, I must say I have ceased to admire their feet myself. How beautiful are the feet, etc., says the Scripture.

"Eat, drink, and be merry; tomorrow ye die." They say that, too.

More "table talk," the sort of thing I hear daily: "Why do you call General Preston 'Conscript Father'? On account of those girls?" "No indeed. He is at the head of the Conscription Bureau."

General Young says: "Give me those daredevils, those dandies I find in Mrs. Chesnut's drawing-room. I like fellows who fight and don't care what all the row's about." "Yes, and he sees the same daredevils, often enough, stiff and stark, stripped, stone-dead on the battlefield." "Oh, how can you bring all that to our eyes here!" "What, not compliment our drawing-room friends; the fellows who dance and fight with light heads; who take fire and famine, nakedness, mud, snow, frost, gunpowder and all, take it all as it comes."

Mr. Ould says Mrs. Lincoln found the gardener of the White House so nice she wished to make him a major general. Lincoln said to his Secretary: "Well, the little woman must have her way, sometimes." She has the Augean perquisite of cleaning the military stables. She says it pays so well — and she need never touch the President's saddle. "Pays?" someone echoed. "Well, the Roman Emperor found all money of good odor."

Here is a marriage in high life! Senator Johnson of Arkansas — or somewhere out West; I may not locate him properly — explained his marriage to Mrs. Davis. With his foot on the carriage steps, so to speak, he married his deceased wife's sister. He wished to leave her power over his children, to protect them and take care of them while he was away. Mrs. Davis asked: "Pray, why did you not tell us before?" "I did not think it a matter worth mentioning. I only proposed it to her the morning I left home, and it was done at once. And now my mind is easy. I can stay here and attend to my business as a man should. She is quite capable of looking after things at home."

I know now why the English, who find out the comfort of life in everything, send off a happy couple to spend the honeymoon out of everybody's way — or shut them up at home and leave them. Today a beautiful bride and happy bridegroom came to me. They had not one thought to give except to themselves, and the wedding, or their preliminary love affairs. But she did tell a capital story — if I could write it!

Mrs. Wright of Tennessee came for me to go with her on a calling expedition. We found one Cabinet Minister's establishment in a state of Republican simplicity. The servant who asked us in was out at elbows and knees.

Wigfall's speech about our husbandless daughters led Isabella to say: "He is right! Here we are, and our possible husbands and lovers are killed before we so much as knew them. Oh! the widows and old maids of this cruel war."

It is only in books that people fall in love with their wives. Is it not as with any other co-partnership, say travelling companions? Their future opinion of each other and the happiness of association depends intensely on what they really are, not on what they felt or thought about each other before they had any possible way of acquiring accurate information as to character, habits, etc. Love makes it worse. The pendulum swings back further, the harder it was pulled the other way. Mrs. Malaprop to the rescue: "Better begin with a little aversion." What we think of people before we know them is of no weight either way; but did two people ever live together so stupid as to be long deceived?

The Examiner gives this pleasant information to the enemy; that we are not ready, and we cannot be before spring, and that now is their time. Our safeguard, our hope, our trust is in beneficient mud! Impossible mud! So I hail with delight these long, long, rainy days, and longer nights. Things are deluging, sloppy, and up to the ankles in water and dirt, enough to satisfy the muddiest-minded croaker of us all.

Somebody in secret session kicked and cuffed Foote of Mississippi, in the Senate. So ends the old year.

The last night of the old year sent me a cup of strong, good coffee. I drank two cups and so did not sleep a wink. Like a fool I passed my whole life in review, and bitter memories maddened me. Then came a happy thought. I mapped out a story of the war. Johnny is the hero, light dragoon and heavy swell. I will call it FF's for it is the First Families both of South Carolina and of Virginia. It is to be a war story, and the filling out of the skeleton was a pleasant way to put myself to sleep.

JANUARY 1st, 1864. — There are breaking hearts this beautiful New Year's day. Young Frasier, on his way back to Maryland to be married, was shot dead by a Yankee picket.

I read "Volpone" until Mr. Chesnut emerged for his breakfast. He asked me to make out his list for his New Year's calls: Mrs. Davis, Mrs. Preston, Mrs. Randolph, Mrs. Elzey, Mrs. Stanard, Mrs. McFarland, Mrs. Wigfall, Mrs. Miles, Mrs. John Redmond Coxe Lewis.

At the President's, he saw L. Q. C. Lamar. Unconfirmed by the Senate, he has had to come home from Russia. They must have refused to confirm his nomination simply to anger Jeff Davis. Everybody knows there is not a cleverer man this side of the water than Mr. Lamar, or a truer patriot. Lamar is changed so much that at first Mr. Chesnut did not recognize him. Colonels Browne and Ives, in full rig of swords and sashes, received as gentlemen ushers. Mr. Chesnut was in citizen's dress and stood behind Mrs. Davis all the time, out of the way; so he enjoyed the fun immensely, having no responsibility.

The Examiner indulges in a horse-laugh. "Is that your idea, that England will come to the help of a slave power?" Slavery was the sore spot on this continent, and England touched the Yankees they so hated on the raw. English writers knew where to flick. They set the Yankees on us by incessant nagging. Now the Yankees have the bit in their teeth.

"The land of our forefathers is not squeamish, but she looks out for Number One," said the irreverent Wigfall, and then he laid sacrilegious hands on the Father of his Country! He always speaks of him as an old Granny, or as the mother of his country, because he looked after the butter and cheese on Madame Martha's Mount Vernon farm. "There is one thing that always makes my blood rise hot within me," said he. "This good slave owner who set his Negroes free when he no longer needed them, rides his fine horse along the rows where the poor African hoes corn. He takes out his beautiful English hunting watch and times Cuffy. Cuffy, under his great master's eye, works with a will. With his watch still in hand, Farmer George sees what a man can do in a given time; and by that measure he tasks the others, whether they be strong or weak, slow or swift, able-bodied or unable. There is magnanimity for you! George the First of America, the founder of the great United States of America!"

"But Wigfall, you exaggerate! He was the very kindest of men. Everyone knows that. You only talk such stuff to be different from other people." "I get every word of it from his own letters."

After he had gone: "You see, we did not expect Wigfall, who shoots white men with so little ceremony, to be so thoughtful and so tender of the poor and helpless. But it is so; he was in bitter earnest. Did you notice his eyes?"

Dangerfield Lewis and Maria came in, and in another second L. Q. Washington was at their heels. Mr. Chesnut was saying: "Flat blasphemy on Wigfall's part." "How? What?" they asked. "Oh, he says Lamar is as model a diplomat as Mr. Mason!"

"How aggravating Louis Wigfall can be; yet he is the very best husband I know and the kindest father."

JANUARY 4th. — At Mrs. Davis's. The President's arm is stiff with the New Year's shaking, and Mrs. Davis's hand is tender to the touch!

This was a day of disasters. Lawrence got drunk, and the kitchen stove fell in. Molly and Lawrence had a grand row. He will have a fire in his room, and he keeps the key of the coal cellar, to fire up as he pleases. Molly says: "As Master dresses without fire to economize, and he taking a cold bath reglar as the day comes, you might." "Oh," says Lawrence, "Have I got anybody to rub me with a coarse towel till I am red-hot?"

"Who's Lawrence, I like to know?" cries Molly to me. "He can't set by the kitchen fire like the rest of us. You watch your coal hole, that's all! And them across the way, they've lost every mouthful of their provisions for the year, and hit uz hid away up in the garret!" "How?" "Niggers stole it. Nobody else could be that mean but their own niggers. You needn't look scared, missis. You rest easy. Why should we take em in de bulk? We takes em as we wants em. Don't I make things last better than you ever did? Tell you why, we ain't ever going to the Yankees. We is going home to our husband and chillun, when you go home!" Much Lawrence cares for home and wife and chillun, though the Lord knows he's got enough of both. "But why do my things last? You forget to tell me that." "Because here we only want what we can eat ourselves. At home, there's the children. Dey gets a little of all dat's goin."

Mrs. Ives wants Mary Preston and myself to translate a French play. A genuine French Captain came in from his ship and gave us good advice as how to select a play. General Hampton sent another basket of partridges, and all goes merry as a marriage bell!

Mr. Chesnut came in and almost killed us with this piece of latest news. "North Carolina wants to offer terms of peace." We only needed a break of that kind to finish us. I shivered as one does when the first handfull of earth comes rattling down on the coffin in the grave of one we cared for more than all.

JANUARY 5th. — At Mrs. Preston's, met the Light Brigade in battle array, ready to sally forth to conquer. They would stand no nonsense from me about staying at home to translate a French play. Indeed, those which have been sent us are so indecent, I scarcely know where the play is to be found that would do at all.

While at dinner, the President's carriage drove up with only General Hood. He sent up to ask, in Maggie Howell's name, would I go with them. I tied up two partridges between plates with a serviette, for Buckie, who is ill, and then went down. We picked up Mary Preston and Maggie. It was Maggie's drive, as the soldiers say. I was only on escort duty. At the Prestons', Major Venable met us at the door and took in the partridges to Buck.

Found my husband in a bitter mood. It has all gone wrong with our world. The loss of our private fortunes is the smallest part. He intimates that with so much human misery filling the very air, we might stay at home and think. "And go mad?" I protested. "Catch me at it! A yawning grave, piles of red earth thrown on one side; that is the only future I ever see. You remember Emma Stockton! She and I were as blithe as birds that day at Mulberry. I came here the next day, and when I got here, a telegram. Emma Stockton found dead in her bed. It is awfully near, that thought. No, no! I will not stop and think, when there is only death to think of."

JANUARY 8th. — Snow of the deepest! I thought nobody could come, but they did. First Constance Cary trips in, the clever Conny. Hetty is the beauty, so-called, though she is clever enough too. Constance has a classically perfect profile. Then came four Kentuckians and Preston Hampton. He is as tall as they are, and ever so much better looking. Then eggnog. "Toujours" is translated. They speak of taking it for their theatricals.

I was to take Miss Cary to Mrs. Semmes's. Mr. Chesnut inquired the price of the carriage. Twenty-five dollars an hour. Then he cursed by all the Gods — such extravagance, such stupid charades; he said the play was not worth the candle — or the carriage, in this instance. Then he quieted down. In Confederate money it sounds so much worse than it is.

I did not dream of asking him to go with me after that lively overture till he said: "I did intend to go with you, but you do not ask me." "And I have been asking you for twenty years to go with me, in vain. Think of that!" I said tragically. I sent the twenty-five-dollar-an-hour carriage back for him, for we could not stay for him to dress. We were behind time. Lord, in this world, the amount of unhappiness there is from useless fault-finding. Of course, when one deserves a good scolding, let it come!

The beautiful Hetty Cary and her friend Captain Tucker came with him. Major Von Borcke and Preston Hampton were at the Carys'. They were in the drawing-room (Constance dressing) and I challenge the world to produce finer specimens of humanity than these three; the Prussian Von Borcke, Preston Hampton, Hetty Cary.

While I waited for Constance, we spoke to the Prussian officer of a vote of thanks passed by Congress yesterday, "Thanks of the country to Major Von Borcke." The poor man was as modest as a girl, in spite of his huge proportions.

"That is a compliment indeed!" said Hetty Cary. "Yes," he said, "I saw it, and the happiest, the proudest day of my life as I read it! It was at the hotel breakfast table. I try to hide my face with the newspaper, I feel it grow red. But my friend, he has his newspaper too, and he sees the same thing, so he looks my way. He says: 'Why does he grow so red? He has got something there!' and he laughs. Then I try to read aloud to them the so kind compliment of the Congress, but you see I cannot." He puts his hand to his throat. His broken English, and the difficulty of enunciation with that wound in his windpipe makes it all very touching and very hard to understand what he says.

General Preston is no longer diplomatic since he has secured the mission to Mexico; so when someone laughs at some guggling mistake which Von Borcke makes, he roars: "You dare to make game of Gun Buck! (as he calls him). Then never, I swear, will I let a Yankee bullet make a hole in my gullet; no, not to save you!"

Now for the Semmes's party. Their success was all they could have desired. The play was charming. Sweet little Mrs. Lawson Clay had a seat for me, banked up among women. The female part of the congregation, strictly segregated from the male, were planted all together in rows; and they formed a gay parterre, edged by the men in their black coats and gray uniforms. Towards the back part of the room, the mass of black and gray was solid.

Captain Tucker bewailed his fate because he was stranded out there with those forlorn men, and he could see us laughing and fancied what we were saying was worth a thousand charades. He preferred talking to a clever woman to any known way of passing a pleasant hour. "It is like music, when the heavenly maid is young, adored, and pretty!"

On a sofa of state in front of all sat the President and Mrs. Davis. Little Maggie Davis was one of the child actresses. They had a right to be proud of her. With her flashing black eyes, she was a marked figure on the stage. She is a handsome creature and she acted her part admirably.

1. Scene: Peasants drinking in front of house. Girl comes in with glasses. The inevitable kiss — or the attempt — and the equally certain-to-follow box on the ear. This attractive barmaid was Conny Cary, in one of my caps.

The word — Inn.

2. Scene: Mistress and maids, dusting, scolding. Mrs. Webb, whom I had only known as the centre of all sweet charities and Christian self-abnegations at her hospital, was mistress; Conny Cary and Mrs. Ives were her maids. Captain Tucker, out in the dim distance to which the gentlemen were banished, asked: "Who are those ladies?" From the crowd came a melancholy and resigned voice: "The one who scolds so well is my wife."

Inn — Dust.

3. Scene: Judges, lawyers, all a stern array. Cooper De Leon got up as a felon; Mrs. Semmes as the broken-hearted wife of a condemned criminal.

Inn — Dust — Trial.

4. Scene: A school, Mrs. Webb matron. She does everything well.

The whole word "Industrial."

Then they did "harum scarum," and then "Pilgrimage," and that was the climax of the evening's entertainment. The shrine for "Pilgrimage" was beautiful beyond words. The Semmes and Ives families are Roman Catholic, and understand how to get up that sort of thing. The pilgrims were American Indians. Burton Harrison, the President's handsome young secretary, was gotten up as a brave in a costume presented to Mr. Davis by the Indians for some kindness of his to them years ago. It was a complete warrior's outfit — scant as that is — and the feathers stuck in the back of Mr. Harrison's head had a charmingly comic effect. He had to shave himself as clean as a baby to act the beardless chief; so he folded up his loved and lost moustache, this Christianized Indian, and laid it there, the most sacred treasure of his life, the witness of his most heroic sacrifice, on the altar of the shrine.

So ended "Pilgrimage." That ought to have been the wind-up. Jane Eyre is responsible to society for beginning our using "Bridewell" as a charade word. How much the gay world has suffered from it, we know now. Our bride was a beauty, and Mrs. Semmes — the best actress I know in private life — was Rebecca at the well. In the prison scene, Cooper De Leon was beyond praise.

But they have no business to give us such painful scenes. We came here to be amused. This was not quite up to heroic and tragic tears; it was simply unpleasant, and the better he does it, the worse it is. They ought to have things so funny as to create a laugh under the ribs of death. We are there, and we know it.

Senator Hill of Georgia took me in to supper; ices, chicken salad, oysters, champagne. The President came in alone, I suppose; for while we were talking after supper, your humble servant was standing between Mrs. Randolph and Mrs. Stanard, when the President offered his arm and we walked off, oblivious of Mr. Senator Hill. Pray, ladies, forgive me for recording this; but Mrs. Stanard and Mrs. Randolph are the handsomest women in Richmond, and I am no older than they are — nor younger either, sad to say — so I was flattered. The President walked with me slowly up and down that long room, and our conversation was of the saddest. Nobody knows so well as he does the difficulties which beset this hard-driven Confederacy. As he talks of things as they are now, in a melancholy cadence, he has a voice which is perfectly modulated, a comfort in this loud and tough soldier world.

Mr. Chesnut was so utterly charmed with Hetty Cary that he at first declined to accompany me home in the twenty-five-dollar-an-hour carriage. He wanted it sent back for him; but being a good manager, I packed Hetty and Constance and my husband in with me, and left the two other men who came with the party to make their way home in the cold. At our door, near daylight of that bitter cold morning, I had the pleasure of seeing Mr. Chesnut stand and pay for that carriage like a man! Today he is pleased with himself, with me, and with all the world. He says if there was no such word as 'fascinating,' you would have to invent it to describe Hetty Cary.

A queer scene during supper. Someone was asking how Captain Fearn's name was pronounced: "Fern," to rhyme to "her'n," or "Feearn" to rhyme to "Eon." Mrs. Davis turned to Willie Mountford. "I hear you are a poet, or at least you write burlesques. What do you say?" The young man turned white and red, green and grey. He has written for private circulation a burlesque poem dealing satirically with Mrs. Myers's quarrel with Mrs. Davis, and he is Mrs. Myers's champion, so you may imagine how Mrs. Davis is dealt with in that poem. At her question, he knew she had read it and stood dumb with embarrassment. General Preston rushed into the breach in the nick of time. He began shaking hands violently with Willie Mountford, saying: "From your name, my lad, you must be my cousin." Their Virginia cousinship and all its ramifications raised such a fog around us that everything else disappeared in it. But Mr. Willie Mountford had his *mauvais quart d'heure*. We came home to find the doorbell broken, and all the gas given out in some inexplicable way.

JANUARY 9th. — I met Mrs. Wigfall, who wants me to take Halsey to Mrs. Randolph's theatricals. I am to get him up as Sir Walter Raleigh. She showed me a note from Lamar, and I said: "What will you do when he hears it was Louis Wigfall who moved heaven and earth to have him recalled from Russia?" She only smiled.

Now General Breckenridge has come. I like him better than any of them. Morgan,* our escaped hero, is here. I heard the music of his welcoming parade a day or two ago. These huge Kentuckians fill the town. Isabella says: "They hold General Breckenridge accountable for the loss of Chattanooga." When I begin to tell why I like him so well, she shakes her head.

I was marching off to see the parade and hear the music of the Morgan welcome, when I met Mrs. Randolph and Miss Carrie Barton. We saw Major M—— introduce General Morgan to the crowd, and as A. P. Hill could not speak, J. B. Stuart did, with all his voice. Then Governor Moore took the stand, and Mrs. Randolph at once proposed to move on. "We came only for soldiers. They have got down to the Governors." As we were then ankle deep in snow, it seemed a prudent step; but a fine-looking young Kentuckian, as tall and as strong as any general of them all, stood near us. He expressed himself as greatly flattered by our homage to Morgan. In all that brilliant cortège, he seemed to think Morgan the star of greatest magnitude. He had shared the General's imprisonment, and described their escape. I do not remember any peculiarly romantic incident, but never did women enjoy a jollier tramp, or have a pleasanter chat with a totally unknown young soldier. The grey coat is passport enough to our old hearts.

The Preston girls who watched the welcome from their window, when they found out all we had seen and heard, abused me roundly for not fetching them! It was a way I had, always to stumble in upon the real show.

* General John Hunt Morgan in the summer of 1863 led a famous cavalry raid into Ohio, where his force was shattered and he and several of his officers were captured. They were taken to the Columbus penitentiary and there treated not like prisoners of war but as common felons, and their heads and beards were shaved. In November they dug through the floor of a cell into an air chamber below, tunnelled through a wall into the prison yard, scaled the outer wall and escaped.

The Examiner today was down on us all. He gave the government precedence in his abuse, then demolished our Mr. Miles, then failed to respect even our feminine insignificance. He went for the merry-makers, the party-goers, the prompters and attenders of festivities at such a time.

Johnny has been down to Essex to see Mary Garnett. He sent us baskets of partridges, and we returned his baskets filled with books and hams.

The President's man Jim — whom he believed in, as we all believe in our own servants — and Betsy, Mrs. Davis's maid, decamped last night. It is miraculous that they had fortitude to resist the temptation so long. At Mrs. Davis's, the hired servants are mere birds of passage; first they are seen with gold galore, and then they fly to the Yankees. But I am sure they have nothing to tell. It is wasted money to the Yankees.

I do not think it had ever crossed Mrs. Davis's mind that these two could leave, though she knew that Betsy had eighty dollars in gold, and two thousand four hundred dollars in Confederate money. Says my Molly, in amazement: "I like Mrs. Davis, but Betsy did give herself such airs because she was Mrs. President's maid."

January 11th. — Mattie Reedy and I were charmed to meet once more under altered skies. We spent the winter of fifty-nine at Brown's Hotel in Washington, and the Reedys were there. Miss Reedy is a beautiful, Kentucky Belle — and now she is that high-placed woman, Mrs. John Morgan. When we called, Colonel Allston did the honor, General Morgan not being at home.

"At Covington," said Mattie, "after the escape, General Morgan did not know where to turn or whom to trust. He decided upon Mrs. Ludlow. She gave him a warm welcome, and without a moment's hesitation or loss of time ordered two horses saddled for Morgan, and one for her son. She handed Morgan sixty dollars in gold, all she had in the house. 'Now go. Ride for your life.' She did not show any fear of the vengeance Yankees were sure to wreak upon her and hers if they knew the part she played in Morgan's escape." Throughout Kentucky it was the same thing. Men and horses were at his command, and brave women tried to force their money on him and were mortified when he refused.

General Preston told us of the impression the first dead Confederate soldiers' faces, grim in death, lying stiff and stark, made upon him at Shiloh: cold, staring open-eyed. They were all hard frozen, these dead bodies. He will not be able to see his wife and children before he goes to Mexico. He has left the sword he wore at Chickamauga and a sealed letter to be delivered to his son in case of his death or his disappearance.

Everybody who comes in brings a little bad news, not much in itself; but the cumulative effect is depressing indeed.

JANUARY 12th. — Round the corner at the Carys' I found confusion, their rehearsal in full blast. Miss Giles as the "Fair Penitent," was beautiful beyond any words of mine to describe. General Breckenridge asked: "I wonder if she has ever read the play?" "No," answered Isabella. "I am certain she has not. But then, nobody else has either, and so it does not matter here."

Hudson, the ever memorable man who went with me and knelt beside Stonewall Jackson's bier in the Capitol that moonlight night, came to ask me to put Halsey Wigfall in his place. I am making a lace collar for Halsey, for his Sir Walter costume. Halsey is cool, modest, wonderfully well read for his age, and toned down in manners since I saw him last.

Mr. Vizitelli in the play was dandling a screaming baby, while his strong-minded wife wrote and dashed aside page after page of manuscript. The stalwart youths who simulated that crying baby's yells behind the scenes were hoarse the next day; but they cried well, that none can deny.

After Halsey, Hetty Cary's radiant face appeared. She was in the act of gathering up an armful of my velvets, feathers, laces and flowers when a thump was heard on the stairs. It was like the sound of the statue walking, in "Don Giovanni." It was Hood's crutches, and he appeared on the scene. Soon Buck's sweet face peeped in, followed by Isabella and "Simon, the Poet," as they all call General Buckner. Hood is "Sam the Soldier." Then Mrs. Caskie, who announced herself later on as a cousin of Lucy, the well-beloved wife of Governor Pickens.

Tonight there will be a great gathering of the Kentuckians. Morgan gives them a dinner. The city of Richmond entertains John Morgan. He is at free quarters.

The girls dined here. Conny Cary came back for more white feathers. Isabella had appropriated two sets, and obstinately refused Constance Cary a single feather from her pile. She said sternly: "I have never been on the stage before, and I have a presentiment that when my father hears of this I will never go again. I am to appear before the footlights as an English Dowager Duchess, and I mean to rustle every feather and to wear all the lace and diamonds these two houses can compass." (Mine and Mrs. Preston's.) She was jolly, but firm; and Constance departed without any additional plumage for her Lady Teazle. Mr. Chesnut wants to coach Hetty Cary for her part! No doubt!

JANUARY 14th. — I gave Mrs. White twenty-three dollars for a turkey and came home wondering all the way why she did not ask twenty-five, which would have made me back out of the bargain!

I have been wearing an old uniform coat of Mr. Chesnut's made into a sacque for me. It is not pretty, but then it is so comfortable. Its great defect is this; it is so awfully thick and warm that when I must dress up a little, and I change it for my old velvet sacque to go out at night, I take cold. Well then, with such a cold as never was before, I still resolved to go. The Prestons sent their carriage for me. I found their Tudy with a young Louisiana cousin at her feet, making love audibly in the solemn stillness of those nearly empty rooms. Buck, from the opposite side of the room, sent to stop it. Someone called out: "Miss Preston, that is a cruel move of yours." She answered with distinctness: "People ought to control their feelings in a place like this." Said Sam, moving his crutches nervously: "Suppose they can't?"

A bill was handed us. Programme. "Oh, I will be so tired of waiting for matrimony," said an unknown voice in the crowd. There was a titter, till she explained: "Don't you see it is the last charade on the list."

To our amazement, Hood, who is a fighter and no talker, said during the charades: "Oh I do hate to see nice girls so hauled about. They could act without all this clawing, pulling, pawing!"

Ruby Mallory made a perfect Marchioness. She is a truly wonderful child. She had us all wiping our eyes, the other night at Mrs. Semmes's when she recited "Bingen on the Rhine."

JANUARY 15th. — At Mrs. Randolph's, Mr. Hudson desired me to congratulate him because his substitute, Halsey Wigfall, had done so well as Sir Walter Raleigh. That was in the spirit of the men who are so proud of the prowess of their substitutes in the army that they put up monuments to them when they are killed!

Mr. Chesnut was flirting with Mrs. Ives, and the Carys. He goes out so rarely that I was asked several times who he was. "Who is the man always with the Carys? See, there he is!" I looked, wondering what I should think of him if I saw him for the first time, and I came to a very pleasant conclusion. Not without pride I answered: "Oh, that is my husband. Have you never met Colonel Chesnut before?"

Immediately back of us sat Mrs. Stanard. She was telling Maggie Howell over my shoulder how great a favorite she was, and Maggie answered sharply: "I don't like your way of backing the favorite! Your knees are in my back!" What a day the Kentuckians have had. Mrs. Webb gave them a breakfast; from thence they proceeded *en masse* to General Lawton's dinner, and then straight here. It is equal to one of Stonewall's forced marches.

General Lawton took me in to supper. He said: "My heart is heavy. This seems too gay, too careless for such terrible times. It is all out of place in battle-scarred Richmond." "I have heard something of that kind at home," I replied. Hope and fear are both gone,* and it is distraction or death with us. I do not see how sadness and despondency would help us. If it would do any good, we could be sad enough.

We laughed at General Hood. General Lawton thought him better fitted for gallantry on the battlefield than for playing in my lady's chamber. When Miss Giles was electrifying the audience as the "Fair Penitent," someone said: "Oh that is so pretty!" "That is not pretty; it is elegant!" Hood cried, in stern reproachfulness.

Not only was my house rifled for theatrical properties, but as the play went on they came for my black velvet cloak. When the play was over, I thought I should never get away, because my cloak was so hard to find; but it gave me an opportunity to witness many things behind the scenes, that cloak hunt did. Behind the scenes! ! ! I know what that means now.

General Stuart was in his cavalry jacket and high boots. He was devoted to Hetty Cary, and Constance Cary said to me: "Hetty likes them that way; you know, gilt edged, and with stars!"

At supper, Isabella said: "Hetty Cary's beauty lit up the scene, but 'coming through the rye,' there was no rye! Mr. Vizitelli had only painted a sparse piece of oats on the back of a screen, and a group of actors hid that. Then Captain Tucker's kisses were make-believe!" "He came near enough the real thing to like it, judging by his face," said an unknown individual in the crowd.

Mrs. Randolph's comment while that baby cried — and really the young men behind the scene had perfected themselves in the art of crying — "That baby yelled to break any mother's heart. Mr. Vizitelli

* The gaiety in Richmond in this winter of 1863–64 was often criticized. Since Gettysburg there had been little serious fighting on the Virginia front; and Grant's 1864 campaign was still months away. Nevertheless, after Gettysburg, many felt — as did Mrs. Chesnut — that hope was gone.

asked for so many things, first a spoon, then a bottle, then a tea kettle: I wondered what would come next."

A voice: "What babies care for most was there most temptingly exposed." Ball dress must tantalize a baby. Can storied urn or animated bust answer to a baby's scream?

John R. Thompson had written a rhymed programme, and Mary Preston read a verse after each charade. She did not appear. The voice came to us from a distance, but very distinctly. When in one of the rhymes Hood was complimented, he grew so red, and was in an agony of girlish blushing.

January 16th. — Mrs. Preston decided that we should have our French play at her house but there should be no audience. Sudden death of the French play. Then and there it ended.

Now that the no-substitute and conscript bill have both passed, men who had substitutes are all wanting offices that exempt them.

A visit from the President's handsome and accomplished Secretary, Burton Harrison. I lent him "Country Clergyman in Town," and "Elective Affinities." He is to bring me Mrs. Norton's "Lost and Saved." Every Sunday Mr. Minnegerode cries aloud in anguish his Litany: "From pestilence and famine, battle, murder and sudden death." And we, on our knees: "Good Lord deliver us." Yet all the week long we go on as before, hearing of nothing but battle, murder, sudden death. Those are the daily events; but a new book, that is the unlooked-for thing, the pleasing incident in this life of monotonous musing.

At Mrs. Randolph's, Mr. Chesnut complimented Constance Cary, who had amply earned his praise by her splendid acting. She pointed to Burton Harrison. "You see that wretch! He has not said one word to me!" My husband innocently: "Why should he? And why is he a wretch?" "Oh! You know!" Going home I explained this riddle to him. He is always a year behind-hand in gossip. Everyone said those two were engaged last winter. There seems a screw loose, but that sort of thing always comes right.

At breakfast today a card was followed without an instant interlude by Barney Heyward, perhaps the neatest, most particular man in South Carolina. I was uncombed, unkempt, tattered and torn, in my most comfortable, soiled, wadded-green-silk dressing-gown, and a white woolen shawl over my head to keep off draughts. He has not been in the war yet, and now he wants to be Captain of an Engineer corps. I wish he may get it. He has always been my friend, so he shall lack no aid that I can give, and if he can stand the shock of my appearance today, we may reasonably expect to continue friends until death. The fastidious Barney to come in, of all men! He faced the situation gallantly.

Last night Barney Heyward went with us to a reception at the President's. After our obeisance before the highest in the land, Maggie took me from Mr. Mallory. She had promised a wounded knight to lead me to his sofa, where I found him entrenched. He was holding an unwieldly sofa cushion next to him to keep a vacant seat for me. When I had occupied the reserved place, there was the cushion still left in his arms; and he dandled it by no means so gracefully as Vizitelli did the squalling baby a few nights before. In an agony of awkwardness he asked: "What shall I do with this thing?" "Throw it behind the sofa." "Ah!" and a sigh of relief! But the old woman who was at the other end of the sofa? She was submerged by my hoops and flounces, but she was doing battle nobly. Though she was effaced for a while, she soon came to the surface, trying to smile, but very red in the face. I was redder, and more energetic in hammering away at my hoops and flounces.

"The virgin," as these girls call Virginia C—— came up with Colonel Ives. She said in an aside that he always suggested St. Ives in the nursery rhymes, and his seven wives and cats and lives. "St. Ives is not a man, no man at all," suggested a comrade of Ives, who knew something of soldiers' lives!

I met Mr. Davis's new cabinet minister, the brother of Bishop Davis of South Carolina. This man * is a North Carolinian, as was the Bishop. When he was introduced to me I said politely: "I have had the pleasure of meeting Mr. Davis before. I remember seeing him at the Bishop's in Camden." He replied with ponderous dignity: "I do not recollect you at all. It is possible, though, that you may have seen me somewhere." Fancy Mr. Mallory's unholy joy at my receiving such a facer! When I told the girls, they dubbed him at once: "the lout in high life."

I was invited to Dr. Haxall's to meet the Lawtons, and Mr. Benjamin dropped in. He is a friend of the house. Mrs. Haxall is a Richmond leader of society, a devout beauty and a belle, a charming person; and her hospitality is of the genuine Virginia type. Everything Mr. Benjamin said, we listened to and bore it in mind and gave

* George Davis of North Carolina was the Confederate Attorney General from January 2, 1864 till the War's end.

heed to it diligently. He is of the innermost shrine, supposed to enjoy the honour of Mr. Davis's unreserved confidence.

The Carys prefer Mr. Chesnut, my husband, to his wife. I don't mind. Indeed, I like it, for *I do too!*

Lamar was asked to dinner here yesterday — so he came today. We had our wild turkey cooked for him yesterday, and I dressed myself within an inch of my life, with the best of my four-year-old finery. Two of us, Mr. Chesnut and I, did not damage the wild turkey seriously, and today Lamar enjoyed the *réchauffé*, and he commended the art with which Molly hid the slight loss we had inflicted upon its mighty breast. She piled fried oysters over the turkey so skillfully that unless we had told it, no one would ever have known the huge bird was making his second appearance upon the table.

Lamar was more absent-minded and distrait than ever, but my husband behaved like a trump, a well-bred man with all his wits about him; so things went off smoothly enough. Lamar had just read "Romola." Across the water, he said, it was the rage. I am sure it is not as good as "Adam Bede" or "Silas Marner." It is not worthy of the woman who was to "rival all but Shakespeare's name below." "What is the matter with 'Romola'?" he protested, and I said: "Tito is so mean, and he is mean in such a very mean way. And then the end is so repulsive! Petting the husband's illegitimate children and left-handed wives may be magnanimity, but human nature revolts at it in disgust." "You mean, women's nature?" "Oh yes. But here is another test. Two weeks ago, I read this thing with intense interest, and already her Savonarola has faded from my mind. I have forgotten her way of presenting him as completely as I always forget Bulwer's 'Rienzi.' "

"Oh, I understand you now," he commented. "For you, Milton's Devil has obliterated all other devils. You can't fix your mind upon any other. The Devil always must be of Miltonic proportions, or you do not believe in him. Goethe's Mephistopheles disputes the crown of the causeway with him, but soon you begin to feel that Mephistopheles is a lesser Devil, an emissary only. Is there any Cardinal Wolsey but Shakespeare's? Any Mirabeau except Carlyle's? They are stamped into your brain by genius."

This saintly preacher, the woman who stands by Hetty and saves her soul! Those heavenly-minded sermons preached at us by the authoress of "Adam Bede!" Lamar told us about this writer who so well imagines female purity and piety. She was a governess, or something of that sort; perhaps she wrote for a livelihood. At any rate, she had an "elective affinity," to which he responded, for Lewes; so she lives with Lewes! Lamar does not know whether she caused the separation between Lewes and his legal wife; but he says they were living in a villa on some Swiss lake. She is the Mrs. Lewes of the hour; a charitable, estimable, agreeable, sympathetic woman of genius; a fallen woman, living in a contented, nay, a happy state of immorality!

Lamar seemed without prejudice on the subject. At least he expressed neither surprise nor disapprobation. He said something of genius being above law, but I was not very clear as to what he said at that point. As for me, I said nothing, for fear of saying too much. "My idol was shattered — my day star fled."

Lewes is a writer. Some people say the man she lives with is a noble man. They say she is kind and good, even if she is a fallen woman. Here conversation ended.

Here is a grand announcement made by the Yankee Congress. They vote one million of men to be sent down here to free the prisoners they will not exchange. I actually thought they left all these Yankees here on our hands as part of their plan to starve us out. All Congressmen under fifty years of age are to leave politics and report for military duty or be conscripted

Mrs. Ould says the men who frequent her house are more despondent than ever since this thing began. Isabella put in: "We keep company with soldiers only, and they are sanguine, their hearts do not fail them."

A dinner party yesterday at the Prestons' was given to General Morgan, who failed to appear! We found later that he came at half past six, and was sent off by the new servant at the door who said Mr. and Mr. Preston were "not at home." When we came into the drawing-room at ten from the dining-room, there was his card besides Barney Heyward, L. Q. Washington and others, eight of whom had been asked to tea. When the girls were made to understand the blunder of the new man who answered the bell, there was a genuine feminine howl of disgust.

JANUARY 17th. — I met crowds coming away from Mr. Minnegerode's church. No standing room left. I knew the old grey-haired sexton would find me a seat, so I persisted in going in; and he did. He led me up to the President's pew.

Some gentlemen came for Mr. Chesnut to ride round and look at the entrenchments. When he came home, he told me that Mr. Lyons "not wisely but too well" pitched into Breckenridge for his conduct of affairs at Missionary Ridge. "Well sir! How came we to lose Chattanooga?" General Breckenridge coolly responded: "It is a long story," then turned away and began talking to someone else.

Our Congress is so demoralized, so confused, so depressed. They have asked the President, whom they have so hated, so insulted, so crossed and opposed and prevented in every way, to speak to them, and advise them what to do.

Mrs. Grundy came to say she had been robbed of a barrel of sugar; a calamity, surely, at this juncture. When Lawrence ushered her in, my husband and I were both sound asleep, on opposite sides of the fireplace, where two sofas are cosily drawn. He waked at a touch, and behaved beautifully, but I sat up and for a moment could not remember where I was. Indeed I was not wide awake until several others came in. Barney Heyward said of his great kinsman: "Cousin Robert is the best of men, and a wise man too; but he will always give the preference to a low-church man, and promote zealously even up to the post of Cabinet Minister in a War Administration a man that he esteems because he is a Sunday School teacher! No mortal can tell the injury he has done his country by this little peculiarity."

Mr. Heyward was at one of the departments yesterday, when a boy rushed in with a telegram. The man at the desk said to the boy: "Now you are a devil of a fellow! Where have you been loitering?" He turned to Barney and said: "Here is a reprieve coming at one o'clock, for a man who was shot at twelve!" Barney was horrified, but it turned out that the man who had charge of the execution was slower than the telegraph boy, and the poor soldier's execution was an hour behind time and so he was saved.

At the Prestons' door, where the invited company was turned away by the new servant, Mr. Heyward says a messenger from the telegraph office was among the number absolutely refused admittance by the inexorable Charles. I hope that blunder did not hang some other man!

JANUARY 19th. — Yesterday the Kentuckians came *en masse*, led by General Breckenridge. They sent their carriage for the girls, after I had consented to let them make taffy. Breckenridge rarely sat down. He walked up and down my small drawing-room like a caged lion. He says the Army of the West desire the Negroes freed and put in the ranks. They wonder it has never been done before.

JANUARY 21st. — Both of us were too ill to attend Mr. Davis's reception. It proved a sensational one; first a fire in the house and then a robbery, said to be an arranged plan of the usual bribed servant there and some escaped Yankee prisoners. Today the Examiner is lost in wonder at the stupidity of the fire-and-arson contingent. If they had only waited a few hours until everybody was asleep, since after a reception the household would be so tired, and so sound asleep! Thanks to his kind counsel, maybe they will do better next time.

Letters from home have carried Mr. Chesnut off today. Heavens! How glad he was to go, how thankful for a decent excuse to leave us!

Thackeray is dead. I stumbled upon "Vanity Fair" for myself. I had never heard of Thackeray before. I think it was in 1850. I know I had been ill at the New York Hotel, and when left alone I slipped down stairs and into a book store that I had noticed under the Hotel for something to read. They gave me the first half. I can recall now the very kind of paper it was printed on, and the illustrations as they took effect upon me; and yet when I raved of it and was wild for the other half, there were people who said it was slow, that he was a coarse, dull, sneering writer, that he stript human nature bare and made it repulsive!

General Breckenridge said he knew Mrs. Stanard was going to run the blockade, that old C—— had told him, and had then put up his withered old hand and whispered: "But don't tell that I said so, or she will give me a curtain lecture!" He was chuckling, but when I stared, he said: "Now, now, don't try to look shocked! You know, C—— is an old bachelor, and attaches no technical meaning to 'curtain lecture.' He only thinks of it as something behind the curtain, not before the footlights. However, she is going out to buy her trousseau to marry another who is just such an old driveller!"

January 22nd. — At Mrs. Lyons's, I met another beautiful woman, Mrs. Penn, the wife of Colonel Penn who is making shoes in a Yankee prison. She had a little son with her barely two years old, a mere infant. She said to him: "*Faites comme* Butler!" The child crossed his eyes and made himself hideous, then laughed and rioted around as if he enjoyed the joke hugely.

I went to Mrs. Davis's. It was sad enough. Fancy having to be always ready to have your servants set your house on fire, to know they are bribed to do it. Such constant robberies, servants coming and going daily to the Yankees, carrying over silver, etc., does not conduce to make home happy.

I saw Hood on his legs once more. He rode off on a fine horse, though he is disabled in one hand too. After all, as the women said:

"He has body enough left to hold his soul!" "How plucky of him to ride a gay horse like that!" "Oh! A Kentuckian prides himself upon being half horse — half man. "And the girl who rode beside him: did you ever see more beauty? Three cheers for South Carolina!!"

Barney has no end of scandal, which he derived from his grandfather. It is rough on American aristocracy. He does not allow credit anywhere; nobody is anybody, so to speak, except Heywards and a few families into which they have intermarried. Mary Preston said I scored when I adroitly made him tell of the tailor who married into the Heyward family. I had been leading up to the tailor for half an hour. As he let out the skeletons in everybody else's closet, I was carefully stalking the tailor as a fitting retribution to his vanity.

Mrs. Huger, on Butler, says: "Why make a proclamation against Beast Butler? * Is he any worse than the rest of them? By all this nonsense, thousands of good Confederates are rotting in Yankee prisons." She lent me "Martin Chuzzlewit." Now that we separate ourselves in thought from the Yankees whom Dickens laughs at, it will bear a second reading.

Tonight we had General Hampton and Von Borcke and the Kentucky generals, for they move as one body and Brewster is their advance guard. Johnny sent me six wild ducks and a perfect monster of a wild turkey. I imparted a plan of mine to Brewster. I would have a breakfast — a luncheon, a matinée, call it what you please — but I would try and return some of the hospitalities of this most hospitable people. Just think of the dinners, suppers, breakfasts, we have been to. They have no variety in war times, but they make up in exquisite cooking for want of that.

"Variety," he echoed, "you are hard to please. Terrapin stew, gumbo, fish, oysters in every shape, game, wine — as good wine as ever is. I do not mention juleps, claret cups, apple toddy, whiskey punches and all that. I tell you it is good enough for me! Variety would spoil it. Then such hams as these Virginia people cure, such home-made bread. There is no such bread in the world. You can call yours a 'cold collation.' " "Yes. I have eggs, butter, hams, game, everything from home, even fruit." "You ought to do your best. They are so generous and hospitable, and so unconscious of any merit, or exceptional credit, in the matter of hospitality." "They are

* There was a more or less formal threat that if General Butler were captured, he would be hanged.

no better than the Columbia people were to us!" So I fired up for my country.

The former editor of the Mercury denounces Colonel Jordan of Beauregard's staff. He says Charleston people think Colonel Jordan suppresses communications addressed to General Beauregard, and that the obnoxious Colonel openly expresses the hope that he may live to see Charleston in flames once more.

JANUARY 24th. — My luncheon yesterday was a female affair exclusively. Mrs. Davis came early, and found Annie and Tudy making the chocolate. Lawrence went South with Mr. Chesnut, so we had only Molly for cook and parlor maid. After the company assembled, we waited and waited while those girls were making the final arrangements. I made my way to the door which opened into the dining room, and as I leaned against it ready to turn the knob, Mrs. Stanard held me like the Ancient Mariner, telling me how she had been prevented by a violent attack of cramps from running the blockade, how providential it all was. All this floated by my ear, for I heard Mary Preston's voice raised in anger on the other side of the door. "Stop! Do you mean to taste away the whole dish? Buck, if you eat many more of those fried oysters they will be missed! Heavens! She is running away with a palpable plug out of that jelly cake!" I listened to Mrs. Stanard on thorns.

Later in the afternoon, when it was over and I was safe, and all had gone well, and Molly had not disgraced herself before the mistresses of those wonderful Virginia cooks, Mrs. Davis and I went for a walk, and today the President walked home with me from church. He walked so fast I had no breath to talk, so I was a good listener for once. The truth is, I am too much afraid of him to say very much in his presence. After dinner, Hood came for him to ride; and Mr. Hunter walked home with me. He made himself utterly agreeable by dwelling on his friendship and admiration of my husband. He said it was high time Mr. Davis should promote him, and that he had told Mr. Davis his opinion on that subject today.

JANUARY 28th. — I gave my newly arrived friend Mrs. Garnett a party Monday night. I must say that now, at my house, it is a party day and night. No longer in awe of Mr. Chesnut, who is in Carolina, the girls are here always, and when they are — well!

Monday morning, the Clays were here rehearsing for Mrs. Ives's private theatricals. Mrs. Clement Clay is to be Mrs. Malaprop, Mrs. Lawson the maid.

At night, Dr. Garnett brought all of the Kentucky contingent. You do not often find such nice men for a tea party, anywhere. Dr. Garnett tried the supercilious Barney's patience, but he was too well bred to show the slightest annoyance. We were playing Whist. "Hold on there, Major!" said someone to Barney, and Dr. Garnett protested: "Don't promote Mr. Heyward too rapidly. Besides, 'Mr.' is a distinction in this military mob." Barney was calm and imperturable. He might have been deaf and dumb, and blind too, as far as Dr. Garnett was concerned.

Bill of fare for my supper: Wild turkey, wild ducks, partridges, oysters, and a bowl of apple toddy made by Mrs. Davis's recipe.

Tuesday, Barney Heyward went with me to the President's reception, and from there to a ball at the McFarlands'. Breckenridge alone of the generals went with us. The others went to a supper given by Mrs. Clay of Alabama. I had a long talk with Mr. Ould, Mr. Benjamin and Mr. Hunter. These men speak out their thoughts plainly enough. What they said means: "We are rattling down hill, and nobody to put on the brakes." I wore my black velvet, diamonds and point lace. They are borrowed for all the theatricals, but I wear them whenever they are at home.

Mrs. Wigfall said she was afraid Louly would be taken for a young lady. "So she dressed her as an old woman," commented Isabella. Louly is lovely, and she was not crushed by a red poplin with a train trimmed with shabby black velvet. She wore a huge lace collar high up in the neck — all because she was fifteen, and not out! Her black eyes, however, saved her.

Johnny here, gravely explaining the Gougles. It is a cruel injustice to respectable young persons, the way Tom Boykin talked. They live over their father's shop — they do eat cheese at tea — and they give little dances. "The Captain, you know," said Tom, "will go the Devil's for a round dance!" Captain Johnny permitted himself a palpable scowl. Then came Custis Lee and John Rutherford, and Major Cox dropped in. Tom Boykin said: "Cousin Mary, don't you fret about the Gougles! The Army finds Gougles everywhere, and they forget them as soon as Boots and Saddle is sounded."

Barney Heyward came and reports Mr. Myers crushed by the contending powers between the upper and nether milestone. He is ill in bed. The Senate has resolved to confirm anyone Mr. Davis appoints in Myers's place, be he who he may.

January 31st. — Mrs. Davis gave her "Luncheon to Ladies" on

Saturday. Many more persons were there than at any of those luncheons which have gone before. We had gumbo, ducks and olives, *suprême de volaille*, chickens in jelly, oysters, lettuce salad, chocolate cream, jelly cake, claret cup, champagne, etc.

General Hood informed me today that he was ordered to the Army of the Tennessee, that he was now a corps commander. Suddenly his eye blazed as he said this. Said I to myself: "All that ambition still! In spite of those terrible wounds!" Did he read my thoughts? He added: "This has been the happiest year of my life, in spite of all my wounds." Again his eye blazed up. "When I am gone, it is all over. I will not come back." I said quickly: "Are you not threatening the wrong end of the sofa?" He laughed heartily, turned his back to Buck who was on the other end of the sofa, and said to me eagerly: "Will she care?" "How do I know?" And I went away.

There was a star with a diamond centre which looped up Hood's hat. When he was going away, I saw this was missing. He is so helpless. I had put his hat down for him, and I gave it to him again. I said in a fright: "Where is your diamond star?" In a moment I saw I had made a blunder somehow. There was much blushing.

Someone sent up a supper of terrapin stew, oysters and Rhine wine, and a box of sugar plums. I have not the slightest idea who sent it. Everybody stayed till late. There was a nice man here whose name I will not write, for Buck murdered him. "He wants to be introduced to you," she said. "But he is a 'substitute' man!"

General Breckenridge said he heard this statement on the stump out West. "When this cruel war broke out, gallantly I rushed to the front. I hired a substitute and sent him to bleed and die for my country; and now my martyred substitute's bones bleach on the battlefield of my country."

Brewster said, as Hood went off out of hearing: "I want him to go back to the Army. Those girls are making a fool of him." After they were all gone, Buck, the loveliest of them all, advanced with gravity and dignity. Though we were alone she began in a sweet dignified way, then broke down and the staid gravity fled and she was all giggle and blush. "Oh Mrs. Chesnut, you know I have Sam's star. I am to put it on his new hat for him. But how could I explain before all those people?"

Johnny and Tom Burwell went with me to tea at the Prestons'. We met, I think, all of the generals in town. Tom Burwell said: "What suits me about these people; they like me, a simple private, as well as any general of them all!" "Stop there, my dear boy!" cried Captain Johnny. "Not exactly! They are as kind and polite to you, maybe; but not the other thing, never!" The captain grows cynical. He thinks this winter not half so pleasant as the last. The very air is darkened with generals. "What are they all doing here anyhow? Why are they not with the Army? There is enough for them to do there, God knows," growls the Captain, left in the lurch and spiteful.

Today, for a pair of forlorn shoes, I gave eighty-five dollars. Colonel Ives drew Mr. Chesnut's pay for me. I sent Lawrence for it. Mr. Chesnut ordered him back to us, since we needed a man-servant here. Colonel Ives wrote that he was amazed I should be willing to trust a darkie with that great bundle of money, but it came safely.

Mr. Pettigrew says: "You take your money to market in the market basket, and bring home what you buy in your pocketbook." *

February 5th. — When Lawrence handed me my husband's pay (six hundred dollars it was), I said: "Now I am pretty sure you do not mean to go to the Yankees, for with that pile of money in your hands you must have known that was your chance." He grinned, but said nothing.

At the President's reception, Hood had a perfect ovation. Mr. Preston navigated him through the crowd, handling him as tenderly on his crutches as if he were the Princess of Wales's new-born baby that I read about today. It is bad for the head of an army to be so helpless, but old Blucher went to Waterloo in a carriage and with a bonnet on his head to shade his inflamed eyes.

Afterwards at the Prestons' — for we left the President at an early hour — Major Von Borcke was trying to teach them his way of pronouncing his own name, and telling them of the numerous travesties of it in this country, when Charles threw open the door. "A gentleman has called for Major Bandbox!" The Prussian Major acknowledged that to be the worst he had heard yet.

Once a German who wished to give me to understand his social position at home said: "At one time, my sister carried the trail of a dyed queen." After mature reflection, we translated: "Trainbearer of a queen now dead."

Off to the Ives's theatrical. General Breckenridge walked with me, Major Von Borcke with Mary Preston. Isabella, Annie, Buck and Lucy went with General Hood in his carriage.

* This was the most popular and most frequently repeated quip in Richmond during the later years of the War.

Our party kept together, but Buck insisted on taking a seat behind us. Mary after a while turned to Buck angrily. "Don't you see this man is making you more conspicuous, twisting his neck off, looking back, than if you would come sensibly alongside." She spoke in French. "Stop it!" said Buck in her softest voice. "Do you suppose nobody speaks French but you?"

"And if she scolds you in German, I will understand," said Von Borcke.

Buck came as she was ordered, and sat by the man whose head she was ordered not to turn. She was not pleased at the one beside her, and she turned her back to him. He amiably remarked: "Plenty of room, do not be afraid, I do not mind scrouging." The arrangement apparently was satisfactory, however; for we sat there five hours, and in coming away, the General said he was never less tired in his life.

Mrs. Clay as Mrs. Malaprop was beyond our wildest hopes, and she was in such earnest when she pinched Lydia Languish's (Conny Cary's) shoulder and called her "an antricate little huzzy" that Lydia showed she felt it, and next day it was black and blue. Even the back of Mrs. Clay's head was eloquent. "But," said General Breckenridge, "Watch Hood! He has not seen the play before and Bob Acres amazes him." When he caught my eye, General Hood nodded to me and said emphatically: "I believe that fellow Acres is a coward!" "That's better than the play," whispered Breckenridge. But it was all good fun, from Sir Anthony down to Fag.

Between acts Mrs. Clay sent us word to applaud. She wanted encouragement. The audience was too cold. To that hint General Breckenridge responded like a man, and after that, they followed his lead and she was fired by thunders of applause. Those mighty Kentuckians turned *claqueurs* were a host in themselves. Constance Cary not only acted well, but looked perfectly beautiful. Lydia's folly gave her so many opportunities for her favorite trick of posing.

During the farce, Mrs. Clay came in all her feathers and diamonds and took her seat by me. Said General Breckenridge: "What a splendid head of hair you have!" "And all my own!" Afterwards she said they could not get false hair enough, and they put a pair of black satin boots on top of her head and piled hair over them.

Bombastes Furioso was the farce. Mr. Randolph sang a comic opera: "Hope told a flattering tale." Those were the only words, but he gave a few bars of every air from nearly all the well-known operas, and the effect was comic indeed; the repetition of words to a variety of tunes.

We went in before the crowd arrived, and the gentlemen who went in with us, sat by us. Elsewhere the sexes were separated as before, the men banked in a black cloud behind the seats. We were regarded with an evil eye for our presumption in contravening the arrangements. I was punched in the back by a fan, and a solemn old lady told me: "If you laugh so much you will make yourself conspicuous!"

We adjourned from Mrs. Ives's to Mrs. Oulds's where we had the usual excellent Richmond supper. We did not get home until three. It was a clear moonlight night, as light as day. As we walked along, I said to General Breckenridge: "You have spent a jolly evening." "I do not know," he replied. "I have asked myself more than once tonight: 'Are you the same man who stood gazing down on the faces of the dead on that awful battlefield; the soldiers lying there, they stare at you with their eyes wide open. Is this the same world?' "

Last night the great Kentucky contingent came in a body. Hood brought Buck in his carriage. She said she did not like General Hood, and she spoke with a wild excitement in those soft blue eyes of hers — or are they gray, or brown? She then gave her reason, loud and distinct enough for him to hear. "He spoke so harshly to Cy as we got out of the carriage. I saw how he hurt Cy's feelings, and I tried to soothe Cy's mortification." "You see, Cy nearly caused me to fall by his awkwardness, and I stormed at him," said the General, vastly amused. "But she salved it over. She told Cy how good he was, and that I could not do without him." Buck insisted: "I hate a man who speaks angrily to those who dare not resent it!" The General declared himself charmed with her sentiments but seemed to think his wrongdoing all a good joke.

She told me she was sorry she had told him that if her father and mother did not oppose it, she would care for him. She repented it already. "You foolish child! To whom did you tell that?" "I told him so as we came here. I told him so himself, and now I am very sorry I said it, for it is not true." Good Heavens, how I wish the man was gone! This poor child!

At Mrs. Ives's play, while Buck was standing guard, as it were, to prevent the crowd rushing against him as he stood leaning on his crutches in the passageway, General Breckenridge said: "That is a beautiful picture. Will she marry him?" "Half of it is sympathy. The girls are all wild about him. She has always no end of men in love with her. That is about what it amounts to." General Breckenridge growled: "He cares awfully for her, and no wonder. She is so sweet. Poor old battered hero!"

Johnny, here on his way home, says he must have a party; that over and above all we have in the house, the cream Mrs. Allen sent me, etc., it would not cost more than a hundred Confederate dollars.

Another disaster at the President's. Their trusty man Robert is broken out with smallpox, and half Richmond at the reception.

Buck reads my journal. She asked me: "What did you say when General Breckenridge asked you, plump, 'Will she have him?' More than is written there, I know." I gave her that frank interview between the General and myself without reserve. She opened her beautiful eyes in amazement, so little do people know themselves. "He said most men would think themselves engaged upon what those girls at Mrs. Preston's say has passed between you already." "What?" "For one thing, in answer to something said by you, they heard him say: 'Oh you! You are so childish and sweet!' Now, Buck! You know you are not childish! You have more strong, good, common sense than anyone in that house, except your mother. Why are you playing with him in that way? I told General Breckenridge that you had been engaged before, and probably would be engaged again; that you were very kind and sympathetic, and as soon as you found an engagement — so called — fastened upon you, you began to reconsider. Your good sense came to the surface and you tired of it." "Oh, how could you be so cruel, so unfair?" she protested.

"You are so unhappy about so many of these men who cared for you having been killed. It was odd, you say, that Hood* was always lucky till he fell in love with you; that you were ever so sorry for him.

*There was no Southern leader, not even excepting Lee, Jackson or Stuart, whose biography would contain more of human interest than that of John B. Hood. Born in Kentucky in 1831, a graduate of West Point in 1853, a Texan by adoption, it was he who in 1861–62 — at thirty — whipped into shape the famous Texas Brigade, which many held to be the greatest single fighting unit in Lee's army. The Brigade first won fame at Gaines's Mill, when they broke the key position of the Yankee front. There Hood received his first wound; at Gettysburg he was wounded in the arm and for a while it appeared he could not survive; at Chickamauga he lost a leg. Put in command in the West to replace Johnston, he suffered repeated and disastrous defeats; he was retired from the army in January, 1865, at his own request. He died of yellow fever in New Orleans in 1879. Mrs. Chesnut's narrative of his courtship of Sally Buchanan Preston, embellished as it is with incidents illustrative of personal traits, is much more than the chronicle of a light war-time flirtation.

And so many farewells nowadays (with the chances never to meet again softening a girl's heart) end in 'engagements.' Chickamauga is the only real victory we have had since Stonewall Jackson, and this man is the hero of Chickamauga. Our victories are splendid, you know. But then we move back, and women cannot understand that. There is always another army of Yankees, fresh and ready for us behind the one we have just defeated." Thus I wandered away from personalities.

Buck said: "We wondered what you two were about. You were so sad, and in such dead earnest. Hood said it was the war, but I knew it was me. You always look that way when you are talking of me, because you love me, and you love so few people."

"There is nobody in the world like my darling," I assured her. "I told him you had never been in love with anybody; that I doubted if you knew what love meant, and that you were not the least in the world in love now."

"How could you say that?"

"Because, my blessed, you tell every word that passes. Those girls come here and tell me about it, as if it were a game of chess, and each move had to be studied and recorded."

"Say backgammon, instead; for that is a game of chance. All depends upon the throw, you know; lucky or unlucky. You know how I hated him when he lost his temper because poor Cy stumbled. There are two things certain in this world. One is, I will never love anybody as I love brother Willie; and the next is I will never disobey Mamma and Papa. There, are you satisfied?"

"All right, but as soon as another girl takes her seat by Sam, don't go straight there and show you have a right to him!"

An engagement in Richmond means so little. "What are they engaged for? What does 'engagement' mean?" Major Venable says: "For one thing, it does not mean a wedding." He pointed out a handsome woman. "She has been married twice, but I am engaged to her still. We became engaged while I was at college and it was never broken off. I married the loveliest woman in the world, be the others who they may; but when I met my fate, I had half that enchantress over there!"

At Mrs. Davis's breakfast, there was an ancient Dame, bluest-blood-ever, in that assemblage of FF's. If not Pocahontas, some other royal American savage had been her ancestress. A western girl, who had been under the hands of dissectors, was about to leave the house of one of the interlocutors. "Why can't you let the poor thing stay," said the Dame. "She is so gay, so attractive." "But my dear, she screams! She is too nervous! She takes fright at night! Twice she has raised the house with her untimely screams." "A well-brought-up girl never screams," said a lady who would have been hideous without a harelip — which she had. "No young girl should ever be the heroine of an inexplicable affair. She must not be talked of for any affair whatever. Let her hold her tongue. Everything blows over. Scream, and it is all up. Who believes explanations? Nobody."

"Once I was tired," I said, "and so I know how it is myself. It was in New York. I saw a man enter my room. He used a false key. Did I scream? No. To pretend horror that one man should see you in *déshabillé*, and then cry out and bring fifty more? Never! I kept perfectly still. I saw him searching. My purse was under my head. I saw him approaching my bed. I sat up. It was moonlight, but I struck a match. I lit the gas and glared at him. The creature turned to stone. He turned and shot out of the room as if the devil and all his imps were after him. I did not trouble myself to bolt the door. I knew he would lack the nerve to come back after what he had seen."

Mrs. Davis described my behavior. She said I began to laugh, early in the story; and it was as good as a play to watch my face change as I perceived that this was not to be taken as a funny story, but was listened to as a didactic lecture. Not even this shook the foundation of solemn, ponderous Richmond society. "Moral, never scream!" But Mrs. Davis, Mrs. Preston and I were literally screaming with laughter.

Says Johnny, the Captain of Dragoons: "Too many generals here this winter. They have demoralized society. It is not half as pleasant as last winter. Last winter, Auntie, you were on the first floor, and your apartments were South Carolina barracks. Now you have gone up a flight of stairs; and our men say there are too many stars on the soldiers' collars up there for a private to venture up. Then there is Hood; they are sending him out west! The men say that at the head of Fourth Texas, he was as sure to bring the coon down as Captain Scott; but buckled up in a carriage, somebody else will have to lead his Texans. Besides, there are all the generals over whose heads he has stepped with his one leg. Already, every man Jack who was a general while he was a colonel grumbles and says he is going up too fast!"

All this amounts to what we began with. Unless there is self-control, no civilization is possible. At the play the other night, there was a succession of shrill, modest, little screams as Bob Acres took off his dressing-gown. "Heavens, will he undress right here before us?" All this set General Breckenridge roaring with laughter. He approved of the homely old maid's theory: "Never scream until you are hurt — and not then if you are wise."

Here L. Q. Washington came in with a treasure trove. He had found at some shop such nice pocket handkerchiefs. He displayed one, strong, white, and large as a tablecloth. The Captain was in a brown study and paid no heed. "I say," said Mr. Washington, "here are some handkerchiefs that have just run the blockade. Don't you want to know when they are to be bought?" "No. I hope the war will end before I need any more." "Have you any as nice as these?" "Yes." "Let me see," said the incredulous Washington.

The Captain took out of his rusty uniform pocket a neatly folded white mesh, as fine as gossamer. He shook it out and showed Washington his monogram, beautifully embroidered.

"Nonsense! Some girl gave you that one! That's not fair." The Captain left us in disgust, and I explained: "You know, he was in Paris the year before the war, and of course he ordered that sort of thing — dozens upon dozens — and well for us he did, as I make a raid upon his supply in times of need!" "That scrap could scarcely cover his Roman nose," said Washington spitefully. "With his dainty ways, I wonder he is not afraid of being called effeminate!" I laughed. "He is Captain of a set of dare-devil Camden boys, and he rules them. General Young said he wished there were a million like them, fellows who can fight and ride and dance round dances!"

Johnny has no unreasonable estimate of his own merit. He says if he should chance to be ruined after the war, he means to establish a chicken farm; that when he was a boy he used to succeed wonderfully with his own chickens in his mother's yard.

General Breckenridge came to say good-bye. Sam Hood was with him. I asked Sam: "How did you enjoy the ride? I saw you from my window." His eyes blazed. There was no smile on his face, but a lazy queer twinkle of inward delight in his eye.

"Oh, a delicious day. I am dying to tell somebody, and I know for her sake you will be cautious. You see, I asked her if she liked me as well as anybody else. 'Yes.' 'Better than anyone else?' 'Yes.' 'Then will you let me try to make you love me?' 'That's just as you please,' with cool indifference. But I did not want any more today. . . ."

Here General Breckenridge broke in. "They are my cousins, so I determined to kiss them good-bye! So I advanced to the charge gravely, soberly, discreetly, and in the fear of the Lord. The girls stood in a row, four of the very prettiest I ever saw. Sam stood with his eyes glued to the floor, but he cried: 'You are afraid. You mean to back out.' But I did nothing of the kind. I kissed every one of them, honestly and heartily." Mrs. Martin said to me in an audible whisper; "Old Sam dares not look up! He is bursting with envy!"

FEBRUARY 9th. — This party for Johnny was the very nicest I have ever had, and I mean it to be my last. I sent word to the Carys to bring their own men. They came alone, saying they did not care for men! "That means a raid on ours," growled Isabella. Mr. Lamar was devoted to Constance Cary. He is a free lance, so that created no heartburning.

Mr. Venable said: "It is not 'The devil on two sticks'; the farce is now, 'Cupid on crutches'!" General Hood took Mrs. Davis in to supper, and they remained at a small table prepared for her for more than an hour after the rest of us left the supper room.

Mrs. Davis told us afterwards she could hear Buck's clear, ringing, musical voice uplifted. She had gone back to flirting with Johnny. "Absurd! Engaged to that man! Never! For what do you take me?"

Mrs. Davis repeated what General Pendleton said. "If he had been so often hit, he would wince and dodge at every ball!" And poor Sam replied: "Why wince, when you would thank God for a ball to go through your heart and be done with it all?" Mrs. Davis added: "It was high tragedy, and not farce; for there was the bitterness of death in his tone, and the silvery voice from the other room came calm and clear: 'Absurd! Oh, you foolish creatures, to fancy I could. . . .' "

Afterwards, when the whole thing was over, and a success, here trooped in the four girls who stayed all night with me. They were in dressing-gowns. They stirred up a hot fire, relit the gas and went in for their supper; *rechauffé* was the word; oysters, hot coffee, etc. They kept it up till daylight. Maggie Howell put her feet through her night-gown sleeves, and then tied up the skirts of it, leaving a huge bunch at the end to represent a bunchy Shanghai fowls' tail. She was a comical bird as she hopped around, and I came near strangling, so long and violent was my laughter; but I could not keep awake even to laugh so I left them.

Of course we slept very late next day. As they came in to breakfast,

I remarked: "The church bells have been going on like mad. I took it as a rebuke to our breaking the Sabbath. You know Sunday began at twelve last night."

About two, my young people went home. Soon the infant dashed in, done up in soldier's clothes. "The Yankees are upon us! Don't you hear the alarm bells? They have been ringing day and night." Alex Haskell came then, and he explained matters. John Chesnut and himself went off to report to Custis Lee, and to be enrolled among his "locals," who are always detailed for defence of the city. They were gone all day. At night Alex Haskell came back for a while to say it was all a false alarm.

We went to the Webb Ball. Such a pleasant time we had. After a while my pet Major General took his seat in the comfortable chair next to mine and declared his determination to hold that position. Mr. Hunter and Mr. Benjamin essayed to dislodge him. Mr. Stanard said: "Take him into the flirtation room! There he will soon be captured and led away." But I did not know where that room was situated, and besides, my bold Texan made most unexpected delay. "I will not go, and will prevent her from going with any of you." Supper was near at hand. Mr. Mallory said: "Ask him if the varioloid * is not at his house! I know it is!" I started as if I was shot, but I took Mr. Clay's arm and went in to supper.

February 12th. — Here is the love story again. People were whispering: "She treated him shamefully! As she came from riding with him she yawned in his face!" She turned calmly as they left the room. "Idiots! It is all over. As we rode, he held out his hand. I said: 'Ah! don't do that! Let it all rest as it is! You know I like you, but you want to spoil all!' He cried: 'Say yes or say no! I will not be satisfied with less. Yes or no, which is it?' Well, he would keep holding out his hand. What could I do, with Cy riding behind? So I put mine in his. Heavens, what a change came over his face! I pulled my hand away by main strength! The practical wretch said at once: 'Now I will speak to your father. I want his consent to marry you at once.' Did you ever know so foolish a fellow?"

So the tragedy has been played out, for I do not think even now that she is in earnest. Such a beamingly, beautiful, crimson face as she turned to me, her clear blue eyes looking straight in mine.

"Do you believe I like him now?" "No." She did not notice my answer. Her parents wept in despair, and yet a month ago they could

* Varioloid is a mild form of smallpox.

easily have stopped it all. They looked to time and the thousand accidents of time to come between, and they so look still. Buck said now: "I am made nearly as miserable by the discontent at home as if they had refused outright to consent! They say I must not announce my engagement. That is, they expect nothing will come of it. But he is so preposterously sanguine and happy. He is actually alarming. He looks triumphant — and contented. And then I go up to Mamma, and she is so broken-hearted," added the darling child, so wistfully.

At the reception, I said to her father: "Why did you wait until now? Three months ago was your time to warn her, and forbid it all." "How did I know? Who tells a girl's father what is going on?" Then the General himself took possession of me. "I am so proud, so grateful! The sun never shone on a happier man! Such a noble girl, a queen among women." He did not notice that I answered never a word.

John Chesnut had a basket of champagne carried to my house, oysters, partridges, etc., for a supper after the reception. He is going back to the army tomorrow. The Infant came with the girls. He was engaged to be married to an FF of the first water, and was so bereft of his senses as not to speak to her at the reception, when she was with our girls all the time! Next day she sent him a note breaking off the engagement.

Buck came today. "Look here, my engagement is announced in the Charleston Mercury, and Mama blames me! How could I help it?" I knew their sacred engagement was not worth a fig, but I said: "He is too proud of it. He cannot keep the secret if he tries. He tells everybody."

Mr. Chesnut had arrived on Wednesday. Buck asked him what he thought of her engagement, and he answered by giving her his opinion of the propriety of one of her performances last night. She came to our house first, and after a while the General's carriage drove up, bringing some of our girls. They told her that he could not come up, but begged she would go down there for a moment. She flew down and stood ten minutes in that snow, Cy holding the carriage door open. "But Colonel Chesnut, there was no harm! I was not there ten minutes. I could not get in the carriage, because I did not mean to stay one minute. He did not hold my hand — that is, not half the time!" "Oh, you say —" "Well, he did kiss my hands! Where is the harm of that?"

"You ought not to have gone down!" "Did you not hear Auntie? He sent for me!" Then she turned to me. "Now do you believe I care for him? See, I have braved Colonel Chesnut for him, and you know how awfully afraid I am of Colonel Chesnut."

Lawrence has been sent back to South Carolina. At breakfast, in some inscrutable way, he had already become intoxicated. He was told to move a chair, and he raised it high over his head, smashing Mrs. Grundy's chandelier. Mr. Chesnut said: "Mary, do tell Lawrence to go home. I am too angry to speak to him!" So Lawrence went, without another word said. He will soon be back, and when he comes he will say: "Shoo! I knew Mars' Jeems could not do without me!" And indeed he cannot.

Brewster asked me for a bottle of brandy to travel on, said I had promised it to him; and I replied: "Whenever you bring that roll of linen cambric you said you had from a blockade runner for me." Mr. Chesnut said gravely, after Brewster left with the brandy bottle: "Surely you did not ask that man for a bolt of linen cambric?" Alas, surely I had.

Burton Harrison at the executive office has given so lively an account of my parties while Mr. Chesnut was gone that he is riding a very high horse indeed. He would not let me go with Mrs. Ould to the theatre last night, and so I missed her supper afterwards.

Molly came in and reported a queer scene: A husband, having departed, came back saying he had forgotten something. Next day Madame wife gave him a daylight breakfast and sent him off in time for the train. To her amazement, that night he came back once more, and his wife met him in a rage. "Do you expect to stay here until a file of soldiers come and carry you handcuffed away, to be shot as a deserter?" Mr. Chesnut said: "Women are so cruel. No doubt the poor soldier had his reasons, which Madame did not understand." He knew the man and liked him.

Isabella says that war leads to love-making. She says these soldiers do more courting here in a day than they would do at home without a war in ten years.

February 13th. — Mr. Chesnut is writing out some resolutions for the Congress. He is very busy trying to get some poor fellows reprieved. He says they are good soldiers, but got into a scrape. Buck came. She had on her last winter's English hat with the pheasant's wing. My husband kissed her tenderly. She asked for congratulations, and he said he would go and congratulate the General. Then he said: "You know, if I speak of him at all, I must speak handsomely; for he has won his honours like a man." She sat down, so overcome

I had to hand her a glass of water. Just then the person spoken of entered most unexpectedly. She was very quiet, though so flushed. Said the blunt soldier: "You look mighty pretty in that hat. You wore it at the Turnpike that day when I surrendered at first sight."

She nodded and smiled and flew down the steps after Mr. Chesnut, looking back to say she meant to walk with him as far as the executive office. The General walked to the window and watched until the last whiteness of her garments was gone. He said: "The President was finding fault with some of his officers in command," and I said: "Mr. President, why don't you come and lead us yourself? I would follow you to the death! Actually, if you stay here in Richmond much longer, you will grow to be a courtier! You came a tough Texan!"

Then Johnny came to say good-bye too. He had been to the Prestons'. He met Buck on the front steps, and she told him not to whisper to her behind his hat, because two old grey-headed men were watching them from the opposite windows, and took them for what they were not, lovers. "I will never marry, now," said Johnny mournfully. "No, you never will marry. There is one inescapable bar to that. You must first ask some woman to marry you. Nobody is going to ask you, and you know you will never muster up courage to ask that question!" "Now, if I had asked you in time, would you have refused me?" "No!" with a laugh of derision. "You might have spared me that," he said. "You women are like cats; you never tire of tormenting a rat!"

FEBRUARY 14th. — The President said yesterday, as we were driving: "No wonder men were willing to fight for such a country as ours, and such women. They are enough to make heroes of any material." Little Jeff rode on his pony by the carriage, and a mob of little boys ran shouting after him from street to street. He was very red in the face, but he rode on and did not look back.

FEBRUARY 15th. — As we walked to church yesterday, Judy whispered: "The General wants so much to come to church, but he can't, you know." "Why not? He stumps up two flights of stairs at my house." As we took our seats, we heard the thud of crutches behind us; and the Sexton marshalled the man in question slowly by us up to the President's pew. That being empty, the General went to the extreme end to be out of the way. Buck, seated in the Wyndham Robinson pew, was near at hand. Indeed, a slight board partition was all that divided them. She never raised her head or her veil. He told Tudy after church: "I was a little nervous when I saw who it was. It took my breath away!" After the service, the President gave the wounded soldier his arm and slowly helped him down the church steps. The mob of boys said: "That's jolly of the President. If it wasn't Sunday we'd cheer."

The President asked why I began to gather up my things to depart as soon as he came into the room. Then he became very jocular as to the open-mouthed lamentation of those girls at Mr. Chesnut's return: "These girls run from Chesnut, I believe, as you do from me."

Johnny's wisdom about love: " 'He who will not when he may. . .' She would have him fast enough now. She has the prevailing epidemic about his heroism; and there is something awfully taking about that rough Texan wooing. Do you know the witch's charm for making fools of men? No? Well, it is the laugh in her big blue eyes, and the slow way she lifts those long lashes. She is so sympathetic, and her voice is so low and sweet, and she never says anything. She listens and lets the fools do their own talking till they are up to the eyes in a bog. And then all the King's horses and all the King's men can't pull them out again. But take my word, if she don't go with him now it will blow over. If any girl said to me, 'I will have you,' I would not care a snap for her family, not for all the family she could pile on. That's my trouble! The parents are willing enough. They say I am a safe match. But the girls giggle and say: 'Oh, it is only Johnny,' and they won't have me at any price. I'd take her now, Lochinvar fashion. See if I didn't!" But he kept his discussion of tactics for our private benefit, not the General's.

Thus Sam to me: "Parents' ways are incomprehensible. They let me ride with her, drive with her. They asked me to dinner, to breakfast, to tea. When I became engaged to their daughter, I expected to have the run of the house. But far from it. Now I never see them at all; I am never asked there. When I call, or when I go to spend the evening there, I see her only in the drawing-room, where there is always a parcel of giggling girls, listening and watching, and that Brewster setting them on. But I'll kill him. . . ."

Brewster came in, unaware of his friend's bloodthirsty state of mind. He told a long story of two ladies whose high and mighty husbands were to fight a duel after the war, because of their wives' quarrels. Said Sam: "Stop that, Brewster. I never could understand women's rows, but I know if any man talks about my wife, I'll kill him."

Today, a terrible onslaught upon the President for nepotism. Burton

Harrison's and John Taylor Wood's letters denying the charge that the President's cotton was unburnt, or that he left it to be bought by the Yankees, have enraged the opposition.

FEBRUARY 16th. — I saw in Mrs. Howell's room the little Negro Mrs. Davis rescued yesterday from his brutal Negro guardian. The child is an orphan. He was dressed up in little Joe's clothes and happy as a lord. He was very anxious to show me his wounds and bruises, but I fled. There are some things in life too sickening, and cruelty is one of them.

Maggie said: "People who knew General Hood before the war said there was nothing in him. As for losing his property by the war, he never had any. West Point was a pauper's school, after all. His was only military glory, and he has gained all that since the war began."

"Only military glory?" said Burton Harrison. "Now I like that! The glory and the fame that he has gained during the war; that is Hood. What was Napoleon the Great, before Toulon? Hood has the impassive dignity of an Indian Chief. He has always a little court around him of devoted friends. Wigfall himself said he could not get within Hood's lines."

Today in the Senate Wigfall said he believed the President to be an honest and loyal man. The President's neck is in as much danger as Wigfall's, if things go wrong. Wigfall, however, had no faith in the President's judgment, and he said that if Jeff Davis's judgment had been as good as his, neither Vicksburg nor Missionary Ridge need have fallen!

Found everything in Main Street twenty per cent dearer. They say it is the new currency bill.

General Lee told us what a good son Custis was. Last night the house was so crowded that Custis gave up his own bed to General Lee and slept upon the floor; otherwise General Lee would have had to sleep in Mrs. Lee's room. She is a martyr to rheumatism and rides about in a chair. She can't walk. Constance Cary says: "If it pleased God to take poor Cousin Mary Lee — she suffers so — wouldn't these Richmond women campaign for Cousin Robert?" In the meantime Cousin Robert holds all admiring females at arm's length.

I found Lydia and Captain A—— at my house, and Colonel Preston was there with Mr. Chesnut, with firelight only, and one tallow candle. Gas is stopped all over Richmond.

Constance Cary gave me a Parthian shot unconsciously. Her words are often too picturesque for the occasion. She described my parties to Mr. Chesnut as "little orgies." I shook in my shoes. Such a stupid word! Who enjoyed my parties more than Conny Cary?

Mr. Davis calls my husband "High South Carolina," because when he takes on stiffly, he is terrible. South Carolina as a rule does not think it necessary for women to have any existence outside of their pantries or nurseries. If they have no children, let them nurse the bare walls. The pleasures of all the world are reserved for men. Besides, Mr. Chesnut takes words literally, makes no allowance for sensational language. But this blew over.

I asked my husband: "Is General Johnston ordered to reinforce Polk? They said he did not understand the order!" "Yes, after five days delay," he replied. "They say Sherman is marching to Mobile. When they once get inside of our armies, what is to molest them — unless it be women with broomsticks!" General Johnston writes that "the Governor of Georgia refuses him provisions, and the use of his roads." The Governor of Georgia writes: "The roads are open to him and in capital condition," and that he has furnished him abundantly with provisions as he desired them. I suppose both of these letters are placed away side by side in our files.

February 20th. — At Mrs. Davis's I met Mr. Senator Clay. Heavens! He knows how to quarrel! Mr. Clay still professes to be devoted to Jeff Davis. It was a miserable hour for me. I was afraid every moment some word might fall, more than could be smoothed away afterwards.

On Broad Street I gave $280 for twenty-four yards of flannel to make some soldiers' shirts.

Maria Lewis came. She can talk of nothing but the great-grandnephew of George Washington, whom she feels now she has a right to expect. She has no thought, no mind, no heart, no imagination that is not engrossed by this coming event which casts its shadow before.

Mrs. Preston was offended by the story of Buck's performance at the Ives's. General Breckenridge told her "it was the most beautifully unconscious act I ever saw." The General was leaning against the wall, Buck standing guard by him. The crowd surged that way and she held out her arm to protect him from the rush. After they had all passed, she handed him his crutches, and they too moved slowly away. Mrs. Davis said: "Any woman in Richmond would have done the same joyfully, but few could do it so gracefully." Buck is made so conspicuous by her beauty, whatever she does cannot fail to attract attention.

Johnny only stayed at home one day. He went to his plantation, got several thousand Confederate dollars, and in the afternoon drove out with Mrs. K——. Well — *aux premiers amours!* At the Bee Store, he spent a thousand of his money, brought us cream-colored gloves, linen, etc. One can do without gloves, but linen is next to life itself.

Yesterday the President walked home from church with me. He said he was so glad to see my husband at church, had never seen him there before, how well he looked, etc. I replied: "He looked so well because you have never before seen him in the part of the right man in the right place." Mr. Chesnut has no fancy for being planted in pews, but he is utterly Christian in his creed.

Annie had heard so much of the wounded in Richmond hospitals that a few days ago she said to Mrs. Preston: "Auntie, I must go home. I can't stay here, their cries break my heart!" "What cries? Whose cries?" "The poor wounded soldiers! I cannot sleep!" "Nonsense, you cannot hear any such thing. The wounded soldiers are nowhere near us, and they never cry out. When you hear one, call me." Annie came flying in ten minutes. "There! There!" and she clapped her hands to her ears to keep out the cruel sound. "Charcoal! Charcoal!" was being shrieked in tones of agony, like a soul in torment, by a vendor in the street, a sound so familiar to us all in Richmond that we never hear it.

Johnny says T. F. is in the toils. The young lady says he tried playing off and on with her. She means to make him speak out, show his hand, and then she will quickly say: "Truly sorry, but I am engaged." "Besides," adds Johnny, "He is strangely fascinating to girls now, since the story that he is half-married. He was married in fun, by a man who happened to be a magistrate. In fun it was, but by the Scotch Law prevailing in South Carolina, some say it is in earnest and a bona-fide marriage, until death us do part. No fun in that!"

Mrs. Memminger has never called on Mrs. Davis. There is manners for you, and a knowledge of proper etiquette.

The Captain gave us a luncheon at Pizzini's, Maggie, Buck and myself. Buck wore the beautiful gloves he had brought her. Said Maggie: "Poor creature, don't you know she is for another? She never can be thine." "Yes, he knows," says Buck, "and that makes him behave so nicely, doubly kind." He walked home with Maggie. Buck and I came together. He remained four hours with Maggie, came home at a two-forty trot, but could not stop for dinner because he had an engagement to ride with Tudy. He came home after dark, had only time to brush his hair, freshen up a little and rush off to the Carys'. It was twelve before he returned. Truly the life of a young Captain of Dragoons in Richmond calls for active service, indeed.

Next day Mr. and Mrs. Miles called. We were discussing the Captain's fast if pleasant life. Said Mr. Miles with a sigh: "I too once kept late hours, but now Betty requires me to retire early." She said with a nervous laugh: "How can you make me so absurd?" Mr. Miles turned pale when I spoke of his friend Garnett's death. He seems to have found time to stop for a while in all this whirl and grieve for poor Garnett, who was worthy indeed of many tears.

The Prussian, Von Borcke, showed the girls a plain gold ring soon after he came here. "I am betrothed. In Germany a little girl waits for me." We told them the man distinctly felt it necessary to warn them off. They do not seem to mind, however, and he has an emphatically good time.

Johnny, who has transferred his attentions to Tudy, said to her: "I could raise a company of cavalry from among the men I meet every night at your house — and every man of them would be Buck's poor, infatuated, deluded, bereft lovers." "And I would make you Captain of them," promptly responded Tudy.

February 23rd. — At the President's. General Lee breakfasted there. A man named Phelan told him all he ought to do, planned a campaign for him. General Lee smiled blandly the while, though he did permit himself a mild sneer at the wise civilians in Congress who refrained from trying the battlefield in person, but from afar detailed the movements of armies.

Mr. Chesnut said that — to his amazement — General Lee came into his room to pay his respects and have a talk. "Goodness gracious," said I. "That was a compliment, from the head of the army; from the very first man in the world, we Confederates think!"

Some of our friends came to boil taffy. I think they kept it from being sufficiently cooked to be pulled on purpose, for they stayed here the live-long day. They played cards. One man had only two teeth left in front, and they lapped across each other. He maintained a dignified sobriety of aspect, though he told funny stories, till finally one was too much for him and he grinned from ear to ear. Maggie gazed, then called out as the Negro fiddlers do when they call dancing figures: "Forward two and cross over!" Fancy our faces! The hero of the two teeth told us that among the country people, cavalry was called "Critter's Companies" and infantry "web-footed" or "ducks."

He said, relapsing into a decorous arrangement of mouth: "Cavalry are the eyes of an army. They bring the news. The artillery are the boys to make a noise; but the infantry do the fighting — and a general or so gets all the glory."

FEBRUARY 26th. — We went to see Mrs. Breckenridge, who is here with her husband; then we paid our respects to Mrs. Lee. Her room was like an industrial school, with everybody so busy. Her daughters were all there, plying their needles, and also several other ladies. Mrs. Lee showed us a beautiful sword recently sent to the General by some Marylanders now in Paris. On the blade was engraved, "*Aide Toi et Dieu T'Aidera.*" When we came out, I said: "Did you see how the Lees spend their time? What a rebuke to the taffy parties!" But I like our parties, *tout même.*

There is a victory claimed in Mississippi, so no fears are now felt for Mobile, and our papers are jubilant. Beneficent mud! No killed and no killing on hand; no rumbling of wagons laden with dead or dying. We enjoy this reprieve. We snatch a fearful joy. It is a brief interlude of comparative peace.

FEBRUARY 29th. — Leap Year. Mrs. Davis and our party did not agree as to the cause of Memminger's appointment as Secretary of the Treasury. She says the South Carolina delegation recommended him. The South Carolina delegation to a man say they repudiated him, except for Mr. Barnwell alone; so he is Barnwell's sole responsibility. It is one of the Mercury's grounds of complaint against the President that he consulted no one but Mr. Barnwell. Teddy Barnwell says his good uncle chose Mr. Memminger because of his fine Low Church proclivities, and his high standing in the Sunday School! "That always blinds Uncle Robert."

The annals of the Memminger family are sensational and legendary enough near home, but before they reached Richmond — or since — the stories have attained frightfully exaggerated proportions. They read now like a ballad from Percy's "Reliques." I will only record one thing, belonging more to the realistic than to the romantic anecdotes. One lady of the family was an heiress. Why? When she was young, an eccentric, rich bachelor uncle looked at her nose. "It is so short, she'll never find a husband!" So he left her all his fortune in his will, by way of compensation. The better nosed were cut off with a shilling.

Buck told us of the General's visit to "Brother Willie" in camp. Her blue eyes were gleaming and beaming with fun, and I think that smile of hers, after all, does most of the mischief; it is so wonderfully sweet.

Brother Willie says: "As a rule, generals don't call on majors of artillery; but this one did, and said such nice things too. The outsiders who did not understand how the land lay must have been amazed." Hood stayed at Mary McDuffie's and they gave him a state dinner at the old Hampton house, out in that fine old garden. What a splendid place that garden would be for lovers. Such beautiful shade, such comfortable seats in out-of-the-way nooks and corners. I can almost hear Sam say: "How different from Richmond with its little stuffy drawing-rooms, every eye turned on you without blinking, a parcel of giggling girls who know more of your affairs and how you stand with your lady love than you do yourself! When you begin to say the very thing you care most to say, open flies the door and someone announces Major this, or Colonel that, or Captain T'other. Then a general confusion and your girl escapes. If you go to ride, there is the groom at your heels; and when he rides too near, if you lose your temper and cry 'fall back,' Buck will not speak to you the rest of the ride because you have hurt Cy's feelings. Pretty rough on a fellow who has so much to do and so little time to do it in. When you were leaving and said good-bye to your sweetheart, with a sly kiss of her hand, you could see eyes from every window of every house in Franklin Street peering down on you."

Love-making! That is what a garden was first used for. Adam and Eve played at that game until she had the very Devil himself bursting with envy. Bible truth, that!

Annie reports that R. L—— has arrived and that she believes he is the only man Buck really cares for. *Le roi est mort. Vive le roi.* There is hardly a day's interval between the king who goes, and the king who comes.

An arrant FFV came to complain of Mrs. Miles. "What is it?" After an immense amount of laughing and twisting this way, twisting that way: "Oh! Such indelicacy!" "What did she say?" "Oh, when they asked for her sister-in-law, she said right out: 'She is in her confinement.' " I gravely replied: "I do not see the indelicacy, and I do not see the fun!"

Another maimed hero is engaged to be married. Sally Hampton has accepted John Haskell. There is a story that he reported for duty after his arm was off. I suppose in the fury of the battle he did not feel the pain.

General Breckenridge asked: "What's the name of the fellow who has gone to Europe for Hood's leg?" "Dr. Darby." "Suppose it is shipwrecked?" "No matter. Half a dozen are ordered."

Mrs. Preston raised her hands. "No wonder the General says that they talk of him as if he were a centipede. His leg is in everybody's mouth!"

MARCH 3rd. — Mrs. Grundy lent me "Romola." I had had it before, but I was hurried then. Now I will take my time, consider my ways, and not presume to judge George Eliot harshly.

Hetty the Handsome and Constance the Witty came. The former was too prudish to read "Lost and Saved" by Mrs. Norton, after she had heard the plot. I asked Conny: "Why don't your cousin marry that Pegram man who is so daft about her? They say she is engaged to him." "Oh! How can you think of such a thing! She is having such a good time. She is so much admired." "She is not in love with him then; just grateful or something, sympathetic and kind, or she could not refuse to marry because she was having a good time!" Constance seemed to turn this over in her mind. "Hetty will be very angry with us if she hears that we doubt her devoted attachment to General Pegram."

Conny was making a bonnet for me. Just as she was about to leave the house, her friendly labours over, Mr. Chesnut entered and quietly ordered his horse. "It is so near dinner," I protested, and he said: "I am going with the President, I am on duty. He goes to inspect the fortifications. The enemy, once more, are within a few miles of Richmond." *

So we prepared a luncheon for him. Conny remained with me. She told me her life's history. After she left I sat down to "Romola," and I was absorbed in it. How hardened we grow to wars, and war's alarms. The enemy's cannon — or our own — are thundering in my ears; and I was dreadfully afraid some infatuated and frightened friend would come in to cheer, to comfort, and to interrupt me. Am I the same poor soul who fell on her knees and prayed and wept and fainted, as the first guns boomed against Fort Sumter?

Once more we have repulsed the enemy, but it is humiliating that

* This was the Dahlgren raid. The "horrid tablets," of which Mrs. Chesnut presently speaks, purported to be an order to Dahlgren's command, signed by him, and directing his men to release Union prisoners in Richmond, burn the bridges and the city, and capture and execute President Davis and his cabinet. The fact that the memorandum was signed "Dalhgren" rather than "Dahlgren" made its authenticity rather more than doubtful; but most Richmond people accepted the paper as genuine.

he can come and threaten us at our very gates whenever he so pleases. If a forlorn Negro had not led them astray (and they hung him for it) they would have walked into Richmond unmolested. Surely there is horrid neglect or mismanagement somewhere! The home defence battalion saved Richmond, that is the cry now.

MARCH 4th. — The enemy is reinforced and on us again. Met Wade Hampton, who told me Mr. Chesnut was to join him with some volunteer troops; so I hurried home. Such a cavalcade rode up to luncheon; Captain Smith Lee and Preston Hampton were the handsomest, the oldest and the youngest of the party. Alarm bells were ringing, horsemen galloping, wagons rattling. Dr. H—— stopped us to say "Beast" Butler was on us with sixteen thousand men. How scared the Doctor looked. And after all, it was only a notice to the militia to turn out and drill.

MARCH 5th. — Tom Ferguson walked home with me. He told me of Colonel Dahlgren's death, and of the horrid tablets found in his pocket. Dahlgren came with secret orders to destroy this devoted city, to hang the President and his cabinet and burn the town. Fitzhugh Lee was proud that the Ninth Virginia captured him.

Buck shook a roll of something at me: "Thirty pages from Sam!" What would the gossips say? The people who said to me: "What does that soldier creature find to talk about to all of you?" Thirty pages!

I found Mrs. Semmes covering her lettuces and radishes as calmly as if Yankee raiders were a myth; but this last affair has left me sore and disheartened. We have shown our weakness, and the imbecility of our arrangements. And to think, here I sat reading "Romola" at my ease, and I might have been roused at any moment by fire and fury, rapine and murder. While "Beast" Butler holds Fortress Monroe, he will make things lively for us. On the alert must we be now.

MARCH 8th. — Met an antique virgin of vinegar aspect whose mind seemed occupied by the unmentionable horrors we had so narrowly escaped. No one else, as far as I know, had thought of all that!

Bragg is made Mr. Davis's Chief of Staff.*

I am reading "Jean Valjean." What a beastly little ingrate is

* General Bragg had been conspicuously unsuccessful as an army commander; and after Chickamauga his refusal to pursue the beaten enemy so angered his own officers that — in his presence — they unanimously asked President Davis to remove him from command. Few of President Davis's actions were more bitterly criticized than the promotion of Bragg to be Chief of Staff; yet in that capacity Bragg did good service.

Cosette! Only genius can make a hero of a man who has dragged himself through all the sewers of Paris.

Reading "Adam Bede" again, to measure the distance up — or down — to "Romola."

Shopping, I paid thirty dollars for a pair of gloves, fifty dollars for a pair of slippers, twenty-four dollars for six spools of thread, and thirty-two dollars for five miserable, shabby, little pocket handkerchiefs. When I came home, I found Mrs. Webb. At her hospital there was a man who had been taken prisoner by Dahlgren's party. He saw them hang the Negro who had misled them — unintentionally, in all probability. He saw Dahlgren give a part of his bridle to hang him. Details are melancholy. This Dahlgren,* like Hood, had lost a leg.

In the afternoon, Mr. Washington described to us the fight of the department clerks who beat off the Dahlgren raid. He was one of them, though he saw no enemy. "It was pouring rain, cold and pitch dark. Still, we were near enough to hear their words of command. I fired my gun once." He showed us a New York Herald which vaingloriously foretold all that Kilpatrick † was going to do to Richmond. To sack it was the best word in their mouths; that, as the Irish say, was like the man who sold the lion's skin that he was going to hunt.

Constance Cary, in words too fine for the occasion, described the homely scene at my house; how I prepared sandwiches for my husband, and broke with trembling hand the last bottle of anything to drink in the house.

MARCH 8th. — Mrs. Preston, as we walked home, told me she had just been to see a lady she had known more than twenty years before. She had met her in this wise. One of the chambermaids of the St. Charles Hotel in New Orleans told Mrs. Preston's nurse — it was when Mary Preston was a baby — that up among the servants in the garret there was a sick lady and her children. Mrs. Preston went up there, met this lady, had her brought down into comfortable rooms, and nursed her until she recovered from her delirium and fever. She had run away, and was hiding herself and her children from a worthless husband. Now she has one son in a Yankee prison, one mortally wounded, and the last of them dying under her eyes of consumption. This last had married here in Richmond, not wisely, and too soon. He

* Dahlgren was killed, not captured. His body was brought to Richmond for identification; and his wooden leg was briefly on display to the curious. His body had been mutilated by the guerrillas who killed him.

† Dahlgren was of Kilpatrick's command.

is a mere boy, his pay as a private eleven dollars a month; and his wife's family charged him three hundred dollars a month for her board. So he had to work double time, doing odd jobs by night and by day, and so killed himself of exposure to cold in this bitter climate to which his constitution was unadapted.

They had been in Vicksburg during the siege, and during the bombardment they sought refuge in a cave. The roar of the cannon ceasing, they came out for a breath of fresh air; and at the moment they emerged a bomb burst among them, struck the son already wounded, and smashed off the arm of a beautiful little grandchild not three years old. This poor little girl with her touchingly lovely face and her arm gone is here now. This mutilated little martyr, Mrs. Preston said, was really to her the crowning touch of the woman's affliction.

March 11th. — Letters from home. There is one from Mr. Chesnut's father, now over ninety, written with his own hand and certainly in his own mind still. I quote: "Bad times, worse coming, starvation stares me in the face, neither John's nor James's overseer will sell me any corn. I despise your Confederate Government. It cheats."

Now what has the government to do with the fact that on all his plantations he made corn enough to last for the whole year, and by the end of January his Negroes had stolen it all? Poor old man, he has fallen on evil days after a long life of unbroken ease. All his other muscles are relaxed by age, but his grip on his gold is as firm as ever.

I do not believe Lamar, with "Adam Bede" fresh in my mind. I cannot believe the woman who wrote that book is a "fallen woman, living in a happy state of high intellectual intercourse, and in happy, contented immorality." She could not be happy! Her books show that she knows good from evil. Lamar heard all this about some other of those literary ladies, and has confused the name.

Today, I read "The Blithedale Romance." It leaves such an unpleasant impression. I like pleasant, kindly stories now; we are so harrowed by real life. Tragedy is for our hours of ease.

Mr. Chesnut wants me to read for him the papers in the case of a young man who was cashiered for writing a reconstruction article. This cashiered man favors return to the Union.

The enemy tried coming up James River, but Ransom sent them back howling from Suffolk.

March 12th. — Constance Cary went shopping with me. The prices are worse than ever. We found Buck in bed and Dr. Garnett there. She said, with a smile in her eye: "Write to Johnny and tell him

I have been percussed and auscultated after all! Dr. Garnett insisted on doing it!" Dr. Garnett, twisting himself for a look in the mirror, said: "I pronounce her lungs all right; nothing the matter with her." Then, twisting back again, with a second good look at himself in the glass: "Broad chest, noble specimen of physical woman, finest neck and shoulders I ever saw in my life, hand and arm to match. All faultless! Nothing amiss with this girl, though her mind may be troubled about something or other." Says Mary Preston aside to me: "She never talks. She is anxious. No doubt that is the matter with most of us."

Kilpatrick still threatens us. Bragg has organized fifteen hundred cavalry to protect Richmond. Why can't my husband be made Colonel of that? It is a new regiment. No, he must be made a General.

MARCH 12th. — Mr. and Mrs. Preston drive out together every afternoon of their lives. They have done so for thirty years or more. Yesterday they spoke of the antique spinster who dreaded Kilpatrick's and Dahlgren's ravishing raids. Mrs. Preston told him that I only answered "fiddlesticks" to her tirade. He said: "Women who respect themselves will always be respected. Even those infernal tales of the treatment of their women in India, which so maddened the Englishmen, have turned out mostly exaggerations. They were murdered in cold blood, nothing worse. The 'unbridled soldiers' so far have found Negro women to answer all their purposes. White women are safe, even in New Orleans — so far!"

There is love-making and love-making in this world. What a time the sweethearts of that wretch, young Shakespeare, must have had. What experiences of life's delights he must have had before he summoned up the Romeo and Juliet business from his own internal consciousness. Also, that delicious Beatrice, and Rosalind. The poor creature to whom he left his second-best bedstead came in second best all the time, no doubt, and she hardly deserved more. Fancy people wondering that Shakespeare and his kind leave no progeny like themselves. Shakespeare's children were half his, only; the other half was only the second-best bedstead's. What could you expect from that commingling of materials?

Goethe used his lady loves as school books are used. He studied them from cover to cover, got all that could be got of self-culture and knowledge of human nature from the study of them, and then threw them aside as of no further account in his life. Byron never could forget Lord Byron, poet and peer. He must have been a trying lover.

To talk to him would be like talking to a man looking in the glass at himself. But then Lady Byron was just as much taken up with herself; so they struck each other — and bounded apart.

Shakespeare knew all the forms and phases of true love. Straight to one's heart he goes, whether in tragedy or comedy. He never misses fire. He had been there (as the slang goes). No doubt the man's bare presence gave pleasure to the female world, and he saw them at their best. But he effaced himself; he told no tales of his own life. Compare old, sad, solemn, sublime, sneering, snarling, fault-finding Milton; a man whose family doubtless found "*les absences délicieuses.*" That phrase describes a type of man at a touch. It took a Frenchwoman to do it. I have heard that there is an Italian picture of Milton, taken in his youth, and he was as beautiful as an angel. No doubt. But love flies before everlasting posing and preaching, and the deadly requirement that a man must always be looked up to. A domestic tyrant, grim, formal, awfully learned, Milton was still a mere man, for he could not do without women. When he tired out the first poor thing who did not fall down and worship him, obey him, and see God in him, and she ran away, immediately he arranged his creed to take another wife; for a wife he must have. What the seer and prophet wants in such a man is the true morality.

The deer-stealer, Shakespeare, never once thought of justifying theft on the ground that he loved venison and could not come by it lawfully. So I say Shakespeare was a better man; yes, and a purer soul than self-upholding, Calvinistic, puritanic, king-killing Milton! There is no muddling of right and wrong in Shakespeare, and no pharisaical stuff of any sort.

General Hood writes that he dines with General Joe Johnston very often, and finds him cordial and kind. "Oh, that's the game always," says Buck. "But when they find they cannot make an officer take sides against the President, they abuse him as they do everybody who is a friend of Jeff Davis. Wait and see. Hood will soon be sent to Coventry by the Joe Johnston clique."

Mrs. Johnston writes she "is glad to hear that the beautiful Miss Preston has accepted General Hood." She thinks it a capital match for both parties. "Oh dear," said Buck, and then a long sigh. "Too smooth water. I see breakers ahead."

Hetty Cary dashed by us on horseback with her General Pegram. We have generals galore. Franklin Street swarms with them.

George Deas joined us. He is fresh from Mobile. There he left peace and plenty. He went to sixteen weddings and twenty-seven tea parties. For breakfast everything was nice, for in Alabama there are acres of those horrid beasts from which delicious pork and sausages are made.

Lily's fun is strong. She was describing a stuttering man's courtship. He would not care if his desired bride ma- ma- marred his joys in the future, if only . . . But we laughed so much we did not hear the rest. Then Lily told of what she had seen one day at the Spotswood. She was in the small parlor, waiting for someone. In the large drawing-room sat Hood, solitary, sad, with his crutches by his chair. Mrs. Buckner came in, and her little girl spied Hood, and she bounded into the next room and sprang into his lap. He smoothed the little dress down and held her close. She clung round his neck for a while, and then, seizing him by the beard, kissed him to an illimitable extent. The soldier and the child were evidently enraptured with each other. "Prettiest picture I ever saw," said Lily.

John R. Thompson sent me a New York Herald only three days old. They are down on Kilpatrick for his miserable failure before Richmond. Also they acknowledge a defeat before Charleston, and a victory for us in Florida. General Grant is charmed with Sherman's successful movements, and says he has destroyed millions upon millions of our property in Mississippi. I hope that may not be true, hope Sherman may fail as Kilpatrick did. If we had Stonewall or Albert Sidney Johnson where Joe Johnston and Polk are, I would not give a fig for Sherman's chances. The Yankees say that at last they have scared up a man who succeeds, and they expect him to remedy all that is gone, so they have made their brutal Grant a lieutenant general.

Dr. Garnett at the Preston's proposed to show me a man who was not an FFV. "Here he is in this house, and these people seem so fastidious too; and they have such beautiful daughters. He is a low-born loafer, this fellow is." When I told Buck of Dr. Garnett's annoyance at a black sheep having slipped into their fold, she smiled. "Well, until we came here, we never heard of our social position. We do not know how to be rude to people who call. Dear Mrs. Chesnut, did you ever hear of your social position, at home?" "No." "I thought not. To talk of that sort of thing seems so vulgar. Down our way, that sort of thing was settled beyond a peradventure, like the earth and the sky. We never gave it a thought. We talked to whom we pleased, and if they were not *comme il faut*, why we were ever so much politer to the poor things." Buck added: "After all, what harm does he do? To save my life I cannot see a way to get rid of this man, without forgetting one's manners. His manners are as good as anybody else's, and he talks ever so much better than most of these men who are FFV to the core!"

Dr. Garnett from that time desisted from further effort to keep us clear of detrimentals!

Whenever Mr. Minnegerode falls short in his English and finds himself thinking in German, he shouts his battle cry. "Oh Lamp of God, I come!" He gave it to us so often today, I fear he knows we are in critical straits; and so I told the President as we walked out of the pew. He too had remarked how often and how excited that cry came.

Somebody counted fourteen generals in church, and suggested that less piety and more drilling of commands would suit the times better. There were Lee, Longstreet, Morgan, Hoke, Clingman, Whiting, Pegram, Elzey, Gordon, Bragg and I forget the others.

Now that Dahlgren has failed to carry out his orders, the Yankees disown them; they disavow it all. He was not sent here to murder us all, hang the President, and burn the town. There is the notebook, however, at the Executive Office, with the orders to hang and burn.

Mr. Preston walked home with me. We found Mr. Chesnut had gone to see someone at the Adjutant General's office. We sat on the marble steps to wait for him. Frank Parker and Colonel Urquhart came, and found us discussing the propriety of putting twenty thousand Negroes in the army.

March 15th. — Old Mrs. Chesnut is dead. I gave three hundred and seventy-five dollars for my mourning, which consists of a black alpaca dress and a crêpe veil; bonnet, gloves, and all came to five hundred dollars. Before the blockade, these things would not have been thought fit for a chambermaid!

I met General Lee the other day. He spoke of Roony. "Poor boy, he is sadly cut up about the death of that sweet little wife of his." "But we hope," said Smith Lee, who was with him, more cheerfully, "that in a few days he will be brighter." I said to Smith Lee: "How I wish broken glass could be as easily mended as widowers' hearts." "Why?" "Then I would not be left with only three glass tumblers."

Mrs. Grundy came in with a story of a Negro woman who murdered the white child she was nursing.

Mrs. Davis took me to drive. We went to Laburnum to inquire of the Lyons' welfare since the fire. It was really pitiful. Only a few days before, we had been there and found them all taking tea under those beautiful shade trees. And now — smoke and ashes, nothing more. There were crowds of friends there, so I did not get out of the carriage. They lost everything, the library filled with books and papers, even Mrs. Lyons's diamonds. Mr. Lyons, trying to save something, got a horrid fall and knocked out his front teeth. The fire was the work of an incendiary. A few weeks before, they accused a Negro of theft. He was put in jail, and was bailed out just in time to do this thing.

Everybody is in trouble. Mrs. Davis says paper money has depreciated so in value they cannot live within their income, so they are going to give up their carriage and horses.

When I got home, General Hampton came with his troubles. Stuart had taken one of Hampton's brigades and given it to Fitzhugh Lee. General Hampton complained of this to General Lee, who told him curtly: "I would not care if you went back to South Carolina with your whole division." Wade said his manner made this speech immensely mortifying.

While General Hampton was talking to me, the President sent for him. It seems General Lee has no patience with any personal complaints or grievances. He is all for the cause, and cannot bear officers to come to him with any such matters as Wade Hampton had come about.

MARCH 18th. — I went to sell some of my colored dresses. What a scene! Such piles of rubbish, and mixed up with it such splendid Paris silks and satins. A mulatto woman kept the shop, in an out-of-the-way old house. White ladies sell to, and the Negroes buy of, this woman.

Buck had a letter which she read as soon as it was handed to her. She blushed a good deal, laughed, twitched that beautiful little nose of hers, crumpled the letter and threw it in the fire. Then, with a knowing nod: "This man is awfully in love with me. You know R. L. He went to his tailor and chose a fine piece of Confederate gray for a new uniform. The tailor said: 'No, my dear sir, you can't have that. It is laid aside. General Hood asked us to keep that and our best stars for his wedding clothes.' "

After some whispering among us, Buck cried: "Don't waste your delicacy! Sally is going to marry a man who has lost an arm, so he is also a maimed soldier, you see; and she is proud of it. The cause glorifies such wounds." Annie said meekly: "I fear it will be my fate to marry one who has lost his head!" "Tudy has her eye on one who lost an eye! What a glorious assortment of noble martyrs and heroes!" The bitterness of this kind of talk is appalling.

General Lee had tears in his eyes when he spoke of his daughter-in-law, now dead; that lovely little Charlotte Wickham, Mrs. Roony Lee. Roony Lee says "Beast" Butler was very kind to him while he was a prisoner; and the "Beast" has sent him back his war horse. The Lees are men enough to speak the truth of friend or enemy, not fearing consequences.

Mrs. Preston thinks Wade Hampton had better ask to be sent to the Army of the West, after Lee's snub. Johnny, now that summer is coming on, has been ordered to the sickly South Carolina coast to collect recruits.

March 19th. — Molly and Lawrence have both gone home; and I am to be left for the first time in my life wholly at the mercy of hired servants. Mr. Chesnut being in such deep mourning for his mother, we see no company. I have a maid of all work.

Tudy came with an account of yesterday's trip to Petersburg, and Conny Cary gave me an account of the wedding there, as it was given to her by Major Von Borcke. "The bridesmaids were dressed in black; the bride in Confederate gray homespun. She had worn the dress all winter, but it had been washed and turned for the wedding. The female critics pronounced it 'flabby-dabby.' They also said her collar was only 'net,' not lace. She wore a cameo breastpin. Her bonnet was home-made." The bridegroom was a German officer. Whenever a foreigner marries here, the ill-natured begin at once to speculate on the probability of another wife left at home.

Conny also told of a new toy, Fitz Lee's new-found joy. It is a little Negro boy which, when wound up, dances minstrel fashion. Fitz Lee sings corn-shucking tunes, and the toy boy dances. Conny has already made the little boy two suits of clothes. He is the delight of Richmond salons, and is so much handled that his dress soon grows shabby.

March 24th. — Another account of the wedding. First, all hands were called to answer a sort of muster roll in the parlor. Seated there, and asserting her right to be there — as a boarder, and so having paid for her seat — sat a grim old Confederate dame engaged in some sort of intricate needlework. Her nose and chin were well in the air, and a disdainful sniff ever and anon meant: "I am here in my own right. I dare you to try and turn me out! And I will see the wedding, will ye, nill ye!" Major Von Borcke was asked to close the folding doors, where an unpleasant crack was visible, and behind which some giggling girls were seen and heard. He advanced his fine profile to obtain a glimpse of the enemy; the door was closed with a snap from behind; he hastily clapped his hand to his nose. It had barely escaped being snapped off.

The bride called for her opera cloak, and they brought her a red blanket shawl. "Heavens, what a contretemps. But I will not keep you waiting!" So she accepted the shawl and did not institute a further search for her opera cloak. I thought this scene one of the shifts of honest poverty.

Apparently, the Bishop had succeeded in frightening the bridegroom; for he looked sulky and hung his head as he muttered the responses. The bride is an FFV of the first water, and she stood her ground with her head erect and lips apart and ran through the gamut of the two sets of names, responding joyously and with a light heart.

When the Bishop asked for the ring, the bride asked with a smile: "Bishop, won't you bless it?" "Put it on her finger!" said the Bishop emphatically. The half-married lady explained: "Bishop, you do not understand him. He hesitates because he wants you to bless the ring!" Said the Bishop decidedly: "Proceed with the ceremony. Maybe I will bless the ring another time."

General Morgan and his wife were there, and Colonel Allston, from whom I had these melancholy details.

Yesterday we went to the Capitol grounds to see our returned prisoners. First, Frank Huger and Mr. Dobbin walked off with Tudy; then Captain Roberts with Lily. Mary Preston said: "What shall we do? Alone in this crowd." "Have faith!" said I, and our faith was rewarded. The President joined us. We walked slowly up and down until Jeff Davis was called upon to speak to the prisoners. Then I stood, almost touching the bayonets, where he left me. I looked straight into the prisoners' faces. Poor fellows! They cheered with all their might, and I wept for sympathy. Their enthusiasm moved me deeply. Oh, these men were so forlorn, so dried up, so shrunken. There was such a strange look in the eyes of some; others were so restless and wild looking; others again had placidly vacant faces, as if they had been dead to the world for years. A poor woman was too much for me. She was hunting for her son. He had been expected back with this batch of prisoners. She said he was taken prisoner at Gettysburg. She kept going in and out among them with a basket of provisions she had brought for him to eat. It was too pitiful. She was utterly unconscious of the crowd. The anxious dread, expectation, hurry and hope which led her on showed in her face.

The Lees were all there, and stood in a group in full fig; Custis, Roony, Robert, Mary, Agnes, Mildred. Custis will be gazetted Major General in a few days, and put in command of Richmond. General Elzey has been made commander of the Marylanders.

I read Hood's letter to Mr. Chesnut. He commented: "If a captain were to write such a letter, it would be called flat; but everything is permitted a lieutenant general." Spiteful! Buck got her daily letter and read it before his face, all giggle and blush. She twitched her nose and stuffed the letter up her sleeve, as there was no fire.

These Virginians, with their proud names! Miss Page Walker married Captain Lee Page the other day. Now she is Mrs. Page Page. Someone said she had turned over a new leaf, but still she was the same Page.

I paid one hundred and sixty dollars for having a shabby black alpaca made. Mrs. Davis was there with us in the shop. The woman wanted to induce us to buy something very high priced, saying: "The officers' ladies buy them always." "Look," said Mrs. Davis. "See these things. She says our poor officers' wives buy them at any price she chooses to ask!" "No, I didn't! I said no such thing!" The woman tossed her head as she flounced away. "Their wives indeed! I said their ladies! That is a different thing!"

Conny came with a note she wanted Mr. Chesnut to take to Burton Harrison. It snowed, and she stayed a while; but the snow showed no signs of stopping, so she waltzed home with Johnny. He said they had to waltz to keep themselves from freezing. He is here in deep mourning, having heard of the death of his grandmother.

A sister of Mrs. Lincoln * is here. She brings the freshest scandals from Yankeeland. She says she rode with Lovejoy, and that a friend of hers commands a black regiment. Two Southern horrors, a black regiment and a Lovejoy!

March 31st. — My new English maid has come, Mrs. Bones. She says "Lady." I forget who called her "Bones." Mrs. Joe Heyward, who brought her to this country, called her Charlotte, so I determined to call her so too. She was too much a "bag of bones" to adopt so suggestive a name as her patronymic.

* Mrs. Lincoln was Kentucky born, and her brothers served in the Confederate Army. During the War she was sometimes accused by irresponsible gossip of being a spy for the South.

I met Preston Hampton. Conny was with me. She showed her regard for him by taking his overcoat and leaving him in a drenching rain. What boyish nonsense he talked! He said he was in love with Miss Dabney now, that his love was so hot within him that he was waterproof and the rain sizzed and smoked off and did not so much as dampen his ardour or his clothes.

He told about a picnic on board a ship somewhere. It rained cats and dogs, and a sharp March wind added its inclemencies. One girl fell down a ladder, and several had their hoops blown over their heads, but were solaced by the fact of being sure of beautiful underclothes. Everybody was wet through and through, and in the hot, closed cabin they steamed as clothes do when hung out on a clothesline. The men were like wet Newfoundland dogs, made to keep their distance; but the girls danced round dances, their damp and draggled dresses flapping round their damper feet. So vulgar it all was; so rowdy — and so funny!

Custis Lee again has refused to jump over heads. The stride from a colonel to a major general, he says, is too much for him.

APRIL 1st. — Mrs. Davis is utterly depressed. She said the fall of Richmond must come, and when it did, she would send her children to me and to Mrs. Preston. We begged her to come to us also. Mr. Chesnut is as depressed as I ever knew him to be. He has felt the death of that angel mother of his keenly, and now he takes his country's woes to heart.

Dr. Garnett came, and I blamed him for leaving that smallpox case in the President's yard. "How light your attack is," he laughed. "How mild your scolding. It falls feebly on my case-hardened ears. I have just seen a Mrs. Grant who wished herself a man that she might horsewhip me." "Why?" "Because I have sent her son back to the army, cured."

Bones went with me to the Prestons'. They had asked her to come and do their hair. We came back like monks of St. Bernard, wrapped in our waterproofs with cowls over our heads, the wind whistling, the snow blinding us as we struggled and slipped up those Richmond hills of streets. Poor Bones could not see the fun.

APRIL 5th. — Record of the piety of the owners of my hired darky. They could not think of such a thing as letting her break the Sabbath by coming to me that holy day. She has three children, this black woman; and six days of the week she gets the breakfast at home — for they are early birds — and then comes to me and earns two dollars a day. Sundays, Bones and I do our own work — or Bones works double time. Fortunately, she does not mind. Yesterday, Mr. Davis dined here. Bones did give us everything that was nice. Poor Bones, what would I give to take her home with me; but she holds up both hands! Her horror of South Carolina is great indeed.

April 11th. — Drove with Mrs. Davis and all her infant family. They are wonderfully clever and precocious children, but with unbroken wills. At one time there was a sudden uprising of the nursery contingent; they fought, screamed, laughed. It was bedlam broke loose. Mrs. Davis scolded, laughed and cried.

She asked me if Mr. Chesnut would speak to the President about that place in South Carolina which everybody said suited him. "No, Mrs. Davis." "That is what I told Mr. Davis. 'Colonel Chesnut rides so high a horse, you and he will never come to an understanding!' Now Browne is so much more practical; he goes to be General of Conscripts in Georgia, and his wife will stay at the Cobbs'."

Mrs. Ould gave me a luncheon on Saturday. I feel this is my last sad farewell to Richmond and the people I love so well. Mrs. Davis sent her carriage for me, and we went to the Oulds's together. Such good things; oranges, guava jelly, etc. The Examiner says Mr. Ould, when he goes to Fortress Monroe,* replenishes his larder. Why not?

The Examiner took another fling at the President as being haughty and austere with his friends, and affable, kind and subservient to his enemies, the Yankees. I wonder if the Yankees would endorse that sentiment. Both sides abuse him. He cannot please anybody, it seems.

John Thompson sent me a Blackwood's, and John Darby brought me an armfull of books from across the water, all very welcome.

The garrison at Fort Pillow is said to be put to the sword. Tell that to the Marines! † Lincoln threatens to murder all of our prisoners,

* He went regularly, to oversee the exchange of prisoners.

† Fort Pillow was garrisoned by a Union force of nineteen officers and five hundred and thirty-eight men, of whom two hundred and sixty-two were Negroes. On the twelfth of April, General Forrest stormed the Fort. The report that surviving members of the garrison were murdered was investigated by a Congressional joint committee, which reported that at least three hundred Union soldiers were killed "after resistance had ceased." Senator Ben Wade of Ohio, the chairman of that committee, was a violent opponent of President Lincoln; and his son commanded a regiment of colored cavalry; and the committee reported within three weeks after the capture of Fort Pillow, and while the Fort, and any Union prisoners there may

by way of reprisal. If there are any marines more credulous than those you told the first story to, tell them this last!

The female brigade of Memminger's Treasury Department has been moved to Columbia. That looks squally!

Mr. Chesnut is now Brigadier General, and he is sent to South Carolina, to organize and take command of the reserve troops. Clay and Lamar are both spoken of to fill the vacancy made among Mr. Davis's aids by his promotion.

We went to Lucy Haxall's wedding. Ours was a distinguished party, as far as good looks are concerned; Captain Smith Lee was with me, and he is handsome enough to bring up the average. Some people pushed and shoved us, so we gave way at once, thinking they had better right to be there, and probably were part of the affair. Then Smith Lee called my attention to a man with both elbows out, pushing and shoving, who stopped to ask: "Whose wedding is it, anyhow?" After that we held our ground.

The church windows were closed, so that it might be a candle-light wedding. A woman in the gallery had a cataleptic fit, and they were forced to open a window. The mixed daylight and gas was ghastly, and greatly marred the effect below. The poor woman made a bleating noise like a goat. Buckets of water were handed over the heads of the people, as if it was a fire to be put out, and they dashed water over her as fast as the buckets came in reach. We watched the poor woman from below in agony, fearing she might die before our eyes. But no, far from it. The water cure answered. She came to herself, shook her dress, straightened up her wet feathers, and put her bonnet on quite composedly; then she watched the wedding with unabated interest — and I watched her. She fascinated me! The poor woman could not have been gotten out of that jam, unless, like the buckets of water, she had been handed out over the heads of the public.

APRIL 27th. — Today, Smith Lee spent the morning here. I am having such a busy, happy life, so many friends; and my friends are so clever and so charming. But oh, the change to that weary, dreary Camden!

The Governor of North Carolina is making a bolder bid for peace than ever Joe Brown of Georgia has dared do yet.

---

have been, were still in Southern hands. It seems reasonable to question the accuracy of the hurried report of the committee and there appears no evidence of any concerted or directed "massacre."

The Prestons gave me a farewell dinner on my twenty-fourth wedding anniversary; the very pleasantest day I have spent in Richmond.

Maria Lewis was sitting with us on Mrs. Huger's steps, and Smith Lee was lauding Virginia people as usual, when there appeared Frank Parker, riding one of the finest of General Bragg's horses, and by his side Buck, on Fairfax. Fairfax is the most beautiful horse in Richmond, his brown coat looking like satin, his proud neck arched. He moved slowly, gracefully, calmly, with no fidgets, completely aristocratic in his bearing. And there sat Buck, tall and fair, managing her horse with infinite ease, her English riding habit showing plainly the exquisite proportions of her figure. "Supremely lovely," said Smith Lee. "Look at them both," I said proudly. "Can you match those two in Virginia?" "Three cheers for South Carolina," was his answer.

In South Carolina, they received Wade Hampton with a grand ovation. Today Hetty Cary greeted me with a kiss and congratulations on my husband's promotion to be General of Reserves.

XIX

Camden

MAY 8th, 1864. — I am again at Mulberry. My friends crowded round me so, those last days in Richmond, that I forgot the affairs of my country utterly, though I showed my faith in my country by buying poor Bones's Confederate bonds.* I gave her my gold thimble, bracelets, etc.; whatever was gold and would sell in New York or London.

My friends in Richmond grieved because I had to leave them, but not half so much as I did because I must come away. I could not persuade my poor Bones, my best of maids, to come to Carolina. One experience here had cured her. What a story she could carry to Mrs. Stowe! Her tales made my flesh creep!

Those last weeks were so pleasant, before the crash came. Poor little Joe! But till then, no battle, no murder, no sudden death, and all went merry as a marriage bell. Clever, cordial, kind, brave friends rallied around me.

But I must come to little Joe's death. Maggie and I went down the River to see an exchange of prisoners. Our party included Mrs. Buck Allan, the Lees, the Mallorys, and Mrs. Ould. One woman aboard the steamer was so pretty. I had seen her before, at her home in the South. They say her husband beats her; so we said to each other: "Let us look at a creature who stays with a man after a beating." But after listening to her for a while, I was on the husband's side. "Listen to the ever-

* Many patriotic Southerners, even after they knew the cause was lost, bankrupted themselves by buying Confederate bonds.

lasting clack of that foolish tongue," moaned Dr. C——. "I don't blame the man! My God!" Another said: "If I were a striking character, I might box her ears even on so slight an acquaintance. She irritates my nerves almost beyond endurance."

We took aboard Judge Ould and Buck Allan at Curles Neck, and saw the huge ironclads at Drury's Bluff.

In all these years, I have seen no Yankees. All the prisoners, well or wounded, have been Germans, Scotchmen, or Irishmen, and mostly Germans. Now on this Yankee vessel there was the genuine Yankee to be seen.

Among our returned prisoners, when they came on board, was a gentleman with whom I had exchanged letters, though I did not know him. A friend of mine, whose fiancé was killed, wanted her letters returned; and she was told this young officer had charge of them. I gave him her address, and he said he would give them into her own hands. Another man showed me some wonderfully ingenious things he had made while prisoner. He said they were issued rations for a week, but he always devoured his in three days. He could not resist doing so. Then he had the gnawing agony of those inevitable four days remaining.

These men (the prisoners) told us that we could never understand the revulsion of feeling that a simple change of vessels made: under one flag and then the other, on one side, all enemies, and now all friends. Most of them had been wounded, and some of them were maimed for life.

Governor Cummings, a Georgian, late Governor of Utah, was among the returned prisoners. He had been in prison two years. He was a striking-looking person, huge, with snow-white hair, and as fat as a prize ox! No sign of Yankee barbarity or starvation about him.

And this is how the pleasant trip came to an end. As we walked up to Mrs. Davis's carriage, suddenly I heard Maggie scream, and someone stepped back in the dark and said in a whisper: "Little Joe! He has killed himself!"

I felt reeling, faint, bewildered. The chattering woman clutched my arm, firing questions. "Mrs. Davis's son? Impossible! Who did you say? Was he an interesting child? How old was he?" The shock was terrible, and unnerved as I was, I cried: "For God's sake, take her away."

Then Maggie * and I drove silently two long miles, the silence broken

* Maggie Howell was Mrs. Davis's sister.

only by Maggie's hysterical sobs. She was wild with terror at having the news broken to her in that abrupt way at the carriage door. At first she thought it had all happened there, and that poor little Joe was in the carriage!

Mr. Burton Harrison met us at the door of the house. Mrs. Semmes and Mrs. Barksdale were there too. Every window and door of the house seemed wide open, and the wind blowing the curtains. It was lit up, even in the third story. We went in. As I sat in the drawing room, I could hear the tramp of Mr. Davis's step as he walked up and down the room above, but not another sound. The whole house was as silent as death. It was then twelve o'clock, so I went home and waked Mr. Chesnut, who had gone to bed. We went immediately back to the President's. We found Mrs. Semmes still there. We saw no one but her, but we thought some friends of the family ought to be in the house. Mrs. Semmes said that when she got there, little Jeff was kneeling down by his brother; and he called out to her in great distress: "Mrs. Semmes, I have said all the prayers I know how, but God will not wake Joe!"

Poor little Joe. He was the good child of the family, so gentle and affectionate. He used to run in to say his prayers at his father's knee. Now he was laid out, somewhere above us, crushed, killed! Mrs. Semmes said he fell from that high north piazza upon a brick pavement. Before I left the house I saw him lying there, white and beautiful as an angel, covered with flowers. Catherine, his nurse, was lying flat on the floor by his side, weeping and wailing as only an Irish woman can.

As I walked home I stopped to tell the Prestons. Then I met Wade Hampton, who went on with me. Even then, he told me again the story of his row with General Lee. I could see or hear nothing but little Joe and the broken-hearted mother and father, and Mr. Davis's step still sounded in my ear as he walked that floor the livelong night.

We stayed in Richmond one day longer than we expected, in order to attend the funeral. There was an immense crowd, sympathetic, but shoving and pushing rudely. Thousands of children came, and each child had a green bough or a bunch of flowers to throw on little Joe's grave, which was already a mass of white flowers. The morning I came away from Mrs. Davis's, early as it was, I met a little girl with a handful of snow drops. "Put these on little Joe," she said. "I know him so well." Then she turned and fled without another word. I did not know who she was then, nor do I now.

Captain E. M. Boykin came the day before we left Richmond, pleased at his promotion. He said: "We Carolinians owe a great deal to Chesnut. He stays here pushing our claims, watching out for us, seeing we are not overlooked." "Yes," I agreed. "He is at it night and day, and a thankless post it is, for you all believe that you rise by your own unaided merit — and that you don't get half you deserve." He is now Major Boykin, for that was his step up the ladder. He is stout and jolly, and radiant at being sent to the front, the very picture of a debonair, devil-may-care cavalier. But here at home I found his wife the picture of woe, pale, thin, sad, dispirited. Men must fight and women must weep.

General Lee was to have a grand review * the day we left Richmond, and quantities of people were to go up by rail to see it. Mrs. McFarland writes: "They did go, but they came back faster than they went. They found the army drawn up in battle array." How many of the brave and gay spirits that we saw so lately have now taken flight — the only flight they know — and their bodies lie dead upon the battlefield. Poor old Edward Johnston is wounded again, and a prisoner. Jones's Brigade broke first. He was wounded the day before.

At Wilmington, we met General Whiting. He sent us to the station in his carriage and bestowed upon us a bottle of brandy which had run the blockade.

Now they say Beauregard has taken his sword from him! Never! I will not believe it! At the taking of Fort Sumter they said Whiting was the brains, Beauregard only the hand.

We came home with Baron Munchausen in the flesh. Ferdinand Mendez Pinto was but a type of the thee-thou liar of the first magnitude. I thought after four years of war that I knew what men could do, swelling their chests, repeating lying rumors, falsifying the half-true, exaggerating, depreciating, bragging! They fight, but they crow! When it is all crow and no fight, it is more than one can bear. These are but the few, thank God! There are the quiet gentlemen, the mob of gentlemen who went into the army because their country called. I believe half of them did not know or care why. The best and the bravest went first. They die, and make no sign.

At first we took Don Braggadocio for an English gentleman we had

* General Lee reviewed Longstreet's First Corps on April 29. On May 2, Grant's army began the maneuvers which culminated when he crossed the Rapidan, and on May 5 the opening guns of the Battle of the Wilderness were fired.

seen somewhere. The man spoke to Mr. Chesnut and he introduced him to me. He was not even amusing; just flat, tame, lies, all cruelly transparent; and I was not in the mood to have patience.

Dr. Corey was along. In the Judith and Holofernes scene while the private theatrical mania was at its height in Richmond, he had enacted the man with his head cut off. First he spoke of it as an Oriental scene, but then it became fixed in his memory as a Turkish picture. "You see, she was in a Turkish dress, and so was my head!" Judith was holding his head, dripping with gore, just above a table through a hole in which it had emerged; but the deception was complete. At first a dead silence, then a feeble voice, as if remonstrating with her own terror: "Why! It's Doctor Corey!"

Mr. Chesnut and the doctor got out at Florence to procure for Mrs. Miles a cup of coffee. They were slow about it and they got left, but I did not mind so very much; for we were to be all day at Kingsville, and Mr. Chesnut would overtake me there by the next train. My maid belonged to the Prestons. She was only travelling home with me, and would go straight on to Columbia. So without fear I stepped off at Kingsville; but my old Confederate silk, like most Confederate dresses, had seen better days, and I noticed that like Oliver Wendell Holmes's famous shay, it had gone to pieces suddenly and all over. It was literally in strips! I became painfully aware of my forlorn aspect when I asked the telegraph man the way to the hotel and he was by no means respectful. I was alone, and a not too respectable-looking old woman. It was my first appearance in the character, and I laughed aloud.

A very haughty and highly painted dame greeted me at the hotel. "No room! Who are you?" I gave my name. She looked scornful. "Try something else! Mrs. Chesnut don't travel around by herself, with no servants, no nothing." I was, to be sure, dusty, tired, tattered and torn. "Where do you come from?" she insisted. "My home is in Camden." "Come now! I know everybody in Camden."

I sat down meekly on a bench in the piazza, free to all wayfarers; but she followed me: "Which Mrs. Chesnut, I say? I know both!" "I am now the only one," I told her. "What is the matter with you? Do you take me for a spy? I know you perfectly well. I went to school with you at Miss Henrietta de Leon's, and my name was Mary Miller." "Lord's sakes alive! To think you are her! Now I see! Dear, dear me! Heaven's sakes, woman, but you are broke!"

"And tore," I added, holding up my dress, "but I had no idea it was so difficult to effect an entry into a railroad wayside hotel!" I picked up a long strip of my old black dress, torn off by a man's spur, as I passed him getting off the train.

"Where are all your people?" "My husband was accidentally left at Florence. He will be here in a few hours." "Well, you know you do look funny, with that bright Balmoral petticoat grinning through all them rips and rears. And you see we are obliged to be pertickler here, and respectable." You look like it, I thought, looking her straight in the face and wiping my own. She went on: "Molly and Lawrence both went by a month ago. They said you had an English lady for a maid. Where is she?" "I never had a lady for a maid in my life." "They said she was white as anybody. You know, lots come here and call themselves any name they think we know, and then slip away on a train and don't pay. We don't take in no impostors now, nor no stray ladies with no servants and no protectors. But I made an awful mistake not to know you." "It is a new experience," said I coolly, but I was inwardly raging. Then Captain de Pau came to my rescue, looked after my baggage, and showed me how I could walk off at once to the Camden cars and stay in them till Mr. Chesnut came.

Mr. Chesnut did not join us until the trains met at Manchester. After hearing my adventures, he was by no means proud of his performance in leaving me to contend with the "specked peach" alone. I said: "She told me she had not seen me for twenty years, but that she met you constantly!" "God bless my soul, I never saw the woman in my life!" "She says she means to reform the hotel at Kingsville." "The reformatory is the very place for her."

"Remember that scene at the church door in Richmond," I asked him. As we turned a corner suddenly, going to church, we met a very handsome woman. She rushed up to him with hands extended. "So glad to see you — did you know you had come — when did you come — why have you not been to see me — etc." I expected him to introduce me, but he said not a word, only continued to shake her hands. "Who is it?" I asked as we walked on. "Don't know. Never saw the woman before in my life. She evidently took me for somebody else." "How very odd!" The subject was renewed again and again, until it became a screaming farce, but he stuck to his formula. "Never saw the woman before in my life." And my teasing retort: "What a credulous fool you must take me to be!" So on to the end of the chapter.

It was sad enough at Mulberry without Mrs. Chesnut, who was the good genius of the place. It is so lovely here in the spring among the giants of the forest; the primeval oaks, water oaks, live oaks, willow oaks such as I have not seen since I left here. And the flowers, violets, roses, yellow jasmine; the air is laden with perfume. Inside, creature comforts of all kinds, green peas, strawberries, asparagus, spring lamb, spring chickens, fresh eggs, rich yellow butter, clean white linen for our beds, dazzling white damask for one's table. Such a contrast to Richmond — where I wish I was!

John Chesnut is ill here. He rode at a tournament in Columbia and crowned Natalie Heyward queen of love and beauty; then he came home and took to his bed, and there sits Mr. Chesnut by his bedside and they talk from morn to dewy eve. It is all horses, horses, horses! Never have I heard either of them mention the war. John is one of the silent heroes; he is prompt to take his place in front, and then has never a word to say about it.

There is a queer coalition here; Uncle Hamilton, John Manning and Judge Withers are joined in unnatural bonds by their hatred of Jeff Davis. Fighting is going on, and Wade Hampton is frantic; for his laggard new regiments fall in so slowly. It is no fault of the soldiers. They are as disgruntled as he is. Bragg, the head of the War Office, cannot organize in time.

John Boykin died in a Yankee prison. He had on a heavy flannel shirt, and they were lying on an open platform car, on their way to their cold prison on the lakes. A Federal soldier wanted his shirt, and prisoners have no rights, so John had to strip it off and hand it to him. So that was his death. In two days he was dead of pneumonia. Maybe frozen to death.

But then I suppose their men will find our hot sun in August and July as deadly as their cold Decembers are to us. Their snow and ice finish our prisoners at a rapid rate.* Napoleon's soldiers found out all that in the Russian campaign.

I met our lovely relative, the woman who might have sat for Eva's mother in "Uncle Tom's Cabin." Beautifully dressed, graceful, lan-

* The difference in climate, coupled with inadequate medical care and with ignorance, even on the part of physicians and surgeons, of ordinary sanitation caused the death of thousands of prisoners in the North and in the South. Thousands more died of malnutrition both in the North and in the South. There was, of course, plenty of food in the North, but there was also plenty of food in the region around Andersonville, Georgia. A lack of solicitude for the health of enemy prisoners was common on each side.

guid, making eyes at all comers, she was softly and in dulcet accents regretting the necessity of sending out a sable Topsy to her sabler parent, to be switched for some misdemeanor. I declined to hear her regrets as I fled in haste.

The President's man Stephen came bringing Mr. Chesnut's Arabian. He said: "Why Missis, your niggers down here are well off. I call this Mulberry place Heaven, plenty to eat, little to do, a warm house to sleep in, a good church, and a good preacher all here right at hand."

The dreadful work of death is beginning again. John L. Miller, my cousin, was killed at the head of his regiment.

Reverend Stephen Elliott preached in our Negro church Sunday afternoon. This congregation, it "takes a Methodist to fetch 'em!" He preached a capital sermon. It made me cry, and I have no gift that way. Laughing is my forte.

The Secretary of War authorizes General Chesnut to reorganize men who have been hitherto detailed for special duty, and also those who have been exempt. He says General Chesnut originated the plan, and organized the Corps of Clerks which saved Richmond in the Dahlgren raid.

John Witherspoon says the President did wrong when he did not arrest Joe Johnston before Seven Pines, when Johnston was in full retreat, apparently ready to abandon Richmond, with Virginia crying: "If you cannot defend our Capital, we will." General Lee stopped those retreating tactics, but now every newspaper except a few in Georgia is busy as a bee excusing Joe Johnston's new retreats.* He gives up one after another of those mountain passes where one must think he could fight, and is hastening down to the plain. "Yes," says John Witherspoon, growing red with suppressed fury, "if the President had sent him out of the Confederacy, sent him to Sherman and McClellan who admire him so much, it would have saved us! Joe Johnston's disaffection with our President and our policy has acted like a dry rot in our armies. It has served as an excuse for all selfishness, all stay-at-home-a-tiveness, all languid patriotism." After this, for him, long speech he asked: "Did you ever see Joe Johnston and the President together?"

"No, but I did see Mr. and Mrs. Davis and Mrs. Johnston at the Spotswood, and I firmly believe if he could have promoted Joe Johnston consistently with his duty to his country he would have done so. I do

*Johnston was facing Sherman north of Atlanta.

not know how the split began. They were as intimate and as affectionate as people could be when I left them."

"I'll tell you," said John Witherspoon. "He made Joe Johnston a dissatisfied general when he refused to make him Number One in the Confederate Army. The breach has been ruinous!"

MAY 27th. — I hate these constant attacks on Jeff Davis. Old hard-common-sense-Lincoln, the essence of a cute Yankee, says "don't swap horses crossing a stream." In battering down our administration, these people are destroying our last hope of success. In all this beautiful sunshine, in the stillness and shade of these long hours in this piazza, memories haunt me. I see that funeral procession as it wound among those tall monuments up that hillside, and the James River tumbling about below, over rocks and around islands; and I see the dominant figure of that poor old grey-haired man, standing bare-headed, straight as an arrow, clear against the sky, beside the open grave of his son. She stood back, in her heavy black wrappings, and her tall figure drooped. The memory of the flowers, the children, the procession as it moved — these come and go — but these two dark, sorrow-stricken figures rise before me now. I remember that night with no sound but the heavy tramp of his feet overhead, the curtains flapping in the wind, the gas flaring. I was numb, stupid, half dead with grief and terror. Then Catherine's Irish howl! Where was she when it all happened? Her place was to have been with the child. Who saw him fall?

Who will they kill next, of that devoted household?

I read today the list of killed and wounded. One long column was not enough for South Carolina's dead. I see Mr. Federal Secretary of War Stanton says he can reinforce Grant at his leisure, whenever he calls for more. He has just sent him twenty-five thousand veterans. Old Lincoln says in his quaint, backwoods way: "Keep a-peggin'."

But we can only peg out. What have we left of men? Our fighting men have all gone to the front. There are only old men and little boys at home now; and the Joe Johnston disaffection is eating into the very vitals of our distracted country.

Mrs. Phil Stockton has it from the Canteys that the President's personal abuse of John Manning alienated him! Why? Does Mr. Davis know John Manning? He is handsome beyond measure, clever, politically and socially of consequence in South Carolina; but I doubt if Mr. Davis thought of John Manning twice, except as part and parcel of Beauregard's useless and superb staff. But it was the regular thing at

Spotswood to tell people that Mr. and Mrs. Davis said dreadful things of them — when Mr. and Mrs. Davis hardly knew of the persons so abused at all.

Judge Withers says: "Jeff Davis drinks!" "No, he is an austere man, quiet, grave, devoted to his work, and without a vice in the world." "Oh, if he don't drink then, I dare say he takes opium, for his brain is obfuscated!" Words are wasted on them. They have made Jeff Davis the scapegoat. For their sins, he is tied to the altar. We made the altar, or the burning bush, or whatever that goat has to come out of.

It is impossible to sleep here because it is so solemn and still. The moonlight shines in my window, sad and white; and the wind, the soft south wind, comes over a bank of violets, lilacs, roses, and orange blossoms with magnolia flowers thrown in.

Mrs. Chesnut was only a year younger than her husband. He is ninety-two or three, but he retains his senses wonderfully for his great age. I have always been an early riser, and formerly I often saw him sauntering slowly down the broad passage from his room to hers in a flowing flannel dressing-gown; that is, when it was winter. In spring, he was apt to be in shirt sleeves, with suspenders hanging down his back. He had always a large hairbrush in his hand. He would take his stand on the rug before the fire in her room, brushing his scant locks, which were shining fleecy white. Her maid would be doing hers, which were dead-leaf brown. She had not a white hair in her head. He had the voice of a stentor, and there he stood roaring his morning compliments. The people who occupied the rooms above said he fairly shook the window glasses. This pleasant morning ceremony was never omitted.

This morning as I passed Mrs. Chesnut's room, the door stood wide open, and I heard a pitiful sound. The old man was kneeling by her empty bedside, sobbing bitterly. I fled anywhere out of reach of what was never meant for me to hear.

I was telling them today of a woman who came to Mrs. Davis in Richmond, hoping to get her help. She wanted her husband's pardon. He was a deserter. The woman was shabbily dressed, chalk-white and with a pinched face. She spoke very good English, and there was an attempt to be dressed up apparent in her forlorn clothes; knots of ribbon, rusty artificial flowers, and draggled feathers in her old hat. Her hands hung down by her side. She was strong, and her way of telling her story was hard and cold enough. She told it simply, but over and over again, with slight variations as to words and never as to facts. She seemed afraid we would forget. The army had to pass so near her. Her poor little Susie had just died, and the boy was ailing; food was so scarce and so bad. They all had chills, and she was so miserable. The Negroes had all gone to the Yankees. There was nobody to cut wood, and it was so cold. "The army was coming so near. I wrote, and I wrote: "If you want to see the baby alive, come! If they won't let you, come anyhow!' So you see, if he is a deserter, I did it. For they would not let him come. Only colonels and generals can get furloughs now. He only intended to stay one day, but we coaxed and begged him, and then he stayed and stayed; and he was afraid to go back afterwards. He did not mean to be a coward, nor to desert, so instead of going back to his regiment, he went on the gunboats on the river, to serve there; and then some of his old officers saw him, and they would not believe his story. I do not know if he told them anything. He does not talk much any time. They are going to shoot him. But it was I who did it. I would not let him alone. Don't you see?"

Mrs. Davis went to the President. She was gone ever so long, and the stiff, cold woman, as white as a wall, sat there and told it over to me so many times. I wanted to go home, but she clutched me. "You stay! You are sorry for me!" Then Mrs. Davis came in, smiling. "Here it is, all that you want." The creature stood straight up; then she fell down on the sofa, sobbing as if soul and body would come asunder. So I fled, blind with tears.

Mr. Chesnut tells me an anecdote illustrating Lincoln's *savoir faire*. When the Marquis of Hartingdon was presented at the Federal drawing-room, Mr. President Abe asked affably: "Any relation to Mrs. Partington? Your names rhyme."

JUNE 1st. — At Bloomsbury we heard that William Kirkland is wounded. Mary was weeping bitterly, Aunt B—— frantic as to Tanny's danger. I proposed to make arrangements for Mary to go on at once, but the Judge took me aside, frowning angrily. "You are unwise to talk in that way. She can neither take her infant nor leave it. The cars are closed, by order of the government, to all but soldiers." I told of the woman who, when the conductor said she could not go, cried at the top of her voice: "Soldiers! I want to go to Richmond to nurse my wounded husband." In a moment, twenty men made themselves her bodyguard and she went on unmolested.

The Judge said I talked nonsense. I said I would go in my carriage if needs be, and besides, there would be no difficulty in getting her a permit. He answered hotly. In no case would he let her go, and I had better not go back into the house! We were on the piazza, and my carriage at the door. I took it and crossed over to see Mary Boykin. She was weeping too, so washed away with tears that one would hardly know her. "So many killed! My son and my husband, I do not hear a word from them!"

At Bloomsbury I found Armsted waiting for me. He refuses to go with us to Columbia. "Missis, when you let me learn to be a shoemaker, I thought I was done with being your house servant! Now you want to take me away from my shoe shop." Mr. Chesnut thought his impudence intolerable, and said he should go with me and resume his place as my butler, when I went to housekeeping in Columbia. I said: "Never! Never! Dissatisfied servants are not to my taste! I hope never to see Armsted's face again in this world!"

Next day Armsted sent me a nice pair of shoes as a present. Mr. Chesnut asked: "What did you say to him yesterday?" "I told him he was an ungrateful wretch, and to keep to his trade, and that I had had enough of his disagreeable airs. And that pair of cloth shoes ends the chapter!"

JUNE 2nd. — At Miss McEwen's, I met the telegraph operator. It was John Witherspoon, grandson of the signer of the Declaration of Independence, President of Princeton College and all that! The telegraph office is exactly opposite Miss McEwen's, the milliner's. John Witherspoon with the long pedigree is her brother-in-law. As soon as a carriage drives up, he dashes over with the news. Priscilla Perkins said: "John Witherspoon has fairly fattened on news!"

I paid today, for two pounds of tea, forty pounds of coffee, and sixty pounds of sugar, $800.

JUNE 4th. — Mary Boykin's bitter weeping was prophetic. Major Edward Boykin is wounded in the knee. They hope he can be brought home. She was trying to be satisfied that it was no worse.

Poor Aunt B. is so unreasonable. She began arraigning Providence. What good was a victory, when we were all heart-broken? Nobody had such trouble as her household had. There was Doctor B. with only a flesh wound in his knee, and there were all those fat loafers in good comfortable safe offices, while her all were before the enemy's guns.

"Well, nobody of mine is either fat or in a comfortable office," I told her. "Anything more uncomfortable than my husband's positions since the war began, one could hardly conceive."

An amusing drawing: Mr. Davis, seated in the middle of a highway, with a pile of stones which he was in the act of throwing at all comers, and crying aloud at the same time: "All that I want is to be let alone." Now it seems to me that is all that the Confederacy wants. We would soon cease to throw stones if they would let us alone!

A New York paper speaks of General Lee as our representative man. What more could we ask? But then this wiseacre goes on to say that General Lee is as base a liar as Beauregard!

Mary Ford writes for school books for her boys. She is in great distress on that subject. When Longstreet's corps passed through Greenville, there was great enthusiasm; handkerchiefs waved, bouquets and flowers were thrown. In their excitement, her boys — having nothing else — threw the soldiers their school books! That is a mother's laughing complaint of her boys.

Poor Mr. Murray was too candid by far. He was asked: "How do my grandsons look?" "Oh, they look well enough. One has spent a fortune in substitutes. Two have been taken from him, and two he paid to change with him when he was ordered to the front. He is at the end of his row now, for all able-bodied men are ordered to the front. I hear he is going as some general's courier."

XX

Columbia

June 24th, 1864. — We are in Columbia once more, and at the Prestons'. Brewster is here. He treats Buck as his queen, swears allegiance to her. He said Joe Johnston was kept from fighting at Dalton by lack of a plan. "Hood and Polk wanted to fight, but he resisted their council. All this delay is breaking Hood's heart. So much retreating would demoralize even General Lee's Army. Johnston is jealous of the favor shown Hood at Richmond. He hates everybody that Jeff Davis likes."

One night at Mrs. Preston's, it had rained for hours, and showed no signs of ever stopping. When I came down I found two strangers seated on one of those leather sofas near the front door, which was open wide, the broad piazza keeping the rain out. Nobody said who they were. Mr. Chesnut thought we were all neglecting some guests of Mr. Preston, and so he devoted himself to them assiduously. They had run in out of the rain at the first open door, and had met such a charming party, and such unquestioning, frank hospitality.

June 28th. — Buck came over with me. She told me her whole life's story. When she came to the last episode, she always spelled the name, H. O. O. D. "To think I told him all about my affair with Ransom Calhoun; and Oh! if I had only known how intimate he was with Cousin Ransom, and that he had heard it from him, how differently I could have told it! When I said that to H. O. O. D. he laughed in my face."

These Prestons, from the oldest to the youngest, are straightforward, bluntly truthful people. I find them candid, utterly without guile, and yet so kindly courteous. They never do or say an unpleasant thing.

Utterly charming, I call this family; and so clever, so wonderfully good-looking.

If Buck and I had been worth poisoning! It really looked like it! We were both so ill! "Saleratus biscuits or the hot drive over," said the doctor coolly to our miserable suspicions.

Godard Bailey, who is an editor here, has just been distinguishing himself by fighting and brawling with a brother editor who lives here now. They used sticks, knives, and pistols; and yet from the bloody fray no serious damage ensued at all.

Mrs. Kirkland discomfits the natural village curiosity. She will see no one, literally; not even her father. So the sympathizing neighbours are disappointed. They like to go and examine everybody's grief, and tell every peculiar symptom. General Kemper saw poor Kirkland. He was as quiet and composed, in view of certain and immediate death, as he had ever seen him before. He discussed it coolly, knew the end had come, and was glad — as things had turned out — that his wife could not go to him. Kirkland died the 19th, and when people rush across the street to ask the Judge: "How is poor Kirkland's wife?" he answers, "What idle curiosity!" He says it is all nonsense, her refusing to come downstairs; but he refuses to go up to her room, and so they have not met. He is devoted to her children, and his wife brings him full accounts of his daughter. She goes upstairs, dear old soul.

Memminger has succumbed to the storm of his own raising. He resigned and retreated under a cloud of hot shot, poured on him from every point of the compass.

Weeping, wailing women are pitiful enough; but save me, good Lord, from such cold, hard, stony faces as Mary Boykin's. She sits by her wounded husband, her eyes fixed like dead eyes. She is heart-broken but tearless. Tom, her splendid boy; there is her agony! The girls are near at hand for any possible want of her husband's. If the utter self-abnegation of a family could give a man happiness he ought to be so. Their very existence seems swallowed up in the thought of tending the wounded father.

I think he knows more than he tells of Tom's fate, because, though cheerful enough otherwise, if Tom's name is casually mentioned, a queer spasm changes his whole expression. He says Tom was slightly wounded and he ordered him off the field, but he saw him afterwards in his place in the ranks.

Converse Frierson is killed; and his fiancée's face is harder, colder, and as tearless as miserable Mary Boykin's.

JULY 6th. — At the Prestons', Mary was laughing at the complaints of Mrs. Lyons, the person from whom we rented rooms in Richmond. "She complained of Molly and Lawrence's deceitfulness. She said they went about the house as quiet as mice while we were at home, but when we were out, they sung, laughed, shouted and danced. She complained, too, that if any of the Lyons family passed him, Lawrence kept his seat and kept his hat on, too." Of course, I did nothing about her tirade. I was glad the poor things could relieve their feelings while we were away. It must be an awful bore to be deaf, dumb and blind, to go about with those sphinx-like faces. I often pity the awful self-control servants must practise.

Colonel Urquhart and Edmund Rhett dined here, charming men both. There was no brag and no detraction — talk is never pleasant where there is either. And yet Colonel Urquhart is aid to Bragg, or was, "And I am sure Edmund Rhett is aid to General Detraction," said the pungent Isabella. "Chief of staff, I should say," said Mary Preston. If I had never heard a word against Edmund Rhett, and come across him on a desert isle, I believe I should find him awfully agreeable. He is so clever, so witty, so audacious!

A noble Georgian dined here today. He says Hampton was the hero of the Yankee rout at Stony Creek, that he has no use for Fitzhugh Lee, that Roony is all right but lazy. "But then, a son or a nephew of General Lee can do no wrong!" He claims that citizens, militia and lame soldiers kept the bridge at Staunton and gallantly repulsed Wilson's raiders. G. W. Smith, he told us, is now Generalissimo in Georgia, by Governor Joe Brown's appointment; Toombs and Vice-President Stephens are his aides-de-camp. "Oh," shouted the Chorus. "Send Joe Johnston and Wigfall there too. Put all the discontented in one Army, and Joe Brown to lead them! Under Joe Brown's vine and fig tree, they can lie down, and no man can molest them or make them afraid." *

Someone asked Buck: "Is not your lame lover out of place in Johnston's retreating army? A lame man can't reverse — as they call it in waltzing." She only answered: "If they give up Atlanta, we are cut in two! We will have to hunt, like foxes, for holes to hide our heads in!"

Here is a bit of doggerel poking fun at General Johnston:

* After the Conscription Law of 1864 was passed, Governor Brown of Georgia took advantage of the exemption granted state militia officers to issue two or three thousand new commissions to his friends.

The shades of night were falling fast
As through a Secesh village passed
A youth who bore mid corn and rice
A banner with this strange device:
Skedaddle!

"Oh stay," the cullid pussons said.
"Upon this shuck bed rest thy head."
A tear stood in his clear blue eye,
But still he answered with a sigh:
Skedaddle!

When I heard it, I asked what "skedaddle" meant. The explanation: "It is like the western Captain's words of command. In place of Boots and Saddles, played by the trumpet he says: 'Git ready to git! Git!' And then you hear nothing but the thunder of retreating hoofs."

The present rage among the young people is to call everything and everybody by an initial letter only. "Now, my dear Madam," says General Preston in his softest cadences, but with his grandest manner, "You will hear all over my house, H and the D. Do not be alarmed. They do not mean Hell and the Devil, they allude to my sons-in-law-apparent — or expectant."

"Certainly not apparent, Papa," Buck retorted. "For we have not seen them for months. They are backing down into the Gulf of Mexico with Joe Johnston!"

Jack Preston has not his father's imposing presence, but he understands as well all the acts of a gracious hospitality. Jack is such a good fellow; so kind, so witty himself, and so ready to make the most of other people's wit and humour.

JULY 18th. — At Mrs. Slocomb's last night, the sensation of the evening was a frail young invalid who has had hemorrhages without number. The Confederacy is short of clothes, but this fair one was too thinly clad; a peasant's waist, and next to nothing under that. "Weak lungs!" I thought. "No wonder! So exposed!"

She tottered as she walked, so weak was she; but when the round dancing began she was there, and deadly smooth her partner. When the weak one danced up towards us, holding out her dress, "Can Can," whispered Mary Preston.

Asked the invalid: "Why do you suppose I am so ill? Before I dressed to come here this evening, I ate twelve eggs!"

"Dressed? Undressed, you mean," in the same tone as "Can Can" was whispered. Then: "Isn't she common?" "At least, she is unenclosed," I suggested.* How Edmund Rhett laughed.

Mrs. Slocomb came up, saying: "In New Orleans, four people never met together without dancing." Edmund Rhett turned to me. "You shall be pressed into service." "No, I belong to the reserve corps, too old to volunteer or to be drafted as a conscript." But I had to go, *faute de mieux*, and I was led, a resisting victim, to the floor. A woman over forty ought not to dance, particularly if she wears Armsted's clumsy home-made shoes. In a hot, draggled old alpaca dress and those clodhopping shoes, to stumble slowly through the mazes of a July dance was too much for me. Then came Blindman's Buff, but I would not play. My age and infirmities confirmed me in that resolution. So I retreated to a quiet seat in a lonely front piazza. I was making pleasant mental pictures there in the beautiful moonlight when suddenly a black object sprang from a window beyond the piazza and fell fifteen feet or more to the ground. Somebody killed! My heart, as it has a way of doing, stood still. There were shrieks, and the crowd poured out of doors. Edmund Rhett had by that time picked himself up and was walking coolly up the steps. "What's the row?" he inquired. Nothing disturbs the equanimity of that ineffable dandy, not even a fall of fifteen feet. He said, looking around: "This porch, I took it for a piazza extending the whole front of the house; so I stepped out of a window, in the game, and fell to the ground."

He walked home with us. Tudy and Teddy Calhoun were seated in the Preston piazza, likewise enjoying the moonlight. Teddy said hastily: "Johnston has been relieved from the command of the Western Army. Hood replaces him in that command!" Buck, in her flowing white dressing gown, met us at the head of the stairs, her blue eyes wide open and shining black with excitement.

"Things are so bad that they cannot be worse, and so they have saved Johnston from the responsibility of his own blunders, and put Sam in. Poor Sam!"

"Why Buck, I thought you would be proud of it!" said Mary.

"No! I have prayed God as I have never prayed Him before, ever since I heard this. And I went to the convent and asked the nuns to pray for him too!"

July 25th. — We are in a cottage rented from Dr. Chisholm. So

* In towns and villages, "the common" was unenclosed land, common to all for grazing, etc.

much has happened. Hood a full General, Johnston removed and superseded, Early threatening Washington City. Admiral Semmes, of whom we have been so proud, is a fool after all. He risked the *Alabama* in a sort of duel of ships, and now he has lowered the flag of the famous *Alabama* to the *Kearsarge*. Forgive who may, I cannot! Mr. Chesnut has been called to Charleston.

Willie Preston has been killed, his heart literally shot away as he was getting his battery in position.

The girls were at my house. Everything was in the utmost confusion. We were lying on a pile of mattresses in one of the front rooms while the servants were reducing things to order in the rear. We were the saddest three, at the straits the country was in. The state of things in Atlanta was the burden of our talk. Suddenly Buck sprang up. "Mrs. Chesnut, your new house is very hot. I am suffocated. It is not so oppressingly hot at home, with our thick brick walls!" So they left. Isabella came soon after. She said she saw the sisters pass her house, and as they turned the corner there was a loud and bitter cry, and both of the girls began to run at full speed. Isabella hurried over there. They had come to tell Mrs. Preston that Willie was killed. Willie, his mother's darling! No country ever had a braver soldier, a truer gentleman to lay down his life in her cause.

Dick Manning came home with the poor boy's body. He talked Joe Johnstonism run mad. He coupled Lee and Davis and abused them with equal virulence. Lee was a solemn hypocrite; he used the garb of religion to mask his sins, but his iniquities were known! Thus Dick Manning. Never were people who were too sad to talk called upon to hear a greater mass of horror and wicked nonsense.

Alex Haskell told of an arrangement to throw all the blame of the retreat on Jeff Davis. A misunderstanding between the President and one of his generals will serve the General to explain any disaster. But a general who is known to disdain obedience to any order, who refuses to give the President any information for fear the President will betray him to the enemy? If that is not the madness of self-conceit, what is? Seward's little bell would have lodged Joe Johnston within triple walls in the twinkling of an eye, years ago, if he were a Yankee.

We agreed that Jeff Davis believed in Joe Johnston's patriotism and loyalty or he would not have placed him — knowing him to be his fierce personal enemy — in command of the Army of the West. Brewster says Joe Johnston is like the snake blinded by its own venom. He thinks that to spite him, Joe Johnston, his subordinate generals would disgrace themselves and destroy their country. He says he was afraid to risk a battle for fear the Davis generals would betray him. That is the apogee of idiotic conceit.

July 26th. — Isabella went with me to the bulletin board. Mrs. D. asked me to read aloud what was there written. As I slowly read on, I heard a suppressed giggle from Isabella. I knew her way of laughing at everything, and tried to enunciate more distinctly; I read slower, louder, and with precision. As I finished and turned round, I found myself closely packed in by a crowd of Confederate soldiers, eager to hear the news. They took off their caps, thanked me for reading out to them all that was on the Board, and made way for me, caps in hand, as I hastily returned to the carriage.

I found my new house already hospitably open to all comers. Mr. Chesnut had arrived. He was seated at a pine table, on which someone had put a coarse red table cover; and by the light of one tallow candle he was affably entertaining Edward Barnwell, Isaac Hayne and Uncle Hamilton. He had given them no tea, however. After I had remedied that oversight, we adjourned to the moonlit piazza.

We have laughed so at broken hearts, the broken hearts of foolish love stories. Now Buck is breaking her heart for brother Willie. Hearts do break in silence, without a word or a sigh. Mrs. Means, Mary Barnwell, they made no moan. They turned their faces to the wall and died. How many more, that we know nothing of?

When I remember all the true-hearted, the light-hearted, the gay and gallant boys who have come laughing and singing and dancing across my way in the three years past! I have looked into their brave young eyes, and helped them as I could, and then seen them no more forever. They lie stark and cold, dead upon the battlefield or mouldering away in hospitals or prisons. I think if I dared consider the long array of those bright youths and loyal men who have gone to their death almost before my very eyes, my heart might break too. Is anything worth it? This fearful sacrifice, this awful penalty we pay for war?

Willie Preston came to my house on Clay Street in Richmond just one year ago. He was worn out. He had had fever in the West. For once there was no laugh in his bonny blue eyes, shaded like a girl's with the longest, tangled black lashes. "Mrs. Chesnut, what a beastly hole — as the English would say. No ice?" "Indeed? Lawrence has discovered a mine of ice across the 'noble Jeems River.' Mr. Davis says: 'All true FF.'s pronounce it the "raging Jeems." ' At any rate, across the river there is ice in exchange for gold." And I hastened away, to return in a moment with a mint julep, cold within, and the outside of the goblet frosted with ice.

"Dear Mrs. Chesnut, you have saved my life!" he cried, and the old laugh came back, and the blue eyes grew wide and deep in his delight. Heavens, what a handsome fellow he was!

Such queer letters. John Kennedy only wants Mr. Chesnut to help him on his upward path to a generalship, but that blessed Wade Hampton is writing in the maddest way. He says he will be forced to resign because since his tiff with General Lee, that prince and potentate is so prejudiced against him! Did you ever? Mr. Chesnut says: "Let them alone. It will all come right. There is really nothing the matter."

Dick Manning called the Western Army "General Lee's Botany Bay." General Lee never permitted any soldier who was of service to him to leave him. When a man was promoted for gallantry and sent West, it simply meant he was sent to Coventry.

Mrs. Bartow said: "After all, Hood is only expected to hold Atlanta until reinforcements can be got there." "Where are the reinforcements to come from?" Echo answers: "Where?" Hood tells his troops that "It is safest always to be nearest the enemy's guns." Hood is a splendid proof to the contrary, shot to pieces as he is.

Joe Johnston is personally so brave that he dares to be overcautious. They say Marshall Ney did not better deserve the name, "bravest of the brave." But taking care of his Army will not do everything. Serving the Army is not our object just now. It is risk all to save the country. Personal courage in a general goes without the saying. How could a coward rise to the rank of general?

I was amazed that Mrs. Bartow answered me sharply when I said my feeble word with all my strength for our Government. "You are right. It is best always to side with those in power!" It was never so hard, never in all my life, to keep my temper. I thought of how Mrs. Davis stood by her when Bartow was killed.

Edmund Rhett has a heart somewhere about him, much as he keeps it hid. His note to Mary Preston when Willie was killed would draw tears from the stoniest, hardest eye.

At dinner, a soldier on crutches — from typhoid fever, however, for he had no wound; he could not be hurt in his heart; he has none — fancied himself a mimic and a humorist. His idea was to amuse the dinner table by describing the vanity of fixed grins on the faces of the dead on the battlefield. Can the hardening process of war go further than that? What next in the indurating process?

William Mazyck heard General Lovell say on Main Street to a terrified audience: "No country can stand many such victories as Hood's on the 22nd." Allan Green says Johnston was a failure, but now he will wait and see what Hood can do before he pronounces judgment on him. He liked Hood's address to his Army. "It was grand and inspiring, but everybody knows a general has not time to write that kind of thing himself."

Mr. Kelly from New Orleans says Dick Taylor and Kirby Smith have quarrelled. One would think we had a big enough quarrel on hand for one while. The Yankees are enough and to spare. And General Lovell says: "Joe Brown importuned our Government to remove Joe Johnston, with his Georgians at his back; but they are scared now, and wish they had not."

How they dump the obloquy on Jeff Davis now, for no fault of his but because the cause is falling. A ruined country! Who can bear it? In our democratic republic, if one rises to be its head, whoever he displeases defiles the tombs of his father and mother; his father becomes a horse thief and his mother no better than she should be, his sisters are barmaids and worse, his brothers are Yankee turncoats and traitors! All this is hurled at Lincoln or Jeff Davis indiscriminately. Thus our table talk: "Chickamauga is the only battle we have gained since Stonewall was shot by Mahone's Brigade." "Jeff Davis is a tyrant, and Hood is his pet and his minion." "The General has a dangerous new acquaintance, and thereby hangs a tale," says small Isaac. Then come eager, avid questions.

"What is her name?" "Oh, it rhymes to rascal, and fast gal." Then came rhymes upon rhymes, maids and women all forlorn, and Earl van Dorn,* and cows with the crumpled horn. Something about Bonham dashing down the back way because he would not receive so beautiful and so notorious a lady in his Executive Office. "Our General will not go to his office at all, while she hovers round. They must surprise her, these gallant Carolinians, with their wives in sight!"

August 1st. — Line of battle formed before Atlanta. When we asked Brewster what Sam meant to do at Atlanta, he said: "Oh! He means to stay there." We hope he may.

Kit Hampton is out on a warpath. "Our rulers are fools; that we

* General Van Dorn was killed by a husband who thought himself betrayed.

know by the generals they appoint. Our statesmen are fools; that we know by the general's appointments that they confirm." Poor Sam!

I read once more, "Mill on the Floss." The hard way brothers show their love. Brotherly love? Say rather, brotherly hate! But sister's love? I am revolted at the sacrifice. Why give up Stephen Guest to her cousin? Maggie had the right divine to him; but then, right and wrong, morality aside, death is better for Maggie than a life with a thin soul like Stephen Guest. He was too small for her. Death was less painful than life would have been with him.

I went in for the war-like, Scott's "Marmion," and Campbell's stirring odes! I forget to weep my dead. But oh, my Confederate heroes, fallen in the fight! You are not to be matched in song or story! We talk so calmly of them: "Remember so and so? Was he not a nice fellow? He was killed at Shiloh!"

Day after day we read the death roll. Someone holds up her hands. "Oh, here is another of our friends killed. He was such a good fellow."

AUGUST 2nd. — I spent today with Mrs. McCord at her hospital. She is dedicating her grief for her son — sanctifying it, one might say — by giving up her soul and body, her days and her nights, to the wounded soldiers at her hospital. Every moment of her time is given up to their needs and their wants.

Today General Taliaferro dined with us. He served with Hood at Second Manassas, and at Fredericksburg, where Hood won his Major General's spurs. He says: "On the battlefield, Hood has military inspiration!" We were thankful for that word, for our all now depends on that Army at Atlanta. If that fails us, the game is up.

General Taliaferro says his place on the river was burned. "Why not? I am not less patriotic than my forefathers. Our house was burned by the British in the first Revolution, and again by the British in 1812. We are so easy to get at, so near the coast. Now the Yankees have followed suit and burned me out once more."

Mr. Chesnut likes Dr. Chisholm's book on surgery,* but will not bring it home on account of its painful illustrations. What foolishness! Alone in our house, we are very friendly and very confidential. We tell stories to each other — stories not to be repeated. We sit out on the piazza in the bright moonlight and discuss high art and military strat-

* "Chisholm's Manual of Military Surgery" is on the shelves of the library at Mulberry Plantation today. In the passages which deal with camp sanitation and the health of the soldiers, it is so far ahead of the practices of the period as to seem modern; but it had little circulation and made no apparent impression on its times.

egy. Last night it was until after twelve o'clock.

This was such a lucky day for my housekeeping, in our hired house. Mrs. Alex Taylor sent me a huge bowl of yellow butter, and a basket of every vegetable in season. Mrs. Preston's man came with mushrooms freshly out, and Mrs. Tom Taylor's with fine melons.

August 3rd. — I sent Smith and Johnson (my house-servant and a carpenter from home) to the commissary's with our wagon for supplies. They went to the depot and stayed there all day. I needed a servant sadly, in many ways, all day long; but I hope Smith and Johnson had a good time. I did not lose patience until Harriet came in an omnibus, because I had neither servants nor horse to send to the station for her.

With her usual tact, she repaid our hospitality at dinner by asking Mr. Chesnut about the beautiful "rascal fast gal" who said she had travelled from Columbia under his protection, and that he had promised her a recommendation to the Department. "Why such women ever come South I cannot imagine," she said; and he gravely replied: "Because Southern men are such fools about women, so soft, so rash, so easily imposed on — if the woman is only pretty enough." Whereupon he declared himself "in a devil of a passion," which fact then there no gainsaying. Lawrence drove up to the door to say something was wrong about the harness. He stormed at Lawrence, and I made myself further agreeable by saying: "It is not Lawrence you are angry with, but me. Besides, I can't run away, and if you abuse Lawrence he may." At which he laughed and drove off to dine with General Taliaferro.

Stephen Elliott is wounded. His wife and his father have gone to him. Six hundred of his men were destroyed in a mine, and part of his brigade taken prisoners. But at least Stoneman and his raiders have been captured. This news gives a slightly different hue to our horizon. Yesterday it was unmitigated misery.

Mr. Chesnut came home in fine spirits, so sorry he had lost his temper; but I said: "Why scold Lawrence instead of the real offender?" He answered: "It would have been a thousand times worse if I had spoken as angrily as that to you. Besides I gave Lawrence a half-dollar, and he grinned; he knew he was only a safety valve."

Teddy and his beautiful wife and his beautiful sister-in-law came to tea. In spite of all our woes, we had the jolliest evening. They came in my general's ambulance, and so for the first time I recognized the fact that I was a general's wife.

General Lovell told us of an unpleasant scene at the President's last winter. He called there to see Mrs. McLane. Mrs. Davis was in the room, and he did not speak to her. He did not intend to be rude; he said it was an oversight, and told us he called again and tried to apologise, but the President was inexorable, and would not receive his overtures. General Lovell is a New York man. Talk of the savagery of slavery. Fancy one of our men forgetting to speak to Mrs. Davis in her own drawing-room.

Buck came today and read us a letter from Hood, which had been some time on the way. He said they had left all the good fighting ground behind them, that an army by constant retreating loses confidence in itself, that there was talk of some new man to be put in command. He hoped not. God help the new commander, whoever he should be, for he had a rough road to travel.

AUGUST 5th. — Made sand bags all day to be sent to the Coast. Then I asked Toby Gibson to come with me. I was going to a tea party. He agreed, and strange to say Mr. Chesnut offered to go likewise. I was grateful and amazed. He eschews tea-drinking. It was at the Elmores. I warned Toby that five fascinating virgins awaited him.

Everything was cool and comfortable, spacious and handsome; a great point gained in August, when the thermometer is among the nineties. Mr. Chesnut was instantly captured by a mature beauty, and like Kathleen O'Moore's dun cow, from that moment "ne'er offered to stir." A flashy Department girl tackled Toby, who surrendered without a murmur, and in a few minutes they were amicably engaged in a thorough flirtation. I do not see what more he could have done if he had known her for years instead of seconds. This red, red rose from the Department attacked South Carolina men. "They actually wear stays, the stiff things; and they are padded."

An irate South Carolina girl screamed, with pointed finger — which was hardly needed — "And the Virginia women paint their faces!"

Supper was here announced, and it was all that could be desired of an August night; ices, cake, melons. Then of course the talk turned to Buck and Sam Hood.

"She is throwing herself away, to marry a maimed man." "Nonsense! If she has the heart of a woman, she will love and honor him fourfold for his honorable wounds." "Her family are meek as mice. They know he is unfit for this high command, and they are frightened." "Oh, I dare say they know no mortal man can right Joe Johnston's unaccountable and silly vacillating." "Hood will be rash enough for you!" Toby said to me, in horror: "I never heard so many women at it before. It is awful!"

There is a call upon the citizens to furnish General Chesnut with horses to mount his men, in case we are threatened by raiders.

August 6th. — Archer came. He was a classmate of my husband's at Princeton College. They called him Sally Archer there, he was so girlish and pretty. There is no trace of feminine beauty about this grim soldier now. He has a hard face, black-bearded, sallow, with the saddest eyes. His hands are small, white and well shaped. His manners are quiet. He is abstracted, weary-looking in mind and body, deadened by long imprisonment. He seems glad to be here, and Mr. Chesnut is charmed. "Dear Sally Archer!" he calls him cheerily, and the other responds in a far off, faded kind of way.

Hood and Archer were given the two Texas regiments at the beginning of the War. They were Colonels, and Wigfall was their General. Archer comments on Hood: "He does not compare intellectually with General Johnston, who is decidedly a man of culture and literary attainments, with much experience in military matters. Hood, however, has the help of youth, and energy, to counterbalance. He has a simple-minded directness of purpose always. He is awfully shy. He has suffered terribly, but then he has had consolations; such a rapid rise in his profession and then his luck to be engaged to the beautiful Miss Preston."

General Archer's mother and sister were allowed to see him once, during his fourteen months in Fort Delaware prison; literally to see him. They were allowed to stand thirty feet away from him, and then they might look at each other. No word was allowed, nor sign of recognition. While they were transferring him from Fort Delaware to Fort Johnson, he wrote on a scrap of paper and handed it to a passenger, a total stranger, merely saying: "Will you have the kindness to put that in the telegraph office?" It was to ask his mother to meet him where they had been ten years before, at the Marshall house in Philadelphia. Then he persuaded his guard to go past the Marshall house, but it had been pulled down to make way for shops long ago. Afterwards, he heard that the kind Yankee had sent his telegram, and his mother had hastened to the Marshall house, to meet with the same disappointment. There was no such hotel now. Poor old mother!

They tried Archer again and again on the Hood-Johnston controversy but he stuck to his text, though he said too much caution might be followed easily by too much headlong rashness.

Today a Virginia gentleman dined here, a bluff Englishman in appearance, a regular, red, big, strong John Bull — or descendant of one. This Colonel Carter is a cousin of General Lee, but has been on Joe Johnston's staff, and he actually considers him superior to his kinsman Lee. "There is where Joe Johnston's power comes in" says Mr. Chesnut. "He has the qualities which attract men to him. That is a gift of the Gods."

Colonel Carter on the topic of the hour: "Hood's a fine dare-devil of a soldier. I give him all the credit due him. But if he is as smart a man as old Joe, I'm a fool, and if there is a braver man than Joe, I have to meet him yet."

General Archer, who is unmarried, said surely no man asked the same woman twice to marry him! Colonel Carter simply roared! "Twice did he say? Aye, and twice over again! I courted my wife steadily for six years, and I asked her whenever I saw her. It took six persistent years courting to get her to have me!" "It's dogged as does it," says Isabella.

A beautiful Miss Waring from Baltimore, an exile, wants to go with General Archer as far as Richmond. She has been working in one of the Departments here, to earn her daily bread. She wants to run the blockade and go home if she can. Poor thing, no wonder!

AUGUST 10th. — Today General Chesnut and his staff departed. His troops are ordered to look after the mountain passes beyond Greenville, on the North Carolina and Tennessee quarter. Misery upon misery. Mobile is going as New Orleans went. Those western men have not held their towns as we held and hold Charleston, or as the Virginians hold Richmond, and they call us, "Frill shirt!" "Silk-stocking chivalry!" "Dandy Miss Nancies!" They fight desperately in their bloody street brawls, but we bear privation and discipline best. Brag is a good dog, but Holdfast is a better.

Mary Boykin's son Tom is dead, after all. He died on the battlefield at Old Church, the same day his father was wounded and borne from the fight. Tom was shot three times. The last shot in the side was fatal. It was on the 30th of May. Now, in August, they hear for the first time that he is not a prisoner but dead.

AUGUST 14th. — Conflicting testimony. Young Wade Hampton says Hood lost twelve thousand men in the battles of the 22nd and 24th; Brewster, who is on Hood's staff, says not three thousand at the uttermost.* Now here are two people, strictly truthful, who tell things

* Hood, as even his friends feared he would, had rashly tried to break Sherman's lines around Atlanta, and suffered a severe reverse.

so differently. War? In this War, people see the same thing so oddly, one does not know what to believe.

Our respected parent, whose moral maxim, "A fool and his money are soon parted," and his military maxim "Weight will tell in the end," were equally disagreeable to his hearers, now says: "Wait till we see who can hold Atlanta. The proof of the pudding is chewing the bag."

Brewster says when he was in Richmond Mr. Davis said Johnston would have to be removed, and Sherman blocked. He says: "This blow at Joe Johnston, cutting off his head, ruins the schemes of the enemies of the Government. Wigfall said to me: 'Go at once, get Hood to decline to take this command. It will destroy him if he accepts it! He will have to fight under Jeff Davis's orders. That no one can do, now, and not lose caste in the Western Army. Joe Johnston says he dares not let the President know his plans, as there is a spy in the War Office who invariably warns the Yankees.' Now," added Brewster, "I blame the President for keeping a man at the head of his armies who treats the Government with open scorn and contempt!" More Brewsterana: "The day Hood took command, he and General Johnston talked all day. The new commander asked the old one for all his views and plans, and they were freely given. Mr. Davis's mistake was to keep Johnston too long. Three weeks ago there would have been a chance for the country." These are the Delphic oracles of Brewster.

Mobile is stripped for the fight, non-combatants ordered out of the town. Horrid times ahead!

August 19th. — Began my regular attendance in the Wayside Hospital. Today we gave wounded men, as they stopped for an hour at the station, their breakfast. Those who are able to come to the table do so; the badly wounded remain in wards prepared for them where their wounds are dressed by nurses and surgeons, and we take bread and butter, beef, ham, not coffee to them there.

One man had hair as long as a woman's. A vow, he said. He had pledged himself he would not cut his hair until war set our Southern Country free. Four of them had made this vow. All were dead but himself. This poor creature had one arm taken off at the socket. When I remarked that he was utterly disabled and ought not to remain in the army, he answered quietly: "I am of the First Texas. If old Hood can go with one foot, I can go with one arm!"

They were awfully smashed-up objects of misery, wounded, maimed, diseased. I was really upset and came home ill. This kind of thing unnerves me quite. As I came into my room I stood there on the bare floor and made Ellen undress me and take every thread I had on and throw them all into a washtub out of doors. She had a bath ready for me, and a dressing-gown.

I read Dr. Doran's "Queens of the House of Hanover." Pleasant ladies, truly!

AUGUST 22nd. — I hope I may never know a raid except from hearsay. Mrs. Huger describes the one at Athens. She, the proudest and the most timid of women, was running madly in the streets, corsets in one hand, stockings in the other.

I paid a man a hundred dollars too much. "Madame, you are absent-minded. Count your money. You gave me the wrong change!" He handed me back the superfluous hundred. "Who steals my purse, steals trash — if it contains Confederate bills," I laughed in answer.

Mobile is half taken, the railroad between us and Richmond tapped; Grant's dogged stay about Richmond is very depressing to the spirits.

Extract from a letter written by a young lady whose fiancé is abused. "You say with a sneer 'so you love that man.' Yes, I do; and I thank God that I love — better than all the world — the man who is to be my husband. 'Proud of him, are you?' Yes I am, in exact proportion to my love. He is my second self. So utterly absorbed am I in him, there is not a moment, day or night, that I do not think of him. In point of fact, I do not think of anything else." No reply was deemed necessary by the astounded recipient of this outburst of indignation. She showed me the letter and exclaimed: "Did you ever? And she seems so shy, so timid, so cold."

Sunday, Isabella took us to Chapel; the Methodist Chapel, of course, and her father had a hand in building it. It was not clean; and it was crowded, hot and stuffy. An eloquent man preached. He had a delightful voice and wonderful fluency, sometimes eloquent and at times ridiculous. He described his own conversion, and stripped himself naked, morally. All that is very revolting to one's innate sense of decency. Then he tackled the patriarchs; Adam, Noah and so on down to Joseph: "A man whose modesty and purity was so transcendant that it enabled him to resist the greatest temptation to which fallen man is exposed."

"Fiddlesticks! That is played out," Isabella whispered. "Everybody knows old Mrs. Pharaoah was forty!" "Potiphar, you goose! And she was fifty!" "Sh-h!" from the devout Isabella; but she forgot herself too.

At home we met General Preston on the piazza. He was vastly entertaining; gave us Darwin, Herodotus, Livy. We understood him, and were delighted; but we did not know enough to be sure when it was his own wisdom and when it was wise saws and cheering words from authors of whom he spoke.

August 23rd. — all in a muddle; and yet the news, confused as it is, seems good from all quarters. Riots in New Orleans, Memphis retaken, two thousand prisoners captured at Petersburg. The Yankee raid on Macon came to grief.

At Mrs. Izard's, met there a clever Mrs. Calhoun. She is a violent partisan of Dick Taylor; * says Dick Taylor does the work and Kirby Smith gets the credit of it. Mrs. Calhoun described the behaviour of some acquaintance of theirs at Shreveport; one of that kind whose faith removes mountains. Her love and confidence in the Confederate Army was supreme, because she knew so many of the men who composed that dauntless band. When her husband told her New Orleans had surrendered, she did not believe a word of it! When he told her to pack up his traps, that it was time to leave, she determined then to run down to the levee and see for herself. She saw the Yankee gunboats having it all their own way down there; so she fell on her knees and prayed, then she got up and danced with rage, than she raved, and dashed herself finally on the ground in a fit! There was patriotism run mad for you! As I did not know the poor soul, Mrs. Calhoun's fine acting was somewhat lost on me, but the others enjoyed it — *quand même!*

Oh the cross-grained ways of fate. Here is old Edward Johnston sent to Atlanta against his will, and Archer is made Major General, and — contrary to his earnest request — ordered not to his beloved Texans but to the Army of the Potomac.

Mr. C. F. Hampton deplores the untimely end of General McPherson, who was killed in front of Atlanta a month ago. General McPherson believed that General Hampton was the ablest general on our side.

Someone was saying: "Oh, how I wish General Lee had been sent west to stop Sherman." I replied: "Grant needs as much stopping as Sherman. Lee faces worse odds than anyone else, for when Grant has ten thousand slain, he has only to order up another ten thousand and they are there."

I read in an old Blackwood's "Alcibiades," the very cleverest thing! How I wonder who wrote it.

August 29th. — I take my hospital duty in the morning. Most per-

* General Taylor, son of Zachary Taylor, after the war wrote "Destruction and Reconstruction," an absorbing account of his own experiences.

sons prefer afternoons, but I dislike to give up my pleasant evenings; so I get up at five o'clock and go down in my carriage, all laded with provisions. Mrs. Fisher and Mrs. Bryan generally go with me. I am so glad to be a hospital helper once more. I had excuses enough, but at heart I felt a coward and a skulker. I think I know how men feel who hire a substitute and shirk the fight. Something inside me kept calling out: "Go, you shabby creature. You can't bear to see what those fine fellows have to bear!" Mrs. Izard was staying with me last night, and as I slipped away, I begged Molly to keep everything dead still, and not let Mrs. Izard be disturbed until I got home. About ten I drove up, and there was a row to wake the dead. Molly's eldest daughter nurses her baby sister. She had let the baby fall; and Molly, regardless of Mrs. Izard, was giving the nurse a switching in the yard, accompanied by howls and yells worthy of a Comanche! The small nurse welcomed my advent, for in two seconds peace was restored. Mrs. Izard said she sympathized with the mother and so forgave the uproar.

I have excellent servants, no matter for their shortcomings behind my back. They save me all thought as to household matters, and they are so kind and attentive and quiet. They must know what is at hand if Sherman is not hindered from coming here, "Freedom, my masters!" But these sphinxes give no sign, unless it be increased diligence, and absolute silence. They are as certain in their actions and as noiseless as a law of nature — when we are in the house!

I read "Indiana." Altogether worse than I expected, jealousy between mistress and maid! My disgust was unspeakable for a time, and then I forget all that when those eloquent letters from the Isle of Bourbon turned up.

Life was a nightmare even without "Indiana." That fearful hospital haunts me all day long and worse at night. So much suffering, loathsome wounds, distortion, stumps of limbs exhibited to all and not half cured. Then that tumult when I was so tired. Molly, looking more like an enraged lioness than anything else, crying that her baby's neck was broken, and howling vengeance; and the poor little careless nurse's dark face had an ashen tinge of grey terror. She was crouching near the ground like an animal trying to hide, and her mother striking at her as she rolled away. All this was my welcome as I entered the gate. It takes these half-Africans but a moment to go back to their naked savage animal nature. Mrs. Izard is a charming person. She tried so to make me forget it all and rest.

September 1st. — The battle is raging at Atlanta, our fate hanging in the balance.

September 2nd. — Atlanta is gone. Well that agony is over. Like David, when the child was dead, I will get up from my knees, will wash my face and comb my hair. There is no hope, but we will try to have no fear.

Isabella to the rescue: "Be magnanimous! I dare say you never tried the affectionate dodge! Then try it now! If my fiancé had lost a battle, I would —"

"What would you? Eh?" "I'd make love to him, straight out!"

Now to drown thought, for our day is done, I read Dumas's "Maitres d' Armes." Russia ought to sympathize with us. We are not as barbarous as this, even if Mrs. Stowe's word be taken. Brutal men with unlimited power are the same all over the world. See Russell's "India."

They say General Morgan has been killed. We are hard as stones. We sit unmoved, and hear any bad news the day may bring! Are we stupefied? Stephen Elliott is a very silent man, but when he speaks it is to the purpose. Today, Teddy Barnwell told us this. When Colonel McMaster heard that Stephen Elliott was wounded, he rushed over to condole with him. Said Stephen harshly: "Not a word from you! If you had obeyed orders, this would never have happened."

September 19th. — Mr. Preston says Bragg is a lightning rod, drawing off some of the hatred of Jeff Davis to himself.

My pink silk dress I have sold for six hundred dollars, to be paid by installments, two hundred a month for three months; and I sell my eggs and butter for two hundred dollars a month. Does it not sound well? Four hundred dollars a month, regularly? But — in what? "In Confederate money!" *Hélas!*

Mrs. Magill says: "If Bob Allston is a prisoner, the Yankees won't keep him long. He has the pleasant way of making himself so intolerable, they will long to get rid of him.

September 21st. — The President has gone West. He sent for Mr. Chesnut.

I went with Mrs. Rhett to hear Dr. Palmer. I did not know before how utterly hopeless was our situation. This man is so eloquent; it was hard to listen and not give way. Despair was his word, and martyrdom. He offered us nothing more in this world than the martyr's crown. He is not for slavery, he says; he is for freedom, the freedom to govern our own country as we see fit. He is against foreign interference in our state matters. That is what Mr. Palmer went to war for, it appears. Every day shows that slavery is doomed the world over. For that he thanked God. He spoke of this time of our agony; and then came the cry: "Help us, Oh God! Vain is the help of man." So we came away shaken to the depths.

Johnny is here, with his fine pair of carriage horses and finer riding horses.

Isabella went with us to the Wayside Hospital today. She said: "Calline is out on a rampage (she is a hired nurse) because we expect her to attend to her duties on Sunday. That man over there abused Hood so badly I would not put any sugar in his coffee, and in her rage Calline let a secret out of the bag, a cat, I mean! She acknowledged that the hired nurses take the real coffee for themselves, and give the poor soldiers the imitation." "You see now, Isabella, why we must come, rain or shine, Sunday and every day. We feed them for love and not money. The hired nurses look out for number one only."

While I was making this point for Isabella's benefit, a sulky officer sneered: "Is this all you have to give us? Why it is a regular farce! I say Wayside ministrations are played out, a humbug! After this I will always go to a hotel." "Good heavens, are you able to go to a hotel?" cried the irrepressible Isabella. "Then you have no right here! This is a charity, for those who cannot pay. You had better go at once!" But he did not, and ate his breakfast without another snarl.

A citizen's wife here took a handsome Department girl to board with them. "So cheap," she said; but she proved dear in the end, as good bargains often are. The lord and master of the mansion fell into the toils of the siren, and Madame ordered her out of her house. At the charity concert, here were the whole party in a few feet of one another. *Monsieur* sat by his wife, devoted in manner; and *Madame* wife received his blandishments with scorn. *L'Autre* sat near, with her attendant cavalier, gotten up regardless; and she watched the married pair and seemed to enjoy the spectacle of the man's discomfiture.

The end has come, no doubt of the fact. Our Army has so moved as to uncover Macon and Augusta.* We are going to be wiped off the

* President Davis, in a public address, had promised that Hood, having abandoned Atlanta, would move north to cut Sherman's communications. The maneuver not only left Sherman free to march to Savannah unmolested; but it ended, at Franklin and Nashville, in the annihilation of Hood's army.

face of the earth. Now what is there to prevent Sherman taking General Lee in the rear. We have but two armies, and Sherman is between them now.

SEPTEMBER 29th. — These stories of our defeats in the Valley fall like blows upon a dead body. Since Atlanta, I have felt as if all were dead within me, forever. Captain Ogden of General Chesnut's staff dined here today. Had ever a Brigadier with little or no brigade so magnificent a staff? The reserves, as somebody said, are gathered by robbing the cradle and the grave of men too old and boys too young. Ogden seemed so detached. He is from New Orleans, and a man less like New Orleans I never saw. I had heard him say he was barely twenty-four, so how was I to dream that he had a wife and children. Today when I made it plain to him that I expected him to assist Isaac Hayne when there were girls about, he thought it right to explain that he had been married several years.

Today we left Mary Preston's wedding cards. Johnny acted as charioteer, and Isabella went along to show us where the people lived. It was not a bad way to spend a day out of doors in charming weather.

The Mercury is really touching in its account of the President's speech at Macon. More in sorrow than in anger it declares there must be some hoax; it cannot believe he made such a speech.*

Maggie Howell is here, visiting us and the Prestons. She has gone to drive with Johnny. The colts went off on their hind legs, the forelegs straight up in the air. He will bring them back tame enough, poor things.

Last night, Maggie told Captain Bacon, before she knew his position on the staff: "I mean to marry a Commissary. Their wives have plenty of horses, and they have always sugar for their tea." Then a pause, and a shrill voice was heard to say: "One and one make two; but in matrimony two are expected to make one!"

OCTOBER 1st. — Last Wednesday was Mary Cantey Preston's wedding day. Maggie dressed the bride's hair beautifully, they said, but it was all covered by her veil of blonde lace. The dress was tulle and blonde lace with diamonds and pearls. The bride walked up the aisle on her father's arm, Mrs. Preston on the Doctor's. I think it was the handsomest wedding party I ever saw. They certainly are magnificent specimens of humanity at its best. We, General Chesnut and Maggie, Captain Chesnut and myself, marched up to where the Prestons and

* This was the speech in which Mr. Davis announced to his audience — and so to the Yankees — what General Hood's next move would be.

Hamptons were drawn up in battle array. The Darby family was in solid mass on the opposite side of the church, sad of visage "at losing John."

Mary McDuffie made audible and not too complimentary remarks upon the enemy's forces. John Darby had brought his wedding uniform home with him from England, and it did all honor to his perfect figure. I forget the name of the London tailor; the best, of course. "Well," said Isabella, "it would be hard on any man to live up to those clothes."

We were not invited to the house, nor was anybody, so soon after Willie's death; so we came home to a nice little supper of our own.

Now, to the amazement of us all, Captain Chesnut, Johnny, who knows everything, has rushed into a flirtation with Buck such as never was. He drives her every day, and those wild, runaway, sorrel colts terrify my soul, rearing, pitching, darting from side to side of the street. But my lady enjoys it! When he leaves her, he kisses her hand, bowing so low to do it unseen that we see it all. They seem utterly content with one another. She says she does it to keep him out of mischief. And he answers: "You are engaged — even if you do say you are sorry it is so." So there is no deception on either part. Mrs. Slocomb sent an invitation to her party to Mrs. John Darby, accompanied by one addressed to Miss Howell. She wrote a note to Mrs. Darby, saying she could send this invitation or not as she pleased. Maggie Howell was staying with us. We were also all invited to Mrs. Slocomb's, but we preferred to take tea at the Martins'. Now how can anyone be so small as to think an impertinence aimed at Miss Howell could hurt the President.

OCTOBER 7th. — The President will be with us here in Columbia next Tuesday. I began at once to prepare to receive him in my small house. His apartments were decorated as well as Confederate stringency would permit. There were mirrors of the first Wade Hampton, pre-Revolutionary relics, some find old carpets of *ci-devant* Governor Miller, and curtains to match. The possibilities were not great, but I did all that could be done for our honored chief. Besides, I like the man. He has been so kind to me, and his wife is one of the few to whom I can never be grateful enough for her generous appreciation and attention. Maggie laughed because Captain Chesnut went off in the midst of all my bustle of preparation. He could not be induced to show one atom of interest in the mere matter of the President of this great Confederacy.

OCTOBER 11th. — I went out to the gate to meet the President, who met me most cordially; kissed me, in fact. Custis Lee and Governor Lubbock were at his back. At breakfast — for the party had arrived a little after daylight — Governor Lubbock told a Texas story. A man drank a gallon of sizing, thinking it milk, and then pulled a piece of cloth out of his mouth, thread by thread! Appetizing table talk!

Immediately after breakfast, General Chesnut drove off with the President's aids, and Mr. Davis sat out on our piazza. There was nobody there but myself. Some little boys, strolling by, called out: "Come here and look! There is a man in Mrs. Chesnut's porch who looks just like Jeff Davis on a postage stamp." People began to gather on the street, and Mr. Davis then went in.

Mrs. McCord sent a magnificent bouquet. I thought of course it was for the President, but she gave me such a scolding afterwards for not letting her know he was here. Having made that mistake about the bouquet, I thought she knew, and did not send her word.

What a comfort it is, in all this upsetting foolish talk, that Mrs. Preston, one of the most sensible women I know, and Mrs. McCord, the very cleverest, are both Jeff Davis's supporters and friends, heart and soul. I must not forget good and staunch and fearless Miss Mary Stark. Men may be selfish and self-seeking but my noble female friends are purely patriotic.

The President was watching me prepare a mint julep for Custis Lee when Colonel McLean came in to inform us that a great crowd had gathered and that they were coming to ask the President to speak to them at one o'clock.

An immense crowd assembled, men, women and children. About eleven, I saw Mem Cohen ushering a party through my back door; and after that my house was overflowed, upstairs, downstairs and in my lady's chamber. There was not standing room anywhere. I tried to go up to Maggie's room to look at the crowd from the window; but an unknown, strong-minded female stood her ground, parasol in hand, and called out: "Who is this rude woman trying to push her way through the crowd?" There was nobody there to identify me, and as I was not prepared to fight my way against a parasol levelled as a lance, I meekly went back. The President's room, which opened on the front piazza, was sacred.

The Reverend Mr. Martin held his hands over Mr. Davis's head and blessed him with all his heart. Mr. Theodore Stark came back to us for another glass of brandy, and said with the air of a connoisseur:

"Jeff Davis will do. I like that game look the fellow has." When Mr. Davis went out into the piazza to make his speech, we slipped into his room and locked the door; the Prestons, Maggie, Isabella and I.

"If he should come here and find us?" I protested. "Goose! He cannot be in two places at once, and can't we see when he moves this way?" We were looking through the Venetian blinds. A male voice came through the slats. "Mrs. Chesnut is a regular Cassandra, but she can't stay miserable. She is happy as the day is long, now, playing at loyalty to the head of the Southern Confederacy." "Don't Southern men flatter?" whispered Isabella, to tease me. "Listen how they are going on through the cracks of the blinds with this old soul." "Excitement is good for you, Mrs. Chesnut." This from outside. "You look ten years younger than you did yesterday." "How did you know me in here, from the piazza?" I protested. "You have a patent on those eyes. They have never been duplicated!" was the answer, and then said Governor Bonham gallantly: "Her back is turned to me, but I would know her voice in heaven, among the angels." That was the climax! Then we listened to the President.

John Wallace got pushed back near our window. He was as good as a play. He was so utterly in sympathy with the President, who bore him along with his speech, that he wept and prayed and cursed. "Stop that!" I whispered, for I could touch him, so near was he, though the blinds were between us. "Stop that! Fight! Go to the front and fight! Now is your time!" "Ah, Mrs. Chesnut, ten thousand pardons! Not for worlds would I use bad words before you."

"Mrs. Chesnut is flirting with these old greybeards as if she were fifteen!" cried the girls. We frankly fraternized now. We opened the Venetians, and outside and inside were as one party. When the thing was drawing to an end, we fled from Mr. Davis's private apartments. He was thoroughly exhausted, but we had a mint julep ready for him as he finished.

While Jeff Davis stood up for her General, Buck said she would kiss him for that, and she did, he all the while smoothing her down the back from the shoulders as if she were a ruffled dove.

I left the crowd overflowing the house. The President's hand was nearly shaken off. My head was intent on the dinner to be prepared for them, with only the Confederate commissariat; but the patriotic public had come to the rescue. I had been gathering what I could of eatables, and now I found everybody in Columbia, nearly, had sent me whatever they had that they thought nice enough for the President's dinner. We had the sixty-year-old Madeira from Mulberry, and the beautiful old china; Mrs. Preston sent a boned turkey stuffed with truffles, stuffed tomatoes and stuffed peppers. Each made a dish as pretty as it was appetizing. But it would take too long to tell all that was sent him. For a week I was busy returning stray dishes and serviettes.

A mob of boys came to pay their respects to the President. He seemed to know how to meet that queer crowd. At dinner, Governor Bonham who sat at my left hand complimented my cook. I had to own that Mrs. Preston's man dominated the kitchen for the day, and Molly was glad to have him lift from her shoulders the awful responsibility. Likewise, William Walker volunteered to assist Lawrence and Smith, and was welcomed with joy by the dusky fraternity of waiters. Mars' Kit (Mr. Hampton) sent a dozen or two of the choicest wine from Millwood, for the President to take along on the railway. Then they had to go, and we bade them an affectionate farewell.

Custis Lee and I had spent much time gossiping on the back porch. I was concocting dainties for the dessert, and he sat on the banister with a segar in his mouth; but he spoke very candidly and told me many a hard truth about the Confederacy and the bad time which was at hand. What he said was not so impressive as the unbroken silence he maintained as to that extraordinary move by which Hood expects to entice Sherman away from us. Mrs. Preston says: "They do things that our feminine common sense regards as madness, but they talk so well, and we listen until they almost fool us into believing they have some reason for the wild work. But say what you will, this northern movement of the Western Army is against common sense."

When they were gone, I was so tired. The reaction set in, and now I am Cassandra worse than ever, till they protested: "Stop that miserable talk unless you want to set us howling!"

October 18th. — For days I have not touched pen or paper. I gave myself a holiday from sad forebodings, and now one of the pleasantest weeks of my life has slipped away.

Mrs. Malaprop called today. She said: "After all, everybody knows you talk too much." Dead silence, for this was fatal fact. Then she asked Maggie Howell if the report was true that she had once ordered Mrs. Lee out of the President's pew. Fancy Maggie's face! I said: "I wish what you accused me of could as easily be proved a preposterous and stupid slander!"

"Oh, but I can tell you a real scandal," cried Mrs. Malaprop.

"Caroline B., they would not let her marry the man, because he was beneath her socially! Who are the B.'s to be proud? Now they do say he is giving her things to make her miscarry." "I think," cried the impressible Isabella, "He had better make her Mrs. Carry."

All this rubbish was today. My pleasant week I owe to my sister Kate, who descended upon me unexpectedly from the mountains of Flat Rock. We are true sisters. She understands me without words; and she is the cleverest, sweetest woman I know, so graceful and gracious in manner, so good and unselfish in character. But best of all, she is so agreeable. Any time or place would be charming with Kate for a companion. We had dinners, suppers, parties of pleasure. Clancy the clever was here, and that pleasant fellow George Deas. We had elderly people for Kate and gay young ones for Maggie. How happily the days passed by.

Richardson Miles stopped my ponies: "Beauregard *Felix* is put in command of this department." The Cassandra in me had an inward groan at the *Felix*. "And so he is coming out at the same hole he went in at," I said.

Kate brought her little son with her, a bright and beautiful boy about five years old. She came under Mr. Urquhart's care. The carriage broke down in one of those mountain streams and Mr. Urquhart said: "Mrs. Williams, I can carry you out dry shod, if David will sit quietly on this log until I come back for him." Kate said: "Put me on the log and take David first." "No, the log would not bear your weight." "Then, my child, sit here quietly. If you move, you may be drowned before we could get to you." "Bully!" said little David. "I'm all right. Catch me being such a fool as to move." "Maybe he will be frightened?" "You take Mamma. Never mind me!" And then he sat until he was brought safely to dry land.

One day at dinner, someone mentioned that a new number of "Les Miserables" had reached Columbia. "Oh, buy it, Mamma," he cried. "I am so interested in Cosette's fate."

"Are you reading the translation, or do you prefer the original?" asked Maggie gravely, but that he did not understand. "Mamma reads it aloud at night," he said.

General Chesnut was away in Camden, but I could not wait. I gave the beautiful bride, Mrs. Darby, a dinner which was simply perfect. I was satisfied for once in my life with my own table, and I know pleasanter guests were never seated around any table whatsoever in the world. My house is always crowded. After all, what a number of pleasant people are thrown by war's catastrophes into Columbia. I call such society glorious. It is the wind-up, the Cassandra in me says; and the old life means to die royally.

General Chesnut came back, and growled that such a life as I lead gives him no time to think. "Think! If you have to think, still, God help you!" "What do you mean?" "The time is past now for anything but action."

He came home in splendid spirits from a dinner at Governor Bonham's. There he met the Governor of North Carolina and Extra Billy Smith. In some way, he picked up some crumbs of comfort as to our affairs. Godard Bailey announced that these men had been sent for by Joe Brown, Governor of Georgia, who wanted a peace conference. They mean to ignore Jeff Davis and Lincoln and settle our little differences themselves. "If there had been any treason hatching, General Chesnut would not have been asked to meet them," replied his wife quietly.

A letter from Mrs. Kershaw. She is in money difficulties and wants General Chesnut to buy her house; or, if he does not need one, to try and sell it for her to someone else.

Burton Harrison writes to General Preston that supreme anxiety reigns in Richmond.

October 28th. — We have not for any cause missed one day's attendance at the Wayside Hospital. Today a man (a Camden man) just from Point Lookout prison answered, when we asked him what he would have, that he was too weak to eat. Then he ate steadily through two breakfasts. When he called for a smaller spoon to stir his coffee, Calline refused indignantly; but I humored him about the spoon and even gave him the milk and rice he demanded with a sigh of repletion.

October 30th. — Some days must be dark and dreary; but at the mantua-maker's I saw an instance of faith in our future: a bride's paraphernalia and the radiant bride herself. The bridegroom expectant and elect is now within twenty miles of Chattanooga, and outward bound to face the foe. Mrs. Preston continues to say: "Midsummer madness has seized upon the men who guide the go-behind-Sherman action. It lacks common sense."

A fatuous friend of Alex Haskell said he had killed eleven men with his own hand. "Were they in buckram?" inquired the irrepressible Isabella, but she said aside: "A man who has given one eye to his country ought not to be made ridiculous in the house of his friends."

I saw at the Laurens's not only Lizzie Hamilton, a perfect little beauty, but the very table on which the first Declaration of American Independence was written. These Laurenses are grandchildren of Henry Laurens of our first Revolution. Alas, we have yet to make good our second Declaration of Southern Independence from Yankee meddling and Yankee rule.

Hood has written to ask them to send General Chesnut out to command one of his Brigades! In whose place? The Macon paper says: "Hood's brilliant movement will free Georgia from Yankees." Yes, no doubt! It will send them on their way, light-hearted and rejoicing, into the Carolinas. They say both Beauregard and General Lee counselled that strategic reverse waltz of Hood's, but his *vis-à-vis* would not dance to Hood's music. Sherman stays in Atlanta.

The day Mr. Davis dined with us, there was a chair left vacant and Mr. William F. DeSaussure called. Lawrence brought him straight into the dining-room. Soup was being served. "Oh," said Mr. Chesnut. "You know we could not wait. The President takes the train at an early hour this evening." Mr. DeSaussure seated himself, saying polite things in the easiest possible manner. Mr. Chesnut said it was a triumph of good manners on Mr. DeSaussure's part. Nobody could imagine that he was surprised to find us at dinner, or that he was not looked for to fill that vacant chair.

"Old and dried up as he is, he made himself vastly agreeable to me," said Maggie.

When he came in, we were discussing the fast Department girls; and to my surprise, instead of moral disapprobation, he made a grimace of disgust and said with wonderful precision and distinctness: "There is vast amount of ugliness among them!" To think he is still looking out for pretty women. His wife was a famous beauty, so he knows one when he sees one. Then about the wine; he tasted it, thought awhile, tasted it again, smacked his lips and smiled: "Lawrence, this wine came from Camden, from your old Master's cellar." "Yes sir." "Leave the decanter here." "Then," said Maggie, "with awful solemnity he rolled up the whites of his eyes and informed me: 'This is some of Colonel Chesnut's old Madeira.' " He was wise in women and wine, though he did not look it.

Buck was laughing today: "To think that Brewster had quarrelled with and left the Western Army before Johnston was removed! To think of the bunches of Papa's best cigars that I gave him, with Papa not at home; to think of the brandy that I coaxed Mamma to let me have, and the toddies I made and took to him in the piazza where nobody knew! To think how I waved my hair in front and how I wore all of my best dresses, when the other girls went about in their cool calico gowns, all so that he might make a lovely report of me to H. O. O. D. Now they say he has gone to Texas, that Brewster; and I feel actually swindled." Everybody howled with amusement as in that plaintive voice of hers she enumerated her wrongs.

Then Maggie talked about Johnny. "That cool Captain! How he can hold his tongue! When he is in a tight place, he winds up his watch, looks into it, says something is wrong and puts it right. He will certainly ruin that watch, but it tides him over his difficulty. Then if you abuse anyone he likes, — he can't bear to hear people abused — he makes the sorrels stand on end. How they rear and pitch and try to run away! It is all make-believe. Those sorrel colts are as gentle as dogs! He makes them do all that, just when it suits him. They perform a series of circus tricks, that is all; their antics are too apropos. I began today, while we were bowling along as smooth as a rocking chair, to say something disagreeable — and very true — of his last love. In one second they were plunging like mad, and he could hardly hold them. He was a picture, with his face set and his feet braced against the splashboard. How does he do it? This I do know, that white horse he has for Natalie Heyward to ride will do anything, exactly as he tells it to do."

"What language does he use in his horse talk?" "Oh, I don't know. He whispers in its ear. Today he was taking me to see Minnie Hayne's foot. He said it was the smallest, the most perfect thing in America! Now I will go anywhere to see anything which can move the cool Captain to the smallest ripple of enthusiasm. He says Julia Rutledge knew his weakness, and would not show him her foot. His Uncle James had told him of its arched instep and symmetrical beauty. So he followed her trail like a wild Indian, and when she stepped in the mud, he took a paper pattern of her track, or a plaster cast; something that amazed Miss Rutledge at his sagacity. You can get a rise out of him if you only begin to deride Company A–1 Cavalry, or Hampton, or if you remind him that Von Borcke wanted to teach him and his company to swim their horses! Captain Boykin says when they went too far from their wagons, the cool Captain and some of his men — to whom a bath and clean clothes were more than life — used to strip, bathe, wash their clothes, and run about like picked chickens, mother-naked, till the clothes dried."

Nowadays, England and France are never mentioned, yet once we counted so strongly on them for a good stout backing. We thought this was to be a bloodless duel and that we would get out of the Union, because if they hated us so, why should they want to keep us! We are as sanguine as ever, though, desperate as our case seems.

Oh for one single port! If the *Alabama* had had in the whole world a port to which to take her prizes, to refit, etc., I believe she would have borne us through. If we had had one single point by which to get at the outside world and refit the whole Confederacy; if we could have hired regiments from Europe, or even imported arms, ammunition and food for our soldiers. But what did out monster Iron Clads do but blow themselves up? We crippled ourselves by intestine strife!

Today General Chesnut said casually at dinner: "I dare say I have as large a stake in the country as any man, and no man has ever doubted my patriotism, and yet so high does party feeling rage among us that when I was sent by the President to inspect and report, in Johnston's camp and Beauregard's, I was always treated more as a foreign spy than as an *aide de camp* of the President of the Confederacy."

Old Stonewall now! How he would have despised all that nonsense. Alas, if Albert Sidney Johnston had lived! Poor old General Lee has no backing. Sherman will catch General Lee by the rear, while Grant holds him by the head, and while Hood and Thomas * are performing an Indian war dance on the frontier.

Next to our house is a common, green grass and very level. Then there comes a belt of pine trees. On this open space, within forty paces of us, a regiment of foreign deserters has camped. They have taken the oath of allegiance to our government, and are now being drilled and disciplined into form before sending them to our army. They are mostly Germans, with some Irish. Their close proximity keeps me miserable; treacherous once, traitors forever.

Jordan has always been held responsible for all the foolish proclamations, and indeed for whatever Beauregard reported or proclaimed. Now he has left that mighty chief, and Lo! here comes from Beauregard the silliest and most boastful of his military bulletins. He even brags of Shiloh! That was not the way the story was told to us! There he lost all that Albert Sidney Johnston had died to gain; but men will boast of anything!

Tom Boykin, the brightest, bravest, best of Uncle William's boys,

* General Thomas was facing Hood's army in Tennessee.

was killed at Rome. I wrote that awkward uncomfortable thing, a letter of condolence today. When one really feels, it is a hard task to write such a letter to a bereaved father.

It rains in torrents. What cares Maggie? For her solace, she has my novel and General Chesnut has "Joseph II," but "Romola" is in my hands, so without protest or fidgets we let it rain its worst. Can this woman who calls herself George Eliot really be a fallen woman? Can you smother the seventh commandment with genius? There it stands. An unchaste woman must be immodest. We won't go into morals at all. No, No! It is all Lamar's wrong hearing of English scandal! She writes such beautiful things of love and duty, of faith and charity and purity. They even say she is an atheist, that she believes in God as little as she cares for his commandments. It cannot be true.

Today's paper congratulates the country on its Generals, says Beauregard brings us the tact and skill lacking in Hood, and that Hood will lend Beauregard dash and boldness. A Yankee paper's description of Hood: "A man whose want of beauty is further embellished by a wooden leg and a wilted arm and lackluster eyes; sad, weary, baleful eyes. He can only smile by a facial revolution. His is a face that speaks of wakeful nights, and nerves strung to their utmost tension by anxiety." Even his old gray cloak lined with red flannel comes in for a fling.

Every man is being hurried to the front. Today Mr. Chesnut met a poor creature coming from the surgeon's with a radiant face and a certificate. "General, see! I am exempt from service; one leg utterly useless the other not warranted to last three months."

November 6th. — A letter from Mrs. Davis, of which I copy a part: "Thank you a thousand times, my dear friend, for your more than maternal kindness to my sister. As to Mr. Davis, he says the best ham, the best Madeira, the best coffee, the best hostess in the world rendered Columbia delightful to him when he passed through. I do not think he realized how much he cared for the General until called upon to leave him behind in South Carolina. It did his heart good to see your reserved General and you once more. Colonel Lubbock was funny about your breakfast and your stuffed peppers. His eyes dilated and he assured me that there never has been such. We are in a sad and anxious state here now. The dead come in, the living do not go out so fast. However we hope all things, and trust in God. I have only been out of the house twice since Maggie left. Her being with you is a great relief to me, for in looking forward to contingencies I feel she is safe, and — what is better than safe in these times — happy.

"I had a surprise of an unusually gratifying nature a few days since. I found I could not keep my horses, so I sold them. The next day they were returned to me with a handsome anonymous note, to the effect that they had been bought by a few friends for me. But I fear I cannot feed them, so my attention is now turned upon the green satin as a source of revenue. Can you make a suggestion about it? I think it will spoil if laid up, and will go out of fashion. I shall probably never go into colors again, and therefore can never want it. Maggie is not imminent in the matrimonial line, or she might have it.

"And now, dear friend, I must brag a little about my baby. She is so soft, so good, and so very lady-like, and knows me very well. She is white as a lily, and has such exquisite hands and feet, and such bright blue eyes. She is 'Piecake' * still. Jeff is going to dancing school. Maggie is also learning to dance — at a fearful rate of shoe leather. Her grace is undeniable, but she comes out at the toes. If there are any good stockings in Columbia, please send her a dozen pairs.

"Strictly between us, things look very anxious here. *Verbum sap.* I am so constantly depressed that I dread writing, for penned lines betray our feelings despite every care."

Sally Hampton went to Richmond with the Reverend Mr. Martin. The day after she arrived there, her father, Wade Hampton, fought a great battle and narrowly missed a victory. Darkness supervened, and impenetrable woods prevented that longed for consummation. Preston Hampton rode recklessly into the hottest fire. His father sent his brother Wade to bring him back. Wade saw him reel in the saddle, and galloped up to him, and General Hampton followed. As young Wade reached him, Preston fell from his horse; and as he stooped to raise him, Wade was himself shot down. Preston recognized his father, but died without speaking a word. Young Wade, though wounded, held his brother's head up. Tom Taylor and others hurried up. The General took his dead son in his arms, kissed him, and handed his body to Tom Taylor and his friends. He bade them take care of Wade and then rode back to his post. Ahead of his troops, in the thickest of the fray, he directed the fight for the rest of the day. Until night, he did not know young Wade's fate. Now he says no son of his must be in his command.

* The baby, "The Daughter of the Confederacy," was eventually named Varina Anne.

When Wade recovers, he must join some other division. The agony of that day coupled with the anxiety and the duties of the battlefield; it is more than a mere man can bear.

We went to the brave boy's funeral. I loved that splendid young soldier. Buck ran away. "I can't bear to think of Preston," she said. "I can't bear to hear any more moaning and weeping and wailing. If I do I shall die."

Dr. Gibbes, who had gone to Augusta in a powerful uniform, was back already, reporting everything blue. General Hampton had ordered Preston's grave to be dug by that of his mother, but Dr. Gibbes interfered, saying there was no space there for it; so it was dug somewhere near. That night, Mr. Mott Allston heard of this, and went up to make a personal inspection. He found there was room enough for the poor boy by his mother's side, so he had his grave made there; so as we stood there, two yawning graves awaited us. It was sad enough, God knows, without that evil augury. Preston was not twenty.

Isabella in her rage and grief grew light-headed over the omen. She wanted to bury Dr. Gibbes there alive in the grave he insisted on having dug, though he would be so proud to be in the Hampton graveyard!

There is a Boyce party forming. Orr denies that he belongs to it, but they are all tarred with the same stick. Edward Boykin told us how it worked like a dry rot in the Army, all this abuse of the government. "If it is as the newspapers say, and as Mr. Boyce says, why waste our blood?" grumble the soldiers. "Why should we fight and die, when it is no use?" And so they disappear. They quietly desert at night and slip away home.

Mrs. Davis writes again: "Maggie (her daughter) is engaged in a stupendous letter of thanks for the dainty and beautiful diamond ring you sent her. She was more than delighted. She assumed all the airs of a woman who wears her trousseau a little in the country, so as to get the fit of it perfect before or against the grand occasion. She laid it by with a sigh, remarking that after all it was too handsome to wear to school just yet. I assured her it would ruin the shape of her finger, and quietly put it on my own. It fits and looks very well thank you." She adds: " 'Piecake' has been teething for some weeks and is not herself at all. She seems conscious who I am, or rather that I am her supply store, but she is an immense source of comfort to me.

"I was dreadfully shocked at Preston Hampton's fate. I know nothing in history more touching than Wade Hampton's situation at that supremest moment, when he sent one son to save the other, and saw them both fall, and he did not know for some moments whether both were not killed. I went to see Sally Hampton. She, poor thing, does her best to keep up for Wade's sake. You know they are staying at Mrs. Huger's. What a dear old gentleman Mr. Martin is. I delighted in the little I saw of him, but the baby sent for me and I went out of the room to nurse her, and when I returned he was gone.

"Mrs. Pringle and daughter passed through here a day or two since, and Mrs. Stanard brought them to see me. I had undressed for bed, for I am still quite weak, and sent her word so; but she insisted upon my seeing them and I was forced to decline, because there were gentlemen in the only room with a fire. It takes me at best an hour to do my hair and dress, and I could not ask them to wait. I felt really irritated that Mrs. Stanard should make me seem to repulse their civility by insisting on my performing an impossibility. If you see Mrs. Pringle, please explain.

"Maggie is so happy with you that I dread to speak of home to her, but I think she must think a little of returning very soon. I should like to see a little deeper into Mr. Grant's plans before risking her here, however."

Mrs. Alex Taylor told us of an ingenious exchange of prisoners, a most satisfactory arrangement. Mr. Taylor undertakes to look after the brother of an Ohioan who is a prisoner of war here, and in return the Ohio man undertakes to make John Taylor, on Johnson's Island, as comfortable as Mr. Taylor does his brother down here.

Buck and Judy went down to the Hospital with me today. There were several wounded men to be given breakfast, after their wounds were attended to by the surgeons and nurses. Of course we are only in the feeding department. At one time I was detailed to see to the breakfast of four men who could not chew at all, so cat-lap was the word. Hominy, rice with gravy, milk and bread. One was shot in the eye, but his whole jaw was paralyzed. Another, the worse case, had his tongue cut away by a shot and his teeth with it. We worked like galley slaves from five in the morning until half past eight, when the train bore away the whole of them, and we waved our handkerchiefs to them and sat down, tired to death.

There was a table where all the men with crutches were sent, and Judy told Buck to go and wait on them, which she did, her blue eyes swimming in tears all the time. She was so shy, so lovely, so efficient; all the same, I cannot bear young girls to go to the hospitals, Wayside or otherwise. The comments those men made on Buck's angelic beauty!

Mrs. Fiske, the good genius of our Wayside Hospital, had her fine cow stolen by one of her own servants and made into beef before the theft was discovered. "Virtue is not rewarded in this world," said Isabella solemnly, "or Jane Fisher would never have a trouble." Madame Pelletier denounced Calline to us. Poor Calline is a Sandhiller, and rough to the hungry, sick and sore soldiers.

A thousand dollars has slipped through my fingers already this week at the Commissary's. I spent five hundred today for sugar, candles, a lamp, etc. Tallow candles are bad enough, but of them there seems to be an end too. Now we are restricted to smoky terebene lamps. When the chimney of the lamp cracks, as crack it will, we plaster up the place with paper. We use thick letter paper, preferring the highly glazed kind. In that hunt, queer old letters come to light. If you could see the pitiful little bundles this five hundred dollars bought.

Our cool Captain writes from Wilmington that there are no gnats there, but they call his fine horses "critters." Sherman in Atlanta has left Thomas to take care of Hood. Hood has thirty thousand men, Thomas forty thousand now and as many more as he wants. He has only to ring the bell and call for more. Grant can get all he wants, both for himself and for Thomas. All the world is open to them; we are shut up in a Bastille. We are at sea — and our boat has sprung a leak!

November 17th. — Maggie Howell went back to Richmond with the Prestons. Mrs. Davis wrote her to stay if she wished it, and she seemed reluctant to go. She told John Darby it had been one of the happiest times of her life. We tried to make it so. The last weeks were gay enough. The staff did duty nobly.

War comes in everywhere. At a party at the Martin's, supper was cut short because Mrs. McKenzie, the pastry cook and confectioner of Columbia par excellence, heard that her son was killed the very day of the party. Instead of a tray of good things came back that news to the Martins. We must sup on death and carnage, or go empty!

Clancy said we could understand the French prisoners in the reign of terror now. They danced and flirted until the tumbril came for them. Buck came and looked in at the window. As we came out, she pinned me. "You were talking about me to Clancy. I saw you." "I was," I admitted. "Clancy, who raves about you, says you are the noblest specimen of womanhood, that a man might write himself happy if you loved him, even though he lost name, fame, life and limb." The blessed child threw her arms around my neck and nearly smothered me with kisses. Mrs. Martin drew us into her chamber — for our love scene, she said, but it was only an outburst — and we parted gayly.

Mr. Chesnut was angry with me that I let Maggie go. How could I keep her here? Sherman is at Atlanta and he does not mean to stay there.* That means fire and swords for us here!

And now I must begin my Columbia life anew and alone. It will be a short shrift.

General Lovell called today. "If Lincoln is not re-elected," he remarked, "with his untold millions at command, his patronage and his army and his navy, he must be a great fool indeed!"

Captain Ogden came to dinner on Sunday, and in the afternoon asked me to go with him to the Presbyterian church and hear Mr. Palmer. What a sermon! The preacher stirred my blood, my very flesh crept and tingled. A red hot glow of patriotism passed over me. Such a sermon must strengthen the hearts and the hands of many people. There was more exhortation to fight and die than meek Christianity.

Judge Magrath dined here. He is besetting Mr. Chesnut to be a candidate for Governor. I take it for granted he wants to be Governor himself, and to use Mr. Chesnut in the canvass as a sort of lightning rod, to draw off the troublesome opposition of our friends. Then came Mrs. Bartow, bringing me some very good tea that had run the blockade, but it was in a glass shaving-soap case. So powerful is the imagination and so unreasonable the human appetite, I could not drink tea taken from a thing where shaving soap was wont to be.

November 25th. — Went out to drive with Mrs. Izard. Came home and found my nieces, Serena and Mary Williams. Girls are gone and now girls have come! Girls are my fate! Serena is a brunette with glorious brown eyes. She carries her head proudly. She is handsome enough, but more graceful and gracious than pretty. Her mouth and teeth are exquisitely beautiful, her red lips and her white regular teeth, but her mouth is a trifle too broad. Mary is a delicious contrast. She is lovely, I cannot say less. She is fair and feminine, blonde, with blue eyes and the longest black lashes, golden hair, rosebud mouth, a regular Cupid's bow, short upper lip, complexion the purest pink and white, affectionate in temperament, rough and abrupt in manners, audaciously clever, left-handed, near-sighted, rather clumsy in movement, beautifully formed. These charming children — for children they are,

* Although Mrs. Chesnut did not yet know it, Sherman had started the day before on his march through Georgia to the sea; but it would be several months before, moving north through the Carolinas, he reached Columbia.

one sixteen, the other barely fourteen — will be an awful care. I was to have a rest; but no, here are two premature belles on my hands again.

William Matthews asked: "Where did you get your new beauties? Do you keep a reserve corps of them?"

These children are pets of Sally Rutledge's, so I ordered out my ponies and drove with them to see her. We came home to meet the cool Captain driving those aforesaid sorrels through our gate, with two led horses following him. "An unexpected pleasure!" smiled Serena. He began his flirtation with Serena as he took his hat off. He seems overwhelmingly in love with Mary, and can show it without let or hindrance; her fourteen years are still no bar to cousinly kisses.

Sherman is thundering at Augusta's very doors, so my General was on the wing, sombre and full of care but the girls were merry as grigs and the staff, who fairly live here, no better. I am Cassandra, with a black shawl over my head, chased by the gay crew from sofa to sofa; for I avoid them, being full of miserable anxiety. It rains all the time, such rains as I never saw before, incessant torrents. Things seemed dismal and wretched to me to the last degree but the staff and the girls and the youngsters did not see it.

Yesterday, I found an enemy in my own camp. I received a most abusive and insulting letter from Harriet Grant. She sneered at everything Southern. Her unfeeling taunts directed toward Buck by name exceeded anything I ever imagined. She seemed to hold me responsible for Confederate disasters, because I would never join the Cabal to tie Mr. Davis's hands and ruin our own government. "Thank God, I am for our side, come what may for Jeff Davis!" says she. These people only care for those who are successful. It was a brutal letter.

Mrs. Slocomb (born in Connecticut) was radiant. She says exultingly: "Sherman will open a way out at last. I will go at once to Europe, or go North to my relatives there." How she derided our misery and "mocked when our fear cometh." I dare say she takes me for a fool. I sat there dumb, for she was in my own house. I have heard of a woman so enraged that she struck someone over the head with a shovel. Today for the first time in my life, I know how that mad woman felt. I could have given her the benefit of shovel and tongs both! Mrs. Joseph Johnston behaved so differently; for after all, it is the day of her triumph. She was quiet and polite, and carefully avoided awkward topics. She said General Johnston took a gloomy view of affairs. Certainly he is not singular in that. In the small matter of good manners, Mrs. Johnston is a notable example to her understrappers and followers.

When, before sending the girls, Kate came here on an exploring expedition, a sort of skirmisher thrown out to feel for the enemy, I told her plainly: "You see my house is only a barrack, soldiers running in night and day. The place is open at all hours. They come and go. For example, we were seated in our front piazza, which is only a few steps from the street. Some men in uniform asked the way to Mr. Martin's depot of clothes for soldiers. They leaned on the gate. Mr. Chesnut went down and pointed out the way; and then he said: 'Come in and have some supper.' 'No thanks, we have had dinner given us on the cars by some kind ladies.' 'Who are they?' asked Sally Goodwyn as he came back to us. 'I do not know, soldiers asking the way.' 'Do you mean to say you ask men in to supper whom you never saw before, whose very names you don't know? I call that hospitality run mad!' "

I told Kate all this; and besides, I was so tired, so broken-hearted that I could not count on myself. I could not take care of girls now; life had gone out of me. But they came. Their mother must bear the blame if harm comes of it. She knew the risk; and I did not know how beautiful they were, and how young and thoughtless and gay and light-hearted they would be.

I sit here and listen for Sherman's bugles. I know we have nothing to put in his way but a brigade or so of troopless, dismantled Generals.

That splendid fellow, Preston Hampton! Home they brought their warrior dead wrapped in that very Legion Flag he had borne so often in battle. Poor boy!

A letter from Mrs. Davis says Maggie has reached Richmond full of talk of her good times here; but she goes on to say: "Affairs west are looking so critical now that before you receive this, you and I will be in the depths — or else triumphant. I confess I do not snuff success in every passing breeze, but I am so tired of hoping and fearing and being disappointed that I have made up my mind not to be disconsolate even though thieves break through and steal. Some people expect another attack upon Richmond shortly, but I think the avalanche will not slide until the Spring breaks up its winter quarters. The temper of Congress is less vicious, but more concerted in its hostile action. 'State's Rights,' and consequently state's wrongs, are rampant! Perhaps the new wine will burst the old bottles. People do not snub me any longer, for it was only while the lion was dying that he was kicked; dead, he was beneath contempt. Not to say I am worthy to be called a lion, nor are the people here asses.

"Scandal is rife here. God forbid I should repeat such black reports as I was treated to a few days ago. Girls and women are the victims, and to tell you the truth I think the most of it is campfire talk by idle men.

"I generally let out my crazy bone to you, so I must tell you how exquisite my little baby is. She looks like a little rosebud. It is the only point upon which I feel not very sane."

There is a woman that my heart aches for, in the trouble ahead!!!

Johnny's colonel was here today, trying to find out where his regiment is. Things are in a muddle, hopelessly mixed up.

My journal, a quire of Confederate paper, lies wide open on my desk in the corner of my drawing-room. Everybody reads it who chooses. Buck comes regularly to see what I had written last, and makes faces when it does not suit her. Isabella still calls me Cassandra, and puts her hands to her ears when I begin to wail. Well, Cassandra only records what she hears. She does not vouch for it, for really, one never nowadays feels certain of anything.

Becky Wallace dilated upon the doctor's horror of our actual condition. He "wished she was dead and that his daughters had never been born." Mrs. W—— dwelt proudly on what "Uncle Huger" thought of our danger. As for herself, she was calm and serene: she would take refuge in the insane asylum of which her father is the head. She knew no Yankees would venture there, and it was bomb proof. She added: "But Mr. Petigru says all South Carolina is an insane asylum. That will not save us now from fire and sword." Mrs. Cuthbert gave us this contribution to the conversation. "All the troops from the mountainous parts of South Carolina, and from North Carolina's mountains, too, are disaffected. They want peace; they say this is a rich man's war, that they want no part in it, and they would gladly desert in a body. Our returned prisoners are broken-spirited, and say they have had enough of it."

I sat dumb, but then came in Mr. Howell who said, not knowing anything of the preceding talk: "Our returned prisoners come back fired with patriotism, and they will fight this thing through to the death." He was in such excellent spirits that mine rose too. Then he showed us maps and traced with his finger how and where Sherman was sure to be bagged. I absolutely found myself believing him.

The two Wigfall girls dined here today, and a daughter of Senator Hill. Mr. Hill wrote to ask me to take charge of her and keep her with me; but when we went for her at the Convent, she had already left it and was staying at Nickerson's and refuses to leave them. They have a fine turnout, and she drives with them in their landau every evening. He is the hotel keeper. I tried to persuade her to come with me, since her father wished it, but I had no power to coerce her. Maybe it is the new rule now; parents, obey your children. She said: "Leave me to deal with my father. He trusts me implicitly."

My girls thought themselves well read in modern poetry, but little Hill took the wind out of their sails, completely. She had Owen Meredith at her finger ends, and they did not know him at all. I told them: "It's better for you to find out while you are young how much more other people know than you do. Anything is better than the awful self-complacency of the modern American girl." I said not a word of how small was the shame of not knowing Owen Meredith; but I sent to Camden at once for my copy!

NOVEMBER 28th. — We dined at Mrs. McCord's. She is as strong a cordial for broken spirits and failing heart as one could wish. How her strength contrasts with our weakness. Poor Cheves's beautiful young widow was there; not yet twenty, and for more than two years in widow's caps! She has a touchingly pathetic smile. It enhances her beauty wonderfully.

General Hampton's house has been robbed, and all of his wife's jewelry taken. Everything valuable was stolen. Isabella said: "It took her to leave it in an empty house." The robbers left derisive notes behind them: "Hang Hampton," "Damn Hampton," "Rebel," "Cattle stealer," etc. The Foreign Battalion gets the credit of this deed, composed as it is of renegades from every nation, and Yankee deserters; and they are here camped under my nose.

Halcott Green tries to raise our spirits. "Take my word for it, good news, wonderful news is coming." It had better hurry up. Time is short now. We have lost nearly all of our men, and we have no money, and it looks as if we had taught the Yankees to fight. Here we stand, despair in our hearts ("Oh, Cassandra, don't!" shouts Isabella) and our houses are burnt — or about to be — over our heads.

The Yankees have just got things shipshape; a splendid army, perfectly disciplined, and new levies coming in day and night to them. Their gentry do not go into the ranks. They pile up shoddy fortunes cheating their government; they dwell in their comfortable cities, tranquil, in no personal fear. The war is to them only a pleasurable excitement.

Someone said: "If we had only freed the Negroes at first, and put them in the Army, that would have trumped their trick." I remember when Mr. Chesnut spoke to his Negroes about it, his head men were keen to go in the Army, to be free and get a bounty after the War. Now they say coolly that they don't want freedom if they have to fight for it. That means they are pretty sure of having it anyway.

November 30th. — The girls went with Mrs. Singleton and Sally Rutledge to see the Legislature. A legislator, sadly soiled, joined them. He lost an arm at Seven Pines. How can he, poor helpless creature, keep neat and clean? Another, who lost a leg in the service of his country, is likewise a member of the Legislature. What a noble use to make of our wounded veterans. Put them, the disabled ones, in the halls of the Legislature, and turn out the able-bodied ones and send them to the front.

Red-hot resolutions are urged by Trescot and the Rhetts, the temper of the House is roused, State's Rights are rampant. We are about to secede again from the Confederacy! No doubt the Devil raved of "Devil's Rights" in Paradise.

How can we stay disintegration when it once begins? Dr. Gibbes's philosophy, in the Carolinian: Let those fight on who have fought for four years. They know how, they have caught the trick of it. But leave in peace those who have printed and published and fought skilfully for Number One and no other; who have carefully skulked the fight with credit and comfort to themselves. How beastly to interfere with them now!

December 1st. — Through the deep waters we wade! General Chesnut writes from Allendale, wherever that is. At Coosawhatchie, Yankees landing in great force. Our troops down there are raw militia, old men and boys who were never under fire before. "The cradle and the grave" is robbed by us, they say. Sherman goes to Savannah and not to Augusta.

The girls went with the Martins to the State House. The Senate was deliberating how much cotton they would allow a man to plant next year, while the House put off until noon tomorrow a bill to raise men for home defense. While the enemy is thundering at their gates, they can still fool themselves with words; and yet the men who would not join Noah in his Ark-building must have left no descendants. They do not count Sherman among the devastating forces of nature. I do believe they forget his existence.

DECEMBER 2nd. — Isabella and I put on bonnets and shawls and went deliberately out for news. We determined to seek until we found some. We met a man, so very ugly. He was awfully in love with me once. He did not know me, and blushed hotly when Isabella told him who I was. I hope it was just that he had forgotten me — or else I am changed by age and care past all recognition. He gave us the encouraging information that Grahamville was burned to the ground.

We saw some soldiers awkwardly arresting some skulkers or deserters. One man turned as white as a sheet. He was the picture of abject terror. Another, of altogether another mettle, jeered: "Don't you come near me with that gun. I am afraid of a gun!" "I wish I could sketch that scene," said Isabella. "It had its comic side." "And for our cause," I remarked, "It is no laughing matter to have to send ten men to drag in two."

When the call for horses was made, Mrs. McCord sent in her fine bays. She comes now with a pair of mules and looks too long at my ponies. If I were not so much afraid of her, I would tell her those mules would be of far more use in camp than my ponies. In all my life before, the stables were far off from the house, and I had nothing to do with them. Now my ponies are kept under an open shed next the back piazza, lest they be stolen. Here I sit at my desk, or with my book, basking in our Southern sun; and I watch Mat feed, curry, and rub down the ponies and then clean their stalls as thoroughly as Smith does my drawing room. I see their beds of straw comfortably laid. Mat says: "Now Missis, ain't lady business to look so much in de stable." I care nothing for his grumbling. Poor ponies, you deserve every attention and enough to eat. Grass does not grow under your feet; night and day you are on the trot.

Mat has been on the Coast at some fortification there, and as he rubs down a pony he tells war stories — not to me, but he knows I hear. "You see Buckra hard run down there! I didn't mind helping them, but dem overseer so mean. When a bomb came awhiz, awhiz, awhizzzzzzz, we all had to run for de dear life and fall on top de overseer. He lay down flat soon as he hear bomb a-coming, and we pile on him. We mek pile ob niggers high as dish here shed Missis call her stable. Buckra down below, nigger heap on top; dat's de way he try to save he life." "Mat, are we to believe such a foolish tale as that?" "Clar to God, Missis, it's a fac."

Richardson Miles has for us always the best of bad news. Today he was grandly patriotic; he fairly hung his head, so shocked and mortified was he that Sherman had marched unmolested through Georgia.

Today General Chesnut was in Charleston, on his way from Augusta to Savannah by rail. The telegraph is still working between Charleston and Savannah, but Grahamville is certainly burnt. We came home with enough to think about, Heavens knows!

And then all day long we compounded a pound cake for tea. The cake was a success, but was it worth all that trouble? Molly said we did not help, we hindered her, and she threatened if we did not keep out of her kitchen to pin the dish rag to Serena.

Teddy Barnwell came with his wife, to say good-bye on his way to the coast. So far, he had been unable to impress the horses he was detailed to find for the Brigade. He left Dr. Gibbes in tears over his valuable paintings that damp walls were ruining. Teddy comforted him. If fire could dry his walls, he thought Sherman would soon do it for him. Dr. Gibbes said he was packing for a flight in time to save nine.

As we were drinking our tea, Smith handed me a note. "A soldier man brought this to Miss Serena." The young Trezevant, whom we met at Mrs. Slocomb's and who has haunted the house since these girls came, wrote this note to Serena, asking her to go with him to a concert. She was all in a flutter at being written to by a strange young man. I answered the note in the third person: I bade him come to tea with us — and we would see about it. He must have been the "soldier who brought the note," for he walked right in. Young Trezevant opened his eyes as I marshalled the clan he was to escort. He had come to take Serena alone; that is his wild western fashion, he told me.

As my party were driving off to the concert with Mrs. Cuthbert as chaperone, an omnibus rolled up. Enter Captain Leland of General Chesnut's staff, and of as imposing a presence as a field marshall, handsome and grey-haired. He was here on some military errand and brought me a letter. He said the Yankees were repulsed, and down in those swamps we could soon give a good account of them if they would only send us men enough. With a sufficient army to meet them, they would be annihilated.

"Where are the men to come from?" asked Nannie mildly. "General Hood has gone off to Tennessee. Even if he does defeat Thomas there, what difference would that make here? He could not overtake Sherman!" "Sherman," wailed Cassandra, "will soon effect a junction with Grant, and leave us a howling wilderness. Even if General Hood could get to Lee's army, it would be no use now." And I fairly broke down. Mrs. McCord does not weep. She works like a Trojan.

A letter from the cool Captain. Why he has been kept in Wilmington till now is a mystery to him, but he is ordered to Virginia at last. "He must make up his mind to stand up to one of his flirtations," quoth Isabella. "No. The scamp says a sabre cut or a shot from the Yankees may soon solve all of his difficulties in that direction."

DECEMBER 3rd. — Our Foreign Legion here now musters eleven hundred men. The War Office has sent down a corps of youngsters from the Military Institute in Virginia to drill and then muster this battalion into service, and a finer set of young men I never saw. Was Kate mad, after all I made plain to her, to send these beautiful children here? After dress parade, Serena stood surrounded by these splendid six-foot boys, with their clear white and red complexions fresh from the mountains, their bright and laughing faces made irresistible by their uniforms. It was young Trezevant who presented the Virginia contingent. A formidable force, I should say — to anxious mothers of grown daughters.

We drank tea at Mrs. McCord's. She had her troubles, too. The night before, a country cousin claimed her hospitality, one who fain would take the train at five this morning. A little after midnight Mrs. McCord was startled out of her first sleep by loud ringing of bells. An alarm at night may mean so much just now. In an instant she was on her feet. She found it was her guest who thought it was daylight and wanted to go. Mrs. McCord forcibly demonstrated how foolish it was to get up five hours too soon. Once more in her own warm bed she fell happily to sleep. She was waked by feeling two ice-cold hands pass cautiously over her face and person. It was pitch dark. Even Mrs. McCord gave a scream in her fright. She found it was only the irrepressible guest, up and at her; so though it was but three o'clock, to quiet this perturbed spirit, she got up and at four drove her to the station, where she had to wait for hours.

General Chesnut writes from Grahamville: "The attack on this place brought me here. We marched all night Tuesday and reached the battlefield in the morning and found the enemy had been repulsed with great slaughter in proportion to the numbers engaged. The enemy had about five thousand men, we had two thousand five hundred.

"I have not slept since I left Hamburg. General Hardee informed me this morning that I am to be left here in command, with four hundred and fifty reserves and two pieces of artillery to hold this place. The force is in the main undisciplined, broken down, and by itself comparatively worthless."

December 5th. — General Lee has had seven hundred men surprised and taken prisoner — and we cannot spare a man! Down here we are surprised at nothing.

They say G. W. Smith with the Georgia Militia won the fight at Grahamville. Half of the Yankee force was Negroes. It was the bloodiest of fights, a carnage. Before the dead were buried next day the battlefield was awful to see.

I asked Captain Bierne and Lieutenant Brockenbrough, who were so devoted to me at dress parade, to tea. Sally Rutledge hints that so much Foreign Battalion is a mistake on my part. I think so too, but they are at my doors, and I know no way to keep them out. After all, these splendid young fellows have fine old Virginia names, Dinwiddie, Barton, Brockenbrough. Absolutely historic!

Louly Wigfall came to say good-bye. I would like to see more of her and be kind to her; but her Johnston proclivities make her stand aloof. Besides, my young ones fill my carriage now with their cronies; they never leave me a corner for mine. They have elected Lizzie Hamilton and Maggie Martin for their devoted and inseparable friends. Surely they are not afraid of beauteous rivals. Little Lizzie Hamilton is that rare thing, a perfect beauty, and a clever little witch beside.

The Foreign Battalion drills now fairly at my front steps. We sit on the porch or at our windows, near enough to catch the eye of the officers as they step about. We can see their white teeth as they smile in passing us. This is enlivening, even if it is a dangerous proximity for the too-young ladies. Also, they have a capital band of music, which plays every afternoon, and is another distraction. We need all that we can get of that.

Miss Olivia Middleton and Mr. Frederick Blake are to be married tomorrow night. We Confederates have invented the sit-up-all-night wedding. Isabella calls it the wake, not the wedding, of the parties married. The ceremony will be performed early in the evening and then the whole company will sit up until five o'clock, at which hour the bridal couple take the train for Combahee. I hope Sherman will not be so inconsiderate as to cut short the honeymoon.

Arnoldus Vander Horst is a queer kind of old-fashioned gentleman. He can be grateful for a kindness, and is not ashamed to show it. He asked Mr. Chesnut to get him a place on General Whiting's staff. The War Office made no objection, and his appointment was sent by return mail. Now Arnoldus Vander Horst is very attentive and kind to John Chesnut at Wilmington, and tells him also how much obliged he is to Mr. Chesnut. Real thoughtfulness, in all this mad confusion. Of all the hundreds Mr. Chesnut has helped in this business of promotion, no one has ever come back to thank him. Indeed, they seem to grow restive under a sense of indebtedness, and attribute their rise to their unaided military merit.

Our cool Captain's too numerous flirtations are shutting up all streets or places to him. He does not know which belle to avoid most strenuously. Still the comedy may turn to a tragedy, with the bullets flying as they are now.

DECEMBER 6th. — The fortunes of war! A fascinating young man left Serena at the door, and I heard a sentimental murmur. "Ah, it will be six long hours 'ere I see you again. Will you write to me?" Then her ringing laugh, and her answer: "A most modest request." So when he came tonight I asked him when he had last heard from his wife and he told me. When he had gone, Serena's cry of amazement: "And the wretch is married!"

Three men of our Foreign Legion have been taken up for an attempt at garrotting. They were heavily manacled and driven with bayonets pointed at their backs up and down the line. They had put barrel shirts * on some others, and they had to march to the tune of "Rogues March." I could not bear to look. The man in the barrel shirt is an Irishman, born in this country. He seemed to feel his degradation cruelly. Another man was bucked, and another was made to ride the wooden horse. When the other men refused to hoot at these poor things as they were driven along, an officer struck several of them with the flat of his sword. Yet these dumb driven cattle are expected to be heroes in the strife, after such treatment. We have shut all the windows of the house on that side.

Captain Bierne, who is an Englishman, and Lieutenant Trezevant and say a dozen or so of them are here every day. They drink tea here every night and often come to breakfast. Molly thinks our hospitality overdone. "Name o' God, young ladies, give me some warning night before they are coming to breakfast, so I may set more rolls and muffins to rise."

* Mrs. Chesnut witnessed some of the punishments normally used for minor military offenses in both armies during the War.

Governor Bonham has issued a proclamation. If we credit it, things are looking brighter for us. I do not see why. I could understand a brightening of our prospects if we had only some men to watch our generals. We could form a Brigade of Generals any day.

Much talk now of politics. Uncle Hamilton said they would not make Mr. Preston Governor. When they found someone was needed to beat Magrath, they wanted to nominate Mr. Chesnut, but Uncle Hamilton firmly declined for him. The girls were furious. It would have been so nice to be the Governor! I told them: "There was no talk of anything more than being candidate for Governor, little goslings; and thank God no one you care for will be in the Governor of South Carolina's shoes just now." "But why?" "He will walk through the Valley of the Shadow of Death!" "Oh, you screech owl!" Then wailed Cassandra: "Such is our fate! Down, down we go, in manners, morals, and common honesty."

When Uncle Hamilton left, we were very tired and it was late; so to bed. A violent knocking, and in tripped Brewster, with his hat on his head, and both hands extended. He was travel-stained, dishevelled, grimy with dirt. The prophet would have had to send him to bathe many times in Jordan before he pronounced him clean. Thus his views: Hood would not turn and pursue Sherman. Thomas was at his heels with forty thousand men, and could have as many more as he wants for the asking. Between Sherman and Thomas, Hood would be crushed; so he was pushing — I do not remember where or what. I know there was no comfort in anything Brewster said.

Serena's account of money spent:

Paper and envelopes	$12.00
Tickets to concert	10.00
Toothbrush	10.00
	$32.00

December 10th. — Sally Rutledge went with me to hunt for Mrs. Dick Anderson. We met a squad of the Foreign Legion, going to guard the Prestons' house. Is that not putting a cat to take care of the cream?

At a party at Isabella's last night the Virginia contingent came out strong. Captain James sings well, and so does Lieutenant Trezevant. While they were playing "Consequences," another accomplishment developed itself. Another James, cleverer still, sketched all of them. When he ought to have written their names, he drew their heads, admirable likenesses. The girls came home radiant, and found Cassandra moaning on the sofa with her shawl over her head.

Allan Green and Joe Barnwell are wounded. Allan has only a flesh wound in his cheek. It may make an ugly scar, but he is in no danger of his life. Joe is wounded in the knee. Allan insisted on going. He said none of his family were handling a musket for his country, and he could not stand it. The struggle at Honey Hill was a fierce one. Militia do not often stand, and they had elected their officers only the night before the fight. General Chesnut sent Stephen Barnwell to take command of them, but after they had elected their own officers he returned to his own troops.

DECEMBER 12th. — Everybody comes to tea at my house, and every evening, I think. At twelve o'clock I turned them all out, and announced my fixed determination to do so every night. "No more words will be needed. I will say 'twelve o'clock,' and you must go, hereafter." And now the young ones are in bed, and I am wide awake.

It is an odd thing. In all my life how many persons have I seen in love? Not a half-dozen, and yet I am a tolerably close observer, a faithful watcher of men and manners. Society has been for me only an enlarged field for character study. Flirtation is the business of society. That is playing at love-making; it begins in vanity, it ends in vanity. It is spurred on by idleness and a want of any other excitement. Flattery is dashed backwards and forwards, because it is so soothing to self conceit. But it begins and ends in vanity, though vexation of spirit does sometimes supervene. They may burn their fingers, playing with fire; but there are no hearts broken. Each party in a flirtation has secured a sympathetic listener to whom they can talk of themselves and who for the time admires them exclusively. It is a pleasant but very foolish game — and so to bed.

William Evans was here tonight. I asked him why in the House he is always looking up in the galleries? "My future daughters-in-law may be there. I am speculating as to that. I have four sons, no daughters." At any rate, that was an original way of accounting for attentions to pretty girls.

Mrs. Bartow was here with her budget of news. Old Box-plaits went to Richmond for an office for his son, or himself, or maybe both. He did not get it, and he has joined the malignants. Cleburne and Gist are killed. General Hardee telegraphed to Richmond asking whether General Lovell might be recalled to service. Answer: "No." Fancy Mrs. Bartow's face as she told us of this snub to Berrien Lovell;

Mrs. Bartow, *née* Berrien. She went on: "And Mr. Lovell brought us such good news. He said Savannah was safe, that we have men enough there, that Dick Taylor was behind Sherman with another Army."

"Where did he get it?" from the irrepressible Isabella. "How these people manufacture men in buckram. Do you wonder New Orleans fell, with this sanguine person in command of it?"

Had a note from Sue King, and went to Nickerson's to see her; and then I had to walk home this freezing day in slippers, had to get out and send the carriage to the coach maker's. Something the matter with one wheel made it unsafe. At Nickerson's I had a glimpse of hotel life in war times. I saw little Hill, who ought to be staying with me as indeed her father thinks she is; but I see now how life at my house would pall upon her after this free and easy existence. It was an exciting scene, that hotel drawing-room. I fancied some of the men — whose wives I knew — drew away an inch or two, when they saw me, from the sirens beside whom they were lolling on sofas. I do not wonder now that the Department girls living at these Hotels get themselves talked about. The degree of familiarity and intimacy between our noted Legislators and some of these women whose names are in everybody's mouth was unconsciously and frankly exhibited to us. I walked across the room and took my seat by the one most maligned of all. I wanted to show them, there and then, that I did not believe a word of their vile stories.

Hood and Thomas have had a fearful fight, with carnage and the loss of generals excessive in proportion to numbers. That means they were leading, urging their men up to the enemy. One of Mr. Chesnut's sins, thrown in his teeth by the Legislature of South Carolina, was that he procured the promotion of Gist — State's Rights Gist — by his influence in Richmond. What have these comfortable stay-at-home patriots to say of General Gist now!

And how could a man die better than facing fearful odds?

Sue King dropped in and found Mrs. Anderson was to stay to tea. She at once borrowed the carriage to rush home and array herself gorgeously for the fray. My mature matrons unbosomed themselves bravely. They are all as old as I am. Said Isabella: "Their style is the unenclothesed common." We had an excellent salad and sandwiches, the best of old sherry, and eggnog. The young crew, fenced off in another room, had cake and lemonade served out to them.

Plain talk between Sue and me. She spoke of a girl who was said to have refused an old lover, though she was openly and shamelessly in love with him, defiantly in love. "She was *that* willing!" She (Sue) then offered to give the last touch to my salad dressing, for which she has a light hand. As we came back to the drawing-room, I said: "Oh Sue, keep on that shawl!" "Why?" "Well, such shoulders, etc., all bare, makes you look *that* willing; too willing, you know." "Willing for what?" she said angrily. "Another husband," I retorted; and yet I am as afraid of her as death!

Wilmot DeSaussure came to see me, fresh from General Chesnut's camp, and says he is in the saddle from six in the morning until six at night. "What is the use? They will not concentrate men enough to block Sherman's way!" From the girls: "Oh Aunty, don't fret so!" I do not think these girls, or the First Foreign Contingent who haunt my house, ever give Sherman a thought. They are light-hearted and happy as the days are long.

Somebody came in while I had the Lovell-Anderson-King coalition here with a message from Captain Bacon. He could not come because he had a sick baby. Sue King found that a very amusing message. "Women have babies, men only have children!" Then she added: "But it is natural, he wants to save his little Bacon."

Another fort has fallen. Good-bye Savannah! Our Governor announces himself a follower of Joe Brown of Georgia. Another famous Joe!

DECEMBER 19th. — The deep waters are closing over us; and we in this house are like the outsiders at the time of the Flood. We eat, drink, laugh, dance, in lightness of heart!

Savannah was a second Vicksburg business. Troops that could have been so useful in the outside swamps were kept there to capitulate.* When they found they could not hold the place, why did they not silently decamp and come up here? Dr. Trezevant came to tell me the dismal news. How he piled on the agony: desolation, mismanagement, despair; General Young, with the flower of Hampton's cavalry, still in Columbia because horses cannot be found to mount them. Neither the Governor of Georgia nor the Governor of South Caorlina is moving hand or foot. They have given up. Eight hundred such cavalry as Young's might make a change in this campaign, but the country is demoralized. Our Legislature is debating State's Rights and the encroachments of the Confederate Government, with an occasional fling backwards at the Governor and Council; the much abused

* Savannah did not fall till a few days later.

Council who wanted to train the militia, and fortify Columbia, and who did put Negroes to work on fortifications.

Our Governor, Isabella says, was most theatrically inaugurated yesterday.

The Yankees claim another victory for Thomas. I hope it may prove like most of their victories, all brag and bluster. I can't say why — maybe I am benumbed — but I do not feel so intensely miserable. I heard the girls, as Smith opened the door for them, ask: "Is she lying on the sofa with a shawl wrapped around her head?" "Yes'm!" "Then let us run for it!" And they dashed upstairs.

Mrs. F—— (the mother of the too-famous beauty, Boozer) according to Captain James, has left her husband. She has been married three times, and yet by all showing she did not begin to marry soon enough. Witness the existence of Boozer. She is a beauty, that none can deny; and they say she is a good girl.

"But why does she not marry some decent man, among the shoals who follow her, and be off out of this tangle while she has a shred of reputation left?" I asked, and echo answered: "Don't you know her engagement to Willie Capers is just broken off because she stole his watch, and some money he had in his pocket, and he found her out and made her give it back to him?" "I do not believe all that! And listen to me. Your fine Foreign Legion gave the first half of the afternoon to her yesterday, as I saw from the window; and then when Boozer drove off, they sauntered up to my party! Not a word, Isabella! I saw it! No lady feels that sort of thing a compliment. It is an insult, that way of dividing time." I was in a fierce indignation. One of the youths was actually disporting himself, with Enie's red ribbon in his buttonhole; his "colors nailed to the mast," as he presumed to say!

How dumbfounded was Captain James, yes and his companions, at my explosion. They only know the prudish American female who would die before she acknowledged that she saw or that she knew of the improper half of the world. But today I relented and sent breakfast to one of the delinquents who I hear is ill in bed.

December 29th. — We went to Camden, but why? Oh, why? The very dismallest Christmas overtook us there. Miss Rhett went with us; a brilliant woman, and very agreeable, which brilliant women are not always. She said: "The world, you know, is composed of men, women, and Rhetts!"

I took a sad farewell look at Mulberry, that I have always hated.

Now I think perhaps I may have been mistaken. It is a magnificent old country seat, old oaks, green lawns and all.

There was a Camden wedding. The girls insisted upon their chaperon wearing velvet, point lace and diamonds. There was another velvet there, so old that it was fashioned "burst bosom"; a mode unknown now to the oldest inhabitant. These people knew so little of the etiquette of society that they left Miss Rhett and myself, the distinguished strangers, alone as they surged in to supper. We walked humbly at the tail of the procession, sustained by point lace and diamonds, defiance and proper pride. It was bitter cold and all the folding doors were thrown open, and the doors leading out into the freezing open air. One of my old friends was wrapped in a snowy swan's-down *sortir de bal*. She looked like a small Alp, and sat resignedly with her hands clasped upon the highest peak! Her devoted husband gave her so much more than she cared for, she graciously asked him to look after the forlorn ones; that is, Miss Rhett and me. For the first time in my life I was nobody.

The wedding guests were divided. We were of the first night. There was a second night, and the second best did not like it. Said Milly C.: "Am I invited to eat up the scraps? Or do they expect me to put on an apron, roll up my sleeves, and help wash the dishes?"

The bride after supper sat in a chair near the center of the room, and the rejoicing bridegroom knelt by her and put his arms around her — chair and all.

Louis Wigfall is here. He is staunch in his faith. "Make Joe Johnston dictator and all will be well." He continued: "Hood is dead, smashed, gone up forever!" Wigfall himself, from whom we hoped so much, has only been destructive.

A reception at my house last night, the Foreign Battalion in full force. These young Virginia FF's refuse to bring their colonel to our house, they say he is not the sort of person for us to know.

JANUARY 7th, 1865. — Trezevant came, looking a woodpecker in his red cap. Captain James sat by me and "talked so sociable" as Yankee Hill says. The Yankees burned a flour mill for him, for which the Confederate Government paid him $28,000. The Yanks ruined his plantation, but he ran off his Negroes in time.

Sherman is at Hardeeville, and Hood in Tennessee, the last of his men not gone — as Louis Wigfall so cheerfully prophesied. Miss Mary Stark said: "I love and honour my President, and I trust my generals!" A steadfast mind like that is something to thank God for. Mrs. McCord is as true and as devoted, but she gave way to furious anger. Half of our Legislature is, she said, reconstructionist.

Yesterday at dinner, just as Serena was about to carve a fat fowl, a message came from Sally Goodwyn to say she was bringing our Virginia Cousin Boykin here tonight. "Take your fork out of that fowl. We will keep it for salad tonight." Smith removed it to a lock-up safe. We sent for Molly to order some cake. She came to the dining-room door with a fiery face, which she wiped with her apron. "Name o' God, Missis, why don't dey ax you dere? It's cook, cook, cook in dis house from daylight till dark. Yo' time is come to be axed somewhere!" She spoke at the top of her voice. "Molly, you forget yourself!" I said in a low tone. " 'Blige to talk dish here way! You'll soon have nothing left for yo'self to eat." "Never mind, the Yankees are coming and I am going to leave you to keep a cheap boarding house here for them." She laughed aloud. "Missis is always running her rigs."

Not by one word or look do these slaves show that they know Sherman and freedom is at hand. They are more obedient and more considerate than ever, to me. Molly's temper was always violent, and as Buck told her, she has no manners whatever, but then she is the best cook, the best dairy maid, the best washerwoman, and the best chambermaid I know; and she will do all that and more, for me. She has an idea people impose on my good nature.

Sally Goodwyn came with nine females, and the Foreign Battalion came *en masse*. About twelve Mr. Martin thundered at my door, an irate Methodist parson as fiercely angry as such a reverent person ever allows himself to be. As he walked off with his brood I could hear him scold until his growls died away in the distance. It was not all on one side however. He cannonaded in his deep tones; but they shrilly fired back, resolutely, shot for shot.

Enie was gone for a half-hour today to the dentist. Her teeth are of the whitest and most regular, simply perfection, but she fancied it was better to have a dentist look in her mouth before she went back to the mountains. For that look she paid three hundred and fifty dollars Confederate money.

Mars' Kit stopped at our door. "How do you like Hood's defeats?" "They will hardly hurt us more than Johnston's victories. Johnston was tolling them here. Hood has at least stopped Thomas's half of them for awhile in Tennessee."

Brewster was here and stayed till midnight. He described Sherman's march of destruction and desolation. "Sherman leaves a track fifty miles wide upon which there is no living thing to be seen," said Brewster, before he departed. His "Me and General Hood" is no longer comic.

By special request of the town authorities, the Foreign Battalion is ordered away from Columbia. Yesterday, General Preston dined with us and in the afternoon I went with him to dress parade. Their Colonel had to be introduced to me. He and I walked immediately in front of General Preston, looking like two small steam tugs towing a seventy-four-gun ship, we so small, the General so large. They presented arms, and all that, in our honour.

Allan Green said there was a report in the street that Hood was killed, and there was great rejoicing. Sherman will soon disturb the skulkers, hiding here to rejoice at the death of one of our own Generals!

At the Bazaar, General Joe Johnston came up to speak to me. We had a very pleasant conversation. As he walked away, Sally fairly raved about "his noble brow," and Lieutenant Governor McCord, who had listened to our conversation, remarked that a change has come over the spirit of our dream. "Two thirds of the South Carolina Legislature openly avows, other things being equal, that for any office in their gift they prefer a man who is not a soldier. They are awfully tired of soldiers!" So now the fever fit is over and the chill sets in.

"The dirty dogs! The dastards!" howled Isabella. "Never mind, our real men are all in the army!" "Yes, lying stark as stone, in bloody graves." "And what for?" moaned a childless mother.

Sue King will have it she is engaged to Beauregard. She showed his letters and his photograph. Incredulous we were, and openly pronounced the photograph proof worth nothing. Anybody can get that for a small pile of Confederate money. It is in every shop window. Then she took a letter from her pocket. This we read. It was written in the French language. He was kind, and awfully civil. It was the very politest of letters, but there was no love or marriage in it that I could see!

JANUARY 10th. — So much talk, pro and con, of Joe Johnston. You do the Anabasis business when you want to get out of the enemy's country, and the Thermopylae business when they want to get into your country; but we retreated in our own country, and we gave up our mountain passes without a blow! To lose men in good battle brings some comfort. As old Tarquin said, for what were men born but to die for their country. Nobody laments the loss of an arrow if it hits the mark. But there's the rub. In one group today, Mrs. McCord and Mrs. Goodwyn had lost each a son, and Mrs. McCord her only one. Some had lost their husbands, brothers, sons. The thought that their lives had been given up in vain retreating was very bitter to them. The besoms of destruction had swept over every family there.

To the station to see the Foreign Battalion depart. The girls stood up in my wagon and the young officers ran around like beggars, each determined to have the last touch of their fair hands. It was a mad scene, as much hand-shaking as at a Presidential reception. They are gone and not a day too soon; for all the jewelry, silver, etc., stolen from General Hampton's house was found in the tent of one of the soldiers. But it was the splendid young officers, high-born, high-spirited, handsome, agreeable, broad-shouldered, golden-haired, with a complexion as rosy as the dawn, whom I feared; not the rogues and deserters who made up the rank and file.

But last night it was *Le roi est mort, vive le roi!* For the room was crowded with an indefatigable new set of admirers. These fine fellows have been wounded, some are married, and they seem as utterly oblivious of the volcano we stand upon as our girls themselves. Many of them are officers passing through from one command to another. We tolerate nobody in this house but men who have done their duty. A man must wear Confederate uniform, and must have done his due share of fighting, to find favour with this bevy of high-spirited young beauties. These poor fellows are nearly all palpably wounded soldiers.

JANUARY 14th. — Yesterday I broke down and gave way to abject terror under the news of Sherman's advance — and no news of my husband. Today, wrapped up on the sofa, too dismal even to moan, there was a loud knock. Shawls and all, I rushed to the door. Telegram from my husband. "All well. Be at home on Tuesday." It was dated from Adam's Run. I felt as light-hearted as if the war were over. Then I looked at the date-line, Adam's Run! So this ends as it began; Bull's Run, from which their first sprightly running astounded the world, and now Adam's Run.* If we run, who are to run? They ran

* An even more striking coincidence: The first skirmish at Bull's Run occurred on a farm owned by Wilmer McLean, who later became a major in the Confederate army. Lee's surrender to Grant, four years later, took place in a house owned by Major McLean, at Appomattox Court House.

full-handed; but we have fought until maimed soldiers and women and children are all that are left to run.

Today, Kershaw's Brigade, or what is left of it, passed through. Oh, the shouts that greeted it, and the bold shouts of thanks it returned. Our soldiers are not demoralized. Their shouts as they go by gladden my heart.

I went to hear Mr. Palmer, to have my heart lifted up and my hands strengthened; but no, he was demonstrating natural history and family relations from a physical and a Biblical point of view. He was just on the verge, always, of frightful moral and indecent precipices. One difficulty is that in church such unpleasant topics are broached, one does not know where to look. "Sit and stare blankly at the parson, even if he forgets he is a man. You must try and forget it too! Think of him only as a parson," cries the irrepressible.

I opened by mistake a strange letter. As my beautiful niece went off, she said: "Any letters for me, open them. We are expecting mother's final decision, go or stay." When she came back, I had been struck dumb. The letter was in the Precious Darling style, as easy and as affectionate as if this boy had been her betrothed lover for years; and yet we barely knew him. It was directed to my care. She took the letter calmly and read it aloud, not omitting one expression of his fatuous and excessive lovesickness. What a cruel ordeal for her! But she is a proud soul and brave, and she wanted to clear her skirts of complicity. Then Smith ushered in Lieutenant Trezevant, with her red ribbon still in his buttonhole. There was that in his eye, and a hardly repressed smile about his mouth, that made me suspect he had heard my savage comments on this self-complacent love letter. Mr. Trezevant opened the conversation by an anecdote. He had just caught Miss—— at the corner of a back street, reading to a group of friends a love letter which the Miss had concocted for one of their number too shy to write for himself. Miss—— denied the charge that it was poor ——'s letter which she was reading to amuse her friends, but Trezevant knew it — as he had written it himself.

Here was food for thought, after he left us. "That wretch wrote them all. He is a good artillery officer, and calculated where his bomb would explode. He ran up from Kingsville and his luck was wonderful! The bomb actually burst — well, so to speak, in his face."

A man came for Kate's children, but they will not go. "Oh, Auntie, we are having such a good time! We cannot go!" If Kate could see that letter!

My small drawing-room is crammed to its utmost limit, and I am so weary, so full of care, so utterly discomfitted, so stupid, so dead. How can I bear it?

Mary sent Lieutenant Trezevant a pair of gloves. He came last night and said gayly: "I sent you no answer. I dared not risk the shortest note. Of late I have chanced to hear — or overhear — letters so laughed at that I have fairly shuddered to think such a fate might be mine someday."

Today they say Sherman has recrossed into Georgia, and that Hood is between Sherman and Thomas. So go to work the upper and the nethermost milestones.

JANUARY 16th. — My husband is at home, but for how long I do not know; his aids fill the house, and a group of hopelessly wounded haunt the place. It rains a flood, freshet after freshet. The forces of nature are befriending us, for our enemies have to make their way through swamps.

A month ago my husband wrote me a letter which I promptly suppressed, after showing it to Mrs. McCord. He warned us to make ready, for the end had come. It was what we could not bring ourselves to believe; and now he thinks, with the railroad all blown up and the swamps made impassable by freshets (which have no time to subside, so constant is the rain) if we had but an army to seize the opportunity, much might be done. No troops, that is the real trouble!

We seem utterly without a head down here, utterly at sea. If some heaven-born genius would rush in and take command! The pilot in calm weather lets any boy toy with his rudder, but when the winds howl and the waves rise, he seizes the helm himself. And our pilot? Where is he?

Today Mrs. McCord exchanged $16,000 Confederate bills for gold, $300. The Bazaar will be a Belshazzar affair. The handwriting is on the wall. Miss Garnett wailed: "I fear the very worst before they find out — those stupid Yankees — that I am Irish!" The fears of old maids increase in proportion to their age and infirmities and hideous ugliness.

Isabella, white and shining, resplendent in apparel, has gone down to Millwood. "If you mourn as loudly now," she says, "You leave yourself no margin for proper affliction when the time comes."

JANUARY 17th. — The Bazaar opens today. Sherman marches always! All the railroads are smashed, and if I laugh at any mortal thing, it is so that I may not weep. Generals are as plenty as blackberries, but they have no one to command.

"What a blessing that quire of dingy Confederate paper is to Auntie," say the girls. Well, you quit crying about what you write about. The agony of finding a rhyme would divert any sorrow. Borrowing rhymes to sorrowing, pluck to luck, Fibs to Gibbes, laugh to quaff. Gather you roses while you may, old time will still be flying! That's my motto.

In a republic, a general ought to have a staff who can write him up. Newspapers lead public opinion, and their pets win fame when they lose a battle, because it was always somebody's fault in the war office.

Here is startling news. Politely but firmly, the Virginia Legislature requests Jeff Davis and all of his cabinet to resign. Breckenridge is to take Seddon's portfolio. He will be War Minister. If we had had Breckenridge in Walker's place at the beginning, what a difference it might have made; Walker, who ruined us almost before we were underway. Clay of Alabama is responsible for that Walker, for Manassas and all that stupidity in not following up victory.

Isabella came. She says: "These infatuated people are talking of a dancing school, and they want our Cassandra to give a strawberry festival! "For what, oh ye fatuous folk?"

I gave thirty dollars for a bottle of cologne, and fifty for a little French mustard pot; this at the Bazaar.

The town is swarming with troopless generals, Joe Johnston, Lovell, Governor Manning, etc. My husband dines out every day, to meet this lordly party. Now he has gone again. He is rarely here for many days at a time.

At church today, a great railroad character was called out of church. He soon returned and whispered something to Joe Johnston, and they went out together. Somehow the whisper moved around to us. "Sherman is at Branchville."

My husband saw Kate's son, Miller Williams, aged ten, stick on so manfully when the pony tried so hard to throw him that in his pleasure at the boy's fine riding he made him a present of the pony. So now there is one perfectly happy creature in the Southern Confederacy. Miller is to ride his horse up to Flat Rock, in company with Mr. Blake and Mr. Lowndes. Miller tells us in confidence that but for himself and a Negro named Scipio, he does not think they could ever drive all of those horses to Flat Rock.

Hood came yesterday. He is staying at the Prestons', and they sent for us. What a heart-felt greeting he gave us. He can stand well enough without his crutch, but he does very slow walking. How plainly he spoke out these dreadful words. "My defeat and discomfiture!" "My army is destroyed." "My losses!" He said he had nobody to blame but himself.

Isabella, who adores Hood, said: "Maybe you attempted the impossible!" Then she began one of her funniest stories. Sam did not listen. Jack Preston touched me, and we slipped away unobserved into the piazza. "He did not hear a word she was saying. He had forgotten us all. Did you notice how he stared in the fire, and the livid spots which came out on his face, and the huge drops of perspiration that stood out on his forehead?" "Yes, he is going over some bitter hours. He sees Willie Preston, with his heart shot away. He feels the panic at Nashville, and its shame." "And the dead on the battlefield at Franklin, they say that was a dreadful sight," said tender-hearted Jack with a shiver. "And that agony in his face comes again and again. I can't keep him out of those absent fits. It is pretty trying to anyone who has to look on. When he looks in the fire and forgets me, and seems going through in his own mind the torture of the damned, I get up and come out as I did just now." *

Jimmy Dick Hill's carriage was put at the General's service, and he came for us to drive with him, and gave us his reason for asking to be relieved. The Virginia Legislature asked to have Joe Johnston put back in command. That was equivalent to a vote of censure. Hood asked to be sent across the Mississippi, to bring all the troops from there. They might save us still. Then he wants to be in Richmond by the 8th of February. That was his lucky day, he says, and blushes like a girl. After all he is a queer compound.

Brewster left General Hood's wedding clothes here in a trunk, six months ago. Johnny said then: "Why don't he put them on his back and go and be married? If he will not when he may, when he will, he shall have nay! There will be no wedding! You will see. He lost his chance last winter! He made his siege too long! He grew tedious, and since then — too much raw licking!" Thus the cool Captain, who sees more than most persons, with those stony blue eyes of his.

* Franklin, which may fairly be called — like Gettysburg — a drawn battle, was marked by a charge as desperate, and more bloody, than Pickett's; Nashville was a Confederate rout, the enemy having a three-to-one superiority.

The Bazaar lags. It is superfluous, now.

A telegram from Beauregard today to my husband. He does not know whether Sherman means to advance on Branchville, Charleston, or Columbia. Governor Magrath and General Winder talk of preparations for a defence of Columbia. If Beauregard can't stop Sherman down there, what have we got here to do it with?

General Lee is Generalissimo of all our forces. That comes rather late, when we have no forces.

The London Times ridicules us for being such fools as to suppose they would recognize our independence if we abolished slavery. The United States of America is England's sole real rival on earth. Some day she will bitterly repent her lost opportunity. This was her chance to cripple her mortal foe.

Last night, General Hampton came in. I am sure he would do something to save us, if he were put in supreme command here. As it is, he takes no interest, for he has no power. He says Joe Johnston is equal to if not superior to Lee as a commanding officer. Law me! He has not quite forgiven Lee yet that cruel blow to his vanity.

Janney, the hotel man, kept exhorting General Chesnut to seize horses and mount his men — which looked more like a preparation to run than a wish to stand and defend. Finally the true object of his visit came out. He wanted to know if the time had come to pack his valuables and move his females.

That work I have underway. My silver is in a box and delivered for safekeeping to Isaac McLaughlin, who is really my beau ideal of a grateful Negro. I mean to trust him. My husband cares for none of these things now. He lets me do as I please.

A man came who had been detailed for some arduous duty. He wanted to get off from it, and he rattled off his ailments with the glib fluency of a vendor of quack medicines. When he saw General Chesnut's unmoved air, he added: "My daughter is about to have typhoid fever." They made short work of him; and after he was gone, they called him a pusillanimous, lying dog. Mr. Chesnut was not rude to this man, and I kept from laughing at his catalogue of ills, but it was hard.

FEBRUARY 10th. — I have been too tormented to write. Now we are all soon to leave Columbia. Yesterday General Lovell dined here, and then they went to poor old Winder's funeral. Well, Winder is safe from the wrath to come. General Lovell said that if the Yankees had ever caught Winder, it would have gone hard with him.*

Such a nice dinner we had, but at a certain hour General Chesnut had to be off to the funeral, so he sent Mat for his horse, and then he sent Smith off on an errand. Neither returned, and after General Chesnut departed, I had to go and look up somebody. Molly remained in the kitchen and took so long to make herself decent that General Lovell excused himself for not being able to wait any longer. I rushed out again to hurry Molly with that nice pudding, but when I came back, the men were all putting on their hats and swords in the entry, and away they went. Who could stand all that upsetting delay at a regular dinner?

The children are gone, and I have a letter from them, so gay, signed "Small Fry." I copy only a sample:

Mrs. General, Commanding Corps
Reserved Young Ladies.

Dear Mrs. General:

I have the honour to inform you of the safe arrival of the retreating column sent to this place by your order; the right wing of my force being placed under command of General Conversation, the left under General Circumspection, the centre being led by General Indifference.

In this manner we passed safely through the enemy's lines. The column under the command of Princess Brighteyes met with more varied fortune. Soon after leaving Columbia, skirmishing commenced on the right and left; but with her usual tact, she parried all attacks and reached Newberry without damage, where we halted and bivouacked for the night.

An effort was made there by Lieutenant General Breakheart (one of the enemy's most skilful commanders) to take her by surprise; the attack however was repulsed with skill.

In the morning of the next day the march was resumed in order. Through the day the Princess was much harassed by General Breakheart, but being aided by General Recollection and Captain Handsome of the Reserves, she succeeded in reaching Greenville, having sustained slight loss of ammunition, colours and commissary stores. The loss of the latter was very seriously felt before reaching our destination.

* General Winder, a Maryland man, beginning as head of the military police in Richmond and eventually having charge of all Confederate prisons east of the Mississippi, had bitter enemies South as well as North.

At that place the enemy asked for time to bury his dead. The Princess then held a council of war; and knowing her foe to be determined, skillful and with great experience in this kind of warfare, she decided with her usual prudence and foresight to evacuate that town before her plans were known. At four o'clock in the morning the retreat commenced, and was so silently conducted that not a suspicion of it was entertained until hours afterwards.

So they reached Flat Rock, in spite of snow in the mountains, and muddy roads. The letter goes on in the same vein of happy foolery.

Since our arrival here, General Breakheart has brought some heavy guns to bear on the fortress. These projectiles are of extreme length and are composed on the outer surface of paper and ink.

But at least, they are at home, and in Kate's hands. Yet how can they jest? Are the young never afraid?

Tom Archer died almost as soon as he got to Richmond. Prison takes the life out of them. He was only half alive here. He had a strange pallid look and such a vacant stare, until you roused him. Poor, pretty Sally Archer; that is the end of you.

XXI

Lincolnton, N. C.

February 16th, 1865. — My ideas of those last days in Columbia are confused. The Martins left the Friday before I did, and their Mammy refused to go with them. That daunted me. Then Mrs. McCord, who was to send her girls with me, changed her mind. She sent them upstairs in her house and actually took away the staircase; at least that was her plan.

Then I met Christopher Hampton arranging to take away his sisters. They were flitting, but only as far as Yorkville. He said it was time to move on. Sherman was at Orangeburg, barely a day's journey from Columbia, and he left a track as blackened as a fire in the prairies.

So my time had come too. My husband urged me to go home. He said Camden would be safe enough, that they had no spite to that old town as they have to Charleston and Columbia. Molly too. She came in, weeping and wailing, wiping her red-hot face with her cook's grimy apron. She said I ought to go among our own black people on the plantation. They would take care of me better than anyone else.

So I agreed to go to Mulberry, or to the Hermitage plantation, and sent Lawrence with a wagon load of my valuables. Then a Miss Patterson called, a refugee from Tennessee. She had been in a country overrun by Yankee invaders, and she described so graphically all the horrors to be endured by those subjected to fire and sword and rapine and plunder that I was fairly scared, and I determined to come here.

This is a thoroughly out-of-all-routes place, and yet I can go to Charlotte. I am halfway to Kate at Flat Rock and there is no Federal army between me and Richmond. As soon as my mind was finally made up, we telegraphed Lawrence, who had barely got to Camden in the wagon when the telegram was handed to him. So he took the train and came back, and Mr. Chesnut sent him with us to take care of the party.

We thought that no matter how loyal the Negroes were to us, they could not protect me from an army bent upon sweeping us from the face of the earth; and if they tried to do so, so much the worse for the poor things. So I left them to shift for themselves, as they are accustomed to do, and I took the same liberty. My husband does not care a fig for the property question, and never did. Perhaps if he had ever known poverty, it would be different. Now he says he has only one care, that I should be safe and not so harassed with dread. And then there is his blind old father: "A man can always die like a patriot and a gentleman," he said. "With no fuss! It is hard not to envy those who are out of all this — their difficulties ended." "Who?" "Those who have met death gloriously on the battlefield. Their doubts are all solved!"

After New Orleans, those vain passionate impatient little Creoles were forever committing suicide, driven to it by despair and "Beast" Butler. As he read of these things, Mr. Davis once said: "If they want to die, why not kill 'Beast Butler,' rid the world of their foe, and be saved the trouble of murdering themselves." However, that practical way of ending their intolerable burden did not seem to occur to them.

I repeated this suggestive anecdote to our horde of Generals without troops. This very distinguished party rode superb horses and rode to the lines every day. They congregated at our house. They laid their fingers on the maps spread out on the table and pointed out where Sherman was going and where he could be stopped. They argued over their plans eloquently. Every man Jack of them had a safe plan to stop Sherman if . . .

Even Beauregard and Lee were expected, but Grant had double-teamed on Lee. Lee could not save his own; how can he come to save us? Read the list of the dead in those last battles around Richmond and Petersburg, if you want to break your heart.

I took French leave of Columbia, slipped away without a word to anybody. Isaac Hayne and Mr. Chesnut came down to the Charlotte depot with me. Ellen, my maid, left her husband and only child, but she was willing to come, and very cheerful in her way of looking at it. "Who gwine trouble my William? Dey don't dares to! Claiborne (her husband) kin take good care of William! I never travelled round with Missis before, and I want to go this time!" As for Lawrence, he turned the same unmoved face toward our trunks and luggage. Smith grinned farewell.

A woman fifty years old at least, and uglier than she was old, sharply rebuked my husband for standing at the car window for a few last words with me. She said rudely: "Stand aside sir! I want air!" With his hat off, and his grand air, he bowed politely. "In one moment, Madame. I have something of importance to say to my wife."

She talked aloud, and introduced herself to every man, claiming his protection. She had never travelled alone before in all her life. Old age and ugliness are protective, in such cases. She was ardently patriotic for awhile; then she was joined by her friend, a man as crazy as herself to get out of this. From their talk I gleaned she had been for years in the Department. They were about to cross the lines. The whole idea was to get away from the trouble to come. They were Yankees. Were they spies?

Here in Lincolnton I am broken-hearted, an exile. Such a place. Bare floors. For a featherbed, a pine table and two chairs, I pay $30.00 a day. Such sheets! But I have some of my own. At the door, before I was well out of the hack, the woman of the house packed Lawrence out, neck and heels. She would not have him at any price. She said his clothes were too fine for a Nigger. "His airs indeed!" Poor Lawrence was so humble and silent. He said at last: "Miss Mary, send me back to Mars' James!" I began to look for a pencil to write a note to my husband, and in the flurry could not find it. "Here is one," said Lawrence, producing a gold pencil case. "Go away," she shouted. "I wants no Niggers here with pencils and airs." So Lawrence fled before the storm, but not before he had begged me to go back. "If Mars' Jeems knew how you was treated he'd never be willing for you to stay here."

The Martins had seen my well-known travelling case as the hack trotted up Main Street, and they arrived out of breath. We embraced and wept. I kept my room. After dinner, Ellen presented herself, blue-black with rage. She has lost the sight of one eye, so that it is permanently bluish and opaque. The other flamed fire and fury. "Here's my dinner, a piece of meat, and a whole platefull of raw ungins. I never did eat raw ungins and I won't begin now! Dese here Niggers say dis ole lady give 'em to 'em breakfast and dinner! It's a sin and a shame to do us so. She says I must come outen her kitchen, de Niggers won't work for looking at me. I'se something to look at surely!" She threw down her odorous plate. "She say you bring me and Lawrence here to keep us from running away to de Yankees, and I say: 'Name o' God, ole Missis, if dat's it, what she bring Lawrence and me for? She's got plenty more. Lawrence and me, we ain't nothing to our white people!' "

Then came an invitation to tea at Mrs. Munroe's. We wanted to rent part of Mrs. Munroe's house, but Mrs. Ben Rutledge was before us. Then we tried a Miss McLean. She blew hot and cold, she would and then she would not. I was left utterly uncertain.

Mrs. Munroe's husband has been killed in battle. She has one child, a boy of seven. She comes from Abingdon, Virginia, the home of the Prestons, Floyds, Lewises, and Joe Johnston. The latter is expected here daily, so I am in the regular line of strategic retreat. Mrs. Munroe is a violent abolitionist. Isabella says she never saw a true woman who was not — but Mrs. Munroe is a Yankee sympathizer, and that is one too much for us.

She gave us pound cake at tea, and such nice tea. I forgot my beautiful tea caddy on the mantelpiece at my house in Columbia, and it was filled with English breakfast tea! Gone forever.

The Fants are refugees here. They are Viginians, and have been in exile since Second Manassas. They tried to go back to their own house and found one chimney standing.

The day I left home, I had packed a box of flour, sugar, rice, coffee, etc.; but my husband would not let me bring it. He said I was coming to a land of plenty, to unexplored North Carolina, where the foot of Yankee marauders was unknown. Now I have written to send me that box and many other things by Lawrence or I will starve.

The Middletons have come, and Mrs. Ben Rutledge. They describe the hubbub in Columbia, everybody flying in every direction like a flock of swallows. She heard the enemy's guns booming in the distance. The train no longer runs from Charlotte to Columbia.

Mrs. Reed was in a state of despair. I can well understand that sinking of mind and body the first days, as the abject misery of it all closes upon you. I remember my suicidal tendencies, when I first came here.

Our landlady evinces great repugnance still to Ellen, but we begin to laugh at her tantrums; for we hope to get away.

FEBRUARY 18th. — Here I am, thank God, settled at the McLeans's in a clean, comfortable room, airy and cosy, and with a grateful heart I stir up my own bright wood fire. I was glad to get away from our landlady's sharp tongue. The sight of Ellen acted upon her as a red rag to a bull. My bill for four days at that splendid hotel was $240.00, with $25.00 additional for fire. I tried to propitiate the termagant; I was mild, humble, patient, polite. "Do not waste your time! They will never comprehend the height from which we have fallen," suggested Miss Middleton. They had their own hired house and could move at once.

My kind young landlady is a cousin of the Brevards, Haynes, etc., of South Carolina, and also a near relative of Mrs. Stonewall Jackson and of Mrs. D. H. Hill. Once more my lines have fallen in pleasant places. Miss McLean is one of the beauties, the belles, the heiresses of the place. Think of that! Can North Carolina *haute volée* go further!

As we came up on the train from Charlotte, a soldier took out of his pocket a filthy rag. If it had lain in the gutter for months, it could have been no worse. He unwrapped this cloth carefully and took out two biscuits of the species known as "hard tack"; then he gallantly handed me one, and with an ingratiating smile asked me "to take some." Then he explained: "Please take these two. Swap with me. Give me something softer, that I can eat. I am very weak still." Immediately, for his benefit, my basket of luncheon was emptied; but as for his biscuits, I would not choose any.

Isabella: "But what did you say to him when he poked them under your nose?" "I held up both hands. 'I would not take from you anything that is yours!' Far from it! I would not touch them for worlds."

Today, dirt has given me a black eye. I have fought a hard battle with that dread antagonist, and it is rather a drawn battle. Ellen has my washing to do, as well as my cooking, so I have elected to do some housework. I must needs make my own tea, and I did a tremendous day's work, windows to be washed, and then the brass and irons were green and grimy. After we rubbed them bright, how pretty they were! Miss Middleton thinks they have played tobacco juice around the sides of the wall with a hose! No mortal expectoration could have accomplished such a feat. Ellen tied up her clothes, and with bare feet and legs scrubbed the floor. "He! Misses, this is harder than hoeing corn." I sat on the bedside and watched, after I was too tired to work, but she sent me away. "You go, dat's a good Missis. Put on your bonnet and stay to Miss Isabella's till de flo' dry." I am very docile now, and I obeyed orders.

On the way I met a cousin, male, elderly, a *ci devant* fire eater, nullifier, secessionist, extreme in everything. In Columbia he refused to be seen with his son-in-law, who was not in the army. He was a disciple of Judge Withers, who denounced Mr. Chesnut and the Council when they tried to put the state on a war footing in 1862, interfering with State's Rights and citizen's rights by sending Negroes away from their owners' plantations to work on fortifications. Here he is, this violent hero, fleeing before the face of the Yankees; his wife, his children, his Negroes all banked up in one room. One poor Negro woman was taken ill, so the family had to go and camp in the hotel drawing-room, leaving the poor soul to herself and her sister who nurses her, in the sole chamber the landlady would let them have for love or money. At this day, trying to save property! Any man who stays at home to save property may hang his head! Shame on you, Carolinians, if such there be among you!

FEBRUARY 19th. — Mrs. Rutledge does not understand taking favors, and refused to let Ellen make her some biscuits, blushing violently all the time. I went home and sent her the biscuits all the same, and they were nice ones. A few minutes after, a Negro woman came in who absolutely bakes bread. She brought a not-half-bad loaf in her basket, and when she found how delighted I was, she went for more. I sent her with three good, fresh, well-baked loaves of bread to Mrs. Rutledge. I almost felt we had saved her life.

The Fants say all of the troubles at the Hotel came from our servants' bragging. They represented us as millionaires, the Middleton men servants smoked segars, Mrs. Reed's averred he had never done anything in his life but stand behind his master at table with a silver waiter in his hand. So they charged us accordingly; but perhaps she did not get the best of us after all, for we paid her in Confederate money, and Ellen's onions — albeit raw — really were onions, which can't be said of our money. Now they won't take Confederate money in the shops here, and how are we to live? Miss Middleton says quartermasters' families are all clad in good gray cloth, but the soldiers are naked. Well, we are like the families of whom the novels always say, poor but honest. In fact, we are well-nigh beggars, for I do not know where my next meal is to come from. Now we know "Bread is the staff of life." I will never forget my joy at the sight of that loaf!

Mrs. Martin says: "Only genius can create something out of nothing. Neither Lee or Wellington could work without material. Genius, like love, pays its own expenses. Stonewall was one genius; he was inspired, some say a little mad. We had the best fighting material in the world, but it was not properly handled and our men could only die!"

Ellen was singing "Massa's in de cold, cold ground." I almost screamed: "Stop, Ellen! Sing something else!" Isabella was with me. "Well, most of them are," she said.

L—— has lost a leg, so he is a hero. A few years ago it was thought almost a sacrilege that he dared challenge William Shannon — who has now, for three years, been safely housed in a bomb-proof job as a bank president, paying himself three thousand dollars a year in gold, while all the rest of Confederate mankind are starving and dying before the enemy's guns.

February 22nd. — Isabella has been reading my diaries. How we laugh at my sage ratiocinations all come to naught, my famous insight into character proved utter folly. The diaries were lying on the hearth ready to be burned, but she told me to hold on, to wait awhile.

Afterwards we were taking a walk and General Joseph E. Johnston joined us. He explained to us all of Lee's and Stonewall Jackson's mistakes. He was radiant and joyful, but we had nothing to say. How could we? He always impresses me with the feeling that all of his sympathies are on the other side. Still he was neither gruff nor rude today, as he can be when he chooses. He said he was very angry at being ordered to take command again. He might well be in a rage, this on-and-offing is enough to bewilder the coolest head.

My husband writes from Charlotte. He came near being taken prisoner in Columbia, for he was asleep on the morning of the 17th, when the Yankees blew up the railroad depot. That woke him, of course. He found everybody had left Columbia, and the town was surrendered by the mayor, Colonel Goodwyn. Hampton and his command had been gone several hours. Isaac Hayne came away with General Chesnut. There was no fire in the town when they came away. They overtook Hampton's command at Meek's Mill. That night, from the hills where they encamped, they saw the fire and knew the Yankees were burning the town, as we had every right to expect they would.

Molly was left in charge of everything, including Mrs. Preston's cow — which I was milking — and Sally Goodwyn's furniture.

Charleston and Wilmington are surrendered. I have no further use for a newspaper. I never want to see another one as long as I live.

Wade Hampton is made Lieutenant General, but it is too late. If he had been made Lieutenant General and given the command in South Carolina six months ago, I believe he would have saved us. But Achilles was sulking in his tent — and at such a time!

Shame, disgrace, beggary, all at once. They are hard to bear.

Grand Smash!

Rain! Rain outside! Inside, naught but drowning floods of tears. I could not bear it, so I rushed down in that rain storm to the Martins'. He met me at the door. "Madame, Columbia is burned to the ground." I bowed my head and sobbed aloud. "Stop that," he said, trying to speak cheerfully. "Come here, Wife. This woman cried with her whole heart, just as she laughs!" But in spite of his words, his voice broke down; he was hardly calmer than myself.

FEBRUARY 23rd. — I want to get to Kate. I am so utterly heartbroken. I hope John Chesnut and General Chesnut may at least get into the same army. We seem scattered over the face of the earth. Isabella sits there calmly reading. May our Heavenly Father look down on us and have pity.

Mrs. Johnston told me that somebody at the north — sister, aunt, cousin — had sent Mrs. Wigfall one of those dollars * which she at once exchanged for twenty-eight thousand Confederate dollars — and that the Wigfalls were now living like fighting cocks.

"By this time they wish they had not changed that gold," said Isabella.

They say I was the last refugee who came from Columbia; that is, the last allowed to enter the doors of the cars. Government took charge, and women could only be smuggled in by the windows. Stout ones stuck, and had to be pushed, pulled and hauled in by main force. Dear Mrs. Izard, with all her dignity, was subjected to this rough treatment. She was found almost too much for the size of car windows.

FEBRUARY 25th. — The Pfeifers, who live opposite, are descendants of those Pfeifers who came South with Mr. Chesnut's ancestors after the Fort Duquesne disaster. They have been driven out of Eden — the Valley of Virginia — once before; and they may have to go again. This Pfeifer is the great man, the rich man *par excellence* of Lincolnton. They say that it was with something very near unto tears in his eyes that he heard of our latest defeats. "It is only a question of time with us now," he said. "The raiders will come, you know."

General and Mrs. Johnston stay at the Pfeifers'. Mrs. Johnston remarked that she would never own slaves. "I might say the same thing," I replied. "I never would. Mr. Chesnut does, but he hates all slavery,

* This is the word in Mrs. Chesnut's manuscript. It is certainly a mistake — but for a ten-dollar gold piece, at that time, $28,000 Confederate would not have been far out of line, especially in rural North Carolina.

especially African slavery." "Why do you say 'African'?" "Why, to distinguish that form from the inevitable slavery of the world. All married women, all children and girls who live on in their father's houses are slaves!" She was startled. She said Johnston was in the very devil of a bad humour, saying that he was only put back in command so that he would be the one to surrender. She was bitter against Columbia, and I knew she detested me, but I am a philosopher and I found her vastly agreeable and entertaining. In Washington, before I knew any of them except by sight, Mrs. Davis, Mrs. Emory and Mrs. Johnston were always together, inseparable friends; and the trio were pointed out to me as the cleverest women in the United States. Now that I do know them all — well, I think the world was right in its estimate of them.

My friend Mrs. Mason said: "Lydia Johnston will laugh at you, no matter how friendly you may find her." "Is she singular in that? I laugh at everybody friend or foe."

Today I was telling Mrs. Johnston the first time I ever heard the word "nigger" used by people *comme il faut*. Now it is in everybody's mouth, but I have never become accustomed to it.

Mrs. Munroe came in to warn me that Mrs. Johnston did not like me, sneered at my prejudices against slavery, said: "I wonder when she took to that dodge," etc. Mrs. Munroe could not understand my lack of indignation. I handed her what I had written. "You see, I knew all about it." But now I cannot go there again. She must be awfully dismal, left to the Pfeifers.

I met a Mrs. Ancrum, of a serenely cheerful aspect, happy and hopeful. "It's all right now," she said, "Sherman is sure to be thrashed, since Joe Johnston is in command." Johnston, surrendering his command to Hood, said with a smile: "I hope you will be able to stop Sherman. It was more than I could do." General Johnston is not of Mr. Ancrum's way of thinking as to his own powers, for he stayed here several days after he was ordered to the front. He must have known he could do no good — and I am of his opinion. General Johnston actually thinks Mr. Davis would sacrifice wife, children, country and God to satisfy his hate of Joe Johnston. I think it awfully conceited of Johnston to feel himself worthy of so much presidential hate.

Heaven is helping us weep, rain, rain, rain. It has rained for six months.

Yesterday, the wagon in which I was to go to Flat Rock drove up to the door, covered with a tent-like white cloth. Ellen flew to me. "Oh

Missis, for the love of the Lord, don't go off in that there thing! Poke your head out of the end of that wagon and you'll be po' buckra for true. I don't min' rain, not an ole brass cent; but you gwine lef boxes and trunks here, an you lef boxes and trunks in Richmond full o' good clothes, and you lef ever so much in Columbia, and it all done burn up. For Lord sake, Missis, go home an stay dere, 'stead of keep running round 'stributing your things everywhere."

"Ellen, they say we have no home." She threw her apron over her head and howled. The man who owned the wagon was standing in the door. I asked him to walk in, and told Ellen to walk out. I asked the man his name. He showed great hesitation in giving it. At last: "My name is Sherman, and now I see by your face that you won't go with me. My name is against me, these times." Here he grinned. "But at least you would leave Lincolnton." The name was the last drop in my cup, but I gave him Mrs. Glover's reason for staying here. General Johnston told her this might be the safest place of all, after all; for he thinks the Yankees are making straight for Richmond and General Lee's rear, and that they will go by Camden and Lancaster, leaving Lincolnton on their west flank.

The McLeans are kind people. They ask no rent for their rooms, only $20.00 a week for firewood. Twenty dollars! And such dollars, mere waste paper!

Mrs. Munroe took up my photograph book. I have one of all the Yankee Generals. "I want to see the men who are to be our masters." "Not mine, thank God! This was a free fight. We had as much right to fight to get out as they had to fight to keep us in. If they try to play the masters, anywhere upon the habitable globe I will go, never to see a Yankee; and if I die on the way so much the better."

Then I sat down and wrote to my husband, words so much worse than anything I can put in this book; and as I wrote I was blinded by tears of rage. Indeed I nearly wept myself away. In vain. Years, death, depopulation, bondage, fears; these have all been borne.

Governor Vance took a fling at us South Carolinians in his speech. He said we were bound to start this thing, the devil could not stop us, we boasted we were ready to shed the last drop of our blood, to die in the last ditch — etc. And now: "The Yankee rate of march through South Carolina is pretty lively, after such promises." Shame! Shame! But Mrs. Glover endorsed the sentiments of Vance. She said she told everyone she was a North Carolinian, and that her father really is one.

FEBRUARY 26th — Mrs. Munroe offered me religious books, which I declined. I am already provided with the Lamentations of Jeremiah, the Penitential Psalms of David, the denunciations of Isaiah, and above all the patient wail of Job. Job is my comforter now!

And yet I would be so thankful to know that my husband is well, and ordered to join the Great Retreater. I am bodily comfortable, if somewhat dingily lodged; and I daily part with my raiment for food. We find no one who will exchange eatables for Confederate money, so we are devouring our clothes. Ellen is a poor maid, but if I do a little work, it is quite enough to show me how dreadful it would be if I should have to do it all.

Social enjoyments are not wanting. Miss Middleton and Isabella often drink a cup of tea with me. One might search the whole world and not find two cleverer or more agreeable women. Miss Middleton is brilliant and accomplished, she knows everybody worth knowing and she has been everywhere. Then she is so high-bred, so high-hearted, pure and true; and she is so clean-minded, utterly unselfish, a devoted daughter and sister. She is one among the many large-brained women a kind Providence has thrown my way. How I love to praise my friends.

If the rain continues, we must have a deluge. As a ray of artificial sunshine, Mrs. Munroe sent me an "Examiner." Daniels thinks we are at the last gasp, and England and France are bound to step in. England must know if the United States are triumphant, they will tackle her next; and France must know she will have to give up Mexico. He is confident, but my faith fails me. It is too late. There is no help for us now, in God or men.

A rumour that Thomas is now to ravage Georgia; but Sherman, from all accounts, has done that work once for all. They say no living thing is found in Sherman's track; only chimneys, like telegraph poles, to carry the news that Sherman's army passed that way.

In a regular tropical downpour, Mrs. Munroe sent me overshoes and an umbrella with the message: "Come over." I went. As well drown in the streets as hang myself at home to my own bedpost. Oh this dismal, lonely, hole!

At Mrs. Munroe's I met a Miss McDaniel. Her father for seven years was the Methodist preacher at our Negro church, in the grove just opposite Mulberry. She says her father has so often described that fine old establishment. I told her: "But now I dare say there stand only Sherman's sentinels, stacks of chimneys. We have made up our minds to the worst. Mulberry House is no doubt razed to the ground."

She praised us, saying that in most places the Methodist missionary preached to the negroes and then dined with the overseer, but at Mulberry, her father always stayed at the "Big House," and the family were so kind and attentive to him. It was pleasant to hear one's family so spoken of among strangers.

Being so well equipped to brave the weather, I continued my prowl further afield and brought up at the Middleton's. I may have surprised them, but never did a lonely old woman receive such a warm and hearty welcome. They had many rumours. Wheeler's men had found a Yankee hid in a barn, who reported that Hampton had cut off Kilpatrick again, somewhere near Greenville. Another: that Sherman left a Negro garrison in Columbia. Another: that there is no Columbia to garrison, that Sherman marched off in solid column, leaving not so much as a blade of grass behind, but howling wilderness, the land laid waste, all dust and ashes. Another: that Wheeler's cavalry sacked the old Hampton house before Sherman's bummers got a chance at it. Another: Stanley and Radcliffe were the heroes who with a white flag bore the keys of Columbia to the conquerors of women and children. Another: Mrs. Blake and Mr. Rutledge (who is wounded) were in Columbia the night it was fired. So the Middleton household was anxious and sad enough.

Tea at the Munroe's meant more gossip, the same everywhere, and women's chatter. We whimper and whine, they say; we speak in a deprecating voice, and sigh gently at the end of every sentence. Why? "Well, it is plain enough. Does a man ever speak to his wife and children except to find fault? Does a woman ever address any remark to her husband that does not begin with an excuse? When a man does wrong, does not his wife have to excuse herself if he finds out she knows it? If a man drinks too much, and his wife shows that she sees it, what a storm she brings about her ears! She is disrespectful, unwomanly, so unlike her mother, so different from the women of his family. Do you wonder that we are afraid to raise our voices above a mendicant's moan?"

"And yet they say our voices are the softest, sweetest, in the world."

"No wonder. The base submission of our tone must be music in our masters' ears!"

A perfect shriek of rage drowned out our small talk. "Mars' Kit said the man was such a fool, he did not know his campaign in Tennessee was a failure!" No doubt Mars' Kit thought Sam a fool, up there fighting to the best of his poor ability, risking life and limb. Maybe staying home, keeping a whole skin, saving your cotton, is better; but I like the fools, the Confederate martyrs. Maybe I am a fool too, but I like that sort best!

Then gossip, gossip, gossip. "Miss Improper was too smart for them. Have you seen her leading her child. She was to be married, but the man was killed in battle. Horrible! Then that child was born and the married sister said this poor girl must be put out, she had disgraced the family. Then the married sister's husband was killed too, and Miss Improper answers her sister: 'My child is the child of your husband! There! I will behave myself if you let me stay here; but if you turn me out, look out!' So she and little Too Soona stay in the bosom of her family."

Gossip, gossip, gossip! "Did you see that beautiful woman on the train and the Major? We guessed they were a runaway couple in the honeymoon, or an old married couple who had had a tiff and we were witnessing the reconciliation.

"We stopped at Charlotte. A grey-haired old man walked in. Up jumps the lady. 'Oh Uncle, this gentleman has been so kind. Major — I did not catch your name, sir, when I was introduced to you this morning.' 'Oh,' said the grave and dignified Uncle, 'I know the Major. By the way Major, I bring you good news of your wife and children. I saw them two days ago in Richmond.' Oh what a look she gave him then! It was so full of rage. Off went niece and Uncle. The Major lolled back on his seat with a smile of perfect self-satisfaction. 'I would like to kill him,' said one of our party, who had grown restive under all that kissing." When this cruel war is over, those Department girls must go home. Oh, the pity of it; nice girls learning to misbehave that way!

Next came the story of the kleptomaniac. "But she is the richest girl!" "So much the better. Her father pays and hushes it up. They make him pay for more than she takes. He dares not investigate the charges." Surely that was scandal enough for one long rainy evening, but it is with such talk that we avoid all allusion to Columbia. We never say "home." We begin to discuss the sure poverty ahead.

"I say, when Ellen is a lady and driving about in your carriage, won't you miss that tray of nice breakfast she brings to your bedside every morning?" "Oh yes, Ellen does make such nice coffee, but we're not of the cry-baby kind!"

Mrs. Rutledge, that plate of biscuits still rankling, has sent me a tumbler of milk, the very first milk I have tasted since I deserted our

Alderney cow in Plain Street, Columbia. Mrs. Preston's cow, it was.

How it pours! Could I live many days in solitary confinement? Things are beginning to be unbearable. What is the good of being here at all? Our world has gone to destruction.

I mean to go to church, even if it rains cats and dogs. My feet are wet two or three times a day, but we never take cold. Our hearts are too hot within us for that. Mrs. Glover has a carriage, and she came for me to go and hear Reverend Mr. Martin preach. Text: "Why are ye so fearful, Oh ye of little faith." We are all women, so fear is no disgrace; but I do think we possess our souls in wonderful patience. Brother Martin lifts our spirits from this dull earth, but my heart wanders and my mind strays back to South Carolina. Oh vandal Sherman, what are you at there now? Hard-hearted wretch!

Serena, the Princess Brighteyes, suddenly wakes up from her dream to write and ask: "Of what Butlers is Nat? Who was his grandfather," etc. So I answered our beautiful flirt with question for question. "What is Nat Butler to you?" Brockenbrough is with Hardee, and so is General Chesnut. I fain hope Brockenbrough will reconsider his somewhat rash determination to make a confidant of General Chesnut.

I have a letter from General Chesnut, in camp near Charlotte.

My dear Mary:

I thank you a thousand, thousand times for your kind letters. They are now my only earthly comfort, except the hope that all is not yet lost. We have been driven like a wild herd from our country, not so much from a want of spirit in the people or the soldiers as from want of energy and competence in our commanders. Hampton and Butler are the only ones who have done anything. The restoration of Joe Johnston, it is hoped, will redound to the advantage of our cause, and the re-establishment of our fortunes. I am still in not very agreeable circumstances, for the last four days completely waterbound. As soon as a wagon can move I will go in search of General Hardee's corps, the whereabouts of which is still in doubt. He has, I suppose the remnant of my command. All, or nearly all, who were here with the prisoners, left the night before I arrived, and without leave. They were left, unwisely, without officers.

I am informed that a detachment of Yankees were sent from Liberty Hill to Camden with a view to destroy all the houses, mills, provisions, etc., about that place. No particulars have reached me. You know I expected the worst, and am fully prepared for any report which may be made.

If you desire it, I will endeavour to convey a message to Lawrence or Isaac to come up to you, though perhaps it would not be safe to attempt to bring anything with them yet. I had intended to run up to Lincolnton to see you till I received your letter saying you would leave there today.

It would be a happiness beyond expression to see you, even for an hour. I have heard nothing from my poor old father. I fear I shall never see him again. Such is the fate of war.

I do not complain. I have deliberately chosen my lot, and am prepared for any fate that awaits me. My care is for you, and I trust still in the good cause of my country and the justice and mercy of God.

When you write, please do not omit to date your letters. It is satisfactory to know the day they are written. In this horrible spell of weather, I am as wet and uncomfortable as a drenched dog. N'importe! God bless and protect you, dear wife.

JC

It was a lively, rushing young set South Carolina put to the fore. They knew it was a time of danger. The fight would be ten to one, but they expected to win by activity, energy, enthusiasm. Then came the wet blankets. Pickens; old Orr, half-hearted in the cause; Mr. Barnwell, an octagenarian and low-church Episcopalian in his first sympathies; Memminger, and so on. Now the old men are posing, wrapping Caesar's mantle about their heads, ready to fall with dignity, while those gallant youths who dashed so gayly to the front lie mostly in bloody graves. As well for them, maybe; there are worse things than honorable graves.

It is a wearisome thought; that late in life we are to begin anew, with laborious, difficult days ahead.

Contradictory testimony. Governor Aiken passed through, saying Sherman left Columbia as he found it, and was last heard of at Cheraw. But my husband wrote that he saw the fires which burned up Columbia, the first night. His camp was near enough to the town for that. Then came in someone who said the road was open to Columbia; and then Mrs. Munroe's cousin said the enemy were in full force in Chester, halfway to Columbia, thereby blocking the way most effectually.

Miss Middleton and Isabella, looking over this, objected: "Why do you write such contradictory statements? It is all contradiction and counter-statements, absolutely laughable!" "I write what I hear, not what I know. I think what I say at the time, but I am reckless, almost shameless, about changing my mind."

St. Julien Ravenel is here. He left his wife not in travelling trim, so she was obliged to stay. He has not heard a word, says sometimes in his madness he hopes it may be no worse than that a bomb has destroyed them all.

They say Sherman has burned Lancaster; that nightmare, ghoul, hyena! But that I do not believe. He takes his time, there is none to molest him, he does things leisurely and deliberately. Why stop to do so needless a thing as burn Lancaster? The courthouse, the jail and the tavern; as I remember it, that constitutes Lancaster. But they say a raiding party did for Camden.

They showed me a note from General Johnston. He communicates to us the fact that the political horizon is black. Maybe he is like the doctors who represent their patients as lying at death's door, so they may have all the more credit for saving their lives. If Joe saves us, I will throw up my cap for him, in spite of all that is past and gone. Magnanimous me!

I gave today fifty dollars for a small wooden bucket which in better days, or in metallic currency, was worth twenty-five cents.

I heard a Columbia Hospital tale of an Irish nurse smothering a man who was booked to die, because she wanted his bed for a man whose life could be saved. Millions of soldier's clothes were left in Columbia which could have been brought here, instead of the old chairs and tables we see piled everywhere. The last people who came away say the streets were lined with commissary stores, ready to be removed — if Sherman had waited a day or two longer.

MARCH 1st. — No train from Charlotte yesterday. There is a rumour that Sherman is in Charlotte. The natives are quite cool on the subject, content to bide their time. They are Union people, they say, and always were. Sherman will take what he wants, but he will hold out to them the right hand of fellowship. The same people who are so proud of those who went forth to do or die for their country think now they can eat their cake and have it too!

How Mrs. Munroe harried my soul with her tales of the way the Yankee prisoners are suffering at Salisbury.* "But the Yankees froze John Boykin and Mr. Venable's brother to death in cold blood." "Would you be willing to be as wicked as they are?" she demanded. "A thousand times, no; but we must feed our army first. Their soldiers need not have starved if Lincoln would consent to exchange prisoners. But men are nothing to them, a thing to throw away. If they send our men back, they strengthen our army." She went on with her horrors till I cried: "Stop it, Mrs. Munroe! These things can't be wilfully done!" I ran from her blood-curdling tales. It goes to my heart like a stab! Oh how can people be cruel to the helpless.

* Salisbury Prison in North Carolina had as unsavory a record as Andersonville.

Young Brevard asked me to play accompaniments for him. The guitar is my instrument, (or was); so I sang and I played to my own great delight. It was a distraction. Then I made eggnog for the soldier boys, and spent a very pleasant evening. Begone dull care! You and I can never agree.

Ellen and I are shut up here by the rain, rain, everlasting rain. As our money is worthless, are we to starve? Heavens; how grateful I was today when Miss McLean sent me a piece of chicken! Ellen said: "Missis, aint you shame, crying for joy like a beggar 'oman? You dat had turkey and eberything home, if you only woulda gone home." I think my empty larder has leaked out, for today Mrs. Munroe sent me hot cakes and eggs for my breakfast. I sent the Fants some good old brandy for their wounded soldier. They say he must die.

I met another Mrs. Johnston. "Where are the Carolina chivalry?" she said with a sneer. "With Lee or Johnston! Where did you suppose they were?" "Oh — I meant the Rhetts and all that." "A good many Rhetts have fallen in battle," I said. "Of those who are alive, I know nothing." The Fants interfered, piously wishing they had some sacred ashes to put on their foreheads, for Ash Wednesday. So we lack even ashes. I have no wood to burn, and cannot afford sackcloth to wail in. We are below the luxury of woe and sackcloth and ashes. Only blockaders can do the thing in that style!

These people are proud of their heroic dead and their living soldiers, but are prepared to say with truth that they always preferred to remain in the Union, and are ready to assure the first comers of Yankees that they have always hated South Carolina seceders and nullifiers as much as the Yankees do.* We discussed fashions of speech. FF's have a dialect. They say, "Mighty little," for very small; they call a ball or a tea party "only a little company." Another form of the simple word "very" is "right such." But Mrs. Mat Singleton uses English as pure as that of Victoria Regina; such clean-cut sentences, every word distinctly enunciated. She is the delight of her friends, the terror of her foes. Sometimes those words dropped one by one with such infinite precision are drops of vitriol!

March 5th. — Is the sea drying up? It is going up into mist and coming down on us in this water spout, the rain. It raineth every day, and the weather represents our tearful despair on a large scale. It is

* North Carolina, like Virginia, stood about two to one against secession until Lincoln's program of coercion made it certain that they must either fight for the seceding states or against them.

also Lent; quite convenient, for we have nothing to eat, so we fast and pray and go draggling to church like drowned rats, to be preached at.

To think there are men who dare so defile a church, a sacred sanctuary dedicated to God. We have to hold up our skirts and walk tiptoe, so covered is the floor, the aisle and pews, with the dark shower of tobacco juice.

My letter from my husband was so — well, what in a woman, you would call heart-broken — that I began to get ready for a run up to Charlotte. Then a tap on the door, and Miss McLean cried in a triumphant voice: "Permit me to announce General Chesnut!" We went after luncheon to see Mrs. Munroe. He wanted to thank her for all her kindness to me. We had been seeing the rough side of life so long, the seamy side, that I was awfully proud of him. I once thought everybody had the air and manners of a gentleman; I know now it is a thing to thank God for. Mr. Chesnut knew Mr. Munroe in our Legislature long ago, so it was all very nice. Father O'Connell was there, fresh from Columbia. Sherman's men had burned the Convent. Mrs. Munroe had pinned her faith to Sherman, because he was a Catholic, and now! Father O'Connell saw the fire. The nuns and girls marched to the old Hampton house and so saved it. They walked between files of soldiers. Men were rolling tar barrels and lighting torches to fling over the house when the nuns came. Columbia is but dust and ashes, burned to the ground. Men, women and children are left there houseless, homeless, without a particle of food. They are picking up the corn left by Sherman's horses in their picket ground and parching it to stay their hunger.

General Chesnut said he had sent Isaac Hayne with a party of scouts to go to Columbia and come back by Camden; so we will hear something definite from home through Isaac Hayne.

How kind my friends were on this my fête day. Mrs. Rutledge sent me a plate of biscuits, Mrs. Munroe sent nearly enough for an entire dinner, Miss McLean sent in a cake for dessert, and Ellen cooked and served up the materials so happily at hand, very nicely indeed. There never was a more successful dinner. My heart was too full to eat, but I was quiet and calm and at least spared my husband the trial of a broken voice or tears. As he stood at the window with his back to the room, he said: "Where are they now; my old blind father, and my sister? Day and night, I see her leading him out from under his own roof tree before they burn the house. That picture pursues me persistently. But come, let us talk of pleasanter things."

He took off his heavy cavalry boots and Ellen carried them off to dry, and to wash the mud off. She brought them back just as Miss Middleton walked in. In his agony, struggling with those huge boots to get them on, he spoke to her volubly in French. She turned away from him instantly, as she saw his shoeless plight, and said: "I had not heard of your happiness — I did not know the General was here." Not until next day did we have time to remember and laugh at that outbreak of French. Miss Middleton answered him in the same language. He told her how charmed he was with my surroundings, and that he would go away with a much lighter heart since he had seen the kind people with whom he would leave me.

I asked him what that correspondence between Sherman and Hampton meant. That was while I was preparing something for our dinner, and his back was still turned as he gazed out of the window. He spoke in the low and steady monotone that characterized our conversation the whole day, and yet there was something in his voice that thrilled me. "The second day after our march from Columbia, we passed the M——'s. He was a bonded man, and not at home. His wife said at first that she could not find forage for our horses. Afterwards she succeeded in procuring some for us. I noticed a very handsome girl who stood beside her as she spoke to me. I suggested to her mother the propriety of sending her daughter out of the track of both armies; there was so much straggling, so many campfollowers, and no discipline on the outskirts of an army. The girl answered quickly: 'I will stay with my mother.' That very night, a party of Wheeler's men came to our camp. They had passed the house later and found horror and destruction, the mother raving of what had been done. This outrage was done before her very face, she being secured first. This straggling party of the enemy, after their crime, moved on. There were seven of them, and the women said they had been gone but a short time. Wheeler's men went off in pursuit at full speed, overtook them, cut their throats, and marked upon their breasts: 'These were the seven.' " "But the girl?" I whispered. "Oh, she was dead!"

When I could speak, trying to forget this horror and to make him forget, I asked: "Are his enemies as violent as ever against the President?" He nodded.

"Sometimes I think I am the only friend he has in the world. At these dinners which they give us everywhere, I spoil sport, for I will not sit there and hear Jeff Davis abused for things he is no more responsible for than any man at table. I lost my temper. I told them it sounded arrant nonsense to me, and that Jeff Davis was a gentleman and a patriot, with more brains than the assembled company." "You lost your temper truly," I said. He smiled. "Yes, I did not know it. I thought I was as cool as I am now. In Washington, when we left it, Jeff Davis ranked second to none. Now they rave that he is nobody and never was." "And she?" "Oh, you would think to hear them that he found her yesterday in a Mississippi swamp!" "Well, in the French Revolution it was worse. When a man failed he was guillotined. Mirabeau did not die a day too soon, even Mirabeau!"

Now he has gone. With despair in my heart, I left that railroad station. Allan Green walked home with me. I met his wife and his four ragged little boys, a day or so ago. She is the neatest, the primmest, the softest of women; her voice is like the gentle cooing of a dove. In her dulcet accents she murmured, without the slightest excitement of manner: "You see me! I am going around like a raging lion, seeking what I may devour." A man she had introduced as a faraway cousin of her stepfather interposed. "She talks that way because they would not take Cousin Sarah's money. But one of the storekeepers paid for Cousin Sarah's something-to-eat in yarn!" Mr. Chesnut gave me his last cent. It was a sad parting, though his words were cheerful enough. That lowering black future hangs there, all the same. The end of the war brings no hope of peace or security to us. But I forced myself to listen to Allan, and to say: "Yes, yarn is our circulating medium. It is the current coin of the realm. At a factory here, Mrs. Glover traded off a Negro woman for yarn. The woman wanted to go there as a factory hand, it suited all round." "That's nothing. Yesterday a Negro man was sold for a keg of nails."

General Chesnut said many people were light-hearted at the ruin of the great slave owners. He quoted someone: "They will have no Negroes now to lord it over! They can swell and peacock about and tyrannize now over only a small parcel of women and children, those only who are their very own family."

A letter from Quinton Washington. "I have given up," he writes. "The bitterness is over. I will write to you no more. I have not the heart."

General Manigault told Miss Middleton that Sherman burnt out all families whose heads had signed the secession ordinance. Members of Legislature's houses were burned. "And if he had thrown in the members of the Legislature themselves, nobody would mind," she said. "They are in bad odor, but to burn them would have created worse," I suggested.

I had a little piece of bread and a little molasses today for my dinner. Jack Middleton writes from Richmond: "The wolf is at the door here. We dread starvation far more than we do Grant or Sherman. Famine; that is the word now!"

I saw a sister of Captain Corrie, the anachronism who tried in the 19th century to reopen the African slave trade. He was the Captain of the *Wanderer*, which was wrecked when she tried to land her black cargo.

March 6th. — Today, a godsend. Even the small piece of bread and the molasses were things of the past. My larder was empty. A tall mulatto woman walked in with a tray, covered by a huge white serviette. Ellen ushered her in with a flourish. "Mrs. McDonald's maid." She set down the tray upon my bare table and uncovered it with conscious pride. Fowls, ready for roasting; sausages, butter, bread, eggs, preserves. I was dumb with delight. After silent thanks to Heaven, my powers of speech returned, and I exhausted myself in messages of gratitude to Mrs. McDonald. Ellen scolded me afterward. "Missis, you oughtn't to let her see how glad you was. It was a letting of yourself down."

Mrs. Glover gave me some yarn and I bought five dozen eggs with it from a wagon. Eggs for Lent! And to show that I have faith yet in humanity, I paid her in advance, in yarn, for something to eat which she promises to bring tomorrow. Dr. Brumby has been at last coaxed into selling me some leather to make me a pair of shoes, else I should have had to give up walking. He knew my father well. He intimated that in some way my father helped him through college. Mr. William C. Preston and my father advanced funds sufficient to let him be graduated, and then my Uncle Charles Miller married his aunt. I listened in rapture. All this tended to leniency in the leather business, and I bore off the leather gladly.

March 7th. — We go to church every day. The air today was clean and bracing, a sniff of snow from the mountains and such a blue, unclouded sky. After so much rain, how refreshing.

Maggie pointed out a shop and the sign over it. "Anywhere else than in North Carolina, when a man rises to be a Congressman, he pulls down his name from off his little shop door and begins to get up a pedigree from Adam, or William the Conqueror." Here a Lincolnton lady halted us to ask Maggie: "Did your mother really give ten dollars a dozen for eggs." "No, the woman asked us five, and we were not such fools as to give even that." I was the real delinquent, with my yarn, but I did not incriminate myself. She asked me $20 for five dozen eggs, and then said she would take it in "confederick." I would have given her $100, as easily; I haggle in yarn for the millionth part of a thread! When they ask for Confederate money, I never stop to chaffer; I give them $20 or $50 dollars cheerfully for anything.

MARCH 8th — Colonel Childs gave me a letter from my husband, and a newspaper containing a full account of Sherman's cold-blooded brutality in Columbia. Then we walked three miles to return the call of my benefactress. McDaniel is her name, not McDonald. They were kind and hospitable, but my heart was like lead. My head ached and my legs were worse than my head, and then I had a nervous chill; so I went to bed and stayed there until the Fants brought me a letter saying my husband would be here today. So I got up and made ready to give him a cheerful reception. Soon a man came in, Troy by name, the same who kept the little corner shop so near my house in Columbia, and of whom we bought things so often. He looked in my face pitifully. We seemed to have been friends all our lives. He says they stopped the fire at the Methodist College, perhaps to save old Mr. McCready's house. Our house still stands, being next to McCready's. Mr. Sheriff Dent, being burnt out, has taken refuge in our house. He contrived to find favour in Yankee eyes. Troy heard Molly hotly disputing the possession of my house with the Dents. "Lord," said Troy, "What a row she did make!" She had saved our Alderney cow, and loved it as a brand snatched from the burning. She was loath to part with it to the Dents. He says a Yankee General, Logan by name, snatched a watch from Mrs. McCord's bosom. The soldiers tore away bundles of clothes and belongings that the poor wretches tried to save from their burning houses and dashed them back into the flames. They were howling round the fires like demons, these Yankees, in their joy and triumph at our destruction. Well, we have given them a big scare, and kept them miserable for five years; just the little handfull of us. They overhauled the Halcott Greens at Lancaster, stripped them bare and threatened to shoot Allan before her very eyes. Some Yankee soldier to whom he had been kind in Charleston recognized him and saved his life. Virginia has a gift of eloquence. Poor darling, no doubt she tried it then.

Mrs. Childs and the Hokes here ride a high horse. It seems they have been living in Columbia, and I did not call on them, did not so much as know they were there; so they say to the Lincolnton folk that they have no reason to come and see me here. But Colonel Childs is magnanimous, and bears no malice for my neglect of his womenkind. He comes every day and patronizes me.

Colonel Fant has turned up. He is a handsome, big Virginian. He is his own man, and he knows the laws and his rights and dares maintain them. The landlady at the Hotel got into one of her tantrums because they wanted eggs in Lent and tried to expel them. He calmly says he won't go, that he has a right to stay. They are three in family. They pay $80 a day, with fires extra, in Confederate currency.

They told me a fearful thing. That family who came like the patriarch — man-servants, maid-servants, wife and children — were huddled into one room by the greedy landlady; then their Negro woman was taken sick, and they all had to camp out in the drawing-room while they nursed her with faithful kindness. Now the poor woman is dead and laid out in their one room, and they still camp in the drawing-room. Old Mrs. Graspall makes them pay their $100 a day in Confederate brown paper.

A woman we met on the street stopped to tell us a painful anecdote. A general was married, but he could not stay at home very long after the wedding. When his baby was born, they telegraphed him. He sent back a rejoicing answer and asked: "Is it a boy or a girl?" Then he was killed before he got the reply. His poor young wife says: "He did not live to hear that his son lived." The kind woman added sorrowfully: "He died and did not know the sect of his child." "Let us hope it will be a Methodist," said Isabella the irrepressible. She is of the Methodist persuasion.

She was asked to supper last night at the Michaels'. They had venison steak and chicken salad. Isabella confessed that when she viewed the spread, she had some difficulty in controlling her feelings. Mrs. Glover, to prove to us the plenty that reigned here in peaceful times, described an "Infair" which she attended here in the early years of the war. An "Infair" means a table standing for days against all comers. At this one, they began to dine at two o'clock in the day, and dined on continuously. As soon as one relay were glutted, another came. Table or tables were constantly replenished. There were two tables in separate rooms; one for beef, bacon, turkeys, fowls, all meats and vegetables and the other for sweets. Everybody fared alike and all fared sumptuously. Without haste, without rest, on flowed the crowd of eaters. Mrs. Glover heard ravenous soldiers aver with delight that they had dined three times that day, and that the last dinner was as good as the first. I record this because I have never known of an "Infair" before.

At the venison feast, Isabella heard a good word for me, and one for General Chesnut's air of distinction. That is a thing people cannot give themselves, try as ever they may. Lord Byron says everybody knows a gentleman when he sees one and nobody can tell what it is that makes a gentleman. In the same way there are some French words which cannot be translated, and yet we all know their meaning: words like *gracieuse*, and *svelte*, applied to a woman. Not that anything was said of me like that! Far from it! I am fair, fat, forty, jolly; and in my unbroken jollity, they found my charm. "You see she don't howl, she don't cry, she never never tells anybody what she was used to at home and what she has lost!" High praise, and I mean to try and deserve it, ever after.

Isabella makes an Irish Bull, saying "We have lost what we never had." We have never had any money, only unlimited credit; for Mr. Chesnut's richest kind of a father ensured us all manner of credit. It was only a mirage; and now at last it has gone, just as we drew nigh to it.

MARCH 10th. — Went to church, crying to Ellen: "It is Lent, we must fast and pray." When I came home, my good fairy, Colonel Childs, had been here bringing rice and potatoes, and promising flour. He is a trump. He pulled out his pocketbook and offered to be my banker. He stood there on the street, Isabella and Miss Middleton witnessing the generous action, and straight out offered me money. "No," I said. "I am not a beggar, and I never will be. To die is so much easier." But, after that flourish of trumpets, when he came with the sack of flour I accepted it gratefully. I receive things I cannot pay for, but money is different. There I draw a line, an imaginary line perhaps. Once before the same thing happened. In 1845, when we left unexpectedly for Europe and our letters of credit were to follow us, I was a poor little inoffensive bride. Our letters were delayed, and a British officer who guessed our embarrassment — for we did not tell him — asked Mr. Chesnut to draw on his banker until our letters came — we did not do it, but it was a nice thing for a stranger to do.

Colonel Childs says the mob runs after Joe Johnston and curses Jeff Davis. When you give the mob its choice, it selects Barrabas and crucifies our Saviour. Of course, a mob murders those who fail, or who appear to do so. They do not wait to find out the truth.

Colonel Childs had news of the beautiful Boozer. "She went off with flying colours. She has married a Philadelphia officer." "No doubt," said Isabella. "And by this time she has married one from Boston, and from New York indiscriminately. Will she marry the entire Yankee army?" And to me: "Your defense of Boozer in Columbia was a mistake, you see!" The Boozer talk was *sotto voce*, not for Colonel Childs to hear.

The Colonel said a ray of light had penetrated inwards from Lincoln, who told Judge Campbell that Southern land would not be confiscated. He told us, too, that Hetty Cary married General Pegram, and in two weeks after the marriage he was killed in the trenches around Petersburg.

Tonight I had fever without stint, the highest fever going.

MARCH 12th. — Better today; a long, long weary day. I suppose General Chesnut is somewhere; but where? That is the question. Only once has he visited this sad spot which holds, he says, all that he cares for on earth. Unless he comes or writes soon, I will cease — or try to — this wearisome looking, looking, looking for him. Mrs. Michael thinks — or says — that I am like sunshine in a house. What a compliment in this cold, damp, dismal, cloudy, rain-forever place.

The last day I was out, Colonel Childs stopped me to present a Mr. Stowe. "Who keeps a sto? " he whispered in an aside. "Now do be pleasant with him." To please Colonel Childs, I did my best; I went in for "the frisky old girl" style. Colonel Childs said Mr. Stowe, even if he did keep a sto', was a millionaire; and he was trying to induce him to let me have a bag of flour. The flour came, and also a tray of butcher's meat, provisions for more than a week. Very kind of Mr. Stowe, as I had no money but only smiles, which are cheap. "No, no!" yells Isabella. "Money is ever so much cheaper than forced smiles."

In Columbia, Childs tells me, our friends are following horses to pick up grains of corn to parch.

There is here the handsomest of men, Thomas by name and a Marylander. He married a girl from New Orleans who died here. The poor young thing died without the consolations of her religion. They were staying with people who were devotedly, tenderly kind to her in all things but one. The severe Calvinistic dame, her hostess, would not let a touch of holy water or sacred oil come into her house, so she died unsprinkled.

Thomas would look well in Confederate gray. That fascinating mouth, that divine complexion of his begins to madden the female world again. He is sublimely handsome — if only he were in uniform. But everyone says: "That you will not see! He has had enough of it. He is on his way across the Mississippi, to avoid the draft!"

My husband did come, for two hours, and brought Lawrence, who had been to Camden and was there indeed during the raid. Mr. Chesnut is ordered to Chester. We are surprised to see by the papers that we had behaved heroically in leaving everything we had to be destroyed, without one thought of surrender. We had not thought of ourselves from the heroic point of view. Isaac McLaughlin hid and saved everything we trusted him with. A grateful Negro is Isaac.

A letter from Quinton Washington in Richmond says: "Our friends the Prestons are well. General Hood is here and says he and Buck are ere long to be married. The report is apparently well founded. I see the Prestons quite often. I have seen little of the ladies at the President's lately. Mr. Hunter is in fine health. Mr. Seddon has been forced out of the Cabinet by the general spirit of calumny and detraction which obtains nowadays."

MARCH 15th. — Lawrence says Miss Chesnut is very proud of her presence of mind and her cool self-possession in the presence of the enemy. She lost, after all, only two bottles of champagne, two of her brother's gold-headed canes, and her brother's horses — including Claudia, the brood mare that he valued beyond price — and her own carriage. A fly-brush boy called Battis, whose occupation in life was to stand behind the table and with his peacock feathers brush the flies, was the sole member of his dusky race at Mulberry who deserted "old Marster" to follow the Yankees.

Now for our losses at the Hermitage, added to the gold-headed canes and Claudia. We lost every mule and horse. Some of John's were there too. My Light Dragoon and heavy swell is stripped light enough for the flight now. Jonathan, whom we trusted, betrayed us. The plantation house and mills, and Mulberry House were saved by Claiborne, that black rascal who was suspected by all the world! He told the Yankees that to burn the place would only hurt the Negroes, that Mars' Jeems hardly ever came there and only took a little something to eat when he came.

Discussing our dinner to the General's wives in Columbia, Isabella said Clancy wanted to be out of it. He said fat old women's big bare arms always looked like legs to him. Poor old "unenclosed commons!"

I was ill again, and the fever continuing, I sent for St. Julien Ravenel. That means "little raven." He justifies his name. How he does croak! He is not "Ravenous," however. Ellen had something nice to offer him, thanks to the ever bountiful Childs; but he was too angry to eat. He gave us an anti-slavery tirade. He was very violent at first — but from the high pillows of my very high bed, I launched my bolts. I out-Heroded Herod. When he began on Mr. Davis: "Jeff Davis is a disciple of John C. Calhoun," I said. This was the red rag shaken before the mad bull. He fairly plunged at it. "I never had any faith in this frantic movement. Now I look back and see we had every chance to free ourselves forever from any connection with New England; but this man's heavy-headed stupidity, his abiding self-conceit, his everlasting wrong-headedness has ruined us. He puts the money of the Confederacy in the hands of a man who would not be trusted with a five-dollar bill by those who know him at home. Northrop! Mallory! Moore! I will not waste words on them."

Then this ill person, me, with the wisdom of the Serpent, began to wail over the injustice which had been done the patriot Wigfall and the daring Joe Johnston. Instantly he fell foul of the faults of those two; and almost before he knew it, he lauded Mr. Davis who would have none of them. Then he pitched into Ellen, who stood glaring at him from the fireplace, her blind eye nearly white, and her blue eye blazing like a comet. On Sunday he gave her some Dover's Powder for me, directions written on the paper in which it was wrapped. He told her to show this to me, and then put what I gave her in a wineglass and let me drink it. Ellen put it all in the wineglass and gave it to me at one dose. "It was enough to last you your life time," he cried to me. "It was murder." Then, turning to Ellen. "What did you do with the directions?" "I never see no directions. You never give me none." "I told you to show that paper to your Missis." "Well, I fling dat ole brown paper in de fire. What you making all dis fuss for? Soon as I give Missis de physic, she stop fretting and flinging about wid fever. She go to sleep, sweet as a suckling baby; and she sleep two days and nights and now she heap better!" Thus Ellen withdrew from the controversy.

"Well all's well that ends well," he told me. "You took opiate enough to kill an army. You were worried and worn out, and you wanted rest. You came near getting it, thoroughly!"

The comic side of my being able to stand that horse-size dose has since given us both some hearty laughs. He says I will die hard, that it is not easy to kill me, and that I have a sturdy constitution. Maybe I was saved by the adulteration so often complained of, in all Confederate medicine.

Sally Green came. As meek, gentle, refined and low-voiced as ever, she began at once to relate her good fortune. She had been again asked to a Lincolnton dinner. "I took the goods the gods provided! Roast turkey, stuffed, and plenty of gravy. Rice as white as snow, every grain standing out separate; no gummy stuff without salt, as if the washerwoman had dropped her bag of blueing in it. Sweet potatoes, browned with butter and sugar. A pound-cake pudding, with wine sauce!" She grew more excited at every item, gloating over the feast. "And oh! to see my boys have enough to eat once more," she murmured softly.

Mrs. Middleton and Isabella stayed to tea. "Ellen, you make delightful cakes." Ellen glowed with pride at the compliment. She is very useful now. She has learned to save me from thinking. She even knows when to let me alone; but last night she gave me a fright. Lying there asleep before the fire, she screamed again and again in a nightmare. "What is it?" I asked. "Nothing, only I was dreaming somebody was troubling my William!" As neither of us could go to sleep any more, she fell into discourse. "Missus, nex time you is bound for de Yallerbam, take me in place of Molly. I want to see my ole mother."

If these people are freed, won't somebody get good servants; those we have been training all these years. Then the man who can hoe cotton is trained for the business in hand. A good hand hires for one hundred dollars, his clothes and food. Do I know a young planter who can earn one hundred dollars by the labor of his own hands? So the Negroes can earn their living at once, when they are freed.

Rony Cameron, a Scotch overseer, a rugged old Covenanter, used to say as he passed old Cunningham's plantation, "That man owes his Negroes sixty thousand dollars for food and clothes!" The General says his Negroes owe him thirty thousand which he has furnished to the plantation, while drawing nothing from it. Joe Cunningham is a born fortune-maker. This millionaire makes shoes. They say neither his family nor his Negroes have ever worn a shoe unless he made it for them. Yet, he eats out of a wooden bowl; and they have no light but firelight, go to bed with the chickens.

My husband writes from Chester Court House: "In the morning I send Lieutenant Ogden with Lawrence to bring you down here. I have three vacant rooms, one with bedsteads, chairs, washstand, basins and pitchers, and the other two bare. You can have half of a kitchen for your cooking. If you can get your friends in Lincolnton to take charge of your valuables, only bring such as you will need here; but perhaps it will be better to bring bed and bedding and other indispensables.

"I wish you would ask Colonel Childs if he would like to buy my cotton, or can sell it for me."

Isabella made a list of the things sent me in my time of need: a bag of flour, bacon, beef, sausages, cranberries, bunches of flowers, blue pills, sole leather and calfskin, morphine, Dover's Powders, camphor, biscuits, bread, milk, plates of dinner, back bones, spare ribs. Then Ellen supplemented in haste; "Oh Miss Isbel, don't forget the two picked chickens Mis. McDaniel just this minute send." I added: "And don't let us forget Moonshine and Stickies." Moonshine is a sort of paste, light and fairy-like, white as snow, twisted and twining, shining, intangible, mystic, wonderful. It crumbles under one's fingers when touched. Stickies are, as their name denotes, cakes which are sticky with sugar or molasses.

Dr. Miles told us that Mrs. Lewis, *née* Vander Horst, died of fright during the Columbia fire. Another lady — a born lady — who shall be nameless here for very shame, went off with the Yankees. Mrs. Guignard, whom I knew years ago as Anna Coffin, when her house was burned, ran out with her family and stood shivering with cold in the woods. Some Yankee soldiers saw them and in rude horse play derided them. "Are you cold? Go in there and get warm. There's fire enough there to warm you all. We have made it hot for you!"

I see that Colonel Young has captured many horses. I hope Mr. Davis's Arabian was among them, and that Johnny's beautiful creatures are once more between Confederate knees.

More of St. Julien's raving. "From the strong minded, the young, the stout hearted, the able-bodied, the active, the energetic, the wide awake, the ardent spirits, did they choose anyone to put in command? No! No, but every old loggerhead that did not so much as believe in the thing stepped to the front. The weight of metal was on the other side, but our mettle did not have a fair showing." Listen to him; their metal, our mettle!

XXII

Chester

MARCH 21st, 1865. — Chester, South Carolina. Another flitting. Captain Ogden came for me. The splendid Childs was true as steel to the last. Surely he is the kindest of men. I saw Captain Ogden was slightly incredulous, when I depicted the wonders of Colonel Childs's kindness; so I skilfully led out the good gentleman, who walked to the train with us. He offered me Confederate money, silver, gold; finally he agreed to buy our cotton and pay now in gold. Of course I laughed at his overflowing bounty and accepted nothing, but begged him to come down to Chester or Camden and buy our cotton of General Chesnut there.

As the train left Lincolnton, and I waved my handkerchief to Mrs. Middleton, Isabella, and my other devoted friends, I could but wonder, will fate throw me again with such kind, clever, agreeable congenial friends? The McLeans refused to be paid for their rooms. No plummet can sound the depths of the hospitality and kindness of the North Carolina people.

Everything went wrong with the train. We broke down two miles from Charlotte and had to walk that distance. That was pretty rough on an invalid, barely out of a fever; and my spirit was further broken by losing an invaluable lace veil which I had worn because I was too poor to buy a cheaper one.

Mr. Chesnut had ordered me to a house kept by some great friends of his. They put me in the drawing-room, a really handsome apartment, and they made up a bed there and put in a wash-hand-stand, plenty of water, everything refreshingly clean and nice. But it continued to be a public drawing-room, open to all; and I was half dead, and wanted to go to bed. The piano was there, and the company played.

The hostess told me she was keeping supper back till Paw and Sis came home. Paw came, politer and more affable still. He walked up to the mirror and took a long look at himself, then washed his face and hands in what I thought was my basin and water. I sat as one in a dream. The landlady announced proudly that for supper there were nine kinds of custard. Custard sounded nice and light, so I sent for some and found it a heavy potato pie. We barricaded ourselves in the drawing-room and left next day at dawn to take the Chester train. Arrived at the station to meet another disappointment; the train was behind time and there we sat on our boxes nine long hours. The cars might come at any moment, we dared not move an inch from the spot.

Then came the train, overloaded with paroled prisoners. Heaven helped us. A kind mail agent took us with two other forlorn women into his comfortable, clean mail car. Mr. Chesnut was at the Chester station with a carriage. We drove at once to Mrs. Da Vega's.

My life has again fallen in pleasant places. Mrs. Da Vega is young, handsome, agreeable, kind, a perfect hostess; and the house and my room leaves nothing to be desired. Again it is the drawing-room, suddenly made into a bedroom for me; but it is my very own. We are among the civilized of the earth once more.

Then I was ill — and they gave me an overdose of morphine. I seem fated to die of opium in some shape, and life seems a senseless repetition of the same blunders.

March 27th. — Moved again. Now I am looking from my window high, with something more to see than "the sky." We have the third story of Dr. Da Vega's rooms, and it opens on the straight street that leads to the railroad about a mile off. This is another Mr. Da Vega, who has a drugstore on Main Street.

Mrs. Bedon is here, the loveliest of young widows. At church, Isaac Hayne nestled so close to her cap strings that I had to touch him and say: "Sit up!" Mrs. Bedon was the wife of Josiah Bedon that we knew so well. He was killed in that famous fight of the Charleston Light Dragoons. Having no orders to retire, they stood still to be shot down in their tracks. They were doubtless forgotten, and scorned to take care of themselves.

Again I am surrounded by old friends. People seem to vie with each other to see how good they can be to me. Today Smith appeared laden with a tray, covered by a snow-white napkin; my first help toward housekeeping. Mrs. Pride had sent by him a boiled ham, a loaf of bread, a huge pound cake, coffee already parched and ground, a loaf of sugar already cracked, candles, pickles, and all the things for which one now must trust to love, since such money as we have avails us nothing, even if there was anything left in the shops to buy.

Teddy Barnwell scented the battle from afar. That is, he saw that heavily laden messenger with his white flag over all, bearing down our way; and he followed until it was all uncovered on my dinner table. He said: "Why, the man asked me where you lived? What could I do but show him!" We had a jolly luncheon. Then James Lowndes came, the best of good company. He said of Buck: "She is a queen! She ought to reign in a palace. No man has ever approached her that I think half good enough for her."

Then Mrs. Prioleau Hamilton, *née* Levy, came, with a report of their progress — not a royal one — from Columbia here. "Before we left home, Major Hamilton spread a map of the United States on the table, and showed me with his finger where Sherman was likely to go. Woman-like, I demurred: 'But suppose he does not choose to go that way!' 'Pooh, pooh! What do you know of war?' So we set out — my husband, myself and two children — all in one small buggy; and straight before Sherman's men for five weeks we fled together. By incessant hurrying and scurrying from pillar to post, we succeeded in being a sort of *avant courier* of the Yankee Army." The first night their beauty sleep was rudely broken into by an alarm: "Move on, the Yanks are on us!" So they hurried on, half awake, to Winnsboro. There they had to lighten the ship and put on all sail, for this time the Yankees were only five miles behind. Ride for your life, was the cry. "Sherman's objective point," said she, "seemed to be our buggy. When we got to Lancaster, Sherman was expected there! We lost no time and soon we were in Cheraw, clearly out of the track; and at midnight General Hardee himself aroused us. In mad haste we made for Fayetteville. There they said: "Why, God bless your soul, this is where Johnston and Sherman are to try conclusions." So we cut across the country, aiming for this place." I was snug and comfortable, all that time, in Lincolnton.

Today, Stephen D. Lee's corps marched through. The camp songs of the men were a heartbreak, so sad and so stirring. I sat down as women have done before and wept. Oh, the bitterness of such weeping! There they go, the gay and gallant few; the last gathering of the flower of Southern manhood. They march with as airy a tread as if they still believed the world was all on their side, and that there were no Yankee bullets for the unwary.

A woman here, high and mighty, with money and a large house, said: "Society is too mixed here. A line should be drawn somewhere." But she was a nursery governess, he is an ex-policeman; so it is not all as sweet as the garden of Eden here, after all.

But I can defy fate now. My darling Preston girls are here. Mrs. Lawson Clay was with them, and unknowingly she let me into one thing. The Hood melodrama is over, though the curtain has not fallen on the last scene. Hood stock going down. When that style of enthusiasm is on the wane, the rapidity of its extinction is miraculous, like the snuffing out of a candle; one moment here, then gone forever.

Lee and Johnston have each fought a drawn battle, so there are a few more dead bodies stiff and stark on an unknown battlefield, a few more women weeping their eyes out — and nothing whatever decided.

Went with Mrs. Pride to a Columbia milliner. She was in Columbia with Sherman; I mean, at the same time. She says that all day — indeed until the fires began — Colonel Goodwyn fraternized with the Yankee generals freely. But when they burnt his house over his head, a change came o'er the spirit of his dream. Old Colonel Chesnut refuses to say grace — but as he leaves the table, he audibly declares: "I Thank God for a good dinner!" When asked why he did this odd thing, he said: "My way is to be sure of a thing before I return thanks for it." Major Goodwyn said grace; that is he fraternized — and had nothing to return thanks for.

Our milliner was handsome. From her own showing, she had been a heroine in the strife. She made eyes shamelessly at my Generals. She said Generals did not come in her way everyday — here she giggled — and that she was bound to improve the occasion.

March 29th. — I was wakened by a bunch of violets from Mrs. Pride. Violets always remind me of Kate, of the sweet south wind that blew in that Garden of Paradise part of my life; and then it all came back, the dread unspeakable that lies behind every thought now.

Dear old Box-plaits came. After I had given him cake with his tea, he departed because I forbade all cursing of Jeff Davis under my hired roof. One thing he said, with that laugh of his which seems to open his countenance to the back hinge like a pair of nut crackers: "Oh, as I wandered in front of Sherman's vandals, there was three weeks that I did not see my own face." And he added how shocked he was at his own appearance when he once more beheld himself, and then he arranged his lips to the size of an ordinary human mouth once more and quoted Scripture. "He had forgotten what manner of man he was!"

No wonder the sudden reminder of a look in the glass was a blow. I composed my face as best I might, bending over my teacups.

I find I have not spoken of the box car which held the Preston party on their journey from Richmond to York.* There were Mr. and Mrs. Lawson Clay, General and Mrs. Preston and their three daughters, Captain Rodgers, Mr. Portman — whose father is an English Earl connected financially and happily with Portman Square — Cellie and her baby and her wet nurse, and no end of servants male and female. In this ark, they slept, ate and drank. Mr. Portman was said to have eaten three luncheons, and the number of his drinks — toddies — were counted too. His contribution to the larder had been three small pigs, but they were run over by the train and made sausage meat before their time.

Wigfall is on his way to Texas. When the hanging begins, he will step over to Mexico. But I am plucking up heart. Such troops as I see go by every day, they must turn the tide. Surely they are going to do something more than surrender!

It is very late. The wind flaps my curtain. It seems to moan "too late." All this will end by making me a nervous lunatic.

General Chesnut has established a hospital here. The night he came, on the floor of the barroom lay one soldier dead and another dying, and men stepped in and out regardless. Against the wall were some so fortunate as to find a bench or a chair to die decently upon. People here were prompt to aid, and the hospital was instantly set going.

Isaac Hayne says Harriet, at Bloomsbury, is wailing: "And they have not hanged Jeff Davis yet!" She had better wait a while. The man she means to marry, will he, nill he, though born in New Jersey, took our side of his own free will. What is the use of being a grandson of a Signer if one is not a loyal gentleman and true to the colors he enlisted and fought under. No doubt he will be disgusted with her disposition to kick the dead or dying lion.

My husband has gone with a wagon train to Columbia.

MARCH 30th. — As I sat disconsolate, looking out, ready for any new tramp of men and arms, the magnificent figure of General Preston hove in sight. He was mounted on a mighty steed worthy of its rider, and

* York, South Carolina, is about twenty-four miles north of Chester. The Prestons, though they passed through Chester on the way, were staying there.

followed by this trusty squire, William Walker, who bore before him the General's portmanteau. When I had time to realize the situation, I perceived at General Preston's right hand Mr. Christopher Hampton and Mr. Portman. Soon Mrs. Pride in some occult way divined or heard that they were coming here, and she sent me at once no end of good things for my tea table. General Preston did come, and with him Mr. Clement Clay of Alabama, the latter in pursuit of his wife's trunk. I left it with the Rev. Mr. Martin, and have no doubt it is perfectly safe — but where? We have written to Mr Martin to inquire. Then Wilmot DeSaussure came in. "I am here to consult with General Chesnut. He and I always think alike." Then he added emphatically. "Slavery is stronger than ever."

"If you think so, you will soon find that for once you and General Chesnut do not think alike. He has held that slavery was a thing of the past, this many a year."

I said to General Preston: "I pass my days — and my nights, partly — at this window. I am sure our army is silently dispersing. Men are going the wrong way all the time. They slip by now with no songs nor shouts. They have given the thing up. See for yourself! Look!" For a while the streets were thronged with soldiers, and then they were empty again; but the marching now is without tap of drum. I told him of the woman in the cracker bonnet at the depot at Charlotte who squalled to her husband as they dragged him off: "Take it easy, Jake. You desert again, quick as you kin. Come back to your wife and children." And she continued to yell: "Desert, Jake! Desert agin, Jake!"

General Chesnut told a story of Wheeler's men in Columbia. Either they did not know Hampton, or they were drunk, and angry at his being put over Wheeler's head. Hampton was sitting on his horse, alone, and beset by about twenty of them. He called out to my husband: "Chesnut, these fellows have drawn their pistols on me!" He is a cool hand, our Wade. General Chesnut galloped up. "Fall in there! Fall in!" By instinct the half-drunken creatures obeyed. Then Chesnut saw a squad of infantry, and brought them up swiftly, and the drunken cavalry rode off. Wade was quite tranquil about it all. He insisted that they did not know him, and besides they were too much intoxicated to know anything. He did not order any arrests, or want any notice whatever to be taken of this insubordination.

A letter from Mary Williams says the Princess Brighteyes is kept busy writing explanatory letters. She can't say Yes, and she will not say

No; hence the waste of paper and penmanship. "Her B's are buzzing around her in swarms. It is becoming troublesome. One B (the giant of the Brockenbrough) is getting angry. She is all serene, however."

Men forever pass under my window. If they were only going to Johnston's camp, all these fine-looking men and fine horses, this crowd of soldiers in Confederate uniform; But they are slowly moving west, by twos and threes. If they were going the right way, I would have hope yet. They might give a good account of themselves.

The Honorable Clement Clay spent the day here, and I have had to talk sensibly and to listen to sense until I am exhausted! Hardee is his scapegoat. He says Hood would have won the battle of Atlanta, but for Hardee. He left me with my spirit prostrate.

MARCH 31st. — My birthday, aged 42. I was on my way to dine at Mrs. Bedon's when Governor Bonham halted me, at the head of a troop of men. "I will not be interviewed in this manner," I told him, and left them planted there.

Mr. Prioleau Hamilton told us of a queer adventure. Mrs. Preston was put under his care on the train. He soon found that the only other women along were what Carlyle calls "unfortunate females," beautiful and aggressive. He had to communicate the unpleasant fact to Mrs. Preston and was lost in admiration of her silent dignity, her quiet self-possession, her calmness, and her deafness and blindness and thorough-bred ignoring of all that she did not care to see. "You know some women, no matter how lady-like, would have made a fuss; but Mrs. Preston dominated the situation, and possessed her soul in innocence and peace."

Mrs. Hamilton reproved him vehemently for the impropriety of his anecdote, said he was always bringing up risky subjects, and then she told one infinitely worse — which I omit. Also she said there were a certain class here who were everlastingly asking you to set, or to lay. "They think we are fowls! Hens lay before they set; but men lie, and sit down on that." I am afraid I have made some mistake in recording their wit!

In the evening, Mr. Clay came again. He said the Senate were inclined to pity Hood after his failure, until his report came out. Then Wigfall fell foul of him savagely. "Hood did not write that report," said Mr. Clay. "That is the disgrace of it."

"Why?" I protested. "I know Beauregard did not write his reports. Jordan and others wrote them for him, and I have no doubt some of those very clever aids of General Lee write his, Marshall, Venable, etc. So little do I know about military matters, I thought it was the aid's business to do it."

April 1st. — * I read some George Sand. Teddy Barnwell dined with me and said he found comfort in my white tablecloth, my white rice and mealy potatoes. He said they gave him nice bread and meat, but seemed not to know that vegetables were a desirable adjunct to a good dinner.

Met Robert Johnson from Camden. He was taken prisoner there. The Yankees robbed Jack Cantey of his forks and spoons. When Jack did not seem to like it, they laughed at him; when he did not seem to see any fun in it, they pretended to weep, and wiped their eyes with their coattails. All of this maddening derision, Jack said, was as hard to bear as to see them ride off with his favorite horse. They stole all of Mrs. Jack's jewelry and silver. The Yankee general later wrote her a very polite note, saying how sorry he was that she had been annoyed, and returned to her a bundle of Jack's love letters written to her before they were married.

Mrs. Reynolds lost nothing. A Lieutenant McQueen of the Yankee Army had befriended the William Reynolds's in Camden. Lieutenant McQueen made his headquarters at her home, so she saved everything of hers. The young ladies were infatuated with Lieutenant McQueen. He even lent his horse to bury Mrs. Sam Capers. In the same cause we lost Claudia. She was safely hidden from the Yankees, but Miss Chesnut sent for her to be put into the hearse, and she was stolen at sight. She was a beauty. Poor Claudia! Robert Johnson said Miss Chesnut was a brave and determined spirit. A Yankee officer came in while they were at breakfast and sat down to warm himself at the fire. "Rebels have no rights," Miss Chesnut said to him politely. "But I suppose you have come to rob us. Please do so and go. Your presence agitates my blind old father." The man jumped up in a rage: "What do you take me for? A thief?" And for very shame he marched out empty-handed.

Robert Johnson married a granddaughter of old Adam McWillie, or McGillie as they call the name now. The old Adam is said still to ride around Camden, a veritable ghost. He was in the flesh a slave owner

* On this April first, the Confederate defeat at Five Forks forced Lee to evacuate his lines around Petersburg and begin the desperate and futile flight that ended at Appomattox Court House.

and a savage. He put Negroes in hogsheads, with nails driven in all around, and rolled the poor things down hill. The Negroes say they know the devil would not have him in Hell, so his spirit is roaming around where he made a little Hell of his own while he was alive. All that, however, was long, long ago. My nurse told me. The son, William McWillie, was an amiable person.

APRIL 3rd. — Mr. Preston came to tell me good-bye. He looked like a crusader on his great white horse, with William, his squire at his heels. How different these men look on horseback. They are all consummate riders. With their servants, as well mounted as themselves, riding behind them and carrying their cloaks and traps, it's hard to think of the same men packed like sardines in dirty railroad cars, which are usually floating inches deep in liquid tobacco juice.

At this late day, General Bonham has been given his longed-for Cavalry Brigade. They are moving the departments to Cokesbury. Oh ye of great faith! General Bonham came to dinner, quite pleased that he has his brigade. He said Lovell meant to come with him, but he heard Lovell say he did not know the way to my house, so he dodged him, as he — General Bonham — meant to stay to dinner. Ellen did her best. She has her hands full. Yesterday it was a *tête-à-tête* dinner with General Preston; today, Governor Bonham.

The latter, as we sat at the window which overlooks two thoroughfares, said: "All this marching and countermarching, this changing of generals and all, it is but Caesar's death scene. He is drawing his mantle around him to die decently."

"See how the stream westward never ceases. Lee's Army must be melting like a Scotch mist."

"Mist! Mist! Yes," he answered. "Yes, these men will be missed, if there is another battle soon."

Without any concert of action, everybody in Columbia seems to have suppressed the first letters written by them after Sherman's fire-arson-burglary called a raid. Miss Middleton sent me a letter from Sally Rutledge, hardly alluding to Sherman. She said she had written a folio in the first red-hot wrath, indignation, disgust and despair; but upon sober second thoughts she had thrown it in the fire. Mrs. McCord's letter was, like herself, cool and business-like, but in a postscript she said she had written a letter in her first futile rage at the senseless destruction but that letter she thought it wisest to destroy. Mrs. St. Julien Ravenel's first letter which I received alluded to the burning of

Columbia only by saying that the letter telling of it she had decided not to send, for reasons she would some day tell me. A strange coincidence. Why?

For the kitchen and Ellen's comfort, I wanted a pine table and a kitchen chair. A woman sold me a chair today for three thousand Confederate dollars.

Robert Johnson told me that Mr. A. H. Boykin camped out all the time the Yankees were in Camden. He said he liked the life, was always happiest in the woods or hunting. Prioleau Hamilton says the man to whose house they expected to move today came to say he could not take boarders for three reasons; first, they had smallpox in the house. "And the other two?" "Oh, I did not ask for the other two reasons."

April 5th. — Miss Middleton writes, in answer to my letter telling of the good things we have had to eat here: "It sounded as if you had landed on one of the Happy Islands, rather than on any part of this Confederate world of ours. We agreed it would be wise to pack up at once and ask the way to Chester. A still more moving argument was Stoneman, with his six thousand only twenty miles off! But today they say he has turned his face toward Salisbury and Greensborough, Danville being his goal. There is an Italian proverb: " 'They say' is a liar," and nowadays no one will dispute this assertion. When we can, we will go back to Columbia. We long for our own small sufficiency of wood, corn, and vegetables. We have fallen upon a new device. We keep a cookery book on the mantelpiece, and when our dinner is deficient, we just read a pudding, or a crême. It does not entirely satisfy the appetite, this dessert in imagination, but perhaps it is as good for the digestion."

Mrs. Prioleau Hamilton was in my parlor on high when Richardson Miles came to say General Hood had sent an orderly to find out where my house was. He said he could make an excuse for me, if I did not want to receive General Hood. "Ask him up!" was my answer, and there we sat on pins for two mortal hours, expecting Hood, and also Mrs. Bedon, who was coming for me to go down to the station to meet Mrs. Davis. At this late day, and as things stand now, not for worlds would I fail in any outward show of my deep reverence and respect for the President and Mrs. Davis. In the days of their power, they were so kind to me.

As I was ready to go, though still upstairs, they came to say General Hood was there. Mr. Hamilton cried: "Send word you are not at home!" "Never!" "Why make him climb all these stairs when you must go in five minutes?" "If he had come here with Sherman dragging a captive at his chariot wheels I might say 'not at home,' but not now!" And I ran down and greeted him on the side walk, in the face of all; and I walked with him as he toiled up those weary three stories. He was so well dressed, so cordial, and not depressed in the slightest. He calls his report self-defence, says Joe Johnston attacked him and so he was obliged to state things from his point of view. An English officer defends his campaign. Humphrey Marshall will answer Wigfall's attack upon him in the Senate. Mr. MacMahon, the author of "Cause and Contrast," is to say something in his favor in some paper, I forget what. And a New Orleans editor whose name likewise escapes me is writing on the Hood side of things. General Hood thinks it is all winding up. He says he was offered a command in Western Virginia, but General Lee thought as he and Joe Johnston were not on cordial terms, and as the fatigue of a mountain campaign would be too great for him, trans-Mississippi was better, and he jumped at the chance. Texas was true to him and would be his home. They had voted him a ranch somewhere out there. Then he spoke comically of his fear of York, to which he was wending his way, where the Hampton and Preston ladies were drawn up in battle array!

Mrs. Davis did not come and Hood stayed to dinner. We had a good glass of wine for him. General Chesnut brought from Camden, when he went there the other day, some of the best wine the Mulberry cellars still contain.

Mrs. Munroe writes from Lincolnton: "The description you give of your present style of living and the wonderful donations you receive have so astonished us here that we fear that your fever has returned, that this is all the ravings of delirium, and these feasts are merely wild phantasmagoria. Bowls of white sugar! Hams baked in biscuit dough! Trays of innumerable delicacies! I can't bear to think of it!

"Did you hear of our threatened raids? The inevitable Yankees seemed surely coming at last. Such burning, burying, packing things away in inconceivable places — to a rational mind the very places the Yankees would go to look for them. Women hurried from house to house repeating every absurd rumour, screaming children followed at the heels of their mothers, infuriated nurses rushed after and captured the straying children, men gathered in ominous groups in the streets! And after all, the Yankees did not come!"

I met Mr. Clarke from Columbia. All unshaven, he was brandishing a chair, holding it aloft like a banner by its one remaining rung. "This is all I have left of my Columbia house, and all my earthly possessions!" Mr. Clarke was one of the rich men of Columbia.

Late yesterday evening, when I was tired to death — my small parlour had been crammed all day — and just as Judge Upshur was handing Hood his crutches, I found a new man turning an immense ear trumpet in my face. A woman with a voice to raise the dead was singing to the guitar on the landing below, and it came up louder than life, but my deaf friend did not hear this reverberating din. He talked affably but the only sound I heard was that singing, and suddenly he stopped, said good night, and departed. He realized that I was growing distracted under his very eyes, I suppose. If he asked me what was the matter with me, I could not hear him.

They say General Lee is utterly despondent, and has no plan if Richmond goes — as go it must.

April 7th. — Richmond has fallen,* and I have no heart to write about it. Grant broke through our lines, Sherman cut through them, Stoneman is this side of Danville. They are too many for us. Everything is lost in Richmond, even our archives. Blue-black is our horizon. Buck writes to me, peremptorily: "Keep Sam in Chester!" To him she writes: "I leave it to your discretion!" The discretion of a man madly in love? He will go! What can I say that will keep him away.

Bonham took tea here. His beautiful command of three regiments of cavalry is not yet visible to the naked eye.

Madame F., the milliner, wants to go West, and General Hood said: "You will all be obliged to go West to Texas. Your own country will be overrun." In an unexpected pause of the conversation, we heard someone ask: "Is his engagement broken?" He understood in an instant, and very significantly answered: "Is my neck broken, did you ask?"

Poor Mrs. Middleton has paralysis. Has she not had trouble enough? How much she has had to bear, their plantation and home on Edisto destroyed, their house in Charleston burned, her children scattered, starvation in Lincolnton, and all as nothing to the one dreadful blow — her only son was killed in Virginia.

With this storm of woe impending, we snatched a moment of reckless gayety. Major and Mrs. Hamilton, Captain Barnwell and Captain Ogden, patriots supposed to be sunk in gloomy despondency, came and

* The telegraph lines had been cut, and Mrs. Chesnut's news continued to be several days late.

we played cards, and the stories told were so amusing. I confess I laughed to the point of tears! I knew trouble was all around us, but we put it out and kept it out, let it bang at the door as it would.

William Matthews, who married Miss Perroneau, says his wife was in her confinement when Columbia was burned; but she had to get out of bed or be burned in it. She sat with her new baby all night in the woods, and yet they are alive! She has never left her bed since. She was carried back to some of the houses left standing. A kind Yankee officer begged her to stay in her house and said he would protect it, but she found he could not do it even if he tried.

Fontaine in his newspaper is on the old cry: "Now Richmond is given up, because it was too heavy a load to carry, so we are stronger than ever!"

Stronger than ever? Nine tenths of our army are under ground! Where is another to come from? Will they wait until we grow one?

A forlorn Confederate came by with his head sticking out of a hole in the middle of a blanket, Indian fashion. This man had been a high functionary. "He looks as if the very crows had picked him," said one spectator, and then at sight of his wife, in deep mourning, with her high Roman nose and fierce black eyes: "And there is the crow that did it!"

APRIL 15th. — Hood brought Mary Darby and Buck with him from York. He sent Judge Upshur here to herald their advent. Hood was awfully proud of that feat. He had never dreamed they would come back with him.

What a week it has been; madness, sadness, anxiety, turmoil, ceaseless excitement. The Wigfalls passed through on their way to Texas. Louly told Hood they were bound for the Rio Grande, and intended to shake hands with Maximilian, Emperor of Mexico. Yankees were expected here every minute.

There was a money train, so many boxes of specie. Teddy Barnwell said adventurous spirits tapped it here; it seemed folly to send it on to the Yankees, who were bound to get it if it went much further. These patriots were disappointed. It had been saved from the Yankees before it got here. There was no specie in those boxes.

Mrs. Davis came. We went down to the cars at daylight to receive her. She dined with me. Lovely little "Piecake," the baby, came too. Buck and Hood were here, and Mary Darby. Clay behaved like a trump. He was as devoted to Mrs. Davis in her adversity as if they had never quarrelled in her prosperity. Some people sent me things for Mrs. Davis, but there were people here so base as to be afraid to befriend Mrs. Davis, thinking that when the Yankees came, they would take vengeance on them for it. She left here at five o'clock. My heart was like lead, but we did not give way. She was as calm and smiling as ever. It was but a brief glimpse of my dear Mrs. Davis, and under altered skies. One of the staff did not rise from his chair when she entered the room. Could ill manners go further?

Hood has gone. He held his hat off while he was in sight of the house. "Why did he remain uncovered so long?" I asked. "In honor of my being here," said Buck quietly.

April 19th. — Mrs. Davis told me that she had horrid reports about Richmond, that all below Ninth Street to Rockett's has been burned by the beggars who mobbed the town.

John Darby tells of a most culpable negligence on the part of Longstreet. General Lee sent him written orders for the next day's fight at Gettysburg. Longstreet left them on his table. When he struck tent, they were swept off and fell on the ground. The Yankees found them the same day, and with that key to his plan of battle were able to forestall every movement that he made.* Old Peter was always too slow, though a bulldog to fight.

Mrs. Middleton writes: "You remember I dared not give you a cup of tea before our Lincolnton visitors. If they saw us with tea, they would not send us bread. They will not tolerate luxuries in pauper exiles. Our men-servants sauntering around the yard with cigars in their mouths, brought us near starvation. We were utterly dependent on these kind folk for our daily bread. Shopkeepers are so different from what we thought them in our insolent prosperity; often well educated, well-mannered, well-dressed, and positively agreeable in conversation."

I remember how Joe Heyward astonished people in Washington when he said he had never known anybody but planters.

Just now Mr. Clay dashed up stairs, pale as a sheet. "General Lee has capitulated." I saw the news reflected in Mary Darby's face before I heard him. She staggered to the table, sat down, and wept aloud.

* This tale, completely false as far as Longstreet is concerned, is an echo of the actual incident before Antietam-Sharpsburg, when a copy of General Lee's orders to his corps commanders was found by McClellan's soldiers and put into McClellan's hands. It may also echo the fact that Lee's plan of action if the Petersburg line were broken, which the Confederate Congress required him to put in writing, was left behind by Jefferson Davis in the hurried evacuation of Richmond, and was delivered to Grant in time to let him anticipate Lee's every move during the week that preceded Appomattox.

Mr. Clay's eyes were not dry. Quite beside herself, Mary shrieked: "Now we belong to Negroes and Yankees." Buck said: "I do not believe it!"

Edward Barnwell was here last night. He was hilarious at my attentions to the Royal Family in Exile, at the way I ran after little Maggie, little Jeff and darling little Billy, and tried to make them happy. Billy is Mr. Chesnut's special pet. I faced the fun gallantly. I would do tenfold more for them now than I would have done in the days of their prosperity and power.

General Preston is very bitter. He says General Lee fought just well enough to make the Yankees more conceited and self-sufficient than ever, when they found they were too much for him. They pay us a compliment we would never pay them. We fought to get rid of Yankees and Yankee rule. How different is their estimate of us! To keep the despised and iniquitous South as a part of their country, they are willing to enlist millions of men at home and abroad and to spend billions, and to have three killed for our one. We hear they have all grown rich. Genuine Yankees can make a fortune trading jack knives!

Someone said we will have to pay the piper, but I say blood cannot be squeezed from a turnip. You cannot pour anything out of an empty cup. We have no money, even for taxes, or for their confiscation.

While the Preston girls are here, my dining-room is given up to them, and we camp on the landing, with our one table and six chairs. Beds are made on the dining-room floor. Otherwise there is no furniture, but there are buckets of water and bathtubs in their improvised chamber. Night and day this landing, and these steps are crowded with the *élite* of the Confederacy, going and coming; and when night comes, or rather bedtime, more beds are made on the floor of the landing for the war-worn soldiers to rest upon. The whole house is a bivouac. My husband is rarely at home. I sleep with the girls, and my room is given up to soldiers too. General Lee's men from the South and West, sad and crestfallen, pass through Chester; and many of the discomfited heroes find their way up these stairs. They say Johnston will not be caught as Lee was. He can retreat, that is his trade.

The plucky way our men bear up is beyond praise. No howling! Our poverty is made a matter of laughing. We deride our own penury. Of the country, we try not to speak at all.

And those gallivanting heroes! Some of these chaps did console themselves a little, and now they go back, rampantly faithful, to their foolish wives who were so faithful and so anxious about them.

April 22nd. — This yellow Confederate quire of paper, blotted by my journal, has been buried three days with the silver sugar dish, the teapot, milk jug, and a few spoons and forks that follow my fortunes. With these valuables was Hood's silver cup, which was partly crushed when he was wounded at Chickamauga. It has been a wild three days, aids galloping around with messages, Yankees hanging over us like the sword of Damocles. We sat up at Mrs. Bedon's, dressed, without once going to bed for forty-eight hours, and we were aweary.

Colonel Cadwallader Jones came with a dispatch, sealed and secret. It was for General Chesnut. I opened it. Lincoln, Old Abe Lincoln, killed, murdered! Seward wounded! Why? By whom? It is simply maddening. I sent off messenger after messenger for General Chesnut. I have not the faintest idea where he is, but I know this foul murder will bring down worse miseries on us.

Mary Darby says: "But they murdered him themselves! There are no Confederates in Washington." "But if they see fit to accuse us of instigating it?"

Met Mr. Heyward. He said the army is deserting Joe Johnston, said: "That is the peoples' vote against a continuance of the war. And the death of Lincoln, I call that a warning to tyrants. He will not be the last president put to death in the Capital, though he is the first." Joe Johnston's army, that he has risked his reputation to save, deserting? He saved his army by retreats, and now they are deserting him! Stonewall's tactics were the best. Hard knocks, blow after blow in rapid succession, quick marches, surprises, victories. But watch, wait, retreat; these ruined us.

Now look out for bands of marauders, black and white; lawless, disbanded soldiers, from both armies.

An armistice, they say, is agreed on.

I take stock, as the shopkeepers say. We have heavy debts for the support of Negroes during the War, and before; but to think of Camden for life, that is worse than the galleys for me.

At Mrs. Bedon's, Buck never submits to being bored. The bores come to tea, and then sit and talk; so prosy, so wearisome was the discourse, so endless it seemed. We envied Buck, mooning on the piazza. She rarely speaks now. Serene she seems, but in deep reveries ever.

Once, softly, she came in from the piazza with face unmoved and devoid of all expression and said quietly: "Guns in the distance! Don't you hear?"

Our guests were off at a bound, hardly taking time to say good night. "Buck, did you hear anything?" "No!" We laughed. "Well, all the same, you saved our lives. I was nearly dead." She smiled in the same listless, unconcerned way, and went back to her post in the piazza.

APRIL 23rd. — My silver wedding day, and I am sure it is the unhappiest day of my life. Then from the piazza sang Buck:

"And from our window high,
Which looks out on the sky,
John Chesnut I do spy!"

Johnny looked up from the pavement below, and we saw the gleam of his white teeth as he caught our eyes and shouted joyfully: "Oh, so you live up there! I am coming." He stopped to kiss his hand to her, and then dashed up half a dozen steps at a time. "Heavens, is this the cool Captain?" asked Mary Darby, and he answered: "Yes, but then I do love you girls so!" "Both?" "Certainly!" He says: "We are not conquered! We are on our way to Maximilian, in Mexico!"

With his philosophical foot foremost, General Chesnut has argued in the most aggravating manner that the Yankees would be after Mexico next, that they would leave no Austrian Prince down there! The French and English, by leaving us in the lurch had solidified and glorified the Yankees, and now their turn would come. We gave them a chance — and they threw it away forever. We told Johnny this, and Mary Darby said: "They left us in the lurch because of slavery, you know."

"That is all rubbish!" cried Johnny. "Virtue in a nation is a matter of latitude and longitude. Look at the English in India, the French in Algiers; and the Yankees hug the Mormons to their Puritan bosoms. Polygamy flourished under the Stars and Stripes. Yankees recoil in horror at the passion Negroes have for marrying, or for doing without it, so it must be polyandry they dislike!"

No wonder he is bitter! Mulberry has been destroyed by a corps commanded by General Logan.*

Poor Nat Butler is here, his right arm gone. John Chesnut, basking at Buck's feet, is jealous of Nat Butler. Someone asked coolly: "Will General Chesnut be shot as a soldier, or hung as a Senator?"

"I am not of sufficient consequence," he answered. "They will stop short of Brigadiers. And then I resigned my seat in the Senate weeks

* This proved untrue. The house was damaged, but not destroyed.

before there was any secession." But after all, it is only a choice between drum head court-martial and a short shrift, and a lingering death at home from starvation.

The Negroes seem unchanged. Ellen has had my diamonds to keep for a week or so. When the danger was over, she handed them back to me with as little apparent interest as if they were garden peas.

While the cool Captain was here, riding in the opposite direction with Buck, an officer sent to John's camp for horses. When John went out to the camp, his servants told him that Confederate soldiers had just impressed his horses and gone off with them. Every horse was missing but the one he rode. Without a word he galloped after the horse-thieves. He saw a man on one of his horses and shot at him. Cried the man: "Do you shoot before you hail a fellow?" "Yes, if he is riding off on one of my horses." "You are brave enough, firing at an unarmed man!" "Well," said the cool Captain, "I see you all have your pistols. If any of you doubt my willingness to shoot at an armed man, let him try to stop me from taking back my horses." Some of John's men came galloping up in hot haste, and they led their horses back without let or hinderance.

"You see," Buck commented. "He loves his horses better than his life."

A man told Mr. Portman, when he stopped and asked for lodging, that two travellers stopped there a day or two before and asked to stay all night. They were such unnatural fire-eaters that the man grew suspicious. While they slept, he overhauled their papers and found they were Yankees. He cut their throats and buried them. Seeing that Mr. Portman did not believe a word he said, the man offered to go and show him the spies, half-buried in the bushes. They took care not to trust themselves to the tender mercies of such a landlord.

Mr. Davis has gone, they say, by Abbeville. Gone where? Said Mary Darby vengefully: "One thing I respect in those awful Yankees. If they did choose a baboon to reign over them, they were true to him; they stuck to him through weal and through woe."

"When they print his life, I wonder if they will put in all of the dirty stories his soul delighted in?" "Faugh!" said Mary Darby, whose darling Darby had enlightened her in many ways. Now most of the anecdotes, funny as they were, which were told me as coming from Lincoln, were so eminently calculated to raise a blush upon a young person's cheek that I had never been able to repeat them.

Our soldiers pass daily. Yesterday these poor fellows were heroes, today they are only rebels, to be hung or shot at the Yankee's pleasure. One year ago, we left Richmond. The Confederacy has double-quicked down hill since then. Burned towns, deserted plantations, sacked villages!

"You seem resolute to look the worst in the face," said General Chesnut wearily.

"Yes, poverty, no future, no hope." "But no slaves, thank God!" cried Buck.

"How does our famous Captain, the Great Lee, bear the Yankee's galling chain?" I asked. "He knows how to possess his soul in patience," answered my husband shortly. "If there was no such word as subjugation, no debts, no poverty, no Negro mobs backed by Yankees; if all things were well, you would still shiver and feel benumbed," he went on, pointing a finger at me. "For your sentence is pronounced. Camden for life!"

MAY 1st. — In Chester still. I climb these steep steps alone. They have all gone. One day just before they began to dissolve in thin air, Captain Gay was seated at the table, halfway between me on the top step and John in the window with his legs outside. Buck went into her room to prepare for the afternoon ride. Captain Gay said, nodding toward her door: "They are engaged, Captain Chesnut and herself."

"No!" came emphatically from the window, and the Captain brought his legs inside. "I have been barking up that tree a long time, but ——" "I saw you put a diamond ring on her hand." "She showed me her engagement ring, and I put it back on her hand. She is engaged, but not to me."

"Well," said Captain Gay, "I have seen many a man do far less courting, and get married on it."

Vizitelli, whom I had not seen since our theatricals in Richmond, came charging up those many stairs and handed Mary Darby a roll of Confederate bills as big as his head. "These I give you for your hospital, for any charitable object!" "How kind, how generous!" said Mary, profuse in thanks. "But after all he might as well keep them to light his pipe, for all they are worth," murmured the sensible Buck.

Mrs. Huger says: "In Richmond, a too grateful and affectionate fat, greasy Negro barber threw his arms around a Yankee general and hugged him in a close embrace. The Yankee freed himself and shot him dead. 'It was time to stop that damned nonsense,' he said."

General Preston came to say good-bye. He will take his family abroad at once. Burnside in New Orleans owes him some money and will pay it.

This very day a party of Federals passed in hot pursuit of our President.

A terrible fire-eater, one of the few men left in the world who believes we have a right divine, being white, to hold Africans who are black in bonds forever, came here today. He is six feet two, an athlete, a splendid specimen of the animal man; but he has never been under fire. His place in the service was a bombproof office. With a face red-hot in its rage, he denounced Jeff Davis and Hood. Now Teddy Barnwell is always ready for a shindy, and does not care very much who he attacks or defends. "Come now," said Edward the handsome, "the men who could fight and did not, they are the people who ruined us. If the men who are cursing Jeff Davis now had fought with Hood and fought as Hood fought we'd be all right now." The fire eater departed.

Mrs. Huger told a story of Joe Johnston before he was famous, in his callow days. After an illness, the Johnston hair all fell out. Not a hair was left on his head, and it shone like a fiery cannon ball. One of the gentlemen from Africa who waited at table sniggered so that he was ordered out, and General Huger, feeling for the agonies of young Africa as he strove to stifle his mirth, suggested that Joe cover his head with his handkerchief. A red silk one was produced, and placed like a turban on his head; but this finished the gravity of the butler. He fled and his guffaw outside of the door was painfully audible. General Huger then suggested, as they must have the waiters back or dinner could not go on, that Joe should eat in his hat — which he did.

XXIII

Camden

MAY 2nd, 1865. — I am writing from the roadside below Blackstock's, *en route* to Camden. Since we left Chester, solitude; nothing but tall, blackened chimneys to show that any man has ever trod this road before us. This is Sherman's track! It is hard not to curse him.

I wept incessantly at first. "The roses of the gardens are already hiding the ruins," said Mr. Chesnut, trying to say something. Then I made a vow. If we are a crushed people, I will never be a whimpering, pining slave.

We heard loud explosions of gunpowder in the direction of Chester. I suppose the destroyers are at it there. We met William Walker. Mr. Preston left him in charge of a carload of his valuables. Mr. Preston was hardly out of sight before poor helpless William had to stand by and see the car plundered. "My dear Missis, they have cleaned me out, nothing left," moaned William the faithful.

MAY 4th. — From Chester to Winnsboro, we did not see one living thing, man, woman or animal, except poor William trudging home after his sad disaster. The blooming of the gardens had a funereal effect. Nature is so luxuriant here; she soon covers the ravages of savages. The last frost occurred the seventh of March, so that accounts for the wonderful advance of vegetation. It seems providential to these starving people; so much that is edible has grown in two months.

At Winnsboro, to my amazement, the young people had a May Day amidst the smoking ruins. Irrepressible youth! The fidelity of the Negroes is the principal topic everywhere. There seems not a single case of a Negro who betrayed his master; and yet they showed a natural and exultant joy at being free. In the fields we saw them plowing and hoeing corn as always. The fields in that respect looked quite cheerful.

May 9th. — Anne Bailey said Godard had gone North. "Where he ought to have stayed," she added venomously. "For we are behaving down here like beaten curs." The cool Captain wants to go across the Mississippi with Hampton. "I do not think Hampton will go," said Dr. Boykin. "They could only fight as partisans, guerillas."

Mary Kirkland had an experience with Yankees. When they came, Monroe, their Negro man-servant, told her to stand up and keep her children in her arms. She stood against the wall with her baby in her arms, and the other two as closely pressed against her knees as they could get. Mammy Selina and Lizzie stood grimly on each side of their young missis and her children. For four mortal hours the soldiers surged through this room, and the Yankee soldiers reviled the Negro women for their foolishness in standing by their cruel slave owners and they taunted Mary with being glad of the protection of her poor ill-used slaves. Monroe had one leg bandaged, and pretended to be lame, so that he might not be enlisted as a soldier. He kept making pathetic appeals to Mary. "Don't answer 'em back, Miss Mary. Let them say what they want to. Don't give em any chance to say you are impudent to 'em."

Finally poor Aunt Betsey fainted from pure fright and exhaustion. Mary put down her baby and sprang to her mother, lying limp on a chair, and called to them: "Leave this room, you wretches! Do you mean to kill my mother!" Without a word, they all slunk out, ashamed.

Mrs. Bartow drove with me to our house at Mulberry. On one side of the house, every window was broken, every bell torn down, every piece of furniture destroyed, every door smashed in. The other side was intact. Maria Whitaker and her mother explained this odd state of things. "They were working like regular carpenters, destroying everything, when the General came in. He said it was a shame, and he stopped them; he said it was a sin to destroy a fine old house like this, whose owner was over ninety years old. He would not have done it for the world. It was wanton mischief."

They carried off sacks of our books and our papers, our letters were strewed along the Charleston road as far away as Vance's ferry.

This was Potter's raid. Sherman only took our horses. Potter's raid, which was after Johnston's surrender, ruined us. He burned our mills and gins, and a hundred bales of cotton. Indeed, nothing is left now but the bare land, and debts incurred for the support of these hundreds of Negroes during the War.

A. H. Boykin was wiser in his generation. The troops who were sent to defend Camden, he without any authority crossed at a ferry opposite his plantation and that of Mr. John DeSaussure. Potter, to evade these troops, came up by the Black River road and destroyed the town — and our fortunes with it — a few hours before a courier came to declare peace. So by being at home to look after their own interests, Hamilton Boykin and John DeSaussure have saved their cotton and their estates, their mills and farming utensils. The Negroes are a good riddance. A hired man is far cheaper than a man whose father and mother, his wife and his twelve children have to be fed, clothed, housed, nursed, taxes paid and doctors' bills.

If our cotton had been saved, we would be in comparatively easy circumstances.*

The raids were regularly organized. First, squads demanded arms and whiskey; then came the rascals who hunted for silver and ransacked the lady's wardrobes. Then came some smiling, suave, well-dressed officers, who regretted it all so much. And then, outside the gate, officers, men and bummers divided share and share alike the piles of plunder.

"Write under any story † you tell about me in your journal, 'this is translated from Balzac!' " She rambled on, not knowing the meaning of half she said. The music, and the moonlight, and that restful feeling of her head on my knee, set her tongue in motion. She accounted for her unwonted fit of confidence thus, because she is as silent as the grave about her own affairs.

"I think it began with those beautiful, beautiful silk stockings that fit so nicely. I have been afraid to warm my feet on the fender ever since. You ought to hear him rave about my foot and ankle. Before that, he was so respectful; he kissed my hand to be sure, but that is

* Mr. Boykin sold his cotton in New York in November and December for "ten thousand dollars in gold and twenty thousand in currency in the hands of Ravenel and Company, and the balance in gold in New York." The price averaged fifty cents a pound.

† This passage in the Diary contains no names; but "he" and "she" are readily identified.

nothing. Sometimes, when he kissed my hand, he said I was his queen, and what a grateful fellow he was that I liked him; and I was proud of that very respectful style he adopted.

"But as I stood by the fender warming my feet, he seized me 'round the waist and kissed my throat. When he saw how shocked I was, he was frightened and so humble, and so full of apologies. He said it was so soft and white, that throat of mine, he could not help it. It was all so sudden. I drew back, and told him I would go away, that I was offended. In a moment I felt a strong arm so tight around my waist I could not move. He said I should stay until I forgave his rash presumption, and he held me fast. I pretended to be in a rage. He said that after all, I had promised to marry him, and that made all the difference in the world; but I did not see it. So I wear boots, and I never warm my feet, and I wear a stiff handkerchief close up around my throat!"

"Lead us not into temptation," I thought; but when people are opening their hearts, I never say a word. In one thing I heartily agree with the late-lamented Lincoln. "I hate a fellow who is interruptious."

"You see I never meant to be so outrageously treated again," she continued. "It was a shame. Yet now, would you believe it, a sickening, almost an insane longing comes over me just to see him once more, and I know I never will. He is gone forever. If he had been persistent, if he had not given way under Mamma's violent refusal to listen to us, if he had asked *me!* When you refused to let anybody be married in your house, well I would have gone down on the sidewalk, I would have married him on the pavement, if the parson could be found to do it. I was ready to leave all the world for him, to tie my clothes in a bundle and, like a soldier's wife, trudge after him to the ends of the earth. Does that sound like me? It was true that day!"

"And now, how you flirt! Nothing but the love of you keeps him here. He is not flirting! He is badly hurt. He is in bitter earnest!"

"Now let us talk of something else! Imagine that we have been translating from the French!"

When we crossed the river coming home, the ferryman at Chesnut's Ferry asked for his fee. Among us all, we could not muster the small silver coin he demanded. There was poverty for you! Nor did a stiver appear among us until Molly was hauled home from Columbia, where she was waging war with Sheriff Dent's family, and as soon as her foot touched her native heath, she sent to hunt up the cattle. Our cows were found in the swamp. Many of them, like Marion's men, were *non comeatabus* in swamps for the Yankees. Now she sells butter for us on shares.

Old Cuffey, head gardener at Mulberry, and Yaller Abram, his assistant, have gone on in the even tenor of their way. Men may come and men may go, but they dig on forever, and they say they mean to, as long as old Marster is alive. So we have green peas, asparagus, lettuce, spinach, new potatoes and strawberries in abundance; enough for ourselves and plenty to give away to the refugees.

My husband and Captain John laugh at my peddling butter; but I notice all of my silver money that General Chesnut fails to borrow on Saturday is begged or borrowed by Captain Chesnut by Monday.

Old Mr. Chesnut had a summer resort for his invalid Negroes, and especially for the women with ailing babies. Myrtilia, an African, was head nurse there. She went off with the Yankees, and now from Orangeburg come the most pathetic letters. Old Myrtilia begs to be sent for. She wants to come home. Miss Chesnut, who feels terribly any charitable distress which can be relieved by others, urges us to send for "poor Old Myrtilia." "Very well," says her brother. "You pay for the horses and the wagon and the driver, and I will send." And that ended the Myrtilia tragedy as far as we were concerned. But poor old Myrtilia, after the first natural frenzy of freedom subsided, knew well on which side her bread was buttered; and she knew too, or found out, where her real friends were. So in a short time old Myrtilia was on our hands to support once more. How she got back, we did not inquire.

Mrs. Barnwell Boykins's coachman had always seen such devoted attention and care bestowed upon Negro children that he made an over-estimate of their worth. Quantities of Negro mothers, running after the Yankee Army, left their babies by the wayside. They left them, and did not spring from block of ice to block, as Mrs. Stowe fondly imagines they do. So the coachman came in exultant. "Oh Missis, I have saved a wagonload of babies for you. Dem niggers run away and lef dem chillun all long de road." I fancy how sorely tried even Aunt Sally's Christian charity must be by such an ill-timed gift.

Johnny went over to see Hampton. His cavalry are ordered to reassemble on the 20th, a little farce to let themselves down easily. They know it is all over.

Isabella writes, and really seems to believe it, that Sherman at once offered Hampton a command in the United States Cavalry.

Had a message from Buck. After a long ride with Rollins Lowndes, she was too tired to write. *Le Roi est mort — vive le Roi.*

We have had our present position defined. General Lovell sent General Chesnut an order, showing that he considered him a paroled prisoner.

Floride Cantey heard an old Negro say to his master: "When you'all had de power you was good to me, and I'll protect you now. No niggers nor Yankees shall touch you. If you want anything, call for Sambo. I mean, call for Mr. Samuel — that's my name now."

May 10th. — A letter from a Pharisee, who thanks the Lord she is not as other women are. She writes: "I feel that I will not be ruined, come what may. God will provide for me." But her husband had strengthened the Lord's hands, and — for the Glory of God, doubtless — invested a hundred thousand dollars in New York, where Confederate money did not corrupt, nor Yankee bummers break through and steal. She goes on to tell us: "I have had the good things of this world, and I have enjoyed them in their season. But I always held them as steward for God. My bread has been cast upon the waters and will return to me."

E. M. Boykin is awfully sanguine. His main idea is joy that he has no Negroes to support, and can hire only those that he really wants.

Minnie Frierson tells a story as of an eye witness, a pendant to Adam's present of the Negro babies to his mistress by the wagonload. Minnie says: "Eighteen Negro women have been found along the road, stabbed by the retreating army. The Yankee soldiers could not rid themselves of these pests any other way. Poor animals."

Stanton has telegraphed to Georgia: "Let no rebel legislature stand." Take care of yourself, shifty old Joe Brown.

Johnny, though his country is in mourning, with as much to mourn for as country ever had, still keeps that cold, calm, unmoved air of his. He is as volatile, as inconsequent, as easily made happy as any light-hearted son of the South. To my amazement, he wants me to give a picnic at Mulberry. Just now I would as soon dance on my father's grave!

Molly tells me all of the men on our plantation have Enfield rifles. The whites are disarmed, or are supposed to be and ordered to be. Now will come the long hoped for rising against former masters and murdering them, missing which our enemies have been so unhappy.

Mr. Chesnut says quietly: "I could take twenty men and clear this country * of armed Negroes to the Santee line."

Upwards of a thousand Confederate soldiers have come here. A man named Latta, a Commissary agent, took it upon himself to invite them here to divide Confederate stores. This rabble alarmed us, but our handfull of gentlemen privates reassured us. "There will be no disorder. Half a dozen of us could clear away this crowd." "Rascality," says Carlyle, "has always outnumbered gentility a hundred to one, and yet . . ."

Said Henrietta: "That old fool Dick Taylor will not disband and let his nasty Confederacy smash and be done with it." I rose. "Excuse me. I cannot sit at table with anybody abusing my country." So I went out on the piazza, but from the windows came loud screams of vituperation and insult. "Jeff Davis's stupidity, Joe Johnston's magnanimity, Bragg's insanity." So I fled. Next day she flew at me again, and raved until I was led out in hysterics, and then I was very ill. They thought I was dying, and I wish I had died.

Sally Reynolds told a story of a little Negro, a pet of Mrs. Kershaw's. The little boy clung to Mrs. Kershaw and begged her to save him. The Negro mother, stronger than Mrs. Kershaw, tore him away from her; and Mrs. Kershaw saw the mother chasing the child before her as she ran after the Yankees, whipping him at every step. The mother soon came back but Mrs. Kershaw would not allow any of them to enter her yard again.

MAY 16th. — We are scattered, stunned, the remnant of heart left alive in us filled with brotherly hate. We sit and wait until the drunken tailor who rules the United States of America issues a proclamation and defines our anomalous position.

Such a hue and cry, everybody blamed by somebody else. Only the dead heroes left stiff and stark on the battle field escape. I cry: "Blame every man who stayed at home and did not fight, but not one word against those who stood out until the bitter end, and stacked muskets at Appomattox." †

MAY 18th. — Colonel Chesnut, ninety-three, blind and deaf, is

* It was common practice in the South for a man to refer to his state and sometimes to his county as his "country."

† The phrase became an honorable badge. To have been paroled at Appomattox was not enough, since many of those paroled were weaponless stragglers. But to have "stacked muskets at Appomattox" meant that men had not only endured, but had carried their weapons and had kept themselves in fighting trim to the last.

apparently as strong as ever and certainly as resolute of will. African Scipio walks always at his side. He is six feet two, a black Hercules and as gentle as a dove in all his dealings with the blind old master, who boldly strides forward, striking with his stick to feel where he is going. The Yankees left Scipio unmolested. He told them he was absolutely essential to his master; and they said: "If you want to stay so bad, he must have been good to you." Scipio was silent. He says: "It made them mad if you praised your Master."

Partly patriarch, partly *grand seigneur*, this old man is of a species that we will see no more; the last of the lordly planters who ruled this Southern world. His manners are unequalled still, but underneath this smooth exterior lies the grip of a tyrant whose will has never been crossed.

Sometimes this old man will stop himself, just as he is going off in a fury because they try to prevent his attempting some impossible feat. He will stop, and say gently: "I hope that I never say or do anything unseemly — sometimes I think I am subject to mental aberrations."

At every footfall he calls out: "Who goes there?" If a lady's name is given, he uncovers and stands hat in hand until she passes. He has still the Old World art of bowing low and gracefully. He came of a race that would brook no interference with their own sweet will by man, woman, or devil; but then such manners would clear any man's character, if it needed it.

Old Mrs. Chesnut used to tell me that when she met him at Princeton, in the seventeen-nineties, they called him the Young Prince. He and Mr. John Taylor of Columbia were the first Up Country youths whose parents were wealthy enough to send them off to college. When a college was established in South Carolina, Colonel John Chesnut, the father of the aforesaid young Prince, was among the first trustees. Indeed I may say that since the Revolution of 1776, there has been no convocation of the notables of South Carolina, whether in times of peace and prosperity or in times of war and adversity in which the representative man of this family has not appeared. The estate has been kept together until now, because there has always been an only son.

They have a saying here — on account of the large families with which people are usually blessed in these parts, and the subdivision of property consequent upon that fact, besides the tendency of one generation to make and to save and of the next to idle and to squander — that there is rarely more than three generations between shirt sleeves and shirt sleeves. But these people have survived four, from the John Chesnut who was driven out from his father's farm in Virginia by the French and Indians when that father was killed at Fort Duquesne, to the young John Chesnut who saunters along here now, the very perfection of a lazy gentleman who will scarce move unless it be for a fight, a dance, or a fox hunt.

The first comer of that name to this State was but ten when he got here. Being penniless, he went to Mr. Joseph Kershaw's grocery shop as a clerk; and the Kershaws, I think, have that fact on their coat of arms. Our Johnny, as he was driving me down to Mulberry yesterday, declared himself delighted with the fact that the present Joseph Kershaw had so distinguished himself in our War that they would let the shop of a hundred years ago rest for awhile. "Upon my soul," cried the cool Captain. "I have a desire to go in there and look at the Kershaw tombstones. I am sure they have put it on their marble tablets, boasting that we had an ancestor one day, a hundred years ago, who was a clerk in their shop." In the second generation, the shop was so far sunk that the John Chesnut of that day refused to let his daughter marry a handsome, dissipated Kershaw; and she, a spoiled beauty who could not endure to obey orders when they were disagreeable to her, went up to her room and there stayed, never once coming out of it for forty years. Her father let her have her own way in that, provided servants to wait upon her and gave her every conceivable luxury that she desired, but neither party would give in.

Among my father's papers — he was a lawyer at the time of our present Joe Kershaw's father, and filed a bill in equity against Colonel John Chesnut's estate — there is a letter from my father advising the Kershaws not to go to law; and then there is a letter from Joe Kershaw's father, asking Colonel James Chesnut not to go to law with them, as by doing so he would beggar Miss Mary Kershaw, the only daughter left alive of the original Joseph. She still owned a few Negroes and some land and was highly respected by all the Camden world. Colonel Chesnut dropped the suit, and it must be remembered to his credit, for he did not part with money easily. How could he? His one moral was: "A fool and his money are soon parted." Colonel John Chesnut had been kindly treated by the Kershaw of the shop before the Revolution, and he would never allow anything to be done when the family lost their property which would any way annoy them. ("Barring marrying them!" cries Johnny, as he finished reading this.)

MAY 21st. — Harriet is radiant. She has heard that Jeff Davis has been captured, and that Columbia has been garrisoned at last. We are threatened with a mob. The law and order men, General and Captain Chesnut and Cousins Haskell and Boykin, sallied forth to protect Commissary stores. Who for? It will be the private property soon, of the commissary. They say Governor Magrath has absconded, and the Yankees said: "If you have no visible governor, we will send you one." And if we had one, and they found him, they would clap him in prison instanter.

How the Negroes flocked to the Yankee squad which has recently come here. They were snubbed, these rampant freedmen. "Stay where you are," say the Yanks. "We have nothing for you." The Negroes have picked up the word "peruse" and they use it in season and out. When we met Mrs. Preston's William and asked: "Where are you going?" he answered: "Perusing my way to Columbia!" The Negro women, dressed in their gaudiest array, carried bouquets to the Yankees; but in this house, there is not the slightest change. I do not see one particle of alteration. They are more circumspect, politer, quieter; but that's all. Every day I expect to miss some familiar face, but so far, none has gone. I have been disappointed.

Mrs. Huger we found at the Hotel here. She told us that Jeff Davis was travelling leisurely with his wife, twelve miles a day, and utterly careless whether he were taken prisoner or not. Also that General Hampton is paroled.

Dr. Lord was here. Mr. Davis attended his church in Mississippi. Dr. Lord is a Princeton man, married a Miss Stockton. Here are his words describing the much-abused martyr, Jeff Davis. "I have never had a parishioner that I liked better. He is one of the purest and best of men, one of the kindest hearted." Then he went on to discuss our military matters, and General Chesnut began to give his far from orthodox views of theology. Miss Chesnut wished to stop that, but I said: "No, let him go on. The parson seems an oracle on war and its ways; let the General enlighten him as to creed and dogma."

We heard of Jeff Davis's capture. Fighting Dick Anderson, and Stephen Elliott of Fort Sumter memory are quite ready to pray for Andy Johnson, and to submit to the powers that be. But not so our belligerent clergy. "Pray for people when I wish they were dead?" cries Mr. Trapier. "No! Never! But I will pray for President Davis till I die." I replied by my tears. "Taken in woman's clothes!" *

* The report that President Davis was clad in woman's garments when he was captured was soon denied by the Union officers who captured him.

exploded Mr. Trapier. "Rubbish! Stuff and nonsense! If Jeff Davis has not the pluck of a true man, then there is no courage left on this earth."

John Witherspoon was in agony. "What might the Yankees not do to Mr. Davis?" "Not hang him, not they. They are too cute for that! They won't have his blood crying to Heaven against them, and make him a martyr on the scaffold, like Charles I, for us to worship down here forever. Look at Lincoln now! How we used to hate him, or to abuse him, anyway; and now who is so base as to utter a word against the murdered President. No, the Yankees will fling him back among us, our beloved Jeff Davis; and in the house of his friends, the Mercury, Rhett, Joe Johnston and company, he will be mangled *con amore*."

We asked Mrs. Kershaw if she had heard from her husband. "From the general, do you mean?" I was near laughing, but I spoke politely. When we parted, Johnny said: "Aunt Mary, I will drive you on one of the back streets so that you may have your laugh out. You who moaned that generals were so cheap and privates so dear!" "Yes, I have been for four years snowed under by generals!"

Dr. Mark Reynolds said today: "I admire the Yankees so as a nation that I find it difficult to quarrel with them individually, even when they come to rob me. Our girls will soon be marrying Yankees, and then the thing will blow over." Oh, the arrows of scorn these people shoot at our country, in her day of humiliation and sorrow. He went back to his nieces and called me a fiery Southerner and said I folded my hands behind me when he tried to help me in the carriage, that I would not let him touch me.

JUNE 1st. — Edward Stockton escaped on a British vessel. The captain passed him off as his steward. He met in New York men who had served with him in the old Navy, but he kept out of their way. He met his father, who greeted him kindly on the street, but said: "Do not go to my house. There they are bitter against the South."

Mrs. Williams is off for New York, to sell four hundred bales of cotton, and a "square," or something which pays tremendously, near the Central Park, and to capture and bring home her *belle fille* who remained North during the War. She knocked at my door. I was in bed, and as I sprang up I discovered that my old Confederate night gown had to be managed, it was so full of rents. I am afraid I gave undue attention to the sad condition of my gown, and could nowhere see a shawl to drape my figure. She was very kind. In case my husband was arrested and needed funds, she offered me some British securities.

We were very grateful, but we did not accept the loan — almost the same as a gift, so slim was our chance of repaying it. It was a generous thought on her part, I own that.

We went to the Hermitage yesterday and saw no change, not a soul absent from his or her post. I said: "Good coloured folks, when are you going to kick off the traces and be free?" In their furious, emotional way they swore devotion to us to their dying day. All the same, the moment they see an opening to better themselves, they will move on.

William, my husband's foster brother, came up. "Well, William, what do you want?" "Only to look at you, Master. It does me good." Both parties, white and black, talked beautifully.

Edward Adamson, without money, has set out for Florida. He has a barrel of whiskey to pay his way on the journey.

Mrs. Huger told us of her brother-in-law, Alfred Ravenel, and his adventures in Charleston with the Yankee officers. He went to the place where people take the oath of allegiance to the United States, and found it surrounded by applicants for that honour several squares deep. The individual there installed to listen to all that "swearing in" is a New York butcher, and no ornament to the butchers as a class. His manner to Mr. Ravenel was insulting in the extreme. "Hey, you! Sir, you are a spy!" And when Mr. Ravenel denied the soft impeachment: "You lie, you rascal! If you are not a spy, why have you changed your dress? You are not in the clothes you had on yesterday. I had you watched!" "The clothes I had on yesterday were of white linen, and easily soiled. I changed them because they were no longer clean." Frank Ravenel, in his quiet grave on Malvern Hill, has the best of it.

The New York Herald today quotes General Sherman, who says, "Columbia was burnt by Hampton's sheer stupidity." * But then who burned everything before they got to Columbia? We came down for three day's travel on a road laid bare by Sherman's torches. There were nothing but smoking ruins left in Sherman's track; that I saw with my own eyes. No living thing left, no house for man or beast. They who burnt the countryside for a belt of forty miles, did they not burn the town?

* General Sherman in his *Memoirs* says: "In my official report of this conflagration, I distinctly charged it to General Wade Hampton, and confess I did so pointedly, to shake the faith of his people in him." The South — and the ordinarily intelligent reader — will read this as the confession of a lie. The fire itself seems to have been the more or less natural result of the looting and disorder which Sherman's officers did not control.

This Herald announces that Jeff Davis will be hung at once, not so much for treason as for his assassination of Lincoln.

The Negroes want to run with the hare, but hunt with the hound. They are charming in the professions of loyalty to us, but declare that they are to be given lands and mules by those blessed Yankees.

JUNE 4th. — Wild tales fly. John Kershaw came with "the very latest," he said. "Jeff Davis has taken the oath, and the Negroes are not to be emancipated!" Another story to match: Mrs. A—— saw a Yankee soldier strike a woman, and she prayed God to take him in hand. The soldier laughed in her face, swaggered off, stumbled; his revolver went off and shot him dead.

The black ball is in motion. Mrs. DeSaussure's cook shook the dust off her feet and departed from her kitchen today, and the washerwoman is packing to go. Eben dressed himself in his best and went at a run to meet his Yankee deliverers. At the gate, he met a squad coming in. He had adorned himself with his watch and chain. "Hand over that watch!" Minus his fine watch and chain, Eben returned a sadder and wiser man. He was soon in his shirt sleeves whistling at his knife board. "Why did you come back so soon?" "Well, I thought maybe I better stay with old Marster that give me the watch and not go with them that stole it."

Went up to my old house, "Kamtchatka." The Trapiers live there now; and in the drawing-rooms where the children played "Puss in boots," and where we have so often danced and sung, Mr. Trapier held his prayer meeting. I do not think I ever did as much weeping, or as bitter, in the same space of time. I let myself go. It did me good. I cried with a will.

President Davis is in a dungeon, and in chains. Men watch him day and night. By orders of Andy, the bloody-minded tailor, nobody above the rank of colonel can take the amnesty oath, and nobody who owns over twenty thousand dollars, or who has assisted the Confederates. Howell Cobb and R. M. T. Hunter are arrested. Our turn next, maybe. Not among the Negroes does fear dwell now, nor uncertainty nor anxiety. It dwells here, haunting us, tracking us, running like an accursed discord through all the music tones of our existence.

JUNE 12th. — Andy, made lord of all by the madman Booth, says "destruction only to the wealthy classes." Better teach the Negroes to stand alone, before they break up all they leaned on. After all, the number of us who own over $20,000 is comparatively small.

My husband will remain quietly at home. He has done nothing

that he had not a right to do, nor anything that he is ashamed of. He will not fly his country, nor hide anywhere in it; these are his words. He has a huge volume of Macaulay, which seems to absorb him.

I have been ill, since I wrote last. I had a letter from Serena. They have been visited by bushwhackers, the roughs who always follow in the wake of an army. My sister Kate, they forced back against the wall. She had Katie, the baby, in her arms. Miller, the brave boy, clung to his mother, though he could do no more. They tried to force brandy down her throat. They knocked Mary down with the butt end of a pistol, and Serena they struck with open hand, leaving the mark on her cheek for weeks. When they struck Mary, Serena seized the Captain's arm. "Do you let your men do that?" and she showed Mary's bleeding head. "No, no!" he said. "That's too bad. You keep all together, and I will get them away for tonight, and then you go off at once." They went that night to the Kings', the next day to Greenville. Next day, while Mary had her head bound up, Confederate prisoners passed. "What is the matter with your head?" "A soldier struck me." All the blood in the man rushed up into his face. "Struck you!" That there could be men found on this earth so brutal as to strike either of these two!

Colonel Chesnut's bank stock, his bonds, his railroad stocks as well as his hundreds of Negroes are now all given up. Nothing but land remains, and debts. The Negroes say Aunt Sally has barrels of money hid away in the cellar, gold and silver money. If it is Confederate, it will be funny. She is just the woman to do it.

Captain Barnwell came to see us. We had a dinner for them at Mulberry. Stephen Elliott was there. He gave us an account of his father's plantation at Beaufort, from which he has just returned. "Our Negroes are living in great comfort. They were delighted to see me, and treated me with overflowing affection. They waited on me as before, gave me beautiful breakfasts and splendid dinners; but they firmly and respectfully informed me: 'We own this land now. Put it out of your head that it will ever be yours again.' "

Edward Barnwell said all the Rhetts had taken the oath. He met Edmund Rhett, who as usual opened the conversation by a volley of oaths against Jeff Davis. "I dare not listen to you," said Edward Barnwell. "Good heavens — why?" "Read this general order: All Confederates are forbidden to discuss their affairs with loyal citizens. You have taken the oath of allegiance to the United States of America.

You are a truly loyal citizen. I am a poor disabled Confederate still." For once the ready-witted Edmund was silenced.

A Yankee general, one Hartwell, issues a proclamation to the Negroes; he urges them to respect henceforth the marriage tie. Says Molly, to whom I read the proclamation: "One garrison in a town will ——" "That will do, Molly. I do not want details!" "But Missis, Mr. Whittemore's marrying all the old niggers over again, tho they was married by a regular preacher in church, and he makes every one pay him two dollars fifty cents; and them that he divorces, he asks three dollars!"

I met Mr. John M. DeSaussure. He said: "I will take the oath gladly, joyfully. I have never willingly sided or abetted the Rebellion." To hear such as Mr. John DeSaussure, these Yankees have poured out all this blood and money to put us just where we were before!

Kit Hampton says in New York they were simply intoxicated with the fumes of their own glory. Military prowess was a new delight to them. They pay us the kind of respectful fear the British meted out to Napoleon. Of course the Yankees know and say they were too many for us, and yet they would prefer not to try it again. Kit Hampton says that in some inscrutable way everybody in the North has contrived to amass fabulous wealth by this War.

Here was jealousy as rough as the moor of Venice's. Adam Team saw Molly heat a red-hot poker and go for a Negro woman to whom her husband Lige had given one of Molly's calico frocks. She knocked the woman down the first blow, and proceeded to burn the frock off her back with the red-hot poker before help came, and the victim was "put out." And then it was she came to me, to swear allegiance anew. "I never lef my Missis, for no husband and children in this world."

Ellen went off for a day or two. While she was gone her husband, Claiborne, came to bargain for her. "White people want a heap of waiting on, you know, ma'am." "I do not mean to give her one cent — for the best of all reasons. I have none to give her. You and your child are living in one of our houses free of rent. Ellen can go or stay as she pleases." When Ellen came back, she said, "Claiborne is an old fool, always meddling and making. I don't care for money. I gits money's worth."

There are two classes of vociferous sufferers in this community: those who say: "If people would only pay me what they owe me," and those who say: "If people would only let me alone. I cannot pay them!" We belong to both classes. Heavens, what people owe us and will not or can not pay would settle all our debts ten times over — and leave us in easy circumstances for life. But they will not pay. How can they?

We are shut in here, with our faces turned to a dead wall; no mails except that a letter is sometimes brought by a man on horseback travelling through the wilderness made by Sherman. All the railroads are destroyed, the bridges gone. We are cut off from the world, to eat out our own hearts. And yet from my window, I look out on many a gallant youth and maiden fair. The street is crowded, and it is a gay sight. Camden is thronged with refugees from the Low Country, and here they disport themselves.

Today H. Lang told me that poor Sandhill Milly Trimlin was dead; that as a witch she had been denied Christian burial. Three times she was buried in consecrated ground at different church yards, and three times she was dug up by a superstitious horde and put out of their holy ground. Where her poor old ill-used bones are lying now I do not know. I hope her soul is faring better than her body. She was a good, kindly creature. Everybody gave Milly a helping hand. She was a perfect specimen of the Sandhill tackey race, sometimes called country crackers. Her skin was yellow and leathery, and even the whites of her eyes were bilious in color. She was stumpy and strong and lean, hard-featured, horny-fisted. Never were people so aided in every way as these people are! Why do they remain Sandhillers, from generation to generation. Why should Milly never have bettered her condition? My grandmother lent a helping hand to her grandmother, my mother did her best for her mother, and I am sure the so-called witch could never complain of me. As long as I can remember, gangs of these Sandhill women traipsed in with baskets to be filled by charity, ready to carry away anything they could get. They were treated as friends and neighbours, not as beggars. They were asked in, asked to take seats by the fire; and there they sat for hours, stony-eyed, silent, wearying out human endurance and politeness. Their husbands and sons, whom we never saw, were citizens and voters! When patience was at its last ebb, they would open their mouths and loudly demand whatever they had come to seek.

One, called Judy Bradley, a one-eyed virago who also played the fiddle at all of the Sandhill dances and fandangoes, made a deep impression on my youthful mind. Her list of wants on one visit was rather long, and my grandmother grew restive and actually hesitated. Judy demanded: "Woman, do you mean to let me starve?" My grandmother then attempted a meek lecture as to the duty of earning one's bread. Judy squared her arms akimbo and answered: "And pray, who made you a Judge and the criterion of the world. Lord, Lord, if I had er knowed I had ter stand all this jaw, I wouldn't a took your old things." But she did take them, and came again and again.

There are Sandhillers born, and Sandhillers who have fallen to that estate. Old Mrs. Simons, now; Mr. Chesnut says she was a lady once. They are very good to her. She pays no rent for her house and the fields around it. She knits gloves, which are always bought for her sake. She has many children, all grown and gone, only one son left and he is a cripple. Once a year he has a drive in a carriage. Some uneasy candidate is sure to drive by there and haul the lame man to the polls. Everybody remembers that Mrs. Simons has seen better days. In coming from Society Hill once, Sally had Mrs. Simons's house pointed out to her. She stopped the carriage, got out and knocked at the door. All was silent as death. The old creature was locked in and barricaded, but after a parley she opened her door. When she saw it was Sally, she fell upon her neck and wept aloud. "Why honey, to think you've come to see me." I asked Sally: "How did it all look there?" "Sad and sorrowful, empty, clean, faded, worn out, just as poverty stricken and old as Mrs. Simons looks in that old shawl and bonnet of hers."

My mother had a protégée who had also fallen from a higher station. She was once a handsome young girl, of good family. A dashing young doctor in a gig fascinated her. He was to marry her and did not. She was ruined, and her severe parents turned her out of doors. Then began her Sandhill life. She lived alone with her child for awhile, and then she lived with a Sandhill man. She always spoke of him as "He." She came always with a half dozen daughters, all alike, gaunt, pale, freckled, white hair or sandy; and they sat in their oak-split bonnets all in a row. They all clutched bags and glared at us, but never a word spoke they. The eldest girl was named for my mother. The others we thought had no fixed names, but they were called Betsey, Sally, Charlotte, Amelia, according as the people happened to be present whose namesakes she claimed them to be.

One day she drew my mother to the window. We saw her clutch my mother's arm and say something; then they shook hands, and tears were in the eyes of both of them. Afterwards my mother said to us: "Did you hear her? She gripped me and said: 'Woman! He has married me!' Neither of us said another word, but Fanny knew I felt for her."

At another time, these old friends met at church, a big meeting with more politics than religion in the wind. My mother proposed to take Fanny home in her carriage. "No, no! Never mind me. I'm done in this world. Take your namesake. Let 'em all see my girl setting by you in your carriage."

JULY 4th. — Saturday I was ill in bed with one of my worst headaches, but I came down when callers arrived. They talked of Negroes who flocked to the Yankees and showed them where the silver and valuables were hid by the white people; lady's maids dressing themselves in their mistress's gowns before their very faces and walking off. Before this, everyone has told me how kind and faithful and considerate the Negroes had been. I am sure, after hearing these tales, the fidelity of my own servants shines out brilliantly. I had taken it too much as a matter of course.

Yesterday there was a mass meeting of Negroes. Thousands of them were in town, eating, drinking, dancing, speechifying. Preaching and prayers were also a popular amusement. They have no greater idea of amusement than wild prayers, unless it be getting married and going to a funeral. But our people were all at home, quiet, orderly, respectfull, and at their usual work. There was nothing to show that any one of them had ever seen a Yankee or knew that there was one in existence.

JULY 26th. — I do not write often now, not for want of something to say but from a loathing of all I see and hear. Why dwell upon it?

Colonel Chesnut, poor old man, was worse, more restless. He seems to be wild with homesickness. He wants to be at Mulberry. He says he feels that he is there as soon as he hears the carriage rattling across the bridge at the Beaver dam.

I am reading French with Johnny. Anything to keep him quiet. We gave a dinner to his company, or the small remnant of them, at Mulberry house. About twenty idle Negroes, trained servants, came without leave or license and assisted; so there was no expense. They gave their time and labour for a good day's feeding, and I think they love to be at the old place.

Yesterday, John saw Dr. Charles Shannon lying drunk on a Yankee's bed. All of the men about town go in and drink with them. Johnny took the Yankee Captain with him to Knight's Hill. That ceremony is necessary now, when making a contract * with plantation hands. Johnny said to me: "Aunt Mary, after all, the Yankee was not half a bad fellow."

I went up to nurse Kate Withers. Now that lovely girl, barely eighteen, is dead of typhoid fever. Tanny Withers wanted his sweet little sister to have a dress for Mary Boykin's wedding — Kate was to be one of the bridesmaids — so Tanny took his horse, and rode one and led one thirty miles in the broiling sun to Columbia. He sold the led horse and came back with a roll of Swiss muslin. When he entered the door, he saw her lying there, dying. She died praying that she might die. She was weary of earth. She wanted to be at peace. I saw her die. I saw her put in her coffin. No words of mine can tell how unhappy I am. Six young soldiers, her friends, were her pall bearers. As they marched out with that burden, sad were their faces; and yet, that night, all save one danced at a ball given by Mrs. Courtney from Charleston.

AUGUST 2nd. — I am old, old, old; the weight of the years that hangs upon my eyelids is of lead. But there is youth in even our world still. I have another letter from my precious little Serena.

Dear Aunty —

Tristy Trezevant arrived here last week and says I can send you a letter by Mrs. Johnson. I am in Greenville. Mamma was obliged to send Mamie and me away. Flat Rock was no longer a place for us, after the bushwhackers. Mamma writes me now what a relief it is for her to know that we are safe from such treatment as we received that night. She says such another night would kill her. However a great many of the wretches have been captured, and I hope something may be done to them.

Miss Louisa King seems glad to have us, and two more in this crowded house does not make a great difference. Dr. King's girls are here too. We are all in

* After the surrender, contracts between planters and their former slaves were required by the Freedman's Bureau. In such contracts, the Negroes agreed to "continue in the discharge of their duties as heretofore," to stay on the plantation, and to behave themselves; the planter agreed to supply lodging and sustenance, medicines and medical attendance, preaching, funerals and taxes, and to pay to the Negroes one third of the crop. The Negroes were to be mulcted or otherwise punished for any failure to fulfil their contract. Of the 126 Negroes who on July 6, 1865, signed such a contract — attested by Major S. D. Shipley of the 30th Massachusetts Volunteers — on the Hamilton plantation adjoining Mulberry, not one could write; they all signed with an "X, his mark." Naturally, they had no understanding of the contract; and the efforts of the Freedman's Bureau to compel "specific performance" had many ludicrous results.

the depths of despair — but we manage with a party of thirteen young people to keep pretty merry. Our amusements are playing chess, and going to walk every evening. But this house is no place for flirting, as what is said in one room is sure to be heard in half a dozen of the others. And Tristy talks so distinctly! He is staying with his Uncle, our semi-detached neighbour. Tristy steps with such nonchalance into Miss Louisa King's drawing-room that everybody laughs at the sight of him, and everybody likes him. He still wears that identical red (dirty brown it is now) ribbon of mine at his button hole.

Give my love to Johnny. Tell him I saved his pictures for the future Mrs. C. He might at least write and thank me for it.

Love to Uncle and you —
Your affectionate
Enie

P.S. In future, Mamma says Johnny is not to read her letters to you; and you know I have already positively forbidden such liberties to be taken with mine!

And here is one Serena wrote to Isabella.

Dear Miss Isabella:

Think of it; I am trying to write in the same room with Mamie, and she and a talkative man both talk at once, and I have no place to retire to. Rolly Lowndes and Captain James Lowndes are still here. You know how pleasant they are. Those two delightful little Captains King, the life and soul of the round dances, have returned to Flat Rock with their sisters.

Papa thinks with a strong escort we might venture home in September. The same men are still there who attacked our house, but now they roam by day and not by night! Here we have a Yankee garrison to protect us. The officers of this garrison find this the dullest place they were ever in, and want the ladies to get up some amusement for them. The Lowndeses want us to continue our weekly dances, but it is too hot.

What has become of Hood, Miss Isabella? We have not heard a word of him since the surrender, nor of our first Foreign Battalion friends; that is, since Tristy described their pathetic parting in North Carolina. Do you still receive letters from Captain James? I am so anxious to see some of them. Do you mind being questioned? No? Well I shall go on then, and ask you a goodly number. Why do you call T. T. "Treacherous Tim." He owned to you he found the ground soft, did he not? Before he left here, he was quite in a bog. I hope he will get safely out of it, for I was really sorry for him. Dear Miss Isabella, do not feel uneasy about me. I have no idea of making a goose of myself yet! So never mind my B's, as Mamie calls them; Brockenbroughs and all. However before going farther down the alphabet, what do you mean by

RLB's "surroundings"? In case I should ever meet him again, I need to be — or I mean I should like to be — armed for resistance at all points.
Goodbye. I must lay the table for dinner.

Yours truly —
Enie

Serena will be sixteen in September, Mary was fourteen in May. Precocious children.

I cannot write, but others can. Here is one from Isabella.

Dear Mrs. C.—

*I have heard from our friends abroad. The Darby * party is in London after a tour through Holland and Northern Germany. They are all going back to Paris for the winter except Mr. Preston, who comes home on a visit. They report Von Borcke in London, splendidly handsome, and twice as big as Mr. Preston. Von Borcke † creates a sensation. He is writing papers for Blackwood's on our War, and he is well paid. John R. Thompson corrects the proof sheets, and gets a third of the pay. Mary and Buck do not like the articles, but I do not see why. Wouldn't you like to see them?*

General Hampton has returned with his arm broken, or badly dislocated. How the return of this season must bring back the tragedy of last year, which closed forever the blue eyes of that glorious boy Preston. Outside I hear them striking up a serenade to General Ames, the Yankee Commander here. General Hampton tells us that Mrs. Davis is still a prisoner in Georgia. They have allowed her to write one letter to her husband and to receive one. Maggie Howell has gone to Mississippi. This time last year we were moving Heaven and Earth for men to tea-fight her.

I have begun my small school. It is the only way to make brains available. What do you think; I have been requested to write a history of the war, the requestor to pay all expenses. If I only could, would I not? I'd give some people such a showing! Your last letters have been of the meagerest. What is the matter?

Toujours —
Isabella

What is the matter? Enough! I will write no more!

* The Darby party included Buck; the Hood romance was ended. After the War General Hood went into business in New Orleans; and he married in 1868 Anna Marie Hennen.

† Von Borcke, six feet two and weighing two hundred and fifty pounds, must have been a heavy burden for his charger. His memoirs have some vivid descriptive passages — for which Mr. Thompson was no doubt responsible — but they were often inaccurate.

Index

Index

Abbeville, S. C., 524
Abingdon, Va., 481
Adam Bede, George Eliot, 389, 390
Adam's Run, 470
Adams, Governor, 29
Adams, Wirt, 15
Adamson, Edward, 538
Adamson, John, 162–63
Adamson, Martha (servant), 162–63
African Scipio, 534
African slave trade, 138, 498. *See also* Negroes; Slavery
Aiken, Governor, 492
Aiken, Mr., 322
Aiken, Miss, 276; wedding to Burnet Rhett, 306–7
Alabama, 286, 343
Alabama Convention, 14
Alabama (ship), 275, 421, 445
Albert, prince consort of England, 177
Albion (newspaper), 125
Alcohol, 153. *See also* Whiskey
Alexandria, Va., 54, 74, 92
Algiers, La., 295
Allan, Buck, 404
Allan, Mrs. Buck, 403
Allan, Mrs. John, 327
Allen, Willie, 334
Allendale, S. C., 456
Allston, Ben, 63, 71
Allston, Mr. Mott, 448
Allston, Colonel Robert, 301, 309–10
Allston, Washington, 44
Allston, Willie, 35
Alms house, 116
Ames, General Adelbert, 547
Ammon (Reynolds' butler), 159
Ancrum, Tom, 58
Ancrum, Willie, 58
Ancrum, Mrs., 486
Anderson, Robert, 10, 31, 34, 41, 68, 126; moves into Fort Sumter, 4; refuses to capitulate, 36; surrenders, 39; report of Sumter, 45–46; offered Kentucky regiment, 61
Anderson, Richard H., 47, 260, 267, 293, 300, 536
Anderson, Mrs. Richard, 462, 464
Andersonville, Ga., 409, 493
Anne (Chesnut's servant), 282
Antietam-Sharpsburg, encounter, 97, 520
Appomattox, Va., 533
Appomattox Court House, 470, 514
Archer, Tom, 120–21, 428, 429; made major general, 432; death, 477
Arlington House, 98, 102, 107, 109, 130, 131
Armistice, 522
Arms and ammunition, 37, 74, 149–50, 208, 212, 237, 278, 445. *See also* Gunpowder
Armsted (Chesnut's butler), 24–25, 157, 292, 414
Army,
— at Atlanta, 425. *See also* Confederate Army; Union Army
— of Northern Virginia, 189;
— of the Potomac, 300, 432;
— of the West, 362;
Art of Making Saltpetre, The, 212
Ashby, Turner, 250
Ashmore, Mr., 257
Athens, Ga., raid, 431
Atlanta, Ga., 53, 316, 418, 421, 423, 424; fall of, 79, 434, 436
Atlantic, 162
Augusta, Ga., 108, 435, 448
Axson (of carslina), 102
Ayer, Miss (Mrs. Gibson), 234

Bacon, Captain, 67, 436, 465
Bailey, Anne, 528
Bailey, Godard, 239, 417, 442, 528

Baker, Mr. 13
Baldwin, Colonel, 83
Ballard house, 279
Baltimore, Md., 9, 40, 45
Banks, A. D., 107, 114
Banks, Nathaniel Prentiss, 117
Barbier de Séville, Le, Beaumarchais, de, 190
Barker, Theodore, 88, 120
Barksdale, Mrs., 405
Barnwell, Edward, 385, 422, 434, 458, 509, 514, 519, 521, 540
Barnwell, Joe, 463
Barnwell, Robert, 7, 13, 45, 53, 76, 82, 90, 99, 102, 108, 110, 111, 112, 113, 117, 125, 164, 168, 217, 220–21, 231, 385, 492
Barnwell, Robert (the younger), 224; death, 305–6
Barnwell, the Reverend Robert, 249, 259
Barnwell, Mrs. Robert (*née* Mary Singleton), 422; death, 305–6
Barnwell, Mrs. Robert, 272
Barnwell, Stephen, 463
Barrel shirts, 461
Barron, Commodore, 105, 127, 129, 130, 136
Barron, Imogene, 131
Barron, Jenny, 130
Barton, Miss Carrie, 353
Bartow, Colonel, 7, 70, 225; killed at Manassas, 86, 89
Bartow, Mrs., 70, 86, 87, 203, 219, 225, 232, 256, 257, 263, 269, 423, 451, 462–63, 528
Battery, the (Charleston), 39, 244, 308
Battery, invented by Jack Hamilton, 37
Battis (fly-boush boy), 503
Battle Flag, of Confederacy, 90
Battle of the Wilderness, 406
Battle of Young's Branch, 97. *See also* Manassas
Bay, Miss, 231–32, 243, 250, 251
Bazaar, 472–73, 474
Beacon (newspaper), 231 *n.*
Beaufort, 158, 168, 184, 540
Beauregard, Pierre Gustave Toutant de, 14, 31, 33, 34, 35, 48, 57, 58–59, 62, 67, 69, 74, 76, 77, 79, 80, 82, 83, 84, 86, 92, 99, 102–3, 106, 112, 120, 121, 136, 143, 157, 190–91, 215, 220, 225, 228, 230, 234, 249, 308, 336, 406, 411, 441, 469, 475, 479, 513; Headquarters of, 39, 62, 445; in Norfolk, 53; report of Fort Sumter, 58; telegraphs General Johnston for aid, 84; at Manassas, 88; at Nashville, 211; refusal to take orders from Davis, 224; illness and death of wife, 229–30, 247; retreating, 237; evacuates Corinth, 241; at Shiloh, 247; in Charleston, 307; on Hood's move north, 443; military bulletins, 445; newspaper reports of, 446
Bedon, Josiah, 508
Bedon, Mrs. Josiah, 508, 516, 522
Bee, Colonel, 86
Bee Store, the, 383
Beecher, Henry Ward, 144
Benjamin, Mr., 359–60, 376
Berrian, Dr., 70, 104, 230, 258
Bethel, battle, 58, 59, 67, 80, 261
Bibbs, Judge, 7, 8
Bierne, Bettie, engagement to William Porcher Miles, 301–2, 326. *See also* Miles, Mrs. William Porcher
Bierne, Oliver, 301
Bierne, Captain, 460, 461
Binney, Horace, 60
Black River (Camden), 529
Blackwood's Magazine, 162, 331, 338, 400, 432, 547
Blair, Montgomery, 68
Blair, Mrs. Montgomery, 68
Blaire, Rochelle, 26
Blake, Daniel, 223, 277–78
Blake, Cissy (Mrs. Phoenix), 279
Blake, Frederick, 460
Blake, Mrs. Frederick, 489
Blake, Mr., 473
Blake, Walter, 263
Blind Factory (Charleston), 174
Blithedale Romance, The, Nathaniel Hawthorne, 390
Blockade, Northern, 52, 105, 139, 149, 154, 173, 200, 204, 235, 278, 287–88, 294
Bloomsbury, 413–14
Bodisco, Madame, 11
Bombs, 237
Bonaparte, Jerome Napoleon, 102, 103, 106, 109, 110, 136, 252
Bonaparte, Napoleon I, 235
Bonaparte, Napoleon III (Louis Napoleon), 252
Bonds; *see* Confederate bonds
Bones, Charlotte, 398, 399, 403
Bonham, General, 13
Bonham, Governor, 279, 440, 442, 462, 465–466, 513, 515, 518
Bonham's Brigade, 84, 85
Bonney, Sue, 137
Bonney's store, 153
Boomerang, 37
Booth, John Wilkes, 539

Borcke, Major Von, 340
Boyce, Mr., 5, 76, 100, 107, 448
Boya, Mr. (of South Carolina delegation), 343
Boyer, Mr., 73
Boykin, A. Hamilton, 36, 58, 98, 140–41, 143, 161, 168, 229, 266, 422, 444, 462, 516, 529
Boykin, Amanda, 18
Boykin, Mrs. Barnwell, 531
Boykin, Burwell, 101, 138
Boykin, Edward M., 16, 18, 26, 53, 101–2, 134, 194, 195, 196, 218, 266, 293–94, 406, 414, 448, 528, 532
Boykin, Elizabeth, 6. *See also* Withers, Mrs. Thomas J.
Boykin, James, 289
Boykin, John, 127, 409, 493
Boykin, (Uncle) John, 138
Boykin, Mary, 414, 417, 429, 545
Boykin, Tom, 54, 193, 366, 417, 429
Boykin, Tom (son of William Boykin), 445–46
Boykin, William, 445
Boykin's Rangers, 75, 98, 109, 140–41, 251
Bradford, Louisiana, 61–62
Bradley, Judy, 542–43
Bragg, Braxton, 204, 224, 268, 299, 307, 327, 328, 402, 434, 533; at Pensacola, 56; at Chickamauga, 316; rumored defeated, 327; promoted to Chief of Staff, 388, 409; organizes cavalry to protect Richmond, 391
Branchville, S. C., 473, 475
Brandon, Mr., 315
Brandy Station, battle, 303, 305
Bratten, Mrs. (*née* Mann), 240
Breckenridge, John C., 317, 353, 355, 361–62, 363, 366, 367, 368, 369, 370, 371, 374, 375, 382, 386–87, 473
Breckenridge, Mrs. John C., 385
Brevard, Alfred, 260
Brewster, Mr., 9, 10, 11, 71, 76, 77, 78, 79, 80, 81, 85, 90–91, 100, 115, 130–1, 335, 336, 337, 338, 339, 364, 367, 378, 380, 416, 424, 429, 430, 443–44, 462, 469, 474
Bright, John, 117
British Legation, 238. *See also* England
Brockenbrough Mansion (White House of the Confederacy), 63, 101, 164, 233–34
Brockenbrough, Lieutenant, 460, 461
Brooks, Preston, 72
Brown, Joe, 343, 401, 418, 424, 442, 465, 532
Brown, John, 1, 92, 93, 163, 176, 264–65, 268, 286
Brown, Manning, 148, 171
Browne, Sir Thomas, 160
Browne, Colonel, 266, 347
Browne, Mr., 7, 16, 18, 25, 46, 70, 268, 271, 400
Browne, Mrs., 16, 18, 25, 73, 264, 270–71
B. (Browne?), Eliza, 30
Brownfield, Mrs., 273
Browning, Robert, 194
Brown's Hotel (Washington), 354
Brumby, Dr., 498
Bryan, Mrs., 433
Buchanan, James, 14, 16, 17–18, 271
Buchanan, Captain, 110
Buckner, Simon Bolivar, 190–91, 340–41, 355
Buell, Don Carlos, 210
Bull Run, 97. *See also* Bull's Run; Manassas; Second Manassas
Bull's bay, S. C., 154
Bull's Run, 59, 84, 116. *See also* Manassas
Burnet, Mr., of Kentucky, 201
Burnside, Mr., 215, 234, 526
Burroughs, Mrs., 253
Burwell, Tom, 367, 368
Butler, Benjamin Franklin, 224, 246, 252, 253, 333, 364, 388, 396, 479; proclamation, 230–31 *n.*
Butler, Nat, 491, 523
Butler, Senator (of South Carolina), 72
Byron, Lord, 195, 391–92, 501

Cadwallader, General, 67, 74
Calhoun, John C., 16, 93, 238, 504
Calhoun, Pat, 301
Calhoun, Ransom, 102, 181, 280–81, 342, 390, 416
Calhoun, Teddy, 420
Calhoun, Mr., 145
Calhoun, Mrs., 432
Cambridge, Mass., 115
Camden, S. C., 2, 26, 108, 181, 307, 316, 318 *ff.*, 401, 466, 478, 491, 493, 522, 542
Camden Hotel, 24
Cameron, Senator, from Pennsylvania, 72; issues Proclamation, 92
Cameron, Rony (Scotch overseer), 505
Camilla (aunt of Wade Manning), 202
Campbell, John Archibald, resigned from Supreme Court, 14; family, 76; 314, 331, 502
Canada, 174
Camp songs, 509; Negro hymns, 149
Cantey, Jack, 514
Cantey, Mary, 247

Cantey, Sally, 127
Cantey, Zack, 194
Cantey (Family), 411
Cantey, Floride, 532
Capers, Mrs. Sam, 514
Capers, Willie, 466
Capitol Square (Richmond), 78, 397–98, 313, 315
Carolina Institute, 173
Carolinian, 212, 456
Carrington, Mrs., 270
Carroll, Judge, 210
Carter, Colonel, 429
Carter, Mr., 303
Carter, Shirley, 335, 337
Carter, Mrs., at Miss Sally Tompkins' Hospital, 109, 112
Carter, Gibbes, 171
Cash, E. B. C., 67; interview with Congressman Ely, 110
Cary, Constance, 311, 333, 349, 350, 351, 352, 355–56, 357, 358, 369, 375, 381–82, 387, 389, 390, 396, 398, 399
Cary, Hettie, 311, 312, 350, 352, 355, 356, 357, 387, 392, 402; Starvation Party; — Marriage to General Pegram —
Cary, Jennie, 311
Casino; *see* Games
Caskie, Mrs., 303, 355
Castle Richmond, Anthony Trollope, 182
Catherine (nurse of little Joe Davis), 405, 411
Cause and Contrast, MacMahon, 517
Cedar Keys, Fla., 190, reported lost
Chancellorsville, battle, 277, 313
Charades; *see* Games
Charleston, S. C., 1, 2, 3, 10, 20, 27, 56, 57, 78, 149, 220, 226, 232, 237, 240, 365, 429, 478; fortification of, 160; fire, 173, 174; bombardment, 234, 327; Union defeat, 393; surrender, 484, 538. *See also* Sumter
Charleston press, 243. *See also* the *Mercury;* Newspapers
Charleston Bar, 38
Charleston Harbor, 4
Charleston Hotel, 37
Charleston Light Dragoons, 508
Charlotte, N. C., 478, 484, 493, 507; depot, 479, 512; trains no longer run to Columbia
Charlottesville, Hospital, 103
Chase, Colonel, 1, 2
Chattanooga, Tenn., 299, 316, 363, 442
Chester, S. C., 505, 527; enemy reported in, 492; James Chesnut ordered to, 503; Mrs. Chesnut goes to, 507 *ff*.
Chesnut, James Jr., resigns seat in Senate, 3; member of Secession Convention, 6; aide-de-camp of Beauregard, 35; at Fort Sumter, 35–36, 39; plan to save country, 52; joins Beauregard, 57; letters, 59, 67–68, 73, 74–75, 79–80, 459–60, 484, 491–92, 505–6; in Senate, 108, 112; speech against confiscation, 113; on office-seekers, 135, 200, 423, 461; investigates Witherspoon murder, 139; defends Ammon, 159; on Davis-Beauregard controversy, 160; on coast defense, 161; musters regiment, 161; loss of Senate seat, 168, 169, 170, 174; Council of Safety, 182, 483; on Manassas, 98, 196; address to South Carolinians, 198; on student enlistment, 199; on enlistment of Negroes, 203–204; Nitre Bureau, 212; refuses place on Davis' staff, 216; military strategy, 220–21; brigadier general, 239; appointed to Davis' staff, 279, 310; rescues Laurence, 296; and General Lee, 354; Dahlgren raid, 387; Corps of Clerks, 410; inspection tours, 316, 317, 321, 361, 445, 456; defense of Columbia, 425; at Adam's Run, 470; rescues Hampton, 512, considered paroled prisoner, 532
Chesnut, Mrs. James (Mary Boykin), 153, 164, 346, 407–8, 422; birthday, 30; during attack on Fort Sumter, 35–36; at Mulberry, 161–162; and Family, 290–91, 310–11, 321–22; views on George Eliot, 360–61, 387, 390, 466. *See also* Women; Slavery
Chesnut, John, 23–24, 59, 154, 161, 192, 218, 219, 225, 243, 256, 257, 263, 266, 298, 312–13, 321, 340, 354, 364, 366, 367–68 *ff*., 380, 383–84, 398, 409, 435, 436, 437, 450, 452, 459, 461, 485, 523, 524, 525, 528, 531, 532, 535, 536, 544–45, 546; private in Gregg's regiment, 54, 55; private in Boykin's Rangers, 75; First Lieutenant of Boykin's Rangers, 98; in Whiting's brigade, 251; Captain of the Dragoons, 281; at Brandy Station, 303; description of, 318–20, 338, 444
Chesnut, Miss Sally, 173, 257, 503, 514, 536, 540, 543
Chesnut Light Artillery, 258
Chesnut's Ferry, 530

Cheves, Edward, 263
Cheves, Langdon, 27–28, 29, 35, 37, 197, 258
Cheves, John, 231, 263
Chickahominy, battle, 240 *n.*, 242, 248, 259. *See also* Seven Pines
Chickamauga, battle, 299, 307, 316, 340, 355, 424
Childs, Mrs. (*née* Mary Anderson), 15–16
Childs, Colonel, 500, 501, 502, 504, 506, 507
Chisholm's Manual of Military Surgery, Dr. Chisholm, 425 *n.*
Christy Minstrels, 220
Cincinnati, Ohio, 115
Circuit rider (Negro church), 170
Claiborne (servant), 503, 541
Clarke, Mr., 517–18
Claremont, Mr., 315
Clay, Clement, 50–51, 78, 107, 331, 376, 382, 401, 473, 512, 513, 519, 520
Clay, Mrs. Clement, 304, 365, 366, 369
Clay, Lawson, 511
Clay, Mrs. Lawson, 335, 336, 340, 350, 365, 510, 511
Clayton, Mr., 109, 110, 117, 118
Cleburne, Patrick Ronayne, 463
Clemens, Jere, 10, 224
Cleveland, Grover, 151 *n.*
Clinch, Tatty, 276
Clingman, Mr., 39, 76, 90, 91, 93, 94, 394
Clothing, for soldiers, 210, 278; selling old, 395, 434
Clyburn, Mr., 24
Cobb, Howell, 5, 15, 19, 65 *n.*, 107, 137, 196; Cabinet Minister under Buchanan, 271; arrested, 539
Cobb, Tom, 16
Cockran, John, 192
Coffee, scarcity, 186–87, 341
Coffey, Captain, 326
Cohen, Isabel, 231
Cohen, Miriam, 224, 225, 228, 231, 235–36, 237, 239, 244, 250, 251, 308, 438
Cohen, Dr., 236
Cokesbury, S. C., 515
Colcock, Colonel, 2
Colquitt, Mr., 110
Columbia, S. C., 2, 3 *n.*, 174, 178, 188, 215, 226, 229, 242, 254, 279, 416, 475, 478, 481; seige, 484, 485, 489, 495, 502, 510, 513–16, 536; burning, 519, 538
Columbia Hospital, 493
Columbia junction, 270
Combahee, 4, 195, 460
Comet, 78
Commissioners, from Virginia, 47 *n.*
Company A-1 Cavalry, 444
Confederate Army, 132 *n.*; target practice, 31; troops, 39, 376, 398, 454, 471, 521, 525; desertion, 294, 412–13, 448, 512; substitutes, 294, 358; lists of killed and wounded, 411; draft avoiding, 503. *See also* Generals
Confederate bonds, 225 *n.*, 403 *n.*; bond cutting, 228, 269
Confederate currency, 186, 331, 332, 329, 349, 368, 371, 383, 383, 389, 394, 395, 398, 414, 431, 434, 450, 467, 472, 473, 482, 485, 487, 493, 499, 500, 516, 519, 525. *See also* Gold
Confederate Flag, 11–12, 54; first, 90 *n.*
Confederate States of America, 7, 14 *n.*, 215, capital, 4, 61, 81; Constitution, 5; Congress, 6, 19, 30, 85, 130, 191, 193, 209, 285, 330, 350, 362, 453, 456, 465–66; War Department, 62, 74, 77, 115, 435, 443, 464, 480. *See also* Confederate Army; Confederate bonds; Confederate currency; Confederate Flag
Confiscation, 502
Congaree House, 187, 188, 201, 209, 229, 270
Congress, *see* Confederate States of America
Congress (ship), 198
Conrad, Mr., 13
Consequences, *see* Games
Conscription, 204, 222–23, 242, 278, 361; bill passed by Congress, 212, 358
Conscription Bureau, 345
Conscription Law of 1864, 418
Council of Safety, 179, 194, 195, 205, 217, 220, 222–23, 225, 231, 232, 242, 259, 264, 267, 278–79, 465–66, 483
Cool Spring (plantation), 60, 137 *n.*
Cooper, Jenny, 130
Cooper, General, 82, 84, 107, 110, 155, 206, 256
Cooper, Mrs., 107
Cooper's Naval History, 60
Coosawhatchie, S. C., 456
Corcoran, Mr., 130
Corey, Dr., 407
Corinth, Miss., campaign, 216, 241, 252
Cornhill Magazine, 162, 329
Cornwallis, Charles, 74
Corps of Clerks, 410
Corrie, Captain, 498
Cotton, 170, 172, 173, 204, 307–8, 490, 506; shipping to England, 52 *n.*, 294;

price, 197; burning, 201, 331, 381; weaving during war, 278; Senate deliberation, 456; price, 529 *n.*; selling in New York, 537
Cotton States, 4
Country Clergyman in Town, "A Country Parson," 358
Covington, Ohio, 353 *n.*, 354
Cox, Mary, 141
Cox, Major, 366
Coxe, Esther Maria, 326
Crawford, Mr., 247
Creoles, 252–53, 479
Crittenden, George Bibb, 205
Crossed Path, The, Wilkie Collins, 71
Cuffey, Old (Chesnut servant), 531
Culpepper, Va., hospital, 79, 96
Cumberland (ship), 198
Cummings, Governor of Utah, 404
Cunningham, Joe, 505
Cunningham, Mrs., 147
Cunningham's plantation, 505
Curles Neck, 404
Custis, Nelly, 94, 141, 303
Cuthbert, George, 275–76, 277
Cuthbert, William, 275

Dabney, Miss, 399
Dahlgren, Colonel, 394; raid, 387 *n.*, 410, death, 388, 389 *n.*
Dallas County, Ala., 50
Dalton, Ga., 416
Daniels, editor of the *Examiner*, 285 *n.*, 286, 488
Danville, Va., 516, 518
Darby, John, 281, 282, 296–97, 298–99, 312–13, 326, 338, 400, 450, 520; 547 *n.*; Surgeon of the Hampton Legion, 53; thought killed at Manassas, 88; goes to Europe for Hood's wooden leg, 386–87; wedding to Mary Preston, 436–37
Darby, Mary (*née* Preston), 437, 441, 519, 520–21, 522, 523, 524, 525, 547. *See also* Preston, Mary
"Daughter of the Confederacy," *see* Davis, Varina Anne
Da Vega, Mrs., 508
Davin, music master, 55, 56
Davis, Bishop, 359
Davis, George, 359
Davis, Jefferson, 5, 7, 13, 36, 45, 46, 47, 50, 52, 61, 69, 70, 71, 75, 82, 85–86, 88, 89, 91, 93 *n.*, 96, 99, 100, 103, 106, 108, 109, 114, 115, 117, 119, 132, 155, 157, 213, 217, 219, 220, 231, 234, 262, 265–67, 280, 292, 312, 316, 322, 328, 329, 331, 333–34, 335, 336, 343, 347, 348, 350, 352, 359, 360, 365, 368, 371, 379, 380, 382, 383, 395, 397, 400, 410–11, 427, 434, 446, 479, 511, 520 *n.*, 521, 524, 533, 536; criticism, 59, 65, 137, 157, 164, 189, 190, 193, 198, 205, 207, 213, 217, 219, 380–81, 392, 400, 409, 410, 411–12, 421, 424, 496–97, 501–2, 504, 511, 520 *n.*; inauguration, 6; Provisional President of the Confederacy, 65 *n.*; Flag presentations, 73, 98; health, 84, 130, 143, 314; sends Johnston to Beauregard's aid; caricatured, 93, 415; coalition against, 107, 114; second inauguration, 191, 193; appoints Chesnut on Staff, 279; conflict with Confederate Congress, 285; fire and robbery at White House, 362–63; and the Senate, 366; appoints Bragg Chief of Staff, 388 *n.*; death of Little Joe, 405; described by Mrs. Chesnut, 411; pardons deserter, 413; sends Hood north after Atlanta, 435 *n.*; speech, visits Chesnuts in Columbia, 437–40; ignored by peace movement, 442; requested to resign by Virginia Legislature, 473; on removal of Johnston, 430; pursued by Federals, 526, 535–36; capture 536–37, 539; prisoner in Georgia, 547
Davis, Mrs. Jefferson, 9, 12, 19 *n.*, 20, 32, 45, 47, 50, 51, 63, 66, 67, 68, 69, 70, 75, 78, 79, 82, 84, 85, 86, 89, 92, 96, 98, 101, 106, 108, 114, 117, 120, 229, 280, 282–83, 304, 307, 311, 314, 326, 327, 329, 333, 334, 335, 342–43, 345, 347, 348, 350, 352, 363, 365, 372, 373, 375, 381, 385, 394, 395, 398, 399, 410–11, 412–13, 427, 446–47, 448–49, 450, 453–54, 486, 516, 517; birth of William Howell Davis, 174; "Luncheon to Ladies," 366–67; death of Little Joe, 404; in Raleigh, 256; matinée musicale, 283; visits Mrs. Chesnut in Chester, 519–20
Davis, "Little Jeff," 379, 521
Davis, Joe, Jr., 70, 83, 85, 89
Davis, Little Joe, 334, death, 403–5
Davis, Maggie, 350–51, 448, 521
Davis, Nathan, 205–6, 208, 274, 275
Davis, Nick, 10
Davis, Lila, 144
Davis, the Reverend Thomas, 278, 321
Davis, Varina Anne, 477 *n.*, 448, 454, 519
Davis, William Howell, 144, 521
Dead March, 87, 88, 89

Deas, George, 10, 12, 75, 127, 134, 301, 392, 441
Deas, Dr., 143, 144
De Kalb, S. C.,74
De Leon, Cooper, 351
Dent, Sheriff, 499, 530–31
Derby, Lord, 195
De Pass, Captain, 177
DeSaussure, Henry, 158, 159, 161, 266, 267
DeSaussure, Ida, 189
DeSaussure, John MacPherson, 156, 160, 173, 529, 541
DeSaussure, Mrs. John, 64
DeSaussure, Mary (Mrs. Henry DeSaussure), 161, 183, 267, 273
DeSaussure, William S., 443
DeSaussure, Wilmot, 88, 104, 114, 119, 149, 225, 237, 465, 512
DeSaussure, Mrs. Wilmot, 150
De Treville, Mr., 13
Desertion, 294, 412–13, 448, 512
Destruction and Reconstruction, General Taylor, 432 *n.*
Dick (Miller's butler), 291, 292–93
Disraeli, Benjamin, 195
Dobbin, Mr., 397
Dogan, Bill, 324–25
Dorn, Earl van, 424 *n.*
Douglas, Stephen A., 9, 56
Dover's Powder, 504–5
Draft, *see* Confederate Army
Dranesville, victory, 176
Drayton, Tom, 132, 159, 164, 205
Drury's Bluff, 239, 297, 315, 404
Du Guesclin, Betrand, 51
Duelling, 26, 27, 281
Duncan, Blanton, 206, 273
Duncan, Mrs. Henry, 194, 207
Dundas, Lord, 105
Dunavant, at Port Royal, 158
Dutch, assist North, 270

Early, Jubal Anderson, 421
East Indians, 111
Edgefield, S. C., 279
Edgefield Band, 269
Edisto Island (S. C.), 518
Edmonston, Mr., 47–48
Education, free school, 89
Edwards, Mrs., 145
Elective Affinities, 218, 358
Eliot, George, 360–61, 387, 390, 446
Ellen (Mrs. Chesnut's maid), 479 *ff.*, 504–5, 506, 524
Elliot, Stephen, 327, 540; wounded, 426, 434
Elliot, the Reverend Stephen, 410
Elliott, Mrs., 158
Ellis, Mrs., 49
Elmore, Elbert, 276
Elmore, Grace, 211
Elmore (Family), 427
Ellsworth (in command of Zouaves), shot at Alexandria, 54
Ely, Alfred, 87 *n.*–88, 110, 117, 136
Elzey, 90, 95, 313–14, 335, 394; at Manassas, 90; Commander of the Marylanders, 398
Emerson, Ralph Waldo, 60, 163
Emory, Tilly, 50, 57, 105, 486
Emory, Major, 56–57
Enfield rifles, 216, 532
England, 11, 52 *n.*, 73, 92, 103, 112, 123 *n.*, 137, 187, 247, 286, 347, 445, 475, 488, 523; Mason and Slidell affair, 160–61, 174, 175
English, Frank, 176
Enlistment, student, 198, 199
Eothen, 213
Eugénié, 177
Eugénie Grandet, 268
Eustis, Loulou (*née* Corcoran), 119, 129
Evan Harrington, 8, 11
Evans, "Shanks," 154
Evans, William, 463
Ewell's Brigade, 84, 300
Examiner, the, 118, 137, 152, 159, 161, 233, 285, 286, 331, 347, 354, 400, 488

F. ——, Boozer, 466, 502
Fair, Dr., 239
Fair Grounds (Richmond), 98
Famine, 498, 502, 518
Fanny, 254
Fanny, Sandhill tackey, 543–44
Fant (Family), 481, 483, 494, 499, 500
Farmers' Hotel, 275
Fauquier White Sulphur Springs, 76, 227
Fayetteville, N. C., 509
Fearn, Captain, 335, 352
Ferguson, Tom, 388
Fifteen Decisive Battles of the World, Sir Edward Shepherd Creasy, 194
Fisher, Mrs. (of Philadelphia), 251
Fisher, Mrs., establishes hospital, 270
Fiske, Mrs., 450
Fitzpatrick, Governor, 12–13, 331
Fitzpatrick, Mrs., 6, 15, 331
Five Forks, Va., 514 *n.*
Flag; *see* Confederate Flag
Flag of Truce boat, 315
Flat Rock, N. C., 160, 274, 277–88, 287, 441, 473, 477, 478, 486, 545, 546
Florence, S. C., 407

Florida, 1, 2, 294, 393
Floyd, John B., 198 *n.*, 202, 271
Floyd (Family), 481
Fontaine, newspaper reporter, 519
Foote, Senator, 346
Ford, Mary, 415
Foreign Battalion, the, in Columbia, 455, 459, 460, 461, 462, 465, 469, 470, 546
Foreign enlistments, in Federal Army, 145, 241, 252, 270, 404, 445
Forrest, General, 400
Fort Donelson, battle, 189, 190, 198 *n.*
Fort Hattaras, 130, 150
Fort Henry, 187
Fort Jackson, 253
Fort Johnson, 428
Fort Delaware, prison, 428
Fort Moultrie, 4 *n.*, 41, 237, 260
Fort Pickens, 1, 2, 45, 130
Fort Pillow, 240, 252, 400 *n.*
Fort Sumter, 4 *n.*, 6, 7, 10, 18, 31, 38, 41, 45–46, 47, 56, 60 *n.*, 60–61, 93 *n.*; attack, 14 *n.*, 35–36; Beauregard's report, 58
Fortress Monroe, 130, 388, 400
Fourth Texas (Hood's regiment), 373
Framley Parsonage, Anthony Trollope, 329
France, 73, 92, 102, 112, 174, 247, 252, 445, 488, 523
Franklin (Family), 83
Franklin Tenn., battle, 79 *n.*, 435 *n.*, 474 *n.*
Franklin Street (Richmond), 299, 303, 314, 386
Fraser Trenholm and Company, 278 *n.*
Frasier, Mr., 346
Fredericksburg, Va., battle, 280, 425
Freedman's Bureau, 545 *n.*
Freeland, Maria, 110, 326; wedding to John Lewis, 334–35. *See also* Lewis, Maria.
Freeland Rose, 284–85, 340
Frémont, John Charles, 235, 242
French Frigate, 328
French man-of-war, in Charleston Harbor, 261
Frost, Henry, 204
Frierson, Converse, *death*, 417
Frierson, John, 186
Frierson, Minnie, 532
Frost, Tom, 29
Frost, Judge, 51

Godsen (Family), 2
Gaillard, Mrs., 232
Games: Casino, 282, 298–99, 334, 335–36; charades, 350–51, 355, 356, 357–58, 365, 369–70; Consequences, 462; whist, 221, 329, 366
Garden, Hugh, 96
Garnett, Mary, 7, 354
Garnett, Dr., 66, 282, 314, 328, 329, 331, 366, 390–91, 393–94, 399
Garnett, Miss, 472
Garnett, Mrs., 365
Garnett, General, killed at Cheat Mountain, 85 *n.*, 126, 384
Garnett (brother of Dr. Garnett), 115
Gay, Captain, 525
Gazette (newspaper), 109
Generals, competence of, 343–44
Geneviève, La martiné, 153
Georgetown, S. C., 224–25
Georgia, Ala., 87, 443; Presidential candidates, 65; attitude, 343
Georgia Legislature, 191
Georgia Militia, 460
Georgia Scenes, Augustus B. Longstreet, 81–82 *n.*
Gettysburg, Pa., campaign, 287, 295 *n.*, 520 *n.*
Gibbes, Dr. Hampton, 29, 34, 92, 95, 100, 103, 106, 186, 188, 207, 214, 229, 234, 263, 266, 267, 269–70, 448, 456, 458
Gibbes, Mrs., 33, 229
Gibson, Claude, 280–81, 285
Gibson Toby, 427–28
Gibson, Dr., 116, 124, 258
Gibson, Mrs., 229, 234, 239, 256
Gidière, Mrs., 4
Giles, Miss, 355, 357
Gish, Governor, 186–187
Gist, General, 195, 208, 209, 463, 464
Gladden, Colonel, 212
Glover, Judge, 195
Glover, Mrs., 497, 500
Goethe, Johann Wolfgang von, 391
Gold, 403
Gold Branch (Chesnut plantation), 184
Gonzales (Cuban leader of rebellion), 108, 111, 115, 132, 205, 206
Goldsboro, N. C., 201
Goodwyn, Artemus, 26, 191
Goodwyn, Sally, 453, 468, 470, 484
Goodwyn, Colonel, 287, 288–89, 484, 510
Gourdin, Robert, 28, 34
Gourdins (Family), 2
Gordon, General, 394
Gordon, Mr., 294–95
Grahamville, 457, 459–60
Grant Harriet, 273, 452
Grant, Ulysses Simpson, 88 *n.*, 406,

411, 432, 445, 449, 450, 459, 520 *n.*; campaign up the Tennessee, 204 *n.*; character, 344; lieutenant general, 393; before Richmond, 431, 479; fall of Richmond, 518
Grant, Mrs., 399
Granville hotel (Greenville), 274
Greeley, Horace, 114, 144, 163, 173
Green, Allen, 33, 231, 424, 469, 497; at Manassas, 97; wounded, 463
Green, Mrs. Allen, 34
Green, John, 35, 105
Green, Halcott, 195, 204, 268, 455, 499
Green, Sally, 505
Greenhow, Mrs. Rose, 121, 124, 168, 226, 238–39.
Greensborough, N. C., 516
Greenville, S. C., 274, 429, 489, 545
Gregg, Maxcy, 33, 54, 68, 75, 92, 102, 104, 108, 242–43, 248
Gregory, Mr. (in England), 60
Grélaud, Mrs., boarding school of, 127
Grundy, Mrs., 325–26, 332, 362, 394
Guardian (newspaper), 242
Guerard, Lieutenant, 98
Guingnard, Mrs. (Anna Coffin), 506
Gulf of Mexico, 419
Gunboat Fair, 210, 211, 212
Gunboats, naming, 214; captured on the Santee, 265
Gunpowder, 199, 252, 237. *See also* Arms and Ammunition
Gwynn, Lucy, 264
Gwynn, Mr., 211

Haile, Edward, 144
Halleck, Henry Wager, 225, 261
Haliburton, Thomas Chandler, 131
Hamilton, Dan, 33
Hamilton, Jack, 37
Hamilton, Lent, 37
Hamilton, Lizzie, 442–43, 460
Hamilton, Louisa (Mrs. Jack Hamilton), 37, 275
Hamilton, Prioleau, 513, 516–17
Hamilton, Mrs. Prioleau (*née* Levy), 513, 509, 516
Hamilton, Sally, 57
Hamilton, Major, 509
Hamilton plantation, 545 *n.*
Hammersmith, Miss, 283
Hammond, Mr., 107
Hammond Huzzars, 164
Hammy, Mary, 63, 66, 70 *ff.*, 87, 104, 108, 111, 112, 125, 129, 130, 133, 226–27.
Hampton, Anne, 259
Hampton, Christopher, 218, 333, 334, 424–25, 432, 440, 490, 478, 541, 512
Hampton, Frank, 242, 305, 325
Hampton, Mrs. Frank, 39, 40, 41, 125, 233, 324
Hampton, Preston, 40, 218, 318, 329, 333, 349, 350, 388, 399; death, 447, 448–49, 453
Hampton, Sally, 386, 447, 449
Hampton, Wade (1), 41–42, 437
Hampton, Wade (2), 45, 81, 105, 175, 191, 202–3, 206, 218, 224, 240, 245, 252, 255, 256, 258, 259, 270, 305, 327, 334, 335, 348, 364, 388, 409, 432, 444, 448, 455, 465, 470, 475, 489, 491, 496, 512, 528, 531, 532, 538 *n.*; wounded at Manassas, 86, 87, 90; wounded at Chickahominy, 230, 243; made lieutenant general, 484; death of son on battlefield, 447–48, 449; and General Lee, 395, 396, 405, 423; paroled, 536; wounded, 547
Hampton, Wade (3), 318, 429; wounded, 447–48
Hampton, Mrs. Wade (1), 41–42
Hampton, Mrs. Wade (2); *see* McDuffie, Mary
Hampton (Family), 252, 437, 517
Hampton House, 218, 271, 386, 489, 495
Hampton Gardens, 192
Hampton Legion, 75, 84
Hampton Roads, Va., 212
Hardee, William Joseph, 181–182, 463, 491, 509, 513; declines command of Western Army
Hardeeville, S. C., 467
Harlan, Senator, 89
Harns, Mrs. Lafayette Borland, 8
Harper's, 162
Harper's Ferry, Va., 1, 53–54, 59, 62, 93 *n.*
Harriett Lane (ship), 36
Harris, Arnold, 91
Harrison, Burton, 286, 311 *n.*, 333, 334, 335, 351, 358, 378, 380–81, 398, 405, 442
Harrison, Dr., marriage, 284–85; death, 340
Hartstein, Captain, 28, 35, 70
Hartwell, General, proclamation to Negroes, 541
Haseltine, Captain, 112
Haskell, Alexander Cheves, 108 *n.*, 248–49, 258, 259, 260, 263, 268, 341, 376, 421, 442
Hastings, Francis Rawdon, 74, 137

Haskell, Decca (Mrs. Alexander C. Haskell, wedding 248–49; death, 258–59, 260
Haskell, John, engaged to Sally Hampton, 386
Haskell, William, 29–30, 33
Haskell, "Cousin," 536
Haxall, Lucy, engaged to Captain Coffee, 326; wedding, 401
Haxall, Dr., 359
Haxall, Mrs., 359
Hay, the Reverend Mr., 164
Hayne, Isaac, 29, 32, 63, 220, 237, 422, 424, 436, 479, 484, 495, 508, 511
Hayne, Minnie, 444
Hayne, Paul (poet), 238, 244, 250, 251, 268, 272
Hayne (Family), 35, 203, 267
Haynesworth (wounded soldier), 134
Hemphill, John, 47, 48, 69, 100
Hennen, Anna Marie, 547 *n.*
Henry Esmond, William Makepeace Thackeray, 9, 182
Hermitage (Chesnut plantation), 24, 137 *n.*, 478, 503, 538
Herbemont, Mrs., 179, 210, 243
Herbert, George, 54–55
Hetty (Miller's servant), 50, 290–91, 292–93
Heyward, Barnwell, 60, 276, 358–59, 361, 362, 364, 366
Heyward, Joe, 106–7, 276, 520, 522
Heyward, Mrs. Joe, 31, 39, 398
Heyward, Natalie, 409, 444
Heyward, Savage, 24
High Hills (home of General Sumter), 206
Hill, A. P., 353
Hill, Senator (of Georgia), 9, 10, 11, 352, 455
Hill, Mrs. D. H., 482
Hill, Jimmy Dick, 474
Hill, Miss (daughter of Senator Hill), 464
Hilton Head, S. C., Federal Forces land at, 68
Hinson (soldier), 67
Hobkirk, 74
Hoedown (Negro Dance), 275
Hook, Theodore Edward, 194–95
Hoke, General, 394
Hoke (Family), 499–500
Holcombe, Lucy, 240. *See also* Pickens, Mrs.
Hollins, Captain, 234
Holt, Mr., 10, 23
Huney Hill, encounter, 463
Hood, John Bell, 104, 297, 298, 307, 316, 326 *ff.*, 334 *ff.*, 369 *ff.*, 374, 385, 386, 395, 398, 416, 435 *n.*, 425, 427–28, 429–30, 440 *ff.*, 450, 468, 469, 473–74, 486, 489–90, 503, 516, 518, 519, 520, 526, 529–30; Colonel of the Fourth Texas, 296–97; wounded at Gettysburg and at Chickamauga, 299; ordered to Army of the Tennessee, 367; biography 371 *n.*, 372; engagement to Buck Preston, 376–77 *ff.*, 510; and Johnston, 392; replaces Johnston; 420–21, 430; at Atlanta, 423, 513; address to Army, 424; Tennessee campaign, 435 *n.*, 458, 464, 467, 472; requests release, 474; marriage to Anna Marie Hennen, 547 *n.*
Horses, scarcity, 231, 257, 302, 402, 428, 457, 458, 465, 475, 506, 514, 524, 528
Hospitals, 79, 96, 104 *n.*, 103, 109, 114, 116, 119, 124, 125, 150, 270 *n.*, 430–31, 432–33, 435, 442, 449, 450, 493
Houston, Governor, 71
Howard, Colonel, 74
Howell, Maggie, 63, 75, 108, 226–27, 304, 328, 335, 349, 357, 359, 375, 381, 383, 403, 404–5, 436 *ff.*, 450, 453, 547
Howell, Mr., 454
Howell, Mrs., 336
Hudson, Mr., 329, 355, 356
Huger, Alfred, 2, 174–76, 252
Huger, Mrs. Alfred, 252
Huger, Ben, 45, 231, 263, 266, 270, 327 *n.*, 344
Huger, Mrs. Ben, 264, 327
Huger, Frank, 397
Huger, Tom, 33, 250
Huger, Meta, 176, 177, 178, 250
Huger, Mrs. William, 174–75
Huger, Mrs. (?), 170, 176, 177, 178, 264, 327, 449, 333, 364, 402, 431, 525, 526, 536, 538
Hunter, R. M. T., 50–51, 53, 90, 100, 280, 282, 302, 334, 343–44, 365, 366, 376, 503, 539
Huntsville, 225
Hunter, Mrs., 8

India, 111
India, Russell, 272, 434
Indiana, 433
Indians, 138
"Infair," 500–1
Ingraham, Duncan Nathaniel, 6, 7, 8, 11–12, 32, 41, 51, 67, 75, 88, 94, 102, 105, 130, 204, 234
Inquirer (newspaper), 144
Intelligencer (newspaper), 60

Irish, assist North, 270
Iron Clads, 445
Iron Flotilla, 234
Iroquois (ship), 250
Island Forts, (Charleston Harbor), 29, 31, 33, 35, 36
Ives, Colonel, 274, 326, 331, 347, 359, 368
Ives, Mrs., 348, 351, 356, 365, 382
Izard, Lucy (Mrs. Barney Heyward), 276
Izard, Mrs. 29, 94, 203, 273, 432, 433, 485; establishes hospital, 270

Jackson, Thomas Jonathan, 54(?), 231, 235, 241, 242, 244, 251, 252, 257, 261, 270, 297, 336, 344, 393, 445, 482, 483, 484; gains sobriquet "Stonewall," at Manassas, 88; at the Seven Days, 259; death, 329, 424; character, 330–31, 332
James, Captain, 462, 467
James Island, 160, 237, 240, 246; Northern Forces land at, 244; abandoned by South
James River, 390, 411
Jamison, Mr. (President of Secession Convention), 51
Jerome, Prince; *see Bonaparte*, Jerome Napoleon
Johns Island, S. C., 237, 240
Johnson, Andrew, 533, 536, 539
Johnson, Mrs. Bradley, 69
Johnson, John, 135
Johnson, Robert, 514, 516
Johnson, William E., 57–58, 141
Johnson, Colonel, killed at Manassas, 86
Johnson, Senator, 345
Johnson's Island, 449
Johnston, Albert Sidney, 190–91, 198–99, 261, 336, 344, 393, 445; death, 211 *n.*, 245
Johnston, Edward, 299–300, 301, 315, 344; wounded and taken prisoner, 406; sent to Atlanta, 432
Johnston, Joseph Eggleston, 62, 66–67, 74, 75, 77, 86, 90, 174, 175, 189, 228, 238, 252, 260, 270, 285, 306, 307, 318, 336, 343, 393, 410 *n.*,–11, 416, 418–19, 421–22 *ff.*, 445, 452, 467, 469, 473, 475, 481 *ff.*, 491, 493, 501, 504, 509, 510, 513, 517, 522, 526, 533, 537; reinforces Beauregard, 84; strategy 79*n.*; at Manassas, 88; wounded at Seven Pines, 239 *n.*; wounded at Chickahominy, 242–43; childhood, 248; Commander in Chief of Army of the West, 335; reinforces Polk, 382; and Hood, 392; replaced by Hood, 420–21; surrender, 528–29
Johnston, Lydia (Mrs. Joseph E.), 50, 75, 84, 85, 106, 107, 133, 144, 344, 392, 410, 452–53, 485, 486
Johnston, Preston, 305, 327, 328
Johnston, Sidney, 175
Johnston's Paladins, at Manassas, 238
Jonas (servant), 49
Jonathan (Chesnut's servant), 244–45
Jones, Cadwallader, 522
Jones, William E., 132 *n.*
Jones, "Commissary," 240
Jones, Mrs. James Alfred, 109
Jones, Mrs. Sam, 106
Jone's Brigade, 406
Jordan, Thomas (?), 102, 109, 365, 445, 513–14
Jourdin (Family), 187

Kamtchatka (Chesnut plantation), 539
Kearsarge (ship), 421
Keith, Dr., murdered by his Negroes, 139, 151–52
Keitt, Ashman, 343
Keitt, Lawrence, 5, 65, 66, 73, 76, 85, 107, 179, 182, 327
Kelly, Mr., 424
Kemper, General, 417
Kennedy, Anthony, 114
Kennedy, John, 423
Kentucky, 48, 136; Kentuckians fêted in Richmond, 355, 357
Kershaw, John, 539
Kershaw, Joseph, 6 *n.*, 13, 26, 58, 95, 96, 103, 105, 109, 112, 120, 182, 287, 308
Kershaw, Joseph (the first), 535
Kershaw, Miss Mary, 535
Kershaw, Mrs., 58, 442, 531, 537
Kershaw Camp, 62
Kershaw District, 6, 188, 190
Kershaw's Brigade, 471
Key, Phil Barton, 132, 247
Kilpatrick, Hugh Judson, 389, 391, 393, 489
King, Henry, killed at Secessionville, 253
King, Mrs. Henry, 35
King, Louisa, 545, 546
King, Sue, 211, 212, 464–65, 469
King, the Captains, 546
King, Dr., 545
King, Judge, 275
King, Mr., Minister to France, 49
King (Family), 540
Kingsville, S. C., 3*n.*, 60, 266, 267, 308, 322–23, 407

Kirkland, Mary (Mrs. William), 413–14, 417, 528
Kirkland, William, 164; aid to Ripley, 275; death 413, 417
Kirkland, Mrs., 4
Kirkland, Mr., 59
Kirkwood, 73, 74, 170, 177, 256
Kirkwood Rangers, 101, 134, 218
Knight's Hill (Chesnut plantation), 137 *n.*, 544–45
Knitting, war work, 121, 130, 143
Knox, Mrs. William, 9
Koszta, Martin, 12 *n.*

La Bord, Dr., 274
Laburnam (Lyons' home), destroyed, 394–95
La Cousine Bette, Honoré de Balzac, 188
Ladies Aid, 96, 115, 137, 143
Lamar, L. Q. C., 347, 353, 360–61, 375, 390, 401, 446; biography, 151 *n.*
Lamar, Mr., 67, 70, 71–72, 81–82, 137
Lamar, Mrs., 82
Lancaster, S. C., 493, 499, 509
Lane, Miss, 93
Landowners, 144
Lang, H., 542
Lang, Murray, 172
Lang, Susan, 172
Lang, Tom, 53, 172
Lang, William, 49
Last Man, The, Mary W. Shelley, 155
Laurens, Henry, 442, 443
Lawrence (Chesnut's manservant), 67, 38, 83–84, 104, 120, 125, 154, 209, 213, 281–82, 295–96, 304, 378, 440, 443, 478 *ff.*, 503, 505
Lawton, General, supersedes Colonel Myers, 330, 357
Lay's cavalry, 88
Le Conte, Professor, supervisor of manufacture of gunpowder, 199, 252, 278
Ledyard, Mr., 17
Lee, Agnes, 335, 398
Lee, Mrs. Ben, 154
Lee, George Washington Custis, 104, 107, 121, 292, 303, 311, 314, 366, 376, 381, 398, 399, 438, 440
Lee, Emma, marriage to Barney Stewart, 340
Lee, Fitzhugh, 107, 132 *n.*, 333, 388, 395, 396
Lee, John Boykin, 135
Lee, Henry (Light Horse Harry), 107, 132 *n.*, 137
Lee, Mary, 329, 398
Lee, Mildred, 398
Lee, Robert E., 58 *n.*, 59, 70, 82, 94–95, 105–9, 114, 121, 131, 155, 157 *n.*, 164, 195, 231, 261, 266, 280, 292, 297, 301, 303, 306, 311, 327, 333, 335, 336, 344, 381, 384, 394, 395, 396, 398, 403, 406 *n.*, 410, 415, 423, 429, 432, 436, 443, 445, 460, 479, 483, 484, 487, 510, 513–14, 517, 521, 525; succeeds Johnston, 239; "Old Spade Lee," 252; the Seven Days, 259, 262; surrender to Grant, 470 *n.*, generalissimo, 475; evacuates lines around Petersburg, 514 *n.*, capitulation, 520 *n.*
Lee "Little" Robert, 335
Lee, Mrs. Robert E., 94, 124, 129–30, 132, 303, 381
Lee, Roony, 94, 107, 394, 398; prisoner, 303, 341, 342, 396
Lee, Mrs. Roony (Charlotte Wickham), 342
Lee, Smith, 20, 23, 94, 95, 105, 315, 316, 388, 394, 401, 402
Lee, Mrs. Smith (*née* Mason), 104, 107, 109, 119
Lee, Stephen D., 509
Lee (Family), 109, 328
Lee's Army, 416, 515
Leesburg, victory, 153–54, 155
Legislature, *see* Confederate Congress
Leisure Hours in Town, "A Country Parson," 327
Leland, Captain, 458
Leon, Edwin de, 231
Leon, Miss Henrietta de, school, 135, 407
Leon, Miriam de, 225; *see also* Cohen, Miriam
Les Miserables, Victor Hugo, 441
Letcher, Governor, 85, 121, 329
Levy, Martha, 274, 275
Lewis, Dangerfield, 347–48
Lewis, John, 326
Lewis, Maria (*née* Freeland), 347–48, 382, 402
Lewis, Mrs. (of Audley), 284
Lewis, Mrs. (*née* Vander Horst), 506
Lewis (Family), 481
Liberty Hill, S. C., 491
Library of the Capitol, 100
Lincoln, Abraham, 1, 6, 9, 11, 13, 14 *n.*, 34, 57, 60, 68, 73, 78, 114, 235, 268, 303 *n.*, 343, 345, 400–1, 411, 413, 424, 451, 494, 502; election and inaugural, 3, 7, 12; journey through Baltimore, 9, 18–19; on slavery, 208; assassination, 522, 539
Lincoln, Mary Todd, 345, 398; economy measures, 16, 17

Lincolnton, N. C., 478; Mrs. Chesnut's opinion of, 480
Lone Star flag, 98
Logan, John Alexander, 499, 523
Logan Street (Charleston), fire, 174
Lomax, Colonel, 2, 238
London *Post,* 120
London *Times*, 47, 39, 475
Long, Mrs., 86, 97
Longstreet, Augustus Baldwin, 81–82 *n.*
Longstreet, James, 240, 301, 307, 327, 330, 336, 394, 520 *n.*
Longstreet's Brigade, 84, 308, 406 *n.*, 415
Lord, Dr., 536
Lorena (ballad), 304 *n.*
Louisiana (ship), 216, 223
Lovejoy, Mr., 398
Lovell, Berrien, 463–64
Lovell, Mansfield, 215, 217, 424, 427–28, 451, 473, 475–76, 515, 532; Fall of New Orleans, 253
Lovell, Mrs., 311
Low Country, 2, 164, 193, 542
Lowndes, Charles, 275
Lowndes, Mrs. Childs, 4
Lowndes, James, 88, 117, 120, 509, 546
Lowndes, Rollins, 532, 546
Lowndes, Mr., 473
Lowndes (Family), 238
Lubbock, Governor, 438, 446
Ludlow, Mrs., 354
Luryea, Albert, 237, 246
Lynchburg regiment, at Manassas, 86
Lynching, 140
Lyndsey, Mr., 60
Lyon, Mr., 73, 105
Lyons, Lord, 174, 175, 195
Lyons, Rachel, 266, 272
Lyons, Mr., 361–62
Lyons, Mrs., 280, 418
Lyons (Family), 281, 285, 394–95

McCaa, Burwell Boykin, 296
McClellan, George Brinton, 62, 67, 85 *n.*, 101, 125–26, 156, 218, 223, 251, 256, 257, 261, 263, 264, 265, 266, 327, 410, 520; Peninsular campaign, 204 *n.*, 214, 217 *n.*, 229; routed, 260
McCord, Cheves, 191, 240, 279
McCord, Mrs. Cheves, 455
McCord, Lieutenant Governor, 469
McCord, Mrs., 211, 213, 215, 220, 235, 240, 279, 438, 455; raises company for son, 197; defends Davis, 198; hospital work, 242, 243, 245, 250–51, 256, 261–62, 268–69, 425, 457, 459, 468, 470, 472, 478, 499, 515
McCord (Family), 274
McCullock, Ben, 48, 136, 264
McDaniel, Miss, 488–89
McDaniel, Mrs., 498, 499, 506
Mac Donald, Squire (well digger), 143
McDuffie, Mary (Mrs. Wade Hampton), 41, 196, 223–24, 238, 242, 243, 255, 386, 437
McEwen, Miss, 58, 156, 414
McFarland, Mr., 302
McFarland, Mrs., 302, 346–47, 406
McFarland (Family), 281, 366
McGillie, *see* McWillie
McIlvaine's Cavalry, 161
McKenzie, Mrs., 450
McLane, Mrs. (*née* Sumner), 49, 67, 83, 84, 85, 86, 89, 90, 91, 316, 427
McLaughlin, Isaac (Chesnut servant), 321, 323, 475, 503
McLean, Mr., 438, 470 *n.*
McLean, Miss, 481, 482
McLean (Family), 481–82, 487, 507
McMahon, Mr., author of *Cause and Contrast*, 517
McMahon, Mr., 263, 268
McMahon, Mrs., 209, 210, 214, 263, 267–68, 274
McMahon (Family), 229, 231, 265
McMaster, Colonel, 434
McPherson, General, 432
McQueen, General, 39
McQueen, Lieutenant, 514
McRae, John, 190
McRae and Company, 294
McReady, Mr., 499
McWillie, Adam, 514–15
McWillie, William, 515
Macon, Ga., raid, 432, 435
Magill, Mrs., 434
Magnolia Cemetery, 29
Magrath, Judge, 2, 3, 451, 475
Magruder, John Bankhead, 58, 67, 228, 230, 261, 266
Mahone's Brigade, 424
Maine, 289
Maîtres d'Armes, Alexandre Dumas, 434
Mallory, Ruby, 356
Mallory, Mrs. Stephen Russell, 57, 87, 332
Mallory (Family), 403
Malvern Hill, 538
Manassas, battle, 66, 67, 73, 77, 87 *n.*, 89, 90, 91, 92, 96, 97, 99, 105, 106, 113, 114, 121, 124, 130, 204, 229, 238, 261, 299, 473. *See also* Second Manassas
Manassas Junction, 279
Manassas Station, 58–59

Manchester, S. C., 408
Manigault, Arthur, 229, 497–98
Manigault pamphlet, 336
Mann, Beverly, 240
Mann, Miss, 240
Manning, Dick, 101, 421, 423
Manning, John, 27, 28–29, 30–31, 34, 35, 36, 38–39, 41, 48, 101, 106, 107, 112, 168, 179, 190, 227, 409, 411, 473
Manning, Wade, 194, 202
Marauders, 522
Maria (servant), 77, 79, 84, 87, 162, 171
Mariage de Figaro, Le, de Beaumarchais, 190
Marmion, Sir Walter Scott, 425
Martin Chuzzlewit, Charles Dickens, 364
Marriage law, in South Carolina, 383
Marshall, Henry 68, 110, 218
Marshall, Humphrey, 517
Martin, Isabella, 211, 213, 223, 326, 335, 338, 346, 353, 355–56, 357, 366, 368, 375, 378, 421, 422, 429, 431, 434, 435, 436, 437, 439, 442, 448, 455, 457, 462–63, 464, 469, 472, 473, 474, 482, 484, 485, 488, 500, 501, 503, 505, 506, 507, 546–47
Martin, Maggie, 460
Martin, Mrs., 450–51, 483
Martin, the Reverend Mr., 7, 438, 447, 449, 453, 468, 478, 480, 485, 491, 512
Maryland, 51, 56–57, 67, 95
Maryland Regiment, 73
"Maryland, my Maryland," Hetty and Jennie Cary, 311 *n.*
Mason, George, 107
Mason, James Murray, 92, 97, 99, 109, 116–17, 123 *n.*,–24, 127, 130, 149, 150, 160, 174–75, 343–44
Mason, Mrs., 486
Massachusetts, 152–53, 246
Massey, Mr., of Lancaster, 161
Matthews, John Raven, 165
Matthews, William, 452, 519
Maum Mary (servant), 205, 206
Maximilian, Emperor of Mexico, 519, 523
Mazyck, William, 261, 424
Meade, George Gordon, 344
Means, Emma, 37, 278
Means, John, 34, 35, 112, 271, 272; killed at Sharpsburg, 278
Means, Mrs., 37–38, 422
Means, Stark, 37
Medical care, of soldiers, 409 *n.*, 425 *n.*
Medical College in Philadelphia, 53
Meek's Mill, S. C., 484
Memminger, Christopher Gustavus, 223, 417, 492; appointed Secretary of the Treasury, 385; move Department women to Columbia, 401
Memminger, Mrs. 383
Memoirs, W. T. Sherman, 538 *n.*
Memphis, Tenn., 240, 250, 252, 432
Mercer, General, 228, 243
Mercier, Count, 214
Mercury (newspaper), 57, 63, 108, 118, 120, 135, 143, 144, 150, 152, 161, 175, 190, 207, 219, 231, 240, 242, 275, 365, 436 *n.*, 537
Meredith, Owen (E. R. Bulwar Lytton), 455
Merrimac (ship), 198, 212 *n.*; success at Newport News, 195 *n.*; named the *Virginia*, 205; sunk, 222
Methodist church, 44, 431
Methodist College, in Columbia, 499
Mexico, 211, 488, 523
Meynardie, the Reverend Mr., 63, 105
Micanopy, Indian, 43
Middleton, Harry, 210
Middleton, Mrs. Harry, 180, 195, 209, 210, 214, 505, 507, 518, 520
Middleton, John Izard, 230, 498
Middleton, Olivia, wedding to Frederick Blake, 460
Middleton, Mrs. Tom, 29
Middleton, Miss, 482, 488, 496, 516
Middleton (Family), 238, 481, 483, 489
Miles, William Porcher, 13, 34, 35, 36, 41, 42, 51, 86, 92, 104, 112, 116, 117, 131, 139, 150, 152, 157, 279, 282, 326, 330, 340, 354, 384 and Congressman Ely, 136; engagement to Bettie Bierne, 299–300, 301–2
Miles, Mrs. William Porcher (*née* Bettie Bierne), 384
Miles, Richardson, 441, 458, 506, 516
Miles, Mrs., 346–347, 386, 407
Military Institute of Virginia, 459
Mill on the Floss, George Eliot, 425
Miller, Charles, uncle of Mary Boykin Chesnut, 498
Miller, John L., cousin of Mary Boykin Chesnut, 410
Miller, Stephen, brother of Mary Boykin Chesnut, 1, 2, 9, 212
Miller, Stephen Decatur, father of Mary Boykin Chesnut, 3, 6 *n.*, 293, 437
Miller, Mrs. Stephen Decatur, mother of Mary Boykin Chesnut, 294, 310–11
Mills House, 32, 41
Millwood, 252, 472
Milly Chesnut's (servant), 213
Milroy, General, 284, 299
Milton, John, 223, 392
Minnegerode, Mr., 313, 358, 361, 394

Minnegerode, Mrs., 313
Missionary Ridge, 362, 381
Mississippi, 65, 151 *n.*, 203, 385, 393
Mississippi (ship), 223
Mississippi fleet, 250
Mississippi Regiment, 155
Mississippi River, 187, 215, 241, 474, 503, 528
Missouri, 111
Mitchell, Maggie (actress), 8
Mobile, Ala., 385, 392–93, 429, 430, 431
Modeste Mignon, 268
Moise, Mr., 241–42
Molly (Chesnut's servant), 60, 148, 164–65, 209, 229, 230, 243–44, 274 *ff.*, 295–96, 306, 316, 323 *ff.*, 348, 418, 458, 461, 468, 477, 478, 484, 499, 530–31, 532, 541
Money; *see* Confederate currency; Confederate bonds
Monitor (ship), 198
Montagu, Lady Mary Wortley, 122
Montgomery, Ala., 4, 13, 23, 25, 30, 45, 50, 51, 57, 78, 226, 289, 294, 307
Montgomery Blues, 1, 2, 9
Montgomery Hall, 26
Monumental Church, 339
Moore, Dr., Surgeon General, 95
Moore, Governor, 2, 8, 10, 15, 23, 46, 353, 504
Morgan, John Hunt, 210, 354, 355, 309, 361, 394, 397, 434; in Kentucky, 273; escapes from Columbus penitentiary, 353 *n.*; and Mattie Reedy, 310
Morgan, Mrs. John (*née* Mattie Reedy), 354
Mormons, 200, 523
Morris Island (Charleston harbor), 33, 39, 259, 307
Morrow, Mr., 47, 161
Moses, Anna de Leon, 246
Moses, Franklin, J., 178, 187
Moses, Franklin J., Jr., 187, 213, 257, 258
Moses (Family), 134
Moultrie, William, memoirs, 137
Mount Vernon, 59
Mountford, Willie, 305, 352–53
Mulberry (Chesnut plantation), 3, 10, 24, 26, 34, 41, 134, 158, 165–67, 169–70, 193–94, 318, 320, 322, 403, 425 *n.*, 440, 478, 488–89, 544; Negroes, 142–43; 148–49, 410; life, 169–70, 228; description, 408–9, 466–67; damage to, 503, 523, 528, 531, 540
Munroe, Mr., 495
Munroe, Mrs., 481, 486, 487, 488, 493, 494, 517
Murray, Mr., 415
Murfreesboro, Tenn., 97 *n.*
Myers, Colonel, 285, 302, 330, 366
Myers, Mrs., 279, 302, 328, 352
Myrtilia (head nurse at Mulberry), 531

Napier, Lord, 238
Napoleon; *see* Bonaparte
Nashville, Tenn., 190, 193, 473
National Flag, *see* Confederate Flag
Negroes, 38, 64, 92, 116, 122, 140, 142, 158–59, 163–64, 176, 179, 197, 199–200, 216, 225, 269, 278, 292, 295, 308, 389, 540; sale, 10–11, 18, 229, 293, 321, 497; loyalty, 91, 167, 244–45, 479, 527–28; camp-meeting hymns, 149; plantation life, 142–43, 165–66; church, 148, 170, 171; wedding, 170–71; value of labor, 197; runaway, 182, 184, 261, 263, 413; whipping, 202–3; offer to fight in Confederate Army, 203, 204; conscription, 222–23, 259, 394, 483; hired, 399–400; freedom, 456, 531, 532–33, 536, 538, 539, 541, 544, 545; in Union Army, 460
Nelson, Jim (driver at Mulberry), 148
Nelson, Warren 200–1
New England, 163, 165, 504
New Orleans, 223, 231 *n.*, 234, 241, 547; Zouaves, 67; fall of, 215, 216–17, 252–53, 432
New York City, 110, 299; cotton market, 529, 537, 541
New York *Herald*, 7, 8, 11, 17, 45, 103, 112, 114, 144, 231, 389, 393, 538, 539
New York Hotel, 363
New York Seventh Regiment, 40
New York *Tribune*, 97, 108, 113–14, 173
Newbern [New Bern], N. C., 201
Newport News, 195 *n.*
Newspapers, 160, 193, 211, 231 *n.*, 246, 415, 443, 446, 519
Nickersons, 455, 464
Ninth Street (Richmond), 520
Ninth Virginia Regiment, 388
Nisbett, Judge, 87
Nitre bed, 278
Norfolk, Va., 53, 220; burned, 222
North, 8, 103, 204 *n.* *See also* United States
North Carolina, 39, 130, 185, 189 *n.*, peace efforts, 348, 401; on secession, 494 *n*
Northrop, Commissary General, 99, 114, 205, 285, 504
Nott, Henry Dean, 110–11
Nott, Dr., 81, 87–88, 102

Nott (Family), 280–81
Nuns, 181

Oath of allegiance, to United States, 538, 540–41
Ogden, Captain, 436, 451, 505, 507
Oliver Twist, Charles Dickens, 111
O'Neal, Judge, 247
Orange Court House, 73, 75
Orangeburg, S. C., 478
Orr, Senator, 157, 168, 340, 343, 448, 492
Osceola, 43
Ossoli, Sarah Margaret Fuller, 33
Ould, Mr., 82, 314, 366, 400, 404
Ould, Mrs., 77, 84, 298, 328, 333, 345, 361, 370, 400, 403
Owens, General, 46, 191

Page, Captain Lee, 398
Palmer, Dr., 434–35, 451, 471
Palmetto Cockades, 77
Palmetto Flag, 2
Palmetto Guards, 61, 212
Paris, Johnny, 171
Parker, Frank, 394, 402
Parker, Sarah, 255
Parker, Mr., 159
Parkman, Mrs., 302
Partisan, Beverly Tucker, 221
Patrick Henry (ship), 85
Patterson, Robert, 74, 75
Patterson, Miss, 478
Patton, Colonel, 305, 313
Patton, Mrs., 313
Pau, Captain de, 408
Peace conference, 8
Peau de Chagrin, 220
Pegram, General, engagement to Hetty Cary, 312, 387, 392, 394; death, 502
Pelissier, Marshall, 29
Pelletier, Madame, 450
Pemberton, John Clifford, 217, 243, 244, 315
Pendelton, General, 375
Peninsular Campaign, 213–24, 271 *n.*, 218
Penn, Colonel, 363
Penn, Mrs., 363
Pennsylvania, 287
Pensacola, Fla., 56
Penny (Salmond's servant), loyalty, 167
Perkins, Caroline, 139–40
Perkins, Priscilla, 139–40, 414
Perkins, Mr., 140
Perroneau, Miss (Mrs. William Matthews), 519
Perry, Governor, 247
Petersburg, Va., 115, 314, 323, 396; battles near, 432, 479, 502; Lee's evacuation, 514 *n.*
Petigru, James Louis, 28 *n.*, 37, 58, 71, 173, 238, 247, 454
Petticola, Mrs., 305
Pettigrew, Johnston, 201–2, 230, 231, 232–33, 238
Pettigrew, Mr., 368
Pfeifer (Family), 485
Philadelphia, Pa., 141, 231, 303
Phillips, Mrs., 10, 23, 124, 266
Phoenix, Mr., 279
Pickens, Francis Wilkinson, 4, 7, 14 *n.*, 31–32, 34, 68, 157, 158, 160, 170, 190, 207, 210, 211, 213, 217, 224, 235, 242, 244, 264, 265, 266, 267, 269, 492; Council of Safety, 179
Pickens, Mrs. Francis Wilkinson (*née* Lucy Holcombe), 32, 106, 193, 206, 210, 214, 220, 224, 233, 240, 258, 274, 355; reception for General Hampton, 257
Pictures from Italy, Charles Dickens, 161
Pillow, Gideon J., 158, 198 *n.*
Pickney, Charles Cotesworth, 33–34
Pickney, Miss, 33
Pickney Island, Negro colony, 179
Pine knots, illumination, 153
Pinto, Ferdinand Mendez, 406–7
Pizzini (Italian confectioner), 119
Plain Hill (plantation), 143
Planters, 238
Planter (ship), 33
Poe, Edgar Allan, 327
Point Lookout prison, 442
Polignac, Prince Charles Ludovic Marie de, 73
Polk, Leonidas, 316, 382, 393, 416
Pollard, Mr., 7
Polly (servant), 15, 57
Porchers, 2, 114–15
Port Royal, Va., 135, 143, 154, 159 *n.*, 196, 225; battle, 150, 156, 158
Portland, Ala., 49, 287, 289, 307
Portman, Mr., 511, 512, 524
Potomac River, 83, 97, 312
Potter's raid, 528–29
Power, David, 121
Prentiss [Seargent Smith?], 110
Presbyterian church, 451
Presidential Mansion, *see* Brockenbrough Mansion
Preston, Artie, 231, 246
Preston, Sally Buchanan Campbell (Buck), 211, 280 *ff.*, 285, 300, 312, 332, 333, 341, 349, 355, 356, 365, 367, 368–69, 382, 383, 385–86, 390–91,

393–94, 402, 416, 418, 420, 421, 422, 428, 439, 443–44, 448, 449, 450, 452, 454, 509, 519, 520 *ff.*, 547; loyalty to Jefferson Davis, 283; and General Hood, 298, 326, 334, 336–37, 341–42, 370–71, 375, 376–78, 388, 392, 395, 398, 427, 518; described, 338–39; character, 371–72
Preston, Ellie, 327
Preston, Jack, 35, 263, 344, 419, 474
Preston, John S., 81, 84, 139, 155, 157, 160, 178–79, 188, 192, 201, 215, 218, 220, 228, 231, 242, 246, 247, 248, 251, 271, 322, 325, 328, 334, 350, 352–53, 354, 381, 394, 419, 431–32, 434, 462, 469, 511–12, 515, 521; heads Conscription Bureau, 345; takes family to Europe, 526, 527, 547
Preston, Mrs. John S., 39, 66, 70, 71, 72, 73, 76, 77, 79, 86, 94, 106, 181, 185, 187, 190, 211, 213, 227–28, 231, 233, 243, 246, 254, 260, 270, 287, 358, 382, 389–90, 421, 426, 438, 442, 513
Preston, Mary Cantey, 181, 187, 193, 196, 200, 202, 207, 211, 215–16, 219, 285–86, 298, 300, 325, 326, 332, 335, 338, 339, 340, 348, 358, 364, 365, 368, 391, 397, 418, 419, 421, 423; marries John Darby, 436–37
Preston, Tudy, 356, 365, 379, 383, 384, 395–96, 397, 420, 449
Preston Willie, 41, 102, 234, 246, 372, 385–86, 437, 474; death, 421; described, 422–23
Preston, William C., 110, 498
Preston (Family), 79 *n.*, 391, 402, 473–74, 481, 503, 511, 517; loss of private fortunes, 215; girls, 277, 280 *ff.*, 353, 510; character, 416–17
Price, Sterling, 143, 247
Pride, Mrs., 509, 510, 512
Prince of Wales, Albert Edward, 271
Princess of Wales, Alexandra, 368
Princeton College, 72, 120, 534
Pringle, Edward, 30
Pringle, John Julius, 251
Pringle, Mrs., 184, 449
Pringle (Family), 30
Prisoners, exchange of, 397–98, 403–4, 449
Privateering, 57
Proclamation, Cameron's, 92; Butler's 230–31 *n.*
Progress of Philanthropy, The, Theodore Edward Hook, 194–95
Property, 331; destruction, 393, 425, 481, 491, 499, 510, 518, 520, 527, 528, 529
Quashie (Chesnut's driver), 193–94
Quattlebaum, Colonel, 195
Queens of the House of Hanover, Dr. Doran, 431

Radcliffe, Mr., 489
Raids, 529. *See also* Union Army Yankee
Railroads, 201
Raleigh, N. C., 229
Randolph, George Wythe, 204
Randolph, Mrs. George, 95–96, 110, 115, 116, 281, 313, 378, 332, 346, 352, 353, 356 *ff.*
Randolph, John, 85
Rapidan River, 406 *n.*
Rappahanock River, 297, 298
Ravenel, Edward, 538
Ravenel, Frank 264, 538
Ravenel, St. Julien, 492, 503–4, 506
Ravenel, Mrs. St. Julien, 515
Ravenel and Company, 529
Rawdon, Lord, *see* Hastings, Francis Rawdon
Revel, Jackson, 137
Reagan, J. H., as Postmaster General, 15
Recollections, Grave and Gay, Constance Cary, 311 *n.*
Reconstructionists, 14, 468
Reed, William B., 121
Reed, Mr., 208
Reed, Mrs., 481, 483
Reedy, Mattie, 310, 354. *See also* Morgan, Mrs. John
Republicans, 30, 74
"Revenue Clippers," 269. *See also* Confederate bonds
Reynolds, Mark, 537
Reynolds, Sally, 533
Reynolds, William, 514
Reynolds, Mrs. William, 24, 159, 514
Rhett, Albert, 223
Rhett, Mrs. Albert, 204
Rhett, Alfred, 281
Rhett, Barnwell, 5, 13, 47, 60 *n.*, 108, 144, 150, 161, 205
Rhett, Burnett, 120, 261, 275; wedding, 306–7
Rhett, Edmund, 186, 207, 418, 420, 423, 541; hostility toward Jefferson Davis, 540
Rhett, John, 85, 204
Rhett, Julius Grimké, 261, 265, 267
Rhett (Family), 352, 434, 456, 466, 467, 494, 540
Rhody (Witherspoon servant), 140, 145, 147, 148

Rice, 225, 230
Rice, Mr., 270
Richland, S. C., troops, 39
Richmond, Va., 54, 56, 65, 66, 77, 78, 80, 81, 99, 191, 203, 217 *n.*, 219, 224, 229 *n.*, 230, 234, 256, 257, 258, 279, 283, 295, 309 *ff.*, 321 *ff.*, 355, 357 *n.*, 393, 429, 442, 453; Confederate capital, 51; social life, 226, 281; evacuation of, 228, 520 *n.*; defense measures, 232, 240, 313–14; raid, 277; battles around, 479; fall of 518, 520
Rickett, Mrs., 106, 107, 116
Rickett's Battery, 97, 106
Rio Grande, 519
Ripley, General, 181, 217, 228, 240, 243, 275
Rivals, The, Richard Brinsley, Sheridan, 275 *n.*
River, Sally, 4
River, Dr. Tom, 4
Roanoke, Va., 187; surrender, 191
Robb, Captain Phil, 315, 316, 337, 338–39
Roberts, Captain, 397
Robinson, Mr. Stephen, 172
Rockett's landing, 316, 520
Rodgers, Captain, 511
Romeo (Chesnut servant), 226
Romeo (Witherspoon servant), 148
Romney (W. Va.?), 187
Romola, George Eliot, 331, 360, 387, 446
Roper, Mrs., 174, 183
Rose, Hugh, 82, 93, 233
Rose, James, 252, 255
Rosencrantz, William Starke, 109 *n.*, 121, 307, 327
Rousseau, Jean Jacques, 329
Rousseau, Lieutenant, 328–29
Ruffin, Edmund, 60 *n.*, 93
Rufus, Dr., 304
Russell, Lord John, 196
Russell, Sir William Howard, 39, 47, 49, 56, 60, 63, 73, 92, 111, 116, 122, 124, 125, 136, 151; on Manassas, 97; on Senator Wilson, 107; entertained by Seward, 109; on slavery, 155–56; on cotton, 170
Russia, 347, 434; Minister, 68
Rutherford, John, 315, 366
Rutledge, Mrs. Ben, 481, 483, 490–91
Rutledge (James?), 77
Rutledge, John, 33, 489
Rutledge, Julia, 306, 444
Rutledge, Robert, 13
Rutledge, Sally, 276, 452, 462, 515
Rutledge, Susan, 98
Rutledge (Family), 29, 30, 238
Rutledge's Mounted Rifles, 269

Safety Council, *see* Council of Safety
St. Andrew's Hall, 32
St. Celia Ball, 32
St. Charles' Hospital (Richmond), 116
St. Charles Hotel (New Orleans), 389–90
St. Lawrence (ship), 198
Salisbury, S. C., 516
Salisbury Prison, 493 *n.*
Salmond, Louisa, 167
Salmond, Maggie, 167
Salt, scarcity, 160
Sand, George, 514
Sandbags, 238, 240, 427
Sanders, George, 10, 14
Sanders, Miss, 11–12, 311–12
Sandhill tackeys, 54 *n.*, 273, 542–43
Sandy Hill (Chesnut plantation), 60, 130, 137 *n.*, 153, 170, 173
Santee River (S. C.), 206, 265, 533
Saratoga, N. C., 247
Sarsfield (Chesnut plantation), 137
Saussure house, 253–54
Savannah (ship), 57, 59
Savannah, Ga., 2, 139, 237, 435, 456, 464; fall of, 465
Savonarola, Girolamo, 331
Saxon, Mrs., 8
Schiller, Johann Christoph Friedrich von, 219
Schools, Free, 233
Scotch, 270
Scott, Captain, 373
Scott, General Winfield, 5–6, 7, 19, 95, 106, 133, 185, 245, 344; resignation, 156
Scott, Mrs. Winfield, 19, 20, 185
Scribe, Augustin Eugène, 190
Seabrook, Captain, 340
Secession, 3, 32
Secession Convention, 6, 29
Secession Ordinance, 4, 497
Secessionville, 253, 254
Second Manassas, 279, 306, 425, 481
Seddon, James Alexander, 289, 314–15, 473, 503
Selma, Ala., 289
Seminole War, 43
Semmes, Admiral Raphael, 275 *n.*, 421
Semmes, Mrs., 349, 351, 388, 405
Semmes, Senator, 275 *n.*, 302, 350
Seven Days, battle, 259 *n.*, 260, 327 *n.*
Seven Pines, battle, 239 *n.*, 261, 295 *n.*, 315, 410
Seventh Regiment, 34
Seward, William Henry, 14, 17, 34, 47,

77, 98, 109, 121, 160–61, 203, 238, 246, 271, 299, 421; trip to England, 268
Shafer and Company (tailors), 80
Shakespeare, William 391–92
Shand, The Reverend Mr., 259
Shand, Nanna (Mrs. Wilson), 214
Shannon, Dr. Charles, 544–45
Shannon, Captain William M., 26, 111, 266, 484
Sharpsburg, N. C., 97 *n.*, 277, 278
Shaw, Colonel, 191
Shelton, Colonel, 43
Sherman, General William Tecumseh, 382, 393, 410, 432, 435 *n.*, 436, 440, 442, 443, 445, 452, 453, 454, 458–9, 462, 469, 470, 472, 473, 475, 478, 486, 487, 488, 489, 493, 496, 497, 509, 510, 518, 538 *n.*, 452; battery, 86; at Atlanta, 450, 451 *n.*; at Augusta, 452; at Hardeeville, 467; at Orangeburg, 428; at Columbia, 492, 499, 515–16; at Lancaster, 493; at Camden, 528
Sherman's Brigade, 54
Shields, James, 242
Shiloh, Tenn., 211, 212, 220, 261, 268, 354, 445
Shipley, Major S. D., 545 *n.*
Ships and shipbuilding, 38, 154, 200, 204, 278. *See also* Blockade
Shuford, Mr., 170–71, 172
Shurtz, Captain, 258
Sickles, Mr., 132, 247
Silvie (Witherspoon servant), 148
Simms, William Gilmore, 42 *n.*, 202
Simon (Chesnut servant) 293
Simons, Mrs., 543
Singleton, Decca (Mrs. Alexander Cheves Haskell), 108, 248–49, 254
Singleton, Mrs. Mat, 88, 220, 248, 263–64, 305, 494
Sisters of Charity, 116, 124
Slavery, 21, 45, 70, 73, 107, 114, 122–23, 136, 138, 141, 151, 155, 163–64, 194, 195, 218, 229, 247, 265, 347, 434–35, 475, 485–86, 512. *See also* Negroes
Slick, Sam, *see* Haliburton, Thomas Chandler
Slidell, John, 123 *n.*, 137, 149, 150, 160, 174–75
Slidell, Mrs. John, 206
Slocomb, Mrs., 419–20, 437, 452
Smallpox, 371, 376 *n.*, 399, 516; epidemic in Columbia, 3
Smith, E. Kirby, 106, 424, 432; wounded at Manassas, 86, 90; disobeys Pemberton, 243
Smith, "Extra Billy," 442
Smith, G. W., 418, 460
Smith, Gus, 200
Smith, Robert, 7
Smith, Major, 104
Smith (Chesnut servant), 440
Society Hill (Witherspoon plantation), 140, 145–47, 148, 543
Souluque (Haitian slave), 73
South Carolina, 2, 3, 5, 6, 8, 68, 100, 154, 247, 315, 343, 534; delegation, 65; troops, 85, 217, 287; conscription, 242; Negro conscription, 259 *n.*; ovation for Wade Hampton, 407; State House, 456; State Legislature, 174, 469
South Carolina College, 39, 53, 218, 319
South Carolinians, 225
Southern Confederacy, *see* Confederate Congress; Confederate States of America
Southwest, 252
Spann, Ellen, 181
Spann, Ransom, 249–50
Spies, 47, 73, 76–77, 81, 112, 113, 235–237, 257, 270–271, 287–89, 524
Spiritualism, 214
Spotswood Hotel (Richmond) 66, 68, 78, 87, 98, 103, 130, 188, 233, 264, 267, 282, 285, 393, 412
Stanard, Mr., 376
Stanard, Mrs., 94, 109, 279, 281, 333, 335, 346, 352, 357, 363, 365, 449
Stanley, Mr., 489
Stanton, Edwin McMasters, United States Secretary of War, 532
Staples, Mr., 47–48
Stark, Mary, 95, 96, 203, 438, 467–68
Stark, Theodore, 439–40
Starke, Mrs., 212
Starvation Party, 329
States' rights, 138, 453, 456, 465, 483
Statesburg, S. C., 206
Staunton, Va., 305, 418
Stephens, Alexander Hamilton, 8, 9, 46; candidate for Confederate President, 65; Vice-President, 109, 343, 418
Stevens, Mary, 209
Stewart, Barney, 340
Stockton, Edward, 537
Stockton, Mrs. Edward, 320
Stockton, Emma, 340, 349
Stockton, Phil Augustus, 127, 318
Stockton, Mrs. Phil, 411
Stoneman, George, 426, 516, 518
Stoneman's raid, 306, 313
Stone's River (Tenn.), 97 *n.*

Stowe, Harriet Beecher, 114, 122, 163, 169, 202, 226, 403, 434
Stowe, Mr., 502
Street cries, 383
Stuart, James Ewell Brown, 328, 340, 353, 357, 395
Stuart's Brigade of Cavalry, 219, 229, 251
Suffolk, Va., 390
Sugar, scarcity, 96, 317
Suggs, Simon, 13
Sullivan's Island, 114–15, 333
Sumner, Charles, 72, 163
Sumter (Family), 238
Sumter, Frank, 71
Sumter, Thomas, 206

Taber, William, 27, 29
Talbot, 34
Taliaferro, General, 425
Taylor, Mrs. Alex, 426, 449
Taylor, Ben, 190
Taylor, Mrs. Ben, 220, 243
Taylor, Edward, 8
Taylor, James, 263, 267
Taylor, John, 449, 534
Taylor, Richard, 159, 294, 295, 424, 432 *n.*, 464, 533
Taylor, Sally Elmore, 10
Taylor, Tom, 85, 245, 447
Taylor, Mrs. Tom, 426
Taylor, Willie, 223
Taylor, Mrs., 23, 307
Tarleton, Sir Banastre, memoirs, 137
Team, Adam (Chesnut's overseer), 62, 169, 184, 194, 225–26, 321, 323, 324, 541
Tennent, Dr., 254
Tennessee, 160, 185, 198–99, 252
Tennessee River, 187
Terebene lamps, 450
Texas, 81, 98, 511, 517
Texas Rangers, 48
Thackeray, William Makepeace, 363
Thomas, George Henry, 445 *n.*, 450, 458, 462, 468, 472, 488; against Hood, 464
Thomas, Mr., 502–3
Thomson, Colonel "Old Danger," 88
Thompson, Jacob, 17 *n.*, 18, 271
Thompson, Mrs. Jacob, 18
Thompson, John R., 327, 329, 331, 358, 393, 400, 547 *n.*
Thompson, Waddy, 214
Thoreau, Henry D., 163
Thornwell, Mrs., 261–62
Thurston, Lieutenant, 98
Tobin, Captain, 164
Togno, Ascélie, 189, 207, 265; school girls, 220
Tompkins, Sally, 104 *n.*, 112, 118; hospital, 109, 116, 119
Toombs, Robert, 5–6, 65, 99, 102, 104, 115, 137, 191, 230, 242, 418
Toombs, Mrs. Robert, 46, 50, 119
Toombs, Miss, 257
Trapier, General, 205
Trapier, Mr., 536–37, 539
Trapier (Family), 184
Treadwell, Mr., 232
Trenholm, George A., 192–93, 207, 228 *n.*
Trent (ship), 123 *n.*
Trenton Bridge, 303
Trescot, William Henry, 7, 27–28, 35, 68, 91, 96, 97, 103, 211–12, 225, 233, 456
Trezevant, Grimké, 267
Trezevant, Howell, 261
Trezevant, Lucy, 261
Trezevant, Dr., 210, 213, 214, 243, 261, 263, 458, 459, 465, 467, 545, 546; belief in spirits, 214
Trezevant Lieutenant, 461, 462, 471–72
Trimlin, "Sandhill Milly," 542–43
Tucker, Randolph, 85
Tucker, Captain, 350
Turnpike (Richmond), 297
Turpentine, burned, 201
Two Years Ago, Henry Kingsley, 162
Tyler, John, 185
Tyler, Miss, 12
Typhoid fever, 101, 136, 545

Uncle Tom's Cabin, Harriet Beecher Stowe, 199–200, 247
United States of America, 117, 183, 270, 303; Congress, 1, 3, 10, 196, 361, 513; Navy, 6, 105, 145, 173, 243; Army, 241, 252, 270, 404, 445
United States Cavalry, 532
United States Dragoons, 62
United States Military Academy, 99, 235, 296, 381
Up Country, 193. *See also* Low Country
Upshur, Judge, 518, 519
Urquhart, Colonel, 394, 418, 441
Urquhart, Mr., 441

Wabash (ship), 127
Wade, Benjamin Franklin 400 *n.*–401 *n.*
Walker, John (Preston's servant), 226, 227–28
Walker, Mrs. Leroy Page, 47, 119
Walker, Leroy Pope, 71 *n.*, 72, 77, 85, 106, 132, 217

Walker, Maria (Preston's maid), 226–27
Walker, Robert J., 148
Walker, William (Preston's butler), 226, 227, 440, 473, 512, 515, 527
Walker, General "Shot Pouch," 111, 113, 159
Walker, Miss Page (Mrs. Lee Page), 398
Wallace, Becky, 454
Wallace, John, 140, 439
Wanderer (ship), 498
Ward, Mr., 48–49
Wardlaw, Judge, 212
Waring, Miss, 429
Warrenton, Va., 76, 77, 81
Warwick, Braddy, 280–81
Washington, George, 10, 78, 233, 303, 326, 347
Washington, John, 284
Washington, L. Quentin, 47, 213–14, 219, 223, 282, 301, 313, 335, 338, 347–48, 361, 374, 389, 497, 503
Washington, Lake, 218
Washington, Martha, 141, 347
Washington, Septima, 158
Washington, D. C., 5, 7, 13, 16, 30, 68, 76, 90, 91, 100, 107, 109, 112, 226
Waters, John, 91
Wateree River (S. C.), 184, 201
Watkins, Mrs., 20
Watts, Beaufort, 41, 42–43
Watts, Attorney General, 204, 315
Wayside Hospital, 270 *n.*, 430–31, 435, 442, 449, 450
Webb, Mrs., 351, 357, 376, 389
Weddings, war, 306–7, 396–97, 401, 436–37, 460, 467
Weldon, N. C., 323
Welles, Nat, 114
West, John C., 69
West Point, N. Y., *see* United States Military Academy
West Point, Ga., 288
Western Army, 423, 440
Weston, Plowden, 216
Weston, Mr., 216
Westward Ho!, Charles Kingsley, 71
Wheeler, Joseph, 489, 512
Whiskey, sale of, 278, 538. *See also* Alcohol
Whist, *see* Games
Whitaker, Jeems (servant), 43–44, 162
Whitaker, Maria (servant), 43–44, 528
White, Mrs., 356
White House, 271, 345
"White-robed choir," 303
Whiting, General, 33, 194, 394, 406
Whitner, Judge, 29
Wickham, Charlotte (Mrs. Roony Lee), 94, 303, 341, 342, 396
Wife and Ward, 264
Wigfall, Charlotte, 33
Wigfall, Fanny, 98, 100
Wigfall, Halsey, 353, 355, 356
Wigfall, Louis, 31–32, 34, 35, 41, 45, 66, 68, 70, 71, 72, 86, 91, 96, 98, 107, 194, 218, 233, 307, 329–30, 337–38, 346, 347–48, 353, 381, 418, 428, 430, 467, 504, 511, 513; enters Fort Sumter, 39
Wigfall, Mrs. Louis, 31, 32, 33, 34, 38, 55, 70, 72, 83, 84, 89, 92, 96, 98, 106, 107, 307, 329, 337, 346–47, 353, 366, 485
Wigfall, Louisa, 98
Wigfall, Louly, 337, 366, 460, 519
Wigfall (Family), 109, 282, 332, 337, 455, 519
Wilderness, Battle of the, 280
William (Chesnut coachman), 14–15
William (Johnny Chesnut's servant),59
William (Witherspoon servant), 140, 145–47, 148
William (James Chesnut's foster brother), 538
Williams, David, 139, 140, 195, 210
Williams, David (son of Kate), 441
Williams George, 176
Williams, John, 148
Williams, John N., 138
Williams, Kate, 60, 96, 134, 139, 140, 143, 150, 151, 154, 155, 174, 210, 275, 276, 306, 441, 453, 471, 485, 510, 540
Williams, Mary, 139, 451 *ff.*, 472, 476–77, 512–13, 540, 545, 546, 547
Williams, Miller, 473
Williams, Serena, 210, 451 *ff.*, 458, 461, 468, 471, 476–77, 491, 540, 545–47
Williams, Mrs., 537–38
Williamsburg, Va., 228; battle, 132 *n.*, 219, 229
Wilmington, N. C., 3, 4 *n.*, 134, 144, 287, 303, 323, 406; surrendered, 484
Wilson, Senator, 88 *n.*–89, 152–53
Wilson's raiders, 418
Winchester, Va., 62, 96, 117; Yankee raid around, 283–84
Winder, General, 475–76 *n.*
Winder, Miss, 121
Wingate, Mr., 176
Winnsboro, S. C., 509, 527
Withers, Kate, 189, 256, 545
Withers, Mary, 275
Withers, Tanny, 1, 178, 413, 545
Withers, Tom, 94
Withers, Thomas J., 6 *n.*, 7, 8, 13, 17,

27, 28, 35, 55, 56, 140–41, 155, 156, 158, 174, 188, 190, 195, 196, 199, 307–8, 409, 412, 483
Withers, Mrs. Thomas J., 159, 413, 528
Witherspoon, Betsy, murdered by slaves, 138, 139 *n.*, 140, 145–47, 151, 153
Witherspoon, John, 140, 145, 146, 176, 319–20, 410, 414, 537
Witherspoon, Mary, 139, 145–46, 154, 210
Women, position of, 186 *n.*, 199–200, 224, 346
Wood, John Taylor, 380–81
Workman, Mr., 137
Wright, Mrs., 345–46
Wynne, Mrs., 112

Yancey, William Lowndes, 60 *n.*, 196, 208, 221; sent to England, 126–27
Yankee, 91, 237, 265, 404, 455, 521, 537; "damyankees," 89; prisoners, 112, 189; women, 165
Yarn, used as money, 497, 498, 499
Yeadon, Mr., 205, 220, 231, 266
York, S. C., 511
York River (Va.), 67
Yorkville, 478
Young, Lewis, 232
Young, Colonel, 506
Young, Dr., 143
Young, General, 338, 345, 465
Young, the Reverend Mrs., 251

Zouaves (New Orleans), 54, 67, 96